# Present Value Tables

Where:
$P$ = Present Value Factor
$i$ = Interest Rate
$n$ = Number of Periods

$$P = \frac{1 - \dfrac{1}{(1+i)^n}}{i}$$

**Table 2**
**Present Value of $1 Received Periodically for n Periods**

| Periods (n) | 1% | 2% | 4% | 5% | 6% | 8% | 10% | 12% | 14% | 15% | 16% | 18% | 20% | 22% | 24% | 25% | 30% | 40% |
|---|---|---|---|---|---|---|---|---|---|---|---|---|---|---|---|---|---|---|
| 0 | 1.000 | 1.000 | 1.000 | 1.000 | 1.000 | 1.000 | 1.000 | 1.000 | 1.000 | 1.000 | 1.000 | 1.000 | 1.000 | 1.000 | 1.000 | 1.000 | 1.000 | 1.000 |
| 1 | 0.990 | 0.980 | 0.962 | 0.952 | 0.943 | 0.926 | 0.909 | 0.893 | 0.877 | 0.870 | 0.862 | 0.847 | 0.833 | 0.820 | 0.806 | 0.800 | 0.769 | 0.714 |
| 2 | 1.970 | 1.942 | 1.886 | 1.859 | 1.833 | 1.783 | 1.736 | 1.690 | 1.647 | 1.626 | 1.605 | 1.566 | 1.528 | 1.492 | 1.457 | 1.440 | 1.361 | 1.224 |
| 3 | 2.941 | 2.884 | 2.775 | 2.723 | 2.673 | 2.577 | 2.487 | 2.402 | 2.322 | 2.283 | 2.246 | 2.174 | 2.106 | 2.042 | 1.981 | 1.952 | 1.816 | 1.589 |
| 4 | 3.902 | 3.808 | 3.630 | 3.546 | 3.465 | 3.312 | 3.170 | 3.037 | 2.914 | 2.855 | 2.798 | 2.690 | 2.589 | 2.494 | 2.404 | 2.362 | 2.166 | 1.849 |
| 5 | 4.853 | 4.713 | 4.452 | 4.329 | 4.212 | 3.993 | 3.791 | 3.605 | 3.433 | 3.352 | 3.274 | 3.127 | 2.991 | 2.864 | 2.745 | 2.689 | 2.436 | 2.035 |
| 6 | 5.795 | 5.601 | 5.242 | 5.076 | 4.917 | 4.623 | 4.355 | 4.111 | 3.889 | 3.784 | 3.685 | 3.498 | 3.326 | 3.167 | 3.020 | 2.951 | 2.643 | 2.168 |
| 7 | 6.728 | 6.472 | 6.002 | 5.786 | 5.582 | 5.206 | 4.868 | 4.564 | 4.288 | 4.160 | 4.039 | 3.812 | 3.605 | 3.416 | 3.242 | 3.161 | 2.802 | 2.263 |
| 8 | 7.652 | 7.325 | 6.733 | 6.463 | 6.210 | 5.747 | 5.335 | 4.968 | 4.639 | 4.487 | 4.344 | 4.078 | 3.837 | 3.619 | 3.421 | 3.329 | 2.925 | 2.331 |
| 9 | 8.566 | 8.162 | 7.435 | 7.108 | 6.802 | 6.247 | 5.759 | 5.328 | 4.946 | 4.772 | 4.607 | 4.303 | 4.031 | 3.786 | 3.566 | 3.463 | 3.019 | 2.379 |
| 10 | 9.471 | 8.983 | 8.111 | 7.722 | 7.360 | 6.710 | 6.145 | 5.650 | 5.216 | 5.019 | 4.833 | 4.494 | 4.192 | 3.923 | 3.682 | 3.571 | 3.092 | 2.414 |
| 11 | 10.368 | 9.787 | 8.760 | 8.306 | 7.887 | 7.139 | 6.495 | 5.938 | 5.453 | 5.234 | 5.029 | 4.656 | 4.327 | 4.035 | 3.776 | 3.656 | 3.147 | 2.438 |
| 12 | 11.255 | 10.575 | 9.385 | 8.863 | 8.384 | 7.536 | 6.814 | 6.194 | 5.660 | 5.421 | 5.197 | 4.793 | 4.439 | 4.127 | 3.851 | 3.725 | 3.190 | 2.456 |
| 13 | 12.134 | 11.348 | 9.986 | 9.394 | 8.853 | 7.904 | 7.103 | 6.424 | 5.842 | 5.583 | 5.342 | 4.910 | 4.533 | 4.203 | 3.912 | 3.780 | 3.223 | 2.469 |
| 14 | 13.004 | 12.106 | 10.563 | 9.899 | 9.295 | 8.244 | 7.367 | 6.628 | 6.002 | 5.724 | 5.468 | 5.008 | 4.611 | 4.265 | 3.962 | 3.824 | 3.249 | 2.478 |
| 15 | 13.865 | 12.849 | 11.118 | 10.380 | 9.712 | 8.559 | 7.606 | 6.811 | 6.142 | 5.847 | 5.575 | 5.092 | 4.675 | 4.315 | 4.001 | 3.859 | 3.268 | 2.484 |
| 16 | 14.718 | 13.578 | 11.652 | 10.838 | 10.106 | 8.851 | 7.824 | 6.974 | 6.265 | 5.954 | 5.668 | 5.162 | 4.730 | 4.357 | 4.033 | 3.887 | 3.283 | 2.489 |
| 17 | 15.562 | 14.292 | 12.166 | 11.274 | 10.477 | 9.122 | 8.022 | 7.120 | 6.373 | 6.047 | 5.749 | 5.222 | 4.775 | 4.391 | 4.059 | 3.910 | 3.295 | 2.492 |
| 18 | 16.398 | 14.992 | 12.659 | 11.690 | 10.828 | 9.372 | 8.201 | 7.250 | 6.467 | 6.128 | 5.818 | 5.273 | 4.812 | 4.419 | 4.080 | 3.928 | 3.304 | 2.494 |
| 19 | 17.226 | 15.678 | 13.134 | 12.085 | 11.158 | 9.604 | 8.365 | 7.366 | 6.550 | 6.198 | 5.877 | 5.316 | 4.843 | 4.442 | 4.097 | 3.942 | 3.311 | 2.496 |
| 20 | 18.046 | 16.351 | 13.590 | 12.462 | 11.470 | 9.818 | 8.514 | 7.469 | 6.623 | 6.259 | 5.929 | 5.353 | 4.870 | 4.460 | 4.110 | 3.954 | 3.316 | 2.497 |
| 21 | 18.857 | 17.011 | 14.029 | 12.821 | 11.764 | 10.017 | 8.649 | 7.562 | 6.687 | 6.312 | 5.973 | 5.384 | 4.891 | 4.476 | 4.121 | 3.963 | 3.320 | 2.498 |
| 22 | 19.660 | 17.658 | 14.451 | 13.163 | 12.042 | 10.201 | 8.772 | 7.645 | 6.743 | 6.359 | 6.011 | 5.410 | 4.909 | 4.488 | 4.130 | 3.970 | 3.323 | 2.498 |
| 23 | 20.456 | 18.292 | 14.857 | 13.489 | 12.303 | 10.371 | 8.883 | 7.718 | 6.792 | 6.399 | 6.044 | 5.432 | 4.925 | 4.499 | 4.137 | 3.976 | 3.325 | 2.499 |
| 24 | 21.243 | 18.914 | 15.247 | 13.799 | 12.550 | 10.529 | 8.985 | 7.784 | 6.835 | 6.434 | 6.073 | 5.451 | 4.937 | 4.507 | 4.143 | 3.981 | 3.327 | 2.499 |
| 25 | 22.023 | 19.523 | 15.622 | 14.094 | 12.783 | 10.675 | 9.077 | 7.843 | 6.873 | 6.464 | 6.097 | 5.467 | 4.948 | 4.514 | 4.147 | 3.985 | 3.329 | 2.499 |
| 30 | 25.808 | 22.396 | 17.292 | 15.372 | 13.765 | 11.258 | 9.427 | 8.055 | 7.003 | 6.566 | 6.177 | 5.517 | 4.979 | 4.534 | 4.160 | 3.995 | 3.332 | 2.500 |
| 35 | 29.409 | 24.999 | 18.665 | 16.374 | 14.498 | 11.655 | 9.644 | 8.176 | 7.070 | 6.617 | 6.215 | 5.539 | 4.992 | 4.541 | 4.164 | 3.998 | 3.333 | 2.500 |
| 40 | 32.835 | 27.355 | 19.793 | 17.159 | 15.046 | 11.925 | 9.779 | 8.244 | 7.105 | 6.642 | 6.233 | 5.548 | 4.997 | 4.544 | 4.166 | 3.999 | 3.333 | 2.500 |
| 45 | 36.095 | 29.490 | 20.720 | 17.774 | 15.456 | 12.108 | 9.863 | 8.283 | 7.123 | 6.654 | 6.242 | 5.552 | 4.999 | 4.545 | 4.166 | 4.000 | 3.333 | 2.500 |
| 50 | 39.196 | 31.424 | 21.482 | 18.256 | 15.762 | 12.233 | 9.915 | 8.304 | 7.133 | 6.661 | 6.246 | 5.554 | 4.999 | 4.545 | 4.167 | 4.000 | 3.333 | 2.500 |
| ∞ | 100.000 | 50.000 | 25.000 | 20.000 | 16.667 | 12.500 | 10.000 | 8.333 | 7.143 | 6.667 | 6.250 | 5.556 | 5.000 | 4.545 | 4.167 | 4.000 | 3.333 | 2.500 |

# Managerial Accounting: *Manufacturing and Service Applications*

**Fourth Edition**

**Arnold Schneider, PH.D., C.P.A.**
**Professor of Accounting**
**Georgia Institute of Technology**

**Harold M. Sollenberger, D.B.A., C.P.A.**
**Professor of Accounting**
**Michigan State University**

**THOMSON** ™

Australia • Canada • Mexico • Singapore • Spain • United Kingdom • United States

# Managerial Accounting:
## *Manufacturing and Service Applications, 4e*

## Arnold Schneider & Harold Sollenberger

**Project Development Manager:**
Greg Albert

**Marketing Coordinators:**
Lindsay Annett and Sara Mercurio

**Production/Manufacturing
Supervisor:**
Donna M. Brown

**Project Coordinator:**
David Lyons

**Pre-Media Services Supervisor:**
Dan Plofchan

**Sr. Pre-press Specialist**
Kim Fry

**Rights and Permissions Specialist:**
Kalina Hintz and Bahman Naraghi

**Cover Image**
Getty Images*

**Cover Designer:**
Phoenix Creative, LLC

**Compositor:**
Integra Software Services Pvt. Ltd.

**Printer:**
Courier - Kendallville

The Adaptable Courseware Program consists of products and additions to existing Thomson products that are produced from camera-ready copy. Peer review, class testing, and accuracy are primarily the responsibility of the author(s).

Managerial Accounting:
Manufacturing and Service Applications
Arnold Schneider & Harold M. Sollenberger–Third Edition
**ISBN 0-759-35042-6**

Library of Congress Control Number
2005930772

### International Divisions List

**Asia (Including India):**
Thomson Learning
60 Albert Street, #15-01
Albert Complex
Singapore 189969
Tel 65 336-6411
Fax 65 336-7411

**Australia/New Zealand:**
Thomson Learning Australia
102 Dodds Street
Southbank, Victoria 3006
Australia

**Latin America:**
Thomson Learning
Seneca 53
Colonia Polano
11560 Mexico, D.F., Mexico
Tel (525) 281-2906
Fax (525) 281-2656

**Canada:**
Thomson Nelson
1120 Birchmount Road
Toronto, Ontario
Canada M1K 5G4
Tel (416) 752-9100
Fax (416) 752-8102

**UK/Europe/Middle East/Africa:**
Thomson Learning
High Holborn House
50-51 Bedford Row
London, WC1R 4L$
United Kingdom
Tel 44 (020) 7067-2500
Fax 44 (020) 7067-2600

**Spain (Includes Portugal):**
Thomson Paraninfo
Calle Magallanes 25
28015 Madrid
España
Tel 34 (0)91 446-3350
Fax 34 (0)91 445-6218

# DEDICATIONS

To my wife, Marcy, and my children, Julie, Evan & Amy
—Arnold Schneider


To Lois, my wife
—Harold Sollenberger

# PREFACE

The service sector of the economy (including merchandising) accounts for over 75 percent of employment in the U.S. Also, about 70 percent of the GNP of the world's leading economies come from the service sector. In addition to the dominance of the service sector in the economy, students (and probably instructors as well) can relate more easily to service organizations. Most students have never been in a factory, but they have had interactions with banks, airlines, restaurants, etc.

This textbook places service organizations on equal footing with manufacturing organizations. Applications involving the service sector are at least as numerous as those involving manufacturing. These applications include opening chapter vignettes, chapter examples, contemporary practice illustrations, review problems, and end-of-chapter exercises, problems, and cases.

## THE BASIC PREMISES OF THE TEXT

The text's core question is: How do managers use management accounting information? The answer is: To make decisions. Every page of this text is devoted to help managers make the best decisions to achieve the goals of their organizations. All decisions concern the future. Today's decisions affect future results. Much more time is given to managing future costs and revenues, and less time is devoted to historical reporting. In today's environment, the emphasis is on customer service, throughput, higher quality, reduced waste, continuous improvement, and global sourcing and marketing.

While managerial accounting is changing dramatically, many fundamentals are still key underpinnings of today's and tomorrow's decision making. The text integrates relevant traditional and leading edge topics into a flow that teaches basic cost analysis, decision definition, relevant information formatting, and decision making itself.

Students must understand that questions cannot be answered "yes" or "no" and that problems cannot be solved merely by calculations. The words "why," "explain," and "justify" appear frequently in exercises, problems, and cases. The student is lead from definition and concept, to mechanical demonstration, to managerial analysis, and to strategy and policy development. Our writing approaches and teaching philosophies are aimed at users of managerial accounting information—future managers. The manager must use all quantitative tools and techniques available but must also apply logic, insight, judgment, and common sense.

Learning should be fun. We attempt to include subtle humor, interesting examples, real-world cases, and student-oriented concerns.

## NOTEWORTHY FEATURES IN THE TEXTBOOK

We have incorporated the latest developments in management and management accounting into this textbook. Among the key features are:

### Service Applications

While most managerial accounting concepts are transferable across manufacturing and service organizations, unique requirements and special adaptations must be recognized and discussed. Each chapter includes a wide variety of service applications, including merchandising and non-profit settings.

### Activity-Based Costing (ABC), Just-in-Time, (JIT) and Activity-Based Management

In addition to Chapter 6 that focuses on ABC and JIT costing, we discuss in nearly every chapter the ramifications that these ideas and other new manufacturing and service developments have on decision making and cost management.

### International Dimensions

Because doing business in Europe, Asia, Africa, South America, and Australia is almost as common as operating on the North American continent, we must be able to think, deal, and calculate in foreign currencies, understand the impacts of European quality standards for example, and make decisions in increasingly complex global markets. We have included international sections in numerous chapters and have several international-based exercises and problems at the end of every chapter.

### Ethics and Ethical Issues

Chapter 1 sets the stage for emphasis on ethical issues. Virtually every chapter has a special section to highlight particular ethical concerns. Each chapter also has end-of-chapter exercises and problems that have a strong ethical base and require students to evaluate ethical dilemmas.

### Critical Thinking Requirements in End-of-Chapter Materials

As we attempt to challenge the student with qualitative and policy issues, we have included numerous exercises, problems, and cases that require the student to think critically. We challenge the student to explain, to justify a viewpoint, to present arguments on both sides of an issue, to provide support for quantitative answers, and to question the basic assumptions and data provided in the exercise, problem, or case. We are convinced that students will understand better and retain more from these challenges.

### Leading Edge Topics

Chapter 14 addresses recent costing developments. These include the costs of quality, target and kaizen costing, value-added and nonvalue-added activities, nonfinancial performance measures, balanced scorecards, and strategies to enhance productivity. Elsewhere, we discuss benchmarking, economic value-added, and life-cycle costing.

## End-of-Chapter Materials

The end of each chapter has questions for review and discussion, exercises, problems, and cases. Icons indicate applications relating to:

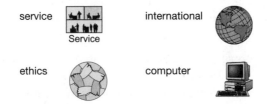

service    Service

international

ethics

computer

## Contemporary Practice Applications and Illustrations

In every chapter, we present live examples from real-world settings or from recent literature. Our intent is to show how concepts we discuss in the text are applied directly in real settings. We also use these Contemporary Practice examples to show the variety of practices that currently do exist.

## THE STRUCTURE OF THE BOOK

The text is divided into five parts. **Part One, Management Accounting Framework**, includes Chapters 1, 2, and 3. Chapter 1 sets the stage for managerial uses of accounting data, business environment changes, decision-making steps, organizational structure, and ethical conduct. Chapter 2 presents the basic definitional material needed for managerial accounting. This is a critical chapter for students in establishing a firm base for moving into costing and decision-making areas. Chapter 3 expands cost behavior into cost estimation and cost/volume/profit relationships.

   **Part Two, Product Cost Framework**, includes Chapters 4, 5, and 6. Chapter 4 sets the cost determination stage by explaining how costs are attached to products and services. Chapter 5 discusses both job and process costing, using the new manufacturing environment as a base. Chapter 6 presents activity-based costing and management and extends the discussion in JIT and automated manufacturing processes.

   **Part Three, Planning and Control Framework**, brings the planning and evaluation tools together in Chapters 7, 8, and 9. Chapter 7 focuses on budgeting and the planning and control system. Chapters 8 and 9 emphasize variance analysis to measure performance by explaining standard costs, contribution margin analysis, and absorption and variable costing.

   **Part Four, Decision-Making Framework**, includes Chapters 10, 11, 12, and 13. Incremental decision-making (Chapter 10) is perhaps the core of decision-making in managerial accounting. Capital investments decisions (Chapters 11 and 12) are important to the complete understanding of incremental decisions but are sometimes covered in other courses. Chapter 13 looks at segmental performance evaluation and internal transactions.

   **Part Five, Extension in Managerial Analysis**, includes Chapters 14 and 15. Chapter 14 is devoted to leading-edge management accounting topics such as costs of quality, target and kaizen costing, activity analysis, and nonfinancial performance measurement. Chapter 15 involves financial statement analysis, a topic that overlaps both financial and managerial accounting. Inclusion of this topic in this course depends on curriculum and course designs.

   Within each chapter, the sequence of presentation reflects the extensive testing in large enrollment principles courses, stand-alone managerial accounting courses, MBA-level managerial accounting courses, and executive-MBA managerial accounting courses. Examples, illustrations, and end-of-chapter materials have largely come from in-class use by the authors and other managerial accounting professors or from real-world examples provided by working managers or adapted from recent business articles.

# CHAPTER FORMAT

Each chapter follows a format or pattern to assist in learning and teaching.

**Learning Objectives.** Learning objectives identify what the student should be able to do upon completing the end-of-chapter materials. They provide a guide to the study of each chapter and a teaching outline.

**Vignette.** We start each chapter with a realistic business situation or problem that focuses on topics covered in the chapter. These vignettes provide a framework for why the chapter topics are important to managers. Many of the vignettes are bases for discussion in the chapter or in end-of-chapter materials.

**Contemporary Practice.** These are examples inserted carefully in each chapter to illustrate current practices, either in survey or summary form from a newspaper, business periodical, or academic journal.

**Chapter Summary.** A brief synopsis of each chapter helps the student organize, review, and integrate key concepts. We have structured the summary around the learning objectives so the student can ascertain if all learning objectives were covered.

**Review Problems.** Problems with suggested solutions enable the student to test the level of understanding of chapter material and obtain immediate feedback about appropriate answers.

**Terminology Review.** Important terminology, definitions, and concepts appear in bold type throughout each chapter. These key terms and concepts are listed at the end of the chapter.

**Questions for Review and Discussion.** Approximately 20 questions are framed to spark class discussion and to help students confirm their understanding of the text materials.

**Exercises.** Exercises usually emphasize one or two simple concepts with basic computations and straightforward "why" or "explain" questions. Each chapter has between 15 and 20 exercises.

**Problems.** Problems have either more than one issue, challenging situations, complex computations, and/or interpretative issues. Each problem is based on a real-life setting. Each chapter contains between 15 and 20 problems.

**Cases.** Most chapters have two cases. Cases have greater depth and complexity than problems. They are designed to help students integrate various concepts within the chapter and across several chapters. The complexity and comprehensiveness help students to develop analytical skills.

The lead-in materials, the chapter contents, and the end-of-chapter materials combine to create a powerful learning and teaching package.

# WHERE AND HOW TO USE THE TEXT

*Managerial Accounting: Manufacturing and Service Applications* is structured with a great deal of flexibility. This text can easily be used in a number of settings: a second semester principles course, a junior-level course between principles and cost accounting, a junior-level non-accounting major managerial course, and MBA-level managerial accounting courses. The variety of chapters and the mix of materials within chapters allow a course to be structured around a plan for student learning consistent with specific curriculum and course needs.

While we believe that the chapter order as presented is the strongest teaching and learning sequence, many other models can be selected. Most chapters are designed so that they are partially or completely independent of other chapters. Consequently, you have an opportunity to design a unique course for different types or levels of students. Also, we have consciously applied illustrations and end-of-chapter materials to both manufacturing and service organizations.

The material within each chapter has a mix of conceptual, analytical, interpretative, and management behavioral issues. The text attempts to balance the fine edge of providing a solid reference of what, how, and why, while challenging students to think for themselves. Extensive end-of-chapter materials allow the selection of simple exercises for beginning students and for in-class teaching examples. More difficult problems and cases should challenge students to interrelate concepts, pragmatic issues, and real-world common sense. These materials are easily adapted to both undergraduate and graduate students.

## LEARNING AND TEACHING AIDS

### For the Instructor

**Solutions Manual.** The solutions manual contains answers to all review and discussion questions and detailed solutions for every exercise, problem, and case. Additional clarifying notes and suggestions are presented where appropriate.

### For the Student

**Check Figures.** Key figures for solutions to the majority of exercises and problems are provided at the end of the text as an aid to students as they prepare their answers.

## ACKNOWLEDGMENTS

This book was completed with the input and assistance of many people. Of special note is Lois Sollenberger, who edited many drafts of all chapters.

Arnold Schneider
Harold M. Sollenberger

# About the Authors

**Arnold Schneider** is Professor and Area Coordinator of Accounting at Georgia Institute of Technology, where he teaches and does research in auditing, managerial accounting and cost accounting. Professor Schneider is a bachelor's graduate of Case Western Reserve University and holds masters and doctoral degrees from Ohio State University. He was an auditor with the U.S. General Accounting Office in Washington, D.C. He is a CPA and is a member of the American Accounting Association.

Professor Schneider has also served as a Visiting Fellow in Accounting at Macquarie University in Australia and as a Visiting Associate Professor at Emory University. He has published over 30 articles in various journals such as *Journal of Accounting Research, Accounting Review, Decision Sciences*, and *Contemporary Accounting Research*. Professor Schneider has served on the editorial boards of the *Accounting Review, Behavioral Research in Accounting, Advances in Accounting, Issues in Accounting Education*, and *Southwest Business Review*. In 1986, Georgia Tech's College of Management gave Professor Schneider the Young Investigator Award for his research.

Professor Schneider has taught undergraduate, masters, and doctoral courses. In addition, he has taught financial and managerial accounting courses to working managers. For several years, he lectured to Chinese executives in the China/U.S. Professional Exchange Program at Georgia Tech. Professor Schneider has served as a consultant with various organizations, including as an expert witness for court cases. He has also held officer and board of director positions for several nonprofit organizations.

**Harold M. Sollenberger** is Professor of Accounting at Michigan State University. He holds MBA and DBA degrees from Indiana University and a bachelor's degree from Shippensburg University. He is a CPA and a member of the Financial Executives International, the Institute of Management Accountants, and the American Accounting Association.

At Michigan State University, Professor Sollenberger has served as Chairperson of the accounting and finance faculties and as Associate Dean for MBA Programs. Over the years, he has served as a consultant to CPA firms, governmental units, professional associations, and industrial firms. He has taught at Indiana University and University of Southern California, and in the People's Republic of China.

He has led numerous management study groups to Europe, Japan, Korea, and the PRC.

His teaching experience spans all levels of accounting instruction from introductory courses, to doctoral research seminars, and to executive manager seminars. He taught managerial accounting to executive MBA students and to undergraduates in large lectures and via live instructional television. Outside the university, Professor Sollenberger has taught for over twenty years in a wide variety of banking and credit union financial management schools. He has taught many continuing education programs. Known for his energetic, humorous, and participatory teaching style, he has received numerous awards for his teaching at both the undergraduate and graduate levels. He has also served as treasurer for several state-wide political campaigns.

Professor Sollenberger has written over 15 books and over 30 articles dealing with management information systems, cost analysis, financial institution management, and assets/liability management.

# CONTENTS IN BRIEF

# TABLE OF CONTENTS

## PART TWO:    PRODUCT COST FRAMEWORK

# PART THREE:    PLANNING AND CONTROL FRAMEWORK

## PART FOUR:    DECISION-MAKING FRAMEWORK

# PART FIVE:    EXTENSION IN MANAGERIAL ANALYSIS

# MANAGERIAL ACCOUNTING FRAMEWORK

# MANAGERIAL ACCOUNTING AND MANAGEMENT'S NEED FOR INFORMATION

**LEARNING OBJECTIVES**

After studying Chapter 1, you will be able to:

1. Understand the main uses of management accounting information.
2. Explain the changes taking place in the business environment and their impacts on managerial accounting.
3. Identify the major transaction systems and data files in an organization that generate and organize accounting information.
4. Identify the steps in the decision-making process.
5. Understand the typical organizational structure of a firm and the controller's responsibilities.
6. Explain how service organizations differ from manufacturing organizations.
7. Distinguish between financial accounting and managerial accounting.
8. Recognize the primary ethical responsibilities of the management accountant.

## The Controller's Work Day: Where Did the Time Go?

*It's early October; and Sarah Baker, Controller of Olson Software Products, has just arrived at her office at about 7:30 a.m. She scans her e-mail messages, checks her electronic calendar, and looks through her in-basket. She says, "Wow, another 'normal' day!" She wonders if she'll make her tennis date with her husband at 6 p.m. Her calendar shows:*

9:00    *Meet with division head of Customer Support to discuss next year's budget numbers. Review preliminary budget numbers before meeting.*

10:00    *Meet with accounting systems analysts to discuss status of a project to improve the firm's monthly management "plan versus actual" reporting system.*

11:30    *Hold a quick session with Marketing Vice-President, Stacy Huffman, to discuss pricing negotiations with new customer.*

12:15    *Have working lunch with corporate attorney to discuss customer contract wording for a new product being introduced early next year.*

2:00    *With budget manager, review September's actual results and budget comparisons and identify problem areas. Also, review third quarter results before her presentation to the President at Friday's staff meeting.*

4:00    *Review a special cost-volume-profit study of Olson software products, relative to the firm's strategic plan's profitability goals.*

*She also knows that she needs to:*

- *respond to four e-mail questions about product costs and operating expenses;*
- *talk to Travis Souza, New Product Development Vice-President, about a serious cost-overrun problem with a new product project;*
- *prepare a presentation on cash flows for the firm's strategic planning meeting next month; and*
- *write a memo supporting the spending of $100,000 by the Marketing Vice-President on media contracts.*

*Every meeting, discussion, and decision that Sarah has today and every day use accounting information. She must generate relevant data in the right form and at the right time. She and her fellow managers must understand cost behavior, cost/benefit analyses, plan versus actual comparisons, and how to use information to achieve Olson Software Products' long-term and short-term goals.*

MANAGERS MAKE DECISIONS. Managers select one alternative from a set of choices. Making the best choice depends on the manager's goals, the expected results from each alternative, and the information available when the decision is made. Decision-making information is the focus of this text. Collecting, classifying, reporting, and analyzing relevant information are fundamental to every action that managers take. Management accountants prepare information for decision makers. In this chapter, the stage is set for discussing how managers use information, how the firm is organized, what changes are occurring in business environments, how decisions are framed, and how management accountants are involved in decision making.

Management accountants transform data into information. Data are the raw materials of decision making. Most business data are captured in the transaction systems of the firm. Information is data that are organized for some purpose or objective.

## HOW MANAGERS USE MANAGEMENT ACCOUNTING INFORMATION

How do managers use management accounting information? The answer is: to make decisions. The major decision areas are:

- Forecasting and planning,
- Performance evaluation,
- Cost determination, pricing, and cost management,
- Operations control and improvement,
- Incremental decision making,
- Financial reporting, and
- Motivation of managers.

Every page of this text is devoted to these topics and their interaction. Each decision area uses different information in various formats. This is management accounting.

### Forecasting and Planning

Decision making always deals with the future. While historical data are useful in helping to understand past relationships, forecast data are critical. A financial plan common to most organizations is the budget. It sets a plan of action for the coming year. This plan or budget also motivates managers to achieve and creates a basis for evaluating actual results.

### Performance Evaluation

After decisions have been made and actions taken, actual results flow in. How did we do? Comparing actual to plan tells a story. Analyzing differences helps evaluate the performance of managers, business segments, or even the entire firm. Comparing actual to plan may also give insights into where changes should be made–perhaps into where and how to improve resource use.

### Cost Determination, Pricing, and Cost Management

What is the "true" cost of a product or service? The answer depends on why the question is asked. **Cost determination**, also known as product costing, deals with measuring the resources used to complete an activity or unit of output. **Pricing** can be market based or cost based. For products with market-based prices, pricing must still consider cost in determining profits and returns on investments. For products with cost-based prices, recovering costs is a key management concern for measuring profits. **Cost management** is finding ways to control activities that incur costs more efficiently. Also, by more careful cost analysis, managers can identify opportunities for cost reduction.

### Operations Control and Improvement

By using various accounting tools, we can measure how well operating activities were managed. Tools such as flexible budgets, standard costs, and cost control charts allow managers to monitor operating activities. Yet the real goal is to improve performance in all activities. **Continuous improvement** is a strategy that examines every aspect of a process and of entire processes for increased efficiency, cost reduction, and higher quality. In so-called "new manufacturing" environments, almost revolutionary views of production management are evolving to achieve significant improvements. Cost systems must change with the processes.

## Incremental Decision Making

Underlying most decisions is an evaluation of the decision's costs and benefits. Many action-oriented decisions can be grouped by the decision objective: where and when to sell and at what price, whether to make or buy, where to use resources, or whether a segment should be added or deleted. Each decision type has specific information needs, an analysis format, and decision rules. Future incremental revenues and costs are relevant; past costs are irrelevant. Sorting relevant from irrelevant information is a responsibility of every manager.

## Financial Reporting

While focusing on assisting managers, the management accountant must remember that financial results are reported to both internal and external users. Financial statements are important internally as indicators of how segments of the business and their managers are performing. In addition, executives report to boards of directors, shareholders, and others on the financial status of the firm. The performance of managers is measured in the light of how investors, shareholders, creditors, tax authorities, and, in the public sector, voters view their results.

## Motivation of Managers

The last item listed is far from the least important. As we will see, messages are sent through accounting numbers–some subtle, some blunt and harsh, and others tempered by intent to motivate, encourage, and reward strong performances. Managerial psychology and attitudes are influenced in important ways by information and how it is presented and used.

Contemporary Practice 1.1 reports where decision makers, responding to a survey, indicate that they use costing systems and cost data within their firms.

## Contemporary Practice 1.1
### Decision Makers' Needs and Expectations

*In a recent study, decision makers and the decision enablers (those people responsible for generating decision making data) agree on the priorities of management accounting. Top on the list was* *generating cost information that would improve the corporation, change employee behavior, or manage costs more efficiently. The chart below shows the main concerns:*

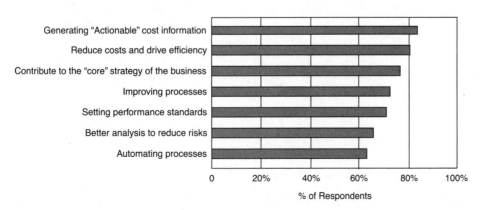

*Source: Ashmish, Garg, Debashis Ghosh, James Hudick, and Chuen Nowacki, "Roles and Practices in Management Accounting Today," Strategic Finance, July 2003, pp. 30–35.*

# THE OBJECTIVE OF MANAGEMENT

For accounting information to fulfill its roles, management's goals must be clear. The financial goal of a firm is to maximize the long-term wealth of shareholders or, express differently, to maximize the present value of shareholders' future cash flows from the firm. Corporate managers have a strong interest in profit. But many organizations do not attempt to produce a profit. The success of a nonprofit enterprise, for instance, is measured by realizing a common goal rather than economic objectives. A governmental agency, for example, is primarily concerned with providing services to its citizens.

In the vast majority of decision-making situations, the same basic decision rules apply to all types of organizations. Economic realities are important in all organizations. At a minimum, management must use its resources in a manner that attains desired goals in an efficient manner.

Contemporary managers recognize that the business enterprise is also responsible to many diverse groups, both inside and outside the organization. Employees depend on the business for a means of livelihood. In addition, the community expects a business to be a positive contributing neighbor. Most businesspersons acknowledge that the goals of each group are best served by the harmonious reconciliation of all interests. Hence, the objective of maximizing profits must be accomplished within socially and legally accepted bounds.

# MANAGEMENT ACCOUNTING INFORMATION: USERS AND SYSTEMS

Organizations create or cause events, referred to as economic activity. A manager in a company within any industry will spend large chunks of time organizing personnel and arranging resources to be productive. A manager faces numerous choices, conflicting priorities, organizational politics and culture, and the normal burdens of bureaucracy.

## Levels of Management

Top, middle, and lower-level managers need different information. A rough parallel exists between a manager's level in the organization and the type of accounting information needed. Executive or top managers generally face unstructured or semistructured problems common to strategic planning. Strategic planning deals with market positioning, the economy, competitors, sources of capital, and other outside factors that affect the long-term well-being of the company. Therefore, much information comes from external sources.

Middle management deals with semistructured problems relating primarily to obtaining and using resources effectively and efficiently. Here, managers want information to formulate operating budgets; create capital investment plans; choose product strategies; plan personnel levels; and measure, evaluate, and improve performances of subordinates.

Supervisory or lower management faces more structured tasks. How many control boards are needed on Monday? When should Order 345 be produced? Each manager typically has authority to operate within a particular department or category of work. Decisions, needed information, and decision rules are clearly identified. Supervisors' information needs are detailed, time dependent, and reported routinely.

## Sources of Management Accounting Data

In today's world, you can often be data rich but information poor. Internal accounting systems exist as a source of financial and nonmonetary data and convert these data into meaningful information. Accounting systems accumulate, classify, store, and report relevant information in ways that meet

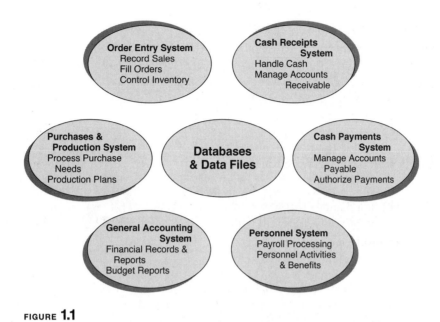

**FIGURE 1.1**

Major Transaction Systems Found in Most Business Organization

each manager's needs. These systems capture transaction data. The common transaction systems in the typical company are illustrated in Figure 1.1.

These six systems generate the vast majority of data used in most firms for accounting, marketing, production, and general management purposes. The data that managers read in reports and analyses depends on how these systems are designed. In the following chapters, the data we use come from these systems.

Figure 1.2 shows the major data files that exist in many organizations. Depending on the sophistication of data processing systems, databases are accessed by these transaction systems.

**FIGURE 1.2**

Major Databases Found in Most Business Organizations

In nonautomated environments, these databases are file cabinets and manually maintained journals and ledgers. Today, a customer record can be accessed via computers by marketing, shipping, order entry, billing, cash receipts, market research, and any other internal user that needs information on that customer. Today's enormous hardware and software capabilities eliminate most constraints that in the past limited managerial accountants' ability to generate relevant information.

## A CHANGING BUSINESS ENVIRONMENT

The business environment is changing rapidly, both domestically and globally. These changes influence the way managers conduct business. Consequently, they also affect information that managers use.

### Global Competition

The world is now one market. Materials, labor, and technical know-how come from all parts of the world. Markets for our products and services are likewise transnational. It is fair to say that every business has seen competition heighten in the past decade. Shifts in the competitive situation cause managers to identify ways to reduce product and service costs while supplying improved product quality and customer service.

Perhaps the most obvious change is the globalization of business activity. **Globalization** can be defined as being world-wide in scope or application. Apart from this geographical application, globalization can also be defined as becoming universal. This second meaning implies both a harmonization of rules and a reduction of barriers to allow a free flow of capital, goods, and services and to permit all firms to compete in all markets. GATT (General Agreement on Tariffs and Trade) and NAFTA (North American Free Trade Agreement) are important treaties promoting increased international trade.

A related movement is called **world-class manufacturing**. It emphasizes higher quality, lower inventory investment, faster processing, automation, and organizational flexibility to meet changing needs and advances in information technology. Many business people view companies with world-class manufacturing as pioneers who are on the "cutting edge" of better ideas.

### The Value Chain and Value-Added Activity

One way to view a firm's activities is to identify its value chain. A **value chain** looks strategically at each part of the firm's operations and asks what key contribution each part makes to the competitive strength of the firm as a whole. For example, being the low-cost producer in a market gives that firm an advantage. Having the ability to fill a customer order faster than its competitors gives another advantage. Managers are planning and working to develop strength in each link of its business chain. Each link should add value to the firm's operations. Management accountants' challenge is to measure the costs and benefits of adding value.

**Value added** is the increase in the worth of the firm, its products, and its activities. Often, the target of managers is the elimination of nonvalue-added activities. **Nonvalue-added activities** are essentially wasted effort. Why do something, if no value is added? Reduction of waste has helped many firms become more competitive and much more productive.

### Quality Assurance

In the past decade, quality has become an obsession in many firms. Customer dissatisfaction with American-made cars, electronic equipment, and many other products paved the way for competitors that delivered high-quality products at low prices–mainly from Japan. Japanese firms, using various quality enhancing techniques including quality circles (QC), statistical quality control, total quality management programs (TQM), continuous improvement programs, and employee empowerment processes, proved that high quality and high productivity are natural allies.

Management accountants focus on the **costs of quality** which come in two forms: voluntary and failure costs. Voluntary quality costs include prevention costs, such as training and quality promotion efforts, and appraisal costs, which include quality inspections and testing. Failure costs are either internal, such as scrap and lost work time due to failures, or external, such as warranty costs and lost sales–the most damaging cost. Better training and greater attention to prevention costs should reduce failure costs. Initially, a total quality management program should increase voluntary costs and reduce failure costs.

Over time, failure costs decline; voluntary costs also drop; productivity increases; customer satisfaction grows; sales jump; and profits multiply. This scenario has been proven. The common cry is "Quality is free." The reverse is also true–poor quality, higher costs, lower sales, and financial losses. We measure the quality costs to help managers attack waste and improve quality.

## Just-in-Time Management

**Just-in-time (JIT)** is a method of management that stresses delivering the product or service when its needed–not before (creating inventory) or after (causing customer dissatisfaction). Often JIT means holding inventories to a minimum. This is a "pull" system, in which sales pull products through the production process. Inventory is expensive. Annual inventory holding costs often run at least 25 percent and as high as 40 percent of inventory value. Thus, a million-dollar inventory costs at least $250,000 just to handle, store, and finance annually.

But JIT is more than just inventory control. It is sometimes called "synchronous manufacturing." The objectives of JIT are to obtain materials just in time for production, to move work in process from one work center to another just in time to meet the needs of the next work center, and to provide finished goods just when the customer wants it.

## Technical Evolution

The technical evolution has impacted every business but perhaps manufacturing the most. Phrases like focused production, flexible manufacturing, and computer-aided design and manufacturing highlight the changes. **Focused production** attempts to decrease the variety of products made in a plant and to manufacture products and provide services that result in the highest contribution margins. Some companies even organize their plants into cells that focus groups of machines and people on producing a particular product line.

**Flexible manufacturing** is a move to increase the variety of products that a given machine or group of machines can produce. The purpose is to reduce space, machinery investment, and setup time and cost, which increases total throughput. By doubling the variety of products that the same machinery can manufacture, a company can substantially cut the equipment required.

**Computer-aided design (CAD)** is the use of high-quality graphics and software to create new products or to change existing products. CAD leads directly to **computer-aided manufacturing (CAM)**. CAM occurs when machines or entire production lines are run and coordinated by computers. **Computer-integrated manufacturing (CIM)** is a term that ties engineering, production planning, and production processes themselves into a linked process. Reduced lead times for meeting a customer order is one result. The wall between the "people that design" and the "people that make" is torn down and replaced by a team effort.

**Management information systems (MIS)** handle the major information technology tasks in organizations. MIS allows information to be literally on the desktop of every manager. In addition, telecommunications technology can move vast amounts of data to any place in the world. For example, in a automotive plant, as a car is started on the assembly line, an electronic message to begin building the seats for that car is sent to a nearby vendor plant. The seats are completed, trucked to the assembly plant, and delivered to the needed point on the assembly line just as the car arrives. Thus, JIT, CIM, TQM, and MIS all merge into a powerful, high-quality, and very productive manufacturing system.

In many firms, these production planning and control systems, cost accounting systems, distribution systems, management information systems, and even marketing systems have been merged into firm-wide **enterprise resource planning (ERP) systems** that utilize integrated software to optimize a wide range of business operations. Much managerial accounting data are generated, imbedded in operating reports, and made available to managers on a broader scale than in previous stand-alone information systems.

## Management Complexity

Management complexity is such a broad area that only a few points can be mentioned here. Traditional line and staff alignments are becoming blurred. Functional management responsibility (marketing, finance, production, etc.) is being merged with product line responsibility. Matrix organizations are being created, linking functional and product responsibilities.

**Downsizing** or "rightsizing" is a common approach that many large companies are using to remove entire layers of management and to make the organization "lean and mean." Too many layers of management remove the executive from the day-to-day business. Terms like "reengineering" represent new approaches to conducting business. **Benchmarking** is a method of comparing operations, costs, and productivity with world-class performers. Certainly, carefully examining every process, singularly and comprehensively, can add to the long-run success of the organization.

Team approaches are increasingly the norm in tackling business problems. Committees, task forces, project teams, and study groups are terms indicating that work is done through cooperation and integration. Directing and motivating people are at the core of managing.

## THE DECISION-MAKING PROCESS

A key to effective decision making is a structured approach. Still, the best process or even the best decision does not guarantee a successful outcome. The future determines its own fate, but the best prepared analysis is most likely to produce the desired result.

The following decision steps outline a structure for decision making.

1. **Define the decision issue.** A careful definition of the problem's scope is fundamental to higher quality analysis in later steps. Defining strategic, competitive, and organizational factors helps to focus on key issues.

2. **Specify the decision objective and decision rule.** Often the **decision objective** is the goal toward which the decision maker is working, such as profit maximization. Other situations may require the greatest efficiency, sales maximization, most persons served, or lowest cost. Knowing the overall goal sets the **decision rule**.

3. **Identify the choices. Choices** are the alternatives available to the decision maker.

4. **Collect relevant data on the choices.** Given time and investigation cost limits, data manipulation is a cost and benefit issue. Theoretically, we should stop collecting data when the marginal cost of collecting more data equals the marginal benefit of making a better decision. Practically, we are often constrained by time and available data.

5. **Format and analyze information about each choice.** Organizing the decision data often simplifies the decision task. The managerial accountant's responsibility is to organize the relevant data for analysis. A specific format focuses attention on the decision's relevant revenues and costs.

6. **Make the decision.** Given the decision rule, select the choice that gives the greatest benefit. Having said that, we must recognize that basic quantitative analysis is one part of the decision. Strategic issues, long-run impacts, qualitative factors, and even personal biases may influence the decision maker. But relevant data *must* be the foundation of analysis.

7. **Implement the decision.** Now the obvious should take place. A decision has been made; implement it.

8. **Evaluate the results of the decision.** Feedback on actual results enhances the analysis of similar future decisions. Here we close the control cycle.

Each step helps move the decision maker closer to achieving the best outcome for the firm. Performing all eight steps of the decision-making process completes the plan, act, evaluate, and control cycle.

## ORGANIZATION OF THE FIRM

Often, to understand an organization we can look at its structure. Figure 1.3 presents an abbreviated organization chart for a medium-sized manufacturing firm. The president reports to the board of directors and eventually to shareholders. The board sets general policies for the entity. Responsibility for operating the entity on a day-to-day basis is vested in the president, who in turn delegates authority to vice-presidents of functional areas. Notice that the internal audit function reports to the president. This independent review of internal controls and activities could report to the board of directors.

The marketing organization presents the firm's products and services to customers. It develops marketing strategies, advertises, sends out salespersons, obtains customer orders, and may fill those orders. Production is responsible for all manufacturing activities. The chart in Figure 1.3 shows only basic activities: production planning, purchasing, receiving and moving materials, and production itself. Personnel activities include all hiring, training, and evaluating activities plus deal with labor unions and develop personnel policies.

The positions of controller and treasurer are shown separately. These might be combined into the position of Chief Financial Officer (CFO). The **treasurer** is responsible for granting credit, collecting and disbursing money, and obtaining credit and long-term funds. **Controller** responsibilities include the duties shown in Figure 1.3. Historically, data processing originated in the controller's area. Now, many companies have a vice-president position responsible for management information systems activities.

## SERVICE ORGANIZATIONS

While the manufacturing sector is an important segment of the economy, service organizations account for the majority of national income and employment in the United States. This phenomenon is also true in most parts of the world. Therefore, managers must be able to determine the cost of services with the same degree of accuracy as they determine the cost of manufactured products.

Service organizations include accounting firms, auto repair shops, insurance companies, banks, airlines, restaurants, hospitals, grocery stores, police departments, libraries, and many other types of organizations. These organizations provide services to customers rather than just manufacture

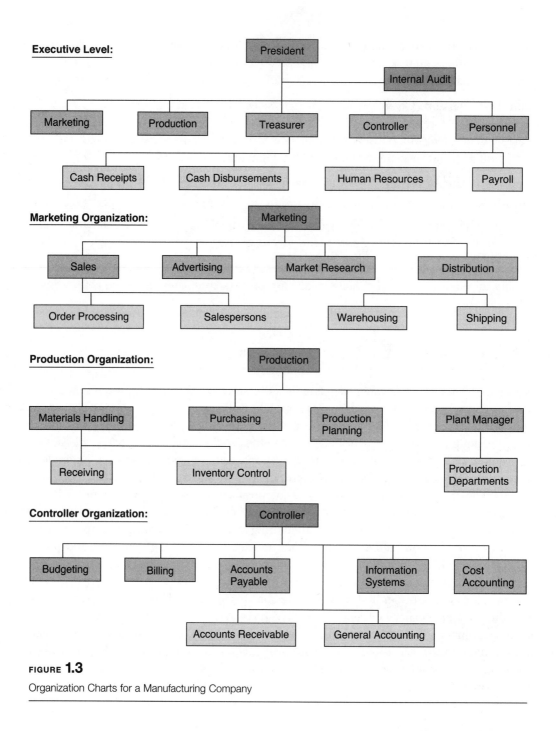

**FIGURE 1.3**

Organization Charts for a Manufacturing Company

products. Some, like restaurants, produce products (e.g., meals) as well as provide services. Others, like grocery stores, sell products which they have purchased rather than manufactured.

## Characteristics of Service Organizations

**Tangible vs. intangible.** We can distinguish between manufacturing and service organizations in several ways. Perhaps the main difference relates to the types of cost object. A cost object is merely the item for which we are trying to determine the cost. A manufacturer puts out a tangible product, while a service organization's "product" is often intangible. We cannot put our hands on an airline flight or insurance coverage. Moreover, service organizations' cost objects are often not easily definable, particularly in nonprofit settings. For instance, a police department offers services dealing with crime prevention and other safety matters. How do we define its output? Should it be the number of cases investigated? Number of criminals apprehended? There is no clear cost object here, so it will be determined by a manager's subjective judgment.

**Customer presence.** Another distinction of a service organization is that the customer is often present when the service is being preformed. In contrast, customers rarely view the processing of manufactured products. A customer is present when a haircut is done, when working out in a health club, and when seeing a theater performance.

**Simultaneous production and consumption.** Related to customer presence is the notion that production and consumption of services are often simultaneous. With manufacturing, the product may be used by the customer long after it has been produced. Hence, the manufacturer can produce adequate quality and inspect for quality prior to sale. This is not the case for a telephone company or amusement park, where the consumer is using the service as it is being performed. In these settings, poor quality of output cannot be tossed aside prior to delivery.

**Perishability.** Another distinguishing characteristic is that many services are perishable. A manufactured product can usually remain in the manufacturer's inventory for some time period. If demand is low, the manufacturer can store it until demand picks up. Services, on the other hand, are usually not inventoriable. If a lawyer has no cases to work on during a particular day because of low demand, the passage of time that day cannot be inventoried–it has perished. If a school has empty classroom seats during a particular semester, those seats cannot be inventoried for use in another semester–the opportunity has perished.

**Heterogeneity.** Finally, services are generally less homogeneous than manufactured products. A customer who buys a particular brand of candy bar will probably find that it tastes the same from on week to the next and from one store to another. In contrast, the customer who stays in a particular hotel chain will probably not experience the same service each time at each location. The one in Kansas City may be cleaner than the one in Denver. The one in Philadelphia may have slow elevator service or a problem with the shower during some stays and no problems during other stays.

## Types of Service Organizations

There are many different types of service organizations, and they can be categorized in a number of different ways. Like most categorizations, the following is not mutually exclusive. That is, a firm can provide services in more than one category. The categories are:

**Business services.** These are professional services that are directly related to commerce. Examples include banking, accounting, consulting, insurance, and advertising. These services are primarily for the benefit of business operations.

**Trade services.** These usually involve the provision of goods, as well as services related to the provision of the goods. Some examples are retailing, wholesaling, rental services, and publishing.

**Infrastructure services.** These services provide the means and resources for conducting commerce. Communications, transportation, and utilities are prime examples of these services.

**Social services.** These services benefit communities and are often provided by nonprofit organizations. Examples would include schools, churches, summer camps, and healthcare organizations.

**Recreation services.** These are services that relate to entertainment and pleasure activities. Some examples are sports activities, concerts, movies, and cruises.

**Personal services.** These generally involve providing services to individuals for their use or consumption. Restaurants, hotels, cleaners, and repair shops would be examples of this types of service.

**Public services.** These are services that are usually provided by governmental agencies since they benefit society at large. Examples include fire protection, garbage collection, libraries, courts, museums, and prisons.

# The Dual Roles of Accounting Information

The accounting system generates the information that satisfies two reporting needs that coexist within an organization: financial accounting and managerial accounting. Figure 1.4 shows the primary interested parties and the typical reports generated to serve these two user groups.

## Financial Accounting

**Financial accounting** is the branch of accounting that organizes accounting information for presentation to interested parties outside of the organization. The primary financial accounting reports are the balance sheet (often called a statement of financial position), the income statement, and the statement of cash flows. The balance sheet is a summary of assets, liabilities, and shareholders' equity at a specified point in time. The income statement reports revenues and expenses resulting from the company's operations for a particular time period. The statement of cash flows shows the sources and uses of cash over a time period for operating, investing, and financing activities.

Most businesses are complex, and guidelines (known as generally accepted accounting principles) are provided for financial reporting. The Financial Accounting Standards Board (FASB), the Security and Exchange Commission (SEC), and the Public Company Accounting Oversight Board (PCAOB) oversee the development of these principles, corporate financial reporting responsibilities, and internal control standards. Internationally, while each country has developed its own accounting principles, the International Accounting Standards Board has taken on an increasing important role.

**Owners, Investors, and Creditors**. Shareholder-owned firms rely heavily on owners, investors, and creditors (providers of short-term credit and long-term loans) for sources of capital. Shareholders and investors use accounting reports to decide whether to buy, sell, or hold the firm's stock. Also, creditors assess whether the firm is able to pay its debts on time.

**Taxing Authorities**. The assessment of many taxes is based on accounting information submitted by the taxpayer. Examples of such taxes include income taxes, sales taxes, use taxes, franchise taxes, excise taxes, property taxes, and gift and estate taxes. In most cases, the dominant taxing authority is the federal government and its tax collection agency, the Internal Revenue Service.

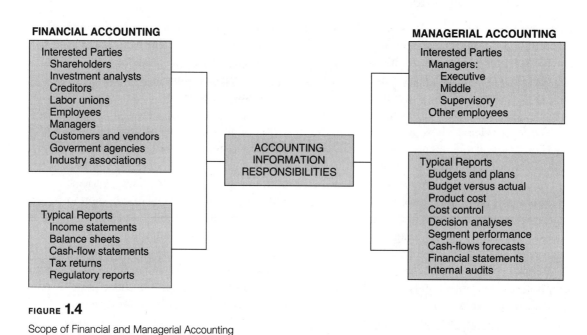

**FINANCIAL ACCOUNTING**

Interested Parties
    Shareholders
    Investment analysts
    Creditors
    Labor unions
    Employees
    Managers
    Customers and vendors
    Goverment agencies
    Industry associations

Typical Reports
    Income statements
    Balance sheets
    Cash-flow statements
    Tax returns
    Regulatory reports

ACCOUNTING INFORMATION RESPONSIBILITIES

**MANAGERIAL ACCOUNTING**

Interested Parties
    Managers:
        Executive
        Middle
        Supervisory
    Other employees

Typical Reports
    Budgets and plans
    Budget versus actual
    Product cost
    Cost control
    Decision analyses
    Segment performance
    Cash-flows forecasts
    Financial statements
    Internal audits

**FIGURE 1.4**

Scope of Financial and Managerial Accounting

**Regulatory Agencies**. Local, state, and federal agencies regulate a substantial portion of business activity in the United States. Much regulation is implemented through or involves accounting reports.

**Industry Associations**. Most industries have an association that gathers important statistics about the national and international industry. A large part of the information they provide comes from accounting reports provided by member firms.

**Managers and Employees**. Managers have direct vested interests in their firms' results. Performance bonuses, stock options, and incentive compensation programs are common. Thus, managers are not passive observers as to how certain transactions are recorded. Firm policies, performance evaluation methods, and compensation systems should encourage managers to act in the best interests of themselves and the firm as a whole.

The firm's executives are responsible to the board of directors and shareholders for the firm's financial results. Numerous examples of changes in high-level executive positions reaffirm the importance of achieving strong profits to remain in power and employed. Based in part on financial statement information, employees make decisions about continued employment, union wage demands and contract negotiations, adequacy of pension plans, and employee stock purchase or savings plans. Profit sharing may encourage employees to want the company to be financially successful.

## Managerial Accounting

**Managerial accounting** is the branch of accounting that meets managers' information needs. Because managerial accounting is designed to assist the firm's managers, relatively few restrictions are imposed by regulatory bodies and generally accepted accounting principles. Therefore, a manager must define which data are relevant for a particular purpose and which are not.

## Differences between Managerial and Financial Accounting

Several important differences distinguish managerial accounting from financial accounting. First, managerial accounting is not subject to the same rules and principles as is financial accounting. In many cases, "common sense" is the most important guide for decision makers.

A second difference is that financial accounting relies on accounting principles structured around the accounting equation. Management reports, on the other hand, are designed to meet managers' needs. These reports often use estimates and forecasts, use different values for the same events, do not balance in a debit/credit sense, and are designed for particular decisions or analyses. The expression *different costs for different purposes* has long been used to describe relevance. Relevant information has an impact on the decision analysis. Irrelevant data have no impact.

Another difference is that managerial accounting focuses on segments of the organization as well as on the whole organization. The primary interest of financial accounting is the company as a whole. In managerial accounting, however, the segment is of major importance. Segments may be products, projects, divisions, plants, branches, regions, or any other subset of the business. Tracing or allocating costs, revenues, and assets to segments creates difficult issues for managerial accountants.

Two important similarities do exist. The transaction and accounting information systems discussed earlier are used to generate the data inputs for both financial statements and management reports. Therefore, when the system accumulates and classifies information, it should do so in formats that accommodate both types of accounting. The other similarity is the manner in which accountants measure costs, define assets, and specify accounting periods. Many concepts underlie accounting information, whether the data are later used for financial or managerial reporting. Recording the results of events is often based on rationales that are common to both financial and managerial accounting. We must understand what is a common thread and what must be independently collected.

# ROLE OF THE MANAGEMENT ACCOUNTANT

Although the top accounting-oriented people in an organization are the chief financial officer and the controller, the accounting and financial management functions contain a range of jobs. A variety of careers are available as shown in Figure 1.5; these careers can frequently be paths to executive management.

## Management Accountant

A **management accountant** maintains accounting records, prepares financial statements, generates managerial reports and analyses, and coordinates budgeting efforts. The management accountant is an advisor, an internal consultant, and an integral part of management. The controller, as shown in Figure 1.3, is responsible for managing the entire accounting function. The controller influences management when answering questions like: What information should be reported? What format best displays the information? How can data be collected and processed? By the nature of the job, the management accountant applies management principles and often is a major player in decision making itself.

## Certified Management Accountant

The Certified Management Accounting program recognizes a person's achievement of a specific level of knowledge and professional skill. Becoming a **Certified Management Accountant (CMA)** is considered an important professional step for anyone desiring to become a management accounting or financial executive. The CMA program was founded on the principle that a management accountant is a contributor to and a participant in management.

To qualify for the CMA designation, candidates must pass a comprehensive examination and meet specific educational and professional standards. To remain a CMA, a person must meet continuing educational requirements and adhere to the program's "Standards of Ethical Conduct." The Institute of Management Accountants (IMA) is the professional organization of management accountants and sponsors the CMA designation.

| | |
|---|---|
| Accounting systems analyst | Internal auditor |
| Bid cost estimator | International controller |
| Budget performance analyst | Labor negotiations cost analyst |
| Capital investment analyst | Master budget coordinator |
| Cash disbursements manager | Payroll accountant |
| Cash flow analyst | Physical asset accountant |
| Cash receipts manager | Plant controller |
| Computer controls auditor | Product cost/profit analyst |
| Corporate financial accountant | Project controller |
| Corporate tax planner | Risk management analyst |
| Cost accountant | Quality cost analyst |
| Cost forecasting analyst | Statistical cost analyst |
| Customer or sales analyst | Strategic planner |
| Efficiency cost analyst | Transfer pricing analyst |

**FIGURE 1.5**

Management Accounting Job Titles

## Ethical Conduct of Management Accountants

In the preceding pages, we discussed managers' needs for accounting information. We assumed that whatever information the accounting system generates is presented and used in an ethical manner. Ethical conduct is a necessary asset of a managerial accountant. The credibility of the information provided, analyses done, and opinions offered depends heavily on the reputation of the responsible accountant. Independence, competence, lack of bias or favoritism, trust, and objectivity are key elements in establishing credibility.

While true for all managers, management accountants in particular must maintain integrity and ethical behavior and must make top management aware of unethical behavior on the part of others within the organization. This does not mean the management accountant is a police officer. Rather, the management accountant promotes and encourages ethical behavior in all aspects of business life.

Ethical standards of businesspersons have been given much more visibility and scrutiny in recent years. Issues which appear again and again in management careers test the ethical standards of everyone. Among common ethical issues are:

- **Business practices and policies.** Practices that seem harmless on the surface may encourage or require employees or managers to be deceitful or dishonest.

- **Objective reporting.** Because situations exist where prejudiced reporting of certain numbers may influence decisions, accountants are guided by goals of unbiased reporting and professional judgment.

- **Colleague behavior.** Even if we have high ethical standards, people around us may not be so blessed. Many policies and internal controls are in place in organizations to prevent wrong doing and to encourage proper behavior. But, your personal integrity should not condone unethical behavior in others.

- **Competitors.** Winning is part of the business "game." But to do so in a fair environment is critical. Using true product and competitor data, following corporate policies, and abhorring bribes, kickbacks, and other similar payments are easy examples. Many firms provide behavior guidelines and policies to purchasing and sales personnel who are at special risk in giving and receiving favors and improper inducements.

- **Tax avoidance and evasion.** Tax burdens can be significant. Proper planning and careful use of tax laws to minimize the organization's tax liability are acceptable. Tax avoidance is legitimate. Inappropriate use of the same laws or use of deceit to hide income or overstate deductions is tax evasion, which is unethical as well as illegal.

- **Confidentiality.** Keeping secrets is still "in." Internal data are developed for managers' use. Disclosures outside the firm often require review and approvals. Privacy of competitive, personnel, and negotiating data is critical. Negative examples of overheard conversations in elevators, on golf courses, and at lunches that lead to lost business, embarrassment, and law suits are unfortunately common. Confidentiality also asserts that "insider" information should not be used for anyone's personal advantage.

- **Appearance of independence.** The accountant should be independent in situations where the resulting information is used for analysis and decision making. Independence applies to both real independence and the appearance of independence. If it appears that the management accountant is biased because of that person's conduct, associations, or vested interests (possible promotion, salary increases or bonuses, or investments), the information provided is tainted and open to doubt by other decision makers.

- **Corporate loyalty and personal advancement.** Many situations exist where, because of an unethical act, the reputation of the firm itself is in danger. Or an unethical act may ensure your personal enhancement in some manner. Also, to report an unethical act may endanger the

## Contemporary Practice 1.2
### *Corporate Greed vs. an Ethics Code*

*The names are infamous: WorldCom, Adelphia, Enron, Tyco, Arthur Andersen, and Martha Stewart, among numerous others. All have suffered unethical behavior at very high levels. The "bad deeds" of managers, auditors, accountants, CEOs, and CFOs in these firms result from simple inappropriate "favors" to outright theft, lies, deceit, and intentional deception. The basic integrity of business itself rests on individual honesty, professional competence, proper accounting, and acceptance of a code of ethical conduct. Codes of ethical conduct cannot prevent unethical behavior, but hindsight definitely points to fundamental violations of the management accountant's code of ethics. The code of ethics presented in Figure 1.6 should set a high standard for managerial reporting and use by both managerial accountants and executives.*

Source: Haywood, Elizabeth M., and Donald E. Wygal, "Corporate Greed vs. IMA's Ethics Code," Strategic Finance, November 2004, pp. 45–49.

future of the person reporting the act. These are all difficult dilemmas pitting right against wrong but not always in an obvious way.

While space and time do not allow us to develop approaches for resolving these problems here, it is clear that ethical issues underlie management accountants' professional and day-to-day activities. Each chapter will raise and discuss ethical issues related to those special topics.

Each person must develop a method of handling ethical problems. Of primary importance is the ability to see an ethical dilemma when it faces us. Once identified, the situation may well cause us to request advice. Numerous sources are available for guidance including:

- **Our own personal values.** We would like to think that our own value system is "ethical" and provides enough guidance. Clearly, this is our main line of defense against "wrong."

- **Corporate policies and ethics statements.** Many firms have statements on expected employee behavior or written policies and procedures on how a range of situations should be handled. These statements do set limits or barriers and may describe expected levels of behavior.

- **Laws.** "If it's legal, it must be okay" is often used a basis for defining ethical behavior. This is absolutely not true. Laws are man-made in a political process, often without much serious consideration for the ethical conduct of any parties involved. But at least if it's illegal, the behavior is very probably unethical.

- **Professional standards.** Most professions have developed a statement of ethical standards for their members. Figure 1.6 presents a statement developed for management accountants. These statements are basic standards of behavior and give professional guidance in many areas.

- **Supervisors, internal auditors, and other company officials.** These are often persons with more experience and broader understanding of conflicting issues and of corporate attitudes. An ethical situation, however, may involve a supervisor or other corporate official, which may make the dilemma much more sensitive and severe. A few companies have created an ombudsperson position to assist employees in handling delicate situations.

- **Counselors from outside of the organization.** This is a last resort and generally violates another ethical consideration–confidentiality. While close friends, a spouse, or a personal counselor may seem like logical sources of advice and support, the nature of the dilemma may well require confidentiality until all other avenues of resolution are exhausted. Merely consulting outsiders presents serious risks of unauthorized disclosure which may only further complicate an issue.

Even though all of these options may exist, we each need to develop a rational approach to identifying, analyzing, and deciding on ethical issues that confront us. Management accountants must be aware of ethical dilemmas, perhaps more than the typical manager, because of their responsibility for decision-making information and their involvement in many decision-making processes.

The Institute of Management Accountants believes ethics is a cornerstone of its organization and recognizes the importance of providing ethical guidance. The IMA has developed *Standards for Ethical Conduct for Management Accounting and Financial Management*. That statement is presented in Figure 1.6. The Standards are broken into four sections: competence, confidentiality, integrity, and objectivity. Competence refers to the skills that the accountant brings to the job. Confidentiality

## Members have a responsibility to:

**Competence**

- Maintain an appropriate level of professional competence by ongoing development of their knowledge and skills.

- Perform their professional duties in accordance with laws, regulations, and technical standards.

- Prepare complete and clear reports and recommendations after appropriate analyses of relevant and reliable information.

**Confidentiality**

- Refrain from disclosing confidential information acquired in the course of their work, except when authorized, unless legally obligated to do so.

- Inform subordinates as appropriate regarding the confidentiality of information acquired in the course of their work and monitor their activities to assure the maintenance of that confidentiality.

- Refrain from using or appearing to use confidential information acquired in the course of their work for unethical or illegal advantage either personally or through third parties.

**Integrity**

- Avoid actual or apparent conflicts of interest and advise all appropriate parties of any potential conflict.

- Refrain from engaging in any activity that would prejudice their ability to carry out their duties ethically.

- Refuse any gift, favor, or hospitality that would influence or would appear to influence their actions.

- Refrain from either actively or passively subverting the attainment of the organization's legitimate and ethical objectives.

- Recognize and communicate professional limitations or other constraints that would preclude responsible judgment or successful performance of an activity.

- Communicate unfavorable as well as favorable information and professional judgments or opinions.

- Refrain from engaging in or supporting any activity that would discredit the profession.

**Objectivity**

- Communicate information fairly and objectively.

- Disclose fully all relevant information that could reasonably be expected to influence an intended user's understanding of the reports, comments, and recommendations presented.

**Source:** *"Standards of Ethical Conduct for Practitioners of Management Accounting and Financial Management, Statement 1C"*, Institute of Management Accountants, Montvale, N.J., April 30, 1997.

**FIGURE 1.6**

Institute of Management Accountants' Standards of Ethical Conduct

defines protecting the access and use of information. Integrity focuses primarily on the personal behavior and interactions of the management accountant. Objectivity as defined here is primarily directed toward disclosure of unbiased information.

## SUMMARY

Managers in all types of organizations need accounting information to aid them in making decisions as efficiently and effectively as possible. Managerial uses of accounting information include forecasting and planning, performance evaluation, cost determination and management, pricing, operations control, incremental decision making, financial reporting, and motivation of managers. All managerial decision making should be made with the mission and the strategic goals of the firm in mind. Frequently, the main goal is profit making. In all cases, a defined and structured decision-making process should be followed.

An organization's structure often can be presented on a chart. The structure of an organization determines responsibility and reporting relationships. The controller is the executive responsible for accounting information, budgets, information systems, cost accounting, accounts payable and receivable, and general accounting.

Accounting information is provided from a system that handles the requirements of two branches of accounting: financial accounting and managerial accounting. Financial accounting presents accounting information to parties outside the organization. Managerial accounting organizes accounting information for internal management. Internal reporting is generally directed to the decision areas mentioned earlier.

The ethical conduct and integrity of the management accountant are critical to the success of the accountant's mission. Ethical situations are common and often complex. Management accountants have a special responsibility to their management colleagues and to themselves to uphold high ethical standards.

## TERMINOLOGY REVIEW

Benchmarking (10)

Cash disbursements system (x)

Cash receipts system (x)

Certified Management Accountant (CMA) (16)

Computer-aided design (CAD) (9)

Computer-aided manufacturing (CAM) (9)

Computer-integrated manufacturing (CIM) (9)

Continuous improvement (4)

Controller (11)

Cost determination (4)

Cost management (4)

Cost object (x)

Costs of quality (9)

Decision objective (10)

Decision rule (10)

Downsizing (10)

Enterprise resource planning (ERP) systems (10)

Financial accounting (14)

Flexible manufacturing (9)

Focused production (9)

General accounting system (x)

Globalization (8)

Just-in-time (JIT) (9)

Management accountant (16)

Management information systems (9)

Managerial accounting (15)

Motivation of managers (x)

Nonvalue-added activities (8)

Order entry system (x)

Performance evaluation (x)

Personnel system (x)

Pricing (4)

Production planning and control system (x)

Purchases systems (x)

Quality assurance (x)

Treasurer (11)

Value added (8)

Value chain (8)

World-class manufacturing (8)

## QUESTIONS FOR REVIEW AND DISCUSSION

1. Explain how forecasting and planning are related to performance evaluation.

2. Identify the major managerial decision areas. What is the main purpose of each?

3. Review the vignette at the beginning of the chapter. Review Sarah Baker's schedule and additional action items. Into which managerial decision area does each item fall?

4. Distinguish between cost determination and cost management.

5. Compare and contrast the characteristics of accounting information needed by top management with accounting information used by lower management.

6. For each transaction system discussed, which of the data files discussed would be used?

7. What is the difference between "value chain" and "value added?" What is a "nonvalue-added activity?"

8. What are TQM, CIM, and JIT? How are they related?

9. What is meant by "world-class manufacturing?"

10. What are the difference among focused production, flexible manufacturing, and computer-integrated manufacturing?

11. What objectives, other than profit, might be important to managers in an organization?

12. Identify the eight steps in the decision-making process. Which steps are primarily information handling activities? Describe the activities.

13. Making the decision may actually be the easiest part of the process. Which part of the decision-making process is the most expensive? Most time consuming? Most difficult analytical process?

14. What groups (both inside and outside an organization) have an interest in financial statements issued by the organization? Give reasons for each group's interest.

15. Briefly describe three ways in which financial accounting and managerial accounting are different. Name two ways in which they are the same or similar.

16. What major activities report to the controller? To the treasurer?

17. Referring to the major transaction systems and the organization chart presented in the chapter, who is probably responsible for each transaction system?

18. How do service organizations differ from manufacturing organizations?

19. Provide one example for each of the following: business services, trade services, infrastructure services, social services, recreation services, personal services, and public services.

20. A management accountant is both an information provider and a part of management. Explain.

21. Carlos Garcia, president of Garcia Food Processors, stated: "The controller in our organization frequently has more influence over the lower-level managers than our upper-level people have. This seems to also be the case with most of our clients." Why would he say this? Do you agree or disagree with the assessment of the president? Explain.

22. Briefly describe the management accountant's responsibility for ethical behavior with respect to competence, confidentiality, integrity, and objectivity.

23. What is the payoff for an organization to have a code of ethics that employees will follow?

24. What are sources of counsel and guidance on ethical dilemmas available to a manager?

25. Give examples of an ethical dilemma that would arise from objective reporting, colleague behavior, confidentiality, tax evasion, and personal advancement.

**26.** Identify the major transactions systems that generate most of the data used in organizations. What is the main purpose of each of these systems?

**27.** What are the major data files that exist in most organizations? What data elements would you expect to find in these files?

**28.** Which of the following areas of decision making is most important? (If management did not do this, the company would be out of business.) Explain.
  **(a)** Forecasting and planning
  **(b)** Performance evaluation
  **(c)** Cost management, pricing, and cost determination
  **(d)** Operations control and improvement
  **(e)** Financial reporting
  **(f)** Motivation of managers

# EXERCISES

**1–1.** **Ethical Dilemma.** You are on your way to lunch and the elevator is packed. Two persons from a firm that competes with your employer happen to be talking about a business deal which involves one of your customers. Your computer-like mind lists your alternatives: plug your ears, tell them that you are with a competitor, listen and then delete the information from your brain, immediately go back to the office and act on the new information, or call their supervisor and report the conversation you just overheard. What should you do?

**1–2.** **Downsizing.** You have been involved in high-level discussions about downsizing. Certain departments will be eliminated. Your best friend is in one of these departments. Should you try to change the downsizing plan to save your friend's job? Should you mention to your friend that a transfer to another department would be wise? Should you tell your friend not to buy a house that he and his wife are considering?

**1–3.** **Ethical Conduct.** Comment on the following frequently heard statements about ethical conduct:
  **(a)** "You can't teach ethics. If people don't know right from wrong by now, they'll never learn."
  **(b)** "It's legal. My attorney says so. Therefore, it's okay."
  **(c)** "Are you trying to impose your values on me?"
  **(d)** "I believe in situational ethics. What's right or wrong depends on the situation."
  **(e)** "I can't be ethical all the time. My competitors would eat me alive!"
  **(f)** "Everyone does it."

**1–4.** **Ethical Analysis.** You have purchased, using company funds, the latest version of SuperSpreadSheet for your work station in your office. Comment on the following situations.
  **(a)** Stan, a friend in another department, is thinking of buying the same product and wants to try yours for several days.
  **(b)** You would like to use the same spreadsheet on your home computer to handle your household budget records.
  **(c)** Mary, your boss, asks for a copy of the diskettes for use on her machine.

# COST CONCEPTS

## LEARNING OBJECTIVES

After studying Chapter 2, you will be able to:

1. Define, distinguish, and illustrate key cost concepts.
2. Understand the differences in cost flows among service, merchandising, and manufacturing enterprises.
3. Explain product cost elements.
4. Describe and formulate a cost function.
5. Distinguish between the behavior of variable and fixed costs.
6. Differentiate among incremental vs. average, planning vs. actual, relevant vs. irrelevant, and controllability cost terms.
7. Introduce the concept of contribution margin and its variations.

## What's It Cost?

*Professor Jacobs enters the classroom a few minutes before the start of the first class of Accounting 202, Principles of Management Accounting. He looks around the room, sees about 40 students, and wonders how this class will evolve. He moves to the front of the room, takes his notes and text from his briefcase, faces the class, and says, "Hi! What does it cost you to take this course?" He pauses and looks for reactions on the faces of the students. He points to the first hand to go up.*

*The volunteer is Karen who says, "Let's see. Tuition is $350 a credit. This is a 3 credit course; so that's about a $1,000."*

*Another person, Sidney, says, "Hey, you forgot this textbook, plus the course packet. That's almost 100 bucks, even for a used book. And, I had to buy a calculator; I lost my other one."*

*Mike, getting a few winks, never heard the question, was jarred awake from of the noise, and asks the woman next to him, "What'd he say?" Professor Jacobs notices Mike's lost look and compliments him on his arrival on the scene. He asks Mike for a cost estimate. Mike replies without much thought, "A lot, probably $5,000."*

*By now, several more hands are up. Randy says, "Being here means I have to eat and sleep. That runs $2,500 a semester in the dorm."*

*Randy's friend reminds him, "You forgot the financial aid package you got. That reduces your out-of-pocket cost by a bunch."*

*Another student, Barb, says, "I quit a good job to come back to school. I was making about 300 a week. Now, I'm getting only 50 a week from my part-time job." But Mike, now aroused, tells Barb, "Yea, but you can't blame all that on Professor Jacobs' class. You're taking four or five courses, aren't you? Average it over all of them."*

*Professor Jacobs asks for any other thoughts. Kim responds, "I've got to have a social life! That costs money–maybe $20 a week. Oh, then there's clothes. Wow, I mean that really costs money–hundreds of dollars every couple of months. I forgot the ordinary stuff like my hair, toothpaste, dues for clubs, and things like that–probably another $100 a month on average."*

*Professor Jacobs smiles and says, "Well, we're off to a great start. These costs are relevant for specific decisions we all make. But, which ones for which decision? Looks like it'll take us the rest of the semester to sort this out."*

*Mike groans, "Looks like sleep in this class is out of the question for a while."*

UNDERSTANDING COST BEHAVIOR and knowing which costs to consider and which to ignore are critical to making business decisions but also in everyday life situations. This chapter explains the terminology needed to analyze these decisions. Most analyses require only basic common sense. Assemble the relevant facts, and make a rational decision. Even when we know the relevant quantitative facts, qualitative and strategic factors may cause us to select an alternative that is economically less attractive on the surface but might help us to achieve other goals.

Managers use cost information in many different ways. Cost data are especially important in these areas:

- **Planning.** Estimating future costs in preparing budgets and in projecting operating activities.
- **Decision making.** Selecting and formatting costs relevant to a wide variety of decision-making processes.

- **Cost control.** Measuring costs incurred; comparing these costs with budgets, goals, targets, or standards; and evaluating differences or variances.
- **Income measurement.** Determining the costs of products and services sold to determine this time period's profitability for the entire business or some segment of the business, such as a contract, a product, or a customer.

## THE NATURE OF COST

**Cost**, broadly defined, is the amount of resource given up to gain a specific objective or object. Generally, cost refers to the monetary measurement (exchange price) attached to acquiring goods and services consumed by some activity. Cash outlays are monetary measurements; but occasionally, goods and services are also obtained by exchanging other assets, such as receivables or property, or by taking on debt.

The **cost objective** is defined as any purpose for accumulating costs. A cost objective is the reason for making decisions, costing products, planning spending levels, or evaluating actual performances. It is the "why" of cost analysis.

Businesspersons undertake activities to achieve some output or result. Often these activities incur costs–purchasing materials, hiring people, and renting space–and are known as **cost drivers**. To achieve a cost objective, activities occur and resources are used. And resources cost money. Determining a product's cost means finding the cause-and-effect connection between inputs and outputs. A cost driver links activities that create outputs and resources that are used.

Figure 2.1 presents the fundamental relationship among resources, activities, and products. Activities are at the core of all we do in business. Activities drive the use of resources; and, from the activities, come products. This is the traditional input to output cycle, understanding that work is done in the middle box–meaning tasks are performed with labor, machines, or hired resources. Costs are incurred by cost drivers and are attached to the products, given whatever cost objective managers have in mind for particular decision. These linkages will be used over and over as we progress through our costing analyses to aid decision making–particularly in Chapter 6.

Cost, in many respects, is an elusive term. It is a noun that needs an adjective, such as incremental, average, or avoidable. Cost has meaning only for a particular purpose and situation. Consequently, meaningful use of the term "cost" requires an adjective to define its use. Each adjective indicates certain attributes, and those attributes dictate the relevance of each cost.

Since costs are resources given up to obtain a specific good or service, that good or service may be consumed; or it may still be an asset at the end of an accounting period. In many managerial analyses, the distinction among cost, expense, and asset is clouded. The words *cost* and *expense* are used interchangeably, as is done throughout this text. Yet for profit measurement, cost dollars imply assets; and expenses are subtracted from revenues.

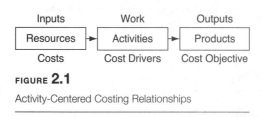

**FIGURE 2.1**

Activity-Centered Costing Relationships

# COMPARING SERVICE, MERCHANDISING, AND MANUFACTURING ORGANIZATIONS

Many similarities exist when we compare service, merchandising, and manufacturing organizations. Providing a service to a client in a law firm or repairing a washing machine in a fix-it shop has strong similarities to manufacturing calculators in spite of different physical and business settings. In service industries, resources are brought together to provide the service, just as they are brought together to create a product in a factory environment.

Differences in measuring profits are largely a function of inventoried costs. Service firms have only supplies inventories. Merchandising firms buy and sell products and hold merchandise inventories. Manufacturing firms buy materials and convert these inputs into saleable products. Inventories here include yet-to-be-used materials, work in process inventory (partially complete products), and finished goods inventory (completed and ready-to-sell products). Figure 2.2 compares income statements and selected balance sheet accounts for the three business types.

| **Income Statements For the Year** | | | |
|---|---|---|---|
| | Service Firms | Merchandising Firms | Manufacturing Firms |
| | Szott Consultants | Rodriguez Supermarket | Audretsch Products |
| Sales | $8,000,000 | $8,000,000 | $8,000,000 |
| Cost of goods sold: | | | |
|   Cost of goods manufactured: | | | |
|   Purchases of direct materials | | | $2,300,000 |
|   +Beginning direct materials inventory | | | 360,000 |
|   −Ending direct materials inventory | | | (310,000) |
|   Materials used | | | $2,350,000 |
|   +Direct labor | | | 920,000 |
|   +Manufacturing overhead | | | 2,300,000 |
|   Total manufacturing costs | | | $5,570,000 |
|   +Beginning work in process | | | 320,000 |
|   −Ending work in processm | | | (340,000) |
| Cost of goods manufactured | | | $5,550,000 |
| Purchases | | $7,000,000 | |
|   +Beginning finished goods inventory | | 510,000 | 600,000 |
|   −Ending finished goods inventory | | (480,000) | (620,000) |
|   Cost of goods sold | | $7,030,000 | $5,530,000 |
|   Direct client expenses | 5,800,000 | | |
| Gross margin | $2,200,000 | $970,000 | $2,470,000 |
| Operating expenses: | | | |
|   Selling expenses | $610,000 | $550,000 | $980,000 |
|   Administrative expenses | 1,270,000 | 260,000 | 1,030,000 |
|   Total operating expenses | $1,880,000 | $810,000 | $2,010,000 |
| Net operating income | $320,000 | $260,000 | $460,000 |
| **Selected Balance Sheet Information For Yearend** | | | |
| Accounts receivable | $1,350,000 | $80,000 | $1,020,000 |
| Materials inventory | | | 310,000 |
| Work in process inventory | | | 340,000 |
| Finished goods inventory | | 480,000 | 620,000 |
| Accounts payable | 220,000 | 110,000 | 460,000 |

**FIGURE 2.2**

Measuring Income in Service, Merchandising, and Manufacturing Firms

## Service Organizations

A service business performs an activity for a fee. Costs of performing the service may include salaries of professionals and support personnel, supplies, purchased services, and routine costs such as rent and utilities. In Figure 2.2, the expenses of Szott Consultants, a public relations firm, are reported as either direct client expenses or operating expenses. Some service organizations report all expenses as operating expenses.

Essentially, all operating costs incurred by the firm are **period costs**; they become expenses of the time period in which the costs are incurred. Only receivables, payables, supplies, depreciation, and perhaps costs not yet billed to clients would cause accrual net income to differ from operating cash flow.

In a service organization, the problems of measuring performance, such as the profitability of specific contracts, and matching direct costs with specific revenues are surprisingly similar to manufacturing cost analyses.

Internally, financial reports for service firms often separate revenues and expenses by type of service or customer. For example, hospitals track revenues by procedure type and attempt to measure costs of those procedures. Professional firms, such as accountants, lawyers, and architects, measure the direct costs of performing services by client. Lawyers record time spent on each case, both for billing purposes and for tracing salary costs. In Figure 2.2, Szott Consultants apparently serves multiple clients and can identify professional time, service costs, and other traceable costs with specific client contracts.

## Merchandising Organizations

A merchandising business purchases products for resale. Generally, a merchandising firm is a link in the physical distribution chain, acting as a wholesaler or retailer. Figure 2.2 introduces cost of goods sold to the income statement of Rodriguez Supermarket, a retail grocery store. Again, supporting the reported totals would be detailed revenues and costs of sales for various segments such as produce, hardware, meat, and grocery departments.

Merchandise costs are inventoriable or **product costs**, meaning that they are an asset until sold. All other expenses in the supermarket operation are treated as **period costs**.

## Manufacturing Organizations

Manufacturing generally occurs in a factory, defined as a place where resources are brought together to produce a product. Examples include:

Soft-drink bottling company–mixing batches and filling bottles of red pop
University dorm cafeteria–preparing and serving "gourmet" food
Print shop–printing a variety of requests from customers
Breakfast cereal manufacturer–processing grains into "grrrrreat" cereal
Automotive assembly plant–joining parts and subassemblies to create a minivan

But, after some thought, you can see how many service firms really do "produce" the service using our definition of a factory.

Telephone company–processing local, long-distance, and information calls
Pharmacy–filling prescriptions
Tax return preparation firm–preparing tax returns
Hospital surgery department–performing heart by-pass operations

As Figure 2.2 illustrates, manufacturing firms have more complexity in determining cost of goods sold. A new income statement section, **cost of goods manufactured**, is introduced. It includes:

- the costs of inputs to the manufacturing process: direct materials, direct labor, and manufacturing overhead and
- direct materials inventory and work in process inventory needed for factory activities.

The sum of the product inputs is **total manufacturing costs**, the total cost of resources used in production during a time period.

Figure 2.3 compares a factory to a large bucket. When the whistle blows to start the production period, the bucket already has resources in it–beginning work in process inventory. During the period, more resources are poured into the bucket–total manufacturing costs (materials used, direct labor, and factory overhead). Flowing out of the bucket are all products that are finished during the period and either sold or added to finished goods inventory. This is cost of goods manufactured. When the whistle blows to end the period, ending work in process inventory remains in the bucket.

Figure 2.4 illustrates a flow of costs through the T-accounts of Audretsch Products. To calculate the cost of goods manufactured, it is important to understand how costs are accumulated. Flows of physical resources and their costs are parallel and end in finished goods inventory with their costs attached.

| **Transaction** | **Events** |
|---|---|
| (a) | Purchase $2,300,000 of production materials. |
| (b) | Issue $2,350,000 of materials to production–work in process. |
| (c) | Pay $920,000 to production workers, including most employee benefits. |
| (d) | Add cost of production workers to work in process. |
| (e) | Pay $2,300,000 for all other production costs, such as utilities, supervision salaries, and supplies. |
| (f) | Add all other production costs to work in process. |
| (g) | Complete and transfer products costing $5,350,000 to finished goods inventory. |
| (h) | Sell products costing $5,380,000 to customers for $8,000,000. |

Certain account balances from Figure 2.2 are included.

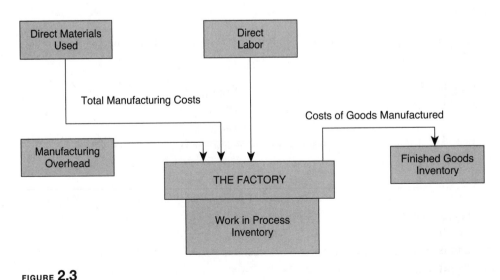

**FIGURE 2.3**

The Factory as a "Bucket" of Costs

| Accounts Payable | | | Direct Materials Inventory | | | | Work in Process Inventory | | | |
|---|---|---|---|---|---|---|---|---|---|---|
| | | — | 1/1 | 360,000 | | | 1/1 | 320,000 | | |
| — | (a) | 2,300,000 | (a) | 2,300,000 | (b) | 2,350,000 | (b) | 2,350,000 | | |
| | 12/31 | 460,000 | 12/31 | 310,000 | | | (d) | 920,000 | (g) | 5,550,000 |
| | | | | | | | (f) | 2,300,000 | | |
| | | | | | | | 12/31 | 340,000 | | |

| Cash, Accrued Payables, & All Other Accounts | | | Payroll | | | | Finished Goods Inventory | | | |
|---|---|---|---|---|---|---|---|---|---|---|
| — | | — | (c) | 920,000 | (d) | 920,000 | 1/1 | 600,000 | | |
| — | (c) | 920,000 | | | | | (g) | 5,550,000 | (h) | 5,530,000 |
| | (e) | 2,300,000 | | | | | 12/31 | 620,000 | | |

| | | | Factory Overhead | | | | Cost of Goods Sold | | |
|---|---|---|---|---|---|---|---|---|---|
| | | | (e) | 2,300,000 | (f) | 2,300,000 | (h) | 5,530,000 | |

| Accounts Receivable | | | | | | | Sales | | |
|---|---|---|---|---|---|---|---|---|---|
| | | — | | | | | | (h) | 8,000,000 |
| (h) | 8,000,000 | — | | | | | | | |
| 12/31 | 1,020,000 | | | | | | | | |

**FIGURE 2.4**

Manufacturing Cost Flows Through T-Accounts For Audretsch Products

---

We use T-accounts in many situations throughout the text to illustrate the flows of costs through a firm's accounts. It is a convenient learning approach to visualize the flows of physical resources through various processes and the flows of costs and revenues through the accounting system.

Figure 2.5 illustrates a simplified version of the Audretsch Products factory. Here resources are brought together for producing aircraft components. An assembly line in the factory is the focus of "manufacturing" activities.

Materials (primarily parts and components) are purchased for production, and factory employees work to convert parts into finished products. Many support services are used; and expenses are incurred for materials handlers, equipment maintenance people, heat, power, employee benefits, factory accountants, supervisors, and depreciation on equipment and the building.

In Figure 2.5, the business is divided into office and factory areas. Obviously, this example is simplified and avoids many business complexities. But, it shows:

- **Product and period costs.** In general, any expense incurred in the office area is an operating expense and a period cost. Any cost incurred in the factory is a manufacturing cost, an inventoriable cost, and a product cost. All other costs are period costs or expenses.

- **Location of inventories.** Manufacturing requires three production inventories–materials, work in process, and finished products. Materials purchases are received and stored in the materials warehouse, and their costs recorded in **Materials Inventory**. When materials are requisitioned for use on the factory floor, direct materials costs are transferred to **Work in Process Inventory**. This is production that is started but not completed. Completed products are physically sent to the finished goods warehouse; and their work in process costs are moved to **Finished Goods Inventory**. These products are ready for sale to customers. And when a sale occurs and is shipped, finished goods product costs are moved to **Cost of Goods Sold**, an expense account.

- **Flow of costs and products.** Figure 2.5 assumes an assembly process, but many different production systems exist. Materials are added, workers process, and other activities support; a physical flow and a cost flow coexist.

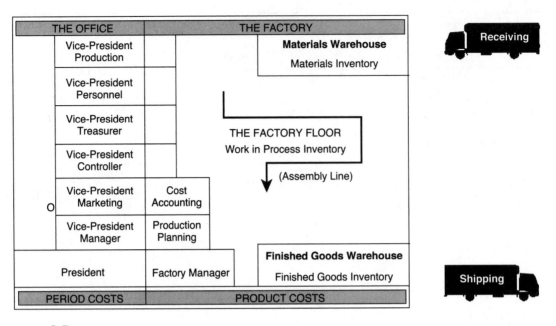

**FIGURE 2.5**

The Audretsch Products Factory

## Traditional Groupings of Product Costs

Figure 2.2 illustrates the income measurement for Audretsch Products. Product cost accounting combines three groups of manufacturing costs–direct materials, direct labor, and factory overhead. While automated manufacturing and cost systems can create many more or fewer cost groups, these three have historically been used in nearly all manufacturing costing.

**Direct materials costs** are costs of physical components of the product. The range of materials includes natural resources, such as oil, flour, or lumber, to partially processed components (another company's finished product). Often, a complete list of all materials used in a product is prepared and is called a **bill of materials**. Materials issued to production are **direct materials used**. To find materials used, take materials purchases, add beginning inventory, and subtract ending inventory. Supplies like nails, glue, lubricants, and paints could be included in direct materials or, more commonly, called indirect materials, which are factory overhead costs.

**Direct labor costs** are wages paid to workers who directly process the product. In Figure 2.5, assembly line workers would be direct labor. Direct labor costs could include fringe benefit costs, such as health insurance, pension costs, and various employer payroll taxes. For example, a $20 per hour wage rate can easily grow to $35 per hour when all employer-paid benefit costs are added.

**Factory overhead costs** include all manufacturing costs that are not materials or direct labor. Manufacturing overhead, factory burden, and indirect manufacturing costs are other names for these costs. Obviously, a wide variety of costs fall into this category, such as maintenance staff wages, factory managers' salaries, factory utilities costs, and factory equipment depreciation and repair costs. Hundreds of different cost accounts could be grouped under manufacturing overhead. Certain workers' tasks could be overhead in one company and direct labor in another. For example, materials handlers and quality control personnel costs could be accounted for as either direct or indirect labor. Generally, if the worker has direct contact with the product or the production process, the cost is direct labor. Generally, support tasks are indirect labor–part of overhead.

Historically, the three cost groups were assumed to be about equal portions of total product cost. Today, automation reduces direct labor and causes factory overhead to increase. As more production is generated from the same capacity, materials as a percentage of total cost may also increase. In a recent internal cost study in a major automaker, these percentages were found:

|  | *Type of Plant* | | |
|  | *Stamping* | *Assembly* | *Machining* |
|---|---|---|---|
| Materials | 59 % | 41 % | 42 % |
| Direct labor | 6 | 10 | 11 |
| Manufacturing overhead | 35 | 49 | 47 |
| Total product costs | 100 % | 100 % | 100 % |

Thus, managers' have paid more attention to materials and overhead costs because they have grown as a portion of total manufacturing costs.

## Types of Product Costs

Materials and direct labor costs are often viewed as **direct product costs** since they are easily identified with specific products and units of product. Factory overhead is usually thought of as **indirect product costs**. Factory overhead is not easily traced to specific products or units. For example, the plant manager's salary cannot be tied to specific product units in a multiproduct factory, since the manager is responsible for all activities in the factory. An exception may exist for a few overhead costs that may be traced to specific products and be considered direct costs. Figure 2.6 illustrates these concepts and shows a dotted line between manufacturing overhead and direct costs to indicate this possibility. In more sophisticated costing systems, more of these direct overhead costs might be identified, as we discuss in Chapter 6.

Direct materials and direct labor are also known as the **prime costs** of a product. These costs are easily traceable to a specific product. Direct labor and factory overhead are called **conversion costs**. In the factory, materials are "converted" into finished product using labor and all of the factory's supporting resources–overhead costs

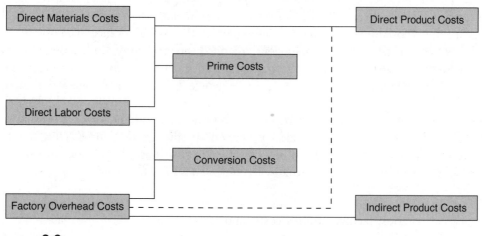

**FIGURE 2.6**

Product Costs and Product Cost Groups

## Calculating Unit Costs

**Product costing** attaches costs to units of product. The simplest approach is to divide the number of units produced into total manufacturing costs. For example, a highly automated factory produces a variety of handheld calculators. The same production processes are used for all models with minimal changeover costs. Three million calculators roll off the line every month. Different circuit boards distinguish the models. March production data by product line are as follows:

|  | Business | Scientific | General Purpose | Total |
|---|---|---|---|---|
| Direct materials costs | $3,600,000 | $4,200,000 | $1,500,000 | $ 9,300,000 |
| Indirect other costs |  |  |  | 6,000,000 |
| Total costs |  |  |  | $15,300,000 |
| Units produced | 1,200,000 | 1,200,000 | 600,000 | 3,000,000 |
| Direct materials costs per unit | $3.00 | $3.50 | $2.50 | $3.10 |
| Indirect other costs per unit | 2.00 | 2.00 | 2.00 | 2.00 |
| Product cost per unit | $5.00 | $5.50 | $4.50 | $5.10 |

The easiest costing approach is to divide the total costs of $15,300,000 by 3,000,000 calculators. However, the $5.10 average cost hides the different direct costs of each model of circuit board. A second approach identifies materials costs as direct to each model and averages all other costs over all units. This produces a high cost of $5.50 for Scientific models and a low cost of $4.50 for General Purpose models. More complex costing is needed if different models use different amounts of resources. The goal is to find the most detailed unit cost, given our decision-making needs.

# COST BEHAVIOR

To say that a cost "behaves" in a certain way is somewhat misleading. Costs result from taking actions or from the mere passage of time. Something drives a cost–some activity, decision, or event. Selling one more hamburger involves a burger, a bun, a container, a napkin, and any condiments used. But selling one more hamburger has no impact on supervision, equipment rental, or advertising costs. Building lease expense will not change unless the lease includes a rental payment based on a percentage of sales. **Cost behavior**, then, is the impact that a cost driver has on a cost.

Which costs can be expected to remain constant when the amount of work activity increases or decreases? Also, which costs increase as more work is performed? If costs are to be estimated and controlled, we need to know whether or not costs will change if conditions change and, if so, by what amount.

Cost behavior is often viewed as a dichotomous pattern–either variable or fixed. But in the real world, many behavior patterns exist since most costs are not strictly variable or fixed. Thus, the concepts of semivariable and semifixed costs add complexity to cost behavior studies. It may oversimplify the analysis, but a split between variable and fixed is common and is used frequently.

## Variable Costs

A **variable cost** changes in total in direct proportion to changes in activity or output. A decrease in activity brings a proportional decrease in total variable cost, and vice versa. For example, direct materials costs are usually variable costs since each unit produced requires the same amount of materials. Thus, materials costs change in direct proportion to the number of units manufactured.

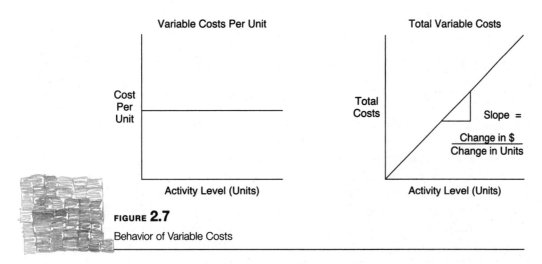

**FIGURE 2.7**

Behavior of Variable Costs

A proportional relationship between activity and cost has these important characteristics:

Variable cost is a rate per unit of activity or output. A variable cost per unit remains constant across a reasonable range of activity. And, the slope of the total variable cost curve is the variable cost per unit–the added cost divided by the added units.

For example, if a product costs $4.00 per unit, the expression $4X yields the total variable cost at X level. Figure 2.7 shows the behavior of variable costs on a per unit basis and in total and also highlights the variable cost line's slope.

## Fixed Costs

A **fixed cost** is constant in total amount regardless of changes in activity level. Costs such as the plant manager's salary, depreciation, insurance, and rent usually remain the same regardless of whether the plant is above or below its expected level of operations. Important characteristics of a fixed cost are:

Fixed cost is a lump of costs that is not normally divisible and does not change as activity or volume changes. A fixed cost remains constant across a reasonable range of activity. The fixed cost per unit decreases as activity or volume increases and increases as activity or volume decreases.

For example, March's rent is quoted as a dollar amount for that month, not as an amount per unit of output or even per hour of use.

By definition, total fixed costs are constant, causing the fixed cost per unit to vary at different levels of activity. Figure 2.8 shows the behavior of fixed costs on a per unit basis and in total. When a company

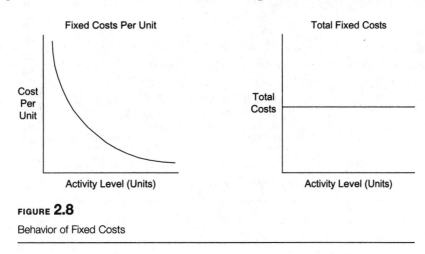

**FIGURE 2.8**

Behavior of Fixed Costs

---

## Contemporary Practice 2.1
### *Outsourcing Converts Fixed to Variable*

*Why not consider bringing in another firm to partner in computer hardware maintenance, desktop management, applications management, or networks and distribution channel management? A major reason that a recent study of the financial services industry gives for considering outsourcing in the information technology business was the reduction of operating costs. Outsourcing allows a company to convert fixed costs to variable costs, meaning that a company can pay on a usage-only basis instead of having the fixed cost of structuring a department's*

*staff and equipment. Tied to this is the ability to react quickly to surges and drops in demand and to reduce the risk of obsolescence because of the huge investment required in ever newer technology. In the study, 81 percent of chief information officers thought that better financial management and cost predictability made outsourcing worthwhile. And, 70 percent thought that outsourcers had better recommendations for cost savings.*

*Source: "When Outsourcing Is Appropriate,"* Wall Street & Technology, *July 1998, p. 96.*

---

produces a greater number of units, the fixed cost per unit decreases. Conversely, when fewer units are produced, the fixed cost per unit increases. This variability of fixed costs per unit creates problems in product costing. The cost per unit depends on the number of units produced or on level of activity.

Certain fixed costs can be changed by management action. These are discretionary fixed costs. **Discretionary fixed costs** are expenditures that managers can elect to spend or not to spend. For example, a company might budget the cost of consultants at $20,000 per month for the coming year. But the contract states that the company can cancel the contract at any time. Management maintains discretionary control over the spending. On the other hand, if the contract guarantees the consultant a 12-month relationship and the contract has been signed, a committed fixed cost has been created. A **committed fixed cost** is one over which a manager has no control and must incur.

An interesting observation is necessary here. Managers can, with time and intent, change the cost behavior of certain activities. For example, variable direct labor costs can be converted into a fixed cost by guaranteeing full-time employment for some period, such as a three-year union contract. Or equipment could be leased on a short-term basis (day-to-day or even hourly) instead of purchased—converting a fixed cost into a variable cost. Also, automated equipment with a fixed rent or depreciation could replace variable cost manual labor. Thus, we recognize that managers can act to change certain cost behavior, particularly over time.

### Expressing Variable and Fixed Costs–A Cost Function

Since a variable cost is a rate, it is a function of an independent variable—an activity or output level. Variable costs can be converted into total variable costs only by knowing the activity or output level. Fixed costs are first expressed as an amount, a constant. Fixed costs can be converted into a rate per unit only if the activity or output level is known. In the following example, the cost per unit of $7 and total costs of $700,000 can be found only if the output of 100,000 units is known.

|  | Costs of 100,000 Units | | Costs of 120,000 Units | |
|---|---|---|---|---|
|  | *Cost Per Unit* | *Total Costs* | *Cost Per Unit* | *Total Costs* |
| Variable costs | **$4.00** → | $400,000 | **$4.00** → | $480,000 |
| Fixed costs | 3.00 ← | **300,000** | 2.50 ← | **300,000** |
| Total | $7.00 | $700,000 | $6.50 | $780,000 |

If the production level increases to 120,000, both the cost per unit and total costs change. A decrease in the cost per unit from $7 to $6.50 results from spreading fixed costs of $300,000 over more units–120,000 instead of 100,000. The increase in total cost equals the variable costs for the additional 20,000 units. A decrease in volume has similar reverse impacts–the cost per unit increases, but total costs decline.

Three factors must generally be known to perform analyses:

**1.** The variable cost rate,

**2.** The fixed cost amount, and

**3.** The level of activity or output.

Notice that if we know the bold numbers in the example above and the activity level, we can calculate all other numbers.

These factors can be brought together in a **cost function**—an expression that mathematically links costs, their behavior, and their cost driver. In the example, the expression is:

Total costs = $300,000 + $4 ($X$), where $X$ is the number of units produced.

This expression can be symbolically shown as:

Total costs = **$a$ + $b$ ($X$)**, where $a$ is fixed costs and $b$ is variable costs per unit.

This is an important formula in managerial accounting. Understanding these relationships can give insight into cost behavior for planning, control, and decision making. By knowing the activity level and cost function, we can find either total costs or costs per unit. The reverse is also true.

## Finding the Cost Function Using Total Costs and Activity Levels

In this example, let's assume we know the total costs ($700,000 and $780,000) at both activity levels (100,000 and 120,000 units). How do we find the cost function? First, we calculate the variable cost per unit as follows:

$$\frac{\text{Change in cost}}{\text{Change in activity level}} = \frac{(\$780,000 - \$700,000)}{(120,000 - 100,000)} = \frac{\$80,000}{20,000} = \$4 \text{ per unit}$$

This is $b$ in our cost function. The change in cost from a change in activity yields the **slope** of the total variable cost line.

To find the fixed cost, which is $a$ in the cost function, we take the total costs at either activity level and subtract the variable costs at that level as follows:

$$\$780,000 - (\$4 \times 120,000 \text{ units}) = \underline{\underline{\$300,000}}$$

**or**

$$\$700,000 - (\$4 \times 100,000 \text{ units}) = \underline{\underline{\$300,000}}$$

We now have both $a$ and $b$. The cost function is $300,000 + $4 ($X$).

## Finding the Cost Function Using Per Unit Costs and Activity Levels

Using the same example, per unit costs were $7 at the 100,000 units activity level and $6.50 at 120,000 units. First, we find total costs at each level by multiplying the cost per unit by the activity level as follows:

$$\$7 \text{ per unit} \times 100,000 = \underline{\underline{\$700,000}} \quad \textbf{and} \quad \$6.50 \text{ per unit} \times 120,000 = \underline{\underline{\$780,000}}$$

Second, we follow the same procedure as shown previously in converting total costs into the cost function. The same calculations could be applied separately to total variable costs for $b$ and to total fixed costs for $a$. Calculations at both levels produce the same cost function.

One danger in converting fixed cost lumps into cost per unit is that the unit cost can be misinterpreted. It might be assumed that $7 is the variable cost–forgetting that the $300,000 is a fixed cost. At different activity levels, the per unit cost will be different. Even in solving homework problems, students are in danger of missing the impact of volume changes on total costs and unit costs if only costs per unit or total costs are used.

## Relevant Range

In Figures 2.6 and 2.7, activity is assumed to start at zero and go to very high levels. Realistically, the cost function holds only for a much narrower range of activity–a relevant range. **A relevant range** is the normal range of expected activity. Management does not expect activity to exceed a certain upper bound nor to fall below a lower bound. Production activity is expected to be within this range, and costs are budgeted for these levels. In cost analysis, costs are expected to behave as defined within the relevant range. The cost function is assumed to be valid for this range of activity. Usually, past experience establishes the relevant range.

Fixed costs are fixed and variable costs are variable within the relevant range. In the above example, the volume range was between 100,000 and 120,000 units. The cost function of $300,000 plus $4 per unit is valid between 100,000 and 120,000 units as shown in Figure 2.9. If planned production was 130,000 units, our cost function may not be valid or useful.

## Semivariable and Semifixed Costs

Figure 2.10 illustrates cost functions that are neither strictly variable nor fixed. In the real world, very few costs are truly variable or fixed. **Semivariable costs** change but not in direct proportion to the changes in output. Some semivariable costs, called **mixed costs**, may be broken down into fixed and variable components, thus making it easier to budget and control costs. Using the cost function techniques shown previously, fixed and variable parts can identified. In Example A of Figure 2.10, telephone expenses may include a monthly basic connection fee (fixed) plus a charge for each local call (variable).

**Semifixed costs** or **step-fixed costs** are typified by step increases in costs with changes in activity as shown in Example B. Activity can be increased somewhat without a cost increase. However, at some activity level, additional fixed cost must be incurred to expand capacity. If many narrow steps exist, a step-cost pattern may approximate a variable cost. Or with wide steps, one step may encompass the entire relevant range; and the step cost appears as a fixed cost.

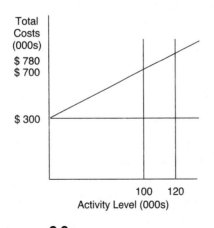

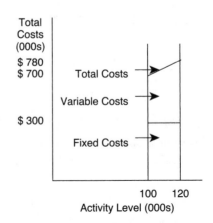

**FIGURE 2.9**

Cost Patterns Using a Relevant Range

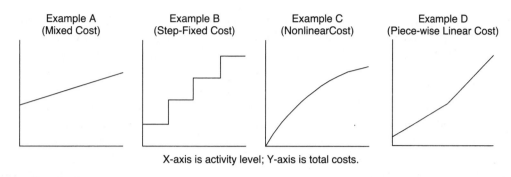

X-axis is activity level; Y-axis is total costs.

**FIGURE 2.10**

Examples of Semivariable and Semifixed Cost Patterns

## Contemporary Practice 2.2
### *Cost Benchmarking: Commercial Aircraft Operating Cost Comparisons*

*Managing operating costs of aircraft is a major task in the commercial aircraft industry. By using industry-wide cost data managers can budget future costs and analyze their actual results by making comparisons. Costs are gathered by six aircraft types (largely by size) and classified by five mission types (largely by flight length). Mission variable costs include fuel, service maintenance, scheduled parts, and other trip expenses. This yields an estimated cost per mile for a mission. Fuel expense, for example,*

*includes jet fuel (averaging $2.71 per gallon in July 2002) and consumption rates for taxi, take-off, climb, cruise, descent, and landing. Aside from mission costs, annual flight management, periodic (overhauls and inspections), personnel (pilot and first officer salaries), training, and facilities costs are calculated and published.*

Source: *"Aircraft Operating Costs Guide; A Benchmarking Tool to Help Flight Department Managers Draft and Analyze Budgets for 2003,"* Business & Commercial Aviation, *August 2002, p. 72–74.*

Example C shows a cost that increases but at a lower cost per unit as activity increases. An example is increased worker efficiency as activity increases, resulting in a lower per unit cost. This is a **nonlinear cost**. Example D shows a **piece-wise linear cost**. It is a constant variable rate until a certain activity level is reached, then the variable cost per unit increases. Perhaps an electric utility offers a low per kilowatt rate for the first 500 kilowatts and a higher rate beyond that level.

Many expenses have both fixed and variable components. Chapter 3 examines techniques that can help separate the fixed and variable portions and that can quantify the cost function.

## COST CONCEPTS FOR PLANNING AND CONTROLLING

Often, cost terms can be explained using contrasts. In other situations, great care must be exercised to distinguish different cost meanings, even subtle differences. For others, similar terms can be substituted for each other.

### Direct Costs Versus Indirect Costs

Costs are often defined as being direct or indirect with respect to a cost objective–an activity, a department, or a product. If a cost can be specifically traced to the cost objective, it is a **direct cost** of that objective. A direct cost is also called a **traceable cost**. The cost of installing a sunroof on a Pontiac Grand Prix is a direct cost of that Grand Prix because it is traceable to that model. If no clear link between a cost and the cost objective is apparent, the cost is an **indirect cost**. For example, the heating costs for a physical therapy center is a direct cost of the physical therapy operation but an indirect cost to each patient being served there.

Thus, the same cost can be direct for one purpose and indirect for another. As another example, the salary of the St. Louis office manager is a direct cost of that branch. But within the branch office where numerous products are sold, the manager's salary is an indirect cost of specific products.

## Common and Joint Costs

An indirect cost is often called a common cost or a joint cost. A **common cost** is incurred to benefit more than one activity. In a university setting, the college of business dean's salary is a direct cost to the college; however, the dean's salary is a common cost to all departments and all courses offered within that college.

The term **joint cost** is applied to situations where multiple outputs are derived from one resource. For example, a barrel of crude oil can be processed into literally thousands of products. The crude oil and the initial refining process costs are joint costs of the products produced. It is impossible to trace specific portions of crude oil costs to specific products; therefore, allocations of the joint costs must be made to those products.

## Cost Allocations

Indirect costs not traceable to particular products or departments may need to be allocated to those objectives. A cost objective may use a resource, but the amount used may not be easily measured. For example, a shoe department occupies 2,000 square feet of a 50,000 square foot store and accounts for 10 percent of sales and 6 percent of profits. If the rent for the entire store is $300,000 per year, how much should be allocated to the shoe department–$12,000 (space), $18,000 (profits), $30,000 (sales), or some other amount? No cost allocation is absolutely correct, and different viewpoints will argue for different allocations. The allocation process should attempt to link the cost, the use of the resource, and the activity or output.

## Incremental Costs Versus Average Costs

A basic distinction in cost analysis is made between the cost of adding one more unit and the average cost of all units produced. **Incremental costs** are the costs incurred by adding more activity—more sales, another project, or a new department. **Marginal cost**, a similar term, is the increase in costs from adding one more unit of output or doing one more task. Incremental or marginal costs are often variable costs but can include any additional fixed costs that result from increased activity.

The concept also applies to deleting a segment. An **avoidable cost** will be deleted if a specific segment or activity is eliminated. An **unavoidable cost** cannot be eliminated. In a retail bakery chain, the Wealthy Street store has revenues and direct expenses. If that store is closed, most operating expenses can be eliminated or avoided. However, if two years remain on the lease, the lease payments are unavoidable.

The per unit **average product cost**, or **full cost**, generally includes production costs for all units, including materials, direct labor, and manufacturing overhead costs. The average cost will generally decline as production volume increases since the same fixed costs are spread over more units.

The incremental cost concept extends the cost behavior discussion. Which costs will change if a change in activity occurs? For example, if a supermarket manager considers adding a pharmacy to the store, what costs will change? Incremental costs will include:

- one-time costs of preparing facilities (equipment and remodeling);
- annual fixed costs of salaries of pharmacists and trained assistants, advertising, and security; and
- variable costs, including costs of sales, utilities, and supplies.

If no space is added to the store, another department will lose space and presumably sales. To make the decision, all expected changes in revenues and costs must be included. This is **incremental cost analysis**.

## Relevant Costs Versus Irrelevant Costs

The key to incremental costing is knowing which costs are relevant and which are irrelevant to a particular decision. To be a **relevant cost**, a cost must:

- differ when decision choices are compared. If a cost increases, decreases, appears, or disappears as different actions are evaluated, it is relevant.
- be a current or future value.

The definition of irrelevant should be obvious. An **irrelevant cost** is one that does not change across alternatives. Being irrelevant does not mean that this cost can be forgotten. Merely, it will not quantitatively affect this particular decision.

A **sunk cost** is an irrelevant cost, a past or committed cost, and an irreversible cost. We cannot go back and change a sunk cost. Also, any future payments that we must make are committed and sunk costs. All historical costs are sunk costs.

To illustrate relevance, assume that Meridian Township owns certain obsolete parts that originally cost $10,000. The maintenance manager is considering selling the parts for $5,000. Or, he could spend an additional $9,000 to modify them for use, saving $20,000 of operating costs this year. Note that the filter's $10,000 cost has already been incurred, does not affect the decision of whether to use or dispose of the filter, is a past cost, and can (must) be ignored as a sunk cost. The analysis is:

|  | Include All Costs | | Exclude Irrelevant Costs | |
|---|---|---|---|---|
|  | Use | Dispose | Use | Dispose |
| Reduced treatment expenses | $20,000 |  | $20,000 |  |
| Proceeds from sale of parts |  | $5,000 |  | $5,000 |
| Refurbishing costs | (9,000) |  | (9,000) |  |
| Original cost of parts | (10,000) | (10,000) |  |  |
| Net benefit | $ 1,000 | $(5,000) | $11,000 | $5,000 |

The economic advantage of using the parts instead of selling them is $6,000, whether the parts' historical cost are included or excluded.

Historical costs, common to most balance sheets, have little or no significance in managerial analysis. Only current and future values have meaning. Even tax effects based on historical costs impact only current and future taxes. The temptation to continue to use historical costs in decision making is great. But using past costs will quickly distort the decision-making process.

## Indifference Points and Opportunity Cost

The **indifference point** is the activity level where a decision maker would accept either alternative. For example, if Alternative A's cost function is $1,000 plus $5 per unit and Alternative B's cost function is $500 plus $10 per unit, the indifference point would be 100 units, found as follows:

| Alternative A | | Alternative B |
|---|---|---|
| $1,000 + $5 (X) | = | $500 + $10 (X) |
| X | = | 100 units |

When $X$ equals 100, we are indifferent between the two alternatives. To choose the lower cost alternative, select Alternative B if volume is less than 100; and select Alternative A if volume is greater than 100.

An opportunity cost is another version of differential cost. An **opportunity cost** is the benefit foregone by selecting another alternative. It is generally the value of the best alternative not taken. For example, we might have three job offers with salaries of $40,000, $35,000, and $28,000 per year. By selecting the best offer of $40,000, our opportunity cost is $35,000, the next best alternative. We give up $35,000 to gain $40,000. The general decision rule is that the opportunity cost should not exceed the value of the option selected.

## Controllable Costs Versus Noncontrollable Costs

Another important aspect of cost is the distinction between costs that can and cannot be controlled by a given manager. This cost classification, like the direct and indirect cost classification, depends on a point of reference. If a manager is responsible for a cost, that cost is a **controllable cost** with respect to that manager. If that manager is not responsible for incurring a cost, it is a **noncontrollable cost** with respect to that manager. The entire cost control system rests on who can control each cost.

All costs are controllable at some level of management. Every cost in an organization is controllable by some manager in that organization. Costs should be planned or budgeted by the manager who has responsibility for that cost.

## Planned Costs Versus Actual Costs

The plan sets the course of action. A plan, also known as a **budget**, shows what and how resources are to be used to achieve certain goals. Actual results are compared to the plan. The very essence of

### ALTMAN FABRICS, INC.
### Monthly Cost Report

**Plant:** Hong Kong     **Period:** June 2005
**Manager:** DaQing Qi

| | June | | | Year-to-Date | | |
|---|---|---|---|---|---|---|
| | Budget | Actual | (Unfav.) Fav Variance | Budget | Actual | (Unfav.) Fav Variance |
| Plant supervision: | | | | | | |
| Salaries & wages | $ 8,830 | $ 9,460 | $ (630) | $ 53,550 | $ 55,320 | $ (1,770) |
| Employee benefits | 760 | 710 | 50 | 4,870 | 4,880 | (10) |
| Insurance | 250 | 250 | 0 | 1,500 | 1,500 | 0 |
| Utilities | 430 | 320 | 110 | 2,680 | 3,290 | (610) |
| Miscellaneous | 1,680 | 1,880 | (200) | 10,160 | 10,800 | (640) |
| Total costs | $ 11,950 | $ 12,620 | $ (670) | $ 72,760 | $ 75,790 | $ (3,030) |
| | | | | | | |
| Department 1 | 68,210 | 68,970 | (760) | 386,420 | 385,280 | 1,140 |
| Department 2 | 46,300 | 49,500 | (3,200) | 263,140 | 278,230 | (15,090) |
| Department 3 | 23,970 | 23,920 | 50 | 143,810 | 143,670 | 140 |
| Total plant costs | $150,430 | $155,010 | $4,580) | $866,130 | $882,970 | $(16,840) |

**FIGURE 2.11**

Management Control Report Comparing Actual to Plan

control rests on the knowledge that actual results will be compared to the plan, used to revise the ongoing plan, and used to evaluate managers.

Periodic control reports monitor the plan-versus-actual status. Generally, this month's actual results are compared to this month's budget as are year-to-date results. Expense variances are shown as over (unfavorable) or under (favorable) budget. What caused the variance? Will the variance recur in the future? What actions will reduce future variances? The budget itself may need revision. Control reports are like flashing warning lights to get management's attention.

As an example, DaQing Qi is plant manager of the Hong Kong Plant of Altman Fabrics, Inc. He has three department supervisors reporting to him. Each month he receives a report similar to Figure 2.11 showing summary costs incurred by him and his departmental supervisors. The June report is converted into U. S. dollars. If Qi believes that costs incurred in Department 2 are excessive, he can review that department's detailed cost report. After an analysis, the Department 2 supervisor and Qi may find that materials costs were excessive. At this point, he would ask the supervisor to explain why the variances occurred and to find ways to control future materials costs.

Each manager receives a similar report, showing costs controlled by that manager. A network of reports showing a comparison of controllable costs with budget extends from the lowest level of management to the president's office.

## CONTRIBUTION MARGIN AND ITS MANY VERSIONS

Thus far, we have defined cost terms. But managerial responsibility for profit measurement is even more important. Revenue is added to the analysis. While net profit evaluates the entire firm, measuring profitability of parts of a firm requires more finely tuned profit yardsticks. The term we use is **contribution margin**, which is the revenue minus certain costs, a margin. This margin contributes to covering all remaining costs and to earning a net profit. Figure 2.12 shows five versions used in different situations.

### Variable Contribution Margin–Per Unit, Ratio, and Total Dollars

The basic and most common definition of contribution margin is sales minus variable costs. **Variable contribution margin** is a more explicit term because only variable items (revenue and costs) are included in the calculation. This contribution margin pays for fixed costs and includes any net profit. We use this definition of contribution margin in Chapter 3.

---

**Variable Contribution Margin:**

| Total sales | Sales price per unit | Sales percentage |
| - Total variable costs | - Variable cost per unit | - Variable cost percentage |
| Variable contribution margin or Contribution margin | Contribution margin per unit | Contribution margin percentage or Contribution margin ratio |

**Controllable Contribution Margin:**                    **Direct (or Segment) Contribution Margin:**

| Total sales | Total sales |
| - Controllable costs | - Direct (or Segment) costs |
| Controllable contribution margin | Direct (or Segment) contribution margin |

---

**FIGURE 2.12**

Versions of Contribution Margin

As an example, a salesperson is selling a product for $20 per unit. The firm buys the item for $12 per unit and pays the salesperson a 10 percent commission. The firm expects to sell 10,000 units. Variable contribution margin can be shown as follows:

| | Variable Contribution Margin | | |
| --- | --- | --- | --- |
| | *Per Unit* | *Ratio* | *Total Dollars* |
| Sales (10,000 units) | $20 | 100 % | $200,000 |
| Variable costs: | | | |
| Cost of sales and commissions ($12 plus 10 % of $20) | 14 | 70 | 140,000 |
| Variable contribution margin | $ 6 | 30 % | $ 60,000 |

Thus, the contribution margin can be expressed as either $6 per unit, 30 percent of sales, or $60,000. Depending on the analysis needed, we may use one, two, or all three versions. From total variable contribution margin, we subtract fixed expenses–the remaining expenses–to arrive at net profit.

## Controllable and Direct Contribution Margins

The next contribution margin concept looks at managerial control and is used when a manager has revenue and cost responsibility. Costs controllable by the manager are typically variable costs and controllable fixed costs. These costs are subtracted from sales to yield **controllable contribution margin** or controllable margin. This represents the money available to pay any noncontrollable expenses and includes any company net profit. Note that the definitions of controllable and noncontrollable developed previously are used for both revenue and costs. Controllable contribution margin is used to evaluate managerial performance. However, this is not the net profit that the manager generates for the company, since noncontrollable costs must be paid before any net profit is earned.

**Direct** or **segment contribution margin** or segment margin is a segment's revenue minus its direct costs. A segment might be a product, a region, or a division. Definitions of direct and indirect were discussed earlier and focus on traceability. As an example, the direct contribution margin of

## Contemporary Practice 2.3
### *Contribution is the Key*

Tom Lewis, President of T. W. Lewis Co. and a Phoenix builder, builds homes in the $160,000 to $400,000 price range. He attributes his success to planned, disciplined, and targeted growth. He says that many of his business decisions are made using variable contribution margin. Lewis gains three key benefits. First, contribution margin is used to forecast profitability for the coming six months. Second, contribution emphasizes the value of a production line. "If we don't start 20 homes in October, then we won't have the closings in March." Finally, Lewis uses contribution to analyze the financial performance of individual floor plans and options. If a floor plan isn't contributing its share, he can tweak it or phase it out.

Source: Donohue, Gerry, "1998 America's Best Builders: T.W. Lewis Company," Builder, January 1998, pp. 258–262.

**Contemporary Practice 2.4**
*Sell a Lube, Generate Contribution Margin*

*In 1990, 28 franchisers operated 4,000 fast lube outlets in the U. S. A survey shows that a typical service package offers an oil change, checks of other fluids, and maybe a car wash for about $24. Direct contribution margin is estimated at $15 to $16 per vehicle. A recent study shows that to be profitable a*

*lube center has to service over 50 vehicles a day and have a population of 80,000 with an average household income of $26,000 within a 3-mile radius.*

Source: Strischek, D., "Lending to Quick Lube Shops," Journal of Commercial Lending, Volume 73, pp.40–47.

a product line is sales less product-line cost of sales, product-line advertising costs, and any other costs traceable to that product line. The product line's direct contribution margin is the revenue remaining to pay for company common costs and to earn company profits.

## Illustration of All Contribution Margin Concepts

Celeste Rudd owns three Burgers Plus locations. Figure 2.13 presents a summary income statement, expanded for the Grand Avenue location. Variable contribution margin is shown in total dollars for each store and also as a ratio for the Grand Avenue store. **Direct controllable fixed expenses** include assistant managers' salaries, maintenance services, and other fixed costs that the store manager controls. The controllable contribution margin is the profit on which the Grand Avenue manager will be evaluated and rewarded (a bonus for meeting profit goals or profit improvement). **Direct noncontrollable fixed expenses** include rent on the building and the outlet manager's salary which are probably controlled by Rudd.

This direct or store contribution margin is used to measure the profit performance of each store. Measuring store profitability stops at the direct contribution margin. Direct contribution margin is

### Contribution Analysis by Store for the Month of September

| | River Road | Pine Street | Grand Avenue | | Totals |
|---|---|---|---|---|---|
| Sales | $120,000 | $96,000 | $185,000 | 100% | $401,000 |
| Variable food expenses | $ 55,500 | $46,000 | $ 85,100 | 46% | $186,600 |
| Other variable expenses | 6,000 | 4,500 | 11,100 | 6 | 21,600 |
| Total variable expenses | $ 61,500 | $50,500 | $ 96,200 | 52% | $208,200 |
| Variable contribution margin | $ 58,500 | $45,500 | $ 88,800 | 48% | $192,800 |
| Direct controllable fixed expenses | 12,600 | 13,900 | 20,400 | | 46,900 |
| Controllable contribution margin | $ 45,900 | $31,600 | $ 68,400 | | $145,900 |
| Direct noncontrollable fixed expenses | 24,400 | 21,300 | 38,900 | | 84,600 |
| Direct contribution margin | $ 21,500 | $10,300 | $ 29,500 | | $ 61,300 |
| Common corporate expenses | | | | | $ 36,900 |
| Net profit | | | | | $ 24,400 |

**FIGURE 2.13**

Contribution Margin Analysis By Store

the finest tuned profit measure that is free of allocations. Common corporate expenses, which include Rudd's salary and other corporate expenses, cannot be traced to the three locations.

Contribution margin per unit requires more detail. Rudd has set target contribution margins for her three main burger products as follows:

| | Cheap Burger | Double Burger | Triple Burger | Average for All Burgers |
|---|---|---|---|---|
| Selling price per unit | $1.00 | $2.00 | $3.00 | $1.95 |
| Variable food costs per unit | .65 | 1.20 | 1.50 | 1.15 |
| Variable contribution margin per unit | $ .35 | $ .80 | $1.50 | $ .80 |
| Variable contribution margin ratio | 35 % | 40 % | 50 % | 41 % |

Note that the Other Variable Expenses (probably supplies and condiments) in Figure 2.13 cannot be traced accurately to each product. Now, actual burger margins can be compared across all stores and to margin targets.

Ms. Rudd has numerous versions of profitability for each location. She will use each to answer specific questions about her products, managers, and stores.

Common use of the term contribution margin frequently means variable contribution margin. But play it safe—define which contribution margin you are using.

## SUMMARY

Cost analysis and income measurement are equally important to service, merchandising, or manufacturing firms. Tracing cost flows is important to understanding the conversion of materials, direct labor, and overhead into a product or service. The cost driver is the link between resources used and outputs.

Different decisions need different costs. A "cost" must have an adjective attached to give it meaning. In general, costs have many attributes, but the three most important ones for using cost concepts are cost behavior, traceability, and controllability.

Variable and fixed costs behave differently when activity levels change. Variable costs are naturally expressed as a rate; fixed costs are naturally a lump of costs. Fixed and variable costs can be expressed as a cost function, such as $a + b(X)$, where $a$ is the fixed cost, $b$ is the variable rate, and $X$ is the level of activity.

Direct costs are traceable; indirect costs are nontraceable. Controllability refers to a specific manager's authority to incur the cost and responsibility to use the resource generating the cost.

Contribution margin is revenue minus a subset of costs. Variable contribution margin can be expressed as an amount per unit, a ratio, or total dollars. Controllable contribution margin is used to evaluate the manager, and direct or segment contribution margin is used to evaluate the segment.

## PROBLEMS FOR REVIEW

### Review Problem A

Ballou Corporation operates sales, administrative, and printing activities from a facility in Dayton. It prints, prepares, and mails a wide variety of promotional materials. The following selected costs relate to the firm's activities and particularly to the factory's Mail Preparation Department.

(a) Production paper used in Mail Preparation Department
(b) Hourly wages of production personnel in Mail Preparation Department
(c) Factory property taxes and insurance
(d) Supplies used which changes with printing volume in Mail Preparation Department
(e) Contract signed by Mail Preparation Department manager for an annual maintenance fee on postage application machinery
(f) Equipment depreciation in Mail Preparation Department
(g) Building depreciation
(h) Sales commissions
(i) Advertising agency contract costs for a special program
(j) Annual computer staff; uses the same number of staff all year—half for operations which includes the Mail Preparation Department and half for administrative work

**Required:**

Based on reasonable assumptions about Ballou Corporation, classify each cost as:

1. Variable or fixed cost.

2. Controllable or noncontrollable by the supervisor of the Mail Preparation Department.

3. Direct or indirect product costs or period costs.

**Solution:**

| Cost Item | Cost Behavior | | Under Control of Department Manager | | Product Cost | | |
|---|---|---|---|---|---|---|---|
| | Variable Cost | Fixed Cost | Yes | No | Direct Cost | Indirect Cost | Period Cost |
| (a) | X | | X | | X | | |
| (b) | X | | X | | X | | |
| (c) | | X | | X | | X | |
| (d) | X | | X | | | X | |
| (e) | | X | X | | | X | |
| (f) | | X | | X | | X | |
| (g) | | X | | X | | X | |
| (h) | X | | | X | | | X |
| (i) | | X | | X | | | X |
| (j) | | X | | X | | X* | X* |

$ An allocation between the operations and administration is required.

## Review Problem B

Wild Eddie's Appliances operates in 15 states and has 45 outlets. February data from Store 13 have just arrived at headquarters as follows:

| | |
|---|---|
| Sales | $300,000 |
| Cost of goods sold | 166,000 |
| Other variable expenses | 17,000 |
| Direct controllable fixed expenses | 25,000 |
| Direct noncontrollable fixed expenses | 30,000 |
| Allocated headquarters expenses | 22,000 |

The store manager reported selling 1,000 appliances in February.

**Required:**  Identify as many versions of contribution margin as possible.

**Solution:**

|  | Total Dollars | Ratio | Per Unit |
|---|---|---|---|
| Sales | $300,000 | 100 % | $300 |
| Variable costs: |  |  |  |
| Cost of goods sold | $166,000 |  |  |
| Other variable expenses | 17,000 |  |  |
| Total variable expenses | $183,000 | 61 | 183 |
| **Variable contribution margin** | **$117,000** | **39 %** | **$117** |
| Direct controllable fixed expenses | 25,000 |  |  |
| **Controllable contribution margin** | **$ 92,000** |  |  |
| Direct noncontrollable fixed expenses | 30,000 |  |  |
| **Direct (or Segment) contribution margin** | **$ 62,000** |  |  |

Three different definitions of contribution margin are variable, controllable, and direct (or segment) contribution margin. Variable contribution margin can be expressed three ways: total dollars, ratio or percentage, and per unit. Notice that allocated headquarters expenses are not used.

## TERMINOLOGY REVIEW

| | |
|---|---|
| Average product cost (38) | Direct product costs (31) |
| Avoidable cost (38) | Discretionary fixed costs (34) |
| Bill of materials (30) | Factory overhead costs (30) |
| Budget (40) | Finished goods inventory (29) |
| Committed fixed cost (34) | Fixed cost (32) |
| Common cost (38) | Full cost (38) |
| Contribution margin (41) | Incremental cost analysis (39) |
| Contribution margin ratio (xx) | Incremental costs (38) |
| Controllable contribution margin (42) | Indifference point (40) |
| Controllable cost (40) | Indirect cost (38) |
| Conversion costs (31) | Indirect product costs (31) |
| Cost (25) | Irrelevant cost (39) |
| Cost behavior (35) | Joint cost (38) |
| Cost drivers (25) | Marginal cost (38) |
| Cost function (35) | Materials inventory (29) |
| Cost objective (25) | Mixed cost (36) |
| Cost of goods manufactured (28) | Noncontrollable cost (40) |
| Cost of goods sold (29) | Nonlinear costs (37) |
| Direct contribution margin (42) | Opportunity cost (40) |
| Direct controllable fixed expenses (43) | Period costs (27) |
| Direct cost (37) | Piece-wise linear cost (37) |
| Direct labor costs (30) | Prime costs (31) |
| Direct materials cost (30) | Product costing (32) |
| Direct materials used (30) | Product costs (27) |
| Direct noncontrollable fixed expenses (43) | Relevant cost (39) |

## QUESTIONS FOR REVIEW AND DISCUSSION

1. Define the terms "cost objective" and "cost driver." How do they relate to resources and resource costs?

2. Why must "cost" have an adjective attached for it to have meaning to a manager?

3. Refer to Figure 2.1. Explain this diagram to a friend that has not studied accounting.

4. What does the mathematical expression $100,000 + $12X mean in terms of measuring product cost?

5. What characteristics distinguish accounting for revenues and expenses for service, merchandising, and manufacturing organizations?

6. Distinguish among the following terms: cost of goods manufactured, cost of goods sold, and total manufacturing costs.

7. Period costs differ from product costs. How do they differ? Why is the distinction important?

8. Name the three traditional cost elements in a manufactured product. How can these elements be attached to the product?

9. Describe the basic cost behaviors of variable, fixed, and semivariable costs, both in total amount and on a per unit basis.

10. Identify at least two ways in which fixed costs pose difficulties for cost accountants and managers.

11. A fixed product cost is a lump of dollars. A variable product cost is a rate per unit. What other data do we need to know or calculate to find total product costs or the cost per unit?

12. (a) Controller, Maria Burroughs, in a recent speech said, "I rarely see a real variable cost or a truly fixed cost." What did she mean?

    (b) She also commented, "Some of my friends define semivariable costs, semifixed costs, step costs, and mixed costs differently. Other friends often use these terms interchangeably. And I like all of my friends." Was she just trying to be funny, or is there truth in her quip? Explain.

13. Comment on the validity of the following statements:

    (a) All sunk costs are irrelevant.
    (b) All irrelevant costs are past costs.
    (c) All relevant costs are present or future amounts.
    (d) All future costs are relevant costs.
    (e) A cost can be relevant for one decision and irrelevant for another decision.

14. How can an individual cost be both a direct and an indirect cost? A controllable and a noncontrollable cost? Give examples.

15. Assume that you are a student in a managerial accounting course. You are analyzing your costs of taking this course. Give an example of a direct cost, common cost, indirect cost, controllable cost, variable cost, fixed cost, opportunity cost, avoidable cost, and out-of-pocket cost.

16. Assume that you are the Department of Accounting chairperson at a college. You are considering hiring an instructor and offering an advanced managerial accounting course. Give an example of a direct cost, common cost, indirect cost, controllable cost, variable cost, fixed cost, opportunity cost, avoidable cost, and out-of-pocket cost of offering the course.

17. Will an indirect cost be reduced by eliminating a product? Explain. Give an example of where an indirect cost might be reduced and of where it might not be reduced.

18. Use the letters for the following product costs to create a formula for each term listed.

    A. Fixed factory overhead
    B. Variable factory overhead
    C. Total factory overhead
    D. Beginning work in process
    E. Beginning finished goods inventory

    F. Direct materials purchases
    G. Direct materials used
    H. Direct labor
    I. Ending work in process
    J. Ending finished goods inventory

    **Terms:** Prime costs, conversion costs, direct costs, indirect costs, total manufacturing costs, costs transferred to finished goods inventory, and cost of goods sold.

19. Glenda Minor supervises the Admissions Department at Tender Care Hospital. The hospital accountant includes Glenda's salary among the direct expenses in her departmental expense report. Glenda claims she cannot control her own salary; and, therefore, it should not be in Admissions Department's expense report. Is Glenda correct? Explain.

20. What is contribution margin? How is variable contribution margin used? How is controllable contribution margin used? How is direct contribution margin used?

21. We have 15 subsidiaries. All corporate costs are allocated to the subsidiaries. In evaluating the profitability of our French subsidiary, we find it generates a net loss. Why might this number not be a good indicator of the profit contribution that this subsidiary makes to the corporation as a whole?

## EXERCISES

2–1. **Cost Flows in Manufacturing.** The following data are from the Krueger Company for August production activities:

| Inventories: | August 1 | August 31 |
|---|---|---|
| Direct materials | $18,000 | $10,000 |
| Work in process | 12,000 | 16,000 |
| Finished goods | 45,000 | 38,000 |

| | Month of August |
|---|---|
| Factory overhead | $120,000 |
| Cost of goods manufactured | ? |
| Direct materials purchased | 80,000 |
| Direct labor | 30,000 |

**Required:**
1. What was the cost of direct materials used during August? What was the cost of goods manufactured?
2. Use T-accounts to show the flows of costs through the appropriate accounts for August.

**2–2.** Cost Classification. Selected costs associated with a variety of business situations are shown below:

**(a)** Sales commissions of the marketing staff.
**(b)** Salary of the plant manager.
**(c)** Lubricating oils for machines.
**(d)** Brass rods used in making plumbing products.
**(e)** Property taxes on a building that includes both the factory and home office.
**(f)** Labor in the repairs and maintenance section.
**(g)** Salary of the supervisor in the grinding department.
**(h)** Crude oil used in a refining process which results in numerous products.
**(i)** Wages of artists preparing ads for a grocery chain, working for the grocery chain.
**(j)** Depreciation on administrative office furniture.
**(k)** Salaries of quality assurance personnel who test products during production.
**(l)** Salaries of software engineers in a production plant using robots.
**(m)** Wages of union auto assembly workers guaranteed 2,000 hours of work per year.

**Required:**
Create columns to classify each item by cost behavior (variable, semivariable, or fixed) with respect to activity; as a product or period cost; and, if it is a product cost, as a direct or indirect product cost.

**2–3.** **Cost of Goods Manufactured.** The following data are available about the Woods Company:

|  | 2006 | 2007 | 2008 |
|---|---|---|---|
|  | Balances | Balances | Balances |
| Beginning materials inventory | $10,000 | $ ? | $15,000 |
| Ending materials inventory | 8,000 | ? | 11,000 |
| Beginning work in process inventory | 30,000 | ? | 18,000 |
| Ending work in process inventory | 24,000 | ? | 21,000 |
| Direct labor |  | 20,000 |  |
| Factory overhead |  | 40,000 |  |
| Materials purchases |  | 30,000 |  |

**Required:** Find cost of goods manufactured.

**2–4.** **Finding Production Costs.** Jean Smith knows the following about the production process in her plant:

**Department 1:**  Conversion costs are $200,000.
Prime costs are $300,000.
Materials purchases are $200,000.
Increase in materials inventory is $20,000.
Decrease in work in process inventory is $40,000.

**Required:** Find factory overhead costs.

**Department 2:**  Direct product costs are materials and direct labor.
Conversion costs are 300 percent of materials.
Indirect product costs are 50 percent of conversion costs.
Total manufacturing costs are $600,000.

**Required:** Find materials costs.

**Department 3:**    Conversion costs are 40 percent of total manufacturing costs.
Direct labor is 25 percent of conversion costs.
Factory overhead is $600,000.

**Required:** Find total manufacturing costs.

**2–5.    Cost Measurement in Manufacturing.** Dong Manufacturing Company of Hong Kong used materials costing HK$200,000 in the production of 10,000 units of product. No materials were on hand at the beginning or at the end of the year. Labor costs of HK$50,000 were incurred. Other costs of manufacturing, such as factory supervision, utilities, taxes, and insurance, are all fixed costs and amounted to HK$250,000 for the year. Administrative and marketing costs were HK$60,000. No finished goods inventory existed at the beginning of the year, and 8,000 units of product were sold during the year.

**Required:**
**1.** Find the cost per unit to manufacture the product. Break down the cost by traditional product cost elements.
**2.** Show where total manufacturing costs are at the end of the year.

Service

**2–6.    Cost Functions.** Consider each of the following cases.
**A.** On Kramer's Turkey Farm, Kramer produced one batch of 8,000 turkeys at a cost of $25,000. Another batch of 6,000 turkeys cost $22,000. Estimate the firm's cost function.
**B.** Bradburn Laboratories handled 120,000 tests this year. Total costs are $600,000; and fixed costs are $240,000. If volume is expected to be 140,000 tests next year, what is Bradburn's forecast of next year's costs using this year's cost function?
**C.** For Slowik Services, Inc. the cost function is $3,000 per service contract plus $30,000 per month. What is the average cost of handling a service contract this month if the activity level is 50 contracts? 30 contracts?

**2–7.    Indifference Point.** Joyce and Diana each operate local french-fry shops. Joyce's place is called AutoFries and is highly automated. She pours potatoes into one end of an expensive machine, and fries come out at the other end. Her costs are $20,000 per month plus $0.10 per box of fine fries.

Diana's place is called Human Touch Fries. She uses manual peelers and ethnic frypersons. Her costs are $2,000 per month plus $0.40 per box of fine fries.

**Required:**
At what volume of boxes would the cost per box be the same for both? What if sales were higher than this volume? Lower? Comment on their relative profits.

Service

**2–8.    Classifying Cost Behavior.** Keith Piwko operates a pizza shop near a major university. During critical periods like registration and final exams, he is open 24 hours a day. Half of his business is takeout. He has these expenses:
**(a)** Cost of supplies (i.e., napkins, toothpicks, and pizza boxes).
**(b)** Cost of dough used in pizzas.
**(c)** Salary of the supervisor of the overnight shift when needed.
**(d)** Wages of the delivery persons.
**(e)** Straight-line depreciation on equipment.
**(f)** Power costs to operate the ovens.
**(g)** Monthly lease partially based on sales.
**(h)** Cost of drinks served.

**(i)** Insurance premiums covering his equipment.

**(j)** Equipment maintenance costs.

**(k)** Cost of supplies (i.e., napkins, toothpicks, and pizza boxes).

**Required:**

Classify each cost as variable, fixed, semivariable, or semifixed costs. Add any assumptions or comments you need to clarify your answers.

**2–9.** **Relevant Inventory Costs.** Wild Side Clothes manufactures designer jeans. At the end of the current year, one line of jeans was out of style. These jeans were carried in inventory at $50,000. Amber DeClercq, a product line manager, estimates that, with a little rework costing $8,000, she could sell the entire lot to a discount clothing outlet for $15,000. Or, Amber figures, the jeans could be sold "as is" to a company in northern Mexico for $6,000, although Wild Side would have to pay $750 freight charges. She could also sell the jeans as waste material to a recycling firm for $2,200.

**Required:**

**1.** What is the sunk cost in this situation?

**2.** Which is the best choice? Why?

**3.** Amber could store the jeans for a cost of $200 per month. She says, "I think this style will return in, oh, maybe eight or ten years." She guesses that the jeans might be sold for "up to $30,000" then, assuming no storage damage and no inflation. Does this information affect your analysis? Explain.

Service

**2–10.** **Cost Behavior Using Cost Functions.** The following situations have been observed by a services industry cost consultant:

**A.** Mydlowski Co. moves equipment. Costs for Week 1 were $28,000 when 700 units were moved. In Week 2, $36,000 was spent to move 1,100 units. Based on this info, what was the cost function?

**B.** Coppo Credit Checking Agency's cost function is $5 per credit check plus $2,000. How well did the actual costs follow the cost function if $13,200 was spent and 2,100 credit checks were performed?

**C.** Puidokas Lub Services does lubrication jobs on cars. Volumes and costs for two recent months are 1,000 units and $18,000 in August and 1,200 units and $21,000 in September. Apparently, what is the cost function?

**2–11.** **Find the Cost Function.** Thelen Corporation has collected data on the cost of supplies and machine hours for the past 2 months:

| | Supply Costs | Machine Hours |
|---|---|---|
| August | $20,000 | 6,000 |
| September | 15,000 | 4,000 |

**Required:**

**1.** What is the company's estimated cost function for supplies?

**2.** What should the controller expect to spend in October if budgeted machine hours is 4,300 hours?

**2–12.** **Finding Unit Costs at Different Levels.** The estimated costs of making "Good Stuff" in the Nakolan Factory is $500,000 for 200,000 gallons. Fixed costs are $300,000.

**Required:**
1. What would be the marginal cost per gallon based on the above information?
2. What would be the average cost per gallon if 180,000 gallons were made?
3. What would be the average cost per gallon if production grew to 220,000 gallons?

**2–13.  Finding a Cost Function.** Otley Corporation, located in London, UK, has collected the following data on the costs of electricity and machine hours used for three months:

|  | Cost of Electricity | Machine Hours |
|---|---|---|
| October | £17,000 | 3,000 |
| November | 22,000 | 4,000 |
| December | 12,000 | 2,000 |

**Required:** The production manager thinks that a pattern exists for electricity costs.
1. Using the approach discussed in the chapter, does a cost function exist for electricity?
2. If so, does one cost function work for all three months? Explain.
3. If the plant manager expects fixed costs to increase by £1,500 per month and variable cost to increase by 5 percent, what total costs should be expected for next year, if machine hours are expected to average 3,500 hours per month?

Service

**2–14.  Opportunity Cost and Relevant Costs.** Cynthia Golden already has credits toward a MBA degree from Edgewater University and thinks that she can finish the degree requirements in one year. To do this, however, she must give up her job that pays a salary of $25,000 per year. Living costs, whether or not she returns to complete the degree requirements, are estimated at $16,000 for the year. In addition, the costs of tuition and books at the university will amount to $9,000.

**Required:**
Write a memo to Golden highlighting her opportunity cost if she decides to return to school. What are the relevant and irrelevant costs of the decision? Include comments on any information that is missing that is critical to her decision.

**2–15.  Cost Flows in Manufacturing.** Analyze the following cases:
  A.  Work-in-process inventory of Baldree Corporation changed from $21,000 to $23,500 during November. Costs incurred during November were $42,000 for materials used, $33,000 for direct labor, and $51,000 for overhead. Find cost of goods manufactured for November.
  B.  In the Hoisington Company, costs incurred during November were $25,000 for materials purchased, $50,000 for direct labor, and $60,000 for overhead. Materials inventory changed from $24,000 to $18,000. If cost of goods manufactured in November was $129,000 and beginning work in process inventory was $16,000, find the ending work in process inventory.
  C.  In the Rickman Company, the cost of goods sold for November was $186,000, finished goods inventory decreased from $30,000 to $21,000, and work in process inventory increased from $21,000 to $33,000. Find the total manufacturing costs for November.

**2–16.  Searching for Unknowns in Manufacturing Costs Flows.** Three Japanese firms–Kumamoto, Kawasaki, and Kanazawa–produce musical products. Operating results for 2006 follow (all numbers are in millions of yen):

|  | Kumamoto Co. | Kawasaki Co. | Kanazawa Co. |
|---|---|---|---|
| Sales | ¥ ? | ¥90,000 | ¥ ? |
| Materials used | 15,000 | ? | 22,000 |
| Direct labor | 25,000 | 20,000 | 15,000 |
| Factory overhead | 60,000 | 25,000 | ? |
| Total manufacturing costs | ? | ? | ? |
| Beginning work in process | 4,000 | 9,000 | 9,000 |
| Ending work in process | 12,000 | 4,000 | 6,000 |
| Cost of goods manufactured | ? | 69,000 | 61,000 |
| Beginning finished goods | 6,000 | ? | 8,000 |
| Ending finished goods | 21,000 | 22,000 | ? |
| Cost of goods sold | ? | ? | 68,000 |
| Gross margin | ? | 24,000 | 24,000 |
| Operating expenses | 25,000 | ? | 13,000 |
| Net income | 6,000 | (6,000) | ? |

**Required:**

Find the missing values. Helpful hint: Format a manufacturing cost of sales section, and insert the known amounts.

**2–17.   Product Line Profits.** The Kraus Protective Products Company has divided its business into three product lines. Product Line Green is expected to generate sales revenue of $900,000 a year, with costs of sales amounting to $490,000. Product Line Pink should yield sales of $600,000 a year, with costs of sales of $390,000. Product Line Purple should have sales of $1,500,000, with costs of sales of $1,040,000. Traceable fixed costs of each line are $250,000, $200,000, and $350,000, respectively. Costs common to all product lines are $300,000.

**Required:**

1. Measure the profit performance of each product line.
2. Which of the three product lines earns the best profit level? How did you measure "best?"
3. Would your answer change if the common costs were allocated on the basis of sales dollars? In equal shares (1/3 each)? Explain.

**2–18.   Cost Flows Through T-Accounts.** Use T-accounts to show the flow of costs and revenues through the accounts of Westenbroek Corporation during July for the transactions listed. Accounts, with beginning balances, include:

| | | | |
|---|---|---|---|
| Cash | $ 36,000 | Accumulated depreciation | $56,000 |
| Accounts receivable | 122,000 | Accounts payable | 49,000 |
| Direct materials inventory | 128,000 | Sales | 0 |
| Supplies inventory | 65,000 | Cost of goods sold | 0 |
| Work in processing inventory | 82,000 | Direct labor cost | 0 |
| Finished goods inventory | 172,000 | Factory overhead costs | 0 |

Transactions:

1. Materials and supplies purchased on account: $346,000 and $98,000, respectively.
2. Direct materials requisitioned for production: $385,000.
3. Supplies used in production: $93,000.

4. Direct labor wages paid: $155,000.
5. Depreciation expense on factory building and equipment: $22,000.
6. Indirect labor wages and supervisory salaries paid: $186,000.
7. Utilities costs paid: $26,000.
8. Other factory costs paid: $83,000.
9. Completed production: $845,000.
10. Sales on account recorded: $1,262,000.
11. Accounts receivable collected: $1,195,000.
12. Cost of goods sold: $860,000.
13. Cash payments made to vendors: $424,000.

Service

**2–19.** **Variable Contribution Margin.** Peterson Testing performs soil tests for toxic chemicals in its laboratory. Data from the third quarter of 2007 include:

| | |
|---|---|
| Selling price | $15 per test |
| Variable lab costs | $8 per test |
| Variable administrative and shipping expenses | $3 per test |
| Total fixed lab costs | $25,000 per quarter |
| Total fixed administrative expenses | $15,000 per quarter |
| Tests performed | 15,000 tests |

**Required:**
Prepare an income statement showing several forms of variable contribution margin plus net income.

**2–20.** **Cost Term Definitions.** For each definition, indicate what cost term is being defined.
   (a) Product costs that are not materials or direct labor.
   (b) Cost per unit that decreases as more units are made during a time period.
   (c) Activity levels within which the firm is expected to operate.
   (d) Costs that are not inventoried.
   (e) Costs that management has obligated itself to incur in the future.
   (f) Costs that will go away if an activity is eliminated.
   (g) Profit that is given up by accepting a different alternative.
   (h) Costs that are the responsibility of a specific manager.
   (i) Costs incurred while producing more than one product but cannot be easily traced to each product.
   (j) Total product costs divided by total units produced.
   (k) Costs of adding one more unit of output.
   (l) Costs that are traceable to a particular cost objective but cannot be controlled by the manager responsible for that cost objective.

**2–21.** **Finding Cost Functions.** For each case below, find the cost function or use it to answer the question.
   **Case 1:** On Nicol's Egg Farm, total cost of producing 400,000 dozen eggs was $240,000 in 2005; and the total cost of producing 500,000 dozen was $250,000 in 2006. What was the cost function?
   **Case 2:** Kazmirowski pots plants. Last month, 5,000 plants were potted. Costs were $20,000. Of that, it is thought that fixed costs were $10,000. This month, sales are running at a rate of 6,000 plants. Based on last month's costs, what should production costs be this month?
   **Case 3:** Miller's office expenses for 2006 when she had $2,000,000 in sales are shown below. What is her cost function?

| Cost | Behavior | Amount |
|------|----------|--------|
| Commissions and travel expense | Variable | $90,000 |
| Sales salaries and office expenses | Fixed | 80,000 |

**2–22.** **Direct and Controllable Costs.** Marie Heltzel is manager of Morec Services in the Frankfurt, Germany office and has the authority to buy supplies, hire labor, and maintain equipment for the office. Costs in euros for January appearing in the Frankfurt office performance report are:

| | |
|---|---|
| Home office general manager's salary allocated to Frankfurt office | €3,000 |
| Home office operating expenses allocated to Frankfurt office | 2,200 |
| Home office marketing costs allocated to Frankfurt office | 1,700 |
| Equipment maintenance charges–Frankfurt office | 2,600 |
| Supplies used–Frankfurt office | 1,400 |
| Salary–Marie Heltzel | 2,500 |
| Labor cost–Frankfurt office | 14,600 |
| Home office depreciation allocated to Frankfurt office | 1,000 |
| Equipment depreciation–Frankfurt office | 2,300 |
| Total | €31,300 |

**Required:**
1. Identify costs that can be controlled by Marie Heltzel.
2. Identify costs that can be traced directly to Frankfurt office.
3. Identify costs allocated to Frankfurt office from the home office. Suggest a cost driver that might have been used to allocate these costs at the home office for each cost.

**2–23.** **Managing By Contribution Margin.** We know the following about March's results for Location # 32 for Cristina's Diners, a franchise operation operating in Southern states:

| | |
|---|---|
| Sales | $480,000 |
| Variable cost of food | 185,000 |
| Other variable costs | 55,000 |
| Controllable fixed costs | 100,000 |
| Direct noncontrollable fixed costs | 85,000 |
| Home office allocated costs | 50,000 |

**Required:**
1. Based on what contribution margin number would you evaluate the Location # 32 manager?
2. Based on what contribution margin number would you evaluate Location # 32?

**2–24.** **Ethics in Cost Control.** Carla Freed, regional manager of Gold Medal Sports Shops, is reviewing the results of 15 stores in her region. Store managers are moved annually. Each store manager's income is very dependent on the direct contribution margin of that store. For the past year, Store 9 has been managed by a person who has operated several other profitable stores in recent years and is about to be promoted to a larger store. Carla notices several items that bother her.
1. Store 9 has almost no personnel training expenses relative to other stores.
2. Store 9 has stopped participating in numerous community events that gave the store significant visibility but did incur substantial expenses.

3. Store 6, where this store manager worked the prior year, has had a severe drop in profits due to higher operating expenses.
4. The advertising budget was spent almost entirely in the first four months of the year, with almost nothing spent in the last several months.

**Required:**
Comment on a possible negative managerial scenario that the regional manager may be sensing. Might the manager of Store 9 be an exceptional manager? Explain.

**2–25.** **Contribution Margin.** As a recent marketing graduate of Big Time University, you landed a job with Food Mills, Inc. as product manager for Red Pop. Recent operating results are:

| | |
|---|---:|
| Sales of Red Pop | $2,000,000 |
| Variable costs of Red Pop | 600,000 |
| Direct noncontrollable fixed marketing expenses | 500,000 |
| Variable selling expenses | 300,000 |
| Direct controllable fixed marketing expenses | 100,000 |
| Allocated corporate marketing expenses (percentage of sales) | 400,000 |
| Allocated corporate office costs (per employee) | 200,000 |

**Required:**
1. Evaluate the profitability of Red Pop.
2. What data should be used to evaluate you as manager of Red Pop?

# PROBLEMS

**2–26.** **Identifying Cost Patterns.** Match the following graphs with the numbered descriptions. Indicate any assumptions you are making. The X-axis is activity; the Y-axis is total dollars of cost.

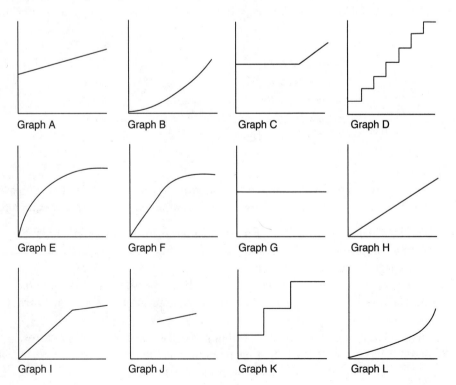

| Graph A | Graph B | Graph C | Graph D |

| Graph E | Graph F | Graph G | Graph H |

| Graph I | Graph J | Graph K | Graph L |

— **1.** a + b (*X*), where "a" and "b" are not equal to zero.

— **2.** Straight-line depreciation expense (a classic fixed cost).

— **3.** Shift supervision salaries (shifts added as demand increases).

— **4.** Municipal utility costs where the rate increases as usage increases. Usage increases with activity increases.

— **5.** Sales commissions paid to salespersons.

— **6.** Workers wages plus overtime premium. Overtime is needed after a certain activity level is reached. Workers are less efficient when they work a lot of overtime.

— **7.** Water and waste water costs with a fixed-cost base charge plus a per-gallon rate beyond a certain level.

— **8.** Payroll taxes that are based on the first $30,000 of each employee's wages. All employees earn more than this at high activity levels.

— **9.** Mixed costs within a relevant range.

— **10.** Cost of hourly messenger service for a regional bank with a reduced rate after 2,000 hours of chargeable time.

— **11.** Wage costs as more hourly telephone callers are added in a tele-marketing campaign.

— **12.** Materials costs where cost per pound decreases as we purchase larger quantities.

 **2–27. Income Statement Formatting.** A partial list of account balances for the Rizwan Corporation follows:

| Revenue and expenses: | | January 1 inventories: | |
|---|---|---|---|
| Purchases of raw materials | $140,000 | Raw materials | $ 45,000 |
| Direct labor | 225,000 | Work in process | 30,000 |
| Indirect labor | 40,000 | Finished goods | 105,000 |
| Rent–factory | 84,000 | | |
| Depreciation–machinery | 35,000 | December 31 inventories: | |
| Insurance–factory | 18,000 | Raw materials | $ 40,000 |
| Salespersons' salaries | 72,000 | Work in process | 35,000 |
| Maintenance–machinery | 12,000 | Finished goods | 110,000 |
| Administrative salaries | 50,000 | | |
| Miscellaneous–factory | 26,000 | | |
| Miscellaneous–office | 40,000 | | |
| Sales | 850,000 | | |

**Required:** Prepare an income statement with a cost of goods manufactured section.

 **2–28. Determining Unknowns.** Find the missing values in the following manufacturing income statement:

| | 2005 | 2006 | 2007 |
|---|---|---|---|
| Sales | ? | $118,700 | $        ? |
| Cost of goods sold: | | | |
| Direct materials inventory 1/1 | $  8,000 | $      ? | $       ? |
| + Direct materials purchases | ? | 20,000 | 30,000 |
| Direct materials available | $      ? | $ 26,000 | $       ? |

| | | | |
|---|---|---|---|
| − Less direct materials inventory 12/31 | ? | − 9,000 | − 12,300 |
| Direct materials used | $    ? | $    ? | $    ? |
| Direct labor | 20,000 | 23,500 | ? |
| Factory overhead | 16,000 | ? | 24,000 |
| Total manufacturing costs | $53,000 | $    ? | $ 90,900 |
| + Work in process inventory 1/1 | 2,000 | 18,000 | ? |
| − Work in process inventory 12/31 | ? | − 16,300 | − 22,300 |
| Cost of goods manufactured | $    ? | $ 63,500 | $ 84,900 |
| + Finished goods inventory 1/1 | ? | ? | ? |
| Goods available for sale | $62,000 | $ 84,500 | $103,200 |
| − Finished goods inventory 12/31 | − 21,000 | ? | ? |
| Cost of goods sold | $    ? | $    ? | $ 78,200 |
| Gross profit | $60,000 | $    ? | $ 46,800 |

Service

**2–29.  Unit Cost and Volume.** Fischer Utilities refurbishes utility meters in older neighborhoods. Estimated costs for a low-activity month and a high-activity month are:

| Meters serviced | 500 | 800 |
|---|---|---|
| Labor costs | $15,000 | $24,000 |
| Replacement parts | 10,000 | 16,000 |
| Other variable refurbishing expenses | 6,000 | 9,600 |
| Fixed refurbishing expenses | 20,000 | 20,000 |
| General and administrative expenses | 15,000 | 21,000 |

**Required:**
1. Using only refurbishing costs, what does it cost to refurbish a meter at each activity level? Prepare a cost function.
2. How do the general and administrative expenses appear to behave? Analyze this cost.
3. What is the firm's average total cost per meter at each level?

**2–30.  Cost Identification of Product Costs.** A regional bakery, Aunt Bird's Goodies, normally produces 200,000 pies per year in the Pie Department. The cost report for the pie department for the year is:

| | |
|---|---|
| Direct materials | $105,000 |
| Direct labor | 91,000 |
| Supervision | 123,000 |
| Supplies used | 36,000 |
| Depreciation on pie department equipment | 32,000 |
| Telephone expenses | 8,000 |
| Other pie department expenses | 25,000 |
| Utilities, insurance, and taxes | 52,000 |
| Rent | 48,000 |
| Total costs. | $520,000 |

Direct materials, supplies used, and direct labor are the only costs that vary with production. Plant-wide costs (utilities, insurance, taxes, and rent) have been allocated to the pie department based on the space occupied by pie making.

**Required:**

1. Determine the variable cost, direct fixed cost, and allocated cost per unit.
2. If a pie sells for $2.90:
   (a) what is the variable contribution margin? per pie? ratio?
   (b) what is the direct contribution margin?
   (c) what is the gross margin from selling pies?
3. Assume that next year only 150,000 pies will be manufactured. Find the price needed just to cover total product costs.

Service

**2–31. Actual Versus Budget.** April's Resume Service provides the following data for January:

|  | Budget | Actual | Difference |
|---|---|---|---|
| Number of resumes prepared | 5,000 | 4,600 | (400) |
| Variable costs | $7,500 | $7,000 | $ 500 |
| Fixed costs | 2,000 | 2,100 | (100) |
| Total costs | $9,500 | $9,100 | $ 400 |

**Required:** Using April's cost function, comment on each of the following statements.
(a) April spent $400 less than she should have in January.
(b) April spent $100 more than she should have for fixed costs.
(c) April spent $100 less than she should have for variable costs.
(d) April should have spent no more than $9,500, given her January activity level.

**2–32. Finding Cost of Goods Sold.** The McCurry Outfitters makes Artic Hotsuits. The general manager has a special board on his office wall where he writes key statistics. For March, the board shows the following:

| | |
|---|---|
| Production output. | 25,000 suits |
| Materials costs. | $50,000 |
| Direct labor costs | 2,000 hours at $10 per hour |
| Factory overhead | $2 per outfit plus $40,000 per month |
| Selling expenses | $1 per outfit sold plus $50,000 per month |

He heard the sales manager brag about selling 22,000 suits this month.

**Required:**

1. From the data, what was the cost of producing an Artic Hotsuit in March?
2. What was cost of goods sold in March?
3. What are the total product and period costs that will appear on McCurry Outfitters' income statement for March?

**2–33. Product Costs and Control.** Metal barrels, used as containers for roofing asphalt and various industrial materials, are manufactured by MVM Containers Company. Materials cost for each barrel is $6.25, and labor cost per barrel is $2.00. Various supplies used in production cost $1.80 per barrel. Other direct operating costs of the Barrel Department, where these barrels are made, are fixed and estimated for the year as follows:

| | |
|---|---|
| Supervision | $85,000 |
| Equipment operating costs | 6,000 |
| Repairs and maintenance of equipment | 5,000 |
| Total | $96,000 |

The supervisor of this department controls all of these costs with the exceptions of equipment depreciation and the supervisor's own salary of $48,000, which is included in supervision costs. Plant-wide overhead is allocated to departments based on a factor that combines space occupied with the number of employees. The Barrel Department expects to be allocated 30 percent of plant-wide overhead costs of $250,000.

**Required:**
1. What are prime costs per barrel? What are variable costs per barrel?
2. What are conversion costs per barrel if 50,000 barrel are produced?
3. Identify the costs controlled by the department supervisor.
4. What are the total costs per barrel, if MVM produces 40,000 barrel per year? If MVM produces 50,000 barrel per year?

Service

**2–34.** **Product Cost in a Service Business.** Robyn Pike developed an annual budget for her Sun City Pharmacy. Her accounting firm has provided the following report for the first quarter:

|  | Budget | Actual | (Over)/Under |
|---|---|---|---|
| Number of prescriptions filled | 20,000 | 22,000 | (2,000) |
| Pharmacists' salaries | $60,000 | $64,000 | $(4,000) |
| Variable overhead costs | 20,000 | 21,500 | (1,500) |
| Fixed overhead costs | 60,000 | 59,000 | 1,000 |

Pharmacists' salaries are considered fixed, because they receive no overtime pay for extra hours worked.

**Required:**
1. What was the cost function that allowed her to create the annual budget?
2. What was the budgeted and actual average cost of filling a prescription for the first quarter?
3. Using her cost function and the actual first quarter activity level, what amounts should have been budgeted for filling 22,000 prescriptions?
4. Prepare a revised budget and compare it to her actual costs to find a new difference between budgeted and actual expenses. Comment.

**2–35.** **Changing Unit Costs.** Gonzales Metals produces rivets from special alloys in a plant in Guadalajara. Its manufacturing costs in Mexican pesos for the first two months of this year were:

|  | Monthly Budget | Actual Costs | |
|---|---|---|---|
|  |  | January | February |
| Prime costs | M$80,000 | M$75,000 | M$82,000 |
| Utilities for the factory | 20,000 | 22,000 | 23,000 |
| Depreciation of machinery and building | 30,000 | 30,000 | 30,000 |
| Supervision and other factory costs | 60,000 | 60,500 | 62,000 |
| Rivet output (units) | 200,000 | 180,000 | 210,000 |

Prime costs and utilities are considered to be variable costs; and the other costs are fixed costs.

**Required:**

1. What was the budgeted average cost per rivet? Find the cost function.
2. What was the actual average cost per rivet for each month?
3. What is the budget variance for each expense for each month based on the actual rivets produced? Comment on the variances.

2–36.  **Ethics of Contract Costs and "Fairness."** The Bureau of Business and Economics Research (BBER) at Western State University has contracted with the Fiscal Planning Office (FPO) of the state legislature to do economic analyses and forecasting. Most of the work involves computer operations using a large planning model and databases that the state Department of Commerce has assembled. The contract calls for payment of all direct costs of personnel with limits on the amount of chargeable time per quarter. An overhead rate is applied to personnel charges at 60 percent of direct personnel costs. This rate is developed by the university to cover common costs of operating the university plus personnel benefits of the persons working on the project.

Data processing costs are reimbursed on a cost basis and include additional equipment needed to perform the analyses, purchase of modeling software, computer time, and data storage.

An auditor from the state's Auditor General's Office has just finished a routine audit of this contract and has written a report critical of the BBER. Among the items noted are:

1. A large copy machine was leased by BBER to prepare reports for the FPO and charged to the contract. The BBER uses the machine for preparing many other reports for the university, including course materials.
2. Computer time is billed at the "average cost of computing time at priority level." This rate is approximately eight times the rate faculty and students are charged for work done on the university's mainframe. The same rate is used for other outside customers of the computer center.
3. Personnel time was billed to the contract using a rate based on the contracting faculty person's annual salary divided by 250 work days. But the auditor found that the work was actually done by a graduate student earning about 20 percent of the faculty person's salary.
4. The software model purchased for FPO contract use has been adapted at low cost to perform analyses for several other BBER corporate clients. It is also used by two faculty members who are doing outside consulting on their own. Corporate clients are charged for the use of the model. The faculty use the model at nights and on weekends when the model is not otherwise used.

**Required:**

1. Identify the parties that have an economic interest in these issues.
2. Does the BBER appear to be costing the contract with the FPO fairly? Evaluate each issue given the information available.

2–37.  **Cost Behavior.** Plesz Food Corporation makes frozen appetizers from spinach. The president finds that sales and variable costs are consistently proportional. Annual data follow:

| | | |
|---|---:|---:|
| Sales | | $100,000 |
| Cost of appetizers made and sold: | | |
| Spinach and direct labor | $35,000 | |
| Processing overhead: Variable | 6,000 | |
| Fixed | 15,000 | 56,000 |
| Gross margin | | $ 44,000 |

| | | |
|---|---|---|
| Less operating expenses: | | |
| Selling expenses: Variable | $ 4,000 | |
| Fixed | 10,000 | |
| General expenses: Variable | 2,000 | |
| Fixed | 15,000 | 31,000 |
| Net operating income | | $13,000 |

**Required:**

Express the above data as a cost function for her production and then for the firm as a whole. What is the variable contribution margin ratio (percentage) for the firm?

Service

**2–38.** **Estimating Costs.** Ferguson WordPros prepares grant requests for scientific research funding. The firm's relevant range is 300 to 400 requests per quarter. Costs at these levels are:

| | For 300 requests | For 400 requests |
|---|---|---|
| Typists' wages. | $1,200 | $1,600 |
| Rent, supplies, and utilities | 1,500 | 1,600 |
| Total costs | $2,700 | $3,200 |

**Required:**

The firm expects to prepare 320 requests in the fourth quarter. Budget operating expenses.

**2–39.** **Finding Relevant Costs in Personal Decisions.**

**Case 1:** You are considering a move from your dorm room to an off-campus apartment next year. You have collected the following information. $600 per month for apartment rent. You are required to sign a 12-month lease, even though you know you will have an internship for the summer in another city. $400 per month for the dorm room rent and a basic meal plan. $2,000 depreciation expense for next year on a car you now own. $250 for gas to drive between your apartment and campus. $300 for CDs of movies that you have become addicted to over the years. $200 for extra telephone calls to your parents proving that you are studying in your apartment every night. In the apartment, you will likely need to spend $100 per month for food costs more than in the dorm.

**Case 2:** You are deciding whether to trade your 1986 Chevy Nova in on a 2006 Mustang. Both cars provide basic transportation that you need while at school. You have assembled essential data. Trade-in value of Chevy is $500. Undepreciated cost (book value) of Chevy is $400. Annual operating cost of Chevy is $1,500. Annual operating cost of Mustang is $1,250. Insurance on Mustang costs $600 more than the Chevy insurance. Garage rent for car will still be $300 per year. If you keep the Chevy, new tires and transmission repair to use it on the road will cost $900. Based on your past behavior, you estimate a yearly cost of $200 for parking tickets.

**Required:** For each case, identify the relevant and irrelevant costs.

**2–40.** **Relevant Costs.** Escanaba Sheet Metal uses one area of its plant for file storage. The plant superintendent complains that this wasted space should be used productively or at least be rented to some other company. The files could be microfilmed at a one-time cost of $20,000. Annual maintenance and updating would cost $3,000. The space could be leased to Elias Trucking at an annual rental of $25,000.

A second option is to manufacture a new product line in this space. Marketing and cost estimates show that the new product can be expected to produce the following results each year:

| | | | |
|---|---|---:|---:|
| Net sales | | | $268,000 |
| Direct materials costs | | $ 50,000 | |
| Direct labor costs | | 32,000 | |
| Supervision and other costs | | 50,000 | |
| Allocated plant costs (based on space occupied): | | | |
| Plant utilities, taxes, and insurance | $34,000 | | |
| Plant supervision | 52,000 | | |
| Plant maintenance and depreciation | 42,000 | 128,000 | |
| Total costs of new product line | | | 260,000 |
| Income before income tax | | | $8,000 |

The superintendent is disappointed to learn that the new product will contribute relatively little profit and is inclined to rent the space to Elias Trucking.

**Required:**
1. Identify the relevant costs for each alternative.
2. What would each alternative contribute to Escanaba's profits?
3. What questions should the superintendent ask about the cost analysis?

Service

**2–41.  Cost Analysis Without Profit as a Bottom Line.** Three Oaks Public Library has three areas, classified by type of books and services provided. The three areas are Technical, General, and Children. The library board of trustees is reviewing budget data and actual spending. Budget and actual direct costs of operating each area for the first quarter of this year are as follows:

| | Technical | General | Children | Total |
|---|---:|---:|---:|---:|
| Budgeted direct costs | $120,000 | $70,000 | $50,000 | $240,000 |
| Actual direct costs: | | | | |
| Salaries. | $ 78,000 | $50,000 | $43,000 | $171,000 |
| Books and periodicals | 47,700 | 16,300 | 11,500 | 75,500 |
| Supplies. | 2,900 | 2,800 | 4,600 | 10,300 |
| Total actual expenses | $128,600 | $69,100 | $59,100 | $256,800 |

Quarterly administrative overhead costs of operating the library were:

| | |
|---|---:|
| Building occupancy and utilities. | $30,000 |
| Library administrative personnel. | 45,000 |

Other data with respect to library areas are:

| | Recent Monthly Activity | | | |
|---|---|---|---|---|
| | Percentage of Useful Space Occupied | Number of Employees | Number of Customers Serviced | Number of Books Checked Out |
| Technical. | 30 % | 6 | 500 | 1,200 |
| General. | 30 | 5 | 2,800 | 2,000 |
| Children | 30 | 4 | 1,700 | 1,800 |
| Administration | 10 | 5 | | |
| Total. | 100 % | 20 | 5,000 | 6,000 |

**Required:**

1. Compare the actual results relative to budgeted direct costs.
2. Why would a cost analysis be important to the library board of trustees?
3. Discuss alternative ways of analyzing operating costs and services provided.
4. Would allocating the administrative overhead costs to the three areas be helpful to your analysis? Comment.

## CASE 2A—WALT'S BUS ROUTES

Illinois Transportation runs passenger and freight services between Chicago airports and downstate cities. The owner, Walter Johnson, is an operations-wise manager. He recently heard about a "segment contribution margin" approach at a university continuing education program. His actual results for the first half of this year have just arrived.

Total revenue was $5.0 million, of which $3.5 million was freight traffic and $1.5 million was passenger traffic. Of the passenger revenue, 60 percent was generated by Route 1, 30 percent by Route 2, and 10 percent by Route 3.

Total direct controllable fixed costs were $600,000, of which $500,000 was spent on freight traffic. Of the remainder, $40,000 could not be traced to specific routes, although it was clearly applicable to passenger traffic in general. Routes 1, 2, and 3 incurred costs of $30,000, $18,000, and $12,000, respectively.

Total direct costs not controllable by segment managers were $500,000, of which 80 percent was traceable to freight traffic. Of the 20 percent traceable to passenger traffic, Routes 1, 2, and 3 should be charged $40,000, $20,000, and $15,000, respectively. The balance was not traceable to a specific route.

Total variable costs were $3.2 million, of which $2.0 million was freight traffic. Of the $1.2 million traceable to passenges traffic, $670,000, $400,000, and $130,000 were incurred by Routes 1, 2, and 3, respectively.

The common fixed costs not clearly traceable to any part of the company amounted to $500,000. Walt has always allocated these costs using a percentage of sales basis.

**Required:**

1. Walter asks you to prepare an earnings statement that shows the performance of each segment of the firm by various types of contribution margin.
2. Comment on what the results tell Walt.

## CASE 2B—HOLIDAY GRAMMY

Holiday Grammy has a part-time business of producing and selling gingerbread houses at holiday craft shows. Production starts in late October and runs four consecutive weeks. To meet health codes, she rents a kitchen at a nearby preschool and bakes and decorates the houses there. She can only use the kitchen on Friday evenings and all day on Saturdays and can produce 300 houses in one weekend. The rent per weekend is $60. Consequently, Holiday Grammy can produce, at most, 1,200 houses for the season. Materials and labor costs amount to $2.50 per house.

The houses are sold at various bazaars throughout the community. Holiday Grammy charges whatever the market will bear at each bazaar. Four bazaars have been announced this year. For some reason, all of this year's bazaars are being held at the same time, thus forcing her to choose which bazaar she will attend. A description of each bazaar with the anticipated selling price and specific costs is as follows:

**Alternative A:** A private athletic club with an elite membership sponsors this two-day bazaar. It charges a flat fee of $25 per day for each seller. Holiday Grammy feels a selling price of $6.75 per house is appropriate. From past experience, she knows she can sell 200 houses with followup orders for 150 houses.

**Alternative B:** A two-day neighborhood bazaar is held in the lower-middle income section of the city. She will charge $5.95 per house and must pay a flat fee of $15 per day. She can sell, at most, 400 houses.

**Alternative C:** This two-day bazaar is held in a community center in another lower-middle income section of the city. Here the price of each house would be a bit lower at $5.45. The center charges $12 per day for each seller. Based on last year's records, she thinks she can sell 500 houses in the two days.

**Alternative D:** The local university sponsors a three-day bazaar and charges each seller 10 percent of the gross revenue from sales as a fee. Because of the student population, she will charge $5.00 per house. But she thinks she can sell 600 houses during the three days.

She has already determined that it is not worthwhile to be in business if she cannot make a minimum of $1.25 per house, since other income options would give her at least that income.

**Required:**
1. Prepare an analysis showing which bazaars, if any, Holiday Grammy should pick to attend this year.
2. If Holiday Grammy could hire someone to handle the next most attractive (profitable) bazaar for her, what is the maximum amount she could pay and at least break even (after her minimum profit per house)?
3. If Holiday Grammy could hire other people to handle additional bazaars and pay them 50 percent of any profits over $1.25 per house as their wage, to which bazaars should she commit?

# COST ESTIMATION AND COST-VOLUME-PROFIT RELATIONSHIPS

## LEARNING OBJECTIVES

1. Understand the significance of cost behavior to decision making and control.

2. Identify the interacting elements of cost-volume-profit analysis.

3. Explain the break-even formula and its underlying assumptions.

4. Calculate the effect on profits of changes in selling prices, variable costs, or fixed costs.

5. Calculate operating leverage, determine its effects on changes in profit, and understand how margin of safety relates to operating leverage.

6. Find break-even points and volumes that attain desired profit levels when multiple products are sold in combination.

7. Obtain cost functions by account analysis, the engineering approach, the scattergraph approach, and the high-low method.

8. Estimate and examine cost functions using regression and correlation analyses (Appendix).

---

## "Can You Lose a Little on Each One, But Make It Up on Volume?"

*David Scott, owner of Baker Cruise Lines, began his cruise business fifteen years ago. During that time, he enjoyed a number of upswings and weathered several downturns in the economy. Generally, the business has had profitable years and has provided a high standard of living for David and his family.*

*But times are changing. Personnel costs continue to rise, particularly fringe benefits like medical insurance premiums. Other costs continue to rise as well. At the same time, because of increased competition from new competitors, prices of cruises have fallen dramatically. David has begun to slash operating costs, but he still faces shrinking profit margins.*

*Because of high profitability in the past, David never analyzed how his costs change in relation to changes in activity levels; nor did he analyze the relationships among revenues, costs, and passenger volume to see how they relate to profit levels. Now, David is wondering how far revenues can drop before he sees the red ink in losses. With that information, he hopes to identify what changes will keep operations profitable. David sees many other businesses closing their doors and is fearful he will have to follow suit someday. He just doesn't know what factors will influence his future costs and revenues.*

---

MANAGERS LIKE DAVID Scott of Baker Cruise Lines need to understand cost behavior and cost estimation to be in a better position to plan, make decisions, and control costs. As we discussed in Chapter 2, cost behavior describes the relationship between costs and an activity as the level of activity increases or decreases. Determining cost behavior is important to management's understanding of overhead costs, marketing costs, and general and administrative expenses and for proper implementation of budgets and budgetary controls. With knowledge of cost behavior, managers can also estimate how costs are affected as future activity levels change, which can lead to better decisions. In addition, knowledge of cost behavior can assist managers in analyzing the interactions among revenues, costs, and volume for profit-planning purposes. These interactions are covered later in this chapter.

## SIGNIFICANCE OF COST BEHAVIOR TO DECISION MAKING AND CONTROL

To understand more fully the significance of a manager's analysis of cost behavior, we look at three areas: decision making, planning and control, and trends in fixed costs.

### Decision Making

Cost behavior affects the decisions management makes. Variable costs are the incremental or differential costs in most decisions. Fixed costs change only if the specific decision includes a change in the capacity requirement, such as more floor space.

Cost-based pricing requires a good understanding of cost behavior because fixed costs pose conceptual problems when converted to per unit amounts. Fixed costs per unit assume a given volume. If the volume turns out to be different from what was used in determining the cost-based price, the fixed cost component of the total cost yields a misleading price. Managers must know which costs are fixed, as well as anticipated volume, to make good pricing decisions.

## Planning and Control

A company plans and controls variable costs differently than it plans and controls fixed costs. Variable costs are planned in terms of input/output relationships. For example, for each unit produced, the materials cost consists of a price per unit of materials times the number of units of materials; and the labor cost consists of the labor rate times the number of labor hours. Once operations are underway, levels of activities may change. The input/output relationships identify changes in resources necessary to respond to the change in activity. If activity levels increase, this signals that more resources (materials, labor, or variable overhead) are needed. If activity levels decrease, the resources are not needed; and procedures can be triggered to stop purchases and reassign or lay-off workers. In cases where more materials or labor time are used than are necessary in the input/output relationship, inefficiencies and waste are in excess of the levels anticipated; and managers must investigate causes and eliminate or reduce the financial impact of the unfavorable variances.

Fixed costs, on the other hand, are planned on an annual basis, if not longer. Control of fixed costs is exercised at two points in time. The first time is when the decision is made to incur a fixed cost. Management evaluates the necessity of the cost and makes the decision to move forward or reject the proposal. Once fixed costs are incurred, another point of control enters, that being the daily decision of how best to use the capacity provided by the cost. For example, a university makes a decision to build a new classroom and faculty office building. That decision is the first point of control. After construction, control is implemented in using the building to its maximum capacity. This will occur if classes are scheduled throughout the day and evening.

Another difference in the planning and control of variable and fixed costs is the level at which costs are controllable. Variable costs can be controlled at the lowest supervisory level. Fixed costs are often controllable only at higher managerial levels.

## Trends in Fixed Costs

Organizations are finding that an increasing portion of their total costs are fixed costs. The following are a few of the more critical changes taking place.

Implementation of more automated equipment is replacing variable labor costs and a major share of the variable overhead costs. Thus, fixed costs are becoming a more significant part of total costs. Costs such as depreciation, taxes, insurance, and fixed maintenance charges are substantially higher. Some industries, like steel and automobile, are becoming essentially fixed cost industries, with variable costs playing a less important role than was once the case.

Another factor that has helped to increase fixed costs significantly is the movement in some industries toward a guaranteed annual wage for production workers. Employees who were once hourly wage earners are now becoming salaried. With the use of more automated equipment, the workers of a company may not represent "touch labor," that is work directly on the product. Instead, the production worker may merely observe that the equipment is operating as it should and is properly supplied with materials or may monitor production by means of a television screen. The production line employee is handling more of the functions normally associated with indirect labor, and the cost is a fixed cost.

# COST–VOLUME–PROFIT (CVP) ANALYSIS

The separation of fixed costs from variable costs contributes to an understanding of how revenues, costs, and volume interact to generate profits. With this understanding, managers can perform any number of analyses that fit into a broad category called **cost-volume-profit**

**(CVP) analysis** or, more commonly, **break-even analysis**. Examples of such analyses include finding the:

1. number of unit sales required to break even;
2. dollars of sales needed to achieve a specified profit level;
3. effect on profits if selling prices and variable costs increase or decrease by a specific amount per unit;
4. increase in selling price needed to cover a projected fixed cost increase.

CVP analysis, as its name implies, examines the interaction of factors that influence the level of profits. Although the name gives the impression that only cost and volume determine profits, several important factors exist that determine whether we have profits or losses and whether profits increase or decrease over time. The key factors appear in the *basic CVP equation*:

$$\text{Sales} = \text{Fixed costs} + \text{Variable costs} + \text{Profit}$$

**or**

$$(\text{Price per unit})(\text{Units sold}) = \text{Fixed costs} + (\text{Variable cost per unit})(\text{Units sold}) + \text{Net income before taxes}$$

The basic CVP equation is merely a condensed income statement, in equation form, where variable costs are separated from fixed costs. This equation, as well as other variations that will be discussed later, appears as formula (1) in Figure 3.1.

The excess of total sales revenue over total variable cost is called the **contribution margin** or, more precisely, variable contribution margin. From the basic CVP equation, we see that the contribution margin contributes to covering fixed costs as well as generating net income. The contribution margin, as well as the **contribution margin ratio**, often plays an important role in CVP analysis. The latter measure is the ratio of the contribution margin to total sales revenue (or, equivalently, the ratio of the contribution margin per unit to the selling price).

Before proceeding, several fundamental assumptions are made to strengthen CVP analysis:

1. Relevant range–CVP analysis is limited to the company's relevant range of activity;
2. Cost behavior identification–fixed and variable costs can be identified separately;
3. Linearity–the selling price and variable cost per unit are constant across all sales levels within the company's relevant range of activity;
4. Equality of production and sales–all units are produced and sold and inventory changes are ignored;
5. Activity measure–the primary cost driver is volume of units;
6. Constant sales mix–the sales of each product in a multiproduct firm is a constant percentage.

Assumptions 1, 2, and 3 are straightforward. Assumption 4 is required because if sales and production are not equal, some amount of variable and fixed costs are treated as assets (inventories) rather than expenses. As long as inventories remain fairly stable between adjacent time periods, this assumption does not seriously limit the applicability of CVP analysis. Regarding assumption 5, factors other than volume may drive costs, as we have discussed earlier in this chapter, and as we will discuss further in later chapters. Costs that vary with cost drivers other than volume can be added to the fixed-cost component. Assumption 6 is discussed in detail later in this chapter. In many cases, these assumptions are and must be violated in real-world situations; but the basic logic and analysis adds value. While our discussion may appear to presume that CVP analysis is applicable only to companies that sell physical products, these techniques are just as applicable to service organizations.

1. Basic CVP equation: $S = FC + VC + P \quad = FC + VC\% (S) + P$

1a. Basic equation further developed $p(X) = FC + v(X) + P$

2. Basic break-even equation: $BES = FC + VC\% (BES)$

2a. Break-even point in units: $BES\ units = \dfrac{FC}{(p - v)} = \dfrac{FC}{CM}$

2b. Break-even point in dollars: $BES = \dfrac{FC}{((p - v) / p)} = \dfrac{FC}{CM\%}$

3. Break-even in units including a target profit: $S\ units = \dfrac{(FC + P)}{CM}$

3a. Break-even in dollars including a target profit: $S = \dfrac{(FC + P)}{CM\%}$

4. Break-even in units including a desired net income after taxes as a lump-sum target profit
$$S\ units = \dfrac{FC + \dfrac{NIAT}{(1 - TR)}}{CM} = \dfrac{FC + NIBT}{CM}$$

4a. Break-even in dollars including a desired net income after taxes as a lump-sum target profit
$$S = \dfrac{FC + \dfrac{NIAT}{(1 - TR)}}{CM\%} = \dfrac{FC + NIBT}{CM\%}$$

4b. Break-even in dollars including a desired net income after taxes as a percentage of sales (or per unit)
$$S = \dfrac{FC}{CM\% - \dfrac{NIAT\%}{(1 - TR)}} = \dfrac{FC}{CM\% - NIBT\%}$$

Where:

- $S$ = Sales
- $FC$ = Fixed cost dollars
- $VC$ = Variable cost dollars
- $VC\%$ = Variable cost dollars as a percentage of sales dollars (or variable cost per unit as a percentage of sales price per unit)
- $P$ = Desired or target profit (Generally acts like a fixed cost)
- $p$ = Selling price per unit
- $v$ = Variable cost per unit
- $CM$ = Variable contribution margin per unit $(p - v)$
- $CM\%$ = Contribution margin ratio $(p - v)/p$
- $BES$ = Break-even sales
- $NIAT$ = Net income after taxes
- $NIAT\%$ = Net income after taxes as a percentage of sales
- $NIBT$ = Net income before taxes (Generally the same as P above)
- $NIBT\%$ = Net income before taxes as a percentage of sales
- $TR$ = Income tax rate
- $X$ = Sales volume in units

**FIGURE 3.1**

Formulas for CVP Analysis

## Contemporary Practice 3.1
### CVP in Australia

A survey of 78 manufacturing companies in Australia revealed that 86 percent of them were using cost-volume-profit analysis in some manner.

Source: Chenhall, R.H. and Langfield-Smith, K., "Adoption and Benefits of Management Accounting Practices: An Australian Study," Management Accounting Research, March 1998, pp. 1–19.

## Basics of CVP Analysis

CVP analysis is often called **break-even analysis** because of the significance of the **break-even point**, which is the volume where total revenue equals total costs. It indicates how many units of product must be sold or how much revenue is needed to at least cover all costs. All break-even analysis can be approached by using Formulas 1 and 1a and by creating their derivations shown in Figure 3.1.

Each unit of product sold is expected to yield revenue in excess of its variable cost and thus contribute to the recovery of fixed costs and provide a profit. The point at which profit is zero indicates that the contribution margin is equal to the fixed costs. Sales volume must increase beyond the break-even point for a company to realize a profit.

Let's look at CVP relationships in the context of Felsen Electronics, a wholesale distributor of calculators. Assume that price and costs for its calculators are as follows:

|  | Dollars Per Unit | Percentage of Selling Price |
|---|---|---|
| Selling price | $25 | 100% |
| Variable cost | 15 | 60% |
| Contribution margin | $10 | 40% |
| Total fixed cost | $ 100,000 | |

Each calculator sold contributes $10 to covering fixed costs and the creation of a profit. Hence, the company must sell 10,000 calculators to break even. The 10,000 calculators sold will result in a total contribution margin of $100,000, equaling total fixed cost.

The break-even point can be calculated by using the basic CVP equations that appear as Formulas 2 and 2a in Figure 3.1. For Felsen Electronics, the break-even point is determined as follows:

2. Break-even sales = Total fixed costs + Variable costs percentage (Break-even sales)
   = $100,000 + 0.60 (Break-even sales)

   Break-even sales (0.40) = $100,000
   Break-even sales = $250,000

**or**

2a. Break-even point in units = Total fixed cost / Contribution margin per unit
    = $100,000 / $10 per unit
    = 10,000 units

A break-even point measured in sales dollars can be computed by Formula 2 as done above, or it can be computed directly using Formula 2b of Figure 3.1, as follows:

Total fixed cost / Contribution margin ratio = Break-even point in sales dollars
$100,000 / 0.40 = $250,000

## A Desired Pretax Profit

In business, only breaking even is not satisfactory, but the break-even relationships do serve as a base for profit planning. If we have a target profit level, we can insert that number into the basic CVP equation. This yields the following general formulas, which appear as Formulas 3 and 3a in Figure 3.1:

3. (Total fixed cost + Net income before tax) / Contribution margin ratio = Sales dollars required
3a. (Total fixed cost + Net income before tax) / Contribution margin per unit = Unit sales required

Continuing with the Felsen Electronics illustration, suppose that Enoch Goodfriend, the president, had set a profit objective of $200,000 before taxes. The units and revenues required to attain this objective are determined as follows:

$$(\$100,000 + \$200,000) / \$10 = 30,000 \text{ calculators}$$

**or**

$$(\$100,000 + \$200,000) / 0.40 = \$750,000$$

## A Desired Aftertax Profit

The profit objective may be stated as a net income after income taxes. Rather than changing with volume of units, income taxes vary with profits after the break-even point. When income taxes are to be considered, the basic CVP equation is altered using Formulas 4, 4a, and 4b in Figure 3.1. Formula 4 works as follows:

4. Break-even units = (Fixed costs + (Net income after tax / (1 – Tax rate))) / Contribution margin per unit

Formula 4a yields the sales dollars needed to earn the desired aftertax profit. Formula 4b approaches profit planning from a different angle–setting a desired after-tax profit goal as a percentage of sales itself.

Suppose Enoch Goodfriend had budgeted a $105,000 aftertax profit and that the income tax rate was 30 percent. We use the above general formulas to obtain the following volume and sales:

$$(\$100,000 + (\$105,000 / (1 – 0.30))) / \$10 = 25,000 \text{ calculators}$$

**or**

$$(\$100,000 + (\$105,000 / (1 – 0.30))) / 0.40 = \$625,000$$

## Desired Profit as an Amount Per Unit or a Percentage of Sales

Managers sometimes state the profit objective as either an average profit per unit or as a percentage of sales revenue (also called profit margin). Suppose Enoch Goodfriend had stated the profit objective as 14 percent of sales on an aftertax basis. Assume a 30 percent tax rate. We can use the basic CVP equation to determine the number of calculators to be sold to meet this target:

Break-even in units = Fixed costs / Contribution margin per unit − (Net income aftertax per unit / (1 − Tax rate))
= $100,000 / ((\$25 − \$15) − \$25 ° (0.14 / (1 − 0.30)))
= 20,000 calculators

Suppose instead that Enoch Goodfriend had stated the profit objective as a $1.40 per unit profit after taxes. Again, we use a CVP equation as follows:

Break-even in units = Fixed costs / (Contribution margin per unit − (Net income after tax per unit / (1 − Tax rate)))
= $100,000 / ((\$25 − \$15) − (\$1.40 / (1 − 0.30)))
= 12,500 calculators

## GRAPHICAL ANALYSIS

Total sales dollars and total costs at different sales volumes can be estimated and plotted on a graph. The information shown on the graph can also be given in conventional reports, but it is often easier to grasp the fundamental facts when they are presented in graphic or pictorial form. Let's look at two common forms of graphical analysis—the break-even chart and the profit-volume graph.

### The Break-Even Chart

Dollars are shown on the vertical scale of the **break-even chart**, and the units of product to be sold are shown on the horizontal scale. The total costs are plotted for the various quantities to be sold and are connected by a line. This line is merely a combination of the fixed and variable cost diagrams from Chapter 2. Total sales at various levels are similarly entered on the chart.

The break-even point lies at the intersection of the total revenue and total cost lines. Losses are measured to the left of the break-even point; the amount of the loss at any point is equal to the dollar difference between the total cost line and the total revenue line. Profit is measured to the right of the break-even point and, at any point, is equal to the dollar difference between the total revenue line and the total cost line. This dollar difference equals the contribution margin per unit multiplied by the volume in excess of the break-even point.

In Figure 3.2, a break-even chart has been prepared for Felsen Electronics using the following data associated with sales levels between 5,000 and 30,000 calculators.

| | | **Number of Calculators Produced and Sold** | | | | |
| | *5,000* | *10,000* | *15,000* | *20,000* | *25,000* | *30,000* |
|---|---|---|---|---|---|---|
| Total revenue | $ 125,000 | $ 250,000 | $ 375,000 | $ 500,000 | $ 625,000 | $ 750,000 |
| Cost: | | | | | | |
| Variable | $75,000 | $ 150,000 | $ 225,000 | $ 300,000 | $ 375,000 | $ 450,000 |
| Fixed | 100,000 | 100,000 | 100,000 | 100,000 | 100,000 | 100,000 |
| Total cost | $ 175,000 | $ 250,000 | $ 325,000 | $ 400,000 | $ 475,000 | $ 550,000 |
| Profit (loss) | ($  50,000) | 0 | $  50,000 | $ 100,000 | $ 150,000 | $ 200,000 |

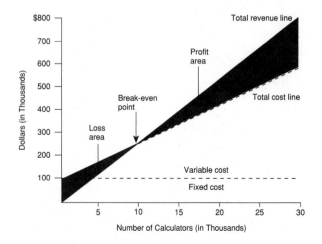

**FIGURE 3.2**

Break-Even Chart

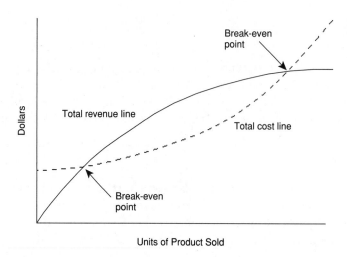

**FIGURE 3.3**

Break-Even Chart With Two Break-Even Points

## Curvature of Revenue and Cost Lines

In some cases, revenues and costs cannot be represented by straight lines. If more units are to be sold, management may have to reduce selling prices. Under these conditions, the revenue function is a curve instead of a straight line. Costs may also be nonlinear depending on what changes take place as volume increases. The cost curve may rise slowly at the start, then more steeply as volume is expanded. This occurs if the variable cost per unit becomes higher as more units are manufactured. Also, fixed costs might change as volume increases. For example, volume increases might cause a jump in supervision, equipment, and space costs. Therefore, it may be possible to have two break-even points as shown in Figure 3.3.

## The Profit-Volume Graph

A **profit-volume graph**, or **P/V graph**, is sometimes used in place of, or along with, a break-even chart. Data used in the earlier illustration of a break-even chart in Figure 3.2 have also been used in preparing the P/V graph shown in Figure 3.4. In general, profits and losses appear on the vertical

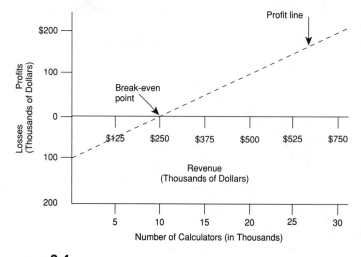

**FIGURE 3.4**

Profit-Volume Graph

scale; and units of product, sales revenue, and/or percentages of capacity appear on the horizontal scale. A horizontal line is drawn on the graph to separate profits from losses. The profit or loss at each of various sales levels is plotted. These points are then connected to form a profit line. The slope of the profit line is the contribution margin per unit if the horizontal line is stated as units of product and is the contribution margin ratio if the horizontal line is stated as sales revenue.

The break-even point is the point where the profit line intersects the horizontal line. Dollars of profit are measured on the vertical scale above the line, and dollars of loss are measured below the line. The P/V graph may be preferred to the break-even chart because profit or loss at any point is shown specifically on the vertical scale; but the P/V graph does not clearly show how cost varies with activity. Break-even charts and P/V graphs are often used together, thus obtaining the advantages of both.

## ANALYSIS OF CHANGES IN CVP VARIABLES

Break-even charts and P/V graphs are convenient devices to show how profit is affected by changes in the factors that impact profit. For example, if unit selling price, unit variable cost, and total fixed cost remain constant, how many more units must be sold to realize a greater profit? Or, if the unit variable cost can be reduced, what additional profit can be expected at any given volume of sales? The effects of changes in sales volume, unit variable cost, unit selling price, and total fixed cost are discussed in the following paragraphs. In all these cases, the starting point for analysis is the CVP formulas in Figure 3.1.

### Sales Volume

For some companies, substantial profits depend on high sales volume. For example, if each unit of product is sold at a relatively low contribution margin, high profits are a function of selling in large quantities. This is more significant when the fixed cost is high.

For an illustration, consider a company that handles a product with a selling price of $1 per unit. Assume a variable cost of $0.70 per unit and a fixed cost of $180,000 per year. The contribution margin, therefore, is $0.30 per unit ($1 − $0.70). Before any profit is realized, the company must sell enough units for the total contribution margin to recover the fixed cost. Therefore, 600,000 units must be sold just to break even:

$$\$180,000 \div \$.30 = 600,000 \text{ units}$$

For every unit sold in excess of 600,000, a $0.30 profit before tax is earned. In such a situation, the company must be certain that it can sell substantially more than 600,000 units to earn a reasonable profit on its investment.

When products sell for relatively high contribution margins per unit, the fixed cost is recaptured with the sale of fewer units, and a profit can be made on a relatively low sales volume. Suppose that each unit of product sells for $1,000 and that the variable cost per unit is $900. The fixed cost for the year is $180,000. The contribution margin ratio is only 10 percent, but this is equal to $100 from each unit sold. The break-even point will be reached when 1,800 units are sold. The physical quantity handled is much lower than it was in the preceding example, but the same principle applies. More than 1,800 units must be sold if the company is to produce a profit.

A key relationship between changes in volume and pretax profit is the following:

Contribution margin per unit × Change in sales volume = Change in net income

This relationship presumes that the contribution margin per unit remains unchanged when the sales volume changes. It also presumes that fixed costs have not been changed. Suppose that Enoch Goodfriend of Felsen Electronics wishes to know how the sale of an additional 500 calculators would impact profits. The above relationship reveals that net income would increase by $5,000 ($10 contribution margin per unit × 500 units).

## Variable Costs

The relationship between the selling price of a product and its variable cost is important in any line of business. Even small savings in variable cost can add significantly to profits. A reduction of a fraction of a dollar in the unit cost becomes a contribution to fixed cost and profit. If 50,000 units are sold in a year, a $0.10 decrease in the unit cost becomes a $5,000 increase in profit. Conversely, a $0.10 increase in unit cost decreases profit by $5,000.

Management is continually searching for opportunities to make even small cost savings. What appears trivial may turn out to be the difference between profit or loss for the year. In manufacturing, it may be possible to save on materials cost by using cheaper materials that are just as satisfactory. Using materials more effectively can also result in savings. Improving methods of production may decrease labor and overhead costs per unit.

A small savings in unit cost can give a company a competitive advantage. If prices must be reduced, the low-cost producer will usually suffer less. At any given price and fixed cost structure, the low-cost producer will become profitable faster as sales volume increases.

The following operating results of three companies show how profit is influenced by changes in the variable cost pattern. Each of the three companies sells 100,000 units of one product line at a price of $5 per unit. Each has an annual fixed cost of $150,000. Company A can manufacture and sell each unit at a variable cost of $2.50. Company B has found ways to save costs and can produce each unit for a variable cost of $2, while Company C has allowed its unit variable cost to rise to $3.

|  | Company A | Company B | Company C |
|---|---|---|---|
| Number of units sold | 100,000 | 100,000 | 100,000 |
| Unit selling price | $ 5.00 | $ 5.00 | $ 5.00 |
| Unit variable cost | 2.50 | 2.00 | 3.00 |
| Unit contribution margin | 2.50 | 3.00 | 2.00 |
| Contribution margin ratio | 50% | 60% | 40% |
| Total sales revenue | $ 500,000 | $ 500,000 | $ 500,000 |
| Total variable cost | 250,000 | 200,000 | 300,000 |
| Total contribution margin | $ 250,000 | $ 300,000 | $ 200,000 |
| Fixed cost | 150,000 | 150,000 | 150,000 |
| Income before income tax | $ 100,000 | $ 150,000 | $ 50,000 |

A difference of $0.50 in unit variable cost between Company A and Company B or between Company A and Company C adds up to a $50,000 difference in profit when 100,000 units are sold. The low-cost producer has a $1 per unit profit advantage over the high-cost producer. If sales volume should fall to 60,000 units per company, Company B would have a profit of $30,000, Company A would break even, and Company C would suffer a loss of $30,000. The same results are shown in the break-even chart in Figure 3.5.

The fixed cost line for each company is drawn at $150,000, the amount of the fixed cost. When 40,000 units are sold, a difference of $20,000 occurs between each total cost line. The lines diverge as greater quantities are sold. At the 100,000-unit level, the difference is $50,000 between each total cost line. Company B can make a profit by selling any quantity in excess of 50,000 units, but Company C must sell 75,000 units to break even. With its present cost structure, Company C will have to sell in greater volume if it is to earn a profit equal to profits earned by Company A or Company B. Company C is the inefficient producer in the group and, as such, operates at a disadvantage. When there is enough business for everyone, Company C will earn a profit but will most likely earn less than the others. When business conditions are poor, Company C will be more vulnerable to losses.

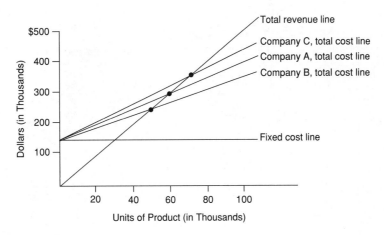

**FIGURE 3.5**

Effects of Variable Cost Changes

## Price Policy

One of the ways to improve profit is to get more sales volume; and, to stimulate sales volume, management may decide to reduce prices. Bear in mind, however, that if demand for the product is inelastic or if competitors also reduce prices, volume may not increase at all. Moreover, even if the price reduction results in an increase in sales volume, the increase may not be enough to overcome the handicap of selling at a lower price. This point is often overlooked by optimistic managers who believe that a small increase in volume can compensate for a slight decrease in price.

Price cuts, like increases in unit variable costs, decrease the contribution margin. On a unit basis, price decreases may appear to be insignificant; but when the unit differential is multiplied by thousands of units, the total effect may be tremendous. Many more units may need to be sold to make up for the difference. Company A, for example, hopes to increase profit by stimulating sales volume; and, to do so, it plans to reduce the unit price by 10 percent. The following tabulation portrays its present and contemplated situations:

|  | Present Situation | Contemplated Situation |
|---|---|---|
| Selling price | $ 5.00 | $ 4.50 |
| Variable cost | 2.50 | 2.50 |
| Contribution margin | $ 2.50 | $ 2.00 |
| Contribution margin ratio | 50% | 44.4% |

At present, one-half of each revenue dollar can be applied to fixed cost and profit. When revenues are twice the fixed cost, Company A will break even. Therefore, 60,000 units yielding revenues of $300,000 must be sold if fixed cost is $150,000. But when the price is reduced, less than half of each dollar can be applied to fixed cost and profit. To recover $150,000 in fixed cost, unit sales must be 75,000 ($150,000 divided by the $2 contribution margin per unit). Thus, to overcome the effect of a 10 percent price cut, unit sales must increase by 25 percent:

$$(75,000 - 60,000) \div 60,000 = 25\% \text{ increase}$$

Similarly, revenue must increase to $337,500 (75,000 units × $4.50 per unit). This represents a 12.5 percent increase, as follows:

$$(\$337,500 - \$300,000) \div \$300,000 = 12.5\% \text{ increase}$$

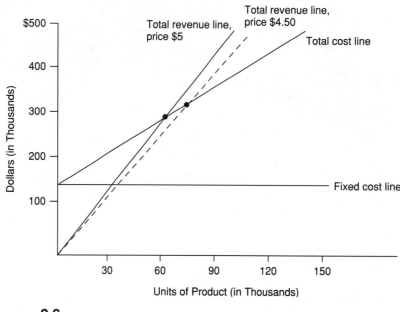

**FIGURE 3.6**

Effect of a Price Reduction

Not only must total revenue be higher, but with a lower price, more units must be sold to obtain that revenue. A break-even chart showing these changes appears in Figure 3.6.

The present pretax income of $100,000 can still be earned if 125,000 units are sold. This is obtained using formula (5) of Figure 3.1:

$$(\$150,000 + \$100,000) \div \$2 = 125,000 \text{ units}$$

## Fixed Costs

A change in fixed cost has no effect on the contribution margin. Increases in fixed cost are recovered when the contribution margin from additional units sold is equal to the increase in fixed cost. Presuming that the contribution margin per unit remains unchanged, the following general relationship holds:

(Contribution margin per unit × Change in sales volume) − Change in fixed cost

= Change in net income

Suppose Enoch Goodfriend estimates that, if he spends an additional $30,000 on advertising, he should be able to sell an additional 2,500 calculators. The above equation reveals that profits would decrease by $5,000 or [($10 x 2,500) − $30,000].

Because fixed cost is not part of the contribution margin computation, the slope of the total cost line on a break-even chart is unaffected by changes in fixed cost. The new total cost line is drawn parallel to the original line, and the vertical distance between the two lines, at any point, is equal to the increase or the decrease in fixed cost.

The break-even chart in Figure 3.7 shows the results of an increase in fixed cost from $100,000 to $130,000 at Felsen Electronics. Under the new fixed cost structure, the total cost line shifts upward; and, at any point, the new line is $30,000 higher than it was originally. To break even or maintain the same profit as before, Felsen Electronics must sell 3,000 more calculators.

Decreases in fixed cost would cause the total cost line to shift downward. The total contribution margin can decline by the amount of the decrease in fixed cost without affecting profit. The lower sales volume now needed to maintain the same profit can be calculated by dividing the unit contribution margin into the decrease in fixed cost.

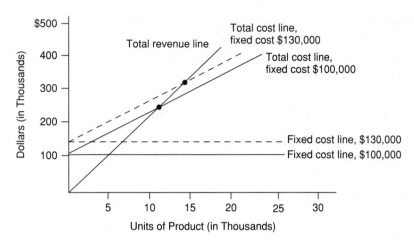

**FIGURE 3.7**

Effect of an Increase in Fixed Cost

## Ethical Considerations When Changing CVP Variables

Managers are often under pressure to reduce costs—both variable and fixed costs. Many companies have downsized in recent years by eliminating jobs and even closing plants. Managers must be careful not to cut costs in an unethical manner. Changing a price can also involve ethical issues. For instance, immediately after a hurricane hit southern Florida several years ago, some sellers of building supplies were accused of "price gouging."

## MEASURES OF RELATIONSHIP BETWEEN OPERATING LEVELS AND BREAK-EVEN POINTS

Companies want to know where they are with respect to the break-even point. If they are operating around the break-even point, management may be more conservative in its approach to implementing changes and mapping out new strategies. On the other hand, if they are operating well away from the break-even point, management will be more aggressive because the downside risk is not as great. Two measures that relate to this distance between a break-even point and the current or planned operating volume are operating leverage and margin of safety. These measures are the subject of the following sections.

### Operating Leverage

**Operating leverage** measures the effect that a percentage change in sales revenue has on pretax profit. It is a principle by which management in a high fixed cost industry with a relatively high contribution margin ratio (low variable costs relative to sales revenue) can increase profits substantially with a small increase in sales volume. We typically call this measure the operating leverage factor or the degree of operating leverage, and it is computed as follows:

$$\frac{\text{Contribution margin}}{\text{Net income before taxes}} = \text{Operating leverage factor}$$

As profit moves closer to zero, the closer the company is to the break-even point. This will yield a high operating leverage factor. As sales volume increases, the contribution margin and pretax profit both increase; and, consequently, the operating leverage factor becomes progressively smaller. Hence, the operating leverage factor is related to the distance between the break-even point and a current or expected sales volume. With an increase in sales volume, profits will increase by the percentage increase in sales volume multiplied by the operating leverage factor.

Suppose Felsen Electronics is currently selling 15,000 calculators. With its unit contribution margin of $10 and fixed costs of $100,000, its operating leverage factor is 3, computed as follows:

$$\frac{(15,000)(\$10)}{(15,000)(\$10) - \$100,000} = \frac{\$150,000}{\$50,000} = 3$$

At a sales volume of 15,000, if sales volume can be increased by an additional 10 percent, profit can be increased by 30 percent:

| Percentage increase in sales volume | | Operating leverage factor | | Percentage increase in pretax profit |
|---|---|---|---|---|
| 10% | × | 3 | = | 30% |

A 10 percent increase in sales volume will increase sales from 15,000 units to 16,500 units. Operating leverage suggests that the pretax profit should be $65,000 ($50,000 × 1.3). Indeed, when we deduct the $100,000 fixed cost from the new contribution margin of $165,000 (16,500 × $10), we obtain a pretax profit of $65,000.

A company with high fixed costs will have to sell in large volume to recover the fixed costs. However, if the company also has a high contribution margin ratio, it will move into higher profits very quickly after the break-even volume is attained. Hence, a fairly small percentage increase in sales volume (computed on a base that is already fairly large) will increase profits rapidly.

## Margin of Safety

The **margin of safety** is the excess of actual (or expected) sales over sales at the break-even point. The excess may also be computed as a percentage of actual (or expected) sales. The margin of safety, expressed either in dollars or as a percentage, shows how much sales volume can be reduced without sustaining losses. The formulas for calculating margin of safety are:

Margin of safety in dollars = Actual (or expected) sales − Break-even sales

$$\text{Margin of safety in percentage form} = \frac{\text{Margin of safety in dollars}}{\text{Actual (or exprected)sales}}$$

For our purposes, margin of safety is the percentage form. Therefore, unless otherwise specified, a reference to margin of safety will mean a percentage.

Recall that the break-even sales level for Felsen Electronics was $250,000. At an actual sales level of 15,000 calculators, its safety margin is one-third, calculated as follows:

$$\frac{[(15,000)(\$25) - \$250,000]}{(15,000)(\$25)} = \frac{\$125,000}{\$375,000} = 0.333 \text{ or } 1/3$$

Note that one-third is the reciprocal of the operating leverage factor computed earlier for Felsen Electronics. The margin of safety will always be the reciprocal of the operating leverage factor.

## THE SALES MIX

When selling more than one product line, the relative proportion of each product line to the total sales is called the **sales mix**. With each product line having a different contribution margin, management will try to maximize the sales of the product lines with higher contribution margins. However, a sales mix results because limits on either sales or production of any given product line may exist.

When products have their own individual production facilities and fixed costs are specifically identified with the product line, cost-volume-profit analysis is performed for each product line. However, in many cases, product lines share facilities; and the fixed costs relate to many products. For such a situation, cost-volume-profit analysis requires averaging of data by using the sales mix percentages as weights. Consequently, a break-even point can be computed for any assumed mix of sales; and a break-even chart or P/V graph can be constructed for any sales mix.

Let's consider cost-volume-profit analysis with a sales mix. Suppose that Bijan's Exotic Catering Service offers three basic dinners for events that it caters: duck, venison, and shark. Assume that the following budget is prepared for these three product lines. Fixed costs are budgeted at $500,000 for the period:

| Product Lines | Sales Volume (Meals) | Price Per Meal | Unit Variable Cost | Contribution Dollars | Margin Ratio |
|---|---|---|---|---|---|
| Duck | 20,000 | $50 | $20 | $30 | 60% |
| Venison | 10,000 | 50 | 30 | 20 | 40% |
| Shark | 10,000 | 50 | 40 | 10 | 20% |
| Total | 40,000 | | | | |

The break-even point in units (i.e., meals) is computed using a weighted average contribution margin as follows:

| Product Lines | Sales Mix Proportions | | Contribution Margin Per Meal | | Weighted Contribution Margin |
|---|---|---|---|---|---|
| Duck | 50% | × | $ 30 | = | $ 15.00 |
| Venison | 25% | × | 20 | = | 5.00 |
| Shark | 25% | × | 10 | = | 2.50 |
| Weighted contribution margin | | | | | $ 22.50 |

$$\frac{\text{Fixed cost}}{\text{Weighted contribution margin}} = \frac{\$500,000}{\$22.50} = 22{,}222 \text{ total units}$$

The detailed composition of this overall break-even point of 22,222 units (and contribution margins at this level) is as follows:

| Product Lines | Sales Mix Proportions | | Total Units | | No. of Meals | | Contribution Margin Per Meal | | Contribution Margin |
|---|---|---|---|---|---|---|---|---|---|
| Duck | 50% | × | 22,222 | = | 11,111 | × | $30 | = | $ 333,330 |
| Venison | 25% | × | 22,222 | = | 5,556 | × | 20 | = | 111,120 |
| Shark | 25% | × | 22,222 | = | 5,556 | × | 10 | = | 55,560 |
| Break-even contribution margin* | | | | | | | | | $ 500,010 |

* Approximately equal to fixed cost of $500,000. Difference is due to rounding.

To obtain the sales revenue at the break-even point directly, we calculate it as we did earlier in the chapter. Simply divide the weighted contribution margin ratio into the fixed costs. Individual product line revenues will be total revenues multiplied by individual sales mix proportions. Continuing with our illustration, we have:

| | Product Lines | | | |
| | Duck | Venison | Shark | Total |
|---|---|---|---|---|
| Units (number of meals) | 20,000 | 10,000 | 10,000 | 40,000 |
| Revenues | $1,000,000 | $500,000 | $500,000 | $2,000,000 |
| Variable cost | 400 000 | 300,000 | 400,000 | 1,100,000 |
| Contribution margin | $ 600,000 | $200,000 | $100,000 | $ 900,000 |
| Less fixed cost | | | | 500,000 |
| Budgeted net income before taxes | | | | $ 400,000 |

As shown in the following calculations, the weighted contribution margin ratio is 45 percent, and revenue at the break-even point is $1,111,111.

$$\frac{\text{Total contribution margin}}{\text{Total revenues}} = \frac{\$900,000}{\$2,000,000} = 45\%$$

$$\frac{\text{Fixed cost}}{\text{Weighted contribution margin ratio}} = \frac{500,000}{45\%} = \$1,111,111$$

Another way to obtain the number of meals needed to break even is by using an equations approach. Let "d" represent the number of duck meals, "v" represent the number of venison meals, and "s" represent the number of shark meals. The following equation is an extension of the basic CVP equation to this scenario with multiple products:

$$\$30d + \$20v + \$10s = \$500,000$$

Next, we need to write the equation in terms of one variable rather than three by using the information from the sales mix proportions. Since there are half as many venison and shark meals as duck meals, we can rewrite the equation as follows:

$$\$30d + \$20(.5d) + \$10(.5d) = \$500,000$$

Solving this equation, we obtain d = 11,111, and therefore, v = s = .5(11,111) = 5,556. These are the same numbers of meals we derived earlier.

If the actual sales mix changes from the budgeted sales mix, the break-even point and other factors of cost-volume-profit analysis may change. Suppose that Bijan's Exotic Catering Service actually operated at the budgeted capacity with fixed costs of $500,000. The unit selling prices and variable costs were also in agreement with the budget. Yet, with the same volume of 40,000 meals and total revenue of $2,000,000, the pretax profit was considerably lower than anticipated. The difference was due to a changed sales mix. Assume the following actual results:

| Product Lines | Sales Volume (Meals) | Unit Contribution Margin | Total Contribution Margin | Revenue |
|---|---|---|---|---|
| Duck | 5,000 | $30 | $150,000 | $ 250,000 |
| Venison | 20,000 | 20 | 400,000 | 1,000,000 |
| Shark | 15,000 | 10 | 150,000 | 750,000 |
| Total | 40,000 | | $700,000 | $2,000,000 |
| Less fixed cost | | | (500,000) | |
| Actual net income after taxes | | | $200,000 | |

Instead of earning $400,000 before taxes, the company earned only $200,000. Sales of venison and shark, the less profitable products, were much better than expected. At the same time, sales of the best product line, duck, were less than expected. As a result, the total contribution margin was less than budgeted, so net income before taxes was also less than budgeted.

One way to encourage the sales force to sell more of the high contribution margin lines is to compute sales commissions on the contribution margin rather than on sales revenue. If sales commissions are based on sales revenue, a sales force may sell a high volume of less profitable product lines and still earn a satisfactory commission. But if sales commissions are related to contribution margin, the sales force is encouraged to strive for greater sales of more profitable products and, in doing so, will help to improve total company profits.

# Cost Estimation

**Cost estimation** is the process of determining a cost relationship with activity for an individual cost item or grouping of costs. We typically express this relationship as an equation that reflects the cost behavior within the relevant range. In Chapter 2, we referred to this equation as a cost function – a + b (X). The **dependent variable** (Y) of the equation is what we want to predict (i.e., costs, in our case). The **independent variable** (X) (i.e., the activity) is used to predict the dependent variable. The cost function can be written as follows:

$$Y = a + b (X)$$

This equation states that Y, the total cost, is equal to a value *a* plus a factor of variability applied to the activity level X. The value *a* represents the fixed cost. The factor *b* represents the change in Y in relation to the change in X, i.e., the variable cost per unit of activity.

Although a number of techniques exist for estimating a cost-to-activity relationship, we will discuss four techniques: (1) account analysis, (2) engineering approach, (3) scattergraph and visual fit, and (4) high-low method. A fifth method, regression analysis, is discussed in the Appendix to this chapter since it requires some knowledge of statistics.

## Account Analysis

In **account analysis**, accountants estimate variable and fixed cost behaviors of a particular cost by evaluating information from two sources. First, the accountant reviews and interprets managerial policies with respect to the cost. Second, the accountant inspects the historical activity of the cost. All cost accounts are classified as fixed or variable. If a cost shows semivariable or semifixed cost behavior, the analyst either (1) makes a subjective estimate of the variable and fixed portions of the cost or (2) classifies the account according to the preponderant cost behavior. Unit variable costs are estimated by dividing total variable costs by the quantity of the cost driver.

As an example, suppose for cost control purposes, the managing partner of Azran & Associates, a stock brokerage firm, wishes to estimate the brokers' automobile expenses as a function of miles driven. Costs for the past quarter, during which 58,000 miles were driven, are classified as follows:

| Item | Cost | Classification |
|------|------|----------------|
| Fuel | $3,200 | Variable |
| Depreciation | 11,200 | Fixed |
| Insurance | 3,900 | Fixed |
| Maintenance | 1,800 | Variable |
| Parking | 2,100 | Fixed |

The fixed costs total $17,200, while the variable cost per mile is 8.62 cents [($3,200 + $1,800) ÷ 58,000]. Hence, the cost function would be expressed as:

$$Y = \$17,200 + \$.0862 \text{ (X)}$$

The managing partner believes that costs should be stable for the coming quarter for which the brokers' auto travel budget would be 65,000 miles. Accordingly, the auto expenses should total $22,803 − $17,200 + ($.0862 × 65,000). The managing partner intends to investigate any significant deviation from this total cost.

Account analysis is fairly accurate for determining cost behavior in many cases. Vendor invoices, for instance, show that direct materials have a variable cost behavior; leasing costs are fixed. A telephone bill is a semivariable cost. One portion is fixed for the minimum monthly charge, and the remainder may be variable with usage.

Account analysis has limited data requirements and is simple to implement. The judgment necessary to make the method work comes from experienced managers and accountants who are familiar with the operations and management policies. Because operating results are required for only one period, this method is particularly useful for new products or situations involving rapid changes in products or technologies.

The two primary disadvantages of this method are its lack of a range of observations and its subjectivity. Using judgment generates two potential issues: (1) different analysts may develop different cost estimates from the same data, and (2) the results of analysis may have significant financial consequences for the analyst, therefore the analyst will likely show self-serving estimates. Another potential weakness in the method is that data used in the analysis may reflect unusual circumstances or inefficient operations, as is likely to occur with new products. These factors then become incorporated in the subsequent cost estimates. This method is also dependent on the quality of the detailed chart of accounts and transaction coding.

## Engineering Approach

The **engineering approach** uses analysis and direct observation of processes to identify the relationship between inputs and outputs and then quantifies an expected cost behavior. A basic issue in manufacturing a product is determining the amount of direct materials, direct labor, and overhead required to run a given process. For a service, the question relates primarily to the labor and overhead costs.

One method of applying this approach to a product is to make a list of all materials, labor tasks, and overhead activities necessary for the manufacturing process. Engineering specifications and vendor information can be used to quantify the units of the various materials and subassemblies. Time and motion studies can help estimate the amount of time required for the tasks to be performed. Other analyses are used to assess the overhead relationships to the process. Once quantities and time are determined, those amounts are priced at appropriate materials prices, labor rates, and overhead rates.

A major advantage of the engineering approach is that it details each step required to perform a task. This permits transfer of information to similar tasks in different situations. It also allows an organization to review productivity and identify strengths and weaknesses in the process. Another advantage is that it does not require historical accounting data. It is, therefore, a useful approach in estimating costs of new products and services. The major disadvantage is the expensive nature of the approach. For example, time and motion studies require in-depth examinations of task and close observations of individuals performing each task. An additional disadvantage is that estimates made by the engineering approach are often based on near-optimal working conditions. Since actual working conditions are generally less than optimal, cost estimates using the engineering approach will generally understate the actual costs.

## Scattergraph and Visual Fit

An approach that yields rough approximations to fixed and variable costs is called **scattergraph and visual fit**. With the advent of personal computers, the mechanical nature of this approach loses its appeal. When the analyst has data, the computer can graph the observations and estimate cost behavior quickly. However, we present the details below because, in many cases, it can be used in a preliminary analysis and can easily be applied.

The first step in applying the approach is to graph each observation, with cost on the vertical axis and activity or cost driver on the horizontal axis. The second step is to fit visually and judgmentally a line to the data. Care should be taken so that the distances of the observations above the line are approximately equal to the distances of the observations below the line. Figure 3.8 shows a graph of maintenance cost and hours of operation for ten weeks of activity. The data for this graph are as follows:

| Hours (X) | Maintenance Cost (Y) |
|-----------|----------------------|
| 50 | $120 |
| 30 | 110 |
| 10 | 60 |
| 50 | 150 |
| 40 | 100 |
| 30 | 80 |
| 20 | 70 |
| 60 | 150 |
| 40 | 110 |
| 20 | 50 |

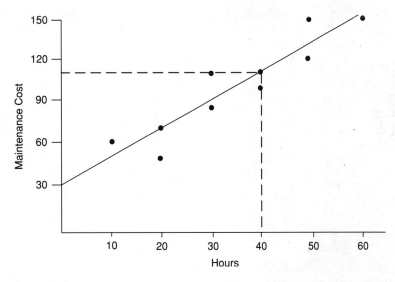

**FIGURE 3.8**

A Visually Fitted Cost Function

The third step is to estimate the cost behavior from the plotted line. The variable cost per hour is indicated by the slope of the line, and the fixed cost is measured where the line begins at zero hours of activity. In the maintenance cost example, the fixed cost is at the Y-intercept and is $30. The variable costs can be calculated by subtracting fixed costs from total costs at some point along the line. Let's select 40 hours of operation. The cost indicated by the line at 40 hours is approximately $110. Compute variable costs as follows:

| | |
|---|---|
| Total costs at 40 hours of operation | $110 |
| Less fixed costs | 30 |
| Variable costs | $80 |

$80 variable costs ÷ 40 hours = $2 per hour of operation

This analysis yields the following cost function:

$$Y = \$30 + \$2\ (X)$$

When used by itself, the scattergraph and visual fit approach is limited by the judgment of the person drawing the line through the data. Even reasonable people will disagree on the slope and intercept for a given graph. However, lines that are drawn visually will tend to be fairly consistent near the center of the data. Therefore, a visual fit may be a useful way to obtain rough approximations near the center of the data. Care should be taken with estimates away from the center. The further from the central area, the larger are the errors that may occur in estimates of fixed and variable costs.

## High-Low Method

Another method for obtaining rough approximations to fixed and variable costs is the **high-low method**. The first step is to list the observed costs for various levels of activity from the highest level in the range to the lowest. This method chooses observations associated with the highest and the lowest activity levels, not the highest and lowest costs. The second step is to divide the difference in activity between the highest and the lowest levels into the difference in cost for the corresponding activity levels to arrive at the variable cost rate. As an example, suppose a manager for Edlin's Pest Control Service wishes to estimate supplies costs as input for bidding on jobs. Its costs of supplies for several recent jobs, along with the hours of activity, are as follows:

| | Hours of Activity | Supplies Cost |
|---|---|---|
| High | 95 | $397 |
| | 90 | 377 |
| | 87 | 365 |
| | 82 | 345 |
| | 78 | 329 |
| | 75 | 317 |
| | 66 | 281 |
| | 58 | 239 |
| Low | 50 | 217 |

The difference in hours is 45 (95–50), and the difference in cost is $180 ($397–$217). The variable supplies cost per hour is computed below:

$$\frac{\text{Cost at highest activity} - \text{Cost at lowest activity}}{\text{Highest activity} - \text{Lowest activity}} = \frac{\$180}{45} = \$4 \text{ Variable cost per hour}$$

The fixed cost is estimated by using the total cost at either the highest or lowest level and subtracting the estimated total variable cost for that level:

Total fixed cost = Total cost at highest activity − (Variable cost per unit × Highest activity)

**or**

Total fixed cost = Total cost at lowest activity − (Variable cost per unit × Lowest activity)

If the variable cost is calculated correctly, the fixed cost will be the same at both the high and low points. For the above illustration, the calculation of total fixed cost is as follows:

$$\begin{aligned} \text{Total fixed cost} &= \$397 - (\$4 \text{ Variable cost per hour} \times 95 \text{ hours}) \\ &= \$397 - \$380 \\ &= \$17 \end{aligned}$$

**or**

$$\begin{aligned} \text{Total fixed cost} &= \$217 - (\$4 \text{ Variable cost per hour} \times 50 \text{ hours}) \\ &= \$217 - \$200 \\ &= \$17 \end{aligned}$$

The cost function that results from the high-low method is:

$$Y = \$17 + \$4 \, (X)$$

If Edlin's manager forecasts that a particular job would require 75 hours, the bid would include an estimate of $317 for supplies cost.

Occasionally, either the highest or lowest activity or the cost associated with one of those points is obviously an outlier to the remaining data. When this happens, use the next highest or lowest observation that appears to align better with the data. Sometimes only two data points are available; and, in effect, these are used as the high and low points.

The high-low method is simple and can be used in a multiplicity of situations. Its primary disadvantage is that two points from all of the observations will only produce reliable estimates of fixed and variable cost behavior if the extreme points are representative of the points in-between. Otherwise, distorted results may occur.

If enough quality data are available, statistical techniques can provide more objective cost estimates than we have discussed thus far. These techniques are covered in the Appendix to this chapter.

## Ethical Considerations in Estimating Costs

All cost estimation methods involve some degree of subjectivity. With account analysis, managers judgmentally classify costs. In the engineering method, the manager must often subjectively adjust data obtained from near-optimal working conditions to normal working conditions. The scattergraph approach involves a subjective fitting of a line to data points. With the high-low method, one must decide whether the high and low points are representative data points.

The subjectivity inherent in cost estimation can lead to biased cost estimates. Indeed in certain instances, incentives exist for managers to bias cost estimates. In developing budgets or cost-based prices, managers may want to overestimate costs. In developing proposals for projects or programs, incentives may exist to underestimate costs. Managers must take care not to use subjectivity as an opportunity to act unethically.

## Other Issues for Cost Estimation

An overriding concern with any cost estimation technique is that of extrapolating beyond the relevant range of activity. Cost behavior may change drastically once the activity falls below or rises above the relevant range. For instance, assume the relevant range of activity for Edlin's Pest Control Service is 40 to 100 hours. We wish to predict the supplies cost for the coming time period during which 130 hours of activity are expected. Since this level is above the relevant range, the cost function we derived earlier may not be appropriate to use.

We have presumed that our cost data are suitably represented by a straight line (linear) and not by a curve. In some situations, the linear relationship may not be appropriate. Costs, for example, may not increase at a constant rate but instead may change at an increasing or a decreasing rate as the measure of activity increases. Hence, the cost data would be represented by a curve rather than a straight line. The shape of the line or curve can be revealed by plotting a sufficient amount of data for various volumes of activity.

## SUMMARY

In planning profit, management considers sales volume, selling prices, variable costs, fixed costs, and the sales mix. When the contribution margin is equal to fixed costs, the company breaks even. A desired profit level can be attained when the contribution margin is equal to the fixed costs plus the desired profit before income taxes. Break-even charts or profit-volume graphs are visual representations of profits or losses that can be expected at different volume levels.

In making plans, management can review various alternatives to see how they will affect profit. For example, what will likely happen if the selling price is increased or if the variable cost is decreased? Often a relatively small change in variable cost per unit will have a relatively large effect on profit. Prices may be cut to increase sales volume, but this will not necessarily increase profit.

Recent developments such as increased automation tend to increase the importance of fixed costs in the total cost structure. With a relatively high contribution margin ratio and relatively high fixed costs, a small percentage increase in sales volume can be translated into a substantial increase in profits. This principle is known as operating leverage. The reciprocal of the operating leverage factor is the margin of safety.

When more than one product line is sold, the relative proportion of total sales for each product line is known as the sales mix. To maximize profit, management will try to maximize the sales of product lines with higher contribution margin ratios. A break-even point and break-even units for each product line can be computed for any given sales mix.

Four methods for identifying variable and fixed cost behavior are account analysis, the engineering approach, the scattergraph and visual fit, and the high-low method. In account analysis, the analyst determines the cost behavior of a specific cost by reviewing and interpreting managerial policies with respect to the cost and by inspecting the historical activity of the cost. The engineering approach uses analysis and direct observation of processes to identify the relationship between inputs and outputs and then quantifies an expected cost behavior. In the scattergraph and visual fit method, the analyst graphs each observation, with cost on the vertical axis and activity or cost driver on the horizontal axis. Then, the analyst visually and judgmentally fits a line to the data. The Y-intercept of the line is the estimate of fixed cost, and the slope of the line is the estimate of variable cost per unit. The high-low method is a simple method in which the rate of cost variability is determined from data taken only at the high and low points of a range of data.

## PROBLEMS FOR REVIEW

### Review Problem A

Rodbell Roofing Co. installs residential roofs throughout Alabama. In 2008, the company installed 145 roofs at an average price of $30,000 per roof. Variable costs were $18,000 per roof and total fixed costs were $1,200,000.

In 2009, fixed costs are expected to increase to $1,350,000, while variable costs should decline to $16,000 per roof due to a new source of materials and supplies. The company forecasts a 20 percent increase in number of installations for 2009; however, the average price charged to customers is not planned to change.

The 2010 forecast is for 20 more installations than in 2009 and fixed costs are expected to jump by $240,000 more than in 2009. The average price and variable cost is not expected to change from 2009.

**Required:**

**1.** For 2008, calculate the number of installations needed to break even.

**2.** For 2009, calculate the operating leverage factor.

**3.** What is expected to be the amount of profit change from 2009 to 2010?

**Solution:**

**1.** For 2009, the break-even point:

$$\frac{\$1,200,000 \text{ (Fixed cost)}}{\$12,000 \text{ (Unit contribution margin)}} = 100 \text{ installations}$$

**2.** For 2009, the operating leverage factor:
Number of installations in 2009    $= 1.2 \times 145 = 174$
Unit contribution margin in 2009 $= \$30,000 - \$16,000 = \$14,000$
Total contribution margin in 2009 $= 174 \times \$14,000 = \$2,436,000$
Pretax profit in 2009                    $= \$2,436,000 - \$1,350,000 = \$1,086,000$
Operating leverage factor in 2009 $= \$2,436,000 \div \$1,086,000 = 2.24$

**3.** Amount of profit change from 2009 to 2010:

Additional contribution margin = 20 additional installations $\times$ $14,000 contribution margin per unit
                                                = $280,000
Additional fixed cost              = $240,000
Additional profit                    = $280,000 - $240,000 = $40,000

### Review Problem B

Elon's Lawn Service incurred the following costs for equipment maintenance and repair during the last eight weeks (Hours worked each week are also given.):

| Week | Hours | Actual Costs |
|------|-------|--------------|
| 1 | 45 | $400 |
| 2 | 60 | 540 |
| 3 | 64 | 560 |
| 4 | 65 | 600 |
| 5 | 55 | 520 |
| 6 | 50 | 470 |
| 7 | 40 | 450 |
| 8 | 35 | 360 |

**Required:**

1. Using the scattergraph and visual fit approach, estimate a cost function from the above data.

2. Using the high-low approach, estimate a cost function from the above data.

3. For each of the methods in parts (1) and (2), predict the cost of equipment maintenance and repair for a week during the following month when 58 hours are expected to be worked.

**Solution:**

1. First, we plot the data and draw a line by visual inspection, as follows:

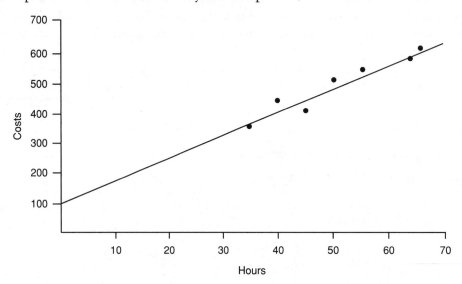

Looking at the graph, it appears that the Y-intercept of line drawn is approximately $100. This is our estimate of the fixed cost. To obtain the variable cost, we arbitrarily choose 30 hours and its associated cost of approximately $300 from the graph. We compute as follows:

| | |
|---|---|
| Total cost at 30 hours | $300 |
| Less fixed cost | 100 |
| Variable cost | $200 |

$200 ÷ 30 = $6.67 per hour

Our cost function is: Y = $100 + $6.67 X

2. We see from the data that the high activity was during week 4 while the low activity was during week 8. Thus, we compute our variable cost per hour as follows:

($600 – $360) / (65 – 35) = $8 per hour

Next, we choose the high point or low point to obtain the fixed cost:

Fixed cost = $600 – 65($8) = $600 – $520 = $80

**or**

Fixed cost = $360 – 35($8) = $360 – $280 = $80

Our cost function is: Y = $80 + $8 X

3. From part (1), the cost prediction would be:

$100 + $6.67(58) = $100 + $386.86 = $486.86

From part (2), the cost prediction would be:

$80 + $8(58) = $80 + $464 = $544

# APPENDIX

## REGRESSION AND CORRELATION ANALYSES

Regression and correlation analyses are statistical techniques that can be used to estimate and examine cost functions. **Regression analysis** fits a line to the cost and activity data using the least squares method. **Correlation analysis** deals with the "goodness of fit" in the relationship between costs and activity as identified by the **regression line**. Both analyses are important in finding relationships and establishing the significance of those relationships.

## Linear Regression

**Linear regression** is a statistical tool for describing the movement of one variable based on the movement of another variable. In determining cost behavior, it is important to know if the movement in costs is related to the movement in activity. The cost behavior is expressed as a line of regression. A line of regression can be fitted precisely to a large quantity of data by the **least squares method**. The high-low method is a rough approximation computed from data taken only at the high and low points of the range, but the least squares method includes all data within the range. The line of regression is determined so that the algebraic sum of the squared deviations from that line is at a minimum.

We will explain the application of linear regression through an illustration. Suppose that the buildings manager of the Atlanta Juvenile Community Center is asked to assist in budgeting for building-related costs. During the past year, electricity costs for various hours of monthly activity in a particular building have been recorded as follows:

| Hours (X) | Electricity Cost (Y) |
|-----------|----------------------|
| 30 | $500 |
| 50 | 650 |
| 20 | 300 |
| 10 | 300 |
| 60 | 900 |
| 50 | 750 |
| 40 | 650 |
| 60 | 700 |
| 30 | 450 |
| 10 | 350 |
| 40 | 600 |
| 20 | 450 |

The advent of the personal computer and spreadsheets has greatly simplified the application of linear regression. By entering data on a spreadsheet and a few function commands, the results appear on the screen. The data for our example of electricity cost and hours of activity yield the following results with a computer spreadsheet analysis:

*Regression Output:*

| | |
|---|---|
| Constant | 200 |
| Std Err of Y Est | 67.08 |
| $r^2$ | 0.886 |
| No. of Observations | 12 |
| Degrees of Freedom | 10 |
| X Coefficient(s) | 10 |

The information necessary to obtain a cost function can be read from the output. The constant is the fixed cost of $200. The $\times$ coefficient is our variable cost per hour, $10. Hence, our cost function is:

$$Y = \$200 + \$10X$$

The number of observations is given as a check. The degrees of freedom are 10 and come from $12 - 2$, where 2 is the number of parameters we are estimating ($a$ and $b$). The remaining terms in the regression output will be discussed later.

The buildings manager can now use the derived cost function to budget the electricity cost. Suppose there is expected to be 35 hours of activity in the building during the next month. In that case, $550 will be budgeted for electricity cost [$200 + ($10 $\times$ 35)].

## Quality of the Regression

In measuring the relationship between the cost and activity, we are interested in more than just an equation for estimating cost. We also want to know the "goodness of fit" for the correlation of the regression line to the cost and activity data and the "reliability" of the cost estimates. This section discusses some of the measures available for assessing "goodness of fit" and reliability.

**Goodness of Fit.** The relationship between cost and activity is called correlation. At times costs may be randomly distributed and are not at all related to the cost driver used in defining the relationship. This is illustrated in Figure 3.9.

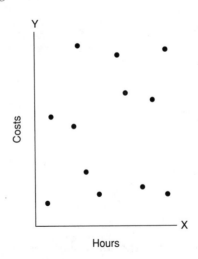

**FIGURE 3.9**

No Correlation

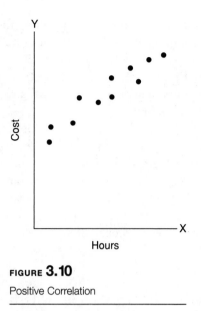

**FIGURE 3.10**

Positive Correlation

At the other extreme, the relationship may be so close that the data can almost be plotted on a line, as shown in Figure 3.10.

Between these extremes, the degree of correlation may not be so evident. A high degree of correlation exists when the regression line explains most of the variation in the data. The above example of electricity costs has all data lying relatively close to the regression line, as shown on the graph in Figure 3.11.

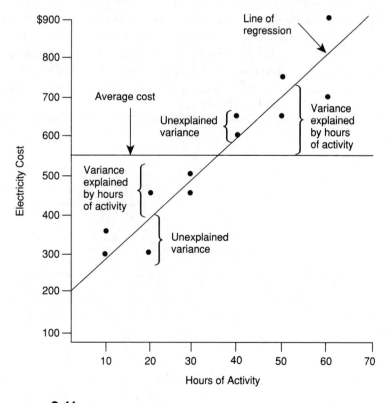

**FIGURE 3.11**

Explanation of Correlation

The average cost is computed in the conventional way by adding the costs and dividing by the number of data points. In this case, the average is $550. Any variance between the line of regression and the average can be explained by hours of activity. The unexplained variances are the variances between the actual costs and the line of regression. In this illustration, a large part of the variance from the average can be explained by hours of activity; only a small amount is unexplained. Hence, a good correlation exists between cost and hours.

The degree of correlation is measured by the correlation coefficient, most frequently designated as r. A related measure, $r^2$, is often used to assess the "goodness of fit" between the data and the regression line. The $r^2$ figure can vary from 0 to 1. An $r^2$ close to 0 would indicate that the regression line does not describe the data. That is, the regression line is nearly horizontal, and little of the variation in Y is explained by the variation in X. If the regression line is very descriptive of the data, the $r^2$ will be close to 1. Such is the case for the above example of electricity cost estimation. Recall that the regression output showed an $r^2$ of 0.886. Thus, 88.6 percent of the variation in electricity costs could be explained by hours of activity.

## Reliability

Because a regression equation will not result in a perfect fit on the data observations, a measure of variability in the data is necessary with respect to the regression equation. The **standard error of the estimate** ($S_e$) is a measure of the deviation between the actual observations of Y and the values predicted by the regression equation. In other words, $S_e$ gives an estimate of the amount by which the actual observation might differ from the estimate. For our example of electricity costs, the regression output showed an $S_e$ of 67.08, labeled as "Std Err of Y Est."

Statistical data often form a pattern of distribution designated as a normal distribution. In a **normal distribution**, data can be plotted as a smooth, continuous, symmetrically bell-shaped curve with a single peak in the center of distribution. We will assume that the cost data in this Appendix are normally distributed. A table of probabilities for a normal distribution shows that approximately two-thirds of the data (more precisely, 68.27%) lie within plus and minus one standard deviation of the mean. In our example, then, approximately two-thirds of the cost observations should lie within plus and minus one standard error of the estimate of the line of regression, or between $67.08 above the line of regression and $67.08 below it. To understand how this works with our data, examine the plot in Figure 3.12 of differences between the actual cost and predicted cost.

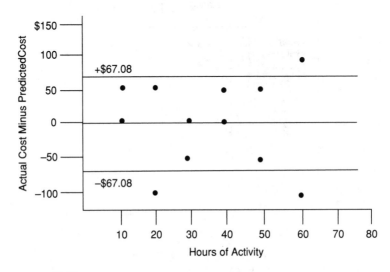

**FIGURE 3.12**

Graph of Differences

An interrelationship exists between $r^2$ and $S_e$. For example, as the deviations between actual cost and predicted cost decrease, our measure for "goodness of fit" ($r^2$) increases in amount and $S_e$ decreases in amount. That is, the higher the $r^2$, the lesser the deviation, the higher the correlation, and the closer actual observations snug the line of regression. The significance of this interrelationship is that the higher the $r^2$ and the lower the standard error of the estimate, the more reliable is our estimate of $b$ (the variable cost per hour).

## Sources of Errors

The cost equation derived from a set of data has a certain degree of error due to imperfections in the data, data collection, and other processing issues. These imperfections will appear in the difference between an actual cost and a cost predicted by the regression equation. Understanding the sources of errors is a step toward eliminating the impact of those errors on the results. The most common sources of errors fall into one of the following three categories: (1) major errors in the original data, (2) errors in keying data, and (3) inappropriate measures of activity.

Major errors in the original data are minimized through (1) reviewing the cutoff procedures that separate costs into periods; and (2) examining the data for procedural errors, such as classification of transactions into the wrong account. For errors in keying data and calculation, look for cost outliers (i.e., observations with large differences between the actual cost and the cost predicted by the regression line). If multiple cost drivers are available in the data, try other cost drivers to locate one with a higher $r^2$ value.

# CONTROL LIMITS

From the data given in our example, the fixed electricity cost is estimated at $200; and the variable electricity cost is estimated to vary at the rate of $10 per hour. For 30 hours of activity, the total cost is estimated at $500. This is a predicted cost, however; and it is unlikely that the actual cost will be precisely $500. Because some variation in cost can be expected, management should establish an acceptable range of tolerance. Costs that lie within the limits of variation can be accepted. Costs beyond the limits, however, should be identified and investigated.

In deciding upon an acceptable range of cost variability, management may employ the standard error of the estimate discussed earlier. Recall that a table of probabilities for a normal distribution shows that approximately two-thirds of the data lie within plus and minus one standard error of the estimate of the regression line. For the electricity cost illustration, the standard error of the estimate amounts to $67.08. At 40 hours of activity, for example, the cost is expected to lie between $532.92 and $667.08 about two-thirds of the time:

|  | Upper Limit (+1 Standard Error) | Lower Limit (−1 Standard Error) |
|---|---|---|
| Regression prediction [$200 + ($10 × 40)] | $600.00 | $600.00 |
| Standard error of the estimate | + 67.08 | − 67.08 |
|  | $667.08 | $532.92 |

If more tolerance is permitted for control purposes, the limits may be extended. For instance, a 95 percent probability (also known as a **confidence interval**) occurs for a range of costs of plus and minus 1.96 standard deviations. From the data given, the 95 percent confidence interval is for a cost range between $468.52 and $731.48 at 40 hours of activity [$600 plus and minus \$131.48 (1.96 × \$67.08)]. Management must make a decision by balancing two alternatives:

**1.** A relatively narrow range of cost variation with a relatively low probability of a cost being within the zone.

**2.** A relatively wide range of cost variation with a relatively high probability of a cost being within the zone.

In other words, the wider the range, the fewer the costs that will be considered for investigation and the higher the likelihood that waste and inefficiencies will go uncorrected.

# MULTIPLE REGRESSION

In many situations, more than one factor will be related to cost behavior. Electricity costs in our example above may vary not only with changes in the hours of activity but also with the number of people using the building, temperature changes, or other cost drivers. Or, telephone service costs may be a function of the basic monthly charge, in-state long distance calls, out-of-state long distance calls, and features such as call waiting or call forwarding. Insofar as possible, all factors that are related to cost behavior should be brought into the analysis. This will provide a more effective approach to predicting and controlling costs. In simple regression only one factor is considered, but in **multiple regression** several factors are considered in combination. The basic form of the multiple regression model is:

$$Y = a + b_1X_1 + b_2X_2 + \ldots + b_mX_m$$

The $X$'s represent different independent variables, and the $a$'s and $b$'s are the coefficients. Any $b$ is the average change in Y resulting from a one unit change in the corresponding $X_1$. Output from a multiple regression analysis with three independent variables might look like the following:

*Multiple Regression Output*

| | |
|---|---|
| Constant | 995 |
| Std Err of Y Est | 146 |
| $R^2$ | 0.724 |
| No. of Observations | 19 |
| Degrees of Freedom | 15 |

| | X1 | X2 | X3 |
|---|---|---|---|
| X Coefficient(s) | 0.735 | 0.121 | 0.885 |

Note that with multiple regression, the "goodness of fit" measure uses a capital $R$ rather than the lower case $r$ we saw with simple regression. Also, note that there are three × coefficients given for the three independent variables. These represent $b_1$, $b_2$, and $b_3$.

## Concerns in Using Multiple Regression

Sometimes a factor affecting the amount of cost is not (or only partially) quantitative in nature. For example, bank charges for various services may be different for senior citizens than for people under 65 years of age. A multiple regression model will have one independent variable that will have a value of 1 for senior citizens and 0 for other customers. These variables are called "dummy variables."

**Contemporary Practice 3.2**
*Regression Analysis for Hospital Overhead Costs*

*A study of overhead costs in hospitals using multiple regression analysis revealed that the following independent variables were important determinants for the cost estimates:*

- *number of patient days*
- *number of discharges*
- *region of the U.S.*

- *whether the hospital was nonprofit, government, or proprietary*
- *percentage of total discharges which are Medicare*

Source: MacArthur, J.B. and Stranahan, H.A., "Cost Driver Analysis in Hospitals: A Simultaneous Equations Approach, Journal of Management Accounting Research, 1998, pp.279–312.

Another concern in using a multiple regression model is the potential existence of a very high correlation between two or more independent variables. The variables move so closely together that the technique cannot tell them apart. We call this situation **multicollinearity**. For example, direct labor hours and direct labor costs would be highly correlated. Multicollinearity is not an issue if we are interested only in predicting the total costs. However, when we need accurate coefficients, a definite problem exists. The coefficients (the $b$'s) in the model are variable costs for that independent variable, and accurate coefficients can be used in pricing decisions and cost-volume-profit analyses.

Multicollinearity, when severe, will be indicated by one or more of the following symptoms:

1. A coefficient is negative when a positive one is expected.
2. A coefficient is insignificant which, in theory, should be highly significant.
3. An unreasonably high coefficient exists that does not make economic sense.

If one or more of the symptoms appear, we need to think through our theory supporting the equation. Remove one of the independent variables that is less critical to the setting. Adding two problem variables together may be a solution in some cases.

## TERMINOLOGY REVIEW

Account analysis (83)
Break-even analysis (69)
Break-even chart (73)
Break-even point (71)
Confidence interval (95)
Contribution margin (69)
Contribution margin ratio (69)
Correlation analysis (91)
Cost estimation (83)
Cost-volume-profit analysis (68)
Dependent variable (83)
Engineering approach (84)
High-low method (86)
Independent variable (83)

Least squares method (91)
Linear regression (91)
Margin of safety (80)
Multicollinearity (97)
Multiple regression (96)
Normal distribution (94)
Operating leverage (79)
P/V graph (74)
Regression analysis (91)
Regression line (91)
Sales mix (80)
Scattergraph and visual fit (85)
Standard error of the estimate (94)

## QUESTIONS FOR REVIEW AND DISCUSSION

1. Identify the interrelated factors that are important to profit planning.

2. When the total contribution margin is equal to the total fixed cost, is the company operating at a profit or at a loss? Explain.

3. If the total fixed cost and the contribution margin per unit of product are given, explain how to compute the number of units that must be sold to break even.

4. Describe the components of a break-even chart.

5. If the total fixed cost and the percentage of the contribution margin to sales revenue are given, explain how to compute the sales revenue at the break-even point.

6. If the total fixed cost and the percentage of the variable cost to sales revenue are given, is it possible to compute the sales revenue at the break-even point? Explain.

7. Can two break-even points exist? If so, describe how the revenue and cost lines would be drawn on the break-even chart.

8. In conventional practice, only one break-even point exists. Why?

9. Is it possible to compute the number of units that must be sold to earn a certain profit after income tax? Explain.

10. How does a P/V graph differ from a break-even chart? Which form of presentation is superior?

11. What does the slope of the P/V graph represent?

12. What is operating leverage?

13. Define margin of safety. How is a margin of safety related to operating leverage?

14. What is the meaning of a break-even point where multiple products are present? Explain the meaning in terms of the individual products.

15. Why is cost estimation so important?

16. Distinguish between the dependent variable and independent variable in a cost-estimating equation.

17. Describe the two major steps involved in the account analysis method of cost estimation.

18. Explain the engineering approach in cost estimation.

19. Describe the steps for preparing an estimate of fixed and variable costs using the scattergraph and visual fit method.

20. When using the high-low method, what criteria should be used in selecting the two points?

21. Describe the high-low method of cost estimation.

22. **(Appendix)** How is regression analysis different from the other methods of cost estimation?

23. **(Appendix)** What is $r^2$? What range of values can it take?

24. **(Appendix)** What does a standard error of the estimate measure?

25. **(Appendix)** In a normal distribution of data, what proportion of the data should lie within plus and minus one standard deviation from the mean?

26. **(Appendix)** What is multiple regression? When would it be used in cost estimation?

27. **(Appendix)** What is multicollinearity? How does it pose problems in multiple regression analysis?

# EXERCISES

Service

**3–1. Break-Even Point and Change in Fixed Costs.** Spira Spirits Store sells each bottle of a particular whiskey for $50. The variable costs are 60 percent of revenue. The fixed costs amounted to $120,000 per year. Last year the store sold 7,500 of these bottles. During the current year, the Spira plans to sell 8,700 bottles, and fixed costs will increase by $36,000.

**Required:**
1. What was break-even point last year?
2. This year, the break-even point will increase by how many bottles?

Service

**3–2. "What ifs" and Target Profits After Taxes.** Wiggins Video Stores sold 20,000 DVD movies at $20 each during the year. Its tax rate is 40 percent, fixed costs are $100,000, and variable costs are $10 per unit.

**Required:**
1. What price must be charged to earn $60,000 after taxes?
2. How many units must be sold to earn $60,000 after taxes?
3. What is the most that fixed costs can be and still allow the firm to earn $60,000 after taxes?
4. What is the most that variable costs per unit can be and still allow the firm to earn $60,000 after taxes?

**3–3. Break-Even Analysis and Cost Changes.** In the Cott Company, the following costs are known for 10,000 units:

| | |
|---|---|
| Selling price | $13 per unit |
| Variable costs | 5 per unit |
| Fixed costs | 6 per unit |

The operations manager, Wendy Solon, is thinking of buying new equipment to automate certain operations. The new equipment will add $20,000 to fixed costs and cut variable costs by $2 per unit.

**Required:**
1. What is the current break-even point in units?
2. By what number of units will the break-even point change and in what direction? Why would you or would you not add this new equipment?

**3–4. "What if" Prices.** The following budget numbers from Cameron Corporation were provided by the controller, Sue Ann Leonard:

| | |
|---|---|
| Sales (12,000 units) | $540,000 |
| Variable costs | (360,000) |
| Fixed costs | (180,000) |
| Net income | $      0 |

**Required:**
1. If Cameron can reduce variable costs by $4 per unit, what price must be charged to earn $90,000? Assume that 12,000 units will still be sold.
2. If Cameron can increase sales revenues by spending $20,000 more on advertising, what price must be charged to earn $120,000? Assume that 12,000 units will still be sold.

**3–5. Changes to Break-Even Variables.** The Aljundi Company sees its profit picture changing. Variable cost will increase from $4 per unit to $4.50. Competitive pressures will allow prices to increase only by $0.30 per unit to $8. Fixed costs ($200,000) and sales volume likely will remain constant.

**Required:**

**1.** What will likely happen to the break-even point?

**2.** To maintain the same profit level, fixed costs will have to change to what amount?

**3.** To maintain the same profit level, volume will have to change to what amount?

**3–6.** **Break-Even Point and Fixed Cost Increase.** Abba Spero operates a health club in Cleveland. Annual memberships are sold, and nonmembers may pay for individual sessions. Spero states that the average revenue amounts to $18 per patron visit. He has estimated the variable cost at $2.20 per patron visit and the fixed cost per year at $42,000. Next year, the fixed cost is expected to increase to $49,500.

**Required:**

**1.** How many patron visits are required this year for Spero to break even?

**2.** Under the new fixed cost structure for next year, how many patron visits are needed to break even?

**3.** How many patron visits above the break-even point are required next year to earn a profit of $13,900?

**3–7.** **Break-Even Point and Variable Cost Increase.** Lydia Perl, the owner of Schloss Hardware Supplies in Frankfurt, Germany, is concerned about increased costs to purchase a hardware item that is sold by the company through one of its retail outlets. This year the variable cost per unit of product was €28. Next year the variable cost is expected to increase to €32 per unit. The selling price per unit, however, cannot be increased and will remain at €39 per unit. The fixed costs amount to €90,000.

**Required:**

**1.** What was the break-even point in units of product this year?

**2.** What was the break-even point in revenues for this year?

**3.** How many units of product must be sold next year to break even?

**4.** How much revenue will generate break-even volume for next year?

**3–8.** **Break-Even Point and Target Profit.** The Marla & Kerry Theatre Group operates five discount movie theatres in the Chicago area. All tickets are priced at $1.75. Variable costs are $1.10 per patron, and the fixed costs per year total $900,000. The fixed costs include concessions, but the variable costs do not. The concessions earn an average contribution margin of $0.60 per patron.

**Required:**

**1.** How many patrons are required to break even?

**2.** If 800,000 patrons are expected for the year, what ticket price would be necessary to earn a profit of $150,000?

**3–9.** **Effects of Changes in Volume and Costs.** Marnie's Boutique sells umbrellas that have a contribution margin ratio of 35 percent of $440,000 annual sales (40,000 units). Annual fixed expenses are $95,000.

**Required:**

**1.** Calculate the change in net income if sales were to increase by 850 units.

**2.** The store manager, Laura Romain, believes that if the advertising budget were increased by $18,000, annual sales would increase by $75,000. Calculate the *additional* net income (or loss) if the advertising budget is increased.

**3.** Laura Romain believes that the present selling price should be cut by 15 percent and the advertising budget should be raised by $12,000. She predicts that these changes would boost unit sales by 30 percent. Calculate the predicted *additional* net income (or loss) if these changes are implemented.

Service

**3–10.** **Revenues and After-Tax Profits.** Filreis Consulting Group has budgeted a 12 percent of revenues aftertax profit. Management has agreed that this level of profit is needed to yield a reasonable return on the owners' investment. Fixed costs have been budgeted at $522,000 for the year, and the contribution margin ratio has been estimated at 30 percent. The income tax rate is 40 percent.

**Required:**
1. How much revenue will be needed to realize the profit objective?
2. By how much does this revenue exceed the break-even revenue?

**3–11.** **Break-Even Point and Profits.** Sheila Hershey has noticed a demand for small tables for personal computers and printers. Retail office furniture outlets are charging from $400 to $600 for a table. Sheila believes that she can manufacture and sell an attractive small table that will serve the purpose for $210. The cost per table of materials, labor, and variable overhead is estimated at $110. The fixed costs consisting of rent, insurance, taxes, and depreciation are estimated at $25,000 for the year. She already has orders for 180 tables and has established contacts that should result in the sale of 150 additional tables.

**Required:**
1. How many tables must Sheila make and sell to break even?
2. How much profit can be made from the expected production and sale of 330 tables?
3. How many tables are needed for a profit objective of $11,000?

**3–12.** **Target Profit and Taxes.** Nimmo had the following results for October:

|  | Fixed | Variable | Total |
|---|---|---|---|
| Sales ($200 per unit) |  |  | $600,000 |
| Cost of sales | $180,000 | $360,000 | (540,000) |
| Net income before taxes |  |  | $ 60,000 |
| Taxes (40 %) |  |  | 24,000 |
| Net income after taxes |  |  | $ 36,000 |

**Required:**
For net income to be $60,000 after taxes in November, what will Nimmo's sales in units need to be?

Service

**3–13.** **Computation of Fixed Cost and Price.** Matlin's Ranch offers horseback riding lessons for children. "Wild Bill" Matlin has figured that break-even revenues are $560,000, based on a contribution margin ratio of 35 percent and variable costs per rider of $6.50.

**Required:**
1. Compute the total fixed costs.
2. Compute the fee charged per rider.

**3–14.** **Effect of a Fixed Cost Increase.** The owner of a Mexican manufacturing company is concerned about increased fixed manufacturing costs. Last year, the fixed manufacturing costs (in pesos) were M$600,000. This year, the fixed manufacturing costs increased to M$750,000. The fixed selling and administrative costs of M$540,000 were the same for both years. The company operated in both years with an average contribution margin ratio of 30 percent. It earned a profit before income taxes of M$910,000 last year.

**Required:**
1. What was the sales revenue last year?
2. How much would sales revenue have had to increase this year for the company to have earned the same profit as it did last year?
3. Calculate the margin of safety for each year. Which year was better?

**3–15.** **Contribution Margin Ratio.** In 2008, Simon's Barber Shop had a contribution margin ratio of 22 percent. In 2009, fixed costs will be $41,000, the same as in 2008. Revenues are predicted to be $250,000, a 25 percent increase over 2008. Simon's wishes to increase pretax profit by $8,000 in 2009.

**Required:**
Determine the contribution margin ratio needed in 2009 for Simon's Barber Shop to achieve its goal.

**3–16.** **Multiple Products.** Bettsak Security Systems installs three types of auto alarm systems. Last year, fixed costs totaled $315,000, and target pretax profit was $190,000. Additional information for the past year:

| Type of Alarm | Unit Contribution Margin | Number Sold |
| --- | --- | --- |
| Best | $50 | 1,000 |
| Better | $45 | 1,100 |
| Good | $38 | 1,300 |

**Required:**
Determine the sales volumes (number of alarm systems of each type) that were needed to achieve the target profit for the past year.

**3–17.** **Multiple Product Analysis.** The Lane Division of Stefan Products, Inc. manufactures and sells two grades of canvas. The contribution margin per roll of Lite-Weight canvas is $25, and the contribution margin per roll of Heavy-Duty canvas is $75. Last year, this division manufactured and sold the same amount of each grade of canvas. The fixed costs were $675,000, and the profit before income taxes was $540,000.

During the current year, 14,000 rolls of Lite-Weight canvas were sold; and 6,000 rolls of Heavy-Duty canvas were sold. The contribution margin per roll for each line remained the same; also, the fixed cost remained the same.

**Required:**
1. How many rolls of each grade of canvas were sold last year?
2. Assuming the same sales mix experienced in the current year, compute the number of units of each grade of canvas that should have been sold during the current year to earn the $540,000 profit that was earned last year.

**3–18.** **Cost Segregation by High-Low Method.** The costs of equipment lubrication for the shops located in the southeastern region of Newmark's Auto Repair have been recorded as follows:

| Hours | Costs |
| --- | --- |
| 18,500 | $61,700 |
| 16,000 | 54,200 |
| 17,200 | 57,800 |
| 18,000 | 60,200 |
| 21,000 | 69,200 |

| Hours | Costs |
|---|---|
| 16,400 | 55,400 |
| 16,700 | 56,300 |
| 15,000 | 51,200 |
| 17,600 | 59,000 |
| 18,100 | 60,500 |

**Required:**

Determine the average rate of cost variability per hour and the fixed cost by the high-low method.

Service

**3–19. Cost Segregation by High-Low Method.** Betty Grus sells various ceramics and crafts at flea markets in the area. She uses a motor home for transportation and lodging. She recognizes that travel costs with the motor home are relatively high and would like to estimate costs so that she can decide how far she can travel and still operate at a profit.

Records from one round trip of 150 miles show that the total cost was $320. On another round trip of 340 miles, the total cost was $472. A local round trip of 50 miles cost $240. She is convinced that the time and cost for trips of more than 300 miles are too high unless the sales potential is very high.

**Required:**

Calculate the variable cost per mile and the fixed cost per trip by the high-low method.

Service

**3–20. Scattergraph and Visual Fit.** Lewyn Financial Advisors uses the scattergraph and visual fit method to estimate its utilities costs. After plotting data for the past 15 weeks, the controller drew a cost function and saw that it hit the vertical axis at $6,500. He then picked a point on the cost function corresponding to $9,700 and 800 hours of activity for further analysis.

**Required:**

What amount of utilities cost would the controller predict for 920 hours of activity?

Service

**3–21. Cost Prediction with Account Analysis.** Muhammed Alley, a bowling alley located in Louisville, had the following costs during a recent month:

| Expenses | Total Amount | Classification |
|---|---|---|
| Wages | $44,500 | Variable |
| Supplies | 9,200 | Variable |
| Rent | 12,000 | Fixed |
| Advertising | 3,700 | Fixed |
| Utilities | 20,000 | Variable |
| Depreciation | 11,300 | Fixed |

During the month, 1,593 customers patronized the bowling alley. Next month, 1,780 customers are expected to come.

**Required:**

Estimate Muhammed Alley's total cost for next month.

**3–22.** **Visual Fit, High-Low Method, and Ethics.** The cost of maintenance for animated exhibits at Auckland Amusement Park in New Zealand is partly variable and partly fixed. Supplies and other materials tend to vary with hours of operation while the salaries of the maintenance workers are fixed. Cost data (in New Zealand dollars) for various hours of operation are given as follows:

| Hours | Total Cost |
|-------|-----------|
| 500 | NZ$ 9,000 |
| 700 | 11,200 |
| 450 | 8,600 |
| 800 | 12,000 |
| 600 | 9,800 |
| 900 | 13,000 |

**Required:**
1. Using the scattergraph and visual fit approach, determine the variable cost per hour and the fixed cost.
2. Compute the variable cost per hour and the fixed cost using the high-low method.
3. Explain why the variable cost per hour and fixed cost are different under the two methods of computation.
4. Suppose that for some reason the cost analyst at Auckland Amusement Park wanted to provide intentionally biased estimates of the variable cost per hour and the fixed cost. Discuss how this could have been done with the visual fit approach versus the high-low method.

**3–23.** **Visual Fit and the Extremes.** The cost of utilities at Harpaz Supply Store varies according to hours of operation, but a portion of the cost is fixed. Hour and cost data for several months are given as follows:

| Hours | Total Cost |
|-------|-----------|
| 100 | $ 800 |
| 200 | 700 |
| 300 | 800 |
| 400 | 900 |
| 500 | 1,000 |
| 600 | 1,100 |
| 700 | 1,200 |
| 800 | 1,300 |
| 900 | 1,600 |

**Required:**
1. Fit a line to the data by visual fit.
2. Using your line, compute the variable cost per hour and the fixed cost per month.
3. Determine the variable cost per hour and the fixed cost per month by the high-low method.
4. In which of the foregoing two variable costs per hour and two fixed cost numbers do you have more confidence for making business decisions? Explain.

**3–24.** **Estimation of Variable Cost.** Quack Clinic contains 500 beds. During April, the occupancy rate was 80%. At that level of occupancy, the clinic's operating costs were $23 per occupied bed per day. This figure contains both fixed and variable costs. During November, the occupancy rate was only 70% and $250,000 of costs (fixed plus variable) were incurred.

**Required:**

Estimate the *monthly* variable operating cost per bed.

Service

**3–25.    Cost Estimation and Break-Even Point.** Water is supplied to Lake Tillem Township by pumping water from a lake to a storage tank at the highest elevation in town, from which it then flows to the customers by gravity. The town council notes that the costs to pump water vary to some extent by the number of gallons pumped, but fixed costs are also included in the pumping costs. A record of gallons consumed per month and total pumping cost per month is as follows:

| Gallons Consumed (000) | Pumping Cost | Gallons Consumed (000) | Pumping Cost |
|---|---|---|---|
| 1,750 | $29,100 | 1,800 | $29,700 |
| 1,900 | 30,800 | 2,300 | 35,900 |
| 2,150 | 34,000 | 2,000 | 31,800 |
| 2,050 | 32,600 | 1,500 | 25,500 |

In addition to pumping costs, 1.1 cents in variable costs and $75,000 in fixed costs are incurred to supply water to the residents. Lake Tillem charges its residents 4.6 cents per gallon consumed.

**Required:**

**1.** Use the high-low method to obtain a cost function for Lake Tillem Township's pumping costs.

**2.** At what level of water consumption would Lake Tillem Township break even?

Service

**3–26.    Describing Regression Results (Appendix).** As controller of Genirberg Enterprises, a long-distance telephone service, you are concerned about the cost behavior of overhead costs. You gathered the appropriate data and asked a statistician friend to perform a regression analysis. You are given the following results:

$$Y = 966 + 6.3\,X$$
$$r^2 = .79$$
$$S_e = 19.2$$

where:    $Y$ = Overhead cost
$X$ = Labor hours

**Required:**

**1.** Explain the meaning of the equation: $Y = 966 + 6.3\,X$.

**2.** What is the percentage of the variance of overhead cost that is associated with changes in labor hours?

**3.** Paula Gris, the president, wants to know what $S_e$ means and how it might be used in evaluating actions. Give a brief answer.

Service

**3–27.    Confidence Interval (Appendix).** The Greenbelt Fire Department wants to examine the costs of operating their fire engines (fuel, maintenance, etc.). Seventeen months of data were obtained on these costs as well as on the number of trips made (actual fires, practice drills, and false alarms). A regression of costs on the number of trips yielded the following results:

| | |
|---|---|
| Mean of X | 22 |
| Constant | 11,000 |
| $r^2$ | .59 |
| X Coefficient | 950 |
| $S_e$ | 3,125 |

**Required:**

Develop a 95% confidence interval for the predicted cost if 18 trips are made.

Service

**3–28.** **Explaining Multiple Regression Results (Appendix).** The Computer Services Department of Herskovits Market Research, Inc. provides services to all other departments. Demand by other departments has grown to a point where the manager wants to bill for services rendered. A decision has been made to analyze computer services operating costs compared to input device time, to CPU time, and to output device time. Operating cost data and the various times were given to a statistician for analysis. The statistician returned the following summary:

| | | |
|---|---|---|
| Constant | | 2,250 |
| Std. Err. of Y Est. | | 221 |
| R² | | 0.95142 |
| Number of Observations | | 12 |
| Degrees of Freedom | | 8 |

| | Input | CPU | Output |
|---|---|---|---|
| X Coefficient(s) | 0.335 | 0.458 | 0.189 |

**Required:**
Explain what information this regression output gives about cost behavior and how management might use it.

Service

**3–29.** **"Goodness of Fit" and Confidence Interval. (Appendix).** Dan White manages a dormitory cafeteria at Tradition University. He has analyzed the actual costs of serving dinners on Tuesday and Thursday nights for the past three years. For a midterm exam night, attendance is lower than normal. Tonight, he estimates that costs will be $830 for the 90 students expected. But with about 95 percent confidence, he thinks that costs will not be higher than $880 nor lower than $780 for that number of students eating. On a more normal night, about 110 students eat with a cost estimate of $970.

**Required:**
1. What cost function underlies Dan White's cost estimates?
2. How did he get the $880 and $780 estimates? (Describe, not calculate.)
3. Dan White tells us that the r² using number of students eating is .75 and that the r² using the total weight of the students eating is .88. What does this say about his approach to budgeting dinner costs above?

# PROBLEMS

Service

**3–30.** **Pricing to Break-Even.** The township of Saylush is inaugurating a youth soccer program. Estimates are that 70 children between the ages of 7 and 9 will enroll and that six teams will be formed. The program will be staffed by volunteer coaches, referees, and administrative personnel, so the only out-of-pocket costs involve the following:

| | |
|---|---|
| Shirts | $4.10 per shirt plus $20 screening charge |
| Balls | $85 (total for all teams) |
| Goals | $120 (total for all teams) |
| Cones | $70 (total for all teams) |
| Shin guards | $9.50 per pair (i.e., $9.50 per player) |

The price obtained for the shirts presume two colors (shirt color and lettering). The program director, Fred Blair, would like very colorful shirts. He has learned that a "rainbow" pattern having several additional colors would cost $1 extra per shirt plus an additional $100 screening charge. The township's recreation director has asked Blair to determine how much to charge each child so that the soccer program fully covers its costs.

**Required:**

If the "rainbow" pattern shirt is selected, what fee per child should Blair suggest to the recreation director?

Service

**3–31.** **CVP with Changes in Prices and Costs.** Data with respect to a basic product line sold by Carson Music Stores are as follows:

| | |
|---|---|
| Selling price per unit | $50 |
| Cost per unit | 30 |
| Contribution margin per unit | $20 |

The fixed costs for the year are $360,000. The income tax rate is 40 percent.

**Required:**

1. Determine the number of units that must be sold in order to break even.
2. If a profit before income taxes of $270,000 is to be earned, how many units of product must be sold?
3. If a profit after income taxes of $180,000 is to be earned, how many units of product must be sold?
4. If the selling price per unit is reduced by 10 percent, how many units must be sold to earn a profit of $8 per unit before income taxes?
5. Assume that the selling price remains at $50. How many units must be sold to earn a profit of $8 per unit before income taxes if the variable cost per unit increases by 10 percent?
6. Why does a 10 percent decrease in the selling price have more effect on the contribution margin than a 10 percent increase in the variable unit cost?

Service

**3–32.** **Costs and Profit Planning.** Alex Gross recently retired from the Coast Guard and plans to use his boat for fishing excursions. He has estimated costs as follows:

| | |
|---|---|
| Per Person: | |
| Pole rental | $    0.75 |
| Bait bucket | 0.75 |
| Per Season: | |
| Fuel cost | $  800.00 |
| Dock rental | 400.00 |
| Boat maintenance | 1,200.00 |
| Depreciation of boat | 3,000.00 |
| Taxes and permits | 400.00 |
| His own salary | 3,000.00 |

A part-time worker is to be hired to dress the fish for the customers. This worker will receive a salary of $1,000 for the season plus a per person fee for each customer. Alex would like to earn a profit of $5,000 each season after his own salary and estimates that the revenue from 4,000 customers will be $46,000.

**Required:**

To meet his profit objective, what is the maximum per person fee that Alex Gross can pay to a part-time worker?

**3–33.   Determining a Selling Price.** Eileen Stewart and her brother, Ralph, would like to make extra money when they have time away from their studies at Wisconsin State University. They are skilled in carpentry and plan to build and sell rustic lawn chairs. Estimates of the cost to make and sell each chair are as follows:

| | |
|---|---|
| Lumber and other materials | $30 |
| Labor (wages to student helpers) | 15 |
| Commission to stores selling the chairs | 8% of selling price |

Radio and direct mail advertising is estimated at $5,000. A pickup truck to transport the chairs can be rented for $1,000. Eileen and Ralph each plan to earn a profit of $4,500 for their efforts. This amount was calculated by considering what they could earn if they used their time in another way.

Eileen believes that 800 units can be made and sold. Ralph is more optimistic and believes that 900 units can be made and sold. Both agree that the price must be less than the commercial price of $98 per chair.

**Required:**
1. Compute a selling price to obtain the desired profit if 800 chairs are sold.
2. Compute a selling price to obtain the desired profit if 900 chairs are sold.
3. Assume that the selling price is based on the sale of 800 chairs but that 900 chairs are actually sold. How much additional profit will each of them make?
4. Assume that the selling price is based on the sale of 800 chairs but that only 700 chairs are actually sold. Will Eileen and Ralph achieve their profit objectives? Explain.

**3–34.   Cost, Volume, and Profit Relationships.** Linder Corporation is reviewing its costs. Currently, variable costs are $7.50 per unit and monthly fixed costs are $72,000. The company expects to sell 50,000 units per month at $10 each. The income tax rate is 40 percent.

**Required:**
Answer the following questions independently.
1. What is the break-even point in units?
2. To obtain a $45,000 before-tax profit, how many units must be sold?
3. To obtain a before-tax profit on sales of 12%, what level of sales dollars is needed?
4. To obtain a $30,000 after-tax profit, how many units must be sold?
5. If a particular advertising campaign will increase sales by 5,000 units, how much could be paid for this campaign without changing the amount of planned profits?
6. To obtain an after-tax profit of $24,000 with the expected sales volume of 50,000 units, what selling price must be charged?
7. To obtain a before-tax profit on sales of 20% with the expected sales volume of 50,000 units, what price must be charged?
8. The company is considering offering its sales reps a 4% commission on sales. What would the total sales dollars need to be to implement the commission plan and still earn a before-tax profit of $70,000?

Service

**3–35.   Break-Even Comparisons.** Dan and Elaine Miller, owners of Evening Star Motel, want to know potential maximum profits and the break-even occupancy for the operation. Evening Star Motel is a low-cost operation to attract business people and families traveling on low budgets. A study of costs shows a difference between summer and winter operations. Swimming pool maintenance adds to summer costs while utilities (heat and light) add to winter costs. Variable costs have been determined on the basis of cost per room occupied per day and are as follows:

|  | Cost Per Room |
| --- | --- |
| Laundry | $ 1.90 |
| Heat and light (summer) | 1.10 |
| Heat and light (winter) | 2.20 |
| Repairs | .75 |
| Supplies | 1.60 |
| Taxes and insurance | 3.60 |
| Maintenance | 1.50 |
| Pool maintenance (summer only) | .60 |

Fixed costs per month have been estimated as follows:

|  |  |
| --- | --- |
| Housekeeping | $ 14,000 |
| Management | 17,000 |
| Desk service | 2,700 |
| Repairs and maintenance | 1,600 |
| Taxes | 1,430 |
| Insurance | 1,120 |
| Heat and light | 1,000 |
| Depreciation–motel | 26,000 |
| Depreciation–furnishings | 12,500 |
| Pool maintenance and personnel (summer only) | 1,800 |

Evening Star has 300 rooms and charges $40 per room per night. Summer is relatively short and is defined as June, July, and August. All other months are designated as winter months. A month consists of 30 days for making calculations. Maximum capacity for a month would be 9,000 room days (300 rooms × 30 days).

**Required:**
1. Compare the maximum operating net incomes that can be expected for a summer month versus a winter month.
2. How do the break-even points (in terms of room days) compare for summer versus winter? Also, state the break-even points as percentages of total capacity.
3. Based on advance reservations and normal expectations, Evening Star Motel plans for 5,000 room days in August. Determine the estimated operating income for August. Also, determine the percentage of capacity expected for August.

Service

**3–36. Operating Leverage and Margin of Safety.** Kay Software Company's vice-president of sales, Joey Fink, observed that the company has operated with a 40 percent contribution margin ratio but that the fixed costs are relatively large at $2,000,000 per year. The income before taxes this year was only $400,000 on sales of $6,000,000. He sees an opportunity to increase sales to $6,300,000 next year but is concerned that such a small increase in sales will have relatively little impact on profits inasmuch as the fixed costs are so high.

**Required:**
1. Compute the degree of operating leverage for both this year and next year. Assume sales revenue for next year can be increased to $6,300,000.
2. Explain why the profits can be increased by a relatively large amount with only a modest increase in revenue.

3. Calculate the margin of safety for both this year and next year, assuming sales revenue can be increased to $6,300,000 for next year.

4. Does the margin of safety give any additional information not available through the operating leverage? Explain.

**3-37.    CVP with a Sales Mix.** Sharon Arts Festival rents four types of booths to exhibitors, providing them with space, tables, chairs, and some pre-festival publicity. Stan Harris, the festival organizer, has indicated that the booth rental fee is three times the amount of variable costs associated with the particular type of booth. Harris expects that the festival will incur fixed costs of $9,200. The number of booths which are expected to be rented this year, as well as the related variable costs, are:

| Booth Size | Variable Cost Per Booth | Number of Booths |
|---|---|---|
| 8' × 10' | $25 | 15 |
| 10' × 12' | 28 | 10 |
| 10' × 15' | 30 | 20 |
| 15' × 15' | 35 | 5 |

**Required:**

Assuming that booths are rented according to the expected mix, determine the number of each type of booth that needs to be rented for the festival to break even.

**3-38.    Change in Sales Mix.** Lindfield Gift Shop in Sydney, Australia, sells three types of stuffed animals: koalas, kangaroos, and crocodiles. Budgeted sales and profits (in Australian dollars) for this year are estimated by the owner, Harry Bleier, as follows:

|  | Koalas | Kangaroos | Crocodiles | Total |
|---|---|---|---|---|
| Sales | A$400,000 | A$900,000 | A$700,000 | A$2,000,000 |
| Variable costs | 300,000 | 450,000 | 510,000 | 1,260,000 |
| Contribution margin | A$100,000 | A$450,000 | A$190,000 | A$ 740,000 |
| Fixed costs |  |  |  | 350,000 |
| Income before taxes |  |  |  | A$ 390,000 |

In reviewing actual results for the year, the manager wonders why the actual profit for the year was less than the budgeted profit, considering that selling prices and costs conformed to the budget and that total sales revenue agreed with the budget. Actual sales by product line were:

| Koalas | A$ 700,000 |
|---|---|
| Kangaroos | 400,000 |
| Crocodiles | 900,000 |
| Total revenue | A$2,000,000 |

**Required:**

1. Compute the sales revenue of each product at the break-even point under the budgeted data.

2. Compute the sales revenue of each product that would be sold at the break-even point under the actual sales mix.

**3.** Calculate the profit before income taxes for the actual sales mix, assuming variable costs maintained the budgeted relationship and actual fixed costs equaled budgeted fixed costs.

**4.** Explain why the actual profit is lower than the budgeted profit.

**3–39. Account Analysis.** The following is a partial list of account titles appearing in the chart of accounts for Lee Caplan Industries:

1. Direct Materials
2. Supervisory Salaries—Factory
3. Heat, Light, and Power—Factory
4. Depreciation on the Building
5. Depreciation on Equipment and Machinery (units-of-production method)
6. Janitorial Labor
7. Repair and Maintenance Supplies
8. Pension Costs (as a percentage of employee wages and salaries)
9. FICA Tax Expense (employer's share)
10. Insurance on Property
11. Sales Commission
12. Travel Expenses—Sales
13. Telephone Expenses—General and Administrative
14. Magazine Advertising
15. Bad Debt Expense
16. Photocopying Expense
17. Audit Fees
18. Dues and Subscriptions
19. Depreciation on Furniture and Fixtures (double-declining-balance method)
20. Group Medical and Dental Insurance Expense

**Required:**

**1.** Discuss each account title in terms of whether the account represents a variable, fixed, or semivariable cost.

**2.** For accounts designated as variable or semivariable, indicate the most likely cost driver with which the cost varies.

**3.** Explain the problems associated with using the account analysis approach to establish cost behavior patterns.

Service

**3–40. Account Analysis.** Your spouse volunteered you as the social chairperson of the local United Way campaign. One of the major activities under your direction is the Christmas dinner and dance for about 220 people. Renting the hall at the local Festive Inn will cost $250. The hall will seat up to 300 people. Decorations for the head table, which will seat 16 people, will cost $50. Decorations for each table will cost $10, and each table will seat up to 8 people. For $25, you can hire the choir director from one of the local high schools to play the piano and sing softly during dinner. The dance band (a prominent college student group) will cost $250. Typesetting and printing 300 copies of the program cost $75. The caterer has offered a full-course meal for $10 per person, but you must guarantee one week in advance. To help serve the meals, you have arranged for the voluntary services of a local Campfire Girls group. You expect 25 people to help serve, and their meal costs will be added to the total costs.

At the time the guarantee was required, you had 205 confirmed reservations for the dinner, including all speakers and dignitaries, but not including servers. You guarantee

224 people plus the servers. Assume that the servers will eat in an adjoining room, which is furnished free of charge, and that their tables will not be decorated.

**Required:**
1. Estimate the total cost of the Christmas dinner and dance for the number of people guaranteed.
2. Estimate the total costs if you had to guarantee 272 people plus servers.
3. Which costs vary with the number of people? Which costs vary with the number of tables (or which costs are fixed per table)? Which costs are fixed for the dinner and dance?

Service

**3–41.** **High-Low and Visual Fit.** Kathleen Otwell, an insurance claims adjuster for Shoenfield Casualty Company, notes that the cost to process a claim has both fixed and variable components. She believes that she can estimate costs more accurately if she can separate the costs into their variable and fixed components. The monthly record of the number of claims and the costs for the past year is as follows:

| Month | Number of Claims | Cost |
|---|---|---|
| January | 120 | $20,600 |
| February | 134 | 20,670 |
| March | 142 | 20,710 |
| April | 156 | 20,780 |
| May | 160 | 20,800 |
| June | 220 | 21,100 |
| July | 250 | 21,250 |
| August | 330 | 21,650 |
| September | 114 | 20,570 |
| October | 280 | 21,400 |
| November | 274 | 21,370 |
| December | 230 | 21,150 |

**Required:**
1. Estimate the variable costs per claim and the fixed costs per month by the high-low method.
2. Estimate the variable costs per claim and the fixed costs per month by the scattergraph and visual fit method.
3. Explain the differences between the two methods in the variable costs per claim and the fixed costs per month.

**3–42.** **High-Low Method.** For years, Bleich Brothers Metals Company paid equipment maintenance personnel on an hourly rate basis. The fixed costs of maintenance labor were relatively low. With the installation of automated equipment, the nature of their work has changed. Now, maintenance personnel monitor the operations and are paid salaries. Therefore, fixed costs have increased, but variable costs per hour have been reduced. Past records show the following monthly information with respect to hours and cost for maintenance labor:

| Hours | Costs | Hours | Costs |
|---|---|---|---|
| 1,500 | $15,000 | 700 | $ 8,000 |
| 800 | 9,400 | 500 | 7,600 |
| 1,200 | 12,600 | 1,100 | 11,800 |
| 1,600 | 15,800 | 1,000 | 11,000 |
| 1,400 | 14,200 | 600 | 7,800 |

Since the installation of automated equipment, costs for monthly maintenance labor are as follows:

| Hours | Costs | Hours | Costs |
|---|---|---|---|
| 1,200 | $17,600 | 1,500 | $17,800 |
| 1,000 | 16,800 | 900 | 17,000 |
| 1,700 | 18,400 | 1,200 | 17,500 |
| 800 | 16,500 | 1,000 | 17,000 |
| 2,000 | 19,000 | 1,400 | 17,700 |

**Required:**
1. Using the high-low method, compute the variable costs per hour and the fixed costs per month under the conditions that existed in the past.
2. Using the high-low method, compute the variable costs per hour and the fixed costs per month under present conditions with automated equipment.
3. How will management now plan and control maintenance labor costs differently with the automated equipment as opposed to past practices?

Service

**3–43.** **Account Analysis and Cost Prediction.** A listing of accounts prepared by Cenker Video Arcade revealed the following data for October, during which time 9,500 video games were played:

| Account | Costs |
|---|---|
| Rent | $1,600 |
| Depreciation on equipment | 70 |
| Wages for part-time help | $1,650 |
| Insurance | 120 |
| Prizes | 200 |
| Supplies | 85 |
| Manager's salary | 2,000 |
| Electricity | 500 |
| Telephone | 100 |
| Heat | 250 |
| Advertising | 150 |

**Required:**
Estimate the cost for November when 11,000 video games are expected to be played.

Service

**3–44.** **Account Analysis and CVP.** Hoepen Company, a Dutch publisher of academic journals, has the following information available pertaining to the 2008 costs of publishing *The Journal of Cost Accounting:*

| Account | Cost (in euros) |
|---|---|
| Paper | 20,000 |
| Binding material | 1,000 |
| Covers | 4,000 |
| Equipment depreciation | 87,000 |
| Rent | 24,000 |
| Production wages | 66,000 |
| Staff and managers' salaries | 220,000 |
| Utilities | 48,000 |
| Printing ink | 13,000 |
| Insurance | 7,000k |

The journal's subscription price is €93, and 8,000 subscriptions were sold in 2008. Hoepen's target pretax profit from *The Journal of Cost Accounting* for 2009 is €250,000. Assume that the number of journals produced is the same as the number of subscriptions sold and that the cost structure will remain unchanged for 2009.

**Required:**
1. Using the account analysis approach, derive a cost function from the above information.
2. How many subscriptions of *The Journal of Cost Accounting* must Hoepen sell to break even with this journal in 2009?
3. How many subscriptions will be needed in 2009 to achieve the target pretax profit?

Service

**3–45.** **Control Limits (Appendix).** Harry Czinn, supervisor of the Maintenance Department at Severn Airport, has estimated that the department's power cost varies at the rate of $0.80 per hour and that the fixed cost for the month is $500. The standard error of the estimate from the line of regression is $60. Czinn investigates the cost of any month that is more or less than one standard deviation from the line of regression. Actual monthly hours and costs for the last year are as follows:

| Month | Hours | Cost |
|---|---|---|
| January | 650 | $980 |
| February | 550 | 970 |
| March | 600 | 960 |
| April | 650 | 1,050 |
| May | 550 | 940 |
| June | 500 | 980 |
| July | 700 | 1,180 |
| August | 800 | 1,150 |
| September | 750 | 1,050 |
| October | 900 | 1,330 |
| November | 850 | 1,180 |
| December | 450 | 900 |

**Required:**
1. Using the formula $Y = a + b(X)$, what should be the cost for each month?
2. Calculate the difference between the actual cost and the predicted cost for each month.
3. Plot the differences in part (2) on a graph, and draw lines that represent the plus or minus one standard error of the estimate.
4. For which month or months should the cost be investigated? Why?

Service

**3–46.** **Cost Estimation with Multiple Regression (Appendix).** Fair Dinkum Painters has gathered data on a random sample of 20 paint jobs. The company's accountant feels that labor costs are related to the surface area painted ($X_1$ = sq. ft. of surface area) and the length of the trim work needed to complete a paint job ($X_2$ = edge trim, in feet). A multiple regression analysis was performed, and the results are as follows:

| | |
|---|---|
| $R^2$ | .83 |
| Constant | 102.50 |
| Coefficient of $X_1$ | .127 |
| Coefficient of $X_2$ | .214 |
| Standard error of estimate | 77.23 |

**Required:**

1. Does the regression line provide a good fit to the data? Briefly explain.
2. How much does it cost to paint an extra 400 sq. ft. of surface?
3. How much does it cost to get set up for a painting job?
4. The cost for a new job needs to be estimated. It will have 8,800 sq. ft. of surface area and 2,900 ft. of edge trim. What is your estimate?

**3–47.** **Varying Control Limits (Appendix).** For the last five years, the management of Kam Fasteners of Singapore has followed the practice of investigating variations if a cost differs by more than one standard error of estimate from the line of regression. One standard error of estimate is S$205 (Singapore dollars).

A new supervisor, hired to manage the machining operation, asks, "Did you ever consider that you may be overdoing it by investigating every cost that is over one standard error from the line of regression? After all, you still have a probability of about 1 in 3 that the variation will be random. Then you have gone to a lot of bother for nothing. For example, last March in this operation you investigated the cost of lubrication and found nothing wrong."

The supervisor of the fabrication operation replies, "I'll grant that we may whip a few dead horses, but your idea of investigating anything over 1.96 standard error would have missed a very important variance for one month that was brought under control."

The cost of lubrication is estimated to vary at S$6 per hour in the machining operation with a fixed cost of S$3,500 each month. The actual costs for last year that the supervisors were discussing are given as follows:

| Month | Hours | Cost | Month | Hours | Cost |
|---|---|---|---|---|---|
| January | 1,200 | S$10,850 | July | 500 | S$ 6,350 |
| February | 1,400 | 12,000 | August | 700 | 7,700 |
| March | 1,000 | 9,800 | September | 900 | 9,100 |
| April | 1,100 | 10,000 | October | 1,000 | 9,850 |
| May | 1,000 | 9,650 | November | 1,200 | 10,600 |
| June | 600 | 7,600 | December | 1,300 | 11,450 |

**Required:**

1. Calculate the difference between the actual cost and the predicted cost for each month.
2. Identify the months which were investigated with the control limit set at one standard error of estimate from the line of regression.
3. Identify the months which would have been investigated if the control limit had been set at 1.96 standard error of estimate from the line of regression.
4. The supervisor of fabrication operation has stated that one very important month would have been missed using the rule suggested by the supervisor of the machining operation. Which month would have been missed? What was the variance for that month?

**3–48.** **Control Limits and Cost Investigations (Appendix).** "You are spending too much to investigate cost variances!" Jonathan Klein exclaims. "Last year we sent someone to the plant four times, and only once did we find a cost difference that should be controlled."

Klein's partner, Ron Green, replies, "It costs nothing to send someone to the plant, and you admit that once we found a cost variance worth looking at."

"But it does cost something to send someone to the plant," Klein persists. "It may not be additional cost, but we lose work that the employee could have done in that time and that has a value or a cost."

The company has been following the practice of investigating the cost of steam treatment whenever the cost is more than one standard error from the line of regression. One standard error is equal to $600. Jonathan Klein wants to investigate costs only when they are more than 1.96 standard error from the line of regression.

A record of line of regression costs and actual costs for last year is as follows:

| Month | Hours | Line of Regression Cost | Actual Cost |
|---|---|---|---|
| January | 600 | $19,000 | $19,350 |
| February | 850 | 22,750 | 22,980 |
| March | 580 | 18,700 | 19,350 |
| April | 740 | 21,100 | 21,600 |
| May | 800 | 22,000 | 21,700 |
| June | 850 | 22,750 | 23,550 |
| July | 900 | 23,500 | 24,700 |
| August | 930 | 23,950 | 23,700 |
| September | 920 | 23,800 | 24,200 |
| October | 870 | 23,050 | 23,750 |
| November | 760 | 21,400 | 21,500 |
| December | 720 | 20,800 | 20,600 |

**Required:**
1. What were the four months in which the costs were investigated with the upper control limit set at a plus one standard error?
2. Assume that the cost that did require control, the cost Ron Green mentioned, was incurred in June. Would this variance have been investigated if the upper limit had been set at plus 1.96 standard error?
3. If the upper control limit had been set at plus 1.96 standard error, for which months would the costs have been investigated?
4. Is Jonathan Klein correct in stating that a cost of lost work occurs even if no added cost is incurred? Explain.

Service

**3–49.** **Linear Regression (Appendix).** Larry Beck has a night job at a ballpark. He manages the late night clean-up crew at Atlanta Stadium. As a student of the game and of garbage, he has selected a sample of 2004 games for study. The attendance figures and clean-up costs, as well as output from a regression analysis, are given as follows.

| Game Date | Attendance | Clean-Up Costs |
|---|---|---|
| April 28 | 25,216 | $5,677 |
| May 10 | 32,566 | 6,381 |
| May 11 | 19,945 | 4,219 |
| June 6 | 26,009 | 5,422 |
| June 10 | 39,856 | 6,722 |
| June 31 | 34,561 | 6,106 |
| July 15 | 19,723 | 4,846 |
| July 19 | 25,924 | 5,533 |
| July 25 | 42,119 | 6,311 |
| July 29 | 38,923 | 6,722 |
| August 21 | 26,912 | 4,909 |
| August 23 | 21,902 | 4,771 |
| September 5 | 36,205 | 6,508 |
| September 7 | 26,931 | 5,456 |
| September 22 | 19,636 | 4,323 |

| Regression Output: | |
|---|---|
| Constant | 2642.63 |
| Std Err of Y Est | 339.05 |
| $r^2$ | 0.85125 |
| No. of Observations | 15 |
| Degrees of Freedom | 13 |
| X Coefficient(s) | 0.10143 |

**Required:**
1. What amount of clean-up cost would Beck budget for the 2005 opening day game which is expected to have an estimated crowd of 50,000 fans?
2. How would you caution Beck about using the estimate obtained in part (1)?

# CASE 3A—JOZEF PLASTICS

The management of Jozef Plastics, Inc. is in the process of preparing a budget for the next year. The company manufactures car mats, dishware, and figures that can be used as decorations or as toys for children. Some changes in prices and costs are expected along with changes in sales volume. Data from operations for the past year are provided by the controller, Erica Eitan, as follows:

| | Figures | Mats | Dishware |
|---|---|---|---|
| Units sold | 550,000 | 1,200,000 | 350,000 |
| Unit selling price | $12.00 | $8.00 | $40.00 |
| Variable costs per unit: | | | |
|   Materials | $3.00 | $3.00 | $12.00 |
|   Indirect materials and supplies | .40 | .40 | 1.00 |
|   Labor | 1.50 | 1.50 | 6.00 |
|   Packing and shipping | .60 | .60 | 1.50 |
|   Utilities | .50 | .50 | .50 |

| Fixed costs: | |
|---|---|
| Supervision | $ 230,000 |
| Employee benefits | 765,000 |
| Postage and telephone | 73,000 |
| Property taxes and insurance | 126,000 |
| Heat and light | 192,000 |
| Repairs and maintenance | 94,000 |
| Depreciation | 86,000 |
| Advertising | 549,000 |
| Travel and entertainment | 162,000 |
| Sales office, other sales expense | 236,000 |
| Office and administration | 372,000 |
| Total fixed costs | $2,885,000 |

The sales volume of figures for next year is expected to be 80 percent of the volume for the past year. The sales volume of mats is expected to remain constant. The volume of dishware sales should increase by 10 percent if the advertising budget is increased by $170,000. The selling price of figures is to be reduced to $10 per unit, and the selling price of mats is to be increased to $9 per unit.

Materials prices per unit of product for next year have been estimated as follows:

| Figures | $ 3.50 |
|---------|--------|
| Mats | 3.50 |
| Dishware | 14.00 |

Labor cost for next year is estimated at $2 per unit for both figures and mats. For dishware, labor is estimated at $7 per unit. The utility costs are estimated at $1 for each unit of each product line. Fixed costs, with the exception of the advertising referred to previously, will probably increase by 10 percent. Income taxes are at 40 percent of pretax income.

**Required:**
1. Compute the contribution margin per unit and contribution margin ratio for each product during the past year.
2. Compute the contribution margin per unit and contribution margin ratio for each product according to the estimates for the next year.
3. Determine the net income for the past year. (Show contribution margin by product line.)
4. Determine the expected net income for next year. (Show contribution margin by product line.)
5. Will the expected volume increase in dishware sales more than compensate for the expected dishware cost increases? Show computations.
6. Compute the break-even point for the given sales mix of each year. Explain the break-even point change between years.

 # CASE 3B—MENDEL PAPER COMPANY

Mendel Paper Company produces four basic paper product lines at one of its plants: computer paper, napkins, place mats, and poster board. Materials and operations vary according to the line of product. The market has been relatively good. The demand for napkins and place mats has increased with more people eating out, and the demand for the other lines has been growing steadily.

The plant superintendent, Marlene Herbert, while pleased with the prospects for increased sales, is concerned about costs:

"We hear talk about a paperless office, but I haven't seen it yet. The computers, if anything, have increased the market for paper. Our big problem now is the high fixed cost of production. As we have automated our operation, we have experienced increases in fixed overhead and even variable overhead. And, we will have to add more equipment since it appears that we need even more plant capacity. We are operating over our normal capacity as it is.

"The place mat market concerns me. We may have to discontinue printing the mats. Our specialty printing is driving up the variable overhead to the point where we may not find it profitable to continue with that line at all."

Cost and price data for the next fiscal quarter are as follows:

| | Computer Paper | Napkins | Place Mats | Poster Board |
|---|---|---|---|---|
| Estimated sales volume in units | 30,000 | 120,000 | 45,000 | 80,000 |
| Selling prices | $14.00 | $7.00 | $12.00 | $8.50 |
| Materials costs | 6.00 | 4.50 | 3.60 | 2.50 |

Variable overhead includes the cost of hourly labor and the variable cost of equipment operation. The fixed plant overhead is estimated at $420,000 for the quarter. Direct labor, to a large extent, is salaried; and the cost is included as a part of fixed plant overhead. The superintendent's concern about the eventual need for more capacity is based on increases in production that may reach and exceed the practical capacity of 60,000 machine hours.

In addition to the fixed plant overhead, the plant incurs fixed selling and administrative expenses per quarter of $118,000.

"I share your concern about increasing fixed costs," the supervisor of plant operations replies. "We are still operating with about the same number of people we had when we didn't have this sophisticated equipment. In reviewing our needs and costs, it appears to me that we could cut fixed plant overhead to $378,000 a quarter without doing any violence to our operation. This would be a big help."

"You may be right," Herbert responds. "We forget that we have more productive power than we once had, and we may as well take advantage of it. Suppose we get some hard figures that show where the cost reductions will be made."

Data with respect to production per machine hour and the variable cost per hour of producing each of the products are given as follows:

|  | Computer Paper | Napkins | Place Mats | Poster Board |
| --- | --- | --- | --- | --- |
| Units per hour | 6 | 10 | 5 | 4 |
| Variable overhead per hour | $9.00 | $6.00 | $12.00 | $8.00 |

"I hate to spoil things," the vice-president of purchasing announces. "But the cost of our materials for computer stock is now up to $7. Just got a call about that this morning. Also, place mat materials will be up to $4 a unit."

"On the bright side," the vice-president of sales reports, "we have firm orders for 35,000 cartons of computer paper, not 30,000 as we originally figured."

**Required:**

1. From all original estimates given, prepare estimated contribution margins by product line for the next fiscal quarter. Also, show the contribution margins per unit.

2. Prepare contribution margins as in part (1) with all revisions included.

3. For the original estimates, compute each of the following:
   (a) Break-even point for the given sales mix.
   (b) Margin of safety for the estimated sales volume.

4. For the revised estimates, compute each of the following:
   (a) Break-even point for the given sales mix.
   (b) Margin of safety for the estimated sales volume.

5. Comment on Herbert's concern about the variable cost of the place mats.

# PRODUCT COST FRAMEWORK

# PRODUCT COSTING: ATTACHING COSTS TO PRODUCTS AND SERVICES

## LEARNING OBJECTIVES

1. Understand why and how costs are attached to products and services.
2. Describe how direct materials, direct labor, and factory overhead are costed to products.
3. Explain why predetermined overhead rates are usually used for product costing.
4. Calculate plant-wide and departmental factory overhead rates.
5. Identify the main differences among alternative measures for the denominator in the overhead rate.
6. Explain why services or products should be costed for pricing purposes by using an overhead rate computed at normal volume levels.
7. Describe how to allocate service center costs so that they can be included in overhead rates of operating departments.

## What is the Cost of a Brake Job?

*As a high school teacher working in Los Angeles, Marty Rosen satisfied his love for automobiles by working as an auto mechanic during the summer months. He also found himself occasionally repairing friends' cars year-round. Demand for his repair expertise began to boom, so Marty used his savings as seed money for a new business, Marty's Auto Repair.*

*Marty started his enterprise with a firm hope of making a profit, and he has realized profits. However, times are changing. Revenues for this year have reached over $2 million and are expected to increase in the future. Costs are, on the other hand, increasing faster than revenues. Marty does not know what his profit margins are for brake jobs, mufflers and body work because he has no idea what it costs him to make repairs. Most of his accounting has been a "shoebox approach" where receipts, deposit slips, and invoices go into a box. Periodically, a local CPA firm, Chester & Wayne, sends a staff accountant to sort the box's contents and prepare financial statements.*

*Marty needs cost information about repairs, and his accounting system does not provide it. For example, he needs to know: What does it cost to make one repair of each type? Are repair costs higher this month than last month? With profits going down, which jobs are losing profit margin? And, behind all of these questions is: How should overhead costs be assigned to jobs? Marty needs an accounting system that will provide cost information for his current needs and for the future.*

COSTS ARE USED to accomplish an assortment of needs: to evaluate the profitability of goods and services; to aid in pricing and bidding decisions; to plan and budget operations; to evaluate performance; to control costs; and to establish inventory values for the balance sheet and cost of goods and services sold for the income statement.

This chapter discusses accounting for production costs and presents ways to identify costs with products. Accounting for direct materials and direct labor comes first. Then, accounting for factory overhead covers simple to more complex situations. Finally, we discuss how service center costs are included in product cost.

## COSTING OF PRODUCTS AND SERVICES

The production of goods and services involves resources. As mentioned in Chapter 2, the costs of these resources are typically classified as materials, labor, and factory overhead. The costs are accumulated by jobs or by departments. Then they are assigned to each unit of output (product or service) based on each unit's use of the resources. These relationships for assigning costs to products or services are depicted in Figure 4.1.

The principles underlying product costing are applicable to manufacturing companies and service organizations. For example, a hospital may be interested in determining the cost of a specific

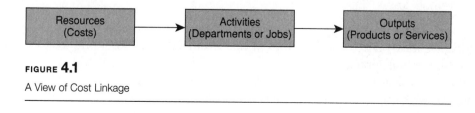

**FIGURE 4.1**

A View of Cost Linkage

medical treatment or the cost of outpatient care. A furniture store may wish to know the costs associated with carrying and selling a particular line of sofas. A building contractor, on the other hand, will accumulate costs by project. If a contractor is constructing a new bridge for the state, for instance, the contractor will identify and trace the costs to the bridge project. A university may be interested in the estimation, measurement, and control of a program to train mathematics teachers. A museum may want to determine the cost of a particular exhibit for a season.

Regardless of the type of organization, costs are identified as direct costs when they can be readily connected to a cost objective. Indirect costs, which cannot as easily be connected to an objective, must be allocated using some reasonable basis for allocation. Because the principles used in tracing costs are more clearly identified in a manufacturing setting, the same manufacturing cost methods can often be adapted to a wide variety of applications.

We can categorize a manufacturing process as yielding commingled products, fabricated products, or assembled products. **Commingled products** exist when one unit cannot be distinguished from any other unit. One pound of sugar is indistinguishable from another pound unless contained in some way. Products in this category include flour, oil, electricity, soft drinks, textiles, processed foods, and paper. **Fabricated products** involve reshaping materials through a cutting, stamping, or molding operation. Examples include tires, nuts and bolts, sugar-coated breakfast cereals, and silverware. **Assembled products** bring parts and subassemblies together for an assembly operation. Each product passes through the same assembly operations. Examples include kitchen appliances, calculators, computers, telephones, and pickup trucks.

## COSTING OF DIRECT COSTS

We now discuss how to determine the costs that are directly traceable to products or jobs. These costs consist of direct materials and direct labor.

### Costing of Direct Materials

Materials include the raw materials, purchased parts, and purchased or subcontracted assemblies and subassemblies. **Direct materials** are those that are identified with the production of a specific product and are easily and economically traced to the product; their costs represent a significant part of the total product cost. All other materials and supplies that become part of a product or are consumed in production are called **indirect materials**, which is part of factory overhead.

The costs associated with acquiring materials and having them ready for production typically fall into five categories:

1. The acquisition cost (purchase price or production cost) of the materials.
2. In-transit charges, such as freight, insurance, storage, customs and duty charges.
3. Credits for trade discounts, cash discounts, and other discounts and allowances.
4. The costs of purchasing, receiving, inspecting, and storing activities.
5. Miscellaneous items, including income from the sale of scrap and spoiled units, obsolescence, and other inventory losses.

Categories 1 through 3 are typically included in the cost of materials, whether direct or indirect materials. Categories 4 and 5 are treated as factory overhead. We allocate those costs to products with one of the several approaches that will be discussed later in the chapter.

The document that lists all materials needed to produce one unit of each product is the **bill of materials**, generated by product design engineers. It lists the sequence in which the materials will enter production. Once a decision is made about the quantity of products to produce, the bill of materials is used to determine the amount of materials to be acquired.

Suppose that Electrika Enterprises, a manufacturer of CD players, purchased materials on account for $75,000. Upon receipt of the materials, we increase Materials and Accounts Payable by $75,000 as follows:

| Materials | | Accounts Payable | |
|---|---|---|---|
| 75,000 | | | 75,000 |

Production managers requisition from the storeroom the materials required for a specific job or product. Thus, each requisition becomes the basis for charging the cost of materials to a specific job or product. Assume that a month's requisitions at Electrika Enterprises show that direct materials costing $60,000 have been transferred from the materials inventory to production. The total of $60,000 is moved from Materials to Work in Process. The latter account is a focal account for the entry of production costs. The costs of the three cost elements—direct materials, direct labor, and factory overhead—are funneled through this account, as will be shown later. It is, therefore, the control account for all in-process activity. The movement of materials used in production for the month is shown as:

| Materials | | Work in Process | |
|---|---|---|---|
| 75,000 | 60,000 | 60,000 | |

The costs included in the $60,000 are also charged to the various processing departments or jobs that used the materials. These itemizations form the subsidiary ledger for the Work in Process control account.

## Costing of Direct Labor

Factory labor is the total labor cost expended for the benefit of production. **Direct labor** can be specifically identified with a product in an economically feasible manner. **Indirect labor** is not readily traced to a product. Because of the changes in the production environment in many companies and the emphasis on a just-in-time philosophy, a new term, value-added direct labor, is being used. **Value-added direct labor** changes materials into a finished product. For example, value-added direct labor fabricates parts, assembles products, and finishes products. Nonvalue-added direct labor moves, inspects, stores, examines, or otherwise handles the product without adding value to the product. For our purposes, we will generally define direct labor as value added and indirect labor as nonvalue added, even though the differences are not always clear.

Labor-related costs include the wages and salaries of the employees plus any additional expenditures made by an employer on behalf of an employee. These typically include bonuses, overtime premiums (i.e., the *additional* wages for overtime), shift differentials, idle time, employer's payroll taxes, and fringe benefits. These additional expenditures are usually treated as part of the factory overhead costs. Some of these expenditures cannot easily be traced to individual production orders. Others such as overtime premiums and shift differentials are treated as factory overhead so those products worked on during overtime hours or late shifts are not unfairly penalized.

Labor time tickets or labor time reports will show how much of the labor time and cost is charged to each job or production order. For the sake of simplicity, we will assume that all of Electrika Enterprises' labor is direct labor. Periodically, factory payroll is recorded by a debit to Work in Process with offsetting credits to Wages Payable, Employees Income Tax Payable, and other liability accounts for payroll deductions. Suppose that during one month, the labor costs for Electrika Enterprises were $10,000 and the workers' take-home pay totaled $7,400. The resulting transaction is shown:

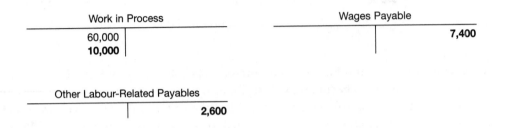

## COSTING FACTORY OVERHEAD

Factory overhead, unlike direct materials and direct labor, cannot be requisitioned or measured directly as a cost of any particular job, production order, or service. Factory overhead consists of a variety of costs such as indirect materials, indirect labor, insurance, depreciation, utilities, repair, and maintenance—all of which are indirectly related to the products. The indirect nature of overhead costs with respect to the products or services creates a difficulty in identifying production costs with each unit. For our purposes at this point, we take an overall, simplified approach to costing of factory overhead to products. This is to convey the concepts involved. Later in the chapter, we explain overhead costs by employing departmental rates. In Chapter 6, we extend the discussion to include activity-based costing.

For the discussion that follows, factory overhead is attached to products or services by means of a cost driver that links costs to products. The cost driver chosen as a basis for overhead allocation should be related logically to both the overhead and the product. If machinery plays an important role in the manufacturing operation, the overhead costs likely consist of power cost, lubrication, maintenance, repairs, depreciation, and other costs closely related to machine operation. The benefits received by the products can probably be best measured against the cost of the machine hours used in their production. Therefore, these overhead costs should be allocated to the products on the basis of machine hours used to produce the products. For other plants whose operations are more labor intensive than capital intensive, direct labor cost or direct labor hours may be more appropriate for overhead allocation.

The most common cost drivers chosen for overhead allocation are direct labor hours, machine hours, and direct labor cost. One survey of manufacturing firms found that over 41 percent of the respondent companies used direct labor (hours or cost) to allocate overhead cost.[1] Another survey found this figure to be 62 percent.[2]

The total cost driver activity for the plant is divided into the total overhead cost to obtain an **overhead rate**. Products then are assigned overhead cost by multiplying the actual quantities of the

[1] Szendi, J. Z., and R. C. Elmore, "Management Accounting: Are New Techniques Making In-Roads with Practitioners?," *Journal of Education*, Spring 1993, p. 66.

[2] Cohen, J. R., and L. Paquette, "Management Accounting Practices: Perceptions of Controllers," *Journal of Cost Management*, Fall 1991, p. 75.

activity by the rate calculated. Suppose that Electrika Enterprises uses direct labor cost to allocate overhead. During the month in the earlier example for which direct labor cost was $10,000, the total overhead for the plant was $15,000. Consequently, the overhead rate would be 150 percent of direct labor cost. During that month, the direct labor cost incurred to produce CD players amounted to $2,700. Hence, $4,050 ($2,700 × 1.5) of overhead cost would be allocated to the CD players.

## Predetermined Overhead Rate

Thus far, we have discussed **actual costing**, where the product costs consist of actual direct materials used, actual direct labor cost, and overhead allocation based on total actual overhead costs and total actual activity. Most companies, however, use a normal cost system or a standard cost system. The latter will be covered in Chapter 8. **Normal costing** differs from actual costing in that overhead is allocated using a **predetermined overhead rate**, defined as:

Predetermined overhead rate = Budgeted factory overhead ÷ Budgeted cost driver activity

With normal costing, the **applied factory overhead** would be determined by multiplying the predetermined overhead rate by the actual cost driver activity for the job or product. Typically, companies use a one-year time horizon to calculate predetermined overhead rates.

Two major reasons exist for the use of normal costing rather than actual costing. The first is the timing of factory overhead cost incurrence. For example, air conditioning costs in the summer for many companies in the sunbelt tend to be higher than heating costs are in the winter. Should we allocate the higher air conditioning costs to products that were manufactured during the summer? The facilities and workers must be maintained regardless of the weather. In addition, discretionary costs may fluctuate widely from month to month. For instance, managers may decide to incur substantial maintenance costs during some months and very little during other months. Because of seasonal and discretionary aspects of overhead, a more stable overhead rate requires a longer time horizon, such as one year.

The second reason for the use of normal costing is the potential fluctuation in the activity represented by the cost driver. Most companies do not have a constant level of activity every month. For example, employees take vacations during the summer months; operations are scaled back to accommodate major repairs and maintenance; production ceases while a changeover in tooling occurs; or the company is closed for the week between Christmas and New Year's Day. Normal costing, by using a one-year time horizon for the overhead rate, averages costs over the units of work regardless of when work is performed. Therefore, a product is not penalized because it is produced during a period of low volume.

Calculating an *actual* overhead rate using a one-year time horizon, prices and other cost-based decisions could not be made until the end of the year. Clearly, companies cannot operate this way. The use of a predetermined overhead rate allows costs of products and jobs to be calculated throughout the year as necessary. Moreover, a predetermined overhead rate helps managers to prepare bids on major orders or to price business from prospective customers.

To illustrate the application of overhead in a normal cost system, suppose that, for 2004, Bodker Publishing Company has budgeted $50,000 for fixed overhead costs and $3 per direct labor hour for variable overhead costs. This is its overhead cost function. These budgeted costs correspond to a budget activity of 10,000 direct labor hours. The predetermined overhead rate would be computed as:

[$50,000 + $3(10,000)] ÷ 10,000 = $8 per direct labor hour

Assume there were 10,000 direct labor hours worked, at a rate of $10 per hour, during 2004. Assume also that $95,000 of direct materials were used. During production, various entries were made to cost the individual jobs. We could quite literally add $8 to Work in Process every time one more hour of direct labor is worked. In normal accounting activity, these transfers to Work in Process are done periodically, perhaps weekly or monthly. If done in aggregate, a summary transfer to Work in Process of all overhead applied to all jobs would show the following:

| Factory Overhead | | | Work in Process | |
|---|---|---|---|---|
| | 80,000 | | 95,000 | |
| | | | 100,000 | |
| | | | **80,000** | |

As each job goes through production, an overhead charge at the predetermined rate of $8 for each direct labor hour is made to the job. Suppose Bodker Publishing Company published an economics textbook (Job 1018) that required $20,000 of direct materials and 2,000 hours of direct labor at $10 per hour. The completed cost for Job 1018 can be summarized as:

| | |
|---|---|
| Direct materials | $ 20,000 |
| Direct labor (2,000 hours at $10 per direct labor hour) | 20,000 |
| Factory overhead (2,000 hours at $8 per direct labor hour) | 16,000 |
| Total cost | $ 56,000 |

At its completion, the cost of a job is transferred from Work in Process to Finished Goods. For Job 1018, the transfer would be:

| Finished Goods | | | Work in Process | |
|---|---|---|---|---|
| **56,000** | | | 95,000 | **56,000** |
| | | | 100,000 | |
| | | | 80,000 | |

## Disposition of the Overhead Variance

While the products are costed using a predetermined overhead rate and by crediting the Factory Overhead account, actual overhead costs are incurred and recorded as debits to Factory Overhead. Suppose Bodker Publishing Company incurred actual overhead costs amounting to $81,500 during 2004. These costs included depreciation of $11,500, expired insurance of $10,000, salaries of $40,000, and utilities of $20,000. The entries to record these actual costs are:

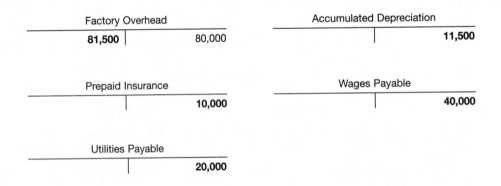

| Factory Overhead | | | Accumulated Depreciation | |
|---|---|---|---|---|
| **81,500** | 80,000 | | | **11,500** |

| Prepaid Insurance | | | Wages Payable | |
|---|---|---|---|---|
| | **10,000** | | | **40,000** |

| Utilities Payable | | |
|---|---|---|
| | **20,000** | |

Notice that expense accounts were not debited because the above items represent product costs rather than period costs, as discussed in Chapter 2. Nonmanufacturing, or selling and administration, costs would be debited to expense accounts. Suppose Bodker Publishing Company had selling expenses of $29,000, office rent of $45,000, executive salaries of $320,000, and office utilities of $33,000. The following entries would be recorded:

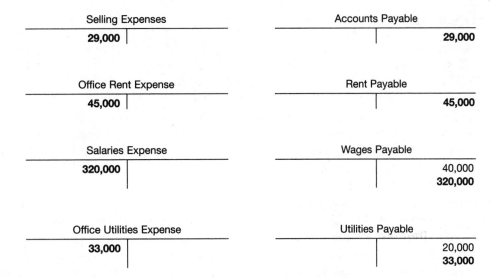

| Selling Expenses | | Accounts Payable | |
|---|---|---|---|
| 29,000 | | | 29,000 |

| Office Rent Expense | | Rent Payable | |
|---|---|---|---|
| 45,000 | | | 45,000 |

| Salaries Expense | | Wages Payable | |
|---|---|---|---|
| 320,000 | | | 40,000 |
| | | | 320,000 |

| Office Utilities Expense | | Utilities Payable | |
|---|---|---|---|
| 33,000 | | | 20,000 |
| | | | 33,000 |

Since only $80,000 of factory overhead was applied during 2004, the total actual factory overhead spent was not charged to jobs. The difference, or variance, of $1,500 can be closed to Cost of Goods Sold at the end of the year or, if desired, can be allocated to Cost of Goods Sold, Finished Goods, and Work in Process on the basis of their account balances. Since these variances tend to be relatively small, most companies simply close them out to Cost of Goods Sold. Using this approach, Bodker Publishing's entry to close out the variance is:

| Factory Overhead | | Cost of Goods Sold | |
|---|---|---|---|
| 81,500 | 80,000 | 1,500 | |
| | 1,500 | | |

Notice that since we did not attach all $81,500 of spending to our production, Cost of Goods Sold is increased by $1,500.

If too little overhead is costed to the products, as in the above example, the variance is called **underapplied** or **underabsorbed overhead**. When this occurs, expenditures for overhead expenses exceed the amount attached to the products during the accounting period. On the other hand, if too much overhead is costed to the products, the variance is called **overapplied** or **overabsorbed overhead**. In this situation, more overhead costs are attached to the period's output than are actually spent for overhead.

Underapplied factory overhead means nothing more than the actual costs were not absorbed by the products manufactured. Underapplied overhead occurs in these situations:

**1.** We produced less than expected, or
**2.** We spent more than expected.

When overhead is overapplied, the variance is credited to (i.e., subtracted from) Cost of Goods Sold. Overapplied overhead occurs in these situations:

**1.** We produced more than expected, or
**2.** We spent less than expected.

In the Bodker Publishing Company example, 10,000 direct labor hours were worked. This was exactly the amount of activity that was budgeted. Therefore, the reason for the underapplied overhead variance was overspending. According to the company's cost function ($50,000 + $3 per direct labor hour), spending should have been $80,000 but was actually $81,500.

More detailed reasons for overhead variances are discussed in Chapter 8.

## Multiple Overhead Rates

Some reasonable, causal, or beneficial relationship should exist among the costs accumulated in factory overhead accounts, the cost driver selected, and the products or services to which the costs will be allocated. Simply stated: The activity (as represented by the cost driver) is the link between the output of products or services and factory overhead spending. The implication is that more output requires more activity and, therefore, more overhead spending. For example, if a company uses direct labor hours as a cost driver, factory overhead costs should consist primarily or exclusively of costs that support direct workers. Such costs may include supervision and facilities for work places, as well as travel, training, and fringe benefits of workers.

In the examples to this point in the chapter, we have assumed that only one cost driver is appropriate for the total factory overhead. However, diversity of products and services will often result in distorted cost allocations when only one cost driver is used. The greater the differences in products, the greater the diversity that exists in the operations. The more diverse the operations, the more likely it is that one cost driver cannot assign costs to all products fairly. In these situations, departmental overhead rates will assign costs more accurately to products than will one plant-wide overhead rate. A plant-wide factory overhead rate can only be justified for a company making few and similar products. Contemporary Practice 4.1 displays results from a survey on types of overhead rates most commonly used by companies in Korea, Japan, and the United States.

For an example, consider Fellman & Associates, a company that finishes furniture for local manufacturers. The furniture passes through two major activity centers that form the two departments in the process: sanding and painting. A summary of direct labor and overhead costs for each department during the last month follows:

|  | Sanding | Painting | Total |
|---|---|---|---|
| Direct labor | $37,000 | $26,500 | $63,500 |
| Overhead | 74,000 | 79,500 | 153,500 |

Overhead is allocated to products on the basis of direct labor dollars. Dividing the overhead costs by direct labor dollars gives the following departmental and plant-wide overhead rates:

Sanding ($74,000 ÷ $37,000)  = 200%
Painting ($79,500 ÷ $26,500)  = 300%
Plant-wide ($153,500 ÷ $63,500) = 241.7%

## Contemporary Practice 4.1
### *Survey on Types Overhead Rates*

| Country | Most Common Type of Overhead Rate |
|---|---|
| *Korea* | *Single plant-wide rate (43% of respondent companies)* |
| *United States* | *Departmental rates (38% of respondent companies)* |
| *Japan* | *Rates for groups of departments (68% of respondent companies)* |

*Source: Kim, I. and J. Song, "U.S., Korea, and Japan: Accounting Practices in the Three Countries,"* Management Accounting, *August 1990, p. 28.*

Using the different rates in allocating overhead costs to a job that has $86 of Sanding direct labor and $32 of Painting direct labor (i.e., a total labor cost of $118) gives the following amounts:

| | | |
|---|---|---|
| Plant-wide overhead rate ($118 × 241.7%) | | $ 285.21 |
| Departmental overhead rates: | | |
| Sanding ($86 × 200%) | $ 172.00 | |
| Painting ($32 × 300%) | 96.00 | $ 268.00 |

The departmental rates allocate costs considering the characteristics of the product or job involved. The plant-wide rate averages all products and jobs.

For Fellman & Associates, the same cost driver was selected for each department. A more common situation is where departments have different cost drivers. For example, a Fabrication Department may use direct labor hours; a Machining Department, machine time; a Production Engineering Department, direct labor cost. As a company considers ways to trace costs to products more accurately, it will look at the production and support activities more closely and choose an appropriate cost driver to allocate the overhead costs.

## Alternative Concepts of Volume

When selecting the denominator for the overhead rate, volume can be measured in one of four ways:

1. Ideal capacity.
2. Practical capacity.
3. Expected volume.
4. Normal volume.

**Ideal capacity** is the maximum amount of product that can be manufactured or the maximum service that can be rendered with available facilities. This is often a too perfect goal to be realized and is generally recognized to be the absolute limit and beyond realistic expectations. Certain interruptions and inefficiencies in production are to be expected.

**Practical capacity** is full utilization of facilities with allowance made for normal interruptions and inefficiencies. For example, production will be slowed or stopped at times because of breakdowns, shortages of labor and materials, or retooling. These possibilities are considered in arriving at practical plant capacity.

**Expected volume** is the level of operation budgeted or estimated for the current period. This may be at or below practical capacity. It is the level at which management expects to operate during the next month or year.

**Normal volume** is generally a balance between practical capacity and sales demand in the long run. Over a period of years, the peaks and valleys of customer demand are leveled by averaging; and the average level of plant utilization is considered to be normal volume.

It may seem, at first, that overhead per unit should be calculated at the expected level of operation for the next year. Indeed, this is the practice of most companies. However, for product pricing purposes, a better approach is to use the normal volume. Why should normal volume be used when you already know that the company may be operating below that level? After all, a rate computed at the expected level of operation will come closer to costing all of the overhead to the products, and product cost will be more in line with actual cost.

The problem with using an overhead rate based on expected, rather than normal volume, is illustrated by the following example. Assume that the normal level of operation for Cherrywood Medical

Laboratory is 200,000 labor hours and that 100,000 items can be analyzed in that time. The fixed overhead for the year is budgeted at $500,000. The normal fixed overhead per item is then $5, computed as:

$$\frac{\text{Budgeted fixed overhead}}{\text{Items analyzed at normal volume}} = \frac{\$500,000}{100,000} = \$5 \text{ Fixed overhead per item}$$

But management expects to operate at only 100,000 labor hours next year and to analyze 50,000 items. An overhead rate at expected volume would be $10 per item:

$$\frac{\text{Budgeted fixed overhead}}{\text{Items analyzed at expected volume}} = \frac{\$500,000}{50,000} = \$10 \text{ Fixed overhead per item}$$

If the lab plans to operate below normal volume, an overhead rate computed at the expected level of operations will result in more fixed overhead being assigned to each item. If prices are set by adding a markup to total cost, the price will be higher when fewer items are analyzed. With a higher price under competitive conditions, customers may be lost, thereby aggravating a condition when volume is already below normal.

For this reason, the objective is not necessarily to assign all overhead costs to products. The products should bear the normal overhead costs, and any unabsorbed fixed overhead should be recognized as a period expense. (Overabsorbed fixed overhead would likewise result in a reduction of period expenses.) Rather than allocating unabsorbed fixed overhead to products produced, this approach treats the costs of idle capacity as the costs of products the company did *not* produce.

## COST OF PROVIDING SERVICES

An entity that provides services instead of tangible products may not operate with a formal cost accounting system that traces costs to jobs. Instead, all service job costs are treated as period costs and are often left in their original cost categories such as supplies expense, labor expense, depreciation expense, etc.

Nevertheless, costs will be used to measure performance by type of service and by customer groups. A hotel, for example, may provide an exercise room for its guests. The cost of supplies used exclusively for the exercise room, such as rubbing lotions and bandages, along with the salaries and wages of the room's employees, such as the manager and exercise class instructors, is identified with the exercise activities. Also, costs of special equipment used, such as depreciation and maintenance expenses, and other overhead costs increased by operating this service will be included. These costs can be used as a basis for deciding how much must be added to a guest's bill to cover all costs and allow for profit. Also, does the amount of customer patronage justify continuance of the service? Can other features be provided at a certain cost to attract more customer attention? Properly assigning costs to the exercise room will give the manager the accounting information needed to answer these questions.

Some service organizations do have formal systems for determining costs associated with jobs. Accounting and legal services are examples where the firm may want costs accumulated by client number or case. In this situation, each client number or case becomes a job, with costs traced to the individual jobs.

In service organizations having formal job cost systems, inventory accounts such as Work in Process Services or Cost of Unbilled Work are used to reflect the cost of resources and effort that have been expended, but where the work is not yet completed for the customer. At year-end, or whenever financial statements are being prepared, the cost of uncompleted work appears in this type of inventory account rather than in an expense account because the related revenue has not yet been earned. Examples of such situations may include:

- A painting contractor is in the midst of a three-week painting job.
- An engineering firm is in the early design stage of a four-month project.
- A web page design firm has another two days of work before presenting the completed work to its client.
- A landscaping company has only partially completed its planting of shrubs and flowers.

When the work is completed, the costs are transferred to an account such as Cost of Completed Jobs or Cost of Services Provided. These accounts are analogous to Cost of Goods Sold for a manufacturing firm. Since most service firms do not have finished goods inventories, there would usually be no account analogous to Finished Goods.

## A PRODUCT COSTING ILLUSTRATION

Summarized cost data are presented in this section for Scher Machine Company to illustrate product costing procedures using a normal costing system. Note that the entries given are in composite form. In practice, many repetitious entries are made to record individual transactions that take place during the year. The sequential order of the cost transactions should also be considered. For example, the preparation of the budget for factory overhead and overhead rate calculations are completed before the beginning of the year. The predetermined overhead rate must be calculated from a budget of factory overhead so that products will be assigned the proper overhead cost. Only at the end of the year will the company know that 220,000 direct labor hours were used and that the actual factory overhead cost was $1,336,200. Throughout the year, the company purchases materials and incurs labor and factory overhead costs as products are continually processed, completed, and sold. At the same time, costs are traced to the products and released as expenses when the products are sold.

Scher Machine Company transactions data for the fiscal year ended April 30, 2004, are as follows:

1. Materials purchased during the fiscal year totaled $840,000.
2. Direct materials requisitioned for production cost $631,400. Indirect materials costing $47,200 were also requisitioned.
3. Factory payrolls amounted to $1,874,000. The income taxes withheld from the employees' wages totaled $393,400, and the deduction for FICA taxes withheld amounted to $106,600. A distribution of the factory labor cost of $1,874,000 shows that $1,760,000 was direct labor while the remaining $114,000 was indirect labor.
4. Factory overhead at the normal operating level of 250,000 direct labor hours results in an overhead rate of $6 per direct labor hour. During the year, direct labor workers recorded 220,000 labor hours.
5. The factory overhead, in addition to the indirect materials and the indirect labor, amounted to $1,175,000. Included in this amount is depreciation of $120,000 and the employer's share of FICA taxes of $106,600. The balance of the overhead was acquired through accounts payable.
6. Jobs completed and transferred to stock during the year had costs of $2,945,200.
7. The cost of orders sold during the year was $2,320,000.
8. The Factory Overhead account is closed to Cost of Goods Sold at the end of the fiscal year.

The transactions are entered in the accounts as follows:

1. **Purchase of materials.** (The cost of each type of materials is also entered on the individual materials inventory cards.)

| Materials | | Accounts Payable | |
|---|---|---|---|
| 840,000 | | | 840,000 |

2. **Materials issued to production.** (Requisitions are the basis for entries reducing materials inventory, for posting direct materials costs to each job, and for posting indirect materials costs to Factory Overhead.)

| Materials | | Work in Process | |
|---|---|---|---|
| 840,000 | 678,600 | 631,400 | |

| Factory Overhead | |
|---|---|
| 47,200 | |

3. **Factory payrolls.** (A classification of labor time by jobs is shown on labor time tickets. These tickets are the basis for distributing direct labor costs to individual jobs and for posting indirect labor costs to the factory overhead subsidiary ledger.)

| Wages Payable | |
|---|---|
| | 1,374,000 |

| Employees' Income Taxes Payable | | FICA Taxes Payable | |
|---|---|---|---|
| | 393,400 | | 106,600 |

| Work in Process | |
|---|---|
| 631,400 | |
| 1,760,000 | |

| Factory Overhead | |
|---|---|
| 47,200 | |
| 114,000 | |

4. **Factory overhead applied.** (Factory overhead applied to products on direct labor hour basis is: 220,000 hours $\times$ \$6 rate = \$1,320,000.)

| Work in Process | | Factory Overhead | |
|---|---|---|---|
| 631,400 | | 47,200 | 1,320,000 |
| 1,760,000 | | 114,000 | |
| 1,320,000 | | | |

**5. Actual factory overhead.** (This is in addition to indirect materials and indirect labor.)

| Factory Overhead | |
|---|---|
| 47,200 | 1,320,000 |
| 1,760,000 | |
| **1,175,000** | |

| Accumulated Depreciation | |
|---|---|
| | **120,000** |

| FICA Taxes Payable | |
|---|---|
| | **106,600** |

| Accounts Payable | |
|---|---|
| | 840,000 |
| | **948,400** |

**6. Work completed during the year and transferred to stock.** (Completed jobs are removed from the file of jobs in process and moved to the subsidiary ledger supporting finished goods inventory. Ending Work in Process is $766,200.)

| Work in Process | |
|---|---|
| 631,400 | **2,945,200** |
| 1,760,000 | |
| 1,320,000 | |
| 766,200 | |

| Finished Goods | |
|---|---|
| **2,945,200** | |

**7. The cost of goods sold.** (Deductions are recorded in the finished goods inventory ledger. Entries are also made in records supporting billings to customers for the sales. Ending Finished Goods is $625,200.)

| Finished Goods | |
|---|---|
| 2,945,200 | **2,320,000** |
| 625,200 | |

| Cost of Goods Sold | |
|---|---|
| **2,320,000** | |

**8. Closing of Factory Overhead.** (Total actual overhead cost from entries in Items (2), (4), and (6), is $1,336,200. Actual overhead amounting to $16,200 is not absorbed as a part of the product cost. The underapplied overhead is closed to Cost of Goods Sold.)

| Factory Overhead | |
|---|---|
| 47,200 | 1,320,000 |
| 114,000 | **16,200** |
| 1,175,000 | |

| Accumulated Depreciation | |
|---|---|
| 2,320,000 | |
| **16,200** | |

## SERVICE CENTER COSTS

Most companies have several departments or functions involved directly or indirectly in producing goods or providing services. The development of departmental overhead rates depends on the interrelationships among these different departments.

**Operating departments** are organizational units most closely tied to the productive effort that results in products or services to customers. In manufacturing organizations, these units are typically called **producing departments**. On the other hand, **service centers** (or **support functions**) provide supporting services that facilitate the activities of the operating departments. Often, service centers provide support services to one another. Service centers include, for example, maintenance, quality control, cafeterias, internal auditing, personnel, accounting, production planning and control, and medical facilities. Although they do not have a direct relationship to output, service center costs support operating departments and, therefore, become part of the cost of a finished product or service. In some

| POSSIBLE COST DRIVERS FOR SELECTED SERVICE CENTERS | |
|---|---|
| *Service Center* | *Possible Cost Drivers* |
| Purchasing | Number of orders, cost of materials, line items ordered |
| Receiving and inspection | Cost of materials, number of units, number or orders, labor hours |
| Storerooms | Cost of materials, number of requisitions, number of units handled, square or cubic footage occupied |
| Personnel | Number of employees, labor hours, turnover of labor |
| Laundry | Pounds of laundry, number of items processed |
| Cafeteria | Number of employees |
| Custodial services | Square footage occupied |
| Repair and maintenance | Machine hours, labor hours |
| Medical facilities | Number of employees, hours worked |
| Factory administration | Total labor hours, number of employees, labor cost |
| Power | Kilowatt hours, capacity of machines |

FIGURE **4.2**

Cost Drivers Used for Service Centers

limited cases, a service center provides support services for operating departments as well as services for outside customers. Examples include engineering consulting, research and development, computer systems design, copying services, and laboratory work.

Service center costs are allocated to operating departments by means of a cost driver. Any one of a number of cost drivers may be appropriate for calculating a rate depending on the nature of the support activity. Examples of cost drivers that could be used are given in Figure 4.2. The allocated service center costs become part of the total overhead costs of the operating departments.

Occasionally, companies may not allocate service center costs to operating departments to ensure that the services are fully utilized by the operating managers. Some examples of this phenomenon include internal audit departments, credit-check services, libraries, and computer services. An illustration of the latter appears in Contemporary Practice 4.2.

Three common approaches are available for allocating the costs of service centers: direct method, step (sequential) method, and reciprocal method.

To illustrate the allocation of service center costs for the first two methods, we will use data from the School of Business at Hardknox University. The School of Business wishes to determine overhead costs per credit hour for its undergraduate and graduate programs. We will treat these as the two operating departments. The School of Business has three service centers: Building Services,

## Contemporary Practice 4.2
### *Cost Allocation in a Data Processing Service Department*

*"For many years, managers of the Corporate Data Processing Services (CDPS) department of the Boise Cascade Corporation did not allocate any of the costs of supporting personal computers (PC), such as purchasing, set-up, and application assistance, to the PC users because they wanted to stimulate PC use. These costs were charged/allocated to all of the other CDPS users, primarily consumers of mainframe computer resources."*

Source: Merchant, K. A., and M. D. Shields, "When and Why to Measure Costs Less Accurately to Improve Decision Making," Accounting Horizons, June 1993, p. 78.

Staff Services (e.g., secretarial support, computer support, and photocopying), and Administration. Budgeted data for the coming year appear as follows:

|  | Square Feet Occupied | Employees | Overhead Costs |
|---|---|---|---|
| Service Centers: |  |  |  |
| Building Services | 1,000 | 30 | $ 165,000 |
| Staff Services | 2,000 | 20 | 90,000 |
| Administration | 8,000 | 20 | 330,000 |
| Operating Departments: |  |  |  |
| Graduate Program | 10,000 | 30 | 265,000 |
| Undergraduate Program | 20,000 | 90 | 420,000 |

Building Services costs are allocated on square footage of classroom and office space. Staff Services and Administration costs are allocated based on number of employees (i.e., faculty and staff). Budgeted credit hours for the year are 20,000 for the Graduate Program and 60,000 for the Undergraduate Program.

## Direct Method

**Direct method** allocations are made from each service center to operating departments in proportion to activity performed for each. Thus, the direct method does not assign costs to other service centers for work performed for other service centers. Allocation of service center costs uses only those cost drivers pertaining to operating departments. Once the service centers have their costs allocated, operating department overhead rates per unit of activity are calculated.

Space associated with the Graduate Program is 10,000 square feet; and, for the Undergraduate Program, the space used is 20,000 square feet. The allocation base, therefore, totals 30,000 square feet. Building Services costs are then prorated over the two programs as follows:

| Graduate Program | 10,000 sq. ft. | 1/3 × $165,000 = | $ 55,000 |
|---|---|---|---|
| Undergraduate Program | 20,000 | 2/3 × $165,000 = | 110,000 |
| Total | 30,000 sq. ft. | Total cost | $ 165,000 |

The Same approach follows for Staff Services and Administration. These are summarized as follows:

| Graduate Program | 30 employees | 1/4 × $ 90,000 = | $ 22,500 |
|---|---|---|---|
| Undergraduate Program | 90 | 3/4 × $ 90,000 = | 67,500 |
| Total | 120 employees | Total cost | $ 90,000 |
| Graduate Program | 30 employees | 1/4 × $330,000 = | $ 82,500 |
| Undergraduate Program | 90 | 3/4 × $330,000 = | 247,500 |
| Total | 120 employees | Total cost | $ 330,000 |

Another way to perform these allocations is to divide the service center costs by the cost driver and apply the resulting rate to the operating department usage amount. For example, Building Services would have a rate of $5.50 per square foot ($165,000 ÷ 30,000).

The results of service center allocations and the subsequent calculation of overhead rates for the operating departments are summarized as follows:

| | Building Services | Staff Services | Administration | Graduate Program | Undergraduate Program |
|---|---|---|---|---|---|
| Costs | $ 165,000 | $ 90,000 | $ 330,000 | $ 265,000 | $ 420,000 |
| Building Services | (165,000) | | | 55,000 | 110,000 |
| Staff Services | | (90,000) | | 22,500 | 67,500 |
| Administration | | | (330,000) | 82,500 | 247,500 |
| | $ 0 | $ 0 | $ 0 | $ 425,000 | $ 845,000 |
| Credit hours | | | | ÷ 20,000 | ÷ 60,000 |
| Overhead rate per credit hour | | | | $ 21.25 | $ 14.08 |

## Step (Sequential) Method

The **step (sequential) method** is an attempt to consider services performed for other service centers. However, recognition of those services is a one-way process. The service centers are arranged in a sequence, and their costs are allocated one after the other. Once a service center's costs are allocated, no other costs are allocated back to that service center even though it may use resources of other service centers. The first service center's costs are allocated to all subsequent service centers and operating departments. The second service center's costs are then allocated to all subsequent service centers and operating departments, but not to the first service center. This process continues until all service centers' costs have been allocated to operating departments. The number of allocation steps will equal the number of service centers.

Since there are three service centers in the Hardknox University School of Business, there are three steps in the allocation process. We begin by allocating the costs of Building Services. The square footage for Staff Services is 2,000; Administration is 8,000; Graduate Program is 10,000; and Undergraduate Program is 20,000. The allocation base, therefore, totals 40,000 square feet. Building Services costs are then prorated over the remaining service centers and operating departments as follows:

| | | | | |
|---|---|---|---|---|
| Staff Services | 2,000 | sq. ft. | 5% × $165,000 = | $ 8,250 |
| Administration | 8,000 | | 20% × $165,000 = | 33,000 |
| Graduate Program | 10,000 | | 25% × $165,000 = | 41,250 |
| Undergraduate Program | 20,000 | | 50% × $165,000 = | 82,500 |
| Total | 40,000 | sq. ft. | Total cost | $165,000 |

Staff Services receives an allocation of Building Services costs. This allocation must be added to the costs already charged to the Staff Services department to determine the allocation of Staff Services costs. The new total Staff Services costs are $98,250 ($90,000 + $8,250). The next step in the allocation process follows:

| | | | | |
|---|---|---|---|---|
| Administration | 20 | employees | 2/14 × $ 98,250 = | $14,035* |
| Graduate Program | 30 | | 3/14 × $ 98,250 = | 21,054 |
| Undergraduate Program | 90 | | 9/14 × $ 98,250 = | 63,161 |
| Total | 140 | employees | Total cost | $ 98,250 |

* This figure has been rounded down.

After allocating Building Services and Staff Services costs, the Administration costs for the next step of the allocation are $377,035 ($330,000 + $33,000 + $14,035). These costs are allocated as follows:

| Graduate Program | 30 | employees | 25% × $377,035 = | $ 94,259 |
|---|---|---|---|---|
| Undergraduate Program | 90 | | 75% × $377,035 = | 282,776 |
| Total | 120 | employees | Total cost | $377,035 |

The results of service center allocations and the subsequent calculation of overhead rates for the operating departments are summarized as follows:

| | Building Services | Staff Services | Administration | Graduate Program | Undergraduate Program |
|---|---|---|---|---|---|
| Costs | $165,000 | $90,000 | $330,000 | $265,000 | $420,000 |
| Building Services | (165,000) | 8,250 | 33,000 | 41,250 | 82,500 |
| | $      0 | $98,250 | | | |
| Staff Services | | (98,250) | 14,035 | 21,054 | 63,161 |
| | | $      0 | $377,035 | | |
| Administration | | | (377,035) | 94,259 | 282,776 |
| | | | $      0 | $421,563 | $848,437 |
| Credit hours | | | | ÷ 20,000 | ÷ 60,000 |
| Overhead rate per credit hour | | | | $   21.08 | $   14.14 |

How do you arrange the order of service centers? The general rule is to sequence service centers according to the amount of services provided to other service centers—going from greatest to least. What constitutes "greatest amount of service?" One interpretation is according to the center serving the greatest number of other service centers. Another is the amount of cost in the service center; the service center with the highest costs goes first. It is not clear which interpretation should be applied. The real issue is to set up a sequence that will provide reasonable and logical allocations.

## Reciprocal Method

Neither the direct method nor the step method of service center allocation recognizes mutual rendering of services among service centers. A third method, the **reciprocal method**, does consider that service centers can perform services in a mutual fashion for each other. The method, however, is more complex than the direct and step methods because it involves solving simultaneous equations. Specifically, the number of simultaneous equations will equal the number of service centers. When this number is large, a computer becomes necessary to solve the equations. For simplicity, we will restrict our analyses to cases of two service centers.

The reciprocal method involves a two-stage procedure:

**Stage 1:** Set-up and solve the following two equations for $S_1$ and $S_2$:

$$S_1 = DC_1 + k_1 S_2$$
$$S_2 = DC_2 + k_2 S_1$$

**where:**    $S_i$ = cost of service center i *after* the reciprocal allocation (i = 1, 2)
$DC_i$ = the direct costs traceable to service center i (i = 1, 2)
$k_1$ = the percentage of $S_2$ cost allocated to $S_1$
$k_2$ = the percentage of $S_1$ cost allocated to $S_2$

**Stage 2:** Allocate the costs of each service center derived in Stage 1 (i.e., $S_1$ and $S_2$) to *all* other service centers and operating departments.

To illustrate, suppose Lubel Brothers, Inc. manages real estate properties for various owners. The firm has two operating departments: Indoor Malls, with directly traceable overhead costs of $200,000 per month, and Outdoor Shopping Centers, with directly traceable overhead costs of $320,000 per month. The departmental overhead rates are based on direct labor hours. There are also two service centers: Storerooms, having directly traceable costs of $48,000 per month, and Custodial Services, having directly traceable costs of $250,000 per month. Storerooms costs are allocated on the basis of number of storeroom requisitions; while Custodial Services costs are allocated on the basis of number of employees. These facts are summarized in the following table:

| Department | Costs | Requisitions | Employees | Labor Hours |
|---|---|---|---|---|
| Indoor Malls | $200,000 | 1,000 | 84 | 13,000 |
| Outdoor Shopping Centers | 320,000 | 8,000 | 12 | 3,000 |
| Storerooms | 48,000 | – | 24 | – |
| Custodial Services | 250,000 | 1,000 | – | – |

First, we set up the two equations for Stage 1:

$$S = \$48{,}000 + .2C$$

$$C = \$250{,}000 + .1S$$

**where:**     $S$ = Cost of Storerooms after the reciprocal allocation
$C$ = Cost of Custodial Services after the reciprocal allocation

The allocation percentages were determined as follows:

$$k_1 = 24/ (24 + 12 + 84) = 24/120 = .2$$
$$k_2 = 1{,}000/ (1{,}000 + 8{,}000 + 1{,}000) = 1{,}000/10{,}000 = .1$$

Notice that the denominators for calculating the allocation percentages consist of all centers and departments other than the one from which the costs are being allocated. This is so because in Stage 2 the costs will be allocated to all other service centers and operating departments.

We now solve the two equations by first substituting the second equation into the first:

$$S = \$48{,}000 + .2(\$250{,}000 + .1S)$$
$$.98S = \$98{,}000$$
$$S = \$100{,}000$$

Now we obtain C by inserting $100,000 into our second equation:

$$C = \$250{,}000 + .1(\$100{,}000)$$
$$C = \$260{,}000$$

Having solved for S and C, we proceed to Stage 2, where we allocate these costs as follows:

**(a)** Of the $100,000 from S, 10 percent (1,000/10,000) is allocated to Custodial Services, 10 percent (1,000/10,000) is also allocated to Indoor Malls, and 80 percent (8,000/10,000) is allocated to Outdoor Shopping Centers.

**(b)** Of the $260,000 from C, 20 percent (24/120) is allocated to Storerooms, 70 percent (84/120) is allocated to Indoor Malls, and 10 percent (12/120) is allocated to Outdoor Shopping Centers.

The resulting allocations, total operating department overhead costs, and departmental overhead rates are summarized in the following table:

|  | Storerooms | Custodial Services | Indoor Malls | Outdoor Shopping Centers |
|---|---|---|---|---|
| Costs | $ 48,000 | $250,000 | $200,000 | $320,000 |
| Storerooms | (100,000) | 10,000 | 10,000 | 80,000 |
| Custodial Services | 52,000 | (260,000) | 182,000 | 26,000 |
| Totals (after allocation) | $          0 | $          0 | $392,000 | $426,000 |
| Direct labor hours |  |  | 13,000 | 3,000 |
| Overhead rate per direct labor hour |  |  | $   30.15 | $  142.00 |

All $298,000 of service center costs ($48,000 + $250,000) have been fully allocated to the operating departments. To confirm: $10,000 + $80,000 + $182,000 + $26,000 = $298,000.

Two other issues influence the way we allocate service center costs: treatment of revenues and allocation of costs by behavior. These issues are presented next.

## Treatment of Revenues

Most service centers simply incur costs and generate no revenues. A few, such as a cafeteria, may charge employees or other outside parties for the services they perform. Any revenues generated should be offset against the service center costs. For both the direct method and the step method, we allocate the costs less the offset. In this manner, other service centers and operating departments will not be required to bear costs for which the service center has already been reimbursed.

## Allocation of Costs by Behavior

Whenever possible, service center costs should be separated into variable and fixed classifications and allocated separately. As a general rule, variable costs should be charged to other service centers and operating departments on the basis of the actual activity that controls the incurrence of the cost involved. The service centers and departments directly responsible for the incurrence of servicing costs are, therefore, required to bear the cost in proportion to their actual usage of the service involved.

The fixed costs of service centers represent the cost of providing capacity. As such, these costs are most equitably allocated to consuming service centers and operating departments on the basis of predetermined amounts. In this way, the amount of costs allocated is determined in advance of the period in which service is provided. Once determined, the amount does not change from period to period. Typically, the amount allocated is based either on peak-period or long-run average servicing needs. This approach of allocating variable costs on the basis of actual activity and fixed costs using predetermined percentages is sometimes referred to as the **dual-rate method** of allocation.

The following example will illustrate undesirable consequences of not separating the allocation of fixed and variable costs. Suppose that Azer Website Designers has an Administration support center that services two operating centers—Domestic and International. Based on needs forecast by these two operating centers, Azer hired staff and incurred other fixed costs amounting to $1,200,000 per year. Sixty percent of this cost derived from the needs of Domestic. In addition, Administration incurs costs that vary with the amount of labor hours worked in the operating centers. This averages about $1 per hour.

In 2004, Domestic worked 400,000 hours and International worked 200,000 hours. If fixed and variable costs are not separated, the allocation rate would be determined as follows:

$$\text{Allocation rate} = \frac{\$1,200,000 + \$1(400,000 + 200,000)}{400,000 + 200,000} = \$3 \text{ per hour}$$

The 2004 allocations to each of the operating centers would be:

Domestic: \$3 per hour $\times$ 400,000 hours = \$1,200,000

International: \$3 per hour $\times$ 200,000 hours = \$600,000

In 2005, International works the same 200,000 hours, but Domestic's work drops off to only 100,000 hours. The allocation rate for 2005 would change as follows:

$$\text{Allocation rate} = \frac{\$1,200,000 + \$1(100,000 + 200,000)}{100,000 + 200,000} = \$5 \text{ per hour}$$

The 2005 allocations to each of the operating centers would be:

Domestic: \$5 per hour $\times$ 100,000 hours = \$500,000

International: \$5 per hour $\times$ 200,000 hours = \$1,000,000

Note that International's share of costs increased by \$400,000 (\$1,000,000 – \$600,000) even though it worked the same number of hours both years. Because fewer hours were worked in Domestic, the allocation rate increased. This resulted in more fixed Administration cost charged to International than in the previous year. To avoid this inequity, each year the dual-rate method would assign \$720,000 in fixed cost to Domestic (.6 $\times$ \$1,200,000) and \$480,000 to International (.4 $\times$ \$1,200,000). These allocations are in accordance with the forecasted needs that generated the total fixed cost of \$1,200,000. For the variable costs, the dual-rate method would assign \$1 per hour each year. Thus, with the dual-rate method, International would be assigned a total cost of \$680,000 each year (\$480,000 + \$200,000), while Domestic would be assigned \$1,120,000 in 2004 (\$720,000 + \$400,000) and \$820,000 in 2005 (\$720,000 + \$100,000).

## ETHICAL ISSUES FOR COST ALLOCATION

Often, a department or division's performance is evaluated on the basis of profits after overhead costs have been allocated. Consequently, the choice of cost drivers can affect performance evaluation. One wishing to reward some managers and penalize others could attempt to do so by unethically selecting cost drivers that would shift overhead costs to the desired entities.

When the prices of certain services or products are cost-based while others are market-driven, managers are often tempted to shift much of the overhead costs to those cost-based services or products. This can be accomplished by:

1. Including in the overhead cost pool items which are not business expenses (e.g., entertainment expenses unrelated to the business).

2. Arbitrary selection of cost drivers.

When using the step method of allocating support costs, another way to shift overhead costs is:

3. Arbitrary ordering of support centers.

Clearly, the inclusion of nonbusiness expenses is unethical. The arbitrary selection of cost drivers or of the order of support centers is not as clear. On one hand, management has an obligation to the

## Contemporary Practice 4.3
### Increasing Revenues by Changing Cost Allocations

*An experiment with individuals in graduate and executive education managerial accounting classes, who averaged about six years of full-time work experience, tested whether they would arbitrarily change an established logically-based cost allocation procedure to one which is more arbitrary in order to increase profits. The scenario was one in which the company was selling one of its products on a cost-plus basis, and by allocating more overhead costs to this product rather than to other products, more revenues could be generated since the revenues for this cost-plus product would be based on the higher cost assigned to it. The study estimated that about 41 percent of the participants would arbitrarily change the cost allocation procedure in order to increase revenues and thereby meet a targeted pretax income figure.*

Source: Schneider, A., "Ethical Decision Making on Various Managerial Accounting Issues," Journal of Applied Management Accounting Research, *Summer 2004, pp. 29–39.*

company's owners to maximize profits using any allowable methods. On the other hand, there is a question of fairness to the parties purchasing the products or services. Moreover, when the government happens to be the other party, the issue extends to one of fairness to taxpayers.

## SUMMARY

One of the objectives in cost accounting is to determine the cost to provide a given service, to manufacture a given quantity of product, or to complete some project. We accumulate the costs of materials, labor, and overhead separately. Materials are identified as direct or indirect. If direct, the materials are charged directly to the specific product. Indirect materials costs are included in factory overhead costs. Labor costs follow the same type of distinctions.

Factory overhead is budgeted and divided by a cost driver that relates overhead costs to the products. This yields a rate that is used to allocate overhead to services or products. If the overhead consists largely of labor-related costs and labor support costs, such as supervision and fringe benefit costs, the cost driver selected may be direct labor hours. The cost driver "direct labor hours" serves as a bridge between the product and the overhead costs. On the other hand, machine hours may be more appropriate if a large part of the overhead is lubrication, maintenance, and other costs generally related to machine operation. Other cost drivers may, however, be better links between costs and outputs. Both overhead costs and the cost driver should be budgeted at a normal level of operations rather than just the expected volume for the coming period. Factory overhead rates can be plant-wide or departmental, depending on the diversity of the products.

Actual costs are accumulated, and comparisons of actual and estimated costs for each product help management to control costs. Actual overhead incurred can be compared with the overhead applied to the services or products. If actual factory overhead is less than the overhead applied to products (or if overhead is overapplied), the variance is usually closed out to Cost of Goods Sold.

The overhead costs of operating departments include allocations of service center costs. The direct method allocates service center costs directly to operating departments without any intervening allocations to service centers. The step method involves a sequence of allocations where service center costs are allocated to other service centers as well as operating departments. The reciprocal method simultaneously allocates service center costs among service centers and operating departments. Any revenues earned by service centers should be deducted from the costs allocated. Ideally, variable costs should be allocated separately from fixed costs.

## PROBLEMS FOR REVIEW

### Review Problem A

Perry Brickman owns and operates Bobo Heating Service. Two overhead rates are used in applying overhead costs to the jobs. One rate is based on direct labor hours, and the other is based on machine hours. The machine is a backhoe used in digging service lines. Overhead costs of operating the backhoe are kept separately, so that only the jobs requiring the use of the backhoe are charged an overhead rate per machine hour. For the year, $126,000 of general overhead costs were budgeted for 6,000 direct labor hours; and $21,600 of backhoe-related overhead costs were budgeted for 1,800 machine hours (hours of backhoe operation).

On February 1, the cost in Work in Process is $440 and consists of only one job, the job for A. Esral. Costs and other data pertaining to jobs worked on during February are:

|  | Direct Materials | Direct Labor | Labor Hours | Machine Hours |
|---|---|---|---|---|
| A. Esral | $    135 | $    320 | 16 | – |
| D. Appelrouth | 246 | 560 | 28 | – |
| M. Spector | 230 | 365 | 12 | 5 |
| S. Vogel | 84 | 60 | 3 | – |
| All other jobs | 842 | 14,000 | 500 | 160 |
| Totals | $  1,537 | $ 15,305 | 559 | 165 |

All orders were finished during February with the exception of the Vogel order which is still in process.

**Required:**
1. Compute an overhead rate per direct labor hour and an overhead rate per machine hour.
2. Prepare a summary of costs incurred for work performed in February.
3. Determine the cost of work completed during February.

**Solution:**

1. $\dfrac{\text{Budget of overhead for direct labor hours}}{\text{Budget of direct labor hours}} = \dfrac{\$126,000}{6,000} = \$21$ per direct labor hour

   $\dfrac{\text{Budget of overhead for machine hours}}{\text{Budget of machine hours}} = \dfrac{\$21,600}{1,800} = \$12$ per machine hour

2. Costs of work performed during February:

| | |
|---|---|
| Materials | $ 1,537 |
| Direct labor | 15,305 |
| Applied overhead—labor (559 hours × $21) | 11,739 |
| Applied overhead—machine (165 hours × $12) | 1,980 |
| Cost of work performed during February | $30,561 |

3. Cost of work completed during February:

| Work in process at February | $    440 |
|---|---|
| Add February costs | 30,561 |
| | $31,001 |
| Less cost of incomplete Vogel job | 207* |
| Cost of work completed in February | $30,794 |

*Work in process at February 28 for Vogel job:

| | |
|---|---|
| Direct materials | $    84 |
| Direct labor | 60 |
| Overhead labor (3 hrs. × $21) | 63 |
| Total cost | $    207 |

## Review Problem B

Gluck's Package Delivery, Inc. has two support centers and three operating departments. The budgeted data for August are:

| | Overhead Cost | Labor Hours | Miles Traveled | Employees |
|---|---|---|---|---|
| Support centers: | | | | |
| Administration | $50,000 | 10,000 | | 20 |
| Personnel | 35,000 | 20,000 | | 25 |
| Operating departments: | | | | |
| National | 225,000 | 25,000 | 200,000 | 150 |
| Regional | 375,000 | 35,000 | 150,000 | 225 |
| Local | 400,000 | 30,000 | 20,000 | 175 |

Administration costs are allocated on the basis of labor hours, and the Personnel allocation is based on the number of employees. The overhead rates in National and Regional are based on miles traveled. The overhead rate in Local is based on labor hours.

**Required:**

1. Using the direct method, allocate the support centers' costs to the operating departments, and calculate overhead rates for each operating department.

2. Using the step method, allocate the support centers' costs to the operating departments, and calculate overhead rates for each operating department. If necessary, round all dollar allocations to operating departments to the nearest dollar. (Allocate support centers in the order of Administration and Personnel.)

**Solution:**

1. Direct Method:

| | Admin. | Personnel | National | Regional | Local |
|---|---|---|---|---|---|
| Total departmental costs | $50,000 | $35,000 | $225,000 | $375,000 | $400,000 |
| Allocation of support costs: | | | | | |
| (25 ÷ 90) × $50,000 | (13,889) | | 13,889 | | |
| (35 ÷ 90) × $50,000 | (19,444) | | | 19,444 | |
| (30 ÷ 90) × $50,000 | (16,667) | | | | 16,667 |
| | $     0 | | | | |
| (150 ÷ 550) × $35,000 | | (9,546) | 9,546 | | |
| (225 ÷ 550) × $35,000 | | (14,318) | | 14,318 | |
| (175 ÷ 550) × $35,000 | | (11,136) | | | 11,136 |
| | | 0 | $248,435 | $408,762 | $427,803 |
| Miles traveled | | | 200,000 | 150,000 | |
| Labor hours | | | | | 30,000 |
| Departmental overhead rate | | | $   1.242 | $ 2.725 | $ 14.260 |

## 2. Step Method:

| | Admin. | Personnel | National | Regional | Local |
|---|---|---|---|---|---|
| Total departmental costs | $ 50,000 | $ 35,000 | $225,000 | $375,000 | $400,000 |
| Allocation of support costs: | | | | | |
| (20 ÷ 110) × $50,000 | (9,091) | 9,091 | | | |
| (25 ÷ 110) × $50,000 | (11,364) | | 11,364 | | |
| (35 ÷ 110) × $50,000 | (15,909) | | | 15,909 | |
| (30 ÷ 110) × $50,000 | (13,636) | | | | 13,636 |
| | $     0 | $ 44,091 | | | |
| (150 ÷ 550) × $44,091 | | (12,025) | 12,025 | | |
| (225 ÷ 550) × $44,091 | | (18,037) | | 18,037 | |
| (175 ÷ 550) × $44,091 | | (14,029) | | | 14,029 |
| | | $     0 | $248,389 | $408,946 | $427,665 |
| Miles traveled | | | 200,000 | 150,000 | |
| Labor hours | | | | | 30,000 |
| Departmental overhead rate | | | $    1.242 | $    2.726 | $  14.256 |

# APPENDIX

## JOINT COST ALLOCATION

For joint products, the costs incurred prior to the split-off point are past costs, and therefore, are not relevant for the sell or process further decision, as noted in the chapter. These **joint costs**, however, are often allocated to the joint products for some product costing purposes such as external financial statement presentation and product pricing. In previous chapters, we have allocated costs using cost drivers that measure inputs such as labor hours or machine hours. However, input measures are not feasible for allocating joint costs since the joint products are not individually distinguishable until the split-off point, and hence, one cannot identify the amount of input associated with each product that emerges at the split-off point. Three common joint cost allocation methods–all based on outputs–are discussed next.

### Physical Measures of Output

Physical measures of output reflect some quantifiable physical characteristics of the joint products. Examples include number of units, weight, liquid volume, and length. The joint costs would be allocated in proportion to each product's output measure. Consider the Vexler Mining Company, which mines ore, and after separating the ore in a smelter, sells the individual outputs to jewelry and industrial manufacturers. Suppose that $400,000 in materials, labor, and overhead was incurred to mine a total of 100,000 ounces of the following three metals:

| Mineral | Amount |
|---------|--------|
| Gold | 10,000 ounces |
| Silver | 20,000 ounces |
| Copper | 70,000 ounces |

The gold would receive an allocation of $40,000 [(10,000 ÷ 100,000) × $400,000], the silver would receive $80,000 of the joint cost [(20,000 ÷ 100,000) × $400,000], and the copper would receive a $280,000 allocation [(70,000 ÷ 100,000) × $400,000].

This method is generally simple to use, but has two potential major drawbacks. First, the outputs may have different units of measure. For instance, consider a dairy farm that produces milk and butter from a joint process. The usual measure for milk, a liquid, would be gallons; for butter, a solid, the usual measure would be pounds.

A second limitation is that physical measures may be unrelated to the profitability of the joint products. Why is this an important consideration? The reason relates to why joint costs are incurred. Since joint costs are incurred because of the value that will be received from selling the joint products, the allocation of these joint costs should be related to the products' values. For Vexler Mining Company, 70 percent of the joint cost was allocated to copper. Suppose, however, that gold accounts for 90 percent of the three metals' total revenues. Clearly, the gold is what motivates Vexler to spend $400,000 to mine the ore, yet it receives only 10 percent of the joint costs, while copper is charged with seven times as much.

## Relative Sales Value

The **relative sales value (RSV)** approach allocates joint costs in proportion to the joint products' total sales values at the split-off point. Assume the following sales values for Vexler Mining Company's joint products:

| Mineral | Sales Values |
|---------|--------------|
| Gold | $500,000 |
| Silver | 200,000 |
| Copper | 100,000 |

Under the RSV method, gold would receive an allocation of $250,000 [($500,000 ÷ $800,000) × $400,000], silver would be charged with $100,000 of joint cost [($200,000 ÷ $800,000) × $400,000], and copper would receive a $50,000 allocation [($100,000 ÷ $800,000) × $400,000].

## Net Realizable Value

A potential problem with the RSV approach is that sales prices at the split-off point may not be readily available. Moreover, there might not even be a market for one or more of the joint products at the split-off point. Further processing may be necessary to sell some products. **The net realizable value (NRV)** method uses approximations of sales values at the split-off point. NRV is the total sales revenue of the product in its final form less any **separable costs**. The latter consist of costs incurred after the split-off point, and as such, can be traced to the individual products. Separable costs include processing costs, selling costs, and disposal costs.

Suppose that after Vexler Mining Company smelts its ore, it incurs some costs to get the metals ready for sale to manufacturers. These separable costs, the products' revenues, and the resulting NRVs are as follows:

| Mineral | Separable Costs | Revenues | NRV |
|---------|-----------------|----------|-----|
| Gold | $10,000 | $550,000 | $540,000 |
| Silver | 12,000 | 252,000 | 240,000 |
| Copper | 15,000 | 135,000 | 120,000 |

For the NRV method, gold would receive an allocation of $240,000 [($540,000 ÷ $900,000) × $400,000], silver would be charged with $106,667 of joint cost [($240,000 ÷ $900,000) × $400,000], and copper would receive a $53,333 allocation [($120,000 ÷ $900,000) × $400,000].

Occasionally, a situation may arise where a product's NRV is negative. When this happens, none of the joint cost should be allocated to that product.

## Byproducts and Scrap

Byproducts and scrap are products that emerge with joint (main) products but have minor sales value compared to the joint products. **Byproducts** are often processed after the split-off point, while **scrap** is usually discarded. The accounting treatment, though, is the same for both byproducts and scrap. Joint costs are not allocated to byproducts or scrap. The rationale for this treatment is that joint costs are incurred to produce the main products–not byproducts or scrap.

Revenue from byproducts or scrap is usually handled in one of two ways:

1. Recognize miscellaneous income from the NRVs of byproducts and scrap.
2. Deduct the NRVs of byproducts and scrap from the joint costs that are allocated to the main products.

The rationale for the second approach builds on the argument we mentioned for not allocating joint costs to byproducts or scrap. That is, the joint production process is undertaken for the profits to be earned from main products–not byproducts or scrap. Therefore, no profit should be recognized on byproducts or scrap. In effect, the second method shifts any profit (NRV) on byproducts and scrap to the main products by reducing the joint costs assigned to the main products.

As an example, suppose that sulphur is a byproduct at Vexler Mining Company. Using the RSV method, together with the RSVs given earlier for the three joint products, suppose now that sulphur could be sold at the split-off point for $8,000 after incurring separable costs of $2,000. With the miscellaneous income approach, $6,000 ($8,000 − $2,000) in miscellaneous income would appear on Vexler's income statement from the sale of sulphur. Under the alternate approach, joint costs of $394,000 ($400,000 − $6,000) would be allocated to the main products. Gold would receive an allocation of $246,250 [($500,000 ÷ $800,000) × $394,000], silver would be charged with $98,500 of joint cost [($200,000 ÷ $800,000) × $394,000], and copper would receive a $49,250 allocation [($100,000 ÷ $800,000) × $394,000].

## TERMINOLOGY REVIEW

Actual costing (127)

Applied factory overhead (127)

Assembled products (124)

Byproducts (148)

Bill of materials (124)

Commingled products (124)

Direct labor (125)

Direct materials (124)

Direct method (137)

Dual-rate method (141)

Expected volume (131)

Fabricated products (124)

Ideal capacity (131)

Indirect labor (125)

Indirect materials (124)

Joint costs (147)

Net realizable value (NRV) (148)

Nonvalue-added direct labor (xxx)

Normal costing (127)

Normal volume (131)

Operating departments (135)

Overabsorbed overhead (129)

Overapplied (129)

Overhead rate (126)

Practical capacity (131)

Predetermined overhead rate (127)

Producing departments (135)

Reciprocal method (139)

Relative sales value (RSV) (148)

Scrap (148)

Separable costs (148)

Service centers (135)

Step (sequential) method (138)

Support functions (135)

Underabsorbed overhead (129)

Underapplied (129)

Value-added direct labor (125)

## QUESTIONS FOR REVIEW AND DISCUSSION

**1.** Explain the distinction between direct and indirect costs.

**2.** What is the distinguishing characteristic of a commingled product?

**3.** What is the difference between a fabricated product and an assembled product?

**4.** Describe briefly how costs flow through the accounts for a manufacturer. How would this change for a service organization?

**5.** What is a bill of materials? Why is it important to the acquisition of materials?

**6.** What are the cost elements associated with the materials acquisition process? Which ones are likely to be included in the cost of materials charged as direct or indirect materials?

7. What are the three criteria for determining whether materials are direct or indirect?

8. What are the cost elements associated with labor? Which ones are likely to be included in the cost of direct or indirect labor?

9. Explain why a budget is used in costing factory overhead rather than assigning actual overhead cost after the end of the year.

10. What is the basis for selecting a cost driver to be used in costing factory overhead?

11. What account is credited when factory overhead is added to work in process?

12. How is the difference between the actual factory overhead and the overhead applied to the products handled at the end of the year?

13. Explain under what circumstances departmental rates are preferred to a plant-wide factory overhead rate.

14. What is the difference between theoretical and practical capacity?

15. Explain the difference between practical capacity and normal volume.

16. If the company does not expect to operate at normal volume during the next year, why should the products be costed by using an overhead rate determined at normal volume?

17. What is the difference between a service center and an operating department?

18. How do service center costs enter into the final cost of products and services?

19. How are service center costs allocated to other service centers and operating departments under the direct method? Under the step method?

20. If a service center generates revenues, how do these revenues enter into the allocation of service costs to other service centers and operating departments?

21. Why is the reciprocal method for service center allocation more justifiable than the step method or direct method?

22. Describe the two stages of cost allocation under the reciprocal method.

## EXERCISES

Service

**4–1.** **Cost of Orders.** Eden Repair Services specializes in the routine maintenance and repair of power lawn mowers and other small machines. Three orders (#721, #722, and #723) were started and completed in March. Materials costing $41 were used on order #721; materials costing $17 were used on order #722; and materials costing $8 were used on order #723. Labor is paid at a uniform rate of $8.50 per hour, and overhead is applied at 80 percent of labor cost. During the month, 3 labor hours were used for order #721, 2 hours for order #722, and 4 hours for order #723.

**Required:**
Compute the costs of each order, showing separately the costs of materials, labor, and overhead.

**4–2.** **Cost of Jobs Completed.** Amy Devorah makes chocolate candies which she sells to local merchants. She applies her overhead costs to jobs each month by adding 20 percent to prime costs. In February, she had the following job activity:

| Job | Beginning Inventory | Materials Added | Direct Labor Added |
|-----|--------------------|-----------------|--------------------|
| 115 | $25,000 | | $10,000 |
| 116 | | $20,000 | 20,000 |
| 117 | | 20,000 | 10,000 |

Job 117 was incomplete at the end of February.

**Required:**
Determine the cost of jobs completed in February.

**4–3.  Entries for Cost Flow.** Svensson Tool & Die Company of Malmo, Sweden, spent Skr6,400,600 for direct materials used in April for the production of various orders. Direct labor cost for the month was Skr2,453,800. Factory overhead is costed to production at 150 percent of direct labor cost. No orders were in process at the beginning and the end of the month. All work was delivered to customers.

**Required:**
Using T-accounts, show how the costs entered production and were transferred to Finished Goods and to Cost of Goods Sold.

Service

**4–4.  Overtime and Late-Shift Labor Costs.** H & L Solomon Computer Supplies operates its stores on a two-shift basis and pays a late-shift differential of 15 percent above the regular wage rate of $18 per hour. The company also pays a premium of 50 percent for overtime work. During the year, work occurred in the following categories:

| | |
|---|---|
| Number of hours worked during the regular shift | 10,000 |
| Number of overtime hours for regular shift workers | 300 |
| Number of hours worked during the late shift | 6,000 |

**Required:**
1. Compute the total cost to assign to direct labor.
2. Compute the amount of labor-related cost to assign to overhead.

Service

**4–5.  Overhead Rates and Normal Volume.** Mavis Maid Service normally operates at 450,000 direct labor hours a year. At this level of operation, variable overhead has been budgeted at $337,500, and fixed overhead has been budgeted at $1,012,500.

**Required:**
1. Compute the total overhead rate per direct labor hour at normal volume.
2. Determine the variable portion of the overhead rate at normal volume. What would be the variable overhead rate if normal volume were 400,000 direct labor hours instead of 450,000 hours? Assume that variable cost varies in direct proportion with hours of operation.
3. Determine the fixed portion of the overhead rate at normal volume. What would be the fixed overhead rate if 400,000 direct labor hours were considered normal volume? Explain why the rate differs depending on the level set as normal volume.

Service

**4–6.  Cost of Jobs.** David Greene's Muffler Shop ("No appointment necessary, we'll hear you coming") uses a normal costing system. Overhead and labor hours were estimated at $42,000 and 6,000 hours, respectively, for 2004. During July 2004, only forty jobs were finished. Materials used on these jobs totaled $3,700 and labor costs were $2,700 (at $20 per hour). During 2004, 5,000 labor hours were worked and $38,000 in overhead costs were incurred.

**Required:**
What is the total cost of the jobs finished during July?

Service

**4–7.   Actual and Applied Overhead.** Valenta Towing Service ("We don't charge an arm and a leg–we want tows") applies overhead on the basis of labor hours. For 2005, the budgeted overhead was $40,000, based on a volume of 10,000 labor hours. Simon Londe, the controller, indicates that the actual overhead amounted to $47,000, and the actual labor hours totaled 12,000.

**Required:**
Was overhead underapplied or overapplied? By how much?

**4–8.   Factory Overhead Account Analysis.** Blatt Company had estimated overhead costs of $400,000 fixed and $600,000 variable for 200,000 units it planned to produce this year. The following T-account represents the company's Factory Overhead account activity for the year:

| Factory Overhead | |
|---|---|
| $1,125,000 | $1,200,000 |

**Required:**
1. What was the company's estimated cost function?
2. How many units were produced this year?
3. How much factory overhead was added to work in process?
4. Was overhead underapplied or overapplied? By how much?

**4–9.   Applied Overhead.** Allan Neal Enterprises produces medical supplies and uses a predetermined overhead rate. The budget for the year included:

| | |
|---|---|
| Direct labor cost | $20,000 |
| Factory overhead | $50,000 |
| Direct labor hours | 1,200 |

During January, the cost sheet for Job #221 indicates that $75 of materials were used plus $100 of direct labor for eight hours of direct labor. Job #221 consists of 44 units of product. The company applies overhead using direct labor costs.

**Required:**
What amount of overhead should be applied to Job #221?

Service

**4–10.   Actual and Applied Overhead.** Parnes Library of Alpert County applies overhead on the basis of direct labor hours. Budget and actual data for direct labor and overhead for the year are as follows:

| | Budget | Actual |
|---|---|---|
| Direct labor hours | 500,000 | 537,000 |
| Overhead costs | $750,000 | $795,000 |

**Required:**
Determine the amount of underapplied or overapplied overheard for the year.

**4–11.  Determination of Actual Overhead.** Four Clothes Mortgage Co. applies overhead on the basis of labor hours. At the beginning of the current year, management estimated that 36,000 labor hours would be worked and $828,000 of overhead would be incurred. During the year, the company actually worked 39,000 hours.

**Required:**
If the overhead was overapplied by $17,000 for the year, what was the actual overhead cost incurred?

**4–12.  Determination of Direct Labor Cost.** Ovadia Company, an Israeli wholesaler of olive wood products, uses a predetermined overhead application rate based on direct labor cost. For the year, Ovadia's budgeted overhead was 900,000 shekels, based on a volume of 50,000 direct labor hours and a budgeted wage rate of 9 shekels per hour. Actual overhead amounted to 963,000 shekels. For the year, the overapplied overhead was 33,000 shekels.

**Required:**
Compute the amount of actual direct labor cost for the year.

**4–13.  Overhead Rate Computation.** Schechter Bakery applies overhead using direct labor cost. The following T-accounts pertain to last year's operations:

| Work in Process | | Overhead | |
|---|---|---|---|
| (a) 10,000 | | 70,000 | 60,000 |
| (b) 50,000 | 120,000 | | |
| (c) 20,000 | | | |
| (d) ? | | | |
| (e) ? | | | |

(a) Beginning balance;   (b) Direct materials;   (c) Direct labor;   (d) Overhead;   (e) Ending balance.

**Required:**
Compute the overhead rate that was used last year.

**4–14.  Flow of Costs.** The Repair Department of Rogin's Gadget Heaven, a consumer electronics store, uses a normal costing system. The following transactions took place during the year:
**(a)** Purchased raw materials (direct and indirect) on credit for $55,000.
**(b)** Used $37,000 of direct materials and $11,000 of indirect materials.
**(c)** Applied $42,000 of overhead.
**(d)** Jobs finished had a total cost of $275,000.
**(e)** Overapplied overhead of $3,000 is closed out to Cost of Jobs Delivered.

**Required:**
Provide entries in T-account form for the Repair Department's transactions during the year.

**4–15.  Closing Out Overhead.** Henry Evans operates a shoe repair shop. At year-end, the following accounts have balances as shown:

| | Account Balance |
|---|---|
| Materials | $5,000 (debit) |
| Cost of Shoes Repaired & Picked Up | 25,000 (debit) |
| Work in Process | 3,000 (debit) |
| Finished Shoes on Hand | 2,000 (debit) |
| Overhead | 450 (credit) |

**Required:**
Mr. Evans has asked you to close out his books. Post to T-accounts the necessary closing entry. Use the method which allocates the underapplied or overapplied overhead to the appropriate accounts.

**4–16.** **Normal Cost Computation.** Muntzie's Ice Cream Shoppe uses a normal costing system. During April, transactions included the following items:

| | |
|---|---|
| Direct labor cost | $17,000 |
| Actual overhead incurred | 45,000 |
| Overhead applied | 41,000 |
| Direct materials used | 37,000 |
| Indirect materials used | 2,500 |

Needless to say, there were no work in process inventories.

**Required:**
Compute the cost of goods completed (and sold) during April.

**4–17.** **Overapplied Overhead and Incomplete Data.** Junko Corporation, a Japanese travel agency, provides the following data for the year:

| | |
|---|---|
| Budgeted overhead cost | ¥20,000,000 |
| Budgeted activity | 20,000 labor hours |
| Actual overhead cost | ¥21,500,000 |
| Overapplied overhead | ¥800,000 |

**Required:**
Determine the amount of labor hours worked at Kyoto Corporation during the year.

**4–18.** **Analysis of Work in Process.** Gelfond's Book Bindery uses a predetermined overhead rate based on labor cost. The following T-account summarizes January 2004 activity relating to work in process:

*Work in Process Inventory*

| 1/1/04 | Balance | 30,000 | 1/31/04 | Jobs completed | 120,000 |
|---|---|---|---|---|---|
| | Materials used | 50,000 | | | |
| | Labor cost | 60,000 | | | |
| | Overhead applied | 40,000 | | | |
| 1/31/04 | Balance | 60,000 | | | |

**Required:**
If jobs in the work in process inventory on 1/31/04 contain $10,000 of materials, how much labor cost is in the work in process inventory on 1/31/04?

**4–19.** **Departmental and Plant-wide Overhead Rates.** Bernhard Toy Company manufactures small battery-powered cars that children under eight years of age can drive in a house or yard. Currently, the company has two models: Speed Demon and Luxury Classic. Both cars sell well. The company processes the cars in three departments: Fabrication, Assembly, and Painting. The departmental budgets for the current year are as follows:

| | Overhead Costs | Machine Hours |
|---|---|---|
| Fabrication | $ 730,000 | 25,000 |
| Assembly | 260,000 | 13,000 |
| Painting | 10,000 | 12,000 |
| Total | $1,000,000 | 50,000 |

The estimated machine hours for 50 units of each model are:

| | Speed Demon | Luxury Classic |
|---|---|---|
| Fabrication | 50 | 90 |
| Assembly | 75 | 40 |
| Painting | 35 | 20 |
| Total | 160 | 150 |

**Required:**
1. Compute overhead rates for each department and for the plant.
2. Compute the estimated overhead cost of 50 units of each model using:
   (a) A plant-wide rate.
   (b) Departmental rates.
3. Explain why a different cost exists for the cars depending on the use of a plant-wide rate or departmental rates.

Service

**4–20** **Divisional and Facility-wide Overhead Rates.** Volova Research Laboratories performs contract research for government and commercial applications. It is located in the Salt Lake Valley where it has access to a labor market with advanced scientific and engineering degrees. Utah has several major universities graduating people who want to pursue careers while remaining in Utah. The company is divided into six divisions with appropriate support and ancillary facilities. Each division is housed in its own building within the industrial complex.

The company bills its customers based on costs of research work. Costs included are for direct equipment, direct labor hours, and overhead. The current overhead rate used for billing purposes is the facility-wide rate which is $31.25 per hour for this year. The overhead costs and labor hours by division are as follows:

| | Overhead (in Thousands) | Labor Hours (in Thousands) |
|---|---|---|
| Thermal | $ 3,760 | 160 |
| Solar | 13,120 | 800 |
| Aquatic | 2,975 | 170 |
| Laser | 113,400 | 2,250 |
| Gases | 16,471 | 910 |
| Mechanical | 37,290 | 1,695 |
| Totals | $187,016 | 5,985 |

Several customers, particularly government agencies, question the overhead rate because it is too high for their projects.

**Required:**

1. Calculate overhead rates for the overall facility and for each of the six divisions.
2. Show how much overhead would be charged to each of the following projects with a facility-wide overhead rate and then with divisional rates:
   (a) Project #96106: *Soil Conservation of Semi-Arid Lands*. (Funded by the U.S. Department of the Interior.) During the year, this project had 31,400 hours of work recorded. Sixty percent of those hours were from the Thermal Division, and 40 percent were from the Solar Division.
   (b) Project #96111: *Coal Gasification Project*. (Funded 30 percent by the State of Utah, 50 percent by the U.S. Department of Energy, and 20 percent by a private utilities company.) This project absorbed 47,500 hours, of which 23,200 were in the Laser Division and the remaining hours in the Mechanical Division.
3. Which of these two project sponsor groups would have a more legitimate complaint about the overhead rate? Explain.

Service

**4–21.  Overhead Application with Departmental Rates.** Maran & Son is a print shop specializing in two types of jobs—brochures and booklets. The 2004 budgets for its three departments were as follows:

|  | Overhead Costs | Labor Hours |
|---|---|---|
| Typesetting | $450,000 | 8,000 |
| Printing | 550,000 | 6,000 |
| Binding | 210,000 | 3,000 |

The labor hours for each type of job in September totaled as follows:

|  | Brochures | Booklets |
|---|---|---|
| Typesetting | 400 | 300 |
| Printing | 500 | 200 |
| Binding | 0 | 350 |

A normal costing system with departmental overhead rates is used.

**Required:**

Compute the overhead applied in September to Brochures and Booklets.

Service

**4–22.  Direct Method and Dual-Rate Allocation.** Karon Realty Company has three operating departments (Commercial Real Estate, Residential Real Estate, Apartment Location Service) and two service departments (Administration, Personnel). The budgeted data for the year are as follows:

|  | Overhead Cost | Labor Hours | Number of Clients | Employees |
|---|---|---|---|---|
| Service departments: |  |  |  |  |
| Administration | $ 55,000 | 12,000 |  | 22 |
| Personnel | 38,000 | 8,000 |  | 10 |
| Operating departments: |  |  |  |  |
| Commerical Real Estate | 250,000 | 35,000 | 200 | 60 |
| Residential Real Estate | 580,000 | 60,000 | 750 | 125 |
| Apt. Location Service | 330,000 | 40,000 | 275 | 90 |

Administration costs are allocated based on labor hours, and the Personnel allocation is based on number of employees. Sixty percent of the Administration costs are fixed; the long-run needs of each of the operating departments were considered as being equal when these costs were incurred. The overhead rates in each operating department are based on the number of clients.

**Required:**
Using the direct method in conjunction with dual-rate allocation, allocate the service departments' costs to the operating departments, and calculate overhead rates for each operating department.

**4–23.** **Direct and Step Methods.** The Gorlin Clinic specializes in treatment of ears and eyes in two separate operating departments (no pun intended!). Information about these departments and the clinic's two service departments follows:

| | Service Departments | | Operating Departments | |
| --- | --- | --- | --- | --- |
| | Custodial | Administrative | Ears | Eyes |
| Number of employees | 4 | 18 | 33 | 40 |
| Square footage | 1,500 | 8,000 | 36,000 | 39,000 |
| Department direct costs | $17,000 | $96,000 | $258,000 | $290,000 |

Custodial costs are allocated based on square footage, while Administrative costs are allocated based on number of employees.

**Required:**
1. Using the direct method, determine the amount of the service departments' costs that are allocated to each of the operating departments.
2. Using the step method (starting with Custodial), determine the amount of the service departments' costs that are allocated to each of the operating departments.

**4–24.** **Direct and Step Method Allocations.** Carl Lee & Sons, a small securities brokerage firm, has two operating departments relating to types of clients—Individual and Corporate. The firm also has two service departments—Research and Secretarial. Estimated direct costs and percentages of services used by other departments are as follows:

| | Used By Department | | | |
| --- | --- | --- | --- | --- |
| Service Dept. | Research | Secretarial | Individual | Corporate |
| Research | — | 10% | 40% | 50% |
| Secretarial | 20% | — | 50% | 30% |
| Direct Costs | $520,000 | $440,000 | $950,000 | $990,000 |

**Required:**
1. Allocate the service departments' costs to the operating departments using the direct method.
2. Allocate the service departments' costs to the operating departments using the step method. Allocate Secretarial costs before Research costs.

**4–25.** **Direct and Step Method Allocations.** Dressler, Inc. operates funeral homes and cemeteries. Data for these two operating centers and for the company's two service centers follow:

| | Costs | Square Feet | Employees |
| --- | --- | --- | --- |
| Funeral Homes | $850,000 | 50,000 | 80 |
| Cemeteries | $980,000 | 150,000 | 20 |
| Legal and Accounting | $275,000 | 15,000 | 30 |
| Building and Grounds | $350,000 | 10,000 | 25 |

Building and Grounds allocates costs based on square feet of space, while Legal and Accounting allocates costs based on number of employees.

**Required:**
1. Using the direct method, what amount of service center costs will be allocated to Funeral Homes and to Cemeteries?
2. Using the step method with Legal and Accounting costs allocated first, what amount of service center costs will be allocated to Funeral Homes and to Cemeteries?

**4–26.** **Reciprocal Method and Overhead Rates.** Manheim County Amusement Park has two operating centers—Rides & Games (R&G) and Concessions. In addition, there are two support centers—Human Resources (H.R.) and Maintenance. The following data have been obtained:

|  | H. R. | Maintenance | R&G | Concessions |
|---|---|---|---|---|
| Overhead costs before allocation | $60,000 | $80,000 | $70,000 | $25,000 |
| Proportions of service by H.R. | — | 30% | 50% | 20% |
| Proportions of service by Maintenance | 10% | — | 60% | 30% |
| Labor hours worked | 5,500 | 5,900 | 6,400 | 5,000 |

**Required:**
Use the reciprocal method to compute overhead rates for R&G and Concessions.

**4–27.** **Reciprocal Method of Allocating Service Center Costs.** Zurich Cheese Company, a Swiss wholesale distributor of cheese products, has two service centers (Maintenance and Utilities) and two operating departments (Domestic and International). Data for October are as follows:

|  | Service Centers | |
|---|---|---|
|  | Maintenance | Utilities |
| Costs (Swiss francs) | 46,000 | 30,000 |
| Services provided to: |  |  |
| Maintenance | — | 10% |
| Utilities | 20% | — |
| Domestic | 40% | 30% |
| International | 40% | 60% |
| Totals | 100% | 100% |

**Required:**
Using the reciprocal method, allocate the costs of the service centers to the operating departments.

**4–28.** **Direct, Step, and Reciprocal Methods.** Beeber Airlines has two operating departments (Freight and Passenger) and two service centers (Maintenance and Administration). The following table shows June data:

|  | Service Centers | | Operating Departments | |
|---|---|---|---|---|
|  | Maintenance | Administration | Freight | Passenger |
| Costs | $630,000 | $950,000 | $1,800,500 | $5,260,470 |
| Labor hours | 8,000 | 9,000 | 30,000 | 51,000 |
| Number of employees | 40 | 50 | 80 | 200 |

Maintenance costs are allocated using labor hours, while Administration costs are allocated using number of employees.

**Required:**
1. Using the direct method, determine the total costs of the operating departments.
2. Using the step method with Maintenance costs allocated first, determine the total costs of the operating departments.
3. Using the reciprocal method, determine the total costs of the operating departments.

**4–29.** **Joint Cost Allocation–Net Realizable Value (Appendix).** Ron Morray & Associates, a CPA firm, provides audit, tax, and consulting services. The firm spent $800 recruiting a particular client, Bernard Birnbaum, who contracted for all three services after a round of golf, a sumptuous meal, and a bottle of fine wine. After the firm's work for Birnbaum was completed, the following information was available:

|  |  | Traceable Costs | |
| --- | --- | --- | --- |
| Service | Fees Charged | Labor | Overhead |
| Audit | $14,000 | $5,200 | $4,000 |
| Tax | 10,000 | 3,000 | 2,300 |
| Consulting | 22,000 | 9,100 | 5,500 |

**Required:**
Using the NRV method, allocate the joint cost to the three services.

**4–30.** **Joint Cost Allocation with a Byproduct (Appendix).** Paul Fay Fisheries spent $11,000 to catch 3,000 pounds of tuna, 12,000 pounds of shellfish, and 500 pounds of various other fish during July. The tuna was sold to Shinderman Industries for $8,000 and the shellfish was sold to Lisa's Diner for $17,000. The other fish was converted to fish oil, which is treated as a byproduct. Separable costs amounted to $200 for the fish oil, which was sold to Uncle Jake's Food Products for $900. Paul Fay Fisheries uses physical output to allocate joint costs.

**Required:**
Explain how the NRV from the byproduct would be treated and determine the joint cost allocations for each of the following two alternatives:
1. Miscellaneous income approach.
2. Reduction of joint cost approach.

# PROBLEMS

**4–31.** **Normal Volume and Expected Volume.** Sylvia Bierman has prepared budgets of overhead costs for the Restaurants Division of Becca Industries, Inc. at the normal level of operations and at the expected level of operations for the next year, shown as follows:

|  | Normal Level | Expected Level |
| --- | --- | --- |
| Direct labor hours | 150,000 | 120,000 |
| Variable overhead | $ 750,000 | $ 600,000 |
| Fixed overhead | 1,200,000 | 1,200,000 |
| Total overhead | $1,950,000 | $1,800,000 |

Bierman states, "We cost our food products by using an overhead rate computed at normal volume; but it seems to me that if we used a rate computed at expected volume, we wouldn't have such a large overhead variance at the end of the year. What makes the variance worse is that we have so much fixed overhead."

During the next year the company operated at 120,000 direct labor hours and incurred overhead costs as follows:

| | |
|---|---|
| Variable overhead | $ 605,000 |
| Fixed overhead | 1,200,000 |
| Total overhead | $1,805,000 |

**Required:**

1. Compute an overhead rate per direct labor hour at normal operating volume.
2. Compute an overhead rate per direct labor hour at the expected level of operations.
3. Determine the underapplied or overapplied amounts when the rate is figured at normal volume and when the rate is figured at expected volume.
4. Point out the fallacy in Bierman's argument.
5. Is Bierman correct in stating that the variance is worse because of the relatively large fixed overhead? Explain.

**4–32.**   **Costs of Individual Orders.** During August, Marmarosher Machine Company started production orders 116, 117, and 118. Order 115 was in process at the beginning of the month with direct materials costs of $35,000, direct labor costs of $21,000, and applied factory overhead of $25,200. During the month, direct materials were requisitioned, and direct labor was identified with the orders as follows:

| Order No. | Direct Materials | DirectLabor |
|---|---|---|
| 115 | — | $26,000 |
| 116 | $39,000 | 45,000 |
| 117 | 53,000 | 47,000 |
| 118 | 47,000 | 16,000 |

Factory overhead is applied to the orders at 120 percent of direct labor cost. Orders 115, 116, and 117 were completed and sold in August. Order 118 was incomplete on August 31.

**Required:**

1. Determine the costs of each order by cost element.
2. What was the total cost of direct materials requisitioned in August and charged to Work in Process?
3. Determine the cost of goods sold in August.
4. What was the Work in Process balance on August 31?

Service

**4–33.**   **Overtime Premium and Shift Differential.** Julie Rachel Interior Designers operates on a two-shift basis, servicing commercial clients primarily from 8 a.m. to 5 p.m., while servicing residential clients primarily between 4 and 11 p.m. The company pays employees who work the evening shift a late-shift differential of 12 percent above the regular wage rate of $25 per hour. The company also pays time-and-a-half for overtime work. During the past week, work occurred in the following categories:

| | |
|---|---|
| Number of hours worked during the regular daytime shift | 650 |
| Number of hours worked during the evening shift | 380 |
| Number of overtime hours for daytime shift workers | 45 |

**Required:**

1. Compute the total cost to assign to direct labor.
2. Compute the amount of labor-related cost to assign to overhead.

Service

**4–34.** **Closing the Overhead Account**. The service department of Collomb's Auto Dealership has underapplied overhead of $222,000 for the year. Before closing the appropriate accounts, ending balances for several accounts were as follows:

| | |
|---|---|
| Revenues | $ 12,860,000 |
| Cost of Jobs Delivered | 8,125,000 |
| Finished Jobs on Hand | 1,230,000 |
| Work in Process | 1,888,000 |
| Materials Inventory | 1,035,000 |

**Required:**

On the income statement, what amount should be reported for Cost of Jobs Delivered? Provide answers for both of the acceptable alternatives of closing out the underapplied overhead.

Service

**4–35.** **Cost of Contracts**. Lefton & Pearl Contracting Company repaves highways and does excavation work. On January 1, 2004, the Eastern Highway Project was in process with costs as follows:

| | |
|---|---|
| Materials | $810,000 |
| Labor | 420,000 |
| Contract overhead | 210,000 |

During 2004, the company incurred costs for various projects as follows:

| | Eastern Highway | State University | Clover Estates | Route 691 | Market Street | Totals |
|---|---|---|---|---|---|---|
| Materials | $ 215,000 | $ 1,780,000 | $ 170,000 | $ 3,720,000 | $ 350,000 | $ 6,235,000 |
| Labor | 170,000 | 1,420,000 | 590,000 | 1,480,000 | 260,000 | 3,920,000 |
| Overhead | 85,000 | 710,000 | 295,000 | 740,000 | 130,000 | 1,960,000 |
| Totals | $ 470,000 | $ 3,910,000 | $ 1,055,000 | $ 5,940,000 | $ 740,000 | $ 12,115,000 |

Contract overhead is costed to the projects at 50 percent of labor cost. Actual overhead cost for 2004 was $2,090,000. The company uses a Contracts in Process instead of a Work in Process account. Projects completed are charged directly to Cost of Contracts Completed.

All projects, with the exceptions of the State University Project and the Market Street Project, were completed during the year.

**Required:**

1. Determine the costs transferred to Cost of Contracts Completed. Use T-accounts to show this transfer.
2. Using T-accounts, close the underapplied or overapplied contract overhead directly to Cost of Contracts Completed.
3. Determine the total cost of the Eastern Highway Project and the costs of each contract in process at the end of the year. (Show detail by project and cost element.)

**4–36.** **Recording Transactions.** A summary of manufacturing cost transactions for Sternbach Motors, Inc. for the year is as follows:

(a) Materials costing $995,650 were purchased from suppliers on account.

(b) Materials were requisitioned during the year as follows:

| | |
|---|---|
| Direct materials | $791,000 |
| Indirect materials (factory overhead) | 147,000 |

Included were direct materials requisitions of $21,000 for Order 115.

(c) The factory payroll for the year amounted to $488,000. FICA taxes withheld was $33,000; income taxes withheld was $87,000; and the amount paid to the employees was $368,000.

(d) The factory labor was utilized as follows:

| | |
|---|---|
| Direct labor | $338,000 |
| Indirect labor (factory overhead) | 150,000 |

Included in the direct labor cost was $22,500 identified by labor time tickets with Order 115.

(e) Factory overhead was applied to production at 150 percent of the direct labor cost.

(f) Factory overhead cost during the year, in addition to the cost of indirect materials and indirect labor previously mentioned, amounted to $173,000. Included in this amount was depreciation of $52,000. Credit the balance of this cost to Accounts Payable.

(g) Orders costing $1,117,000 were completed during the year. Order 115 is included among the completed orders.

(h) Goods costing $944,000 were sold to customers on credit terms for $1,552,000.

**Required:**

1. Record transactions (a) through (h) using T-accounts, and close the factory overhead variance to Cost of Goods Sold.

2. Compute the total cost and cost per unit of Order 115 assuming that 15,000 units were produced for that order.

**4–37.** **Cost Flows.** Kunis Paddle Shop, Inc. keeps accounting and cost records on a personal computer. During the month of January, data were lost as a result of errors made by a new operator. Fortunately, some data were retrieved and are set forth as follows:

(a) The total payroll amounted to $130,000. This balance included $20,000 in indirect labor that was charged to the Factory Overhead account.

(b) The debits in the Factory Overhead account totaled $166,000. This amount included the indirect labor from part (a).

(c) Factory overhead is applied to the products at 150 percent of direct labor cost.

(d) The Work in Process account showed a January 1 balance of $91,000. Materials requisitioned and charged to Work in Process during the period amounted to $98,000. The balance in Work in Process on January 31 was $82,000.

(e) The Finished Goods balance at January 1 was $48,000.

(f) Cost of Goods Sold had a debit balance of $389,000. This amount did not include underapplied or overapplied factory overhead.

**Required:**

1. From the information given, determine the direct labor and the factory overhead applied to production in January.

2. What was the cost of work completed and transferred to the finished goods inventory for the month?

**3.** Determine the finished goods inventory cost on January 31 before factory overhead is closed out.

**4.** Determine the underapplied or overapplied factory overhead in January.

**4–38.  Incomplete Data.** You find that the cost records at Oberman Printing Company have been poorly maintained. Some information has been entered, but other information is missing. Fortunately, the information given is correct.

The costs for jobs 686, 687, and 688 are to be determined. The direct materials cost is $528 for Job 686 and $715 for Job 687. The cost of direct materials requisitioned during the month for all other jobs, except Job 688, is $4,820. No jobs were in process at the beginning of the month. The total cost of direct materials requisitioned during the month was $6,913.

Labor is paid at a uniform rate of $10 an hour. Job 686 required 82 direct labor hours, and job 688 required 43 direct labor hours. A total of 760 direct labor hours were worked during the month. The direct labor cost of all other jobs, with the exception of the three jobs being considered, was $5,850.

Two machine hours are used for each direct labor hour. Overhead is applied at a rate of $4 per machine hour. The actual overhead cost for the month was $6,320. Jobs 686, 687, and 688 were completed during the month.

**Required:**

**1.** Compute the costs for Jobs 686, 687, and 688. Show costs by cost element.

**2.** Determine the amount of overhead applied to all orders during the month.

**3.** What was the amount of the underapplied or overapplied overhead?

**4.** You have received a telephone call from the general manager requesting the total cost per unit on Job 686. There were 50 units (books) on this order. What is the total cost per unit?

**4–39.  Allocations Using Departmental Rates.** Buckeye University, located in northeastern Ohio, has two academic departments, Science and Liberal Arts. The number and types of courses that students take in each department depend on whether they are Science or Liberal Arts majors. The following information is available for the most recent quarter:

|  | Science | Liberal Arts |
| --- | --- | --- |
| Student credit hours | 15,000 | 25,000 |
| Operating costs | $ 467,000 | $ 552,000 |

The credit hour distribution of Science and Liberal Arts majors in a typical quarter is as follows:

| Credit Hours Taken | Science Major | Liberal Arts Major |
| --- | --- | --- |
| Science | 12 | 4 |
| Liberal Arts | 4 | 12 |

**Required:**

Determine the costs per quarter of educating a Science major and a Liberal Arts major.

**4–40.  Departmental and Plant-wide Rates.** Sloman Products, Inc. has one division that makes rollers for printing presses. The rollers vary in size from 1/4 inch to 8 inches in diameter. Fabrication and Finishing are the two departments within this division. The company uses machine hours as the base for allocating factory overhead costs to products. The budgeted data for the two departments for the coming year are:

|  | Fabrication | Finishing | Totals |
|---|---|---|---|
| Machine hours | 90,000 | 30,000 | 120,000 |
| Overhead costs | $2,232,000 | $252,600 | $2,484,600 |

The machine hours for a batch of 100 units for two different products are given as:

|  | Fabrication | Finishing | Totals |
|---|---|---|---|
| 1/2"roller | 4 | 8 | 12 |
| 6-1/2"roller | 9 | 6 | 15 |

The prime costs per batch for these two products are:

|  | 1/2''Roller | 6-1/2''Roller |
|---|---|---|
| Direct materials: |  |  |
| Fabrication | $ 18.90 | $ 33.40 |
| Finishing | 9.70 | 11.50 |
| Direct labor: |  |  |
| Fabrication | 48.10 | 187.30 |
| Finishing | 37.80 | 32.20 |
| Total prime costs | $114.50 | $264.40 |

**Required:**
1. Compute the departmental overhead rates for Fabrication and Finishing using machine hours as the cost driver.
2. Compute a plant-wide overhead rate using machine hours as the cost driver.
3. Compute the overhead cost per batch of product assuming:
   (a) The plant-wide rate.
   (b) The departmental rates.
4. Is the total cost *per unit of each product* distorted by using a plant-wide rate instead of departmental rates? Explain with supporting computations.

**4-41. Departmental Rates versus Company-wide Rates.** Auerbach Enterprises manufactures air conditioners for automobiles. The company designs its products with flexibility to accommodate many makes and models of automobiles. The main products are MaxiFlow and Alaska. MaxiFlow uses a few complex fabricated parts, but these have been found easy to assemble and test. On the other hand, Alaska uses many standard parts but has a complex assembly and test process. The following planning information is available for the next year for each department:

|  | Overhead Costs | Machine Hours |
|---|---|---|
| Radiator parts fabrication | $ 80,000 | 10,000 |
| Radiator assembly, weld, and test | 100,000 | 20,000 |
| Compressor parts fabrication | 120,000 | 5,000 |
| Compressor assembly and test | 180,000 | 45,000 |
| Total | $480,000 | 80,000 |

A production batch of 20 units requires the following number of hours in each department:

|  | MaxiFlow | Alaska |
|---|---|---|
| Radiator parts fabrication | 28 | 16 |
| Radiator assembly, weld, and test | 30 | 74 |
| Compressor parts fabrication | 32 | 8 |
| Compressor assembly and test | 26 | 66 |
| Total | 116 | 164 |

**Required:**
1. Compute the departmental overhead rates using machine hours as the cost driver.
2. Compute a company-wide overhead rate using machine hours as the cost driver.
3. Compute the overhead costs per batch of MaxiFlow and Alaska assuming:
    (a) The company-wide rate.
    (b) The departmental rates.
4. Compute the total costs per unit of MaxiFlow and Alaska assuming:
    (a) The company-wide rate.
    (b) The departmental rates.
5. Is one product affected more than the other by use of departmental rates rather than a company-wide rate? Why or why not?

Service

**4–42. Direct Method, Step Method, and Ethical Analysis.** Sherry & Levy, Inc. is an office supplies wholesaler and retailer. The company shows the following estimated operating statistics for this year:

|  | Personnel Transactions Processed | Number of Employees | Space Occupied Square Feet |
|---|---|---|---|
| Service centers: |  |  |  |
| Utilities | 10 | 80 | 1,000 |
| Cafeteria | 20 | 25 | 8,000 |
| Personnel | 15 | 50 | 2,000 |
| Operating departments: |  |  |  |
| Retail | 80 | 900 | 70,000 |
| Wholesale | 20 | 600 | 30,000 |

Budgeted overhead costs for the year and the cost driver for each department are as follows:

|  | Overhead | Cost Driver |
|---|---|---|
| Utilities | $ 30,000 | Square footage |
| Cafeteria | 20,000 | Number of employees |
| Personnel | 10,000 | Number of personnel transactions |
| Retail | 80,000 | Labor hours |
| Wholesale | 60,000 | Labor hours |

The Retail Department budgeted 20,000 labor hours for the year, while the Wholesale Department budgeted 15,000 labor hours.

**Required:**

1. Using the direct method, allocate the service centers' costs to the operating departments, and calculate overhead rates for each operating department.
2. Using the step method, allocate the service centers' costs to the operating departments, and calculate overhead rates for each operating department. Allocate service centers in the order of utilities, cafeteria, and personnel. If necessary, round all dollar allocations to operating departments to the nearest dollar.
3. Suppose the Wholesale Department sells its products to the government on a cost-plus basis, while the Retail Department sells its products on the open market where the price is determined by supply and demand. Assume the step method of allocation is used and that any ordering of the three service centers is permitted. How might management decide on the ordering of the service centers? Discuss the ethical issues.

 **4–43. Step Method with Revenues.** Chaiken Co. has two operating departments (Fabrication and Assembly) and two service centers (Maintenance and Public Relations). Maintenance costs are allocated based on square footage and Public Relations costs are allocated based on number of employees. Data for December are as follows:

|  | Fabrication | Assembly | Maintenance | Public Relations |
|---|---|---|---|---|
| Materials | $ 8,500 | $ 8,900 | $ 4,200 | $ 5,500 |
| Labor | 6,500 | 8,400 | 3,300 | 3,900 |
| Overhead | 5,100 | 1,800 | 2,500 | 3,700 |
| Totals | $20,100 | $19,100 | $10,000 | $13,100 |

In addition to these costs, Public Relations generated revenues of $705. Other data are:

|  | Fabrication | Assembly | Maintenance | Public Relations |
|---|---|---|---|---|
| Number of employees | 37 | 44 | 22 | 30 |
| Square footage | 2,800 | 3,700 | 2,000 | 1,400 |

**Required:**

Using the step method, determine the total overhead costs of each operating department after allocation of service center costs. Begin the allocation with Maintenance.

 **4–44. Direct Method and Dual-Rate Allocation.** Jeffram Headhunters is an executive search firm that specializes in two areas—financial managers and marketing managers—and has organized its two operating centers around these areas. Data for these operating centers, as well as for three service centers, follow:

|  | Sq. Ft. of Space | Number of Employees | Personnel Transactions |
|---|---|---|---|
| Operating Centers: |  |  |  |
| Financial Managers | 38,000 | 470 | 54 |
| Marketing Managers | 33,000 | 425 | 41 |
| Service Centers: |  |  |  |
| Custodial | 2,700 | 30 | 8 |
| Personnel | 2,900 | 23 | 7 |
| Administration | 4,100 | 50 | 11 |

Budgeted overhead costs for the year and cost driver data are as follows:

|  | Overhead | Cost Driver |
|---|---|---|
| Financial Managers | $158,000 | Labor hours |
| Marketing Managers | 144,000 | Labor hours |
| Custodial | 63,000 | Square feet of space |
| Personnel | 74,000 | Personnel transactions |
| Administration | 59,000 | Number of employees |

Of the Custodial overhead, $20,000 is fixed. According to the controller, Diane Benjamin, the fixed overhead relates to the long-run needs of the two operating centers, as follows:

| Financial Managers | 70% |
|---|---|
| Marketing Managers | 30% |

Each operating center budgeted 12,000 labor hours for the year.

**Required:**
Using the direct method in conjunction with dual-rate allocation, allocate service centers' costs to the operating centers, and calculate overhead rates for each operating center.

**4–45.    Support Function Allocation—Direct and Step Methods.** Slovin Women's Clothing of Manchester, England, specializes in designer skirts which it manufactures to customer order. The budgeted data for its main plant for 2004 are:

|  | Support Functions | | Producing Departments | |
|---|---|---|---|---|
|  | Administration | Maintenance | Cutting | Sewing |
| Overhead cost | £80,000 | £30,000 | £500,000 | £600,000 |
| Labor hours |  | 10,000 | 50,000 | 80,000 |
| Machine hours |  |  | 100,000 | 150,000 |
| Square meters of space occupied | 4,500 | 7,000 | 50,000 | 25,000 |

During the year, Fier Co. placed an order that was started and completed by year-end. Data for this job include the following information:

|  | Cutting | Sewing |
|---|---|---|
| Direct materials cost | £95,000 | £21,000 |
| Direct labor hours | 7,000 | 15,000 |
| Direct labor cost | £56,000 | £120,000 |
| Machine hours | 16,000 | 30,000 |

**Required:**
Treat each of the following requirements independently:
1. The company follows a policy of applying overhead for the entire plant on the basis of machine hours.
   (a) Calculate a plant-wide overhead rate based on machine hours.
   (b) Apply overhead to the Fier job.
2. The company follows a policy of allocating support function costs to the producing departments using the direct method. Administration costs are allocated on direct labor

hours; Maintenance on square meters of space occupied; Cutting on machine hours; and Sewing on direct labor hours.

(a) Allocate support function costs to producing departments.

(b) Calculate overhead rates for producing departments.

(c) Apply overhead to the Fier job.

3. The company follows a policy of allocating support functions' costs to the producing departments using the step method. Administration costs are allocated first using direct labor hours; Maintenance using square meters of space occupied; Cutting using machine hours; and Sewing using direct labor hours.

(a) Allocate support functions' costs to producing departments.

(b) Calculate overhead rates for producing departments.

(c) Apply overhead to the Fier job.

4. Prepare a summary of the results of allocating overhead to the Fier job in each of the three alternatives. Explain why the differences in overhead costs occur.

Service

**4–46.  Reciprocal Method and Overhead Rates.** In recent years, the township of Calibre Woods, Georgia, has attracted many people who are single. Seeing a golden opportunity, Sybil Goldstein formed Sybil's Dating Service, which just completed its third full year of operations and currently serves clients in many nearby towns. The company is organized around three operating departments corresponding to age groups. The operating departments incurred the following overhead costs and labor hours during the past year:

|  | Costs | Labor Hours |
|---|---|---|
| Under 30 | $ 291,000 | 18,500 |
| Ages 30–45 | $ 615,000 | 24,700 |
| Over 45 | $ 710,000 | 26,200 |

Sybil's Dating Service also has two support centers—Secretarial and Administration. The following table indicates the percentages of services used by all of the support centers and operating departments:

|  |  |  | User Department | | |
|---|---|---|---|---|---|
|  | Secretarial | Administration | Under 30 | Ages 30–45 | Over 45 |
| **Support Center** | | | | | |
| Secretarial | — | 40% | 30% | 20% | 10% |
| Administration | 10% | — | 20% | 15% | 55% |

The direct costs incurred in the support centers during the past year were as follows:

Secretarial—$158,000
Administration—$140,000

Sybil's Dating Service uses the reciprocal method to allocate the support centers' costs.

**Required:**

Compute overhead rates per labor hour for each of the three operating centers.

Service

**4–47.  Reciprocal Method and Revenues.** Unterberger's Health Club is organized into two operating departments—Programming & Classes and Individual Fitness. There are also two service centers—Janitorial and Cafeteria. Janitorial costs are allocated based on square footage, while Cafeteria costs are allocated based on number of employees. The costs traceable to the operating and service centers during the year were as follows:

|  | Service Centers | | Operating Departments | |
|  | Janitorial | Cafeteria | Programming & Classes | Individual Fitness |
| --- | --- | --- | --- | --- |
| Materials | $ 10,000 | $ 200,000 | $ 8,000 | $ 5,000 |
| Labor | 100,000 | 300,000 | 265,000 | 150,000 |
| Overhead | 20,000 | 40,000 | 75,000 | 90,000 |
| Totals | $130,000 | $540,000 | $348,000 | $245,000 |

In addition to the above costs, the Cafeteria generated revenues of $480,000. Other data are as follows:

|  | Service Centers | | Operating Departments | |
|  | Janitorial | Cafeteria | Programming & Classes | Individual Fitness |
| --- | --- | --- | --- | --- |
| Square footage | 1,600 | 8,000 | 24,000 | 32,000 |
| Number of employees | 5 | 14 | 19 | 6 |

**Required:**
Compute the total overhead costs for each operating department after allocation of service centers' costs. Use the reciprocal method to allocate the service centers' costs.

Service

**4–48.**   **Joint Cost Allocation and Decision-Making (Appendix).** Strazynski Advertising Agency produced television and magazine ads for a client, Jane Leavy Enterprises. The ads were developed with a common theme, and in so doing, $49,000 in joint costs were incurred. Separable costs totaled $60,000 for the TV ads and $20,000 for the magazine ads. The agency received $95,000 in fees for the TV ads and $42,000 for the magazine ads.

**Required:**
1. Allocate the joint costs using the net realizable value method.
2. Suppose that the magazine ads have been developed (after $20,000 in separable costs were incurred), but they have not yet run. The client has approached the agency and suggested that rather than the magazine ads, it would prefer newspaper ads. Instead of the $42,000 fee previously contracted for the magazine ads, the client is now offering $45,000 for newspaper ads. The agency estimates that it would take $4,500 to convert the magazine ads to newspaper ads because they would need to be modified for a slightly different target audience. Is it advantageous for the agency to accept the new offer made by the client? Show computations.

Service

**4–49.**   **Joint Cost Allocation and Income Statements (Appendix).** Lowenstein Promotions, Inc. produces rock concerts across the country. A recent concert by The Twins was also recorded as a CD. The live concert attracted 9,000 people who paid $35 per ticket and the CD is projected to sell 26,000 units at $11 each. Joint costs of the concert and CD amounted to $300,000. Separable costs are $2 per ticket and $3 per unit for the CDs.

**Required:**
1. Comment on the feasibility of allocating the joint costs based on physical measures.
2. Using the NRV method, compute the amount of joint costs to allocate to the live concert and to the CDs.

3. Prepare product-line income statements for the live concert and for the CDs.

4. LeeJay Company wants to buy 15,000 cassette tapes, for $7 each, that Lowenstein could produce from the master recording of the live concert. Separable costs related to these tapes would be $1.50 per tape.

   (a) Presuming these tapes are produced, use the NRV method to determine the amount of joint costs to assign to the tapes.

   (b) Using only relevant costs and revenues in your analysis, compute the dollar advantage (or disadvantage) for producing the cassette tapes.

## CASE 4—BIRNBREY & BOGART LEGAL SERVICES

Birnbrey & Bogart Legal Services is a large law office in St. Louis. It is organized into three operating departments: Criminal, Civil, and Personal & Family Services. Support functions include a secretarial pool and a research center. An administrative function is responsible for managing the entire company. Birnbrey & Bogart follows the practice of allocating support functions to the three operating departments in order to establish a cost-based charge for pricing the various legal services to clients. Administrative costs are not allocated. (They are treated as period costs in the income statement.) But they are recovered through the profit margin developed as a percentage of all other costs.

Budgeting for the upcoming fiscal year has resulted in the following costs charged directly to all functions and departments:

| | Secretarial | Research | Criminal | Civil | Personal & Family |
|---|---|---|---|---|---|
| Salaries and wages | $80,000 | $120,000 | $300,000 | $400,000 | $100,000 |
| Fringe benefits | 5,600 | 11,200 | 30,000 | 40,000 | 10,000 |
| Depreciation | 8,000 | 16,000 | 24,000 | 32,000 | 8,000 |
| Supplies | 16,000 | 3,200 | 4,500 | 6,000 | 1,500 |

The indirect costs that are prorated to administration, support functions, and operating departments are of four varieties: insurance, leasing, utilities, and janitorial services. The following means are used to prorate indirect costs:

   (a) Insurance costs ($160,000) are for malpractice coverage and for equipment, fixtures, and furniture. The premium ($36,000) representing coverage on equipment, fixtures, and furniture is prorated on the basis of book value. The remainder of the $160,000 is for malpractice. Since malpractice relates to people, the proration is based on the number of people in each department.

   (b) Leasing costs ($96,000) are incurred for the office space occupied by the firm. Therefore, these costs are prorated based on square footage occupied.

   (c) Utilities costs ($60,000) are for heat, light, and water. They are prorated on the basis of square footage occupied.

   (d) Janitorial services ($36,000) to keep the offices clean are contracted out. These costs are prorated on square footage.

In allocating the support functions to the operating departments, Secretarial is allocated on the basis of secretarial time. The Research Center is allocated on the basis of salaries and wages. Overhead rates for the operating departments are determined by using salaries and wages in the

Criminal and Civil Departments, and staff time in Personal & Family Services. The following budgeted data are available for the allocation bases:

| | Administration | Secretarial | Research | Criminal | Civil | Personal & Family |
|---|---|---|---|---|---|---|
| Number of people | 2 | 4 | 6 | 4 | 6 | 2 |
| Book values | $10,000 | $70,000 | $80,000 | $120,000 | $160,000 | $40,000 |
| Square footage | 1,000 | 2,000 | 2,000 | 1,500 | 2,500 | 1,000 |
| Staff time (hours) | 4,000 | 8,500 | 12,500 | 9,000 | 12,500 | 5,000 |
| Secretarial time (hours) | 500 | 200 | 2,000 | 2,000 | 3,000 | 1,000 |

**Required:**

1. Complete the proration of indirect costs to all support functions and operating departments. Show the sum of direct and indirect costs in each function and department.

 2. Explain why the proration of indirect costs is necessary.

3. Using the direct method, allocate the service functions' costs to the operating departments; and develop the overhead rates for each of the operating departments. (Round dollar allocations to the nearest dollar and overhead rates to four decimal places.)

4. Using the step method, allocate the service functions' costs to the operating departments; and develop the overhead rates for each of the operating departments. The secretarial pool is allocated first. (Round dollar allocations to the nearest dollar and overhead rates to four decimal places.)

5. Compare the answers in Part (3) and Part (4) and explain why the differences occurred. Is the direct method used in Part (3) or the step method used in Part (4) preferred? Why?

# PRODUCT COSTING: JOB AND PROCESS COSTING

## LEARNING OBJECTIVES

1. Differentiate among job, process, modified, and hybrid cost systems.
2. Analyze costs in a job cost system for the purpose of cost control.
3. Describe the cost elements and cost flows in a process cost system.
4. Compute the equivalent units of production and unit costs using FIFO.
5. Prepare a cost of production report.
6. List several ways in which management can use departmental unit costs as a tool in evaluating departmental performance.
7. Explain the impact that JIT inventory systems have on process cost accounting.
8. Compute the equivalent units of production and unit costs using the weighted average method (Appendix).

---

### *Where There's a Will, There's a Way of Costing*

*When Stan Stein, an attorney, founded U Will It, he envisioned an enterprise involving the mass production of routine wills with standard wording and little variation. Because he kept his fees low and had clever advertising, his first two years were very successful. Stein was preparing wills for clients throughout Ohio.*

*Periodically, Stein was approached by clients who wished to have more specialized and complex wills prepared. Stein was reluctant to accept these jobs because his practice was near full capacity. Moreover, because these specialized wills required considerable research, client conferences, and other demands made by the clients, Stein did not feel his current practice was amenable to the preparation of specialized wills. Therefore, he would routinely turn down these requests.*

*One day, Stein decided to invest his growing profits into a new venture that would be oriented to preparing specialized wills. One of Stein's many concerns was how he would determine the costs of these customized jobs. He knew that the process costing system used for his current firm would not be suitable for his new venture.*

---

THIS CHAPTER DISCUSSES how to determine the costs of products produced in a process cost environment as well as products produced in a job cost environment. Although we focus on manufactured products, the concepts presented are applicable in service organizations, as was just indicated in the above vignette.

## OVERVIEW OF JOB AND PROCESS COSTING

A **job cost system** identifies costs with individual jobs or products. A separate tracking of costs is associated with each job or product. The costs accumulated for a job in process can be determined at any point in time.

A **process cost system** identifies costs with individual departments for an interval of time such as one month. Costs are not charged to specific units or orders as work is performed, but unit costs are based on costs incurred during a time period and on the volume of output during the same period. The unit cost of a final product will be the sum of all costs allocated to the product by each department that worked on it.

Several other characteristics distinguish job costing from process costing.

### Environment

Job costing is most appropriate in environments where jobs or products are different from one another. These jobs use different types or amounts of materials, labor, and overhead. Examples include building construction, defense contracting, consulting engagements, and printing shops.

Process costing is most appropriate in an environment where products are mass produced or result from continuous processing. Each unit going through the same process is identical to other units. Examples include candy, soft drinks, clothing, chemicals, and most processed foods. In addition, individual operations can be suitable for process costing if every product passing through the operation has the same work performed on it. For instance, various models of televisions and video cassette recorders on an assembly line may have the same operations performed during the assembly process.

In a job cost environment, sales orders usually precede production. Production is for a specific order. In a process cost environment, however, production usually precedes sales. Goods are produced for anticipated sales.

## Materials, Labor, and Overhead Costs

A process cost environment will generally use materials that are standard. In a job cost setting, materials requirements are often unique to each job and perhaps even the types of materials needed are unknown. Hence, process cost companies usually have larger inventories of materials.

Tasks in a process cost environment are generally routine. Less-skilled labor is usually needed than in a job cost environment, where workers need to perform a greater variety of tasks because of the different types of jobs. Automation is found more often in process cost settings. Therefore, the proportion of overhead cost in the total product cost will generally be higher than for job cost settings.

## Focal Point for Cost Accumulation

In process cost systems, we identify materials, labor, and overhead costs with specific departments or operating centers. This differs from job cost systems which identify costs with specific batches or customer orders. In this chapter, the term department will be used as a generic term and will cover the traditional concepts of department, operating or work center, operation, task, activity center, and responsibility center. As a result of charging costs to departments, few detailed records are needed with process costing.

# MODIFIED AND HYBRID SYSTEMS

Classifying an accounting system as a job cost or process cost system is often not easy. This is especially true when companies have a wide variety of products and processes. Modifications and adaptations are made to the accounting system to meet the needs of specific situations. These result in systems we categorize as modified cost systems and hybrid cost systems.

A **modified cost system** has one or more elements of cost using job costing, while the other cost elements use process costing. For example, a manufacturer of shoes will make different sizes and styles and use different grades of leather. However, the operations of cutting and sewing the leather and attaching the heels and soles are essentially the same for each shoe. Consequently, the manufacturer can group the shoes by sizes, styles, and grades of leather and treat the costing of materials using job costing. Then, the labor and factory overhead costs for the operations can use a process cost system.

A **hybrid cost system** exists where one type of cost system (job costing or process costing) is used for one phase of the production process, and another system is used for a subsequent phase. For example in manufacturing cars, the various parts, subassemblies, engines, transmissions, and so forth may be produced where a job cost system is used. In a JIT environment, most parts are produced in small batches only when needed. In assembly, every car, regardless of model, has the same assembly operations performed. Therefore, the labor and factory overhead costs of the assembly operations may be accounted for using a process cost system. Hybrid cost systems can involve various sequences of job and process costing depending on the particular production process.

**Operation costing** is a term often used to refer to modified or hybrid cost systems. Except in the simplest of cases, pure job costing or process costing does not exist. There is usually some modification. Managers need to understand their own organization's cost system in order to evaluate the cost information generated by that system. The remainder of this chapter provides detailed discussions of job cost and process cost systems.

# THE JOB COST SYSTEM

The job cost system accumulates separately the costs of materials, labor, and overhead for each job, whether a job of one unit or a job of many units. Every job is assigned a number which is used for accumulating the costs of that job. Daily, weekly, or monthly cost summaries for each job are generated. These summaries are referred to as **job, work**, or **production orders**. The file of production orders in process constitutes a subsidiary ledger in support of the work in process account in the general ledger. An example of a completed job order (Job Order No. 216) for Hiller's Computer Repair Shop is shown in Figure 5.1.

Chapter 4 discussed the accounting for the cost elements—direct materials, direct labor, and applied overhead—that make up a job. Now, let's look at issues related to job cost control.

## Cost Control in a Job Cost System

Supervisors, in planning their operations, may estimate the direct materials and direct labor costs for each job for which they are responsible. They subsequently measure actual costs and compare them with the estimated costs of each job, taking into account the stage of completion. For example, a report on direct materials for Lasar Company may be prepared as follows:

**Direct Materials**

| Job Number | Estimate | Actual | Dollar Variance Under/(Over) | Percentage of Completion |
|---|---|---|---|---|
| 1017 | $22,000 | $21,000 | $ 1,000 | 100% |
| 1018 | 19,500 | 20,000 | (500) | 100 |
| 1019 | 10,000* | 14,000 | (4,000) | 50 |
| 1020 | 5,000* | 5,000 | -0- | 25 |
| Total | $56,500 | $60,000 | $(3,500) | |

\* Estimates adjusted to percentage of completion basis.

| Hiller's Computer Repair Job Order No: | 216 | | | | | | | |
|---|---|---|---|---|---|---|---|---|
| Customer No: | 3122 | | | Customer Name: | Josh's Fine Gold Jewelry | | | |
| Job Date: | 1/10/07 | | | Job Due: | 1/20/07 | | | |
| Job Started: | 1/11/07 | | | Job Completed: | 1/19/07 | | | |
| Quantity: | 10 | | | | | | | |

| Date | Description | Code No. | Quantity | Price | Materials | Labor | Overhead | Total |
|---|---|---|---|---|---|---|---|---|
| 1/11 | Part #689 | 0052 | 7 | $54.75 | $383.25 | | | |
| 1/11 | Part #337 | 0068 | 5 | 88.50 | 442.50 | | | |
| 1/12 | Payroll | 1004 | 6 | $30.00 | | $ 180.00 | | |
| 1/19 | Payroll | 1005 | 27 | 30.00 | | 810.00 | | |
| 1/12 | Overhead | 2004 | 6 | $20.00 | | | $ 120.00 | |
| 1/19 | Overhead | 2005 | 27 | 20.00 | | | 540.00 | |
| Total | | | | | $825.75 | $990.00 | $660.00 | $2,475.75 |
| Unit cost | | | | | $ 82.58 | $ 99.00 | $ 66.00 | $ 247.58 |

**FIGURE 5.1**

A Completed Job Order

The variance column shows the differences between estimated and actual amounts. The total estimates for each job have been adjusted by the percentage completed so that a valid comparison can be made with the actual amounts. The total direct materials cost of Job 1019 was estimated to be $20,000. Since the job is 50 percent complete as to direct materials, the estimated cost is $10,000 (50 percent of $20,000).

A report that compares actual direct labor hours with the estimated hours will reveal whether more hours are being used on a job than expected. Again, the estimates are made comparable with actual results by determining the percentage of work completed and applying that percentage to the total estimate. For example, Job 1020 is only 10 percent complete for direct labor. The total estimate on that job for direct labor hours must have been 4,500 hours if 450 hours is 10 percent of the total estimate, as shown:

### Direct Labor Hours

| Job Number | Estimate | Actual | Direct Labor Hour Variance Under/(Over) | Percentage of Completion |
|---|---|---|---|---|
| 1017 | 4,450* | 4,000 | 450 | 80% |
| 1018 | 1,800* | 2,000 | (200) | 50 |
| 1019 | 3,300* | 3,500 | (200) | 50 |
| 1020 | 450* | 500 | (50) | 10 |
| Total | 10,000 | 10,000 | -0- | |

* Estimates adjusted to percentage of completion basis.

The report on direct labor hours can be converted to a direct labor cost report by multiplying the direct labor hours by the direct labor hour rate (in this case, $10), as shown in the following report:

### Direct Labor Cost

| Job Number | Estimate | Actual | Direct Labor Dollar Variance Under/(Over) | Percentage of Completion |
|---|---|---|---|---|
| 1017 | $ 44,500* | $ 40,000 | $4,500 | 80% |
| 1018 | 18,000* | 20,000 | (2,000) | 50 |
| 1019 | 33,000* | 35,000 | (2,000) | 50 |
| 1020 | 4,500* | 5,000 | (500) | 10 |
| Total | $100,000 | $100,000 | -0- | |

* Estimates adjusted to percentage of completion basis.

Supervisors are able to use such cost information to follow each job from its inception to completion. As a **cost overrun** (unfavorable variance from estimate) develops, they can take corrective measures. The preceding example shows that Job 1019 is 50 percent complete with respect to both direct materials and direct labor. More materials and more hours were used than anticipated. Knowing what caused the overrun may enable the supervisor to find ways to reduce cost. Or, perhaps the estimate was unrealistically low; in this case, budgets could be revised.

Whereas a job cost system accumulates costs by jobs, a process cost system accumulates costs by departments. This, and other differences, changes the approach to determining unit costs in a process cost environment. However, as outlined in the remaining sections of this chapter, many of the product cost concepts of Chapter 4 apply as well to process costing.

# THE COST ELEMENTS IN A PROCESS COST SYSTEM

The cost elements in a process cost system depend on whether the organization is a manufacturing or service organization. A manufacturer typically has more detailed costs; therefore we focus on manufacturing firms in the following sections. We will discuss the two major elements of manufacturing costs in a process cost system—materials and conversion costs.

## Materials

Materials are requisitioned for use in a specific department, and the materials costs are accumulated by the department for a specific time period. Although materials can be added in any department, they are often issued from the storeroom to the first operating department in the process. The concept of accounting for materials costs does not depend on whether materials are added in the first department or in subsequent departments. Distinguishing between direct materials and indirect materials is not considered critical to obtain accurate unit costs.

Two major differences in accumulating materials costs between the job cost system and the process cost system should be noted. Materials costs are identified first with departments and then assigned to individual units in a process cost system. Materials costs bypass departments and are charged directly to specific jobs in a job cost system. In process costing, materials costs are accumulated for a period of time and averaged over all units receiving materials during the period. This averaging of costs is broader in a process cost system than in a job cost system, where costs would be averaged only over the batch of units comprising a particular job.

## Conversion Costs

Labor and overhead costs are incurred to convert materials into a finished product; hence, labor and overhead costs are called **conversion costs**. Because labor and overhead often enter the process at the same time, we combine them for illustrations throughout the chapter. This assumes that overhead is applied to production using direct labor hours or dollars. Where another cost driver is used, we separate the two cost elements.

Labor cost is measured monthly, by department, and without identifying specific orders. Labor time tickets may be used for payroll accounting but are not needed to measure the time to complete a single order because each unit of product in a process cost setting is presumed to take the same amount of time. Like materials, little emphasis is placed on distinguishing precisely between direct labor and indirect labor.

Overhead costs are accumulated by department. Typically, we record them in a departmental overhead control ledger by type of cost (e.g., depreciation, utilities). Overhead costs are charged to production through predetermined overhead rates for each department. In most of our illustrations, overhead appears to be actual overhead. However, the costs represent charges based on predetermined overhead rates under a normal cost system. Since normal costing was discussed in Chapter 4, we will not repeat the coverage here. We assume that overhead is accumulated and applied using departmental rates.

## Cost Flows

In a process system, a product may flow through several operations before completion. For example, production of cellular phones may start in a fabricating operation, as shown in Figure 5.2.

Both the physical units and costs will be identified for the fabricating operation over a period of time, such as a month. When the inner components of the phones are completed in the fabricating operation, the units with their costs are transferred by automated guided vehicles to the next operation—in this case, the molding operation where the casings are formed. Additional costs will be incurred and accounted for in the molding operation. At the completion of the molding operation, the units and accumulated costs of preceding operations will be transferred to the last operation in this example, the finishing operation.

Because costs need to be identified with departments, a process cost system normally involves accounting transfers between departmental work in process inventory accounts. Each department has its own work in process account; and when goods are completed in one department, their costs are transferred to the work in process account of the next department.

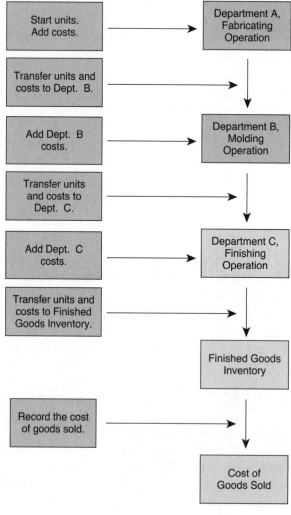

**FIGURE 5.2**

Flow of Units and Costs in a Process Manufacturing System

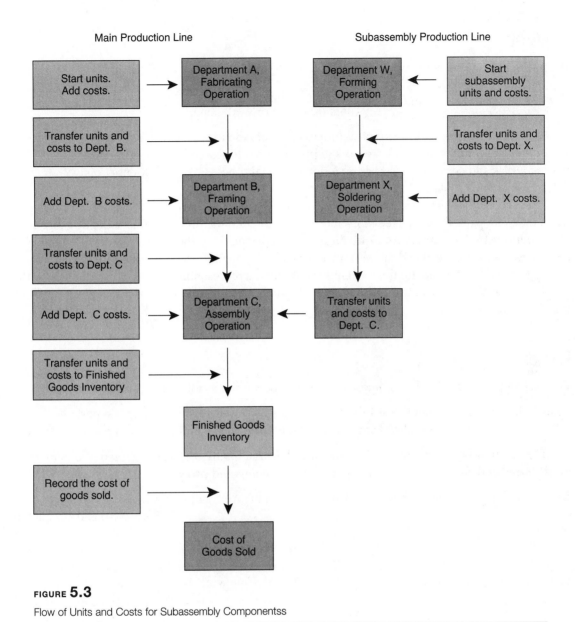

**FIGURE 5.3**

Flow of Units and Costs for Subassembly Componentss

In some types of operations, a subassembly may be produced on a separate production line for addition to the product at a later stage. For example, assume that the main production line for computer disk drives extends from Department A (Fabricating) to Department C (Assembly). A subassembly line, consisting of Departments W (Forming) and X (Soldering), uses numerically-controlled machines to produce a component that converts physical measures like velocity and pressure into digital form. These components are brought into the main line in Department C. A diagram showing the flow of units and costs for this example appears in Figure 5.3.

## THE EQUIVALENT UNIT CONCEPT

A primary goal of any cost accounting system is to identify product costs for determining ending inventories of work in process and finished goods and for establishing the cost of goods sold amount. Costs are attached to units in inventories whether the units are wholly or partially completed. The mechanism for tracing costs to units is a unit cost.

## Unit Costs

When calculating unit costs, we typically think of a formula similar to the following:

$$\text{Unit cost} = \frac{\text{Total costs}}{\text{Units produced or work done}}$$

Applying this formula to the typical process cost situation is complicated by two major factors: (1) the stage of completion of units in work in process inventories; and (2) the different points in time that materials and conversion costs enter a departmental process. We will discuss point (2) in more detail later in the chapter.

The number of units completed is not a good measure for determining an appropriate unit cost when there are partially completed units in beginning or ending inventories. Consequently, an equivalent unit must be identified. An **equivalent unit** represents the theoretical number of units that could have been produced had the resources been applied to units that were started and completed during the period. We can also think of equivalent units as representing the actual work done on the physical units. For instance, two physical units 50 percent complete represent the equivalent of one unit 100 percent complete.

## Flow of Physical Units

For each department, the flow of *physical* units can be viewed as follows:

Units in beginning work in process inventory + Units of product started during the period
= Units completed and transferred out + Units in ending work in process inventory

This relationship among physical units is also shown in Figure 5.4. As diagramed, the number of units started and completed during the period can be computed two ways:

Units completed and transferred out − Units in beginning work in process inventory
= Units started and completed

**or**

Units of product started during the period − Units in ending work in process inventory
= Units started and completed

Knowing where all units are in a production process is an important starting point for calculating unit costs. Figure 5.4 represents the location and flow of physical units through a production process for a given time period.

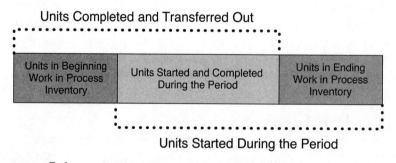

**FIGURE 5.4**

Relationship Among Physical Units Within a Department

## Stage of Completion

In a process cost system, the units in the beginning and ending inventories are usually at different stages of completion. The **stage of completion** is the average percentage of work completed on a unit of product at any point in time. For a department, it is useful to identify three distinct groupings of products when computing equivalent units:

1. Partially completed units in the beginning inventory which are completed during the current period. The work to complete these units is represented by 100 percent less the stage of completion when the period started. We generally assume a first-in, first-out flow.

2. Units started and completed during the period. The work completed is represented by 100 percent.

3. Partially completed units at the end of the period. The work completed is represented by the percentage of completion at the end of the period.

When all three of these groups are summed, the result is equivalent units of output for this time period—the work done by the workers in this department. This is the number of units that could have been produced if all production were started and completed during the period, assuming no beginning or ending work in process inventories.

For example, the Norwich Post Office has a sorting department. On March 1, 15,000 units were in process and were 60 percent completed. During March, the department started work on 200,000 units. On March 31, 20,000 units were in process and were 30 percent completed. From our flow of physical units formula, we calculate the number of units completed as follows:

| | |
|---|---|
| Units in beginning inventory | 15,000 |
| +Units started during period | 200,000 |
| −Units in ending inventory | (20,000) |
| Units completed and transferred | 195,000 |

Next, we compute the units started and completed using both methods described previously:

| | |
|---|---|
| Units completed and transferred | 195,000 |
| −Units in beginning inventory | (15,000) |
| Units started and completed | 180,000 |

**or**

| | |
|---|---|
| Units started during the period | 200,000 |
| −Units in ending inventory | (20,000) |
| Units started and completed | 180,000 |

We now have the three groups of units and their stages of completion which are necessary to find the number of equivalent units. One way to calculate the equivalent units of output for the period, referred to as the "units started and completed method," is as follows:

| *Units started and completed method:* | |
|---|---|
| Current period work to complete beginning inventory [15,000 × (100% − 60%)] | 6,000 |
| +Units started and completed (180,000 units × 100%) | 180,000 |
| +Current period work in ending inventory (20,000 units × 30%) | 6,000 |
| Equivalent units of output (work done during the period) | 192,000 |

Two other methods are available for calculating these equivalent units. One is called the "units completed method," and the other method is the "units started method." They give the same equivalent units results, as follows:

*Units completed method:*

| | |
|---|---|
| Units completed (195,000 units × 100%) | 195,000 |
| +Current period work in ending inventory (20,000 units × 30%) | 6,000 |
| −Prior period work in beginning inventory (15,000 units × 60%) | (9,000) |
| Equivalent units of output (work done during the period) | 192,000 |

*Units started method:*

| | |
|---|---|
| Current period work to complete beginning inventory<br>[15,000 × (100% − 60%)] | 6,000 |
| +Units started (200,000 units × 100%) | 200,000 |
| −Next period work to complete ending inventory<br>[20,000 × (100% − 30%)] | (14,000) |
| Equivalent units of output (work done during the period) | 192,000 |

Any one of these three methods may be used if a manager is working only with equivalent units and unit costs. However, in preparing the cost of production report which we will discuss later, the units started and completed method is most suitable. Hence, this is the approach we will use.

## Timing of Inputs

Materials, labor, and overhead are the inputs to the production process. These inputs may enter at different points during the process. The most common situation is for materials to enter at the beginning of a departmental process and for labor and overhead to be added continuously throughout the process. Consequently, it is possible for some units in process to have all of their materials content but only part of the labor and overhead. In other processes, the materials may be added continuously or at the end of the process. For our purposes, unless otherwise stated, presume that materials are added at the beginning of the process, and labor and overhead enter the process together and are added continuously or evenly throughout the process.

To calculate unit costs when inputs have different timing for entering a process, we need to calculate the equivalent units for each cost input. Therefore, one equivalent unit computation is for materials; and another computation is for conversion costs. The computational steps developed in the next section will show how separate equivalent units quantities are used to establish unit costs.

## Computational Steps

Tracing physical units to a department and accounting for those units are generally clerical functions. Likewise, the identification of the costs charged to a department is a relatively simple function. However, distributing the costs to work completed and ending inventories requires an understanding of several steps. These steps are:

1. Determine flow of physical units.
2. Calculate equivalent units.
3. Compute unit costs.
4. Distribute total costs to units.
5. Reconcile the costs.

The last step checks whether the four previous steps were completed accurately. This step verifies that the total costs distributed to the units equal the total costs charged to the department. Each of these steps will be presented in detail as part of developing a cost of production report.

We assume a **first-in, first-out (FIFO) cost method** in progressing through the five computational steps. The beginning inventory is completed before new units are completed. Costs incurred flow in the same manner. Most companies using process costing use the FIFO cost method.[1] Another frequently used method, the weighted average cost method, is discussed in the Appendix to this chapter.

Under FIFO, the older units and costs are transferred out first, and the more current units and costs are transferred out next. Only the most recent costs are held as ending inventory. With the FIFO cost method, the equivalent units of output are literally the units that could have been completed if all efforts during the period were devoted to starting and completing units, allowing no partially completed units. Usually, however, some units will be in a stage of partial completion at both the beginning and at the end of the month. The beginning work in process units are completed during the month, and a start has been made on the units in ending work in process.

To illustrate the computational steps, consider the current plant of Shirts Unlimited. Sweatshirts are produced in three departments: Cutting, Sewing, and Finishing. Our illustration will focus on the Cutting Department. All cloth material enters production at the beginning of the Cutting Department operations. The cloth is cut there. Both materials and conversion costs are incurred in the Cutting Department. Its activity for May is summarized as follows:

| | |
|---|---|
| Work in process, May 1: | |
| Units | 4,000 |
| Stage of completion: | |
| Materials | 100% |
| Conversion costs | 40% |
| Costs: | |
| Materials | $400,000 |
| Conversion costs | 80,000 |
| Beginning inventory total cost | $480,000 |
| Units started | 12,000 |
| Units completed and transferred | 14,000 |
| Current period costs: | |
| Materials | $1,200,000 |
| Conversion costs | 650,000 |
| Total costs added | $1,850,000 |
| Work in process, May 31: | |
| Units | 2,000 |
| Stage of completion: | |
| Materials | 100% |
| Conversion costs | 30% |

**Step 1: Determine Flow of Physical Units.** Determining the flow of physical units for a department involves identifying the units in the beginning inventory, the units started and completed during the period, and the units in the ending inventory. These are whole units; stage of completion is not an issue here. For the Cutting Department of Shirts Unlimited, we have:

| | |
|---|---|
| Units in beginning work in process | 4,000 |
| Units started and completed: | |
| (12,000 − 2,000 or 14,000 − 4,000) | 10,000 |
| Units in ending work in process | 2,000 |
| Total units | 16,000 |

---

[1] Hauser, R. C., F. R. Urbancic, and D. E. Edwards, "Process Costing: Is It Relevant?", *Management Accounting*, December 1989, p. 53.

**Step 2: Calculate Equivalent Units.** Equivalent units are computed by multiplying physical units by the percentage of work completed on them. For our example, using the units started and completed method, we have the following calculations:

|  | Materials | Conversion |
|---|---|---|
| Current period work to complete beginning inventory: | | |
| 4,000 × (100% − 100%) | 0 | |
| 4,000 × (100% − 40%) | | 2,400 |
| Units started and completed in May: | | |
| 10,000 × 100% | 10,000 | 10,000 |
| May's work in ending inventory: | | |
| 2,000 × 100% | 2,000 | |
| 2,000 × 30% | | 600 |
| Equivalent units (work done during May) | 12,000 | 13,000 |

**Step 3: Compute Unit Costs.** We begin this step by itemizing the costs for which the Cutting Department will be held accountable.

| Costs Charged to Department: | Materials | Conversion | Total |
|---|---|---|---|
| Beginning inventory | $400,000 | $80,000 | $480,000 |
| May's costs | 1,200,000 | 650,000 | 1,850,000 |
| Total costs | $1,600,000 | $730,000 | $2,330,000 |

The unit costs for materials and conversion costs are calculated from the *current* month's costs and equivalent units. Last month's costs and equivalent units of work will be treated separately. Using May's costs and the equivalent units from above, the costs for May are divided by the equivalent units for May to obtain unit costs:

**Unit Costs for May:**

Unit cost for materials = $1,200,000/12,000 = $100

Unit cost for conversion = $650,000/13,000 = $50

The beginning work in process cost provides useful information for managers. These dollars represent costs from the prior period, in this case, the previous month. Thus, unit cost information about the beginning inventory is obtained by dividing the beginning inventory costs by the prior period work (i.e., equivalent units) in the beginning inventory:

**April's Unit Costs in May's Beginning Inventory:**

Unit cost for materials = $400,000/4,000 = $100

Unit cost for conversion = $80,000/1,600 = $50

These unit costs are identical to those for the current period, although such a case will not occur very often.

**Step 4: Distribute Total Costs to Units.** We next show the distribution of costs to units using the unit costs and equivalent units derived earlier.

| Costs Accounted For: | Materials | Conversion | Total |
|---|---|---|---|
| Completed and transferred to Sewing: | | | |
| Work in process, May 1: | | | |
| Prior period costs | $ 400,000 | $ 80,000 | $ 480,000 |
| May: Equivalent units | 0 | 2,400 | |
| Times cost per unit | $ 100 | $ 50 | |
| Costs | $0 | $ 120,000 | $ 120,000 |
| Completed cost of beginning inventory | $ 400,000 | $ 200,000 | $ 600,000 |
| Started and completed: | | | |
| Units | 10,000 | 10,000 | |
| Times cost per unit | $ 100 | $ 50 | |
| Costs | $1,000,000 | $ 500,000 | $1,500,000 |
| Total cost of completed and transferred units | $1,400,000 | $ 700,000 | $2,100,000 |
| Work in process, May 31: | | | |
| Equivalent units | 2,000 | 600 | |
| Times cost per unit | $ 100 | $ 50 | |
| Costs | $ 200,000 | $ 30,000 | $ 230,000 |
| Total costs accounted for | $1,600,000 | $ 730,000 | $2,330,000 |

Note the sequence of computations. First, the old costs in the beginning work in process are listed. Then, we compute the cost to complete the beginning work in process in the current period. Next, we calculate the costs associated with units started and completed. The sum of all of these costs is the cost of goods completed and transferred out. This is also called the cost of goods manufactured. Finally, we determine the costs of the work done on the units still in process on May 31.

Often the unit cost calculations result in the need to round to some decimal place. The more decimal places used, the less the rounding error in total dollars assigned to units completed and units in ending inventory. If rounding errors occur, it is customary to adjust the costs assigned to units completed to compensate for the rounding error.

**Step 5: Reconcile the Costs.** This final step in the computational process is really a check to ensure that all department costs are charged to units completed and units in the ending inventory. As shown in Step 3, the total costs charged to the Cutting Department are $2,330,000. After distributing the costs to the units completed and units in the ending inventory, the sum should also equal $2,330,000. This is confirmed by the total costs accounted for in Step 4. This check shows that materials and conversion costs charged to the department have indeed been distributed to all units.

## Cost of Production Report

The five computational steps provide all of the calculations needed to prepare a **cost of production report** for May. This report, which presents information about units, costs charged to the department, and how the costs are accounted for, is shown in Figure 5.5.

In T-account form, the transactions reflected in the cost of production report would be summarized as shown in Figure 5.6.

We use the same procedures to determine costs for subsequent departments in the processing operation. In departments after the first, however, unit costs must be combined with the accumulated costs of work done in earlier departments. For example, if operations cover 10 departments, Department 10 would obtain a unit cost for the total work done in all preceding nine departments and calculate a unit cost for its own work.

# SHIRTS UNLIMITED
## Cutting Department
### Cost of Production Report for the Month of May

| Units: | Physical Units | Materials Equivalent Units | Conversion Equivalent Units |
|---|---|---|---|
| Beginning work in process: | 4,000 | | |
| Prior month: | | | |
| 4,000 × 100% | | 4,000 | |
| 4,000 × 40% | | | 1,600 |
| May's work: | | | |
| 4,000 × (100% − 100%) | | 0 | |
| 4,000 × (100% − 40%) | | | 2,400 |
| Units started and completed: | 10,000 | | |
| 10,000 × 100% | | 10,000 | 10,000 |
| Ending work in process: | 2,000 | | |
| 2,000 × 100% | | 2,000 | |
| 2,000 × 30% | | | 600 |
| Total units | 16,000 | | |
| Equivalent units of output | | | |
| | | 12,000 | 13,000 |

| Costs Charged to Department: | Materials | Conversion | Total |
|---|---|---|---|
| Beginning work in process: | | | |
| Costs | $ 400,000 | $ 80,000 | $ 480,000 |
| Divided by equivalent units | 4,000 | 1,600 | |
| Cost per unit | $ 100 | $ 50 | |
| May's production: | | | |
| Costs | $1,200,000 | $650,000 | $1,850,000 |
| Divided by equivalent units | 12,000 | 13,000 | |
| Cost per unit | $ 100 | $ 50 | |
| Total costs charged | $1,600,000 | $730,000 | $2,330,000 |

| Costs Accounted for: | Materials | Conversion | Total |
|---|---|---|---|
| Completed and transferred to Sewing: | | | |
| Work in Process, May 1: | | | |
| Prior period costs | $ 400,000 | $ 80,000 | $ 480,000 |
| May: Equivalent units | 0 | 2,400 | |
| Times cost per unit | $ 100 | $ 50 | |
| Costs | $ 0 | $120,000 | $ 120,000 |
| Completed cost of beginning inventory | $ 400,000 | $200,000 | $ 600,000 |
| Started and completed: | | | |
| Units | 10,000 | 10,000 | |
| Times cost per unit | $ 100 | $ 50 | |
| Costs | $1,000,000 | $500,000 | $1,500,000 |
| Total cost of completed and transferred units | $1,400,000 | $700,000 | $2,100,000 |
| Work in process, May 31: | | | |
| Equivalent units | 2,000 | 600 | |
| Times cost per unit | $ 100 | $ 50 | |
| Costs | $ 200,000 | $ 30,000 | $ 230,000 |
| Total costs accounted for | $1,600,000 | $730,000 | $2,330,000 |

FIGURE **5.5**

Cost of Production Report for Cutting Department (FIFO Method)

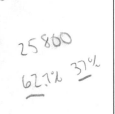

25 800
62.7% 37%

| Work in Process—Cutting | | | | Work in Process—Sewing | | |
|---|---|---|---|---|---|---|
| Beg. Inventory | 480,000 | Completed | 2,100,000 ⟶ | Transferred in | 2,100,000I | |
| Materials | 1,200,000 | | | | | |
| Conversion | 650,000 | | | | | |
| End. Inventory | 230,000 | | | | | |

**FIGURE 5.6**

Flow of Cost From Cutting Department to Sewing Department

## Management's Use of Cost of Production Reports

Internal accounting reports often serve only to attach dollars to the events about which managers already know. For example, managers know about volumes, inefficiencies, and scrap; but they do not know the costs related to them. However, the information provided by a cost of production report can be used by managers in several different ways.

When unit costs for materials and conversion costs change from one period to the next, a manager should ask why. Why is a materials price higher or lower? What causes conversion costs to change? The manager has to find the answers to ensure that the numbers reported represent reality and are accurate. Sometimes managers intuitively know the numbers are either correct or incorrect because of their experiences.

Cost of production reports for several periods in succession can show trends. Here certain questions arise. Are inventories bouncing around, or are they stable? Why? Why are unit costs steadily moving up, or why are they erratic? Are we changing the mix of workers as reflected in labor cost changes? These and many other questions help managers understand their working environment and the company's focus much better.

If unit costs are identified as variable and fixed costs, a manager can perform various cost-volume-profit analyses. Naturally, a sequence of departments that depends on one another must cooperate in some of these analyses for the company to have the greatest benefit.

Many other uses are available. In later chapters, we use these costs to obtain budgeted costs; and we analyze variances from expected costs in detail. These uses are cited only to show that the cost of production reports are more than mere printing on paper.

## Ethical Considerations

As with all financial reports, production reports can easily be manipulated. Estimating the stage of completion of the work in process is an area particularly susceptible to manipulation by production

## Contemporary Practice 5.1
### Estimation of Equivalent Units

An experiment with individuals in graduate and executive education managerial accounting classes, who averaged about six years of full-time work experience, tested whether they would overestimate the degree of completion of ending work in process inventory in a process costing scenario. Overestimations would lower unit costs, thereby lowering cost of goods sold, and in turn, increase the reported profit. The study estimated that about 9 percent of the participants would intentionally misrepresent equivalent units by overstating the stage of completion of ending work in process in order to meet a targeted pretax income figure.

Source: Schneider, A., "Ethical Decision Making on Various Managerial Accounting Issues," Journal of Applied Management Accounting Research, Summer 2004, pp. 29–39.

managers. These estimates are very subjective. Two reasons explain why managers might be motivated to overestimate the stage of completion. First is pressure to meet production quotas of units or equivalent units produced. A second reason relates to minimizing unit costs. A higher estimate for the degree of completion of the work in process inventory results in a greater number of equivalent units of output for the period. This, in turn, generates a lower cost per equivalent unit. Notice, however, that any overestimate in one period results in an opposite impact in the following period. Management accountants, nevertheless, need to be aware that temptations to overestimate the stage of completion may exist.

## SIMPLIFICATIONS OF JIT AND AUTOMATION

For companies adopting a **just-in-time (JIT) philosophy**, the expectation is to reduce or eliminate inventories. If a company implements JIT throughout its operations, the final departments in the process finish the products just in time to be shipped; parts, components, and subassemblies are manufactured just in time to meet the final department's needs and so on back through the process. Even in the beginning, materials are received just in time to enter the appropriate department.

JIT can significantly simplify accounting for a process cost system. Partially completed units within each department will be kept as low as possible. Thus, little difference exists between units completed and work done during the period. Consequently, the costs incurred during the period are largely tied to goods completed. As a result, unit costs are more accurate in a JIT environment because they are less influenced by stage of completion estimates. This is true of automated factories as a whole, since they tend to have fairly uniform amounts of beginning and ending work in process inventories. Thus, work done during the period will be approximately equal to the number of units completed during the period.

In addition, little need exists to transfer costs from one department to the next. The costs of the period can be recorded directly to the cost of goods sold account. Process costs per unit can still be computed but on a daily or weekly basis. The unit costs will be calculated using units produced rather than equivalent units. Further aspects of JIT product costing are discussed in Chapter 6.

Also, in JIT factories, certain departments remain idle until their outputs are needed by the next department. This may cause a particular department to appear inefficient in one period and very efficient in another. Therefore, evaluations of managers and costs in JIT plants need to consider the flow of production and who controls decisions of what and when to produce.

Many managers believe that a system truly operating under JIT will have no inventories and, therefore, no need for a process cost system. Because the process flow time is not zero, some items are always in production in a partially completed stage. Process costing becomes greatly simplified in such a setting, but it is not eliminated.

## SUMMARY

In a job cost environment, costs are identified with specific batches or customer orders. In a process cost environment, products are continuously manufactured through a series of departments. Physical units and costs are identified with the departments. Unit costs are used in tracing the costs through the various departments and to the finished goods inventory account.

Because manufacturing situations will vary from one company to another, modifications and adaptations to the cost accounting system must be made. Modified and hybrid cost systems are common. A modified cost system will have some elements of cost using job costs and other elements of cost using process costs. A hybrid cost system will have one department on a job cost basis and another department on a process cost basis.

For control purposes, actual costs of jobs are compared to estimates, taking into account the stage of completion for each job. If a cost overrun develops before the completion of a job, corrective measures can be taken.

Unit costs in a process cost system are computed by dividing the appropriate current costs by the related equivalent units. The inventory costing method used is the first-in, first-out method. This assumes the beginning inventory is completed before new units are completed. Costs incurred are assumed to flow in the same manner. The cost of production report summarizes the costs charged to departments and how the costs are distributed between completed units and ending work in process.

Changes taking place in the manufacturing environment have an impact on a process cost system. Some changes, such as JIT, can simplify the calculation of unit costs.

## PROBLEM FOR REVIEW

Decatur Tune-Up has 755 auto tune-up shops located throughout the country. The following data pertain to their operations during May:

| | |
|---|---:|
| Work in process, May 1: | |
| Units | 3,000 |
| Conversion costs | $ 6,000 |
| Stage of completion: | |
| Materials | 0% |
| Conversion costs | 10% |
| Units started | 13,000 |
| Units completed | 15,000 |
| May's costs: | |
| Materials | $225,000 |
| Conversion costs | 260,100 |
| Work in process, May 31: | |
| Units | 1,000 |
| Stage of completion: | |
| Materials | 0% |
| Conversion costs | 60% |

**Required:**
1. Perform the computational steps for Decatur Tune-Up.
2. Prepare a cost of production report for May.

**Solution:**
## 1. Computational Steps
**Step 1:** Determine physical flow:

| | |
|---|---:|
| Units in beginning work in process | 3,000 |
| Units started and completed: | |
| (13,000 − 1,000 or 15,000 − 3,000) | 12,000 |
| Units in ending work in process | 1,000 |
| Total units | 16,000 |

**Step 2:** Calculate equivalent units:

|  | Materials | Conversion |
|---|---|---|
| Current period work to complete beginning inventory: |  |  |
| 3,000 × (100% − 0%) | 3,000 |  |
| 3,000 × (100% − 10%) |  | 2,700 |
| Units started and completed: |  |  |
| 12,000 × 100% | 12,000 | 12,000 |
| Current period work in ending inventory: |  |  |
| 1,000 × 0% | 0 |  |
| 1,000 × 60% |  | 600 |
| Equivalent units (work done during the period) | 15,000 | 15,300 |

**Step 3:** Compute unit costs:

$$\text{Unit cost for materials} = \$225,000/15,000 = \$15$$
$$\text{Unit cost for conversion} = \$260,100/15,300 = \$17$$

**Step 4:** Distribute total costs to units:

| Costs Accounted for: | Materials | Conversion | Total |
|---|---|---|---|
| Completed and transferred: |  |  |  |
| Work in process, May 1: |  |  |  |
| Prior period costs | $ 0 | $ 6,000 | $ 6,000 |
| May: Equivalent units | 3,000 | 2,700 |  |
| Times cost per unit | $ 15 | $ 17 |  |
| Costs | $ 45,000 | $ 45,900 | $ 90,900 |
| Completed cost of beginning inventory | $ 45,000 | $ 51,900 | $ 96,900 |
| Started and Completed: |  |  |  |
| Units | 12,000 | 12,000 |  |
| Times cost per unit | $ 15 | $ 17 |  |
| Costs | $180,000 | $204,000 | $384,000 |
| Total cost of completed and transferred units | $225,000 | $255,900 | $480,900 |
| Work in process, May 31: |  |  |  |
| Equivalent units | 0 | 600 |  |
| Times cost per unit | $ 15 | $ 17 |  |
| Costs | $ 0 | $ 10,200 | $ 10,200 |
| Total costs accounted for | $225,000 | $266,100 | $491,100 |

**Step 5:** Reconcile costs:

| Costs Charged to Department: | Materials | Conversion | Total |
|---|---|---|---|
| Beginning inventory | $ 0 | $ 6,000 | $ 6,000 |
| Current month | 225,000 | 260,100 | 485,100 |
| Total costs | $225,000 | $266,100 | $491,100 |

## 2. Cost of Production Report

Steps 1 through 4 provide all of the calculations needed to prepare a cost of production report for May, as follows:

<table>
<tr><th colspan="4">DECATUR TUNE-UP<br>COST OF PRODUCTION REPORT FOR THE MONTH OF MAY</th></tr>
<tr><td>Units:</td><td>Physical Units</td><td>Materials<br>Equivalent Units</td><td>Conversion<br>Equivalent Units</td></tr>
<tr><td>Beginning work in process:</td><td>3,000</td><td></td><td></td></tr>
<tr><td>Prior month:</td><td></td><td></td><td></td></tr>
<tr><td>3,000 × 0%</td><td></td><td>0</td><td></td></tr>
<tr><td>3,000 × 10%</td><td></td><td></td><td>300</td></tr>
<tr><td>May's work:</td><td></td><td></td><td></td></tr>
<tr><td>3,000 × (100% − 0%)</td><td></td><td>3,000</td><td></td></tr>
<tr><td>3,000 × (100% − 10%)</td><td></td><td></td><td>2,700</td></tr>
<tr><td>Units started and completed:</td><td>12,000</td><td></td><td></td></tr>
<tr><td>12,000 × 100%</td><td></td><td>12,000</td><td>12,000</td></tr>
<tr><td>Ending work in process:</td><td>1,000</td><td></td><td></td></tr>
<tr><td>1,000 × 0%</td><td></td><td>0</td><td></td></tr>
<tr><td>1,000 × 60%</td><td></td><td></td><td>600</td></tr>
<tr><td>Total units</td><td>16,000</td><td></td><td></td></tr>
<tr><td>Equivalent units of output</td><td></td><td>15,000</td><td>15,300</td></tr>
<tr><td>Costs Charged to Department:</td><td>Materials</td><td>Conversion</td><td>Total</td></tr>
<tr><td>Beginning work in process:</td><td></td><td></td><td></td></tr>
<tr><td>Costs</td><td>$      0</td><td>$   6,000</td><td>$   6,000</td></tr>
<tr><td>Divided by equivalent units</td><td>0</td><td>300</td><td></td></tr>
<tr><td>Cost per unit</td><td>0</td><td>$20</td><td></td></tr>
<tr><td>May's production:</td><td></td><td></td><td></td></tr>
<tr><td>Costs</td><td>$225,000</td><td>$260,100</td><td>$485,100</td></tr>
<tr><td>Divided by equivalent units</td><td>15,000</td><td>15,300</td><td></td></tr>
<tr><td>Cost per unit</td><td>$      15</td><td>$      17</td><td></td></tr>
<tr><td>Total costs charged</td><td>$225,000</td><td>$266,100</td><td>$491,100</td></tr>
<tr><td>Costs Accounted for:</td><td>Materials</td><td>Conversion</td><td>Total</td></tr>
<tr><td>Completed and transferred:</td><td></td><td></td><td></td></tr>
<tr><td>Work in process, May 1:</td><td></td><td></td><td></td></tr>
<tr><td>Prior Period Costs</td><td>$      0</td><td>$ 6,000</td><td>$   6,000</td></tr>
<tr><td>May: Equivalent units</td><td>3,000</td><td>2,700</td><td></td></tr>
<tr><td>Times cost per unit</td><td>$      15</td><td>$      17</td><td></td></tr>
<tr><td>Costs</td><td>$ 45,000</td><td>$ 45,900</td><td>$ 90,900</td></tr>
<tr><td>Completed cost of beginning inventory</td><td>$ 45,000</td><td>$ 51,900</td><td>$ 96,900</td></tr>
<tr><td>Started and completed:</td><td></td><td></td><td></td></tr>
<tr><td>Units</td><td>12,000</td><td>12,000</td><td></td></tr>
<tr><td>Times cost per unit</td><td>$      15</td><td>$      17</td><td></td></tr>
<tr><td>Costs</td><td>$180,000</td><td>$204,000</td><td>$384,000</td></tr>
<tr><td>Total cost of completed and transferred units</td><td>$225,000</td><td>$255,900</td><td>$480,900</td></tr>
<tr><td>Work in process, May 31:</td><td></td><td></td><td></td></tr>
<tr><td>Equivalent units</td><td>0</td><td>600</td><td></td></tr>
<tr><td>Times cost per unit</td><td>$      15</td><td>$      17</td><td></td></tr>
<tr><td>Costs</td><td>$      0</td><td>$ 10,200</td><td>$ 10,200</td></tr>
<tr><td>Total costs accounted for</td><td>$225,000</td><td>$266,100</td><td>$491,100</td></tr>
</table>

# APPENDIX

## WEIGHTED AVERAGE COST METHOD

An alternative to the first-in, first-out cost method for calculating equivalent units is the **weighted average cost method**. This method averages the beginning work in process inventory (last period's costs) and the current production (this period's costs). The method assumes that the started and completed units for the period are the units completed and transferred out (regardless of when the units were started). In computing unit costs, equivalent units are calculated as the sum of (1) the units completed during the period, and (2) the ending work in process inventory multiplied by its stage of completion. Whereas the equivalent units for the FIFO unit cost represent only work done during the current period, equivalent units for the weighted average method represent all units completed during this period (including work already done in the beginning work in process) plus any work done on ending work in process units.

The weighted average cost method is easier and simpler than FIFO because it does not require tracking the costs in the beginning inventory separately from those costs added during the current period. It is justified on the basis of convenience and simplicity. One can argue that a process which produces identical or similar units should generate the same unit costs from one month to the next. In addition, if beginning and ending inventories do not differ significantly from period to period, the costs per unit are relatively stable. However, the weighted average method commingles costs and production efforts of two time periods. The resulting product costs do not match production management's measures of inputs and outputs. Thus, many managers view the extra effort for FIFO as worthwhile.

## WEIGHTED AVERAGE COMPUTATIONAL STEPS

We apply the same computational steps to the weighted average cost method as we had for the FIFO cost method. A slight difference occurs in the "Costs Accounted for" section of the cost of production report. In this section, costs are distributed to units completed and units in the ending inventory. The weighted average cost method will usually have different unit costs than FIFO.

We continue the example of the Shirts Unlimited illustration in the chapter. For the Cutting Department, we prepared the cost of production report using the FIFO cost method. Now, we apply the weighted average cost method to the data.

**Step 1: Determine Flow of Physical Units.** Determining the flow of physical units for a department is the same as for the FIFO method:

| | |
|---|---|
| Units in beginning work in process | 4,000 |
| Units started and completed: | |
| (12,000 − 2,000 **or** 14,000 − 4,000) | 10,000 |
| Units in ending work in process | 2,000 |
| Total units | 16,000 |

**Step 2: Calculate Equivalent Units.** The weighted average method computes unit costs by aggregating costs to date (for the completed units and ending work in process) and dividing these by work done to date. Thus, to obtain the equivalent units of work done to date on the completed units and

ending work in process, we need only consider the 14,000 units completed (4,000 + 10,000) and the 2,000 units in ending work in process. For our example, we would have the following calculation:

| | Materials | Conversion |
|---|---|---|
| Units completed: 14,000 × 100% | 14,000 | 14,000 |
| Ending inventory: | | |
| 2,000 × 100% | 2,000 | |
| 2,000 × 30% | | 600 |
| Equivalent units of work done to date | 16,000 | 14,600 |

**Step 3: Compute Unit Costs.** The unit costs for materials and conversion costs are calculated from the total costs and the equivalent units. The costs for which the Cutting Department will be held accountable are:

| Costs Charged to Dept. | Materials | Conversion | Total |
|---|---|---|---|
| Beginning inventory | $ 400,000 | $ 80,000 | $ 480,000 |
| Current month | 1,200,000 | 650,000 | 1,850,000 |
| Total costs | $ 1,600,000 | $ 730,000 | $ 2,330,000 |

We calculate unit costs by using the equivalent units from above and dividing them into the total costs:

**Unit Costs for May:**

Unit cost for materials   = $1,600,000/16,000 = $100

Unit cost for conversion = $730,000/14,600   = $50

These unit costs are identical to those calculated using the FIFO cost method because April's unit costs were the same as those for May. Usually, some difference will occur in the numbers but generally not a significant one.

**Step 4: Distribute Total Costs to Units.** The distribution of costs using the unit costs from Step 3 is as follows:

| Costs Accounted For: | Materials | Conversion | Total |
|---|---|---|---|
| Completed and transferred to Sewing: | | | |
| Units | 14,000 | 14,000 | |
| Multiplied by cost per unit | $      100 | $      50 | |
| Costs | $1,400,000 | $700,000 | $2,100,000 |
| Work in process, May 31: | | | |
| Equivalent units | 2,000 | 600 | |
| Multiplied by cost per unit | $      100 | $      50 | |
| Costs | $ 200,000 | $ 30,000 | $ 230,000 |
| Total costs accounted for | $1,600,000 | $730,000 | $2,330,000 |

**Step 5: Reconcile the Costs.** As shown in Step 3, the total costs charged to the Cutting Department are $2,330,000. After distributing the costs to the units completed and units in the ending inventory, the sum of that distribution should equal $2,330,000. This is confirmed by the total costs accounted for in Step 4.

**SHIRTS UNLIMITED**
**Cutting Department**
**Cost of Production Report for the Month of May**

| Units: | Physical Units | Materials Equivalent Units | Conversion Equivalent Units |
|---|---|---|---|
| Units completed: | 14,000 | | |
| 14,000 × 100% | | 14,000 | 14,000 |
| Ending work in process: | 2,000 | | |
| 2,000 × 100% | | 2,000 | |
| 2,000 × 30% | | | 600 |
| Total units | 16,000 | | |
| Equivalent units of work to date | | 16,000 | 14,600 |

| Costs Charged to Department: | Materials | Conversion | Total |
|---|---|---|---|
| Prior period costs | $ 400,000 | $ 80,000 | $ 480,000 |
| Current month costs | 1,200,000 | 650,000 | 1,850,000 |
| Total costs | 1,600,000 | 730,000 | 2,330,000 |
| Divided by equivalent units | 16,000 | 14,600 | |
| Cost per unit | $ 100 | $ 50 | |

| Costs Accounted For: | Materials | Conversion | Total |
|---|---|---|---|
| Completed and transferred to Sewing: | | | |
| Units | 14,000 | 14,000 | |
| Times cost per unit | $ 100 | $ 50 | |
| Costs | $ 1,400,000 | $ 700,000 | $ 2,100,000 |
| Work in process, May 31: | | | |
| Equivalent units | 2,000 | 600 | |
| Times cost per unit | $ 100 | $ 50 | |
| Costs | $ 200,000 | $ 30,000 | $ 230,000 |
| Total costs accounted for | $ 1,600,000 | $ 730,000 | $ 2,330,000 |

**FIGURE 5.7**

Cost of Production Report for Cutting Department (Weighted Average Method)

## Cost of Production Report

The five computational steps provide all of the calculations needed to prepare a cost of production report for May. The report prepared under the weighted average cost method appears in Figure 5.7.

## TERMINOLOGY REVIEW

Conversion costs (177)

Cost of production report (185)

Cost overrun (176)

Equivalent unit (180)

First-in, first-out (FIFO) cost method (183)

Hybrid cost system (174)

Job cost system (173)

Job order (175)

Just-in-time (JIT) philosophy (188)

Modified cost system (174)

Operation costing (174)

Process cost system (173)

Production orders (175)

Stage of completion (181)

Weighted average cost method (192)

Work order (175)

## QUESTIONS FOR REVIEW AND DISCUSSION

1. Distinguish between a job cost system and a process cost system as to the timing of sales versus production.

2. What is the focal point for cost accumulation in a process cost system?

3. Distinguish between a modified cost system and a hybrid cost system.

4. What is the purpose of a job, work, or production order?

5. For job cost control purposes, what amounts are compared with actual costs?

6. List the five computational steps necessary to account for costs in a process cost system.

7. Explain how equivalent units are computed under the FIFO method of process costing.

8. How are the unit costs computed under the FIFO method of process costing?

9. Why are equivalent units for materials usually different from equivalent units for conversion costs?

10. What accounting report is the major document for a process cost system?

11. How can one check to ensure that cost distribution to completed units and ending inventory has been done properly?

12. How can management use a cost of production report?

13. Which aspect of determining unit costs in a process cost system is particularly susceptible to manipulation by production managers?

14. Explain how a just-in-time environment can simplify a process cost system.

15. **(Appendix)** What is the distinction between equivalent units under the FIFO method and equivalent units under the weighted average method?

16. **(Appendix)** Under what circumstances will both FIFO and weighted average yield the same equivalent units?

17. **(Appendix)** On a cost of production report, the costs of units completed and transferred out are treated one way under the FIFO method and a different way under the weighted average method. Explain this difference.

## EXERCISES

Service

**5–1.** **Analysis of Job Orders.** Data from three job orders completed by Koniver Upholstering Shop are as follows:

| | Job Orders | | |
| | --- | --- | --- |
| | 163 | 164 | 165 |
| Direct materials | $ 5,600 | $ 3,800 | $ 2,600 |
| Direct labor | 4,500 | 2,700 | 3,000 |
| Applied overhead | 2,400 | 900 | 1,200 |
| Total costs | $ 12,500 | $ 7,400 | $ 6,800 |
| Direct labor hours | 600 | 300 | 400 |
| Number of units | 1,000 | 500 | 200 |

**Required:**

**1.** What was the direct labor rate per hour on each of the orders?

**2.** What was the overhead rate per hour on each of the orders, assuming this rate was based on direct labor hours?

**3.** Compute the total cost per unit for each order.

Service

**5–2.** **Job Cost Control–Labor.** Silber & Son, an engineering consulting firm, has three jobs in process at the end of the year. The following labor cost information is provided:

| Job Number | Original Estimate | Percentage Complete | Labor Costs to Date |
|---|---|---|---|
| 9611 | $12,000 | 20% | $2,525 |
| 9612 | $17,500 | 40% | $6,080 |
| 9613 | $10,800 | 75% | $8,020 |

**Required:**

Determine which of the jobs in process are underbudget and which are overbudget.

Service

**5–3.** **Job Cost Control–Materials & Labor.** Wyncote Air, an air conditioning installation service, has three jobs in process at yearend. The following cost information for parts and labor is provided:

| | Parts | | | Labor | | |
|---|---|---|---|---|---|---|
| Job Number | Original Estimate | Percentage Complete | Cost to Date | Original Estimate | Percentage Complete | Cost to Date |
| 9936 | $ 960 | 60% | $ 600 | $ 800 | 30% | $ 200 |
| 9937 | 380 | 50% | 210 | 950 | 10% | 150 |
| 9938 | 500 | 90% | 440 | 250 | 60% | 180 |

**Required:**

For both parts and labor, determine which of the jobs in process are under budget and which are over budget.

Service

**5–4.** **Physical Flow.** Rolnick's Protective Coating Service specializes in providing protective coating for eyeglasses. The company's work in process inventory in Operation 1 on July 1 was 2,500 units. During July, 72,000 units were completed in Operation 1 and transferred to Operation 2. The ending work in process inventory in Operation 1 was 3,500 units.

**Required:**

**1.** Compute the number of units started during July.

**2.** Compute the number of units started and completed.

**3.** Why is the stage of completion for the work in process inventories irrelevant for these computations?

Service

**5–5.** **Costs of Finished Units and Work in Process.** Henry's Dry Cleaners uses a FIFO process cost system. Its work in process on December 1 consisted of 8,000 garments which were 20 percent complete; $12,800 in processing costs were incurred last month for these garments.

During December, 82,000 garments were started and 78,000 were completed. Processing costs during December amounted to $124,160. The ending work in process was 80 percent complete.

**Required:**

Determine the cost of the finished garments and the cost of the ending work in process.

**5–6.** **Cost of Finished Units and Work in Process.** Rekant Labs performs routine blood testing for local physicians. The chief accountant, Allen Bentsi, has provided data for April as follows:

| Units: | |
|---|---|
| In process, April 1 (40% complete) | 30,000 |
| Started in April | 230,000 |
| In process, April 30 (20% complete) | 40,000 |
| Costs: | |
| In process, April 1 | $45,000 |
| Incurred during April | 375,000 |

**Required:**
1. Compute the cost of finished units.
2. Compute the cost of ending work in process.

**5–7.** **Cost of Completed Units.** Ninablair Products of Wellington, New Zealand, produces a kiwi fruit drink. The units and equivalent units (in liters), as well as unit costs, for the Initial Mix Department are as follows:

| | Materials | Conversion |
|---|---|---|
| Equivalent units in beginning work in process | 6,000 | 1,200 |
| Units started and completed | 40,000 | 40,000 |
| Equivalent units in ending work in process | 3,000 | 1,800 |
| Unit costs | NZ$0.10 | NZ$0.20 |

**Required:**
1. Compute the current period costs for:
   (a) Materials.
   (b) Conversion costs.
2. If the beginning work in process inventory was valued at NZ$12,600, what would be the cost of units completed?

**5–8.** **Equivalent Units.** Irene Carroll Fisheries raises cutthroat trout for local restaurants. The process involves three ponds: raising, growing, and fattening. Fingerlings are grown after hatching in the raising pond. At a specified point, the fingerlings are moved to the growing pond, where they mature. After maturing, the fish are transferred to the fattening pond. The growing pond had 5,000 fingerlings on April 1 that were 10 percent complete for the growing pond. The fish represent materials. During the month, an additional 30,000 fingerlings were put into the pond. By the end of April, 28,000 fish had been moved to the fattening pond. The fingerlings remaining in the growing pond were 30 percent complete.

**Required:**
1. Determine the equivalent units for fingerlings.
2. Determine the equivalent units for conversion costs.

**5–9.** **Unit Cost Computation.** Kloss Equipment, of Oslo, Norway, manufactures ski poles. On November 1, 15,000 poles were in process in Department 1 that were 100 percent complete for materials and 60 percent complete for conversion costs. Materials are added at the beginning of the process. The cost of the beginning work in process inventory (in Norwegian krone) was NKr150,000 for materials and NKr45,000 for conversion costs. In November, 200,000 units were started in process. Materials costs for the month were NKr2,050,000. Conversion costs amounted to NKr3,700,000. On November 30, 30,000 units were in process that were 30 percent complete for conversion costs.

**Required:**
1. Compute the equivalent units and unit cost for materials.
2. Compute the equivalent units and unit cost for conversion costs.
3. How would the computational process in Part (2) change if labor and factory overhead were not incurred at the same rate?

**5–10.** **Conversion Costs.** In Sanderson Corporation, the following information is known about production for October:

| | Units | Conversion Dollars |
|---|---|---|
| Beginning work in process (40% done) | 500 | $ 4,800 |
| October conversion costs | | $350,000 |
| October equivalent units | 20,000 | |
| Units transferred to finished goods | 18,700 | |

**Required:**
1. What was the conversion cost of one unit produced in September?
2. What was the conversion cost of one unit produced in October?
3. Determine the amount of conversion costs in work in process and finished goods at the end of October.

**5–11.** **Conversion Costs.** The Fabrication Department is the first stage of Viness Company's production process. Conversion costs in beginning work in process for this department were 70% complete, and in the ending work in process they were 40% complete. Conversion costs data in the Fabrication Department for January are as follows:

| | Units | Conversion Costs |
|---|---|---|
| Work in process at January 1 | 28,000 | $ 51,000 |
| Units started and costs incurred during January | 153,000 | $293,000 |
| Units completed and transferred to next department during January | 131,000 | |

**Required:**
1. What was the conversion cost of work in process in the Fabrication Department at January 31?
2. What were the conversion costs per equivalent unit last month and this month, respectively?

**5–12.** **Costs for Two Periods.** Broyde & Berger Manufacturers reported the following data on its April cost of production report:

| | Units | Materials Costs | Conversion Costs |
|---|---|---|---|
| Beginning work in process | 13,000 | $ 23,000 | $ 32,000 |
| Units started | 50,000 | | |
| Ending work in process | 9,000 | | |
| April production costs | | $110,000 | $295,000 |

All materials are added at the beginning of the process. Both the beginning and ending work in process were 60 percent complete as to conversion costs.

**Required:**
1. What were the costs of producing one unit in both March and April?
2. What costs were transferred to cost of goods manufactured for April?

**5–13.  Distribution of Total Cost and Ethics.** There were 5,000 units in process in the Cutting Department of Allen & Marcus, Inc. at the beginning of February. These units had materials and conversion costs of $48,000 and were 60 percent complete for conversion costs. Materials are added at the beginning of the process. During February, 60,000 units were started. The ending inventory for the month totaled 8,000 units, 25 percent complete for conversion costs. The unit cost calculation shows $4 for materials and $8 for conversion costs.

**Required:**
1. Compute the cost of units completed and transferred to the next department.
2. Compute the cost of units in the ending inventory for the month.
3. Why might the production manager wish to inflate the estimate of the degree of completion of the ending inventory from 25 percent to 50 percent? Support your answer with computations.

**5–14.  Cost of Production Report.** Spitalny Chicken Farms raises chicks to the egg-laying stage and then moves the hens to the laying sheds. Information about the Chick Raising Operation for March is:
    **(a)**  Beginning inventory of chicks is 12,000, 100 percent complete for chicks and 20 percent for raising costs.
    **(b)**  Beginning inventory costs are $12,960 for chicks and $1,153 for raising costs.
    **(c)**  Chicks added during March totaled 20,000.
    **(d)**  Costs incurred during the month are $20,000 for chicks and $12,180 for raising costs.
    **(e)**  Ending inventory at March 31, consisted of 2,000 chicks, 100 percent complete for chicks and 70 percent for raising costs.

**Required:**
Prepare a cost of production report for the Chick Raising Operation for March.

Service

**5–15.  Unit Costs in a Bank.** Chittenden Bank of Columbus, Ohio, processes checks in its Check Clearing Department. No materials costs are incurred in this department. On June 1, 4,000 checks in process were 25 percent complete with an associated processing cost of $200. During June, 100,000 checks were started in process. By the end of June, 70,000 checks had been started and completed. The direct processing costs in June amounted to $18,000. On June 30, the checks in process were one-third complete.

**Required:**
Calculate equivalent units and the unit cost of work done during June.

Service

**5–16.  Equivalent Units (Appendix).** Schroeder's Photo Lab began the month with 6,000 items in inventory, which averaged 50 percent complete for materials and 40 percent complete for conversion costs. At the end of the month, there were 7,000 items in inventory, which averaged 60 percent complete for materials and 30 percent complete for conversion costs. During the month, 65,000 items were completed.

**Required:**
1. Using the FIFO method, determine the appropriate numbers of equivalent units needed to compute unit costs for materials and for conversion costs.
2. Using the weighted average method, determine the appropriate numbers of equivalent units needed to compute unit costs for materials and for conversion costs.

**5–17.** **Cost Distribution.** Red, Inc. manufactures a vitamin product. On July 1, it had 8,000 units in process that were 25 percent complete for conversion costs. Materials (a coating) are added at the end of the process. The cost of the beginning work in process was $1,800. July conversion costs were $36,000, and the materials costs were $17,000. Red, Inc. started and completed 60,000 units in July. The work in process inventory on July 31 of 10,000 units was 60 percent complete.

**Required:**

**1.** What was the total cost of work transferred to the finished goods inventory in July?

**2.** Determine the cost of work in process inventory on July 31.

**5–18.** **Cost Distribution. (Appendix).**

**Required:**

**1.** Work Exercise 5-17 using the weighted-average cost method.

**2.** Under what circumstances would the conversion cost per unit be identical to that computed by the FIFO method? Explain.

**5–19.** **Conversion Costs—Weighted Average Cost Method (Appendix).** Uncle Abe's Vineyards grows grapes; and after sorting and crating them, it sells the crates of grapes to S&M Winery ("We whip 'em till they wine."). On December 1, Uncle Abe's Vineyards had 10,000 pounds of grapes that were 40 percent complete for conversion costs. The conversion costs in the beginning work in process inventory were $20,000. In December, 150,000 pounds of grapes were started in process. Conversion costs in December amounted to $790,000. On December 31, 20,000 pounds of grapes were 40 percent complete for conversion costs.

**Required:**

**1.** Compute the equivalent units (pounds).

**2.** Determine the conversion costs per pound.

Service

**5–20.** **Unit Costs—FIFO and Weighted Average (Appendix).** Craig's Diaper Service, located in a medium-sized city in California, is the lone remaining company that cleans cloth diapers in that city. The company currently uses a FIFO method of process costing and has arrived at a unit cost of $0.65. Beth Intro, the owner, wonders what the unit cost would be with the weighted average method. He has obtained the following information from his accountant:

| | |
|---|---|
| Equivalent units for the weighted average method | 5,600 |
| Equivalent units for FIFO method | 5,000 |
| Costs in beginning work in process | $800 |

**Required:**

Compute the unit cost for the weighted average method.

**5–21.** **Cost Distribution—Weighted Average Cost Method (Appendix).** AKC Beef Processing Company ("Let us meat your needs.") had work in process at the beginning and end of 2007 as follows:

| | Percentage of Completion | |
|---|---|---|
| | Direct Materials | Processing Costs |
| January 1, 2007 – 3,000 pounds | 40% | 10% |
| December 31, 2007 – 2,000 pounds | 80% | 40% |

The company completed 41,000 pounds of finished products during 2007. Costs incurred during 2007 were: direct materials, $242,600; processing costs, $456,200. Work in process at January 1, 2007 was carried at a cost of $16,600 (direct materials, $13,000; processing costs, $8,900).

**Required:**
1. Compute the cost of ending work in process using the **weighted-average** method.
2. Compute the cost of finished products using the **weighted-average** method.

Service

**5–22. Equivalent Units with Incomplete Data.** Calculate the equivalent units for the period with respect to  for each of the following independent situations.

**(a)** Dovber Mufflers operates a nationwide chain of muffler installation shops. It had 5,000 units (mufflers) in process on April 1 which were 60 percent complete for conversion costs. Materials are added at the beginning of the installation process, and conversion costs are added uniformly throughout the process. On April 30, the in-process work consisted of 8,000 units that had 25 percent of the work completed. There were 83,000 equivalent units of output for the period with respect to *materials*.

**(b)** Weisman Oil Change & Lube operates throughout the country. At the beginning of July, 12,000 units (cars) were in process, 90 percent complete for materials and 70 percent complete for conversion costs. On July 31, the in-process work was 10,000 units, which were 50 percent complete for materials and 40 percent complete for conversion costs. There were 176,200 equivalent units of output for the period with respect to *materials*.

**5–23. Flow of Costs.** Burmenko Paper Company manufactures paper from pine logs in a continuous process. Its operations are divided into three activity centers: Stripping, Mixing, and Pressing. The Stripping Center strips the bark off the log, and chips the log into small pieces. The Mixing Center mixes the chips with chemicals in a vat. The Pressing Center presses the chemically dissolved pulp into paper.

The process does not change, and the company's operations move at a constant speed so that beginning and ending inventories are always in the same amount and at the same stage of completion. For this reason, costs are transferred out of work in process inventories by the end of each period.

The company completed the following transactions during one week in August:

**(a)** Purchased on credit three car load lots of logs for $2,700 and one tank car of chemicals for $1,000.

**(b)** Placed two car loads of logs and half of the chemicals into process.

**(c)** Labor for the week was as follows:

| | |
|---|---|
| Stripping Center | $1,500 |
| Mixing Center | 700 |
| Pressing Center | 900 |
| Factory indirect labor | 800 |

**(d)** Manufacturing overhead (other than indirect labor) was as follows:

| | |
|---|---|
| Depreciation | $ 400 |
| Machinery repairs | 100 |
| Power | 100 |
| Supplies | 50 |
| Taxes | 100 |

**(e)** The company applies manufacturing overhead to departments on the basis of 50 percent of direct labor costs.

**Required:**

Show the flow of costs for each of the above transactions using T-accounts. Separate work in process accounts exist for each activity center.

**5–24.  Total Costs—FIFO and Weighted Average (Appendix).** Lefkove, Inc. manufactures staplers. Materials are added at the beginning of the process; conversion costs are incurred uniformly. 6,000 staplers were in beginning work in process. These units were 65% complete. During the period, the company began working on an additional 87,000 staplers, and finished the period with 9,000 staplers that were 30% complete in ending work in process.

Costs attached to beginning inventory were $7,500 for materials and $9,500 for conversion costs. Costs added during the period were $74,000 for materials and $22,000 for conversion.

**Required:**

1. Compute the cost of finished products and the cost of ending work in process using the **FIFO** method.
2. Compute the cost of finished products and the cost of ending work in process using the **weighted-average** method.

# PROBLEMS

Service

**5–25.  Job Cost Control.** Pollack & Son Photography Studio has four jobs in process at the end of the year. The following cost information for materials and conversion costs is provided:

| Job Number | Materials | | | Conversion Costs | | |
|---|---|---|---|---|---|---|
| | Original Estimate | Percentage Complete | Cost to Date | Original Estimate | Percentage Complete | Cost to Date |
| K98 | $120 | 10% | $20 | $550 | 20% | $125 |
| L76 | $100 | 75% | $65 | $850 | 80% | $655 |
| T45 | $180 | 50% | $95 | $950 | 70% | $620 |
| P90 | $145 | 20% | $30 | $600 | 25% | $185 |

**Required:**

1. For both materials and conversion costs, determine which of the jobs in process are underbudget and which are overbudget.
2. Does any job have a total cost overrun? Identify.

**5–26.  Cost Flows—Multiple Departments.** Toy trains are manufactured in three operations by David Jared Products, Inc. No work in process existed on August 1 in any of the three operations, but 10,000 units were in process in each operation at the end of August. All costs within each department, including materials, are added uniformly throughout the department's production process. The percentage of the work in process that was completed in each operation at August 31 is as follows:

| | |
|---|---|
| Department 1 | 40% |
| Department 2 | 60% |
| Department 3 | 20% |

Costs in the three departments for August were as follows:

| | Departments | | |
|---|---|---|---|
| | 1 | 2 | 3 |
| Materials | $ 94,000 | $ 0 | $ 0 |
| Labor | 47,000 | 30,000 | 14,400 |
| Overhead applied | 47,000 | 21,600 | 7,200 |
| Total | $188,000 | $51,600 | $21,600 |

During August, 100,000 units were started in process in Department 1.

**Required:**
1. For each department, compute the unit cost of work completed in that department and the cumulative unit cost of work done (i.e., including preceding departments' costs).
2. Using T-accounts for each department, trace the flow of costs through the three departments and into finished goods inventory.
3. Assume that 50,000 units were sold during the month. What amount will appear in the Cost of Goods Sold account?

**5–27.** **Cost Distribution and Cost Flows.** Bao Brothers is a manufacturer of men's neckties in Singapore. Materials are added to production at the beginning of the manufacturing process, and factory overhead is applied to each unit at the rate of 60 percent of direct labor costs. Its operations for June show the following ending inventories of work in process and finished goods as reflected in the general ledger:

| | Units | Costs |
|---|---|---|
| Work in process (50% complete for labor and overhead) | 300,000 | S$870,000 |
| Finished goods | 200,000 | 900,000 |

No finished goods inventory existed on June 1. The operating data for the month are:

| | | Costs | |
|---|---|---|---|
| | Units | Materials | Labor |
| Work in process, June 1 | | | |
| (80% complete for labor and overhead) | 200,000 | S$200,000 | S$315,000 |
| Units started during June | 1,000,000 | | |
| June's materials costs | | 1,300,000 | |
| June's labor costs | | | 1,780,000 |
| Units completed | | 900,000 | |

**Required:**
1. Calculate the unit costs for June for:
   (a) Materials
   (b) Labor
   (c) Overhead
2. Determine the cost of completed units and ending work in process.
3. Using T-accounts, prepare a summary of cost flows from Work in Process Inventory through Finished Goods Inventory to Cost of Goods Sold.

Service

**5–28.    Cost of Production Report and Ethics.** The Lipseyville Municipality uses a process cost system to compute water purification costs. All materials (chemicals) are added at the beginning of the purification process. Data for the month of May are given as follows (units are kiloliters of water):

|  | Units |
| --- | --- |
| Work in process, May 1 | 5,000 |
| Units started in process. | 120,000 |

|  | Costs |
| --- | --- |
| Work in process, May 1: |  |
|    Materials. | $    15,000 |
|    Labor and overhead | 2,500 |
| May's costs: |  |
|    Materials. | $ 360,000 |
|    Labor and overhead | 232,000 |

The beginning work in process was 20 percent complete for labor and overhead. During the month, 115,000 units were completed; and 10,000 units that were 20 percent complete as to labor and overhead were in process at May 31.

**Required:**

**1.** Prepare a cost of production report for the month of May.
**2.** Explain how management might use this cost of production report.
**3.** What might motivate the production manager to inflate the estimate of the degree of completion of the ending work in process from 20 percent to 40 percent? Support your answer with computations.

**5–29.    Cost of Production Report.** McDuffy Robotics, a subsidiary of U.S.-based International Robotics located in Dublin, Ireland, manufactures a small robot which looks like a leprechaun and can be moved by remote control. It can be used as a novelty to serve food and drinks to guests; and, with a special attachment, it can vacuum the carpet.

The materials are all added at the beginning of the Assembly Operation (the first operation). Labor and overhead are added during the month. Data for the month of July in the Assembly Operation are as follows:

|  | Units: |
| --- | --- |
| Work in process, July 1 | 35,000 |
| Units started in process | 250,000 |

|  | Costs (in U.S. dollars) |
| --- | --- |
| Work in process, July 1: |  |
|    Materials | $    240,000 |
|    Labor and overhead | 80,000 |
| July costs: |  |
|    Materials | $3,500,000 |
|    Labor and overhead | 1,457,280 |

The inventory of work in process on July 1 was complete as to materials but only one-fourth complete as to labor and overhead. On July 31, the inventory consisted of 20,000 units that were 40 percent complete with respect to labor and overhead.

**Required:**

1. Prepare a cost of production report for the Assembly Operation for the month of July.
2. Explain how management could use this report.

Service

**5–30.  Explanations About a Cost of Production Report.** Estreicher's Painting Service receives a continuous flow of clear light bulbs from various manufacturers who want their bulbs painted—typically yellow or black. A partial production report for the month of May is as follows for Department 1 (units are packages of eight bulbs):

| Physical units: | |
|---|---|
| Work in process, May 1 (40% complete) | 500 |
| Started and completed | 1,700 |
| Work in process, May 31 (50% complete) | 300 |
| Total units | 2,500 |
| **Costs charged to department:** | |
| Work in process, May 1 | $ 800.00 |
| Production costs, May | 9,020.00 |
| Total costs charged | $9,820.00 |
| **Costs accounted for:** | |
| Transferred to Department 2: | |
| Work in process, May 1 | $ 800.00 |
| Cost to complete work in process, May 1 | 1,258.60 |
| Started and completed | 7,132.09 |
| | $9,190.69 |
| Work in process, May 31 | 629.30 |
| Total costs accounted for | $9,819.99* |

\* Difference caused by rounding.

**Required:**

1. Explain what the above partial cost of production report shows about the quantity flow and the cost flow.
2. Explain why equivalent units are preferred to total units produced in determining costs of units completed and units in ending inventory.
3. What additional information can this report give a manager?
4. Calculate how many units were completed during the month of May.

Service

**5–31.  Cost Accountability—Two Months.** Tinman Alarm Systems installs car alarms for several automobile manufacturers. The data for October and November are:

| | October | November |
|---|---|---|
| Units in beginning work in process | 0 | 600 |
| Units started during month | 12,400 | 13,100 |
| Units completed | 11,800 | 13,300 |
| Costs incurred: | | |
| Materials | $ 258,640 | $ 271,760 |
| Labor and overhead | $ 526,860 | $ 569,770 |
| Units in ending work in process | 600 | 400 |
| Stage of completion for ending work in process: | | |
| Materials | 90 % | 50 % |
| Labor and Overhead | 60 % | 30 % |

**Required:**

1. Prepare a cost of production report for October. Round unit costs to five decimal places and total dollars to the nearest dollar.

2. Prepare a cost of production report for November. Round unit costs to five decimal places and total dollars to the nearest dollar.

Service

**5–32.** **Cost Accountability—Two Months (Appendix).** Work Problem 5–31 using the weighted average cost method.

**5–33.** **A Comparison of Actual and Estimated Unit Cost.** Owen Tu ("The Count") has estimated unit costs at various production stages in manufacturing baseballs. The unit costs of work done in Operation 1, according to budget estimates, should be $2.50, consisting of a unit cost of $1.60 for materials and a unit cost of $0.90 for labor and overhead. All materials are added at the beginning of the operation, and labor and overhead are added as the work progresses. Cost and production data for Operation 1 are as follows for the month of October:

| Quantities: | | |
|---|---:|---:|
| Units in work in process, October 1 (40% complete) | | 10,000 |
| Units started in production | | 150,000 |
| Units in work in process, October 31 (20% complete) | | 5,000 |
| *Costs charged to operation:* | | |
| Work in process, October 1: | | |
| Materials | $ 16,000 | |
| Labor and overhead | 5,400 | $ 21,400 |
| October's costs: | | |
| Materials | $240,000 | |
| Labor and overhead | 182,400 | 422,400 |
| Total costs charged | | $443,800 |

**Required:**

1. Determine unit costs for materials and for conversion costs.

2. Compare the actual unit costs with the estimated unit costs. Identify separately any variance of materials cost and any variance of conversion cost.

**5–34.** **Finished Goods and Work in Process Costs—Weighted Average (Appendix).** The following information is available for the Assembly Department of Merrens Enterprises for August:

| | Units | Costs |
|---|---:|---:|
| Work in process, August 1 (70% complete) | 5,000 | |
| Direct materials | | $ 6,000 |
| Direct labor | | 3,000 |
| Manufacturing overhead | | 4,000 |
| Total work in process, August 1 | | $13,000 |
| Started in production during August | 20,000 | |
| Costs added: | | |
| Direct materials | | $29,000 |
| Direct labor | | 8,000 |
| Manufacturing overhead | | 10,000 |
| Total costs added during August | | $47,000 |
| Work in process, August 31 (80% complete) | 3,000 | |

Materials are added at the beginning of the process.

**Required:**
1. Compute the total cost of goods transferred out using the weighted average method.
2. Compute the total cost of ending work in process using the weighted average method.

**5–35.** **Work in Process Costs—FIFO and Weighted Average (Appendix).** The following data pertain to the Claims Processing Department of Smilgoff Insurance Company, which does not incur any direct materials costs:

| | |
|---|---:|
| Work in process, May 1: | |
| Units (claims) | 3,200 |
| Conversion costs (10% complete) | $    6,900 |
| Units (claims) started in May | 13,500 |
| May's conversion costs | $ 285,000 |
| Work in process, May 31: | |
| Units (claims) | 1,900 |
| Stage of completion for conversion costs | 60% |

**Required:**
1. Using the FIFO method, compute the cost of the May 31 work in process.
2. Using the weighted average method, compute the cost of the May 31 work in process.

**5–36.** **Cost of Production Report—Several Months.** Travis Industries is a bottling company that purchases orange juice from growers in Florida and bottles the juice in one-gallon plastic containers for sale to grocery stores. Only in its second year of operations, the company's accounting system is evolving and has not been fully formalized. A chief accountant, Laura Kahn, has been hired to bring order to the paper shuffling. In the process, Kahn has gathered data to prepare cost of production reports for Activity Center A for the first three months of the current fiscal year (April, May, and June). This information is as follows:

| | April | May | June |
|---|---|---|---|
| Gallons: | | | |
| Beginning inventory | 10,000 | ? | ? |
| Started in production | 80,000 | 65,000 | 70,000 |
| Completed | 70,000 | 60,000 | ? |
| Ending inventory | ? | ? | 20,000 |
| Stage of completion: | | | |
| Beginning inventory | 60% | 30% | 70% |
| Ending inventory | 30% | 70% | 40% |
| Cost data: | | | |
| Beginning inventory: | | | |
| Materials | $10,000 | ? | ? |
| Converstion costs | 20,000 | ? | ? |
| Current period: | | | |
| Materials | $80,000 | $66,000 | $70,000 |
| Converstioon costs | 170,000 | 142,000 | 156,000 |

Materials (orange juice) are added at the beginning of Activity Center A. Conversion costs flow uniformly throughout the process.

**Required:**
1. Compute the physical flows of units (gallons) for each of the three months.
2. Prepare a cost of production report for each of the three months. Round unit costs to four decimal places and total dollars to the nearest dollar.
3. Analyze the cost of production reports for each month, and comment on production stability and unit costs for materials and conversion costs.

**5–37.** **Cost Flows Through T-Accounts.** Niren Manufacturing Company produces a single product. Its operations are a continuous process through two activity centers: Machining and Finishing. Materials are added at the start of production in each department. For November, the following transactions took place:

**(a)** Purchased materials on credit costing $435,400.

**(b)** Started 80,000 units in production in the Machining Center. The direct materials cost $240,000, and indirect materials cost $8,100. The Machining Center had no beginning work in process inventory.

**(c)** Paid the following salaries and wages for the month:

| | Machining | Finishing |
|---|---|---|
| Direct labor | $ 140,000 | $ 141,500 |
| Factory indirect labor | 30,000 | 6,700 |

**(d)** Applied factory overhead at 100 percent of direct labor cost in Machining and at 20 percent of direct labor cost in Finishing.

**(e)** Incurred actual factory overhead costs for Machining, other than indirect materials and indirect labor, of $100,000.

**(f)** Completed 60,000 units in Machining and transferred them to Finishing. The units remaining in Machining were 100 percent complete for materials and 50 percent complete for conversion costs.

**(g)** Added $88,500 of direct materials costs in Finishing. Indirect materials were $2,400. No beginning inventory was in Finishing on November 1.

**(h)** Incurred actual factory overhead costs for Finishing, other than indirect materials and indirect labor, totaling $16,600.

**Required:**

Using T-accounts, trace the costs reflected in the transactions through the appropriate accounts.

**5–38.** **Analysis of a Work in Process Account.** Garber Pharmaceutical Company manufactures a tablet for allergy sufferers. All ingredients are added at the beginning of the Blending Operation. Conversion costs flow uniformly throughout the process. Tableting and Coating are operations downstream from Blending. Information on the Blending Operation for October is as follows:

| Work in Process—Blending Operation | | | |
|---|---|---|---|
| October 1, balance (100,000 units, 40% complete for conversion costs) | $ 151,760 | Completed and transferred to Tableting: | |
| | | | Units – ? |
| | | | Costs – ? |
| Direct materials added (1,000,000 units) | $1,310,000 | | |
| Direct labor costs | ? | | |
| Factory overhead (Applied at 180% of direct labor cost) | $ 396,000 | | |
| October 31, balance (200,000 units, 70% complete for conversion costs) | ? | | |

The October 1 balance consists of the following cost elements:

| | |
|---|---:|
| Direct materials | $128,000 |
| Direct labor | 8,800 |
| Factory overhead | 14,960 |
| Total costs | $151,760 |

**Required:**

1. Compute the amount of direct labor cost for the period.
2. Calculate the unit costs for direct materials, direct labor, and factory overhead for the current month (October). Direct labor and factory overhead should be separate; do not combine them into one figure.
3. Calculate the unit costs for direct materials, direct labor, and factory overhead in the inventory at the beginning of October.
4. Compare the unit costs computed in Parts (2) and (3). Explain what information this comparison gives to a manager.

**5–39.** **Analysis of a Work in Process Account (Appendix).** Work Problem 5-38 using the weighted average cost method.

Service

**5–40.** **Work in Process—FIFO and Weighted Average (Appendix).** The Division of Corporate Taxation processes corporate tax returns for a state located in the northeastern United States. Processing costs for this agency were 70 percent complete as to the beginning work in process and 60 percent complete as to the ending work in process. Information on processing costs for the month of August is as follows:

| | Number of Returns | Processing Costs |
|---|---:|---:|
| Work in process at August 1 | 8,000 | $ 72,000 |
| Returns started and costs incurred during August | 45,000 | $666,000 |
| Returns completed during August | 49,000 | |

**Required:**

1. Using the FIFO method, what amount of processing cost was in work in process at August 31?
2. Using the weighted average method, what amount of processing cost was in work in process at August 31?

Service

**5–41.** **Cost Distribution (Appendix).** Martino's Mailing Service (MMS) does mass mailings for hundreds of companies throughout the country. After receiving the mailing contents and computerized mailing lists, MMS staff members prepare envelopes, stuff them, and mail them. MMS uses a weighted average process cost system.

October 2004 began with 3,700 pieces of mail in process, which were 70 percent complete as to materials (envelopes, labels, etc.) and 40 percent complete as to conversion costs. During October, 44,800 pieces were started. The ending work in process consisted of 5,200 pieces which were 30 percent complete as to materials and 10 percent complete as to conversion costs. The following cost information is available:

| | Beginning Work in Process | Costs Added in October |
|---|:---:|:---:|
| Materials | $1,250 | $14,220 |
| Labor | 9,760 | 99,750 |
| Overhead | 7,000 | 61,140 |

**Required:**

1. Compute the cost of pieces finished during October.
2. Compute the cost of the October ending work in process.

Service

**5–42.  Cost of Finished Units—FIFO and Weighted Average (Appendix).** The Department of Motor Vehicles processes auto tag applications. All materials costs (i.e., tags) are completed when processing begins. The following information was obtained by the controller, Arthur Kurtz, for October:

- The October 1 work in process had 5,000 applications (40 percent completed) and the following costs:

| | |
|---|---|
| Direct materials | $ 2,700 |
| Direct labor | 16,880 |
| Overhead | 31,400 |

- During October, 11,000 applications were completed; the following costs were incurred:

| | |
|---|---|
| Direct materials | $ 5,200 |
| Direct labor | 95,775 |
| Overhead | 159,925 |

- On October 31, there were 2,400 partially processed applications on hand (80 percent completed).

**Required:**

1. Using the FIFO method, determine the cost of completed applications.
2. Using the weighted average method, determine the cost of completed applications.

Service

**5–43.  Converting from Weighted Average to FIFO (Appendix).** Goldie's Package Delivery Service uses weighted average process costing to determine the cost of processing (receiving, sorting, etc.) packages. The following information has been obtained for June:

| | No. of Units (Packages) | Processing Costs |
|---|---|---|
| Work in process, June 1 (40% complete) | 11,000 | $ 9,000 |
| Units started in June | 100,000 | ? |
| Units completed during June | 88,000 | |

At June 30, the controller, Josh Pearl, determined that packages still in process were 70 percent complete with respect to processing. This ending work in process was assigned a cost of $21,735.

**Required:**

1. Compute the processing costs incurred during June.
2. Suppose that the FIFO method had been used. Compute the costs of the ending work in process and the completed units.

# Case 5A—Lerman Hi-Tech Products

Lerman Hi-Tech Products manufactures a product that is accounted for under a process cost system in the Assembly and Finishing departments. Recently, the production superintendent, Ed Irving, was reviewing the April cost of production reports for the two departments. His intuition suggested something was wrong with the reports. He asked the departmental managers if they had reviewed the reports. Both indicated that they had. However, both managers acknowledged that the reports must be in error because they did not agree with the operating facts. One manager, Joyce Bella, suggested the Accounting Department had screwed up again.

You have been asked to review the departmental cost of production report for the Assembly department and determine what adjustments should be made. You have the following information available to you for the Assembly department:

| Units: | |
| --- | --- |
| Beginning inventory | 10,000 |
| Units started | 20,000 |
| Units completed and transferred | 26,000 |
| Ending inventory | 4,000 |
| Costs: | |
| Materials costs | $22,000 |
| Labor costs | 8,000 |

In the Assembly Department, materials are added at the beginning of the process, and conversion costs enter evenly throughout the operation. Beginning work in process was 50 percent complete for conversion costs. Beginning inventories include $6,000 for materials and $2,000 for conversion costs. Overhead is applied at the rate of 50 percent of labor dollars. Ending inventory was 40 percent completed. The FIFO method is used.

Excerpts from the Assembly Department's cost of production report are as follows:

| | | |
| --- | --- | --- |
| Cost of goods completed (26,000 × $1.2667) | | $32,934 |
| Ending inventory: | | |
| Materials (4,000 × $.9333) | $3,733 | |
| Conversion costs (4,000 × $.3333) | 1,333 | 5,066 |
| Total costs accounted for | | $38,000 |

| Additional Computations | Materials | Conversion Cost |
| --- | --- | --- |
| costs in process, beginning | $ 6,000 | $ 2,000 |
| Current period costs | 22,000 | 12,000 |
| | $28,000 | $14,000 |
| Computation of equivalent units: | | |
| Units completed | 26,000 | 26,000 |
| Ending inventory | 4,000 | 4,000 |
| Equivalent units | 30,000 | 30,000 |
| Equivalent unit cost | $0.9333 | $0.3333 |

**Required:**
Prepare a corrected cost of production report for the Assembly Department. Identify the errors, if any, in the original cost of production report.

Service

# CASE 5B—GULF COAST PIPELINES

Gulf Coast Pipelines, Inc. is a liquid petroleum pipeline transportation company. The line running from Corpus Christi to Kansas City is a 30-inch, high pressure line which moves product at an average of 8 miles per hour. A filled line contains 28 million barrels of product which travel an average 192 miles per day. The line speed can be increased safely to about 280 miles per day or slowed to almost a stop. The line can be filled to capacity or be partially empty. Over certain segments, the line moves faster than elsewhere as more product is placed in and taken out. The line carries various products including crude oil of varying weights, home heating oil, and numerous other petroleum products.

As a transportation company, Gulf Coast Pipelines does not own the products transported. Instead, it is paid a fee for its services based on moving 10,000 barrels (420,000 gallons) of product one mile. The variable cost of running the line is for the 30 pumping stations along the line: the higher the traffic, the higher the fuel cost for pumping. The other cost of running the line is overhead cost, which relates to line maintenance. One unit is considered to be moving 10,000 barrels of product one mile.

On April 1, the Corpus Christi to Kansas City line had 1.44 million units in process (18 million barrels that were to be transported an average of 800 miles), which were 60 percent complete. During the month, the line completed 12 million units of delivered product and had ending units in process of two million units (20 million barrels to be transported 1,000 miles) that were 40 percent complete. The beginning units in transit had accumulated costs of $8,800,000 of which $2,400,000 were variable costs. During the month, the Corpus Christi to Kansas City line had $33,420,800 in variable costs and $81,168,800 in fixed costs. The completed deliveries were billed at $134,400,000 for services.

**Required:**

1. What is the nature of the costs incurred as to direct materials, direct labor, and variable or fixed overhead?

2. Why should this application be considered for a modified process cost system?

3. Compute the equivalent units of production for the Corpus Christi to Kansas City line. (Round to four places, if needed.)

4. Compute a cost per unit of output for variable and fixed costs.

5. What were the profits before administrative expenses and taxes during April?

6. What were the costs of the units in transit on April 30?

# ACTIVITY-BASED COSTING AND JUST-IN-TIME COSTING

## LEARNING OBJECTIVES

1. Explain the interrelationships among cost drivers, activities, and products in an activity-based cost system.
2. Describe the key components and cost flows in an activity-based cost system.
3. Distinguish between the two stages of cost allocation in an activity-based cost system.
4. Apply activity-based costing in a manufacturing setting.
5. Understand how activity-based costing is extended to nonmanufacturing settings.
6. Relate activity-based management to activity-based costing.
7. Describe the key elements of a just-in-time cost system.

## Testing . . . Testing

*Cortell Laboratories was formed in 1989 and began its operations in testing various electrical characteristics of integrated circuits sent to it by manufacturers on the west coast. Cortell focused on a strategy of providing quicker turnaround times than currently offered by manufacturers' labs or other outside labs. The strategy was successful and had been marketed well. Within ten years, Cortell had annual revenues of over $30 million. Profit and cash flow, also highly positive, allowed Cortell to self-fund all expansion.*

*In 2002, Cortell began offering tests for transformers. Within one year, transformer testing was so successful that the lab was now running on three full shifts. In the midst of all this success, Harriet Cortell, the company president, is now faced with a dilemma. The marketing manager, Beth Jacobs, has come to her and argued that testing transformers is much more profitable than testing integrated circuits, and therefore, the lab should concentrate more of its resources on marketing and performing transformer tests. To support her argument, Jacobs compiled costs and profit margins for each testing service. These figures showed that transformer testing was over 40 percent more profitable than testing integrated circuits. Cortell looked at the overhead allocated to the two types of tests and could hardly believe that each test was assigned the same amount of overhead per test. She knew that testing transformers involved more job orders and required more setups than testing integrated circuits. "Our costing system is not reflecting the complexity of these tests," claimed Cortell.*

*Several months earlier, Cortell had heard about an activity-based cost approach for assigning overhead costs. She immediately contacted the controller, Bill Kelector, and asked him to do an activity-based cost analysis.*

TWO MAJOR FORCES have combined to put great pressure on managerial accountants like Bill Kelector to provide improved cost information about their firms' products and services. These are global competition and automation in the workplace.

1. **Global competitiveness.** Most companies in nearly every industry face increased competition from direct competitors, whether from across the street or halfway around the world. Whether the technology is old (making iron and steel) or new (making high definition televisions), the needs for accurate and relevant product cost data have grown dramatically. Competitiveness also means knowing the costs of product quality, reliable delivery, and waste (unproductive effort). Cost control takes on new meaning if a competitor can sell an item at a price that is 10 percent lower than another company's production cost and still make money on the sale. Increasingly, companies are realizing that traditional volume-based cost systems are not using the "right" variables or collecting cost data in enough detail.

2. **Automation of the workplace.** Dramatic changes in production have also taken place. Another "industrial revolution" is what some people have called it. Computer power has introduced concepts like computer-aided design (CAD), computer-aided manufacturing (CAM), flexible manufacturing systems (FMS), and robotics. Computer power has allowed precise tasks to be programmed and machines to be designed to do those tasks. Likewise, computer power has enabled production managers to coordinate thousands of events, transactions, and possible courses of action. One outcome is a shift from heavy dependence on labor to technology. Direct labor costs were often a major product cost, and labor activity often reflected general activity in the plant. Now, in many companies, direct labor is a minor portion of a product's total cost. Other production costs have grown tremendously because of equipment costs and support

personnel needed to coordinate production. New activity measures are needed to link resources used with production activities. The traditional approach of allocating overhead costs using direct labor hours or direct labor cost is no longer relevant in companies that are highly automated.

Competition and automation have focused attention on getting more accurate, timely, and relevant costs for products and services. The concepts are very simple and have always been at the heart of cost accounting: Link the cost of resources used to the activity using the resources, and link the activity to the product being produced. Traditionally, the activity measure used most often has been a volume measure—direct labor hours (or dollars). In recent years, there has been a recognition that the complexity of production, rather than volume, is the most important determinant of overhead costs. Cost systems known as activity-based costing reflect this new orientation.

This chapter presents the conceptual foundation for activity-based costing as a means of improving the accuracy of assigning costs to cost objectives—primarily to products and services. Many companies that have adopted activity-based cost systems have also instituted just-in-time inventory systems. Later in the chapter, we discuss how adoption of just-in-time inventory systems has affected product costing.

# ACTIVITY-BASED COSTING

Activity-based costing focuses on finding the cost of producing a product or service. In Chapter 2, we introduced cost of goods manufactured and the three traditional groups of costs—direct materials, direct labor, and factory overhead. At one time, direct materials and direct labor were linked with products because of their obvious direct relationships; all other manufacturing costs were traditionally lumped together as overhead. One activity measure, often direct labor, was used to attach all overhead costs to products. Many different overhead costs were combined and included:

1. Plant supervision salaries.
2. Materials handling costs.
3. Plant engineering costs.
4. Setup or changeover costs.
5. Supplies and indirect materials.
6. Depreciation, taxes, and insurance on equipment.
7. Energy and other utility costs.
8. Repair and maintenance costs.

Ideally, every overhead cost item could be traced directly to specific products. This is just not possible. If we produce a million units of different types and sizes of batteries in a factory, can the manager's $100,000 salary be traced to the different batteries? No. Can we link the manager's salary to certain factory activities, then link the activity costs to the different batteries? Yes, but only with careful analysis and application.

## Issues Influencing Cost Management Systems Design

Product costs are so critical to managerial decisions that greater precision and accuracy are needed today than were demanded in the past. Thus, a major effort is under way in many companies to upgrade their cost systems.

## Contemporary Practice 6.1
### "Let Your Fingers Do the Costing"

*A phone company that sells yellow pages had historically sent salespeople to both small and large towns to sell advertising. After an ABC analysis revealed that it was too costly (in relation to the revenue generated) to send salespeople to the small towns, the company switched to phone sales. Another ABC analysis was performed later, and the company concluded that even phone sales were too costly for the amount of revenue generated from the small towns. So the phone company went to direct mail solicitations; and, even though revenues declined for the small towns, the profit margins increased due to the cost reductions.*

Source: Brimson, J. A., and J. Antos, Activity-Based Management for Service Industries, Government Entities, and Nonprofit Entities, *John Wiley & Sons, NY: 1994, p. 325.*

The level of detail that a cost system needs is based on the following considerations:

1. The competitive environment, which will impact the degree of accuracy needed and the toleration of costing errors.
2. The homogeneity or heterogeneity of the products or services.
3. The complexity of the production process.
4. The volumes of each product or service produced.
5. The costs of measuring and collecting activity and cost data.
6. The impacts that more accurate and relevant data will have on managerial behavior.

Detailed cost systems are expensive to design and to operate. Yet the value of better cost information can also be extremely high. One such anecdote relating to this value appears in Contemporary Practice 6.1.

## Definition of Activity-Based Costing

**Activity-based costing (ABC)** is a system of accounting that focuses on activities performed to produce products or services. Activities become the fundamental cost accumulation points. Costs are traced to activities, and activities are traced to products based on each product's use of the activities. We show these relationships for allocating costs in Figure 6.1.

Under activity-based costing, an effort is made to identify and account for as many costs as possible as direct costs of production. Any cost that can reasonably be traced to a particular product or service is treated as a direct cost. For example, under the traditional cost system, the cost of setup time (the factory downtime incurred in converting from producing one product to another) is included in manufacturing overhead and applied to products on the basis of direct labor hours. Under

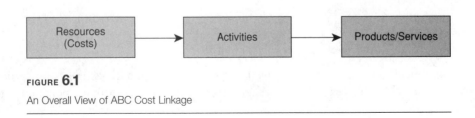

FIGURE **6.1**

An Overall View of ABC Cost Linkage

ABC, setup time might be measured for each product line; and setup costs would be directly assigned to each part or product manufactured.

An ABC system identifies the major activities in a production process, aggregates those activities into activity centers, accumulates costs in activity centers, selects cost drivers that link activities to products, and assigns the costs of activities to products. We show this process in Figure 6.2. An **activity center** is a segment of the organization for which management wants the costs of a set of activities to be reported separately. A mechanism called a **cost driver** is used for linking a given activity's pool of costs. A cost driver is an event, action, or activity that results in cost incurrence. It is any factor that causes costs to change. The basic concept is that cost drivers, such as setup time, measure the amount of resources a specific product uses. A cost function is created from the activity's planned costs and cost driver activity level.

Although not always obvious, several different cost drivers could link an activity's costs and the cost objective. In the materials handling case in Figure 6.2, four possible cost drivers are listed. Assume that *pounds of materials moved* is considered to be the most appropriate cost driver. We therefore divide the planned materials handling costs by the planned pounds to be moved. Cost per pound moved is the cost function. Then, the actual pounds handled in the production of a product times the cost per pound moved is the amount of materials handling costs assigned to that product. Again, the overall process is to identify the best cost driver that links costs and activities and then to use that cost driver to link activities with products (or other cost objectives).

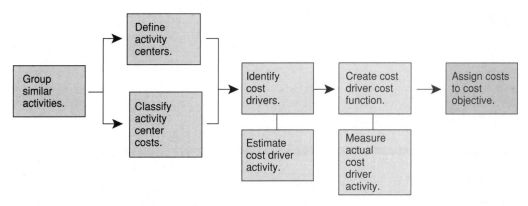

*Example:* Moving and handling materials in the factory:

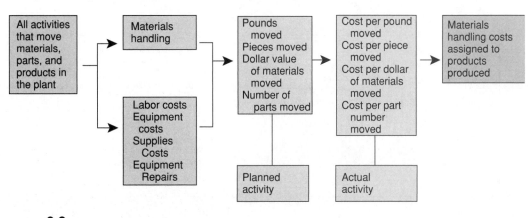

FIGURE **6.2**

An Overall View of ABC Process

## Flow of Costs Under Activity-Based Costing

In applying ABC to a specific organization, we follow five basic steps:

1. Assemble similar actions into activity centers.
2. Classify costs by activity center and by type of expense.
3. Select cost drivers.
4. Calculate a cost function to link costs and cost drivers with resource use.
5. Assign costs to the cost objective—often the product cost.

These steps are consistent with Figure 6.2.

**Step 1: Assemble Similar Actions into Activity Centers.** The number of actions performed in any organization can be quite numerous. Although the ideal is to relate the cost of every action to a cost driver and then to the product, the costs of doing this can far exceed the benefits. Therefore, we combine actions into activity centers. Treating collections of actions as activity centers eliminates the need to measure and track the performance of numerous individual actions and costs.

One meaningful way of grouping actions is to classify them with different levels of activities. A common outline is unit-level activities, batch-level activities, product-level activities, and facility-level activities. Figure 6.3 illustrates the four types. **Unit-level activities** are performed

| Unit-Level Activities | Batch-Level Activities |
|---|---|
| Activities: | Activities: |
|   Assembly |   Batch changeovers (setups) |
|   Stamping |   Materials handling |
|   Machining |   Order processing |
| |   Inspections |
| Resources Used: | Resources Used: |
|   Direct labor |   Labor costs of setups |
|   Direct materials |   Labor costs of materials handling |
|   Supplies |   Labor costs to process orders |
|   Electricity |   Labor costs to inspect |
| Cost Drivers: | Cost Drivers: |
|   Direct labor hours |   Number of batches |
|   Machine hours |   Number of setups |
|   Number of units produced |   Number of orders processed |
| **Product-Level Activities** | **Facility-Level Activities** |
| Activities: | Activities: |
|   Production scheduling |   Plant supervision |
|   Product designing |   Building occupancy |
|   Parts and product testing |   Personnel administration |
|   Special handling and storing | |
| Resources Used: | Resources Used: |
|   Specialized equipment |   Plant depreciation |
|   Labor costs of design |   Insurance and property taxes |
|   Testing facility costs |   Salaries of plant management |
| Cost Drivers: | Cost Drivers: |
|   Number of products |   Number of employees |
|   Number of parts |   Number of units produced |
| |   Labor hours |

**FIGURE 6.3**

Levels of ABC Activity Groups

each time a unit is produced or handled. These are repetitive activities. Direct labor or machining activities are examples. Costs of these activities vary with the number of units produced. **Batch-level activities** are performed each time a batch of goods is produced or handled. Machine setups, order processing, and materials handling are related to batches rather than individual units. The costs of these activities vary according to the number of batches but are common or fixed for all units in the batch. **Product-level activities** are those performed as needed to support the production of each different type of product or service. Maintaining bills of materials and routing information, processing engineering changes, and performing testing routines are examples of activities in this category. **Facility-level activities** are those which simply sustain a facility's general production process. Examples would include plant supervision and building occupancy. These costs are common to a variety of products and are the most difficult to link to product-specific activities. For this reason, many people question whether facility-level costs should be linked to products.

Traditionally, we classify overhead costs as variable or fixed. Relative to volume of outputs, costs of unit-level activities are predominately variable while costs of the other three levels are predominately fixed. However, identifying batch-, product-, and facility-level activity centers helps in selecting cost drivers. Often, the cost perspective changes; many costs that are fixed relative to units of output are now variable relative to the cost driver. This is particularly true for batch- and product-level activities. Costs of facility-level activities remain primarily in the fixed category and are often apportioned or allocated to products in some arbitrary manner.

**Step 2: Classify Costs by Activity Center and by Type of Expense.** Once the actions are grouped into activities, the next step is identifying the costs with the activities. The coding and classifying of cost data at this early point determine the level of detail and the breakdowns of cost data available to management for all cost analysis purposes later. A chart of accounts or a data base classification scheme will identify the type of cost by natural classification: salary, postage, telephone, repair, supplies, etc. A second code will identify the activity center. Often, this is called a cost center. An activity center and a cost center are both commonly defined as the smallest part of an organization for which costs are accumulated. In fact, in most carefully defined cost systems, the terms activity center and cost center can be used interchangeably.

**Step 3: Select Cost Drivers.** Direct costs can be traced immediately to a product without the need for a cost driver. All other costs need links between cost, activity, and product. Cost drivers are the links. A cost driver can link a pool of costs in an activity center to the product. Or a cost driver can link costs in one activity center to activities in another activity center. Multiple layers of activities can exist. One activity relates to another activity, which may relate to still another activity before relationships to products are identified. Figure 6.4 gives an example of the variety of these relationships. The first box at the top is the total costs of manufacturing during a production period. The costs are classified by activity center code and by natural expense type. A manager is responsible for each activity center and the costs incurred in that center.

A **preliminary stage cost driver** links costs of resources consumed (inputs) in one activity center to other activity centers. A **primary stage cost driver** links costs in an activity center directly with products. Some costs, such as batch-level activity center costs in Figure 6.4, are initially assigned to a primary stage activity center and only need a single stage assignment process. These primary stage centers may collect reassigned costs from numerous preliminary stage activity centers—based on cost drivers that reflect activities and resources used.

The activity centers are typically one of four types as described above. Direct costs of unit-level activity centers are assumed in Figure 6.4 to be always traceable to specific products. Batch-level activity center costs should also be traceable to specific products but often use a cost driver. Product-level activity center costs may be related to a specific product or may be grouped by

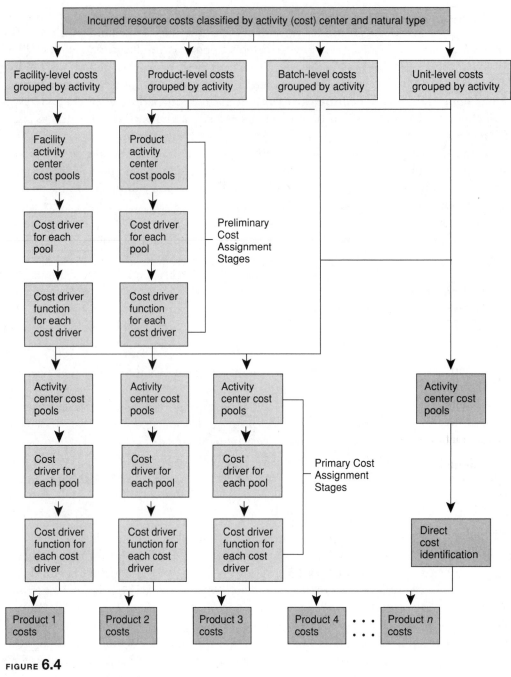

**FIGURE 6.4**

Reationships of Activity Cost Centers Cost Drivers, Cost Funtions, and Processess

activities before being assigned to products at the primary stage. Facility-level activity center costs may go through multiple preliminary stages before being assigned to products.

ABC systems differ from traditional volume-based cost accounting systems in the number and variety of cost drivers used to trace costs. Traditional cost accounting systems use very few drivers—often only direct labor hours or dollars, which are related to volume of production. ABC systems, on the other hand, may use a multitude of cost drivers that relate costs more closely to resources consumed and the activities occurring. In this way, ABC systems reflect the complexity of

| | |
|---|---|
| Number of products or units. | Number of machine hours used. |
| Number of labor minutes per piece. | Number of vendors. |
| Amount of labor cost incurred. | Number of purchasing and ordering hours. |
| Value of materials in a product. | Number of customer options per product. |
| Number of materials moves. | Number of accessories. |
| Number of materials handling hours. | Number of times ordered. |
| Number of times handled. | Number of units scrapped. |
| Number of parts received per month. | Number of engineering change orders. |
| Number of part numbers maintained. | Number of die impressions. |
| Number of part numbers in a product. | Number of units reworked. |
| Amount of hazardous materials. | Volume of scrap—by weight or units. |
| Number of new parts introduced. | Number of customer orders processed. |
| Number of setup hours. | Square feet used by an activity. |
| Number of setups. | Number of employees. |

**FIGURE 6.5**

Cost Drivers Used in Actual ABC Systems

production and not just volume. Although not comprehensive, Figure 6.5 gives examples of cost drivers that might be found in an ABC system.

Accountants must work with management to discover and identify activities and cost drivers. This is done through interviewing, process observation, simulation, diagramming, and analysis of current information systems.

**Step 4: Calculate a Cost Function.** In Figure 6.4, a cost function is used to convert the pool of costs and cost driver data into a rate per cost driver unit, a percentage of other cost amounts, or an allocation percentage. This cost function could be based on either planned or actual costs and activity levels. In Chapter 4, we discussed the creation of predetermined overhead rates using planned costs and activity levels. Using planned activity levels and costs for example, if costs of the setup activity center cost pool totaled $25,000, if setup hours were the cost driver, and if 500 hours were expected, the cost function would be $50 per setup hour. Costs are then distributed to products as setup hours are incurred. This approach is the same as that discussed in Chapter 4, except for the use of a different type of cost driver.

**Step 5: Assign Costs to the Cost Objective.** The final step is distributing costs to the users of the resources. The cost pool, the cost driver, and the cost function now combine to determine how much cost is charged to each resource user. If this is at a preliminary stage, the users are predominately other activity centers. Thus, a group of costs are now reassigned to other cost pools based on use. If the activity center is at the primary stage, the users are the products themselves. In the setup example, if 60 hours of setup time were used for Product A's production, $3,000 would be charged to Product A. All costs entering the manufacturing process during a given time period are eventually assigned to products.

## Influence of Production Complexity

The primary goal of ABC for product costing is to generate accurate product costs. In general, this means the cost accounting system must handle the complexity of production while minimizing possible distortions caused by cost assignment processes. Production complexity plays a significant role in determining whether the costs of two or more activities can be combined and traced to a product by means of a single cost driver and still be assigned accurately. If a company wants more accurate product costs, it must increase the number of activity centers, cost pools, and cost drivers. Since the introduction of a new cost driver in the system has a cost/benefit value, most companies face a trade-off between more cost drivers, greater detail, and more expensive data processing versus more data aggregation and less expensive data processing. Two important issues that affect cost driver selection are product diversity and batch-size diversity.

**Product diversity** refers to the degree to which each product differs in the number of activities (that is, resources or inputs) required. The greater the difference in how two products use resources or inputs, the greater the distortion a single cost driver will make in tracing costs to these products. For example, producing an ornate bathroom faucet fixture may consume labor-intensive production resources while producing a kitchen sink faucet may consume machine-intensive resources. Some products are simply larger than other products. A console model versus a portable model is an example. The size influences how the product is produced and which resources are required.

The complexity of a product is determined by the differences in how a product is manufactured and by the number of options a manufacturer has for its products. Deluxe models and products with many customer options, for example, increase the manufacturing difficulty. Each option adds an extension to the production process. However, supervision and other departmental costs are not necessarily influenced by these options. Materials inputs may differ by product. Some materials may require more handling from the receiving dock through the storeroom to the production floor. In other cases, certain materials may require longer machining time or more time in trimming processes. Some products may have a high degree of vertical integration—from raw materials to finished products. Others are merely assembled from purchased parts.

**Batch-size diversity** occurs when products are manufactured in different-size batches. Batches refer not only to production orders but also to order quantities of raw materials and to shipping quantities of finished goods. In an automotive stamping plant, a weekly run of hood stampings for a popular model may be 3,000 units, while a very similar, but higher priced model hood, may have a biweekly run of 500.

Although we normally think of differing batch sizes when we produce different products, batch-size diversity can also occur with the same product over time. For instance, this week the production order consists of 500 units. Due to an increase in demand, the production schedule for next week calls for 800 units. Just-in-time production encourages producing only what is needed immediately—often smaller batches and more frequently. Frequent batch runs may also require that more attention be given to minimizing setup time and cost. In traditional cost systems, setup costs are added to other overhead costs, losing the separate identity and cost detail of setup activities. In ABC systems, a separate cost pool for setup costs would typically be formed and would be assigned to products using cost drivers such as setup hours or number of setups. Both of these cost drivers reflect batch-size diversity, with the former measure being more detailed and, thus, often more appropriate.

If computer resources were free and if managers had unlimited amounts of analysis time, more and more detail could be captured and evaluated. Since this is not the case, very practical decisions must be made. In large ABC applications, the number of cost drivers (both preliminary and primary) used across an entire facility may be as low as 20 or as high as several hundred. Often, a high percentage of costs are assigned using a small number of drivers. The cost system's design should allow judgments to be made about the number of cost pools and cost drivers and should allow for cost pools and cost drivers to be changed easily when the need arises.

# A COMPREHENSIVE ACTIVITY-BASED COST EXAMPLE

Guttman Cafeterias has just completed the installation of an activity-based cost system. The firm operates cafeterias within office buildings, factories, hospitals, and other institutions. These cafeterias produce and serve three standard meals—breakfast, lunch, and dinner. Activity centers consist of four support centers and two operating centers. The volume for October is as follows:

|  | Breakfast | Lunch | Dinner |
| --- | --- | --- | --- |
| Meals | 22,000 | 15,000 | 12,000 |

The activity centers' traceable costs for October and cost drivers are as follows:

**Activity Center Information**

| Activity Center Code | Activity Center | Materials | Labor | Other Costs | Cost Driver |
| --- | --- | --- | --- | --- | --- |
|  | **Support Centers:** |  |  |  |  |
| 120 | Occupancy |  |  | $ 60,000 | Square feet used |
| 130 | Data Processing |  |  | 30,000 | Transactions processed |
| 140 | Personnel Benefits |  |  | 9,000 | Payroll cost |
| 220 | Materials Handling |  |  | 16,000 | Materials cost |
|  | **Operating Centers:** |  |  |  |  |
| 410 | Cooking | $18,000 | $10,000 | 20,000 | Cooking hours |
| 420 | Serving | 14,000 | 20,000 | 15,000 | Serving hours |
|  | Total | $32,000 | $30,000 | $150,000 |  |

Activities are grouped and activity centers are determined as a result of special studies. Each activity center has one cost driver. For example, the cost driver selected for Occupancy is square feet of space used by each activity.

The materials and labor costs are directly traceable to the three meals as follows:

|  | Materials | Labor |
| --- | --- | --- |
| Breakfast: |  |  |
| Cooking | $ 1,000 | $ 2,000 |
| Serving | 4,000 | 2,000 |
| Lunch: |  |  |
| Cooking | 6,000 | 2,000 |
| Serving | 2,000 | 8,000 |
| Dinner: |  |  |
| Cooking | 11,000 | 6,000 |
| Serving | 8,000 | 10,000 |
| Total | $32,000 | $30,000 |

As for the other costs, cost drivers are selected after analysis of past cost behavior and activity levels within each activity center. First, the other costs of the support centers are assigned to the operating centers. This is the preliminary stage allocation.

## Preliminary Stage Allocation

The cost driver data for the preliminary stage cost assignments are as follows:

**Cost Driver Data—Preliminary Stage Allocation**

| Activity Center Code | Activity Center | Cost Driver | Activity Centers Using Resources | |
|---|---|---|---|---|
| | | | 410 | 420 |
| 120 | Occupancy | Square feet used | 80,000 | 40,000 |
| 130 | Data Processing | Transactions processed | 120,000 | 180,000 |
| 140 | Personnel Benefits | Payroll cost | $10,000 | $20,000 |
| 220 | Materials Handling | Materials cost | $18,000 | $14,000 |

Cost functions for each of the support centers are developed as follows:

| Activity Center | Calculation | Cost Function |
|---|---|---|
| Occupancy | $60,000/(80,000 + 40,000) | $0.50 per square foot |
| Data Processing | $30,000/(120,000 + 180,000) | $0.10 per transaction |
| Personnel Benefits | $9,000/($10,000 + $20,000) | 30% of payroll cost |
| Materials Handling | $16,000/(18,000 + $14,000) | 50% of materials cost |

Using these cost functions, the following costs are assigned to the two operating centers:

Cooking: $0.50(80,000) + $0.10(120,000) + .30($10,000) + .50($18,000) = $64,000

Serving: $0.50(40,000) + $0.10(180,000) + .30($20,000) + .50($14,000) = $51,000

Having made these preliminary cost assignments, the operating centers contain both direct costs and costs to be assigned to meals using primary cost drivers.

## Primary Stage Allocation

The activities and cost drivers are as follows for each meal:

**Cost Driver Data—Primary Stage Allocation**

| Activity Center Code | Activity Center | Cost Driver | Cost Driver Activity Linked to Each Meal | | |
|---|---|---|---|---|---|
| | | | Breakfast | Lunch | Dinner |
| 410 | Cooking | Cooking hours | 2,000 | 3,000 | 5,000 |
| 420 | Serving | Serving hours | 2,500 | 1,500 | 1,000 |

As can be seen, different meals use different amounts of the resources in each activity center. Overhead cost functions for each of the operating centers are developed as follows:

| Activity Center | Calculation | Overhead Cost Function |
|---|---|---|
| Cooking | ($20,000 + $64,000)/(2,000 + 3,000 + 5,000) | $8.40 per cooking hour |
| Serving | ($15,000 + $51,000)/(2,500 + 1,500 + 1,000) | $13.20 per serving hour |

Using these cost functions, the following overhead costs are assigned to the three products:

Breakfast: $8.40(2,000) + $13.20(2,500) = $49,800

Lunch: $8.40(3,000) + $13.20(1,500) = $45,000

Dinner: $8.40(5,000) + $13.20(1,000) = $55,200

Materials and labor costs which are directly traceable are added to determine the total meal costs:

| Cost Item | Breakfast | Lunch | Dinner |
|---|---|---|---|
| Materials | $5,000 | $8,000 | $19,000 |
| Labor | 4,000 | 10,000 | 16,000 |
| Overhead | 49,800 | 45,000 | 55,200 |
| Total Cost | $58,800 | $63,000 | $90,200 |

Note that the total cost assigned to these meals equals the sum of the costs reported by the five activity centers (i.e., $58,800 + $63,000 + $90,200 = $32,000 + $30,000 + $150,000 **or** $212,000). Per unit costs for each meal are:

Breakfast: $58,800/22,000 = $2.67

Lunch: $63,000/15,000 = $4.20

Dinner: $90,200/12,000 = $7.52

## Comparing ABC to Traditional Volume-Based Costing

As discussed, traditional volume-based cost systems unfortunately have paid less attention to the cause-and-effect relationships between resources used and production activities. Assume that the prior cost system in use by Guttman Cafeterias assigned overhead costs to meals using labor dollars. This is a common approach to assigning overhead. Let us also assume that the preliminary cost assignment steps are the same under either approach. Since $150,000 of total overhead cost is incurred and total labor cost is $30,000, an overhead rate of $5 for each $1 of labor is added to each product. The product costs would be as follows:

| | Total | Breakfast | Lunch | Dinner |
|---|---|---|---|---|
| Direct materials | $32,000 | $5,000 | $8,000 | $19,000 |
| Direct labor | 30,000 | 4,000 | 10,000 | 16,000 |
| Overhead costs (500% of labor) | 50,000 | 20,000 | 50,000 | 80,000 |
| Total meal costs | $212,000 | $29,000 | $68,000 | $115,000 |
| Number of meals | | 22,000 | 15,000 | 12,000 |
| Traditional cost per unit | | $1.32 | $4.53 | $9.58 |
| ABC cost per unit | | $2.67 | $4.20 | $7.52 |
| Difference: | | | | |
| Traditional minus ABC cost | | $(1.35) | $0.33 | $2.06 |
| Percentage of ABC cost | | (50.6%) | 7.9% | 27.4 % |

A dramatic picture appears. Using a cost system very common in many companies today, two of the three products have large cost differences—Breakfast and Dinner. Guttman had been using a cost overstated by 27.4 percent for Dinners. This is a far more profitable meal than Guttman's management had thought. Guttman may be losing Dinner business because of its higher than necessary price. Conversely, Breakfast is less profitable than previously thought. With traditional costing, Breakfast received a disproportionately low amount of overhead allocation because its labor cost of $4,000 was much lower than those of Lunch and Dinner ($10,000 and $16,000, respectively). However, Breakfast consumed overhead resources, namely serving hours per unit, comparable to the other two meals. Breakfast prices might need to be raised to cover its actual use of resources.

ABC is also considered superior to volume-based costing when a company's sales mix includes the following two types of products or services:

- high volume, low complexity.
- low volume, high complexity.

To illustrate, suppose Reznick Food Corporation produces 50,000 boxes of "Bland," a breakfast cereal where each piece has the same shape, color, and flavor (high volume, low complexity). The company also produces 10,000 boxes of "Wow!," a cereal having a variety of shapes, colors, and flavors (low volume, high complexity). Setup costs of $2,000 and materials handling costs of $9,000 are to be assigned to the two cereals. The following activity information is obtained:

|  | "Bland" | "Wow!" |
| --- | --- | --- |
| Direct labor hours | 25,000 | 2,500 |
| Production runs | 10 | 20 |
| Materials moves | 50 | 40 |

Volume-based costing, using direct labor hours, would assign the costs as follows:

"Bland": ($2,000 + $9,000) × (25,000/27,500) = $10,000

"Wow!": ($2,000 + $9,000) × (2,500/27,500) = $1,000

An ABC system would use the number of production runs to assign setup costs and the number of materials moves to assign materials handling costs, as follows:

"Bland": [$2,000 × (10/30)] + [$9,000 × (50/90)] = $5,667

"Wow!": [$2,000 × (20/30)] + [$9,000 × (40/90)] = $5,333

After dividing these assigned costs by 50,000 boxes for "Bland" and 10,000 boxes for "Wow!," we obtain the following costs per box:

|  | "Bland" | "Wow!" |
| --- | --- | --- |
| Volume-based costing | $0.20 | $0.10 |
| Activity-based costing | $0.11 | $0.53 |

## Contemporary Practice 6.2
### ABC Applications in the U.K.

U.K. companies who adopted ABC reported the following purposes to which ABC systems were being put to use in 1999:

| Application | Percent |
| --- | --- |
| Cost reduction | 90 |
| Pricing | 81 |
| Performance measurement | 74 |
| Cost modeling | 65 |
| Budgeting | 55 |
| Customer profitability analysis | 52 |
| Output decisions | 52 |
| New product/service design | 42 |
| Inventory valuation | 16 |
| Other | 16 |

Source: Innes, J., F. Mitchell, and D. Sinclair, "Activity-Based Costing in the U.K.'s Largest Companies: A Comparison of 1994 and 1999 Survey Results," Management Accounting Research, September 2000, p. 355.

A recent survey of service companies in ten different industry segments in the U. S. found that 14 percent of the companies already had ABC systems in use, another 14 percent planned to implement ABC, and yet another

14 percent were considering the implementation of ABC.

Source: Martinson, O. B., Cost Accounting in the Service Industry, *Institute of Management Accountants, Montvale, NJ: 1994, p. 68.*

Compared to ABC, volume-based costing has over-costed the high volume, low complexity product ("Bland"), while under-costing the low volume, high complexity product ("Wow!"). This distortion is known as **product cross-subsidization** and has caused companies that use volume-based costing to set high prices for high volume, low complexity products and low prices for low volume, high complexity products. Signals that companies may be experiencing product cross-subsidization include the inability to break into new markets or to maintain current market share as a result of competitors' seeming ability to price below cost.

Whether ABC costs are "correct" or not, they would appear to be more accurate than the traditional costs. ABC makes a greater effort to match resource use, costs, activities, and products.

## ABC AND NONMANUFACTURING ACTIVITIES

Historically, manufacturing-related costs comprised the bulk of a manufacturing organization's total costs. Only manufacturing-related costs are considered product costs for external reporting purposes. In recent times, emphasis on accounting for nonmanufacturing costs such as selling, distribution, general administration, and research and development has grown. One reason is that nonmanufacturing costs are a growing portion of companies' total costs. Another reason is that, due to computerization, it has become less costly to develop alternate accounting systems within a company. Therefore, in

An ABC study was done for 18 orthopedic surgery practices in California, Florida, Illinois, Oklahoma, and Maryland. First, more than 100 tasks were identified that were performed by office and clinical practice staff, such as walking patients to examination rooms, making patient appointments, and working with third-party payers. These were then grouped into 17 activities such as servicing patients in the office, maintaining medical records, and billing. Costs were assigned from the general ledger to activities based on how the activities consume resources. For instance, administrative and clinical support

staff salaries were assigned on the basis of the average percentage of time spent on each activity. To obtain this information, employees estimated the amount of time spent on each of the 17 activities. So, "if an employee worked 50 percent on billing, 20 percent on collections, and 30 percent on obtaining insurance authorization, that employee's salary costs would be assigned accordingly" (p. 47).

Source: Zeller, T. L., G. Siegel, G. Kaciuba, and A. H. Lau, "Using Activity-Based Costing to Track Resource Use in Group Practices," *Healthcare Financial Management,* September 1999, pp. 46–50.

addition to the cost system needed for external reporting, companies now find it worthwhile to maintain alternate systems more useful for internal purposes such as pricing, control, decision making, and performance evaluation. With the growing emphasis on accounting for nonmanufacturing costs, manufacturing firms who have adopted ABC for manufacturing-related activities are increasingly expanding their implementation of ABC to include nonmanufacturing activities.

In addition to manufacturing firms, the usage of ABC is growing in the service sector. Contemporary Practice 6.3 shows the usage and intended usage of ABC in service firms.

Competitive pressures in industries such as health care, financial services, telecommunications, and transportation have led to increased cost consciousness. (See Contemporary Practice 6.4) Not only is ABC being used to assess costs associated with various services but, increasingly, it is being used to determine costs associated with particular customers. Customer profitability analysis is becoming an increasingly important issue with management.

## ACTIVITY-BASED MANAGEMENT

Aside from product costing purposes, ABC systems are also used to improve the operations of an organization. This extension of ABC is often referred to as **activity-based management (ABM)**. The ABM philosophy is that the activities identified for ABC can also be used for cost management and performance evaluation purposes.

One aspect of ABM which evolves from activity analysis is the identification and elimination of **nonvalue-added costs**. Activities and their costs that are eliminated without deterioration of product quality and value can reduce total production time and increase profitability. For instance, many companies have adopted just-in-time production systems in an effort to eliminate activities related to storing and handling inventories.

Another aspect of ABM is the determination of efficiency and effectiveness measures for all cost generating activities. Traditionally, accountants have been concerned only with financial performance measures. With ABM, performance evaluation of activities has been expanded to include many nonfinancial measures. Measures dealing with quality and productivity have become particularly prominent. Indeed, the phenomenon of total quality management is considered part of ABM. Examples of nonfinancial quality measures include product defect rates, number of customer complaints, number of engineering change orders, and amount of rework. Examples of nonfinancial productivity measures include the ratio of value-added time to total production time, amount of production per day per employee, and square footage required per day per unit of output.

ABM also encompasses innovations such as target costing, continuous improvement, employee empowerment, and benchmarking. These cost management and performance evaluation issues are discussed in detail in Chapter 14. The remainder of this chapter covers an ABM topic which deals with product costing—JIT costing.

## JIT COSTING

To reduce nonvalue-added costs, many companies in recent years have adopted **just-in-time (JIT) systems**. These systems generally have the following characteristics:

1. Raw materials, work in process, and finished goods inventories are reduced as much as possible, if not eliminated. Costs associated with inventories, such as storage and moving, are considered to add no value to the product. As such, the production system operates on a **demand-pull** basis. Raw materials are purchased only as demanded by production needs; production is scheduled only as demanded by sales orders.

2. Since little or no inventory buffers exist at various work stations, problems such as defective materials or machine breakdowns not only stop work at that station but also cause shutdowns at subsequent stations. Thus, total quality programs are emphasized in JIT environments.

3. Long-term agreements are negotiated with a small number of suppliers. The criteria for selecting suppliers focus on dependable delivery and quality.

4. Layouts of production facilities are structured in the form of **focused factories**, i.e., "factories within a factory." To simplify activities, especially materials handling, machines are grouped in arrangements that allow a worker or a team of workers to perform a variety of sequential operations. These arrangements are often referred to as **manufacturing cells**.

5. JIT is facilitated by automation in various forms—flexible manufacturing systems, automated materials handling systems, numerically-controlled machines, computer integrated manufacturing systems, etc. Thus, in JIT environments, direct labor cost is usually not significant and sometimes even nonexistent.

Due to these characteristics, firms with JIT systems sometimes record costs differently than was discussed in Chapter 4. **Just-in-time (JIT) costing** differs from traditional costing with regard to the accounts used and the timing of cost recording. Specifically, three major differences exist. First, instead of using separate accounts for Raw Materials and Work in Process, JIT costing combines these into a Raw and In-Process Inventory (RIP) account. The rationale is that the amount of work in process at any particular time will be low.

A second difference is that since direct labor is usually a minor cost item in a JIT setting, no separate account for direct labor in JIT costing is created. Rather, direct labor is combined with overhead into a Conversion Cost account. In some companies, direct labor is actually included in the Overhead account.

The third difference relates to the application of overhead. In traditional environments, overhead is applied to products as they are being produced. As such, overhead is applied to and recorded into the Work in Process account. In JIT costing, overhead is not applied to products until they are completed. No Work in Process account exists to accumulate conversion costs. When products are completed under JIT costing, conversion cost is applied to the Finished Goods account. In more "pure" JIT systems, the conversion cost is applied or added to Cost of Goods Sold, since the goods are sold soon after production is completed. JIT costing is sometimes termed **backflush costing** because the product costs are "flushed" out of the accounting system and are attached to the products only *after* they are completed. This is the reverse of the traditional approach which attaches costs to products, via the Work in Process account, as products are being produced.

Just as the Overhead account is closed out in the traditional cost system, the Conversion Cost account in the JIT system is closed out at the end of the period. In Chapter 4 we stated that Overhead should be closed out to Cost of Goods Sold or prorated among Cost of Goods Sold, Work in Process, and Finished Goods. With JIT costing, Conversion Cost would typically be closed out just to Cost of Goods Sold.

To illustrate JIT costing, suppose that Tex Rubin Tire Center sells, installs, and repairs auto and truck tires. Recently, the company has begun to consider implementing a JIT inventory system. The following transactions occurred during January:

(a) Tex Rubin purchased $17, 000 of materials.
(b) All materials purchased were requisitioned for use.
(c) Tex Rubin incurred direct labor costs of $8,000.
(d) Actual overhead costs amounted to $125,000.
(e) Tex Rubin applied conversion costs totaling $130,000. This includes $8,000 of direct labor.
(f) All jobs were completed. No jobs were in process on January 1.

These transactions would be recorded in a traditional costing system as follows:

| Materials | | Accounts Payable | | Work in Process | |
|---|---|---|---|---|---|
| (a) 17,000 | (b) 17,000 | | (a) 17,000 | (b) 17,000 | (f) 147,000 |
| | | | (d) 125,000 | (c) 8,000 | |
| | | | | (e) 122,000 | |

| Wages Payable | | Overhead | | Finished Jobs on Hand | |
|---|---|---|---|---|---|
| | (c) 8,000 | (d) 125,000 | (e) 122,000 | (f) 147,000 | |

Under JIT costing, no entries are made for transactions (b), (c), and (e). Entry (b) is not necessary because the placement of materials into use is implied in transaction (a) when the materials are first received. No separate entry for (c) is made because direct labor is combined with overhead and recorded as a debit to Conversion Cost as part of entry (d). Finally, entry (e) is omitted because conversion cost is not applied until the jobs are completed. The entry for conversion cost application, therefore, becomes part of entry (f).

The JIT costing system would record the January transactions in the following manner:

| Raw and In-Process Inventory | | Accounts Payable | | Conversion Cost | |
|---|---|---|---|---|---|
| (a) 17,000 | (b) 17,000 | | (a) 17,000 | (b) 133,000 | (f) 130,000 |
| | | | (d) 125,000 | | |

| Wages Payable | | Finished Jobs on Hand | |
|---|---|---|---|
| | (d) 8,000 | (f) 147,000 | |

Note that the JIT costing system is much simpler and less expensive than the traditional system because fewer entries are needed.

# SUMMARY

Activity-based costing is a system of accounting that focuses on activities performed to produce items or services. The activities are the primary building blocks in cost accumulation. Cost drivers are used to identify costs with activities and to identify activities with products. Preliminary stage cost drivers assign support activity costs to other activity centers. Primary stage cost drivers relate costs of activities to products or services.

In designing an activity-based cost system, five basic steps are followed. First, assemble similar actions into activity groups. This process involves categorizing activities as unit level, batch level, product level, and facility level. Second, classify costs by activity group and by expense. Third, select the appropriate preliminary stage and primary stage cost drivers. This process eliminates distortions in cost allocations to products that result from production complexity. Fourth, calculate a cost function to link costs and the cost driver activity. Finally, fifth, assign costs to the cost objective (often the product cost).

ABC can also be applied to nonmanufacturing activities and to service organizations. Activity-based management involves the analysis of activities for cost management and performance evaluation issues.

JIT costing differs from traditional cost systems in three respects. First, JIT costing does not use a Work in Process account. Second, JIT costing combines direct labor and overhead into one account. Third, in JIT costing, overhead is not applied to products until the products are completed.

## PROBLEM FOR REVIEW

Lowy Manufacturing Company makes a variety of backpacks. The activity centers and budgeted information for the year are:

| Activity Center | Overhead Costs | Cost Driver | Activity Center Rate |
|---|---|---|---|
| Materials handling | $300,000 | Weight of materials | $0.300 per pound |
| Cutting | 1,800,000 | Number of shapes | $3.00 per shape |
| Assembly | 4,600,000 | Direct labor hours | $12.00 per labor hour |
| Sewing | 1,200,000 | Machine hours | $8.00 per machine hour |

Two styles of backpacks were produced in December, the EasyRider and the Overnighter. The quantities and other operating data for the month are:

| | EasyRider | Overnighter |
|---|---|---|
| Direct materials weight in pounds | 50,000 | 15,000 |
| Assembly direct labor hours | 7,500 | 1,200 |
| Sewing machine hours | 12,500 | 1,800 |
| Units produced | 5,000 | 1,000 |
| Number of shapes | 35,000 | 15,000 |

### Required:
1. Using the activity center rates, find the total overhead costs charged to each product during the month.
2. Calculate a per unit cost for each backpack.
3. With the information given, compute the budgeted level for each cost driver upon which the activity center rates were based.

### Solution:

| (1) Total overhead costs traced to products: | EasyRider | Overnighter |
|---|---|---|
| Materials handling: | | |
| 50,000 × $0.30 | $15,000 | |
| 15,000 × $0.30 | | $4,500 |
| Cutting: | | |
| 35,000 × $3 | 105,000 | |
| 15,000 × $3 | | 45,000 |
| Assembly: | | |
| 7,500 × $12 | 90,000 | |
| 1,200 × $12 | | 14,400 |
| Sewing: | | |
| 12,500 × $8 | 100,000 | |
| 1,800 × $8 | | 14,400 |
| Total costs | $310,000 | $78,300 |

**(2)** Unit costs:

|  | EasyRider | Overnighter |
|---|---|---|
| Total costs | $310,000 | $78,300 |
| Units | 5,000 | 1,000 |
| Unit costs | $62.00 | $78.30 |

**(3)** Budgeted levels for cost drivers:

| | | |
|---|---|---|
| Materials handling | $300,000 ÷ $0.30 = | 1,000,000 pounds |
| Cutting | $1,800,000 ÷ $3 = | 600,000 shapes |
| Assembly | $4,600,000 ÷ $12 = | 383,333 labor hours |
| Sewing | $1,200,000 ÷ $8 = | 150,000 machine hours |

# APPENDIX

## ECONOMIC ORDER QUANTITY

Many methods have been developed for use in planning inventory levels, timing the cycle for reorders, and estimating optimum order sizes. One frequently used application deals with obtaining the lowest possible cost of ordering and storing inventories. When inventories are stored, the company has to use space that has a rental value, must carry additional insurance, and invests funds in inventories that reduce the availability of funds for other purposes. Ordering costs include costs of placing orders as well as costs of receiving and handling shipments. Also, by placing frequent orders, the company may be losing quantity discounts that could be obtained by purchasing in bulk. Perhaps the savings to be obtained from placing large orders more than compensate for the increased storage costs. Normally, the cost of ordering increases as orders are placed more frequently, but the cost of storage decreases.

### Calculating Order and Storage Costs

The order and storage costs can be tabulated under different assumptions as to the number of orders placed and the inventory investment. Assume that a company predicts that 3,000 units of a certain material are needed next year. Each unit costs $6. Past experience indicates that the storage costs are approximately equal to 10 percent of the inventory investment. The cost to place an order amounts to $9. If only one order were placed for the year, it would be for 3,000 units, and the average number of units held in the inventory during the year would be 1,500 (3,000 divided by 2) assuming a uniform rate of withdrawal. With two orders, 1,500 units would be purchased on each order, and the average inventory would be only 750 units. The cost to order and store the inventory is computed and set forth in the following table. Computations are made for a varying number of orders placed and a varying investment in inventory.

| Number of Orders | Number of Units per Order | Average Inventory | Cost of Average Inventory | Total Storage Cost | Total Order Cost | Total Storage & Order Cost |
|---|---|---|---|---|---|---|
| 1 | 3,000 | 1,500 | $9,000 | $900 | $9 | $909 |
| 2 | 1,500 | 750 | 4,500 | 450 | 18 | 468 |
| 3 | 1,000 | 500 | 3,000 | 300 | 27 | 327 |
| 4 | 750 | 375 | 2,250 | 225 | 36 | 261 |
| 5 | 600 | 300 | 1,800 | 180 | 45 | 225 |
| 6 | 500 | 250 | 1,500 | 150 | 54 | 204 |
| 7 | 429 | 215 | 1,290 | 129 | 63 | 192 |
| 8 | 375 | 188 | 1,128 | 113 | 72 | 185 |
| 9 | 333 | 167 | 1,002 | 100 | 81 | 181 |
| 10 | 300 | 150 | 900 | 90 | 90 | 180 |
| 11 | 273 | 137 | 822 | 82 | 99 | 181 |
| 12 | 250 | 125 | 750 | 75 | 108 | 183 |

The company should place 10 orders each for 300 units. The storage cost of $90 is equal to the total ordering cost at this level, and the combined costs of $180 are at a minimum.

The number of orders that minimizes the sum of the total costs of ordering and storing is called the **economic order quantity** (**EOQ**). At the EOQ level, the total ordering costs equal the total storage costs. EOQ can be computed by use of the following formula:

$$EOQ = \sqrt{2DP/S}$$

Where:    D = annual demand expressed in units of inventory
P = cost per order placed
S = storage cost per unit

In our example, D = 3,000 units, P = $9, and S = $0.60 (10 percent of the $6 materials cost). Hence, we have the following result, which confirms our earlier analysis:

$$EOQ = \sqrt{(2 \times 3,000 \times \$9)/\$0.60}$$
$$= 300$$

## Time to Order

Forecasting the most probable quantity used during a period of time is an important element in the decision about the most economical quantity to order. As a control measure, some flexibility should be allowed in case a quantity larger than was forecast is used. An excessive investment in inventory is certainly not desirable, but some buffer stock may be warranted to guard against not having inventory available when actual use exceeds the estimated use.

When placing an order, recognition should be given to the time that will elapse between the placement of the order and the actual receipt of the quantity ordered. This is called **lead time**. Sufficient quantities of inventory must be on hand to provide for operations during this lead time.

Some companies will physically segregate the inventory estimated for the lead time; it may be marked and placed in a separate box, for example. When the supply reaches the point where this portion of the inventory is to be used, an order must be placed. If estimates are made correctly, the inventory will be received before the special stock is exhausted. Or a computer program may trigger orders when the supply on hand is down to an order point.

## Storage Cost and Changing Production Runs

The EOQ model is only one application used to minimize costs when one cost is increasing while another cost is decreasing. In planning the size of a production run, for example, we incur the equivalent of order costs. We call them set-up costs. These costs include the costs to change machine settings and the costs of idle labor time while the machines are reset to produce another product line. Because set-up costs tend to be high, management may be inclined to operate by producing large batches of a product and storing relatively large quantities as inventory. But, costs are also associated with inventory storage, including financing charges and the risk of breakage and spoilage. With short production runs, the costs to store inventory decrease. With long production runs, the costs to store larger inventories increase. The objective is to minimize the combined cost. As with order and storage costs, the total cost is at a minimum when the two costs are equal.

As an example, assume that the setup is $20 and that the cost to store inventory is 20 percent of inventory cost. Inventory cost is $30 per unit; hence, storage cost is $6 per unit. Annual demand for this product is 24,000 units. How many units should be manufactured in each batch to minimize combined costs of set-up changes and storage cost? We can again use the EOQ formula, but instead of using P to represent ordering costs, we now use C to represent the set-up cost per unit and just substitute C for P, as follows:

$$EOQ = \sqrt{2DC/S} = \sqrt{(2 \times 24{,}000 \times \$20)/\$6} = 400 \text{ units}$$

The optimum production run is 400 units, which would necessitate 60 production runs (24,000 units demanded ÷ 400 units per production run). This would yield a combined set-up and storage cost of $2,400. The following table illustrates this minimum cost in relation to number of production runs above and below the optimum.

| Number of Runs | Number of Units per Run | Average Inventory | Cost of Average Inventory | Total Storage Cost | Tota Set-Up Cost | Total Storage & Set-Up Cost |
|---|---|---|---|---|---|---|
| 50 | 480 | 240 | $7,200 | $1,440 | $1,000 | $2,440 |
| 60 | 400 | 200 | 6,000 | 1,200 | 1,200 | 2,400 |
| 70 | 343 | 172 | 5,160 | 1,030 | 1,400 | 2,430 |

Other factors can also be considered. If the plant is operating at close to capacity, management may prefer to accept some additional storage cost (in order to save the time taken to change the machine settings) and not risk a failure to meet production quotas. However, with some automated equipment, a change in machine setting may require only a simple change in the program. Hence, the problem is relevant only if set-up costs are significant.

## TERMINOLOGY REVIEW

Activity-based costing (ABC) (216)
Activity-based management (ABM) (228)
Activity center (217)
Backflush costing (229)
Batch-level activities (219)
Batch-size diversity (222)
Cost driver (217)
Demand-pull (228)
Economic order quantity (EOQ) (234)
Facility-level activities (219)
Focused factories (229)

Just-in-time (JIT) systems (228)
Just-in-time (JIT) costing (229)
Lead time (234)
Manufacturing cells (229)
Nonvalue-added costs (228)
Preliminary stage cost driver (219)
Primary stage cost driver (219)
Product cross-subsidization (227)
Product diversity (222)
Product-level activities (219)
Unit-level activities (218)

## QUESTIONS FOR REVIEW AND DISCUSSION

1. Describe the relationships among resources, activities, and products.

2. What is a cost driver? What is its role in tracing costs to products?

3. Identify the five basic steps in applying activity-based costing to a costing problem.

4. Why are actions grouped into activities instead of treated individually?

5. Define an activity center. How many activity centers can exist in one production department? Explain.

6. What is the purpose for grouping actions into specific categories of unit-level activities, batch-level activities, product-level activities, and facility-level activities?

7. Describe the differences among unit-level activities, batch-level activities, and product-level activities.

8. How might the definitions of variable and fixed costs be changed in an activity-based cost system?

9. Explain the difference between a preliminary stage cost driver and a primary stage cost driver.

10. Explain the purpose of a cost function that will use cost driver data.

11. What is meant by product diversity? Why is it important in product costing?

12. How can batch-size diversity influence the costs assigned to products?

13. What factors have led to an increased emphasis on accounting for nonmanufacturing costs such as selling, distribution, general administration, and research and development?

14. How does activity-based management relate to activity-based costing?

15. Identify the key characteristics associated with JIT systems (other than cost recording issues).

16. How does JIT costing differ from traditional costing?

17. Why is JIT costing sometimes referred to as backflush costing?

# EXERCISES

6–1.  **Classification of Activities.** Lubin Electronics, Inc. makes avionics equipment for private aircraft manufacturers. The production process takes place in three departments. The following costs were budgeted for February:

| | |
|---|---:|
| Computer programming—production | $27,000 |
| Custodial wages—plant | 4,500 |
| Depreciation—machinery | 95,000 |
| Depreciation—plant | 60,000 |
| Electricity—machinery | 11,600 |
| Electricity—plant | 7,400 |
| Engineering design | 36,000 |
| Equipment maintenance—wages | 14,100 |
| Equipment maintenance—parts and suppliess | 2,900 |
| Heating—plant | 3,200 |
| Inspection—production | 3,800 |
| Insurance—plant | 10,000 |
| Property taxes | 9,300 |
| Raw materials, components, subassemblies | 280,000 |
| Setup wages | 19,000 |

**Required:**

1. Identify each of the costs as one of the following:

   (a)  A unit-level activity.
   (b)  A batch-level activity.
   (c)  A product-level activity.
   (d)  A facility-level activity.

2. Specify an appropriate cost driver for tracing to the products the costs that are associated with the various activity levels previously identified.

**6–2.** **Activity Groupings and Cost Drivers.** Plasker Products, Inc. uses JIT manufacturing and has the production process organized into manufacturing cells where each cell produces either a few products or major subassemblies. Cell workers are responsible for completing a quality product, setting up machinery, and maintaining all machinery in the cell. The following are the costs incurred either within each cell or for the benefit of each cell:

| | | | |
|---|---|---|---|
| (a) | Raw materials | (j) | Oil for lubricating machinery |
| (b) | Direct labor | (k) | Cell equipment maintenance |
| (c) | Salary of a cell supervisor | (l) | Parts for machinery |
| (d) | Salary of the plant manager | (m) | Power |
| (e) | Salaries of janitors | (n) | Costs to set up machinery |
| (f) | Salary of an industrial engineer | (o) | Taxes on plant and equipment |
| (g) | Overtime wages for cell workers | (p) | Insurance on plant and equipment |
| (h) | Plant depreciation | (q) | Pencils and paper for cell supervisor |
| (i) | Depreciation on machinery | | |

**Required:**

1. Indicate the costs that can be identified directly with products without the use of cost drivers.
2. Group the remaining costs by similar activities.
3. Suggest an appropriate cost driver for assigning the costs of grouped activities to the product. (It is possible for some groupings to have a cost driver to trace the costs to another grouping of activities before assigning costs to products.)

**6–3.** **Appropriateness of ABC.** Zalik Industries has identified the following activity centers and cost drivers:

| Activity Center | Cost Driver |
|---|---|
| Purchasing | Number of purchase orders |
| Materials handling | Number of parts |
| Setups | Number of setups |
| Cutting | Number of parts |
| Assembly | Direct labor hours |
| Painting | Number of units painted |

Two customer orders were received for the month. The cost drivers appearing on each order are as follows:

| Cost Drivers | Order 1 | Order 2 |
|---|---|---|
| Number of purchase orders | 3 | 6 |
| Number of parts | 8 | 4 |
| Number of setups | 6 | 2 |
| Direct labor hours | 35 | 15 |
| Number of units painted | 11 | 33 |

**Required:**

Assuming the company traditionally allocated these costs using direct labor hours, how would activity-based costing, with the indicated cost drivers, improve the allocation of costs to products on the two customer orders?

Service

**6–4.    Primary Stage Assignment.** For J. Rosing, Inc., a publisher of magazines, the Materials Handling activity center moved materials for four other activity centers. The cost of materials moved were as follows:

| Activity Center | Cost of Materials Moved |
|---|---|
| Receiving | $45,000 |
| Typesetting | 90,000 |
| Printing | 20,000 |
| Shipping | 15,000 |

Materials Handling had $50,000 of direct costs and $35,000 of costs assigned to it from other activity centers. Cost of materials moved is the cost driver.

**Required:**
Printing will be assigned how much cost from Materials Handling?

Service

**6–5.    Choosing an Activity Base.** Costs and activity levels over the past three months are as follows for Mindi Stuart Enterprises, which operates a national chain of car washes:

|  | December | January | February |
|---|---|---|---|
| Activity center total costs | $20,000 | $30,000 | $40,000 |
| Labor hours | 1,000 | 1,000 | 1,000 |
| Machine hours | 3,000 | 4,500 | 6,000 |
| Pounds of materials used | 10,000 | 12,000 | 14,000 |
| Number of cars washed | 120,000 | 130,000 | 140,000 |

**Required:**
Which activity measure would appear to be the best cost driver for this cost center? Comment.

**6–6.    Basic ABC.** Ratner Glassware, Inc. uses activity based costing and has provided the following data:

| Activity Center | Cost Driver | Amount of Activity | Center Costs |
|---|---|---|---|
| Materials handling | Pounds handled | 55,000 lbs. | $220,000 |
| Painting | Units painted | 40,000 units | $320,000 |
| Assembly | Labor hours | 6,000 hours | $240,000 |

Job #45 contains 400 units. It weighs 880 pounds and uses 950 hours of labor.

**Required:**
Compute the total overhead cost that should be assigned to Job #45.

**6–7.    Overhead Cost Assignment.** Litzman Enterprises manufactures two types of hats, Black and White. The overhead activities, costs and related data are as follows:

|  | Black | White | Activity Center Costs |
|---|---|---|---|
| Receiving orders | 120 | 180 | $9,000 |
| Machine hours | 3,000 | 2,000 | $90,000 |
| Setups | 50 | 25 | $12,000 |
| Shipping orders | 250 | 150 | $22,000 |

**Required:**

Using activity based costing, determine the overhead costs assigned to each of the two hats.

Service

**6–8.    Cost Comparison.** Scott Jacobson, controller of Faber Insurance Company, uses ABC for a new claims processing operation. He has identified the following processing activities needed and their operating costs:

| Activities | Operating Costs |
|---|---|
| Assembly of claims packages | $60,000 |
| Forms preparation | 144,000 |
| Approval steps | 150,000 |
| Quality checking | 150,000 |

The cost drivers and their activity levels are budgeted at the following amounts:

| Activity | Cost Driver | Cost Driver Activity |
|---|---|---|
| Assembly of claims packages | Claims processed | 60,000 claims |
| Forms preparation | Forms processed | Average of 12 forms per each claim |
| Approval steps | Approvals required | Average of 5 approvals per claim |
| Quality checking | Quality hours | Average of 4 claims per hour |

**Required:**

Compare the cost of an average claim to one that has 6 forms, requires 8 approvals, and takes an hour to quality check.

Service

**6–9.    Cost Control with ABC.** The Flying Llama Travel Agency of Lima, Peru, budgets its agents' expenses based on the following activities, cost drivers, and cost functions:

| Activities | Cost Drivers | Cost Functions |
|---|---|---|
| Operations | Kilometers traveled | 0.60 New Sol per kilometer |
| Entertainment | Admission expenses | 15.00 New Sol per passenger |
| Trips | Trip agent costs | 300.00 New Sol per trip |

Juanita Garcia spent 8,200 New Sol in September. She ran 10 trips, had 20 persons per trip, and traveled a total of 4,000 kilometers. Other agents' spending averaged 8,600 New Sol.

**Required:**

Using activity-based costing, comment on Garcia's spending for September. Also, comment on the spending of the other agents.

**6–10.   Product Costing with ABC.** Budgeted unit costs and production for the two products made by Monica's Cat Foods, Inc. are as follows:

|                    | Kitty Gourmet | Cat Yummies |
|--------------------|---------------|-------------|
| Units of product   | 375,000       | 225,000     |
| Direct materials   | $28           | $22         |
| Direct labor       | $75           | $45         |

Other information for the coming year follows:

|          |                   |                | Required Units of Cost Drivers: | |
|----------|-------------------|----------------|-------------------|----------------|
| Activity | Budgeted Costs    | Cost Driver    | Kitty Gourmet     | Cat Yummies    |
| Machining    | $5,550,000 | Machine hours       | 34,000 | 30,000 |
| Inspection   | 51,000     | Number of batches   | 500    | 700    |
| Shipping     | 88,000     | Number of shipments | 100    | 750    |
| Purchasing   | 17,000     | Number of orders    | 35     | 25     |
| Machine setup | 360,000   | Setup hours         | 3,200  | 1,800  |

**Required:**

Using ABC, compute the budgeted unit costs for each of the two products made by Monica's Cat Foods, Inc.

**6–11.   Job Costing with Volume-Based Costing and with ABC.** Bergen Corporation has four categories of overhead, with expected costs for next year as follows.

| | |
|---|---|
| Maintenance        | $820,000 |
| Materials Handling | 180,000  |
| Inspection         | 390,000  |
| Setups             | 315,000  |

Job #58 is scheduled for next year and has the following estimates:

| | |
|---|---|
| Direct materials          | $82,000 |
| Direct labor (2,000 hours) | $97,000 |
| Number of inspections     | 95      |
| Number of setups          | 88      |
| Number of machine hours   | 4,500   |
| Number of materials moves | 185     |

Sixty thousand direct labor hours are budgeted for next year. Expected activity for the activity-based cost drivers that could be used are:

| | |
|---|---|
| Machine hours      | 34,000 |
| Material moves     | 18,000 |
| Setups             | 31,000 |
| Quality inspections | 37,000 |

**Required:**

1. Determine the total cost of Job #58 if direct labor hours are used as the cost driver for overhead.
2. Determine the total cost of Job #58 if activity-based costing is used.

**6–12. Customer Cost with ABC.** The following cost data have been accumulated for Klehr Tuxedo Rentals:

| Activity Center | Cost Driver | Amount of Activity | Center Costs |
|---|---|---|---|
| Selling | Labor hours | 900 hours | $38,000 |
| Alterations | Number altered | 200 units | 6,500 |
| Cleaning & Preparation | Number rented | 750 units | 16,800 |
| General Overhead | Labor hours | 900 hours | $52,000 |

Mitch Davis, a customer, necessitated two hours of selling time. He rented seven tuxedos, and three of them required alterations.

**Required:**

Compute the total cost that should be assigned to Mitch Davis.

**6–13. Activity Center Rates.** The following budgeted activity data and costs are from Chernin Laundromats:

| Activity Centers | Direct Costs | Support Costs | Percentage of Space Used | Number of Employees |
|---|---|---|---|---|
| Preliminary Centers: | | | | |
| Administration | | $64,000 | 20% | |
| Maintenance | | 75,000 | | |
| Primary Centers: | | | | |
| Washing | $123,000 | 45,000 | 60% | 30 |
| Drying | 69,000 | 88,000 | 20% | 20 |

Administration uses number of employees as its cost driver. Maintenance uses percentage of space used as its cost driver. Washing uses machine hours as its cost driver and has budgeted 42,300 hours this month. Drying also uses machine hours as its cost driver and has budgeted 40,100 hours this month.

**Required:**

Find the cost rates that will be used this month in each primary center.

**6–14. ABC Rates and Overall Rate.** The Department of Road Works in Cuyahoga County repairs streets and sidewalks that have holes and cracks. The overhead activities, costs, and related data are as follows:

| Activity | Streets | Sidewalks | Activity Center Costs |
|---|---|---|---|
| Preparation | 100 labor hours | 150 labor hours | $7,500 |
| Machining | 12,000 machine hrs. | 13,000 machine hrs. | 125,000 |
| Removal | 45 tons | 20 tons | 9,750 |
| Resurfacing | 200 miles | 400 miles | 30,000 |

**Required:**
1. Compute an overhead activity rate for each center.
2. Allocate the activity costs to the two types of repair jobs using the rates from Part (1).
3. Assume the total overhead costs of all activity centers are allocated on the basis of machine hours. Calculate the overall rate and allocate overhead costs to the two types of repair jobs using that rate.
4. Explain why the overhead costs allocated to the two types of repair jobs differ between Parts (2) and (3).

**6–15.   Product Costing with ABC.** Linda Irvin, the controller of Sonya Electronics, wishes to use activity-based costing for a new circuit board produced for personal computers. Irvin has identified the following activities associated with circuit board production and the related conversion costs forecast for the period:

| Activity | Conversion Cost |
|---|---|
| Purchasing of parts | $72,000 |
| Starting the product | 90,000 |
| Inserting the components | 150,000 |
| Soldering the boards | 180,000 |
| Testing the quality | 140,000 |

The cost drivers which Irvin intends to use, as well as the amounts of activity forecast for the period, are:

| Activity | Cost Driver | Cost Driver Amounts |
|---|---|---|
| Purchasing of parts | Number of parts purchased | 12 per board |
| Starting the product | Number of boards started | 60,000 |
| Inserting the components | Number of insertions | 10 per board |
| Soldering the boards | Number of boards soldered | 60,000 |
| Testing the quality | Number of testing hours | 2,000 |

Each circuit board has anticipated direct materials costs of $36. In addition, each circuit board takes on average 15 minutes to test.

**Required:**
Determine the cost of a circuit board produced by Sonya Electronics.

Service

**6–16.   Assigning Overhead Costs to Customers.** Skibell Power Company is an electric utility that supplies power to residential and commercial customers. The company uses an activity-based cost approach. The overhead costs have been divided into four cost pools that use the following cost drivers:

| Customers | Kilowatt Hours | Number of Customers | Labor Hours | Maintenance Hours |
|---|---|---|---|---|
| Residential | 4,880,000 | 5,500 | 3,000 | 450 |
| Commercial | 8,560,000 | 4,200 | 2,200 | 390 |
| Cost per pool | $20,500,000 | $1,800,000 | $8,600,000 | $1,350,000 |

**Required:**
Compute the overhead cost allocation to Residential customers and to Commercial customers.

**6–17.  Finding Missing Costs.** Susan Robinson, the operations manager for Flink Towing Service, is unable to locate the 2005 budget. You have managed to recover the following information for her:

| Activity Center | Budgeted Overhead Cost | Cost Driver | Budgeted Cost Driver Level |
|---|---|---|---|
| Dispatching | $14,000 | Number of calls | 350 calls |
| Towing | 42,000 | Towing hours | 600 hours |
| Billing & Collection | 15,000 | Pages of forms processed | 5,000 pages |
| Miscellaneous Overhead | ? | Labor hours | 10,000 hours |

You have also obtained the following information pertaining to the Southern Region, which you learned was assigned an overhead cost of $9,500:

| | |
|---|---|
| Labor hours | 2,000 |
| Number of calls | 50 |
| Towing hours | 55 |
| Pages of forms processed | 430 |

**Required:**
Determine the amount of Miscellaneous Overhead that was budgeted for 2005.

**6–18.  Two Stages and Cost Comparisons.** A new cost system has been implemented in Ludwig Plumbing, Inc. The old system applied overhead to customer jobs using labor dollars as the cost driver. The new cost system uses cost drivers for each activity center to cost customer jobs. Administrative Tasks and Preparation Services are preliminary activity centers. The activity centers and their information are as follows:

| Activity Centers | Labor$ | Overhead | Cost Driver | Occupancy% | Other Activity |
|---|---|---|---|---|---|
| Administrative Tasks | | $100,000 | % of space | | |
| Preparation Services | | 100,000 | Labor dollars | 20% | |
| New Installation | $120,000 | 80,000 | Materials cost | 40% | $200,000 materials cost |
| Renovation & Repairs | 80,000 | 120,000 | Repair hours | 40% | 9,000 hours |
| Total activity | $200,000 | $400,000 | | | |

One large commercial contract, for Roth Corporation, used $28,000 of New Installation materials and $36,000 of labor. The job also used $27,000 and 950 hours of Renovation & Repairs labor.

**Required:**
For the Roth Corporation project, what is the cost difference between the old and new costing methods?

**6–19.  Overhead Cost Assignment.** Helene's Tennis Experts is a company that specializes in installing and resurfacing tennis courts. Using ABC, the company has assigned all overhead costs into five cost pools. The budgeted amounts for these cost pools and their associated cost drivers are:

| Overhead Cost Pool | Budgeted Costs | Costs Driver | Budgeted Level for Cost Driver |
|---|---|---|---|
| Purchasing & materials-related | $230,000 | Materials costs | $1,450,000 |
| Engineering | 97,000 | Engineering hours | 5,300 hours |
| Office & storage rental | 125,000 | Square feet of jobs | 478,500 sq. ft. |
| Equipment depreciation | 150,000 | Direct labor cost | $998,000 |
| General administration | 280,000 | Direct labor hours | 88,000 hours |

The company has just completed resurfacing Thompson Park Tennis Courts, which had the following cost driver data:

| | |
|---|---|
| Materials cost | $39,000 |
| Direct labor cost | $15,200 |
| Engineering hours | 62 |
| Square feet | 4,100 |
| Direct labor hours | 75 |

**Required:**

Determine the total overhead cost that would be assigned to Thompson Park Tennis Courts.

Service

**6–20.** **Preliminary and Primary Stage Allocations.** Krohn Movers has a pricing structure that distinguishes between local and out-of-town moving jobs. During the year, the local jobs involved 175,000 miles; and the out-of-town jobs involved 250,000 miles. The following traceable costs are reported by Anita Stein, the controller, for Krohn's activity centers:

| Activity Center | Materials | Labor | Other Costs |
|---|---|---|---|
| #1100 | | | $75,000 |
| #1200 | | | 60,000 |
| #2300 | | | 25,000 |
| #3100 | $36,000 | $45,000 | 80,000 |
| #3200 | 52,000 | 88,000 | 92,000 |

Data for the preliminary stage cost assignment are as follows (in the order shown):

| | Activity Centers Using Resources and Receiving Costs | | |
|---|---|---|---|
| Activity Center | #2300 | #3100 | #3200 |
| #1100 | 10% | 40% | 50% |
| #1200 | 25% | 60% | 15% |
| #2300 | | 80% | 20% |

Data for the primary stage cost assignment are as follows:

| | Jobs Using Resources and Receiving Costs | |
|---|---|---|
| Activity Center | Local | Out-of-Town |
| #3100 | 75% | 25% |
| #3200 | 35% | 65% |

One-fourth of the materials and labor costs are traceable to local jobs and the remainder to out-of-town jobs.

**Required:**

Determine the per mile costs for local jobs and for out-of-town jobs.

**6–21.** **Preliminary and Primary Stage Allocations.** Maryland Forklift Manufacturing produced 100 electric forklifts and 150 propane forklifts during the year. Andy Weber, the controller, reported the following traceable costs, other than direct materials and direct labor, for its activity centers:

| Activity Center | Costs |
|---|---|
| Plant Administration | $66,000 |
| Setup Operations | 24,000 |
| Materials Handling | 47,000 |
| Machining | 180,000 |
| Assembly | 150,000 |

Data for the preliminary stage cost assignment are as follows:

| | Activity Centers Using Resources and Receiving Costs | | |
|---|---|---|---|
| Activity Center | Setup Operations | Machining | Assembly |
| Plant Administration | 5% | 40% | 55% |
| Materials Handling | | 65% | 35% |

Data for the primary stage cost assignment are as follows:

| | | Cost Driver Activity Linked to Each Product | |
|---|---|---|---|
| Activity Center | Cost Driver | Electric | Propane |
| Setup Operations | Number of setups | 30 setups | 20 setups |
| Machining | Machine hours | 250 hours | 150 hours |
| Assembly | Labor hours | 6,000 hours | 9,000 hours |

**Required:**

Determine the overhead cost per unit assigned to each type of forklift.

**6–22.** **Account Balances Under JIT Costing.** Ian Kippen, general manager of Toba Corporation's Midwest Division, has provided the following information for transactions that occurred during March. This division uses a JIT cost system.

**(a)** Raw materials were purchased at the cost of $104,000.

**(b)** All materials purchased were requisitioned for production.

**(c)** Direct labor costs of $77,000 were incurred.

**(d)** Actual factory overhead costs amounted to $225,000.

**(e)** Applied conversion costs totaled $290,000. This included $77,000 of direct labor.

**(f)** All units were completed.

**Required:**

**1.** Determine the March 31 balance in the Conversion Cost account.

**2.** Determine the March 31 balance in the Finished Goods account.

**6–23.** **Recording Transactions Under JIT Costing.** Hyeun-Suk Rhee, owner of Taegu Supply Company in South Korea, which manufactures chopsticks for restaurants, has recently decided to implement a JIT cost system. Transactions (in South Korean won) for August are as follows:

(a) Raw materials were purchased at the cost of W950, 000.
(b) All materials purchased were requisitioned for production.
(c) Direct labor costs of W2,500,000 were incurred.
(d) Actual factory overhead costs amounted to W6,000,000.
(e) Applied conversion costs totaled W8,100,000. This included W2,500,000 of direct labor.
(f) All units were completed.

**Required:**

Enter the August transactions into T-accounts. Label these entries by the identifying letters.

**6–24.** **Comparing JIT Costing to Traditional Costing.** Hagerty, Inc., a manufacturer of computer diskettes, currently uses a conventional process cost system. During February, Hagerty plans to purchase $50,000 of raw materials. Of this amount, 80 percent will be used for current production, while the remainder will serve as a buffer in inventory. Direct labor cost is expected to be $10,000 during February, and the actual factory overhead is anticipated to total $65,000.

Paul Widman, the owner, has been considering the use of a JIT inventory system. If implemented at the beginning of February, only the materials needed for current production would be purchased.

**Required:**

1. Using T-accounts, enter the February transactions for the purchase and usage of materials under:
   (a) Conventional costing.
   (b) JIT costing.
2. Using T-accounts, enter the February transactions for the labor and overhead costs under:
   (a) Conventional costing.
   (b) JIT costing.
   Do not record the entry for applied overhead.

Service

**6–25.** **JIT Costing and Conventional Costing.** Sinkoe's Optometry Center purchases all raw materials (e.g., lenses, frames, etc.) on credit. During June, these purchases totaled $8,700. Labor and actual overhead during June totaled $24,000 and $35,000, respectively. In addition to the labor cost, the applied conversion cost included an added $38,000. All of the eyeglasses worked on during the month were completed and sold on credit for a total of $80,000.

**Required:**

1. Record these transactions (including any closing entries) into T-accounts, assuming a traditional cost system.
2. Record these transactions (including any closing entries) into T-accounts, assuming a JIT cost system.

**6–26.** **Economic Order Quantity (Appendix).** Steffen Corporation uses a chemical in the production of plate glass and it is purchased in bulk. Over the course of a year, 10,000 tons of this chemical are required. It costs $25 to process and receive each order. Storage costs are equal to 20 percent of the $10 cost per ton.

**Required:**
1. How many orders should be place in a year, and how many tons should be received on each order to minimize the combined costs of ordering and storing the chemical?
2. Prove that this cost is minimal by showing the combined cost of the optimum number of orders, the combined cost for one order more than optimal, and the combined cost for one order less than optimal.

**6–27.** **EOQ and Reorder Point (Appendix).** Capland Robotics has reached its capacity to produce a component part for one of its most popular robots. Purchasing has found a supplier for the part that will meet the anticipated delivery schedule. The contract calls for a total of 2,000 parts over the net year. Order costs will be $18 per order, and the carrying costs are $5 per unit per year. The purchase price is $25 per part. The lead time is 30 days. No stockouts are allowed.

**Requsired:**
1. Find the economic order quantity that minimizes total cost.
2. Determine the reorder point.

# Problems

Service

**6–28.** **Activities and Cost Drivers for an Employment Agency.** Kelsey Relocation Services is an employment agency working specifically with mid-level executives looking for new career opportunities or seeking employment after a layoff. The company views its product as placements. These are identified in four categories: employer-paid fee, applicant-paid fee, out-placement contract, and executive-search contract.

The agency incurs a number of costs in performing its services. Those costs are classified as operating expenses as follows:

| Acct # | Account Title |
| --- | --- |
| 402 | Salaries and Wages |
| 403 | Payroll Taxes |
| 404 | Employee Benefits |
| 408 | Office Supplies (postage, stationery, etc.) |
| 409 | Dues and Publications |
| 410 | Utilities |
| 412 | Rent |
| 413 | Repairs and Maintenance (contracted from outside) |
| 420 | Business Promotion |
| 421 | Auto Expenses |
| 422 | Travel Expenses |
| 430 | Professional Fees |
| 432 | Collection Expenses |
| 435 | License |
| 441 | Property Taxes |
| 444 | Insurance Costs |
| 445 | State Franchise Tax |
| 447 | Bad Debt Expense |
| 448 | Depreciation and Amortization |
| 449 | Miscellaneous |

**Required:**

1. Classify each cost as related to unit-level, batch-level, product-level, or facility-level activities. Indicate an appropriate cost driver for each cost.
2. With the information from Part (1), group costs into logical activity groups and specify a cost driver for each activity group.
3. Explain what differences exist between applying activity-based costing to a manufacturing firm and to an employment agency.

**6–29. Unit Costs with Volume-Based Costing and ABC.** Klarman Company produces two products, Single and Double. Data for last year's production are as follows:

|  | Single | Double |
| --- | --- | --- |
| Direct material cost per unit | $77 | $94 |
| Direct labor cost per unit | $15 | $32 |
| Units produced | 17,000 | 11,000 |
| Direct labor hours per unit | 2 | 4 |

The company's overhead costs of $680,000 can be traced to three major activities as follows:

|  |  | **Cost Driver Numbers** | | |
| --- | --- | --- | --- | --- |
|  | Traceable Costs | Total | Single | Double |
| Machine setups | $120,000 | 1,400 | 800 | 600 |
| Power consumption (KWHs) | 450,000 | 116,000 | 44,000 | 72,000 |
| Shipments | 110,000 | 1,100 | 700 | 400 |
|  | $680,000 | | | |

**Required:**

1. If Klarman allocates overhead on the basis of direct labor hours, compute the total cost to produce one unit of each of the two products.
2. If Klarman allocates overhead using ABC, compute the total cost to produce one unit of each of the two products.

**6–30. Cost Estimation with Volume-Based Costing and ABC.** Neil's Customized Gift Service (NCGS) contracts with corporate clients to print their logos and emblems on small giftware items such as pens, cups, calculators, coasters, etc. Cal Nitz, the controller of NCGS, has provided the following information on overhead cost estimates for 2005:

| Activity | Estimated Cost | Cost Driver |
| --- | --- | --- |
| Supervision | $855,000 | Direct labor hours |
| Power | 450,000 | Kilowatt hours |
| Maintenance | 720,000 | Machine hours |
| Setups | 225,000 | Setup hours |

The following are estimated 2005 and planned January activity levels of the cost drivers:

| Cost Driver | Estimated Activity for 2005 | Planned Level in Jan. 2005 |
| --- | --- | --- |
| Direct labor hours | 300,000 | 35,000 |
| Kilowatt hours | 150,000 | 12,000 |
| Machine hours | 120,000 | 10,000 |
| Setup hours | 100,000 | 8,000 |

**Required:**
1. Estimate overhead costs for January 2005 using direct labor hours as the allocation base.
2. Estimate overhead costs for January 2005 using activity-based costing.

**6–31. Traditional Costing and Two-Stage ABC.** Drukman Enterprises recently changed its costing system. The old system used labor dollars as the plant-wide overhead cost driver. A new, two-stage cost assignment system has one service department and two producing departments, each using different cost drivers. The data follow:

| Department | Labor Costs | Overhead | Cost Driver | Activity | Support Hours Used |
|---|---|---|---|---|---|
| Support | | $200,000 | Support hours | 4,000 hours | |
| Painting | $40,000 | 100,000 | Area painted | 50,000 sq. inches | 1,000 hours |
| Polishing | 60,000 | 300,000 | Polishing compound | 1,000 pounds | 3,000 hours |

To test this new ABC system, the controller, John Jenkins, selected Job #441, which used the following resources:

| | |
|---|---|
| Labor cost–Painting | $3,750 |
| Labor cost–Polishing | 6,740 |
| Materials cost | 7,700 |
| Area painted | 3,890 sq. inches |
| Compound used | 52 pounds |

**Required:**
Prepare a total job cost comparison of the old and ABC systems.

Service

**6–32. Overhead Cost Assignment—ABC and Overall Rates.** Sethlynn Airlines uses activity-based costing for its ground handling department. The department has assigned all overhead costs into seven activity cost pools. The budgeted amounts and the associated cost drivers for these cost pools are as follows:

| Activity Cost Pool | Budgeted Costs | Cost Driver | Budgeted Level for Cost Driver |
|---|---|---|---|
| Loading and unloading cargo | $250,000 | Pounds of cargo | 2,000,000 lbs. |
| Directing planes to and from gates | 110,000 | Directing distance | 5,500 miles |
| Loading and unloading baggage | 300,000 | Bags loaded & unloaded | 100,000 bags |
| Communicating with pilots | 80,000 | Communication time | 2,000 hours |
| Fueling planes | 450,000 | Fueling time | 10,000 hours |
| Deicing planes | 75,000 | Deicing time | 1,000 hours |
| Locating mishandled bags | 200,000 | Number of inquiries | 5,000 inquiries |
| Total | $1,465,000 | | |

A flight has just been completed with the following cost driver information available:

| | |
|---|---|
| Pounds of cargo | 40,000 |
| Directing distance (miles) | 1.5 |
| Bags loaded & unloaded | 200 |
| Communication hours | 0.9 |
| Fueling hours | 2.2 |
| Deicing hours | 0 |
| Number of inquiries | 3 |

**Required:**

**1.** Determine the total overhead cost that would be assigned to the flight.

**2.** Compare the total overhead cost computed in Part (1) with one obtained by using an overall overhead rate based on number of bags loaded and unloaded.

**6–33. ABC with Preliminary and Primary Stages.** Techno Manufacturing has grouped activities into five categories: Building, Repair, Computer, Machine, and Finishing. Building charges its costs to the other groupings based on square footage of floor space used. Repair charges its costs only to Machine and Finishing. Computer has both outside and inside business. It uses computer hours as the cost driver for charging costs of work performed. Currently, 30 percent of the computer service is provided to outside customers, while 70 percent goes to inside users. Machine uses setup hours as the cost driver for 40 percent of its costs. Machine hours is the cost driver for the other 60 percent. All costs of Machine are charged to products. Finishing uses transactions as the cost driver for 70 percent of its costs, and the other 30 percent has product flow time as the cost driver. All costs of Finishing are assigned to products.

The current month's costs for each grouping, prior to charging costs from one grouping to another, are as follows:

| | |
|---|---|
| Building | $864,800 |
| Repair | 500,000 |
| Computer | 300,000 |
| Machine | 400,000 |
| Finishing | 200,000 |

The operating statistics for the month for each category follow:

| | Building | Repair | Computer | Machine | Finishing |
|---|---|---|---|---|---|
| Floor space (in sq. ft.) | | 9,000 | 19,000 | 14,400 | 57,600 |
| Repair hours | 8,000 | | | 22,400 | 9,600 |
| Computer hours* | | | | 16,800 | 4,200 |
| Setup hours | | | | 5,000 | |
| Machine hours | | | | 100,000 | |
| Transactions | | | | | 400,000 |
| Product flow time (hours) | | | | | 20,000 |

\* The total computer hours are 30,000, but 30 percent of those relates to outside work. Therefore, 30 percent of the computer costs should be designated for outside work.

During the month, a number of jobs were active. Two jobs were started and completed during the month. Following are the operating statistics for these two jobs:

| | #TK451 | #RG566 |
|---|---|---|
| Setup hours | 200 | 50 |
| Machine hours | 100 | 300 |
| Transactions | 200 | 100 |
| Product flow time | 80 | 900 |

**Required:**

1. Using the indicated preliminary stage cost drivers, determine the total dollars that will be charged into Machine and Finishing.
2. Using the indicated primary stage cost drivers, determine the total amount of costs charged to each of the two jobs.

Service

**6–34. ABC and Volume-Based Costing for Marketing Studies.** Janet Emerson & Associates, a marketing research firm, uses ABC and has budgeted the following overhead costs and cost drivers (10,000 direct labor hours were budgeted.):

| Activities | Cost Driver | Budgeted Cost | Budgeted Activity Level |
|---|---|---|---|
| Phoning | Number of calls | $25,000 | 80,000 |
| Mailing | Number of mailings | 15,000 | 40,000 |
| Personal visits | Miles driven | 10,000 | 50,000 |

The following data were collected on three market research studies completed:

|  | Study #15 | Study #19 | Study #23 |
|---|---|---|---|
| Direct materials cost | $ 6,020 | $ 5,425 | $4,885 |
| Direct labor cost | $15,660 | $12,235 | $19,650 |
| Direct labor hours | 140 | 110 | 175 |
| Number of calls | 500 | 300 | 700 |
| Number of mailings | 7,000 | 6,000 | 2,000 |
| Miles driven | 900 | 1,300 | 1,600 |

**Required:**

1. Using volume-based costing with direct labor hours as the cost driver, calculate the total cost of each of the three studies.
2. Using ABC, calculate the total cost of each of the three studies.

**6–35. Comparing ABC with Traditional Costing.** In manufacturing roller blades, Radzeli Company's plant used 400 direct labor hours, 500 machine hours, and 20 setups. The following overhead costs were taken from the factory accounts by the cost accountant, Sarah Lewis:

| Overhead Expenses | Cost | Volume of Activities |
|---|---|---|
| Machining center | $120,000 | 20,000 machine hours |
| Setup center | 40,000 | 100 setups |
| Total expenses | $160,000 | 4,000 direct labor hours |

The plant was using a factory-wide overhead rate based on direct labor hours. A new ABC system will use machine hours in the Machining Department and number of setups in the Setup Department as cost drivers.

**Required:**

By what amount would the overhead costs assigned to roller blades differ between the prior system and the ABC system?

**6–36. Two-stage Allocation and Overhead Rates.** Koonin Corp. has provided the following information about overhead costs traceable to its activity centers:

| Activity Center | Overhead Cost | Cost Driver |
|---|---|---|
| Maintenance | $90,000 | Maintenance Hours |
| Receiving | 40,000 | Receiving Orders |
| Fabrication | 150,000 | Labor Hours |
| Assembly | 280,000 | Machine Hours |

The following activities were reported:

| Activity Center | Maintenance Hours | Receiving Orders | Labor Hours | Machine Hourss |
|---|---|---|---|---|
| Fabrication | 200 | 30 | 1700 | 450 |
| Assembly | 800 | 120 | 1300 | 550 |

Overhead allocations involving Maintenance and Receiving are performed in the preliminary stage; overhead costs for Fabrication and Assembly are assigned to products in the primary stage.

**Required:**
Compute the overhead rates for product costing in Fabrication and Assembly.

**6–37.    Impact of Grouping Activities.** Frisch Water Treatment Services has one division that manufactures two models of residential water treatment systems. The controller, Adrian Grant, is considering implementing an activity-based cost system for overhead costs. In looking at the operations for the past year, the following overhead costs were reported:

| | |
|---|---|
| Materials handling | $120,000 |
| Receiving | 40,000 |
| Engineering | 90,000 |
| Depreciation on machinery | 60,000 |
| Power | 30,000 |
| Setups | 84,000 |
| Maintenance | 80,000 |
| Packing for shipment | 35,000 |
| Total | $539,000 |

The controller is looking at two alternative approaches. The first is to find a cost driver for each cost. The second is to group some of the costs and to select a cost driver for each grouping. Tentative groupings and their cost drivers are:
**(a)** Materials-related costs (Cost driver = Materials dollars):
     Materials handling
     Receiving
**(b)** Engineering (Cost driver = Engineering labor hours).
**(c)** Manufacturing overhead (Cost driver = Machine hours):
     Depreciation on machinery
     Power
     Setups
     Maintenance
**(d)** Packing for shipment (Cost driver = Number of orders shipped).

The following activity information is available for the past year for the two models:

|  | Standard | Deluxe |
| --- | --- | --- |
| Units produced | 10,000 | 20,000 |
| Direct labor hours | 10,000 | 20,000 |
| Machine hours | 20,000 | 40,000 |
| Number of moves for materials handling | 2,000 | 4,000 |
| Engineering labor hours | 5,000 | 3,000 |
| Number of orders received | 600 | 400 |
| Number of setups | 70 | 30 |
| Maintenance hours used | 1,500 | 2,500 |
| Kilowatt hours | 15,000 | 30,000 |
| Number of orders shipped | 2,000 | 3,000 |
| Materials | $80,000 | $240,000 |

**Required:**
1. Using the costs and activity information, determine how much of the overhead costs would be charged to each model if costs were traced to products under the controller's first alternative.
2. Using the costs and activity information, determine how much of the overhead costs would be charged to each model if costs were traced to products under the controller's second alternative.
3. Explain how grouping of costs influences the costs traced to the products.

**6–38. Distortion of Product Profitability.** The Chromosome Manufacturing Company produces two products, X and Y. The company president, Gene Mutation, is concerned about the fierce competition in the market for product X. He notes that competitors are selling X for a price well below Chromosome's price of $12.70. At the same time, he notes that competitors are pricing product Y almost twice as high as Chromosome's price of $12.50.

Mr. Mutation has obtained the following data for a recent time period:

|  | Product X | Product Y |
| --- | --- | --- |
| Number of units | 11,000 | 3,000 |
| Direct materials cost per unit | $3.23 | $3.09 |
| Direct labor cost per unit | $2.22 | $2.10 |
| Direct labor hours | 10,000 | 2,500 |
| Machine hours | 2,100 | 2,800 |
| Inspection hours | 80 | 100 |
| Purchase orders | 10 | 30 |

Mr. Mutation has learned that overhead costs are assigned to products on the basis of direct labor hours. The overhead costs for this time period consisted of the following items:

| Overhead Cost Item | Amount |
| --- | --- |
| Inspection costs | $16,200 |
| Purchasing costs | 8,000 |
| Machine costs | 49,000 |
| Total | $73,200 |

**Required:**

1. Using direct labor hours to allocate overhead costs, determine the gross margin per unit for each product.
2. Using activity-based costing, determine the gross margin per unit for each product.
3. How do your answers to Parts (1) and (2) help explain the observations made by Gene Mutation about competitors?

Service

**6–39.    Comparison of Labor-Based and ABC Systems.** In the Loubser Advertising Agency, a new cost system has been implemented. The old system applied Other Costs to customer ad jobs using an overhead rate of 300 percent of Labor Costs. The new cost system uses cost drivers for each activity center to cost customer ad jobs. The activity centers and their information are as follows:

| | | | Activity Center Costs | | |
|---|---|---|---|---|---|
| | Labor | Other | Cost Driver | Occupancy Percentage | Hours Worked |
| Occupancy Services | | $100,000 | % of space | | |
| Support Staff Services | | 100,000 | Labor dollars | 20% | |
| Art Department | $ 40,000 | 60,000 | Art hours | 50% | 5,000 (art) |
| Writing Department | 60,000 | 40,000 | Writing hours | 30% | 2,000 (writing) |
| Total activity | $100,000 | $300,000 | | | |

An ad campaign for Monheit Enterprises used $160 (20 hours) of Art Department labor and $1,500 (50 hours) of Writing Department labor. All labor in a given department costs the same rate per hour.

**Required:**

For Monheit Enterprises' ad work, what is the cost difference between the old costing method and the new method?

**6–40.    Overhead Rates and Cost Comparisons.** Joe Asher's Machine Shop makes replacement parts for automotive transmissions. It produces three basic products: gears, shafts, and casings. The company is budgeting activity for 2005. The activity centers, costs, and cost drivers are as follows:

| Activity Center | Budgeted Cost | Cost Driver |
|---|---|---|
| Materials handling | $312,400 | Direct materials cost |
| Production scheduling | 116,000 | Number of production orders |
| Setups | 144,600 | Number of setups |
| Manual machinery | 986,000 | Direct labor hours |
| Automated machinery | 3,212,000 | Machine hours |
| Finishing | 1,798,000 | Direct labor hours |
| Packaging and shipping | 234,000 | Number of orders shipped |

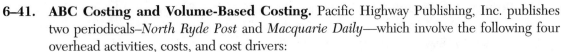

The following data are predicted for 2005:

|  | Gears | Shafts | Casings |
|---|---|---|---|
| Units produced | 10,000 | 2,000 | 700 |
| Direct materials cost per unit | $60 | $80 | $100 |
| Number of production orders | 40 | 20 | 10 |
| Number of setups | 20 | 10 | 14 |
| Direct labor hours | 20,000 | 10,000 | 8,400 |
| Machine hours | 30,000 | 15,000 | 2,800 |
| Number of orders shipped | 1,000 | 1,500 | 70 |

**Required:**

1. Compute an overhead rate for each activity center. Round calculations to four decimal places.
2. Compute an overall rate for the combined activities based on direct labor hours. Round calculations to four decimal places.
3. Show how much overhead is budgeted for gears, shafts, and casings using the activity center rates and the overall rate.
4. Calculate an overall rate for the combined activities based on the total number of units.
5. Show how much overhead is budgeted for gears, shafts, and casings using the rate in Part (4).
6. Explain why the overhead costs differ in Parts (3) and (5).

Service

**6–41.  ABC Costing and Volume-Based Costing.** Pacific Highway Publishing, Inc. publishes two periodicals–*North Ryde Post* and *Macquarie Daily*—which involve the following four overhead activities, costs, and cost drivers:

| Activity | Overhead Cost | Activity Driver |
|---|---|---|
| Design | $275,000 | Number of design changes |
| Receiving | 62,000 | Number of shipments received |
| Setup | 159,000 | Number of setup hours |
| Shipping | 88,000 | Number of outgoing shipments |

Additional information:

|  | Shipments Received | Setup Hours | Design Changes | Outgoing Shipments | Number of Periodicals |
|---|---|---|---|---|---|
| North Ryde Post | 800 | 4,800 | 30 | 4,900 | 140,000 |
| Macquarie Daily | 200 | 800 | 10 | 1,400 | 105,000 |

**Required:**

1. Determine the overhead cost per unit for each periodical if overhead is allocated based on volume of periodicals.
2. Determine the overhead cost per unit for each periodical if overhead is allocated using activity-based costing.

Service

**6–42.  Activity-Based Costing for a Tour Company.** Ozzie Tour Company provides tours in Australia and uses an activity-based cost system. The basic 10-day package covers the east coast, including Sydney, Melbourne, Canberra, Brisbane, and the Great Barrier Reef. The deluxe 21-day package adds the outback, west coast, and other areas including Darwin, Tasmania, Adelaide, Perth, and Alice Springs. Direct labor (drivers, tour guides) and

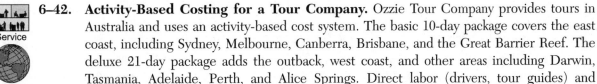

materials costs (e.g., fuel, brochures, various drinks and refreshments, etc.) for 2005 were (in Australian dollars):

|  | 10-day Package | 21-day Package |
| --- | --- | --- |
| Direct labor | A$670,000 | A$1,770,000 |
| Materials | A$10,800 | A$22,400 |

The following additional information for 2005 was provided by the owner, David Rogut:

| | | | Activity (Cost Driver) Level | |
| --- | --- | --- | --- | --- |
| Activity | Overhead Cost | Cost Driver | 10-day Package | 21-day Package |
| Advertising | A$56,700 | No. of ads | 150 | 175 |
| Organizing itinerary | A$89,300 | No. of tours | 55 | 72 |
| Touring | A$380,500 | No. of tourists | 2,725 | 3,130 |

**Required:**
Compute the total cost per tour for each of the two tour packages.

Service

**6–43.**   **Product-Line Profitability Analysis with ABC.** Lefco Supermarket has three main areas within its store: Produce, Packaged Foods, and Nonfood Items. The following information pertains to last year, when store overhead was allocated based on cost of sales:

| | Produce | Packaged Foods | Nonfood Items |
| --- | --- | --- | --- |
| Financial information: | | | |
| Sales | $135,500 | $190,900 | $111,800 |
| Cost of sales | $55,000 | $69,000 | $48,000 |
| Store overhead | $22,000 | $27,600 | $19,200 |
| Activity usage (&cost driver): | | | |
| Ordering (number of orders) | 120 | 50 | 35 |
| Customer support (items sold) | 80,000 | 70,000 | 30,000 |
| Stocking shelves (hours worked) | 720 | 590 | 515 |
| Delivery (number of deliveries) | 310 | 350 | 375 |

An activity analysis revealed that, of total store overhead, 30 percent related to ordering, 20 percent to customer support, 40 percent to stocking shelves, and 10 percent to delivery.

**Required:**
Using ABC, prepare a product-line profitability report for Lefco Supermarket.

**6–44.**   **Analysis of Accounts With JIT Costing.** L.D. Ferreira, general manager of a highly auto-mated coffee production plant in Sao Paulo, Brazil, has provided the following information for transactions that occurred during October. All amounts are in Brazilian real. The production plant uses a JIT cost system.

(a) Raw materials costing R$300, 000 were purchased.
(b) All materials purchased were requisitioned for production.
(c) Direct labor costs of R$200,000 were incurred.

**(d)** Actual factory overhead costs amounted to R$995,000.

**(e)** Applied conversion costs totaled R$1,300,000. This includes the direct labor cost.

**(f)** All units were completed and immediately sold.

**Required:**

1. Determine the October 31 balance in the Cost of Goods Sold account. No adjustment has been made for overapplied or underapplied conversion cost.

2. What was the amount of overapplied or underapplied conversion cost for the month?

**6–45.** **Recording Transactions Under JIT Costing.** Phil's Jewelry Factory manufactures a variety of costume jewelry. The owner, Phil Joseph, has recently decided to implement a JIT cost system. Transactions during September were as follows:

**(a)** Raw materials totaling $45,000 were purchased.

**(b)** All materials purchased were requisitioned for production.

**(c)** Direct labor costs of $11,000 were incurred.

**(d)** Indirect labor costs amounted to $120,000.

**(e)** Utilities costs totaled $15,000.

**(f)** Other actual factory overhead costs amounted to $85,000.

**(g)** Applied conversion costs totaled $221,000. This includes the direct labor costs.

**(h)** All units were completed.

**Required:**

1. Enter the September transactions into T-accounts. Label these entries by the identifying letters.

2. Determine the amount of overapplied or underapplied conversion cost for the month.

**6–46.** **JIT and Conventional Costing.** DeKalb Industrial Products manufactures automated materials-handling systems. The company currently uses a conventional job cost system. During November, the company plans to purchase $96,000 of raw materials. Of this amount, 75 percent will be used for current production, while the remainder will serve as a buffer in inventory. Direct labor cost is expected to be $18,000 during November, and the actual factory overhead is anticipated to total $85,000. The applied factory overhead is expected to be $90,000. By the end of the month, two materials-handling systems should be completed; no systems were in process at the beginning of the month or at the end of the month.

Robert Cohen, the owner, has been considering the use of a JIT inventory system. If implemented at the beginning of November, only the materials needed for current production would be purchased.

**Required:**

1. Using T-accounts, enter the November transactions for the purchase and usage of materials under:

   **(a)** Conventional costing.

   **(b)** JIT costing.

2. Using T-accounts, enter the November transactions for the labor and actual overhead costs under:

   **(a)** Conventional costing.

   **(b)** JIT costing.

3. Using T-accounts, enter the November transactions for the application of overhead costs and the completion of the materials-handling systems under:

   **(a)** Conventional costing.

   **(b)** JIT costing.

**6–47.   JIT Costing Transactions.** Hoffman's Plant Nursery grows many different types of small plants. Bonnie Baseman, the owner, has recently decided to implement a JIT cost system. Transactions during June were as follows:

**(a)**  Raw materials were purchased at a cost of $600.

**(b)**  All materials purchased were used.

**(c)**  Direct labor costs of $4,000 were incurred.

**(d)**  Actual overhead costs amounted to $3,500.

**(e)**  Applied conversion costs totaled $7,950. This included $4,000 of direct labor.

**(f)**  All of the plants were fully grown (i.e., completed).

**(g)**  All of the plants were sold for $9,800 cash.

**Required:**

**1.** Enter the June transactions into T-accounts. Label these entries by the identifying letters.

**2.** Close out the underapplied or overapplied conversion cost.

**6–48.   Optimum Lot Size for Production (Appendix).** Cindy Jaret, a plant supervisor at Kanell Suppliers, believes the company is making a mistake by producing in large lot sizes. She recognizes that there is a cost of $60 (in idle time and other costs) associated with changing a machine setting when a new batch is to be run. But, in her opinion, the cost to store large amounts of product in the warehouse exceeds the cost of changing a production run.

"For example," she stated, "We just completed a run of 1,500 units on a product where annual sales are only 75,000 units. This product has a cost of $500 per unit, and the cost of storage is 20 percent, or $100 a unit."

**Required:**

**1.** How many units should be made on a production run to minimize the combined costs of resetting equipment and storage? What is the minimum combined cost?

**2.** What is the combined cost of resetting equipment and storage when 1,500 units are made on a run?

Service

**6–49.   EOQ and Reorder Point (Appendix).** Schumer's Home Supply Shoppe has a line of kitchen water filtration and treatment systems that the company retails for $240. The purchase price from its supplier, Saralee Industries, is $165 per unit. Annual demand runs about 800 units. Insurance during shipment adds $2 per unit and freight averages $8 per unit. The clerical processing costs of placing an order are $25 per order. The company's cost of capital for its various sources of funds is 16 percent. It takes five days from the time an order is released until the units are delivered. The retail store is open every day except for a few special holidays (assume 360 days). The store currently orders 50 units each time an order is placed.

**Required:**

**1.** Compute the carrying cost per unit. (Hint: determine the cost invested per unit and multiply that amount by 16 percent.)

**2.** How many units should be ordered under economic order quantities? How many orders per year does that result in?

**3.** What is the reorder point?

**4.** Compared to current ordering policies, how much can the company save in carrying and ordering costs if it uses economic order quantities?

# CASE 6A—GLASER HEALTH PRODUCTS

Glaser Health Products of Ranier Falls, Georgia, is organized functionally into three divisions: Operations, Sales, and Administrative. Purchasing, receiving, materials and production control, manufacturing, factory personnel, inventory stores, and shipping activities are under the control of the vice-president for operations, George Gottlieb. Advertising, market research, and sales are the responsibility of the vice-president for sales, Jake Bogan. Accounting, budgeting, the firm's computer center, and general office management are delegated to the corporate controller (Administrative), Charlie Kaplan. The following cost categories are found in the company as a whole:

(a) Depreciation on factory equipment.
(b) Depreciation on office equipment.
(c) Depreciation on factory building.
(d) Advertising manager's salary.
(e) Assembly foreman's salary.
(f) Salespersons' salaries.
(g) Salespersons' travel expenses.
(h) Supplies for the Machining Department.
(i) Advertising supplies used.
(j) Electricity for the Assembly Department.
(k) Lost materials (scrap) in a Machining Department.
(l) Direct labor in the Assembly Department.
(m) Supplies for the sales office.
(n) Sales commissions.
(o) Packing supplies.
(p) Cost of hiring new employees.
(q) Payroll fringe benefits for workers in the Shipping Department.
(r) Supplies for Production Scheduling.
(s) Cost of repairing parts improperly manufactured in the Machining Department.
(t) Paint for the Assembly Department.
(u) Heat, light, and power for the factory.
(v) Leasing of computer equipment for the Accounting Department.

**Required:**
1. Identify each of the costs with the appropriate division: Operations, Sales, Administrative.
2. Identify each of the costs with one of the following:
    (a) Unit-level activities.          (c) Product-level activities.
    (b) Batch-level activities.          (d) Facility-level activities.

   Organize these classifications by division: Operations, Sales, Administrative.
3. Specify an appropriate cost driver for tracing costs associated with the various levels of activities to the next cost objective or products, whichever is appropriate.
4. Glaser Health Products is interested in using activity-based costing to identify as many costs as possible with the products. These costs will be used for planning and control decisions rather than for inventory valuation. The controller decided that all operation costs will be related to products but only those sales and administrative costs that are classified as unit-level, batch-level, or product-level costs should be related to products. Using preliminary stage cost drivers, explain how individual items of costs will be traced to activity groupings.

5. Using primary stage cost drivers, show how the costs should be related to products.

6. Explain why it is necessary to use preliminary stage and primary stage cost drivers.

## CASE 6B—DRUID VALLEY APARTMENTS

Service

Druid Valley Apartments (DVA) has 18 apartment buildings with a total of 600 units—420 two-bedroom units and 180 one-bedroom units. Also, the complex contains a sports area which has a basketball court, exercise room, tennis court, and two activity rooms. The sports area was used by 475 residents this past year. DVA currently has 1,580 tenants—280 in one-bedroom units and 1,300 in two-bedroom units. The one-bedroom apartments occupy 90,000 square feet, while the two-bedroom apartments occupy 275,000 square feet. The sports area occupies 35,000 square feet.

Jerry Siegel, DVA's Chief Operations Officer, oversees the day-to-day operations of the apartment complex. Doug Ross supervises the sports area. He organizes programs, classes and other activities. The facilities are managed by Bruce Gaynes, who oversees the staff for building maintenance and grounds. Sylvia Miller does the bookkeeping and Colleen Weston is the secretary/receptionist.

The following expense report for the past year was given to Jerry Siegel:

| Expense Items | Amounts |
|---|---|
| Administrative salaries | $227,000 |
| Custodial costs | 177,000 |
| Maintenance costs | 90,000 |
| Instructor/trainer costs | 60,000 |
| Grounds costs | 55,000 |
| Heat and electricity | 42,000 |
| Water | 98,000 |
| Office supplies | 13,000 |
| Building depreciation | 795,000 |
| Equipment depreciation | 130,000 |
| Liability and property insurance | 720,000 |
| Advertising | 51,000 |
| Telephone | 17,000 |
| Newsletter | 10,000 |
| Interest | 20,000 |
| Postage | 11,000 |
| Miscellaneous | 27,000 |
| Total Expenses | $2,543,000 |

Siegel wondered what it cost to operate the apartment units and the sports area. He contacted his CPA, Jay Starkman, who convinced him to install an activity-based costing (ABC) system. Siegel engaged Starkman to do this.

After discussions with DVA staff, Starkman developed a list of eight activities that seemed to capture the operations at DVA:

| No. | Activity |
|-----|----------|
| 1 | Attracting new residents |
| 2 | Servicing current residents |
| 3 | Maintaining the buildings |
| 4 | Maintaining the grounds |
| 5 | Cleaning the apartments/sports area |
| 6 | Providing recreational programs |
| 7 | Collecting rent and fees |
| 8 | Sustaining the business |

Activity 6, "providing recreational programs," included classes, personal training, resident meetings, and any other events that took place in the sports area. Activity 8, "sustaining the business," is a catchall that includes tasks such as accounting, purchasing, general office management, and human resource management.

Starkman's next task was to assign costs to the eight activities. He asked all DVA administrative personnel to fill out estimates of how they spent their time, on average, during the past year. These estimates were as follows:

| | Salary | | | | |
|---|---|---|---|---|---|
| Activity: | J. Siegel $67,000 | D. Ross $48,000 | B. Gaynes $44,000 | S. Miller $35,000 | C. Weston $33,000 |
| Attracting new residents | 10% | 5% | | | |
| Servicing current residents | 20% | 20% | | 15% | 10% |
| Maintaining the buildings | 5% | | 30% | | |
| Maintaining the grounds | 5% | | 25% | | |
| Cleaning the apts./sports area | 5% | | 30% | | |
| Providing rec. programs | | 65% | | | |
| Collecting rent and fees | 10% | | | 60% | |
| Sustaining the business | 45% | 10% | 15% | 25% | 90% |
| Total | 100% | 100% | 100% | 100% | 100% |

Some costs were assigned entirely to one activity. These included interest expense, instructor/trainer costs, custodial costs, maintenance costs, and grounds costs. The latter three costs consist of wages to workers as well as various supplies. Office supplies, equipment depreciation, telephone, postage, and miscellaneous expenses were distributed evenly to all eight activities. The remaining costs were assigned as follows:

| Cost | Assignment |
|------|-----------|
| Heat and electricity | 10% to activity 1; 20% to activity 2; 40% to activity 6; 10% to activity 7; 20% to activity 8 |
| Water | 70% to activity 2; 15% to activity 4; 15% to activity 6 |
| Building depreciation | 95% to activity 2; 5% to activity 6 |
| Liability and property insurance | 60% to activity 2; 10% to activity 6; the remainder evenly |
| Advertising | 90% to activity 1; 10% to activity 6 |
| Newsletter | 75% to activity 2; 25% to activity 6 |

After this cost assignment, Starkman decided to allocate evenly the costs that had been assigned to activity 8 to the other seven activities. Having done this, he then assigned the costs of these seven activities to the one-bedroom units, two-bedroom units, and sports area using the following cost drivers:

| Activities | Cost Driver | Cost Objects |
|---|---|---|
| Attracting new residents | Number of units | 1-bedroom units, 2-bedroom units |
| Servicing current residents | Number of residents | 1-br. units, 2-br. units, sports area |
| Maintaining the buildings | square footage | 1-br. units, 2-br. units, sports area |
| Maintaining the grounds | square footage | 1-br. units, 2-br. units, sports area |
| Cleaning the apts./sports area | Number of residents | 1-br. units, 2-br. units, sports area |
| Providing recreational programs | | sports area |
| Collecting rent and fees | Number of residents | 1-br. units, 2-br. units, sports area |

**Required:**

Determine the total costs assigned to the one-bedroom units, two-bedroom units, and the sports area. For the apartment units, also compute the costs per unit. Comment on these costs.

# PLANNING AND CONTROL FRAMEWORK

# BUDGETING FOR OPERATIONS MANAGEMENT

## LEARNING OBJECTIVES

After studying Chapter 7, you will be able to:

1. Identify the major elements of a financial planning and control system.

2. Explain the major purposes of budgeting.

3. Define responsibility accounting including cost, profit, and investment centers.

4. Understand the role of flexible budgeting in planning and control.

5. Identify the major human behavior factors that affect budgets and the budgeting process.

6. Identify independent and dependent budget variables.

7. Understand the basic format and calculation sequences necessary for preparation of budgets and supporting schedules.

8. Prepare and format schedules for all elements of the master budget.

9. Identify the primary components of financial planning models. (Appendix)

10. Understand the need for simulation capabilities in budget preparation and for "what if" analyses. (Appendix)

# Budgeting: The Negatives and the Positives!

*If you mention the words "plans" or "budgets" to Joyce Hengesbach, president of Internet Pathways, you get a reaction ranging from disdain to outright hostility. She has been heard to say:*

*"How can I plan? Things always change so fast!"*

*"My business isn't suited to anything so formal. My managers and I need to be flexible, fast on our feet, and ready to change direction overnight, if we have to do so."*

*"The budget always says we can't do it. I just say, 'Do it!'"*

*"The budget reports tell me where I've been, never where I'm going."*

*"That's the accountant's budget; it doesn't tell me what my problems are and what to do about them!"*

*"We can't wait for approvals and reports. Budgets hold us back!"*

*Joyce even has a coffee cup with "Budgets Are For Wimps!" printed on it. She believes that intuition and drive, not reports, got the company to where it is today.*

*"The easiest way to lose our edge is to start acting like paper shufflers!" she exclaims. Each of her comments has some truth in it; but, more likely, the comments together reflect serious deficiencies in the firm's management process–little or no planning and little ability to measure performance.*

*A close friend says plans and budgets strike terror in Joyce because her "style" is threatened. She likes to operate quickly, often keeping others in the dark. The friend says that she's afraid to admit that she had little idea where the company is going.*

*Recently, a situation arose where Joyce thought employees were making too many "bad calls" on key decisions. She was surprised by the responses she got when she asked several department managers what was wrong. Each complained about lack of direction at the top, how management kept changing its mind, that there was no plan of action, and how employees felt they could not judge how each of them and the company as a whole was progressing.*

A SIMPLE CONCEPT is a key to budgeting: Planning is not deciding what to do in the future; it is deciding what to do now to assure a future. This chapter discusses concepts, tools, and processes used in a planning and control system and illustrates an integrated master budget.

## BUDGETING: A PLANNING AND CONTROL SYSTEM

Planning and control consist of an overall management system. **Planning** can be viewed as a framework within which managers anticipate future events, develop a plan of action, and estimate future revenues and costs. **Control** is the process of using feedback on actual operating results to compare to the plan, to evaluate performance in achieving the plans and goals, and to make changes. A **budget** is a plan showing what and how resources are to be used over a specified time period.

The plan, act, control, and evaluate cycle is shown in Figure 7.1. The master plan is prepared; decisions are made and actions taken; reports are prepared and analyzed; and the plan is reviewed and updated.

A **mission statement** sets the purpose of the organization. **Goals and objectives** are statements about its future position and its long-term direction. They describe specific performance targets within certain timeframes. A profit goal might be, for example, to earn an annual 15 percent

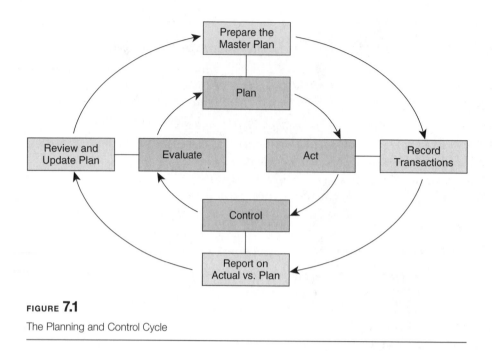

**FIGURE 7.1**

The Planning and Control Cycle

after tax return on shareholders' equity or to generate sales of $1 billion by 2008. Once goals (direction and motivations) and objectives (quantified performance targets) are set, action plans can be defined. The budgeting process determines the inputs needed to achieve the forecast outputs.

A planning and control system includes tools, methods, and attitudes. The following set of common elements appears:

- **Strategic planning process.** This long-range planning effort defines the firm's mission (why the firm exists), the **long-range goals** (what level of achievement it expects), and a **strategic plan** (what markets, price policies, resource needs, and production capabilities the firm will have).

- **Business plan and personal goal setting.** Creating the annual business plan is the task of evaluating the firm's strengths, weaknesses, opportunities, and tactics to build firm-wide priorities for the coming year. Also, each manager develops a personal set of goals and a plan of achievements that are consistent with firm's business plan.

- **Planning process and timetable.** A budgeting schedule includes when to start the process, submit budgets, and review and approve budgets at various management levels—who does what and when.

- **Responsibility accounting system.** This is a planning and control system that combines responsibility centers, control reports, and activity centers and cost drivers from activity-based costing.

- **Reward or incentive system.** Rewards can provide incentives for managers who achieve their unit's budget goals and/or MBO targets. Tying performance to compensation appears to be an increasingly common practice.

- **Financial modeling.** Ability to evaluate alternative or "what if" scenarios is now an expected part of any financial planning system. Simulation can test a plan to assess goal achievement and evaluate alternative actions.

- **Participatory budgeting.** It is assumed that every manager in the firm is involved in planning and control. Often, budget objectives are set at the executive level; but budgets are constructed from the bottom up—sometimes called "grass roots" budgeting.

A budget period may be a week, month, quarter, year, or longer. But normally, a master budget is for a year's activities and is divided into months or quarters. Long-term budgets may be for five or more years.

# RESPONSIBILITY ACCOUNTING

**Responsibility accounting** has no universal definition but does link authority and control. Managers prepare plans for their areas of responsibility and exert control over those activities by making decisions and evaluating results. A responsibility accounting system brings discipline to planning and control tasks. The same basic elements remain visible in accounting systems of small firms to sophisticated planning systems in large, complex organizations. The basic elements of responsibility accounting are:

- **Responsibility center definitions**–to segment the organization into small sets of similar activities.
- **Control reports**–to report actual versus plan for expenses, revenues, and other financial and activity measures such as cost drivers.
- **Roll-up reporting capability**–to summarize lower level activities at higher levels along responsibility channels.

Strictly speaking, cost control is less cost control and more management of people who incur costs. Controllable costs are tied to organizational structure, activities management, and performance assessment.

## Responsibility Centers

From a firm's perspective, planning and control focus on responsibility centers. A **responsibility center** is an organizational unit that has a specific manager with authority and control over spending, earning, or investing. Responsibility centers can be subdivided into three groups—cost centers, profit centers, and investment centers. Figure 7.2 illustrates these responsibility centers.

A **cost center** is a responsibility center where control exists over incurring costs. Often, cost centers are defined by an organization chart and may be further subdivided into more cost centers if costs and activities can be better linked for cost determination and management purposes. It is here that quality costs, setups, and other ABC relationships are integrated into the cost system. A cost center is the smallest unit of an organization within which costs and activities are measured. **Activity centers**, discussed in Chapter 6, are like cost centers.

A **profit center** is a responsibility center where control exists over generating revenue and incurring its related costs. Often, sales organizations are profit centers–with product revenues, cost of sales, and marketing expenses. Managers with product-line responsibility might include both manufacturing and marketing departments. Branch or regional managers often have sales and expense control. The term **revenue center** can be used where a manager has revenue responsibility but controls few expenses, such as in a regional sales office.

An **investment center** is a responsibility center where control exists over costs, revenues, and investments in assets used or managed. Managers must have the authority to acquire or dispose of assets. Typically, divisions of large firms are considered to be investment centers and are viewed by top management essentially as separate business entities.

## Identifying Cost Centers

In many cases, cost centers parallel the boxes on the organization chart. Figure 7.2 illustrates the link between a firm's organization and its cost center coding. Activity groupings should be studied before cost centers are defined. In fact, ABC, TQM, nonmonetary performance measures, and other management needs may well determine the responsibility center structure. A logic is

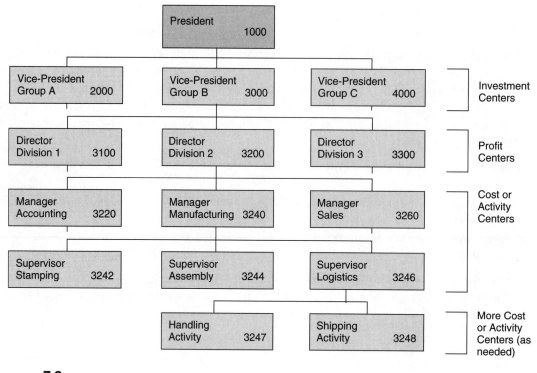

FIGURE **7.2**

Responsibility Centers: Investment, Profit, and Cost Centres

## Contemporary Practice 7.1
### Different Organization and Adjusting the Accounting planning and control system

*Traditionally, organizations have been structured around a functional organizational chart: operations, marketing, accounting, human resources, and research and development. As companies grow, they frequently move to a divisional structure, organized around product lines, world geography, or different customer groupings. Functional activities would be part of each division. To gain efficiencies, a hybrid structure evolves where certain activities are centralized at corporate levels (i.e., finance and R & D) and others are decentralized within divisional groups (i.e., marketing and after-market customer service).*

*Matrix organizations evolve to combine the advantages of both functional and divisional*

*organizations. Marketing may be done at the divisional level but coordinated across all divisions by a corporate marketing function. Now, in specific situations, a manager has both functional and divisional responsibility. The accounting system must be designed to provide relevant information to from both perspectives to make good choices at that decision point, consistent with corporate goals. Accountants must "go back to the drawing board" as we seek to design accounting planning and control systems to serve new organizational approaches.*

*Source: Ritson, Philip, "Accounting for Organizational Design," Australlian CPA, April 2000, pp. 46–51.*

Cost Center:    Stamping  
Cost Center No.:   3242

Period:    September  
Supervisor:   Tatso Kannisoni

| | Monthly | | | Year-to-Date | | |
|---|---|---|---|---|---|---|
| | Actual | Budget | Fav./ (Unfav.) | Actual | Budget | Fav./ (Unfav.) |
| 6110 Total direct labor | 23465 | 24192 | 727 | 206211 | 209520 | 3309 |
| 6160 Total direct materials | 79560 | 80000 | 440 | 712344 | 715000 | 2656 |
| 6211 Machine setup | 3703 | 3424 | (279) | 29920 | 30608 | 688 |
| 6212 Downtime | 1076 | 1680 | 604 | 13357 | 13286 | (71) |
| 6215 Maintenance labor | 430 | 639 | 209 | 4205 | 3016 | (1189) |
| 6245 Hourly overtime premium | 761 | 0 | (761) | 3094 | 0 | (3094) |
| 6271 Hourly fringe benefits | 11222 | 12000 | 778 | 106112 | 103506 | (2606) |
| 6330 Repairs-dies & fixtures | 10671 | 7319 | (3352) | 78971 | 77446 | (1525) |
| 6441 Rework | 68 | 22 | (46) | 479 | 206 | (273) |
| 6443 Scrap | 1247 | 1242 | (5) | 8730 | 13827 | 5097 |
| 6490 Miscellaneous expenses | 118 | 160 | 42 | 1901 | 1434 | (467) |
| Total controllable o/h expenses | 29296 | 26486 | (2810) | 246769 | 243329 | (3440) |
| 6220 Other indirect labor | 2498 | 2389 | (109) | 21111 | 20732 | (379) |
| 6260 Salaries | 2107 | 2045 | (62) | 16914 | 18105 | 1191 |
| 6272 Salaried benefits | 424 | 518 | 94 | 4138 | 4812 | 674 |
| 6320 Repairs-equipment | 7066 | 10069 | 3003 | 82987 | 80253 | (2734) |
| 6420 Factory utilities | 337 | 139 | (198) | 2564 | 3888 | 1324 |
| Total semicontrollable o/h expenses | 12432 | 15160 | 2728 | 127714 | 127790 | 76 |
| 6510 Depreciation-building | 271 | 267 | (4) | 1588 | 962 | (626) |
| 6520 Depreciation-equipment | 4070 | 4070 | 0 | 36630 | 36630 | 0 |
| 6540 Property taxes | 1342 | 1342 | 0 | 12078 | 12078 | 0 |
| 6780 Administrative allocations | 33945 | 27503 | (6442) | 260230 | 244201 | (16029) |
| Total allocated o/h expenses | 39628 | 33182 | (6446) | 310526 | 293871 | (16655) |
| Total cost center overhead | 81356 | 74828 | (6528) | 685009 | 664990 | (20019) |
| Total cost center expenditures | 184381 | 179020 | (5361) | 1603564 | 1589510 | (14054) |
| Activity measures: | | | Diff | | | Diff |
|   Workers | 12.0 | 12.0 | 0.0 | 11.7 | 11.8 | 0.1 |
|   Direct labor hours | 1920.0 | 2016.0 | 96.0 | 16450.0 | 17460.0 | 1010.0 |
|   Number of stampings (000) | 179.7 | 175.0 | 4.7 | 1563.0 | 1575.0 | 12.0 |
|   Operating machine hours | 1145.0 | 1209.6 | 64.6 | 10419.0 | 10476.0 | 57.0 |

FIGURE **7.3**

Example of a Cost Center Control Report

often created by a numbering system–defining different parts of the organization, levels of management, and superior/subordinates links. For example, the first digit indicates a group; the second, a division; the third, a functional area; and the last digit provides even greater detail if needed.

Design of the cost system is critical. If activities are segmented too finely, too many cost centers are created; and key cost information is subdivided too finely. Yet, data aggregation and summarization start here. A greater danger is losing important cost relationships if cost and activity detail are too summarized. Cost centers defined too broadly lose detail needed in later analyses, and this detail can be recreated only at great cost.

## Control Reports and Roll-Up Reporting

Control reports are prepared routinely for each cost center for a specific time period. Figure 7.3 is a cost center report from a metal-forming factory. This is from Cost Center 3242 in Figure 7.2 and uses an account numbering system set up to detail the types of costs that will be tracked. This factory has nearly 40 cost centers and uses approximately four hundred different expense accounts.

Several observations should be made about the control report in Figure 7.3. The breakdown among controllable, semicontrollable, and allocated expenses is an excellent approach to signal which costs and variances are the responsibility of that cost center's manager. Monthly and year-to-date comparisons of actual to budget costs report the current situation, annual trends, and magnitude and direction of variances from budget. Activity measures, including cost drivers that relate overhead costs to outputs, are reported at the bottom of the report.

The overall performance of supervisor Kannisoni in controllable and semicontrollable categories was close to budget for September. But because of an extra large administrative allocation in account 6780, the cost center's total overhead expenses appear to be about $6,000 over budget. While including allocated expenses may be useful for other purposes, it has little beneficial budget impact and violates a basic responsibility accounting rule–account for what you control.

**Roll-up reporting** aggregates results for each higher management level. Middle and upper levels of management receive reports containing summarized results for all cost centers under their control. The report in Figure 7.3 is reviewed by supervisor Kannisoni and his superior. Results from this cost center are summarized at the next higher level–in the control report for the manufacturing manger in Cost Center 3240 from Figure 7.2. All cost centers in Division 2, Profit Center 3200, are summarized in the director's control report. Division 2 is then summarized in Group B vice-president's Investment Center 3000 control report along with all divisions reporting to the Group B vice-president. All responsibility center reports are eventually summarized into one firm-wide control report for the president.

# WHY BUDGET?

Advantages of budgeting nearly always outweigh the costs and efforts required by the process. Although many reasons exist for budgeting, several key purposes are now discussed.

**Formalize the Planning Process.** Perhaps the foremost purpose of budgeting is to compel managers to think about the future. This forces them to set goals, consider future problem areas, and formulate strategies. Budgeting motivates managers to anticipate opportunities, problems, and actions rather than to merely react.

**Create a Plan of Action.** The planning process brings together ideas, forecasts, resource availability, and financial realities to create a course of action to achieve the firm's goals and objectives. Build the plan, then use it!

**Create a Basis for Performance Evaluation.** Actual results lack meaning unless they are compared to some target or a budgeted number. A budget is a **benchmark** against which actual results are measured and managers' performances are evaluated. Significant variances between actual and planned require explanations and, often, corrective actions.

**Promote Continuous Improvement.** Redesigning processes, increasing productivity expectations, eliminating nonvalue-adding activities, and erasing quality problems are integral parts of planning for future performance. The budgeting system is where these improvement processes are quantified and locked into operating plans.

**Coordinate and Integrate Management's Efforts.** Budgeting processes open lines of communication within the organization: (1) up and down organizational lines of subordinates and supervisors and (2) across organizational lines to integrate functional tasks.

**Aid in Resource Allocation.** "We'll do it, if we get budget approval to hire another person." This is a typical comment about resources and budgets. Many resources are allocated during budget preparation time.

**Create an "Aura of Control."** The expression "in control" can mean many things; but, in a management sense, effective controls ensure that managers understand their authority, responsibilities, and limits. A budget system can serve as a fiscal disciplinarian or a "money cop."

**Motivate Managers and Employees Positively.** The motivational "good news" is:

- People who help to prepare budgets for their domain will have a commitment to the budget and take pride in achieving "our" plans.
- Through the budget, managers can see how their parts of the puzzle fit together to form a whole—the firm-wide plan.
- Promotions, raises, and incentives are based on job performance, which includes achieving budget targets.

Budgeting systems can promote improved teamwork, more involvement in process improvement, and greater goal congruency throughout the organization. If management, from the president down, treats budgets as important, each manager and employee will too.

## Behavioral Side of Budgeting

While the goal is to motivate managers positively, budgeting can have a variety of impacts on people and organizations. Budgets have the potential of motivating workers to reach higher levels of efficiency and productivity or creating artificial barriers to progress.

## Top-Management Support

Intense top-management involvement in planning and control processes is correlated with budgeting success at middle and lower management levels. Nothing will destroy the effectiveness of the budgeting process quicker than managers' perceptions that their superiors do not support the process. Top-management actions must cement the impression that a major commitment exists for planning and budget-related performance evaluations.

Demonstration of support involves at least five important steps. First, establish clearly delineated lines of authority and responsibility. Second, involve managers in the planning process. Third, set appropriate goals and objectives that can be easily translated into plans and actions at lower management levels. Fourth, review, critique, and approve budgets thoroughly. And fifth, follow-up and review budget reports with the intent of encouraging budget updates and goal-oriented actions.

## Budget Slack

**Budget slack**, also called "padding the budget," occurs when managers intentionally request more funds than needed. If lower level managers know from past experience that their budget requests will be cut by upper-level managers, the response is to inflate certain expenses or to "low-ball" revenue estimates. In turn, upper-level managers, knowing that lower-level managers pad their budgets, automatically raise estimated revenues and cut budgeted expenses. The result is a vicious circle of lack of trust and counter productivity.

Another problem arises during budget downsizing when upper management requires all segments to cut expenses by some arbitrary percentage, say 10 percent. Managers may make noneconomic decisions or resort to gamesmanship for self-preservation, perhaps creating protective slack for the next cuts. This approach suffers from three weaknesses: (1) organizational differences are ignored; (2) specific resource reallocations needed to support the firm's long-run goals are obliterated; and (3) executive management is viewed as capricious and uncaring. In its defense, if everyone "shares" the pain of budget reductions, a feeling of "together we can solve the problem" can be encouraged.

The most effective weapon against "slack" and "across the board" budget cutting is a careful and rigorous review of budgets by line managers. To be effective, reviewers must know the inner workings of the activities reporting to them. Nonaccounting managers must be able to read and interpret budget data and control reports.

## Human Factors and Budget Stress

Budgets are bases for directing activities and establishing a discipline within an organization. The tightness of budgets necessarily depends on a number of factors, including the ability to predict future results for a given function, the manager's experience, and the closeness of supervision. Some people need close guidance and a "fear of God" approach, while others operate best with broad degrees of freedom. Supervisors and upper-level managers must make careful judgments about how tight budget standards should be for each manager. Remember, the objectives are to generate the greatest benefit from each manager's area of responsibility and to maximize goal achievement for the whole organization.

## Ethics of Budgeting

"Gamesmanship" often rears its head in budgeting. Budgets are future estimates. Management judgment is heavily involved. We expect ethical behavior, objective allocations of resources based on need and returns, and a managerial attitude of fairness and equity to permeate the organization. We have already mentioned the problem of budget slack–budgeting expenses too high or revenues too low to cover anticipated budget cuts. Other problems involve misstating to earn approval of projects, hiding over spending on one project by charging expenses to another project, blaming controllable budget variances on noncontrollable events, and pressuring subordinates which encourages them to act unethically "to meet the budget." In the public sector where budgets are legislated, spending unused appropriations near the end of a fiscal year on nonessential or wasteful activities to help justify budget requests for the next fiscal year is common and borders on unethical use of public funds.

Executive management must be alert to messages that the budget system sends to all employees. The discussions of "aura of control," top-management support, budget slack, and human factors all combine to highlight the importance of a structured control system with clear responsibilities and feedback. Planning and control systems can move a firm to a higher ethical plane and also create more dilemmas. Managers involved in budget-setting process and in the control reporting process are the most effective weapons in upholding the integrity of the planning and control system.

## MASTER BUDGET–AN OVERVIEW

The annual budgeting effort is commonly called the **master budget** or, in some firms, the **profit plan** or financial plan. Although a master budget usually covers a one-year period in detail, it may be prepared on a month-by-month basis for the year and may be extended in summary form for several years.

## Master Budget for a Manufacturer

Master budget terminology and classifications may differ among organizations, but a common set is shown in flowchart format in Figure 7.4 to describe it and its supporting schedules. A comprehensive example follows to illustrate each schedule and its format. Figure 7.4 references the appropriate master budget schedules shown later in the chapter.

**Operating Budgets.** The **operating budget** is a formal document that takes a sales forecast and converts it into a plan of action. Planned operating results are summarized in a cash-flow forecast and forecast financial statements. The day-to-day activities of any business are the interdependent parts of an operating cycle. The **operating cycle** is a circular sequence of events from purchasing on account, paying those bills, generating sales, and collecting cash for the sales. The cycle can be viewed as a "cash-to-cash" process. The cycle continuously repeats itself.

**Cash-Flow Forecast.** Cash-flow forecasting is a key to cash management. **Cash management** is planning and controlling cash balances over time. Often, three timeframes can be identified: long term, annual, and short term which may be daily or weekly. Each fits into the firm's planning process.

**Project Budgets.** While much budgeting uses a 12-month timeframe to plan repetitive activities, a number of activities are project-related and have **project budgets.** Examples include

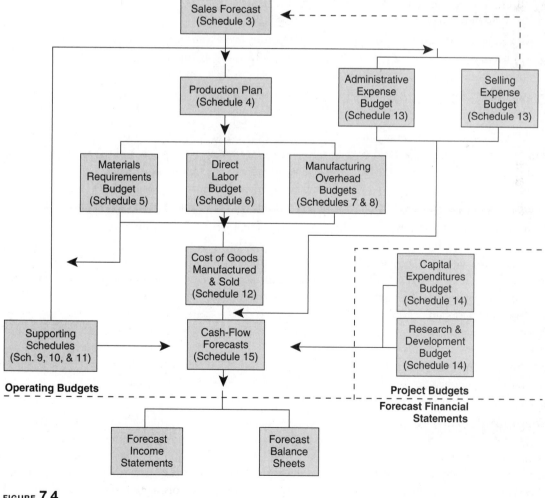

**FIGURE 7.4**

Master Budget Components and Their Relationships

capital spending for new construction and equipment, research and development programs, and information systems development projects. Project costs are planned around resources and the project's time line. Project budgets, however, are integrated into annual plans as well.

**Forecast Financial Statements.** Forecast balance sheets and income statements summarize the financial results from operating, cash-flow, and project budgets for managers. Forecast income statements and balance sheets provide managers with information needed to judge how adequately the master plan achieves the firm's financial goals and objectives. Most financial goals are expressed as ratios of balance sheet and income statement numbers. The forecast financial data then become the basis for management's evaluation of actual results. Information from internal planning processes and released to stockholders and others external to the firm is carefully structured, must meet external reporting requirements, and is called "financial forecasts" or "financial projections."

## Master Budget for Nonmanufacturing Organizations

How does a master budget differ for a merchandising or service organization? The basic budgeting concepts are essentially the same; however, variations do exist.

**Merchandising Organizations.** A merchandiser replaces production with purchases in Figure 7.4. The budget cycle for merchandisers will have the following different traits:

- Often, multiple locations exist and have individual budgets. Budgets for all segments are consolidated into one sales and operating expense budget.
- Revenue and expense budgets for store operations are created.
- If distribution systems and warehousing are involved, these budgets must be linked to sales forecasts and store budgets.
- A greater proportion of managers are profit center managers (product lines, branches, or departments) with both revenue and expense responsibilities.

Most merchandising companies will concentrate on a gross margin or contribution margin plan, which combines sales and cost of sales budgets. Operating expenses may differ in nature in merchandising firms, but the functional classifications of selling and administrative expenses remain.

**Service Organizations.** A service organization often depends heavily on human resources. Planning personnel capacity and staffing levels is critical. In many service organizations, personnel expenses, which include salaries and benefits, account for well over 75 percent of all expenses. This is the case, for example, in school systems and accounting, legal, and consulting firms. Here personnel may be organized by type of service, skill, customer, or project. Staffing plans using headcounts may be more valuable for planning and control than dollar plans.

In complex organizations such as hospitals and banks, budgets develop around services provided. Forecasts of customer or patient work volumes, equipment used, support services required, and revenue generated are developed in responsibility centers and are combined vertically and linked horizontally. In financial institutions, for example, interest income from loans and investments is forecast along with interest expense paid on deposits. Yet, operating expenses for the people who make loans and get deposits require traditional expense budgeting.

**Nonprofit Organizations.** Many nonprofit organizations operate similar to merchandising and service firms. Yet, two characteristics of nonprofit organizations require special attention: (1) lack of clearly defined outputs and (2) fixed or legislated inputs or revenues. These commonly arise with governmental, educational, and philanthropic services. Budgets are determined by a legislative process with legal constraints placed on how much can be spent and what type of spending can be incurred. The outputs might be better fire protection, natural resource conservation, or national defense. In certain areas, workloads can be defined, such as in issuing drivers licenses or processing tax returns. Given the legislated revenue side, the budgeter's tasks are to work with managers to define desirable goals and outcomes, to allocate resources (people and dollars) to the programs that generate the greatest benefit, and to evaluate performance based on comparisons of predefined goals and results for given benchmarks.

## THE STARTING POINT AND BEYOND

The executive team meets to set goals, targets, and assumptions. If executives emphasize planning, updating budgets, and evaluating performances using budget comparisons, all managers see that financial planning and control are major parts of the "corporate culture." The controller sets the wheels in motion by providing time schedules, forecast support data, and forms. But given these basics, where is the starting point of the planning cycle? What is planned first?

### Finding the Controlling Constraint

The starting point of the budget effort should always be the most constraining variable. Generally, this is sales. Most managers work to generate more sales. But other constraining variables might be:

- Machine capacity in a specialized area (plastic extruding equipment in a plastic bottle plant).
- Floor space in a retail outlet (the first floor in a major downtown department store).
- Salespersons' time to make calls on customers (sales reps who must decide on which client to visit).
- Tables in a restaurant (where demand for reservations cannot be met).

When a variable other than sales limits growth, it becomes the starting point for planning. But, for most firms, sales units or revenue is the limiting "resource."

### Sales Forecasting

A realistic sales budget is the foundation of a master budget. The **sales forecast** is based on a variety of interlocking factors, such as pricing policy, economic outlook, industry conditions, advertising, historical patterns, and the firm's strategic market position. A sales forecast is built using data from many sources, including:

- Analysis of historical trends to create a momentum forecast.
- Grass-roots forecasts by products and by customers prepared by salespersons.
- Statistical analysis of sales and economic data.
- Market research analysis of promotion, sales efforts, and market share.

These approaches are not independent. More likely, all are involved in solving the forecasting problem. Each method tests the assumptions and the data of the others. The marketing plan and the sales forecast are interdependent. Figure 7.4 shows the reciprocal relationship by solid and dotted linePart Three

### Using Activity-Based Costing Relationships

Activity-based costing sets formal links among resource inputs and their costs, operating activities, and outputs. The budgeting process must include these relationships in converting expected sales volumes into production and operating expense budgets. A carefully developed ABC system will

*"The sales budget is key to the entire budgeting process, and an accurate sales budget is based on an accurate sales forecast," says a Lowe's executive. Three sales forecasts are prepared and then merged. The controller's forecast is based on historical sales, general economic conditions, industry competition, and market research studies. Individual store managers prepare a local sales forecast. Regional managers make a forecast for their areas of responsibility. The three forecasts are brought together at the corporate offices, and a single approved sales budget results.*

*Source: Howell, K. A., "Lowe's Companies' Statistical Approach to Sales Forecasting," Corporate Controller, May-June 1991, pp. 24–28.*

greatly simplify the budgeting process by using the cost functions developed for product costing to plan expenses. From ABC studies come a much greater understanding of cost-causing relationships.

Quality assessment, JIT performance, and employee involvement and empowerment measures are parts of planning and evaluation processes. These are predominately nonmonetary indicators but still part of budgeting. Financial modeling can include these linkages in a computer-based simulation of operations and operating budgets. Budgeting, benchmarking, and continuous improvement are integrated.

## Independent and Dependent Variables

The planning assumptions, management inputs, product cost and price data, sales forecasts, and all the formula-driven relationships are called **independent variables**; they can be changed by the planner or budget analyst. Most remaining values in budgets come from mathematical relationships, using the independent variables. These calculated values are called **dependent variables**. Independent variables are used to calculate dependent variables. For example, sales units, prices, and the percentage of sales collected in the month of sale are independent variables and combined to find cash collected, a dependent variable. In spreadsheet software logic, independent variables are constants or external inputs. The dependent variables are found by creating a cell formula.

Through modeling, "what if" changes to independent variables will allow alternative scenarios to be tested. The impacts of the changes can be seen on the dependent variables–for example, net income.

## Preparing and Formatting Budget Schedules

Budget preparation uses forecasts, planning assumptions, basic logical and mathematical relationships, and management experience and judgment. A few calculation guidelines help, such as:

- While budgeting does not follow debit and credit rules, a final test of the master budget is whether the forecast balance sheet balances. Are all flows of dollars included?

- Budget relationships are defined quantitatively to allow the same formulas to be repeated in later time periods, such as in spreadsheet cell formulas.

- Ideally, initial planning assumptions, management inputs, and beginning values (the independent variables) should be sufficiently complete to calculate all other variables.

- Prepare schedules in the order of the sequential chain of events, such as the sales forecast, production plan, and then the purchases schedule.

- Align time periods by columns—month by month or quarter by quarter. This pattern allows repetitive calculations to be duplicated easily.

- Put independent variables in an initial schedule for easy access when making "what if" changes for later analyses.
- Avoid circular reasoning. For example, sales may be a function of advertising. Yet, the advertising budget may be a percentage of sales.

Structure and format simplify budget preparation. Frequently, data from one period are needed in the prior or next period. Or, data in one schedule are used in a following schedule. A structure keeps data and calculations organized.

Assume that:

1. Sales for the first four months of 2007 are forecast to be $50,000, $60,000, $80,000, and $70,000, respectively.
2. Cost of sales is forecast to be 60 percent of sales.
3. Beginning inventory is $18,000. Ending inventory is expected to be 40 percent of next month's cost of sales.
4. Cash from sales will be collected as follows: 60 percent in the month of sale and 40 percent in the month after the sale. Uncollectibles are ignored here.
5. Beginning accounts receivable is $40,000, all from December sales.

The format and data for cash receipts forecasting for 2007's first quarter are:

|  | January | February | March |
|---|---|---|---|
| Sales | $50,000 | $60,000 | $80,000 |
| Cash collections of receivables from: |  |  |  |
| December sales ($40,000 receivables) | $40,000 |  |  |
| January sales ($50,000 × 0.6 and × 0.4) | 30,000 | $20,000 |  |
| February sales ($60,000 × 0.6 and × 0.4) |  | 36,000 | $24,000 |
| March sales ($80,000 × 0.6) |  |  | 48,000 |
| Total cash collected from sales | $70,000 | $56,000 | $72,000 |

The January *column* contains all data needed to find cash collections for January. The sales *row* provides the data to find cash collections for January, February, and March. This column/row format can be used in all master budget schedules.

The format and data for forecasting purchases for the first quarter are:

|  | January | February | March | April |
|---|---|---|---|---|
| Sales | $50,000 | $60,000 | $80,000 | $70,000 |
| Cost of sales (60 %) | 30,000 | 36,000 | 48,000 | 42,000 |
| Product needs: |  |  |  |  |
| Cost of sales | $30,000 | $36,000 | $48,000 | $42,000 |
| Ending inventory (40 % of next month's cost of sales) | 14,400 | 19,200 | 16,800 |  |
| Total needs | $44,400 | $55,200 | $64,800 |  |
| Product available: |  |  |  |  |
| Less beginning inventory | 18,000 | 14,400 | 19,200 |  |
| Required purchases | $26,400 | $40,800 | $45,600 |  |

As can be seen from the arrows, organizing data by columns and rows sets a repeating pattern for calculations. Also, an important pattern is established—sales plus ending inventory set the total amount needed, while beginning inventory and purchases meet the need.

## Contemporary Practice 7.3
### What If the Sales Budget is Wrong?

*While many marketing managers can quote their company's forecast accuracy, most cannot quantify value of accurate sales forecasts. Now, managers are looking at quantifying the costs of forecast errors in both operations and in marketing itself. Different costs result from over-forecasting and under-forecasting. Having estimates of these costs places greater priority on investing in quality forecasts at the very beginning of the budget process.*

*Operations costs include the following: (a) producing the wrong product causes inventory levels and inventory storing costs to increase; (b) changing production schedules will increase production costs due to personnel and equipment changes; (c) expediting raw materials create*

*higher inbound raw material costs; (d) shipping to the wrong location incurs extra logistics costs for storing product in the wrong location; (e) trans-shipment costs to get product to the right location; and (f) if necessary, discounting price to get the product sold.*

*Marketing costs include the following: (a) inefficient use of marketing resources; (b) improper allocation of resources across products; (c) reduced or even lost revenue from our inability to deliver; and (d) lost sales opportunities.*

*Source: Kahn, Kenneth B., "How to measure the impact of a forecast error on an enterprise?" The Journal of Business Forecasting Methods & Systems, Spring 2003, pp. 21–25.*

## OTHER BUDGETING TECHNIQUES

So far we have discussed budgeting in terms of a master budget and its components. The concept of budgeting can incorporate other tools where needed.

### Flexible Budgeting

In Chapter 2, we introduced cost functions. We suggested that expense budgets can be based on a variable rate and a fixed amount of costs. By knowing the cost function, we can plan costs for any activity level within our relevant range. This a **flexible budget**. Initially, when the master budget is prepared, an expected activity level is the basis for the expense budget.

For example, Bill Cron provides local area delivery services. He is developing a home delivery service for local restaurants to be called Your Favorite Foods. This would utilize the unused capacity in his delivery services. Activity is the number of deliveries. Following are expense items, which include variable, fixed, and semivariable behaviors.

The cost function is: $5,000 + ($1.80 × deliveries). Bill thought he would handle about 10,000 deliveries this year but only made 9,000. Figure 7.5 presents his original budget, a flexible budget for

| Expense Item | Fixed Expenses | Variable Expenses |
|---|---|---|
| Driver payments | | $1.50 per delivery |
| Supplies expense | | .15 |
| Added management expenses | $3,000 | |
| Depreciation expense | 1,000 | |
| Added communications expenses | 600 | .10 |
| Miscellaneous expenses | 400 | .05 |
| Totals | $5,000 | $1.80 per delivery |

|  | Original Expense Budget | Flexible Budget Based on Actual Deliveries | Actual Expenses | Budget Variances Fav. (Unfav.) |
|---|---|---|---|---|
| Variable expenses: |  |  |  |  |
| Driver payments | $15,000 | $13,500 | $14,050 | $(550) |
| Supplies expense | 1,500 | 1,350 | 1,300 | 50 |
| Fixed expenses: |  |  |  |  |
| Added management expenses | 3,000 | 3,000 | 3,100 | (100) |
| Depreciation | 1,000 | 1,000 | 1,000 | 0 |
| Semivariable expenses: |  |  |  |  |
| Added communication expenses | 1,600 | 1,500 | 1,900 | (400) |
| Miscellaneous expenses | 900 | 850 | 750 | 100 |
| Total expenses | $23,000 | $21,200 | $22,100 | $(900) |

**FIGURE 7.5**

Flexible Budgeting Performance Report For *Your Favorite Foods*

the actual 9,000 deliveries, and a comparison of his actual expenses to the adjusted budget. The original budget is based on 10,000 deliveries and, therefore, cannot be used to evaluate actual results. The flexible budget is based on the actual activity level, 9,000 deliveries. Remember: Fixed expenses are fixed, and variable expenses adjust to the actual activity level. For example, miscellaneous expenses are $400 plus 10,000 times $0.05 or $900 in the original budget and are $400 plus 9,000 times $0.05 or $850 in the flexible budget. The manager is expected to spend no more than $850 for miscellaneous expenses since only 9,000 deliveries were made.

Flexible budgeting can also be tied to applying overhead in product costing. In Chapter 4, we developed rates to apply factory overhead to products. Applied overhead was found by using the cost function and actual activity. Actual overhead minus applied overhead produces either an overapplied or underapplied overhead variance. (See the master budget example later in this chapter.) This variance includes any spending variance and any mismatch in applying fixed overhead. These variances are discussed in detail in Chapter 8.

## Project Budgeting

Project budgets are oriented to specific events or tasks and use time schedules to do annual operating budgets. Project budget examples include construction projects, information systems projects, engineering and design projects, entertainment events, and government defense contracts.

Project management has been a source of many cost and time overruns. Many projects are unique, one-time efforts. Research projects often present another management dilemma—working in technologically unknown areas with no predictable output or timetable. Project budgets link stages and segments of work, timetables, deadlines or decision points, and spending authorizations. Actual costs are compared with budget time and dollar amounts to monitor the project periodically and at specific review points.

Two management concerns exist. How did we do? And, what should we do now? The first is control oriented, and the second is planning oriented. One looks back at resources used, and the other looks forward to completing the project. As an example, assume that a systems development project is budgeted at $90,000 and should take six months to complete. It is now three months into the project, and $40,000 has been spent. The manager in charge estimates that it is one-third done and will take another six months and $80,000 to complete. How should the current status be evaluated? If the project is now one-third complete, the manager is over budget in both time and money as follows:

|  | Performance to Date | | | | Total Project | |
| --- | --- | --- | --- | --- | --- | --- |
|  | Original Budget | Resources Used to Date | Original Budget For Portion Completed | Budget Overrun To Date | Revised Projected Budget | Projected Budget Overrun |
| Costs | $90,000 | $40,000 | $30,000 | ($10,000) | $120,000 | ($30,000) |
| Time | 6 months | 3 months | 2 months | (1 month) | 9 months | (3 months) |

Using the original budget, at this point the project is a month behind schedule and overspent by $10,000. If the total project budget is revised for time and dollars, the project will be $30,000 and three months over budget. Careful monitoring of project status (costs and accomplishment) is needed to meet time and dollar targets.

## Probabilistic Budgeting

Probabilities reflect the likelihood that certain business conditions will occur. When risk exists that a particular variable may move within a range of values, probabilistic expressions of those outcomes help the budget to be more realistic. The sensitivity of profits to changes in variables, such as sales volume and prices, can be tested; then management can focus on sensitive variables.

Randy Hayes, controller of CMU Industries, can calculate **expected values** of sales, costs, and any other budgeted variable from probabilities assigned by senior managers in marketing, production, and other areas. Assume, for example, that CMU plans to sell a product next year for $20 a unit with a variable cost of $14. Probability estimates have been made for three sales volume levels.

|  | Sales Volume (Units) | | Probabilities | | Expected Value (Units) |
| --- | --- | --- | --- | --- | --- |
| Conservative | 150,000 | × | .20 | = | 30,000 |
| Most likely | 200,000 | × | .70 | = | 140,000 |
| Optimistic | 250,000 | × | .10 | = | 25,000 |
|  |  |  | 1.00 |  |  |
| Expected sales volume (units) |  |  |  |  | 195,000 |

The calculation of expected contribution margin is as follows:

| | |
| --- | --- |
| Expected sales (195,000 units × $20) | $3,900,000 |
| Expected variable costs (195,000 units × $14) | 2,730,000 |
| Expected contribution margin | $1,170,000 |

Price, volume, variable cost, fixed costs, and many other variables can be assigned probabilities in many combinations reflecting the levels of uncertainty. Past experience coupled with a careful analysis of the future can serve as a basis for establishing probability estimates. Admittedly, probability estimates will not be precise, but they should represent the best inputs managers can generate and be more accurate than rough approximations or intuitive estimates.

# A MASTER BUDGET EXAMPLE

To illustrate the master budget sequence of planning activity and schedule formats, a comprehensive example is presented. The firm is Linsmeier Products Company, a small manufacturer of wood-based products. In recent years, its primary product is a speaker's podium, which is sold to chapters of the Effective Speakers Society of America (ESSA). Graduates of the Society's speaker training programs are awarded a wooden podium as a symbol of public speaking prowess. Linsmeier produces a high-quality product at a very competitive price. The product is called the "EXEC."

In the Linsmeier Products factory, wood is cut and assembled; a polyurethane finish is applied; and packing and shipping are done. A small sales office and administrative staff completes the organization.

Each year, Linsmeier Products prepares a master budget on a quarterly basis and generally follows the structure shown in Figure 7.3. As in most budgeting situations, Linsmeier Products' dollar amounts are rounded to the nearest dollar. The model used to prepare the budget will track decimal places. When amounts are rounded throughout the budget example, certain columns or rows may appear to add incorrectly; however, overall accuracy is maintained.

## Annual Goals and Planning Assumptions

Linsmeier Products begins its planning process with a meeting organized by the controller at a local resort each August. All managers discuss their areas of responsibility and present strengths, opportunities, problems, and last year's results. Financial and operating goals for 2007 are set; and planning guidelines are agreed upon.

**Planning Assumptions.** Certain data and relationships are needed to begin the planning process. These include beginning balances, product costs and prices, operating assumptions, and financing assumptions.

*Product Cost and Pricing Data.* The first planning data are EXEC quantities and costs. Materials, labor, and overhead are listed by each resource used. A list of materials is often called a **bill of materials**. Direct labor shows costs and hours. Schedule 1 shows these quantities and amounts. Amounts that are **bold** are independent variables throughout the example.

## Schedule 1: Product Quantities, Costs, and Prices

| Product costs | Cost | Quantity | Per Unit |
|---|---|---|---|
| Materials: | | | |
| Plywood (square feet) | **$0.275** | **15.00** | $ 4.125 |
| Trim (feet) | **0.085** | **18.00** | 1.530 |
| Total materials | | | $ 5.655 |
| Direct labor: | | | |
| Preparation and finishing hours | **$12.00** | **1.00** | $12.000 |
| Factory overhead: | | | |
| Variable–Based on direct labor hours | $ 6.50 | 1.00 | $ 6.500 |
| Fixed–Based on machine hours | 12.00 | **0.60** | 7.200 |
| Total manufacturing overhead | | | $13.700 |
| Total product cost | | | $31.355 |
| Sales price | | | $ 49.00 |

Manufacturing overhead is identified as fixed or variable. After analyses of activities and cost behaviors, direct labor hours was selected as the variable overhead cost driver. Much activity in the plant is linked to labor-intensive processes that generate the majority of variable overhead costs. The fixed overhead cost driver is machine hours, because most fixed overhead is generated by equipment costs.

*Operating and Financing Assumptions.* A variety of planning details is needed to prepare budget schedules. Most come from past experience, estimates of beginning balances, and 2007 forecasts. Schedule 2 presents the initial assumptions.

**Operating assumptions** include percentages, specific budgeted amounts for certain accounts to prepare overhead rates, and any other constant that will be needed in calculations. Borrowing details, cash policies, taxes, dividends, and beginning balance sheet figures are the independent variables for **financing assumptions**. These starting points are needed to complete the cash-flow forecast and **pro forma (or forecast) financial statements**.

## Schedule 2: Operating and Financing Assumptions

| Inventory data: | Plywood (sq feet) | Trim (feet) | EXEC |
|---|---|---|---|
| December 31, 2006, inventory | 10,000 | 6,000 | 700 |
| Ending inventory (part of next quarter's usage) | 20% | 10% | 25% |
| **Accounts receivable:** | | | |
| Sales percentage collected this quarter | | | 75% |
| Cash discount percentage for receipt of this quarter's sales | | | 2% |
| **Accounts payable:** | | | |
| Purchases percentage paid this quarter | | | 60% |
| **Manufacturing activity base:** | | | |
| Normal labor hour activity rounded to the nearest 500 hours | | | 11,500 |
| Normal machine hour activity rounded to the nearest 500 hours | | | 7,000 |
| (See Schedule 7 for budgeted variable rates and annual fixed amounts.) | | | |

| | | | |
|---|---|---|---|
| **Selling and administrative expense data:** | | | |
| Sales commissions | 4% | Shipping expenses | $  1.30 per unit |
| (See Schedule 13 for annual budgeted selling and administrative expense amounts.) | | | |

| | | | |
|---|---|---|---|
| **Financial assumptions and balances:** | | | |
| Cash balance: Minimum balance | $5,000 | Maximum balance | $10,000 |
| Borrowing and investment incremental amount | | | 5,000 |
| Quarterly principal payment on notes payable | | | 3,000 |
| Capital stock–Outstanding shares | | | 24,000 |
| Paid-in-capital | | | 240,000 |
| Dividend rate–per share per quarter | | | $   0.05 |
| Income tax rate (federal, state, and local) | | | 40% |
| Interest rate on bank borrowings and investments (annual) | | | 9% |
| (See December 31, 2006, Balance Sheet for beginning balances.) | | | |

| Project expenditures: | First Quarter | Second Quarter | Third Quarter | Fourth Quarter |
|---|---|---|---|---|
| Equipment purchases | $8,000 | $0 | $10,000 | $12,000 |
| Research and development | 0 | 0 | 0 | 4,000 |

## Sales Forecast

The sales forecast is the only remaining independent variable necessary. It is prepared using a rolling five-quarter timeframe. A fifth quarter of sales data is needed to complete a number of fourth quarter schedules. Physical quantities are independent variables. Dollar amounts are found by using the physical units and prices from Schedule 1.

From the sales dollars in Schedule 3 through the end of the master budget, all numbers are calculated using data and instructions in Schedules 1, 2, and 3. All values from this point are dependent variables using the independent variables.

## Schedule 3: Sales Forecast

|  | First Quarter | Second Quarter | Third Quarter | Fourth Quarter | Total | Fifth Quarter |
|---|---|---|---|---|---|---|
| Unit sales | 2,400 | 2,800 | 3,000 | 3,200 | 11,400 | 3,000 |
| Sales dollars | $117,600 | $137,200 | $147,000 | $156,800 | $558,600 | $147,000 |

## Production Plan

A production plan, Schedule 4, is prepared using the beginning finished podium inventory, the sales forecast, and the desired ending inventory levels. In this example, work in process inventory is assumed to be so small and unchanging that it is immaterial to both planning and product costing tasks. Key relationships in this production plan are the percentages of sales that should be on hand at the end of each quarter. Note the format of Schedule 4. Sales plus required ending inventory equal units needed. Then, by subtracting beginning inventory, the needed production volume is found. This sequence is common to many budgeting calculations.

## Schedule 4: Production Plan

|  | First Quarter | Second Quarter | Third Quarter | Fourth Quarter | Total | Fifth Quarter |
|---|---|---|---|---|---|---|
| Unit sales | 2,400 | 2,800 | 3,000 | 3,200 | 11,400 | 3,000 |
| Ending finished goods | 700 | 750 | 800 | 750 | 750 | |
| Total units needed | 3,100 | 3,550 | 3,800 | 3,950 | 12,150 | |
| Beginning finished goods | (700) | (700) | (750) | (800) | (700) | (750) |
| Production needed | 2,400 | 2,850 | 3,050 | 3,150 | 11,450 | |

**Materials Requirements and Purchases Budget.** Quantities of materials used in each unit (the bill of materials) are specified in Schedule 1. Estimated quantities are based on experience or engineering studies and help set standard costs, which are discussed in Chapter 8. Quantities of materials needed to meet production requirements are determined by multiplying the units to be made by the quantities of materials required for each unit.

## Schedule 5: Materials Requirements and Purchases Budget

|  | First Quarter | Second Quarter | Third Quarter | Fourth Quarter | Total | Fifth Quarter |
|---|---|---|---|---|---|---|
| **Plywood requirements (square feet):** | | | | | | |
| Ending inventory | 8,550 | 9,150 | 9,450 | 8,850 | 12,195 | |
| Production requirements. | 36,000 | 42,750 | 45,750 | 47,250 | 171,750 | 44,250 |
| Total needs | 44,550 | 51,900 | 55,200 | 56,100 | 180,600 | |
| Beginning inventory | (10,000) | (8,550) | (9,150) | (9,450) | (10,000) | |
| Purchases in square feet | 34,550 | 43,350 | 46,050 | 46,650 | 170,600 | |
| Dollar cost of plywood purchases | $9,501[1] | $11,921 | $12,664 | $12,829 | $46,915 | |

---

[1] The purchase cost is actually $9,501.25. This number is rounded to the nearest dollar, $9,501. This is the first of many rounded amounts in the comprehensive example. Spreadsheet software tracks all significant digits in calculations and rounds to the specified level. Certain columns and rows which include rounded numbers may appear to add incorrectly. Budgeting rarely needs detail beyond whole dollars.

**Trim requirements (linear feet):**

| | | | | | | |
|---|---|---|---|---|---|---|
| Ending inventory | 5,130 | 5,490 | 5,670 | 5,310 | 5,310 | |
| Production requirements | 43,200 | 51,300 | 54,900 | 56,700 | 206,100 | 53,100 |
| Total needs | 48,330 | 56,790 | 60,570 | 62,010 | 211,410 | |
| Beginning inventory | (6,000) | (5,130) | (5,490) | (5,670) | (6,000) | |
| Purchases in linear feet | 42,330 | 51,660 | 55,080 | 56,340 | 205,410 | |
| Dollar cost of trim purchases | $ 3,598 | $ 4,391 | $ 4,682 | $ 4,789 | $17,460 | |
| Total materials purchases | $13,099 | $16,312 | $17,346 | $17,618 | $64,375 | |

Ending plywood inventory for the first quarter of 8,550 square feet is 20 percent (Schedule 2) of the second quarter's production needs of 42,750 square feet. The 36,000 square feet of plywood needed for production in the first quarter is found by multiplying 15 square feet per unit (Schedule 1) times the 2,400 units to be produced (Schedule 4). Thus, the rules from Schedules 1 and 2 and the quantities from Schedule 4 determine all amounts needed to calculate the purchases requirements in Schedule 5.

In more complex production situations, the accumulation of parts and materials needs is called a **bill of materials explosion**. All uses of the same part in different products are summed to find the total usage across the entire product line for a time period. Computer software for production planning, such as Materials Requirements Planning (MRP), is used to calculate needs and to issue purchase orders when inventory levels reach certain points.

**Direct Labor Budget.** The direct labor budget is estimated first by the direct labor time required per unit (Schedule 1) times the units to be made (Schedule 4). Hours per podium are set by past experience or industrial engineering studies. At one hour per EXEC, the hours per quarter equal the units to be produced per quarter.

Labor cost per hour can be the "straight" wage rate, with all payroll taxes and fringe benefits included in manufacturing overhead. Or the rate could be a "loaded" wage rate, which includes most fringes and expected overtime premiums. The differences can be dramatic. For example, the current United Auto Workers contract with the major U.S. auto companies provided an average straight wage of just over $25 per hour, while the loaded rate was nearly $50 per hour.

## Schedule 6: Direct Labor Requirements

| | First Quarter | Second Quarter | Third Quarter | Fourth Quarter | Total |
|---|---|---|---|---|---|
| Total direct labor hours needed | 2,400 | 2,850 | 3,050 | 3,150 | 11,450 |
| Total direct labor payroll expense | $28,800 | $34,200 | $36,600 | $37,800 | $137,400 |

**Factory Overhead Budgets.** Planning factory overhead takes two forms–creating the expected overhead spending patterns using a flexible budget and budgeting spending and applied overhead levels.

*Cost Estimation Using ABC and Statistical Techniques.* Detailed cost estimates come from several sources already discussed in prior chapters. Cost estimation techniques presented in Chapter 3 (regression analysis, high-low method, etc.) are used by managers and accountants to budget expenses that track well against one or more activity variables. More commonly, the same cost drivers used in Chapters 4 and 6 to build cost functions and assign costs to cost objectives are now applied to another cost objective–budgeting.

*Factory Overhead Flexible Budget.* Selecting activity bases for applying overhead, setting normal activity levels, planning variable and fixed overhead items, and setting the overhead rates are all part of the annual budgeting process. Schedule 7 is the result. Independent variables (bold) are the variable overhead rates and the fixed overhead annual amounts. Separate cost drivers were selected for variable and fixed overhead. The variable overhead cost driver is direct labor hours. Fixed overhead is applied using machine hours. Annual normal direct labor and machine hours are rounded (11,500 labor hours and 7,000 machine hours). Budgets are prepared for various ranges of activity, in both cases in increments of 500 hours around normal levels. Using budgeted expenses and normal activity levels given in Schedule 2, variable and fixed overhead rates are set. These are calculated on Schedule 7 and added to product costs in Schedule 1.

## Schedule 7: Factory Overhead Flexible Budget

| | | **Cost Driver Activity Levels** | | |
| | | | **Normal** | |
| --- | --- | --- | --- | --- |
| Variable cost driver: Direct labor hours | | 11,000 | 11,500 | 12,000 |
| Fixed cost driver: Machine hours | | 6,500 | 7,000 | 7,500 |
| | | | | |
| Variable expenses: | Rate/Hour | | | |
| Supplies and other variable expenses | **$   1.40** | $ 15,400 | $ 16,100 | $ 16,800 |
| Indirect labor and benefits expenses | **5.10** | 56,100 | 58,650 | 61,200 |
| Total variable overhead expenses | $   6.50 | $ 71,500 | $ 74,750 | $ 78,000 |
| | | | | |
| Fixed expenses: | Amount | | | |
| Depreciation expense | **$20,000** | $ 20,000 | $ 20,000 | $ 20,000 |
| Supervision salaries | **41,000** | 41,000 | 41,000 | 41,000 |
| Other fixed overhead expenses | **23,000** | 23,000 | 23,000 | 23,000 |
| Total fixed overhead expenses | $84,000 | $ 84,000 | $ 84,000 | $ 84,000 |
| Total manufacturing overhead expenses | | $155,500 | $158,750 | $162,000 |
| | | | | |
| Overhead Rates: | | | | |
| Variable rate per direct labor hour | | $   6.50 | $   6.50 | $   6.50 |
| Fixed rate per machine hour | | | $ 12.00 | |

*Factory Overhead Operating Budget.* With overhead rates and budgeted activity levels, quarterly budgets for manufacturing overhead and applied overhead are prepared. Again, direct labor and machine hour activity levels come from the hours per unit in Schedule 1 and the production plan. Variable expense budgets for each quarter are the expected spending levels given that activity level. First quarter's supplies and other variable expenses of $3,360 in Schedule 8 result from multiplying $1.40 per direct labor hour (Schedule 7) times 2,400 hours (Schedule 6). Budgeted fixed costs are merely divided equally among four quarters.

Near the bottom of Schedule 8 is the planned applied overhead. This will differ from the budgeted spending level because of the difference between budgeted fixed cost and applied fixed overhead. The quarter's planned activity level for machine hours (1,440 hours) does not equal one quarter of the annual normal activity level (7,000 hours ÷ 4 quarters). Fixed overhead is budgeted at $21,000 for the quarter, one-fourth of $84,000. Using the fixed overhead rate of $12.00 per machine hour developed in Schedule 7, the applied fixed overhead is $17,280. Budgeted fixed overhead is underapplied by $3,720, which is $21,000 minus $17,280 ($12 per hour × 310 hours).

Variable overhead is *budgeted* and *applied* at $6.50 per direct labor hour. Therefore, no budgeted overapplied or underapplied variable overhead exists.

## Schedule 8: Factory Overhead Operating Budget

| | First Quarter | Second Quarter | Third Quarter | Fourth Quarter | Total |
|---|---|---|---|---|---|
| Budgeted direct labor hour activity | 2,400 | 2,850 | 3,050 | 3,150 | 11,450 |
| Budgeted machine hour activity | 1,440 | 1,710 | 1,830 | 1,890 | 6,870 |
| Budgeted variable overhead expenses | $15,600 | $18,525 | $19,825 | $20,475 | $ 74,425 |
| Budgeted fixed overhead expenses | 21,000 | 21,000 | 21,000 | 21,000 | 84,000 |
| Total budgeted factory overhead | $36,600 | $39,525 | $40,825 | $41,475 | $158,425 |
| Budgeted factory overhead cash outflow | $31,600 | $34,525 | $35,825 | $36,475 | $138,425 |
| Applied factory overhead: | | | | | |
|    Variable overhead applied | $15,600 | $18,525 | $19,825 | $20,475 | $ 74,425 |
|    Fixed overhead applied | 17,280 | 20,520 | 21,960 | 22,680 | 82,440 |
|      Total applied overhead | $32,880 | $39,045 | $41,785 | $43,155 | $156,865 |
| Overapplied/(Underapplied) overhead | $ (3,720) | $ (480) | $ 960 | $ 1,680 | $ (1,560) |
| Overapplied/(Underapplied) overhead YTD | $ (3,720) | $ (4,200) | $ (3,240) | $ 1,560 | $ (1,560) |

## Supporting Schedules

Several supporting schedules are prepared by the accounting staff and are important to cash-flow forecasting and in the calculation of costs of podiums manufactured and sold. Assumptions about collections, payments, and ending balances were given in Schedule 2. We can now develop forecasts for accounts receivable (Schedule 9), inventories (Schedule 10), and accounts payable (Schedule 11).

## Schedule 9: Accounts Receivable

| | First Quarter | Second Quarter | Third Quarter | Fourth Quarter |
|---|---|---|---|---|
| Beginning balance | $ 40,000 | $ 29,400 | $ 34,300 | $ 36,750 |
| Net sales | 117,600 | 137,200 | 147,000 | 156,800 |
|    Total receivables | $157,600 | $166,600 | $181,300 | $193,550 |
| Decreases in receivables: | | | | |
|    Collections of prior quarter's sales | $ 40,000 | $ 29,400 | $ 34,300 | $ 36,750 |
|    Collections of this quarter's sales | 86,436 | 100,842 | 108,045 | 115,248 |
|      Total cash collections of receivables | $126,436 | $130,242 | $142,345 | $151,998 |
|    Cash discounts | 1,764 | 2,058 | 2,205 | 2,352 |
|      Total credits to receivables | $128,200 | $132,300 | $144,550 | $154,350 |
| Ending balance | $ 29,400 | $ 34,300 | $ 36,750 | $ 39,200 |

## Schedule 10: Ending Inventories–Cost Basis

| | December 31, 2006 | First Quarter | Second Quarter | Third Quarter | Fourth Quarter |
|---|---|---|---|---|---|
| Materials inventory: | | | | | |
|    Plywood (square feet) | $ 2,750 | $ 2,351 | $ 2,516 | $ 2,599 | $ 2,434 |
|    Trim (linear feet) | 510 | 436 | 467 | 482 | 451 |
|      Total materials inventory | $ 3,260 | $ 2,787 | $ 2,983 | $ 3,081 | $ 2,885 |
| EXEC finished goods inventory | 21,949 | 21,949 | 23,516 | 25,084 | 23,516 |
|    Total inventories | $25,209 | $24,736 | $26,499 | $28,165 | $26,401 |

## Schedule 11: Accounts Payable

|  | First Quarter | Second Quarter | Third Quarter | Fourth Quarter |
|---|---|---|---|---|
| Beginning balance | $ 6,000 | $ 5,240 | $ 6,525 | $ 6,938 |
| Purchases on account | 13,099 | 16,312 | 17,346 | 17,614 |
| Total payables | $19,099 | $21,552 | $23,870 | $24,556 |
| Decrease in payables: |  |  |  |  |
| Payments of prior quarter's purchases | $ 6,000 | $ 5,240 | $ 6,525 | $ 6,938 |
| Payments of this quarter's purchases | 7,860 | 9,787 | 10,407 | 10,571 |
| Total cash payments | $13,860 | $15,027 | $16,932 | $17,509 |
| Ending balance | $ 5,240 | $ 6,525 | $ 6,938 | $ 7,047 |

For accounts receivable, the percentage of net sales collected in the current quarter is 75 percent and cash discounts are 2 percent of collections of the current quarter's net sales. Inventory values use quantities from Schedules 4 and 5 and costs from Schedule 1. For accounts payable, Schedule 2 indicates that 60 percent of purchases are paid in the current quarter.

## Cost of Products Manufactured and Sold Schedule

Now all the elements are in place to prepare a schedule of the cost of goods manufactured and sold. These costs are forwarded in summary form to the income statement.

## Schedule 12: Cost of Podiums Manufactured and Sold

|  | First Quarter | Second Quarter | Third Quarter | Fourth Quarter | Total |
|---|---|---|---|---|---|
| Materials costs: |  |  |  |  |  |
| Plywood used | $ 9,900 | $11,756 | $12,581 | $ 12,994 | $ 47,231 |
| Trim used | 3,672 | 4,361 | 4,667 | 4,820 | 17,519 |
| Total materials used | $13,572 | $16,117 | $17,248 | $ 17,813 | $ 64,750 |
| Direct labor | 28,800 | 34,200 | 36,600 | 37,800 | 137,400 |
| Factory overhead applied | 32,880 | 39,045 | 41,785 | 43,155 | 156,865 |
| Cost of EXECs manufactured | $75,252 | $89,362 | $95,633 | $ 98,768 | $359,015 |
| Plus:Beginning inventory | 21,949 | 21,949 | 23,516 | 25,084 | 21,949 |
| Less:Ending inventory | (21,949) | (23,516) | (25,084) | (23,516) | (23,516) |
| Cost of EXECs sold | $75,252 | $87,794 | $94,065 | $100,336 | $357,447 |
| Overapplied/(Underapplied) overhead | (3,720) | (480) | 960 | 1,680 | (1,560) |
| Adjusted cost of EXCEs sold | $78,972 | $88,274 | $93,105 | $ 98,656 | $359,007 |

Using Schedule 12, a useful proof can be made. With product costs from Schedule 1 and sales from Schedule 3, total costs of EXECs sold can be calculated quickly—$357,447. These numbers can be checked against the sums of materials, labor, and applied overhead and the changes in inventories. For each product in each quarter these numbers should match.

## Selling and Administrative Expense Budgets

Expenses of promoting, selling, and distributing the products are budgeted by combining the costs into a selling or marketing expenses budget (Schedule 13). Administrative expenses are fixed costs and are allocated to the four quarters.

## Schedule 13: Selling and Administrative Expenses Budget

| | First Quarter | Second Quarter | Third Quarter | Fourth Quarter | Total |
|---|---|---|---|---|---|
| Selling expenses: | | | | | |
| Sales commission expenses | $ 4,704 | $ 5,488 | $ 5,880 | $ 6,272 | $ 22,344 |
| Advertising and other sales expenses | 4,000 | 4,000 | 4,000 | 4,000 | **16,000** |
| Sales salaries expenses | 7,500 | 7,500 | 7,500 | 7,500 | **30,000** |
| Shipping expenses | 3,120 | 3,640 | 3,900 | 4,160 | 14,820 |
| Total selling expenses | $19,324 | $ 20,628 | $21,280 | $21,932 | $83,164 |
| Administrative expenses: | | | | | |
| Wage and salaries expense | $15,000 | $15,000 | $15,000 | $15,000 | $ 60,000 |
| Other administrative expenses | 3,500 | 3,500 | 3,500 | 3,500 | 14,000 |
| Total administrative expenses | 18,500 | 18,500 | 18,500 | 18,500 | 74,000 |
| Total selling and administrative expenses | $37,824 | $39,128 | $39,780 | $40,432 | $157,164 |

## Project Budgets

Few project budgets exist in this example. Linsmeier Products has a small capital investment and research and development budget, which is shown in Schedule 14. Equipment purchases are capitalized, and research and development costs are expensed.

## Schedule 14: Capital Investment Project Budget

| | First Quarter | Second Quarter | Third Quarter | Fourth Quarter | Total |
|---|---|---|---|---|---|
| Projects: | | | | | |
| Equipment purchases | $8,000 | $0 | $10,000 | $12,000 | $30,000 |
| Research and development expenses | 0 | 0 | 0 | 4,000 | 4,000 |
| Total project expenditures | $8,000 | $0 | $10,000 | $16,000 | $34,000 |

## Cash-Flow Forecasts

Now that all operating and project budgets are in place, the time for summarizing has arrived. The first summary is the preparation of the cash-flow forecast. Nearly every schedule impacts cash. The basic structure is to list receipts and disbursements, sum to a cash balance, and show any planned investing or borrowing activities. In Schedule 15, a source document for each cash-flow item is cited.

## Schedule 15: Cash-Flow Forecasts

| | Source | First Quarter | Second Quarter | Third Quarter | Fourth Quarter | Total |
|---|---|---|---|---|---|---|
| Cash inflows: | | | | | | |
| Collections from sales | Schedule 9 | $126,436 | $130,242 | $142,345 | $151,998 | $551,021 |
| Interest received | Balance sheet | 0 | 0 | 0 | 0 | 0 |
| Total cash inflows | | $126,436 | $130,242 | $142,345 | $151,998 | $551,021 |
| Cash outflows: | | | | | | |
| Purchases payments | Schedule 11 | $ 13,860 | $ 15,027 | $ 16,932 | $ 17,509 | $ 63,328 |
| Direct labor payroll | Schedule 6 | 28,800 | 34,200 | 36,600 | 37,800 | 137,400 |
| Factory overhead | Schedule 8 | 31,600 | 34,525 | 35,825 | 36,475 | 138,425 |
| Selling & administrative exp | Schedule 13 | 37,824 | 39,128 | 39,780 | 40,432 | 157,164 |
| Interest payments | Balance sheet | 1,125 | 1,125 | 1,058 | 1,103 | 4,410 |

| | | First Quarter | Second Quarter | Third Quarter | Fourth Quarter | Total |
|---|---|---|---|---|---|---|
| Income taxes payments | Balance sheet | 2,000 | (834) | 2673 | 4,323 | 8,162 |
| Dividend payments | Schedule 2 | 1,200 | 1,200 | 1,200 | 1,200 | 4,800 |
| Project budget payments | Schedule 14 | 8,000 | 0 | 10,000 | 16,000 | 34,000 |
| Note payable repayments | Schedule 2 | 3,000 | 3,000 | 3,000 | 3,000 | 12,000 |
| Total cash outflows | | $127,409 | $127,371 | $147,068 | $157,841 | $559,689 |
| | | | | | | |
| Cash inflows minus outflows | | $ (973) | $ 2,871 | $ (4,723) | $ (5,843) | $ (8,668) |
| Plus: Beginning cash | | 6,000 | 5,027 | 7,898 | 8,176 | 6,000 |
| Cash available | | $ 5,027 | $ 7,898 | $ 3,176 | $ 2,332 | $ (2,668) |
| Less: Excess cash on hand | | 0 | 0 | 0 | 0 | 0 |
| Plus: New borrowing needed | | 0 | 0 | 5,000 | 5,000 | 10,000 |
| Ending cash balance | | $ 5,027 | $ 7,898 | $ 8,176 | $ 7,332 | $ 7,332 |
| Cumulative borrowings | | $ 0 | $ 0 | $ 5,000 | $ 10,000 | $ 10,000 |
| Cumulative investments | | $ 0 | $ 0 | $ 0 | $ 0 | $ 0 |

A key part of cash-flow forecasting is to anticipate cash deficits or surpluses. If the cash balance falls below the minimum desired level (given in Schedule 2), bank borrowings or investment sales are needed. If the cash balance exceeds the maximum level, excess cash should be invested to ensure maximum earnings. Calculations at the bottom of Schedule 15 forecast that Linsmeier Products will need to borrow cash.

## The Completed Example: Forecast Financial Statements

The operating data presented determine the forecast financial results. Consolidation of operating numbers into forecast financial statements is frequently the controller's responsibility. These statements are reviewed carefully by the firm's executives. In this example, the source schedule for each account balance is listed to help explain the income statement and balance sheet numbers.

**Forecast Income Statements.** The forecast or pro forma income statement is a summary of the expected revenue and expense budgets. Management can compare its actual income statements with the forecast statements as the year progresses. If budgeted profits are to be realized, adjustments may have to be made. Perhaps the budget itself requires revision.

### LINSMEIER PRODUCTS COMPANY–FORECAST INCOME AND EXPENSE STATEMENTS

| | First Quarter | Second Quarter | Third Quarter | Fourth Quarter | Total | Source |
|---|---|---|---|---|---|---|
| Sales | $117,600 | $137,200 | $147,000 | $156,800 | $558,600 | Schedule 3 |
| Cost of goods sold | $ 75,252 | $ 87,794 | $ 94,065 | $100,336 | $357,447 | Schedule 12 |
| Factory variances | (3,720) | (480) | 960 | 1,680 | (1,560) | Schedule 8 |
| Net cost of goods sold | $ 78,972 | $ 88,274 | $ 93,105 | $ 98,656 | $359,007 | |
| Gross margin on sales | $ 38,628 | $ 48,926 | $ 53,895 | $ 58,144 | $199,593 | |
| Selling & administrative expense | $ 37,824 | $ 39,128 | $ 39,780 | $ 40,432 | $157,164 | Schedule 13 |
| Research & development expense | 0 | 0 | 0 | 4,000 | 4,000 | Schedule 14 |
| Total operating expenses | $ 37,824 | $ 39,128 | $ 39,780 | $ 44,432 | $161,164 | |
| Operating income | $ 804 | $ 9,798 | $ 14,115 | $ 13,712 | $ 38,429 | |
| Other: Interest income | $ 0 | $ 0 | $ 0 | $ 0 | $ 0 | Calculated |
| Interest expense | (1,125) | (1,058) | (1,103) | (1,148) | (4,433) | Calculated |
| Sales cash discounts | (1,764) | (2,058) | (2,205) | (2,352) | (8,379) | Schedule 9 |
| Total other items | $ (2,889) | $ (3,116) | $ (3,308) | $ (3,500) | $(12,812) | |
| Net income before taxes | $ (2,085) | $ 6,683 | $ 10,808 | $ 10,213 | $ 25,618 | |
| Income tax expense | (834) | 2,673 | 4,323 | 4,085 | 10,247 | Calculated |
| Net income | $ (1,251) | $ 4,010 | $ 6,485 | $ 6,128 | $ 15,371 | |

As can be seen, most amounts are summarized from earlier schedules. Only the interest income and expense and income tax expense are computed here from data in Schedule 2 and from amounts already calculated.

**Forecast Balance Sheets.** The forecast or pro forma balance sheet indicates the firm's financial position at a future date. Like the income statement, it is a summary statement that depends on individual budgets that have been prepared. Analyses of budgeted and actual balances show how accounts are affected by operations during the budget year. The forecast balance sheet also serves as a point of reference during the year. Interim statements prepared at various dates can be compared with corresponding budget statements.

### LINSMEIER PRODUCTS COMPANY–FORECAST BALANCE SHEETS

| | December 31, 2006 | March 31, 2007 | June 30, 2007 | September 30, 2007 | December 31, 2007 | Source |
|---|---|---|---|---|---|---|
| **Assets:** | | | | | | |
| Cash | $ 6,000 | $ 5,240 | $ 7,898 | $ 8,176 | $ 7,332 | Schedule 15 |
| Short-term investments | 0 | 0 | 0 | 0 | 0 | Schedule 15 |
| Accounts receivable | 40,000 | 29,400 | 34,300 | 36,750 | 39,200 | Schedule 9 |
| Inventories | 25,209 | 24,736 | 26,499 | 28,165 | 26,401 | Schedule 10 |
| Interest receivable | 0 | 0 | 0 | 0 | 0 | Income Stmt |
| Total current assets | $ 71,209 | $ 59,163 | $ 68,697 | $ 73,090 | $ 72,934 | |
| Building and equipment | $ 360,000 | $ 368,000 | $ 368,000 | $ 378,000 | $ 390,000 | Schedule 14 |
| Accumulated depreciation | (100,000) | (105,000) | (110,000) | (115,000) | (120,000) | Schedule 8 |
| Total assets | $ 331,209 | $ 322,163 | $ 326,697 | $ 336,090 | $ 342,934 | |
| **Liabilities and equity:** | | | | | | |
| Accounts payable | $ 6,000 | $ 5,240 | $ 6,525 | $ 6,938 | $ 7,047 | Schedule 11 |
| Taxes payable | 2,000 | (834) | 2,673 | 4,323 | 4,085 | Income Stmt |
| Bank borrowings | 0 | 0 | 0 | 5,000 | 10,000 | Schedule 15 |
| Interest payable | 1,125 | 1,125 | 1,058 | 1,103 | 1,148 | Income Stmt |
| Total current liabilities | $ 9,125 | $ 5,531 | $ 10,255 | $ 17,364 | $ 22,280 | |
| Long-term notes payable | 50,000 | 47,000 | 44,000 | 41,000 | 38,000 | Schedule 15 |
| Total liabilities | $ 59,125 | $ 52,531 | $ 54,255 | $ 58,364 | $ 60,280 | |
| Capital stock | $ 240,000 | $ 240,000 | $ 240,000 | $ 240,000 | $ 240,000 | Schedule 3 |
| Retained earnings | 32,084 | 29,633 | 32,442 | 37,727 | 42,654 | Schedule 15 |
| Total equity | $ 272,084 | $ 269,633 | $ 282,442 | $ 277,727 | $ 282,654 | & Income |
| Total liabilities and equity | $ 331,209 | $ 322,163 | $ 326,697 | $ 336,090 | $ 342,934 | Statement |

## Master Budget Summary

Several observations should be made about the master budget example. The budget should be tested for reasonableness, including:

- A review of the reasonableness of critical independent variables (most often the sales forecast) as a key evaluation step.
- A sensitivity analysis to determine whether small changes in key variables will cause major changes in profitability or cash flows.
- "What if" analyses to determine whether a better combination of resource inputs could produce a stronger plan.

- A budget review and approval by each manager involved in the planning effort.
- An analysis to determine whether the management's goals and objectives are realized.

Many iterations may be needed to arrive at a budget that managers can accept, meets management's goals, and pushes the firm toward its long-range goals.

## IMPACTS OF NEW MANUFACTURING APPROACHES

The evolution of manufacturing approaches has in some cases had major impacts on budgeting. The following observations can be made:

- Just-in-time systems reduce inventory needs and may even eliminate their role in production budgeting. Some firms have reduced major component inventories to under two hours of production requirements. Shorter lead times place greater pressure on production planning. Small mistakes or delays can cause entire plants to stop—incurring nonproductive costs and lost output.
- Activity-based costing will likely increase the number of cost drivers and cost centers. Budgeting may actually be easier since costs and activity are more closely related.
- Flexible manufacturing and team production activities change the collection of cost data–where, how, and what. Costs will be regrouped for improved planning and control. Also, greater emphasis is placed on certain costs, such as costs of quality, manufacturing cycle times, value-added labor, and manufacturing throughput.

The reduction of lead times and buffers throughout the production process means planning grows in importance.

## SUMMARY

One major management function is to plan and control the activities of an organization. A planning and control system includes a strategic plan, a responsibility accounting system, a master budget, and financial modeling. Cost or activity, profit, and investment centers define a manager's sphere of responsibility. The glue that holds planning activities together is the budget. Purposes of budgeting are outlined.

The master budget is an integrated set of schedules and ties operating, project, and financial budgets together. The operating budget begins with the constraining variable, most commonly the sales forecast. All operating budgets are integrated into the cash-flow budget and forecast financial statements. Understanding how to organize budget data and to format budget schedules can ease the assimilation of the huge amount of budget data brought together to create an operating plan. A master budget example was developed to show the integrative nature of the various budget schedules.

Other budgeting approaches were presented. Flexible budgeting allows managers to be evaluated according to the actual activity they experience. Project budgeting prepares plans that span normal annual timeframes or are nonroutine in nature. Probabilistic budgeting gives managers an opportunity to bring into the budgeting process a range of estimates for key variables.

Consideration is given to managers' budget-related behavior and the impacts that budgets have on people. Areas of particular importance are top-management's support of the budget, budgetary slack, budget stress, and ethical issues.

## PROBLEM FOR REVIEW

The production manager of the Haka Company maintains an inventory of materials equal to production needs for the next month because of potential delays in shipments from his Korean supplier. Each unit takes 4 pounds of materials, which cost $3 per pound. The target for finished goods inventory is 20 percent of the following month's sales. Budgeted sales in units for the first five months of 2007 are:

| Month | Budgeted Sales | Month | Budgeted Sales |
|---|---|---|---|
| January | 12,000 | April | 16,000 |
| February | 16,000 | May | 20,000 |
| March | 15,000 | | |

At December 31, 2006, 60,000 pounds of materials and 3,000 units of finished goods were on hand.

**Required:**

Prepare a budget for production in units and a budget for purchases in pounds and dollars for the first three months of 2007.

**Solution:**

*Production plan in units:*

| | January | February | March | April | May |
|---|---|---|---|---|---|
| Sales | 12,000 | 16,000 | 15,000 | 16,000 | 20,000 |
| Ending inventory (20 % of next month) | 3,200 | 3,000 | 3,200 | 4,000 | |
| Total units needed | 15,200 | 19,000 | 18,200 | 20,000 | |
| Beginning inventory available | 3,000 | 3,200 | 3,000 | 3,200 | |
| Production required | 12,200 | 15,800 | 15,200 | 16,800 | |

Purchases budget:

| | January | February | March | April |
|---|---|---|---|---|
| Production required | 12,200 | 15,800 | 15,200 | 16,800 |
| Pounds per unit | × 4 | × 4 | × 4 | × 4 |
| Pounds required | 48,800 | 63,200 | 60,800 | 67,200 |
| Ending inventory (next month's production requirements) | 63,200 | 60,800 | 67,200 | |
| Total pounds needed | 112,000 | 124,000 | 128,000 | |
| Beginning inventory available | 60,000 | 63,200 | 60,800 | |
| Materials purchases in pounds | 52,000 | 60,800 | 67,200 | |
| Cost per pound | × $3 | × $3 | × $3 | |
| Materials purchases in dollars | $156,000 | $182,400 | $201,600 | |

# APPENDIX

## FINANCIAL PLANNING MODELS

We are living in a rapidly changing environment. The problem is how to cope with change. One tool now widely available for managing change is financial modeling. **Modeling** is a meaningful abstraction of reality where key variables and relationships are mathematically represented. **Simulation** uses a model to test policies, decisions, and alternative forecast scenarios. This appendix defines a financial planning model and examines the uses of financial simulation. A major application, testing plans using "what if" analysis, is illustrated.

### Defining the Financial Planning Model

A **financial planning model** converts an organization's accounting and other processes into a series of equations. These equations represent interrelationships that exist within an organization. The aims are to simulate, using computer power, all significant processes that may affect the decision problem and, thereby, to arrive at realistic approximations of actual results. Successful modeling depends on defining relationships, identifying key variables, and inputting accurate data. The master budget is an excellent example of defining the interrelationships that describe an organization's operating and financial functions, its inputs, and its outputs.

Financial planning models:

- Evaluate and test financial goals and operating and financial policies.
- Perform "what if" analyses to:
  —weigh the results of complex decisions.
  —measure impacts of policy changes.
  —measure impacts of price and cost changes.
- Assess long-range impacts of specific strategies.
- Without incurring costs of decision making in the real world:
  —identify warning signals that may require managerial attention.
  —fine tune decisions to find optimal points.
  —allow advocates of competing strategies to "strut their stuff."
- Speed the budget consolidation task to give fast feedback and more time for decision analysis.

Output from a financial planning model is typically in financial statement form plus analysis schedules of specific decisions. Financial models come in all sizes, modes, and complexity. Usually, a model is used repeatedly. The range of model types includes:

- **Manual calculations** that involve few steps, require limited data and interrelationships, and rarely need many iterations.
- **Spreadsheet software** (generally personal computer based) that is developed or purchased for general use.
- **Stand-alone programmed software** developed for personal computers, networks, and mainframes. These models are more powerful versions of spreadsheet software and operate separately from a firm's accounting transaction and reporting systems.
- **Modeling capabilities integrated into the firm's information systems** designed as an integral part of the accounting systems.

While modeling costs are decreasing, the variety of modeling products is large and growing as are their applications.

## Contemporary Practice 7.4
### *What Makes a Model Work*

*In building a spreadsheet-based financial model for a hospital, two major flaws occur frequently—an inappropriate level of detail and a fundamental structural flaw. The following practical steps are critical to building a model: (1) define the problem, (2) specify the desired output, (3) demarcate the planning horizon, (4) determine the level of detail*

*required, (5) structure the model, (6) define major variables and their interrelationships, (7) review the assumptions, (8) build the model, and (9) test the model.*

*Source: Porter, M., and T. R. Miller, "Uses and Abuses of Financial Modeling,"* Topics in Health Care Financing, *Fall 1992, pp. 34–45.*

### Elements of the Model

A financial planning model consists of three significant elements: inputs, the model, and outputs. These are combined to create a mathematical representation of the organization or task it models. In Figure 7.6, the basic modeling elements are illustrated and linked.

**Inputs.** Inputs are historical databases, economic indicators, operating and financial parameters, management policies, planning assumptions, and model queries. Historical databases include detailed financial statement account information, transaction summaries, statistical relationships, economic data, nonfinancial data, and other databases needed in specific industries and for specific applications. The forecast information may be generated internally, developed externally, or even purchased.

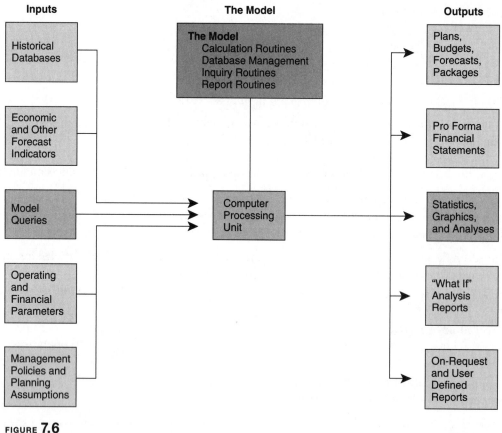

**FIGURE 7.6**

Elements of the Financial Planning Model

Operating factors represent constraints, physical relationships and processes, customer and product data files, purchasing and distribution linkages, and staffing. Financial factors include cash patterns, borrowing and investing policies, capitalization issues, taxes, and accounting policies and practices.

Management policies involve goal setting, pricing, marketing practices, borrowings, dividends, salary and benefits practices, and other decision rules that affect the financial affairs of the firm directly and indirectly. Often guidelines or constraints are needed to serve as **parameters** or boundaries for model variable values and to keep the model "in control." Planning assumptions include the items already illustrated in the master budget example plus anticipated inflation rates, salary and benefits changes, and market growth.

**Model queries** are questions that managers ask the model. The questions often represent changes in independent variables. These are **"what ifs."** The query defines the modeling problem and includes any new assumptions or data required. Also, **management overrides** may be allowed to provide managers with a mechanism to supersede statistical projections or other modeled values that are unrealistic.

**The Model.** The second element is the **model** itself—a core of programs, software routines, and computer power that makes the model work. Calculation routines, file management systems, reporting routines, and user query routines are prime components. While the essential resource is often computer power, models also contain:

- Statistical routines for projections, confidence interval setting, and probability measurement.
- Formulas for expressing constraints, cost and production functions, input/output relationships, and other known interrelationships.
- Optimization routines that define maximums or minimums for particular goals.
- Interactive capability to allow users to perform on-line **"what ifs."**
- Ability to upload and download data from other information systems.
- Report preparation routines.

Most of these tools are not visible to the user. For example, a bank financial planning model needs to know that February 2008 has 29 days and not 28. But few users will consciously think about this minute detail.

**Outputs.** The third element is the model's output: revised plans, pro forma financial statements, statistical summaries, "what if" analyses, and other reports requested by managers. Outputs can be hard copy, screen displays, or computer files. The model's output often moves through a report-generating package that allows managers to create relevant report formats and comparisons.

## Building a Financial Model

Dupere Wholesalers is implementing a financial planning model to aid in its monthly and annual budgeting process. Tom Denomme, controller, has identified the following relationships among key planning variables.

1. Sales volume (in units) is increasing at the rate of 4 percent per month. The selling price is $25 per unit.

2. All sales are on credit. Cash collections are received 40 percent in the month of sale and 60 percent in the month after the sale.

3. Inventory is maintained at 30 percent of next month's unit sales forecast.

4. Purchases are paid 50 percent in the month of purchase and 50 percent in the month after purchase. Each unit costs $13.

5. The operating expenses are both variable and fixed. The variable expenses average 20 percent of each month's revenue. Fixed expenses, including depreciation of $30,000, total $65,000 per month. All expenses are paid in the month incurred.

The following notations have been defined by Tom:

| | | | | | |
|---|---|---|---|---|---|
| $S_t$ | = | Volume for current month (units) | $P$ | = | Price per unit |
| $S\$_t$ | = | Revenue for current month (dollars) | $G$ | = | Growth rate |
| $Pur_t$ | = | Current period purchases in units | $C$ | = | Cost per unit |
| $Pur\$_t$ | = | Current period purchases in dollars | $D$ | = | Depreciation expense |
| $CGS_t$ | = | Cost of goods sold for current month | $t$ | = | Current month |
| $NI_t$ | = | Net income for current month | $t - 1$ | = | Last month |
| $CR_t$ | = | Cash receipts for current month | $t - 2$ | = | Two months ago |
| $CD_t$ | = | Cash disbursements for current month | $t + 1$ | = | Next month |
| $Co_1$ | = | Percentage of sales collected in current month | | | |
| $Co_2$ | = | Percentage of sales collected in next month | | | |
| $Py_1$ | = | Percentage of purchases paid in current month | | | |
| $Py_2$ | = | Percentage of purchases paid in next month | | | |
| $I_t$ | = | Inventory at the end of current month | | | |
| EI% | = | Inventory as a percentage of next month's sales | | | |
| VO% | = | Variable operating expense as a percentage of sales | | | |
| FO$ | = | Fixed operating expenses | | | |

To begin to create a financial model, we can use the above notations for each variable and prepare a series of equations that may be used to calculate the dependent variables needed to construct the model. The model will eventually be able to create forecast financial statements.

1. Sales volume for the current month:      $S_t = (1 + G) * S_{t+1}$

2. Revenue for current month:      $S\$_t = P * S_t$

3. Purchases for current month (units):      $P_t = S_t + I_t - I_{t+1}$; where $I_t = EI\% * S_{t+1}$ and $I_{t+1} = EI\% * S_t$

4. Purchases for current month (dollars):      $Pur\$_t = C * Pur_t$

5. Cost of goods sold for current month:      $CGS_t = C * S_t$

6. Net income for current month:      $NI_t = S\$_t - CGS_t - (VO\% * S\$_t) - FO\$$

7. Cash receipts for current month:      $CR_t = (Co_1 * S\$_t) + (Co_2 * S\$_{t+1})$

8. Cash disbursements for current month:      $CD_t = (Py_1 * Pur\$_t) + (Py_2 * Pur\$_{t-1}) + (VO\% * S\$_t) + (FO\$ - D)$

## TERMINOLOGY REVIEW

## QUESTIONS FOR REVIEW AND DISCUSSION

1. Reread the vignette about Joyce at the beginning of the chapter. Respond to each of her comments about budgeting. Give a possible reason for why she thinks that way. What retort could you give to each comment?

2. List the major components of a planning and control system.

3. Identify and explain at least five purposes of budgeting.

4. Which is a better basis for judging actual results: budgeted performance or past actual performance? Explain.

5. What are the similarities and differences among an activity center, a cost center, a profit center, and an investment center?

6. Since the limiting factor is the starting point for budgeting, identify the most common limiting variable. Explain. Now pick four specific businesses, and identify another variable that might be the limiting factor.

7. What is the difference between an independent variable and a dependent variable in the budgeting process? Give three examples of each.

8. Explain why variable and fixed costs behave differently when a budget is "flexed" from the expected to the actual level of activity.

9. For what kinds of business activities are project budgets useful?

10. When probabilities are estimated for various possible selling prices, sales volumes, or unit costs, what is meant by "expected value of contribution margin?"

11. Why are the human behavioral concerns important in budgeting? Identify and explain the concerns.

12. What is "budget slack?" Is it good or bad? Why "yes" *and* "no?"

13. If Linsmeier Products Company were a wholesaler and not a manufacturer, how would the master budget sequence as presented change?

14. If Linsmeier Products Company provided interior design services and were not a manufacturer, how would the master budget sequence as presented change?

15. From the master budget example, identify the independent variables. Which schedules contain only dependent variables?

16. Why is it important that the balance sheet balance in preparing budgets?

17. Explain why preparing the cash-flow forecast requires that all operating and project budget schedules be completed first.

18. What does "what if" analysis mean?

19. In the Linsmeier Products Company example, trace the following numbers back to independent variables:

    (a) Schedule 5, first-quarter ending plywood inventory: 8,550 square feet.
    (b) On Schedule 6, third-quarter direct labor hours: 3,050 hours.
    (c) On Schedule 8, second-quarter indirect labor and fringe benefits expenses: $14,535.
    (d) On Schedule 11, third-quarter payment of prior quarter's purchases: $6,525.

20. (Appendix) Describe the primary components of the three basic elements of a financial planning model.

21. (Appendix) How can a simulation model be used to create a better budget?

22. (Appendix) A financial planning model should help management perform its functions better. Give an example of how a financial planning model could be helpful to a bank. To a travel agency. To an automotive parts manufacturer.

23. **(Appendix)** John Gaetz, controller of a local hospital, said the following about financial modeling at a recent meeting of the Tri-City Accountants Society: "The first financial model was A = L + OE." Comment.

## EXERCISES

7–1.   **Types of Responsibility Centers.** The list below describes a variety of business situations:
   (a) The parts department of an automobile dealership.
   (b) A convenience store that is owned by a chain organization. The goods to be sold and the selling prices are all determined by the corporate office.
   (c) The wing assembly department of a private airplane manufacturer.
   (d) The janitorial department of an office furniture manufacturer.
   (e) The women's shoe department in a large retail store. The buyer, an assistant department manager, decides which styles, sizes, etc., are purchased. The department supervisor sets selling prices.
   (f) The marketing department of a local TV station.
   (g) The purchasing department for a large electronics company.
   (h) The PC product line of a major computer manufacturer that is organized by product lines.
   (i) The technical support department for a large computer software company. Customers call an 800 number and ask questions about problems they are experiencing with software purchased from the company.
   (j) The car pool operation for a city government. City officials needing cars check them out for the days of travel.

   **Required:**
   For each business segment, indicate how it is most likely to be organized, as a cost center, a profit center, or an investment center. State any additional assumptions you feel are necessary to clarify a situation.

7–2.   **Responsibility Problems.** Refer to Figure 7.3, and discuss the following responsibility situations:
   **Case A:** Notice the September and the year-to-date budget variances in account 6780 Administrative Allocations. Why might these variances occur? Where does control over this expense probably exist? Comment on the budget planning and control implications.
   **Case B:** Assume that the unexpected overtime costs in account 6245 arise from rework that had to be done on several major jobs this month. The cause of the rework is disputed. Mr. Kannisoni claims the materials were either defective when purchased or prepared improperly in the preceding department. He feels this expense should be charged to Materials Preparation or to Purchasing. Comment on his problem.
   **Case C:** The Assembly Department, the next production department after Stamping, has experienced a production problem; and the manager must stop the assembly line. The manager asks Mr. Kannisoni to stop the transfer of stampings to Assembly until the problem is solved. If it stops, the Stamping Department will lose output and incur extra costs to catch up again. If Stamping does not stop, Assembly will have to handle the stampings several times, incurring more costs. Who should do what? Who should bear the additional costs?

**7–3.  Forecast Cash Payments.** Renee's Soft Shoe Shop is preparing its cash budget for the month of November. The following information is available about its operation:

| | |
|---|---|
| November beginning inventory | $18,000 |
| Estimated November cost of goods sold | 90,000 |
| Estimated November ending inventory | 16,000 |
| Estimated November payments for purchases made prior to November | 21,000 |
| Estimated November payments for purchases made in November | 80 % |

**Required:** What are the estimated cash payments in November for Renee?

**7–4.  Materials Requirements.** Miller Co. produces plastic buckets. The following budget data are available:
  **(a)** Ending finished goods inventory: 20 percent of next quarter's sales
  **(b)** Ending materials inventory: 30 percent of next quarter's production
  **(c)** Forecast sales for each quarter of next year are 1,000, 1,100, 1,200, and 1,300 buckets, respectively.
  **(d)** Two pounds of plastic are needed for each bucket. January 1 inventories are at the correct planned levels.

**Required:**
How many pounds of plastic must be purchased for the first two quarters of next year to meet the bucket sales forecast?

 **7–5.  Cash Receipts.** Dale Company, located in Manchester, U. K., prepared the following sales budget for the first six months:

| | January | February | March | April | May | June |
|---|---|---|---|---|---|---|
| Sales units | 6,000 | 7,000 | 7,500 | 8,500 | 7,800 | 8,300 |

Units sell for £20 each. Twenty percent of sales is for cash, and the remainder is on account. The firm forecasts collection of sales on account to be 60 percent in the month of sale with the remainder collected in the next month. Beginning receivables at January 1 is £40,000.

**Required:**
**1.** Find the forecast cash receipts for each month.
**2.** If more customers use credit cards causing cash sales to increase to 40 percent of total sales, by how much is cash increased in the second quarter?

**7–6.  Basic Budget Relationships.** Find the requested amount in each situation.
  **A.** Wille Corporation has a $75,000 balance in its accounts receivable account at the beginning of the budget month. Sales on account this month should be $160,000, and 70 percent of those sales should be collected in the month of the sale. In addition, 60 percent of the beginning balance in accounts receivable is expected to be collected this month. What is expected to be the budget month's ending balance of accounts receivable?
  **B.** Crumbaugh Supply, a wholesaler, estimated sales of $750,000 for the third quarter and $800,000 for the fourth quarter. The estimated gross profit rate is 40 percent. The June 30 inventory is $120,000. The targeted inventory at the end of the third quarter is to be 20 percent of fourth quarter sales volume. What quantity of inventory should be purchased in the third quarter?
  **C.** White's Wholesale Apparel is budgeting for the year. The beginning accounts receivable and partial sales data are given below:

|  |  | First Quarter | Second Quarter |
|---|---|---|---|
| Accounts Receivable | $200,000    Sales | $600,000 | $800,000 |

Sales are all on credit, and 80 percent are collected in the quarter of sale. The remainder is collected in the next quarter. What are budgeted cash collections in the second quarter?

**7–7. Purchases and Payments.** Gaffigan Company sells course note packets for classes with high enrollments at Prestige University. Each packet sells for $10, and the purchase cost is $6 per packet. The firm keeps an inventory of 40 percent of next month's forecast sales. Each month, it pays suppliers 70 percent of the current month's purchases, and the remainder is paid in the following month. The Spring semester's sales budget is:

|  | January | February | March | April | May |
|---|---|---|---|---|---|
| Sales | $6,000 | $4,000 | $3,000 | $6,000 | $1,000 |

**Required:**

1. Calculate Gaffigan's budgeted purchases per month through April.
2. Show Gaffigan's cash payments to suppliers per month from February through April.

**7–8. Flexible Budgeting.** Analyze the following situations:

**A.** In the Whitmyer Company, an activity level of 20,000 clerical hours is planned. A flexible budget for October shows $100,000 of fixed overhead cost and $100,000 of variable overhead cost. The actual activity level during October was 18,000 clerical hours, and the actual overhead cost was $180,000. How did the manager manage the overhead costs in October?

**B.** Thelen prepared the following flexible budget for possible sales of 5,000 and 7,500 units:

|  | 5,000 units | 7,500 units |
|---|---|---|
| Sales | $500,000 | $750,000 |
| Operating expenses | 400,000 | 550,000 |

Sales were actually 6,000 units at an average price of $90 each and spending was $500,000. Using flexible budgeting, find the difference between the budgeted and actual net income?

**C.** Assume that budgeted overhead is made up of variable costs of $4 per hour and fixed costs of $80,000 for 10,000 hours. By how much was the flexible budget overspent or underspent in 2008 if 9,500 hours were worked and $115,000 was spent? Was overhead overapplied or underapplied and by how much?

**7–9. Flexible Budgeting.** The Dan's Bicycle Co. operates a repair shop on Louis Street. Dan, the owner, has calculated his overhead costs per year to be $10,000 plus $10 per bicycle repaired. In late 2006, he prepared a budget for repairing 500 bikes in 2007. He actually repaired 550 bikes in 2007 and spent $15,200 for overhead expenses.

**Required:** Comment on each of the following statements about 2007 activities.

**(a)** His cost function is ($10,000/500) + $10, or $30 per bike.
**(b)** His spending was $300 under his adjusted budget; therefore, he did control costs well.
**(c)** His original budget for 2007 (prepared in late 2006) was $15,500.
**(d)** His spending was $200 over his original budget; therefore, he did not control costs well.

**7–10. Linking Applied Overhead and Flexible Budgeting.** Wegener Steins, a Bavarian ceramic stein maker, has a cost function in euros of €400,000 plus €4 per stein. The original budget for the year used 200,000 steins as its normal capacity. This cost function and the normal capacity are used to cost each stein. Sales were unusually good. Wegener produced and sold 245,000 steins. Variable costs totaled €992,000, and fixed costs were €445,000. Because of the higher volume, extra overtime of €40,000 was incurred and added to variable costs. Also, extra supervision salaries added €40,000 to fixed costs.

**Required:**

1. Looking only at total variable and fixed costs, were Wegener's costs well controlled this year? Explain.
2. If the extra production costs are excluded for the analysis, were Wegener's other costs well controlled? Explain.
3. Show how much overhead cost was added to products. Comment on overapplied or underapplied overhead.

Service

**7–11. Performance Report with a Budget Formula.** Desert Rat Rentals, operating in Quartzite, Arizona, has one department totally dedicated to dune buggies. The company rents them at a daily rate plus mileage. The company's accountant, Dusty Aire, developed the following annual budget formula for each cost related to the dune buggies and the actual costs for this season, which just ended:

| Cost Item | Formula | | This Season's Actual Costs |
|---|---|---|---|
| Fuel and oil | $0.40 per mile | | $ 9,735 |
| Chassis and other lubricants | 0.05 per mile plus | $ 1,000 | 2,190 |
| Repairs | 0.06 per mile plus | 1,200 | 2,705 |
| Depreciation | | 2,500 | 2,500 |
| Licenses, taxes, and fees | | 2,600 | 2,930 |
| Insurance expenses | | 1,600 | 1,735 |
| Total budget formula | $0.51 per mile plus | $ 8,900 | $ 21,795 |

During the season, records of Desert Rat Rentals show that the dune buggies were driven 24,000 miles.

**Required:**

Prepare a responsibility performance report for Dusty that will show the budget, actual results, and variances for the Dune Buggy Department for this season.

Service

**7–12. Project Budgeting.** We have approved a 6-month $200,000 systems project to improve office communications. We are now 4 months into the project. People and equipment expenses have been $160,000, and we think it will take another 3 months and $80,000 to finish the project.

**Required:**

1. From a control perspective, how is the project coming along?
2. From a planning perspective, how does the project look as we view the future?

**7–13. Budget Comments.** Comment briefly on the following quotes about budgeting from a financial planning textbook:

(a) "One major criticism of budgeting is that it is used as a 'cost reduction' tool rather than a 'cost control' tool. The objective of the budget is to control costs at an efficient level of operation."

(b) "There are generally three benefits from allowing employees to participate in developing the budget: (1) Employees tend to accept the budget as their own plan of action.

(2) Participation tends to increase morale among employees and toward management. (3) Employee cohesiveness is increased, and productivity will also increase if dictated by the group norm."

(c) "Even though budgets are quantitative tools, considerable emotion is connected to budgeting. The individual in control often sees the budget as a means of getting things done. People being controlled often have feelings of anxiety because their success and promotion are tied directly to the budget."

**7–14. Expected Value of Profit.** The sales manager of the Zweng Corporation's Economic Forecasting Department has estimated that a 40 percent probability exists that sales volume for next year will be 600,000 units with a selling price of $7 per unit. A 60 percent probability exists that sales will be 500,000 units with a selling price of $8 per unit. Variable cost per unit is estimated at $6 (with a probability of 20 percent) or $5 (with a probability of 80 percent). Fixed costs for the next year have been estimated at $800,000.

**Required:**
1. Compute the expected value of forecast net income for next year.
2. Comment on the resulting net income.

**7–15. Purchases and Cash Payments.** A production plan by quarter for Danielle Company is:

| First quarter | 24,000 units | Third quarter | 32,000 units |
|---|---|---|---|
| Second quarter | 30,000 | Fourth quarter | 42,000 |

Four units of materials are used in producing each unit of product. Each unit of materials costs $0.60. Ending materials inventory is to be equal to 25 percent of production requirements for the next quarter. This requirement was met at the beginning of the year. Production for the first quarter following the budget year is estimated at 28,000 units. Accounts payable for materials purchased is estimated at $38,400 at the beginning of the current budget year. Forecast accounts payable at the end of the quarter should equal 40 percent of the purchases during the quarter.

**Required:**
1. Determine the units of materials to be purchased each quarter.
2. Determine the cost of materials purchases by quarter.
3. Estimate the payments to be made each quarter for materials.

**7–16. Cash Budgeting.** Wuerth Corporation, a Melbourne, Australia, firm, is preparing a cash budget for 2008 using the following data:
(a) Each month, 70 percent of sales is on credit. Of credit sales, 60 percent is collected in the month of sale and 40 percent in the next month.
(b) Cost of goods sold is 70 percent of sales. Of purchases, 60 percent is paid when purchased; and the remainder is paid in the next month.
(c) Planned inventory is 40 percent of the next month's sales. Budgeted purchases in February were A$60,000.
(d) Operating expenses are A$30,000 per month, including A$2,000 of depreciation expense. These are paid when incurred.
(e) Forecast cash balance as of March 1 is A$20,000, which is the target level.
   Budgeted sales, in Australian dollars, for a portion of 2008 are: February A$90,000, March A$120,000, April A$110,000, and May A$100,000.

**Required:**
1. Create a cash forecast for March.
2. If Wuerth plans to buy a computer system for A$20,000, can the firm pay for it and keep a "safe" cash level? What are the main risks?

**7-17.** **Purchases and Cash Receipts.** Olympia Candies is preparing a budget for the second quarter of the current calendar year. The March ending inventory of merchandise was $106,000, which was higher than expected. The company prefers to carry ending inventory amounting to the expected sales volume of the next two months. Purchases of merchandise are paid half in the month of purchase and half in the month following purchase, and the balance due on accounts payable at the end of March was $24,000. Budgeted sales are as follows:

| April | $ 50,000 | July | $ 72,000 |
|-------|----------|------|----------|
| May | 48,000 | August | 56,000 |
| June | 60,000 | September | 60,000 |

**Required:**
1. Assume that a 25 percent gross profit margin is budgeted. Prepare a budget schedule that shows the following for April, May, and June:
   **(a)** Cost of goods sold.
   **(b)** Purchases required.
   **(c)** Cash payments for merchandise.
2. Assume that the accounts receivable balance on April 1 was $35,000 and that three-fourths of all customers pay in the month of sale and one-fourth in the month following the sale. Prepare a budget showing the cash receipts from accounts receivable for April, May, and June.

Service

**7-18.** **Cash Receipts from Sales.** Ponytail Production Shows has forecast revenues as follows:

| July | $ 67,000 | October | $ 75,000 |
|------|----------|---------|----------|
| August | 69,000 | November | 80,000 |
| September | 72,000 | December | 90,000 |

The controller has maintained a record of collections and has estimated the following pattern:

| Month of sale | 60 % |
|---------------|------|
| First month after sale | 30 % |
| Second month after sale | 8 % |
| Uncollected | 2 % |

**Required (Use of spreadsheet software is recommended.):**
1. Calculate the amount of cash receipts the company is budgeting by month in the fourth quarter.
2. If the collection pattern changed to 40, 40, 15, and 5 percent respectively, what is the impact on fourth quarter cash receipts?

**7-19.** **Production Cost Budget.** A manufacturing budget for 2008 was prepared for Sequeira Metals, of Barcelona, Spain, and is as follows:

| First quarter | 48,000 units | Third quarter | 64,000 units |
|---------------|--------------|---------------|--------------|
| Second quarter | 56,000 units | Fourth quarter | 60,000 units |

Budgeted cost estimates in euros are based on the previous year's actual costs. Direct materials cost per unit is estimated at €600. Direct labor cost is budgeted at €400 per unit, and factory overhead is to be applied at 200 percent of direct labor cost. Factory overhead spending is based on a cost function of €200 per unit plus €36,000,000 per quarter. Of the quarter's production, 75 percent is sold in the current quarter, and 25 percent is sold in the next quarter. December 31, 2007, inventory is 12,000 units.

**Required:**

1. Prepare a schedule showing production costs for each quarter and for 2008 in total.
2. Compute estimated cost of goods sold for each quarter and for 2008 in total.
3. Analyze factory overhead.

**7–20.  Adequacy of Cash Flow with "What Ifs."** Jennifer Victor is preparing a budget of cash receipts and disbursements for Gourmet Food Services, Inc. Some sales are for cash, and the remainder is billed on a contract basis. Sales for April to August are:

|        | Cash Sales | Billed Sales | Total Sales |
|--------|-----------|-------------|-------------|
| April  | $ 65,000  | $ 40,000    | $ 105,000   |
| May    | 72,000    | 46,000      | 118,000     |
| June   | 84,000    | 68,000      | 152,000     |
| July   | 88,000    | 72,000      | 160,000     |
| August | 86,000    | 70,000      | 156,000     |

Of the billed sales, 65 percent is collected during the month of sale; and the other 35 percent is collected the next month.

Food costs amounting to 75 percent of sales must be paid during the month of sales. Monthly operating costs are $24,000. The cash balance at May 1 amounted to $7,000. If the cash balance is over $20,000 on August 31, Victor and the other shareholders will receive the excess as dividends.

**Required (Use of spreadsheet software is recommended.):**

1. Prepare a budget of cash receipts and disbursements for each month, May to August, inclusive.
2. Compute the amount, if any, that can be paid in dividends at the end of August.
3. What is the impact on possible dividend payments in the following situations?
   (a) "What if" competitive pressures cause food costs to increase to 80 percent of sales.
   (b) "What if" collections of billed sales slow to 50 percent in the month of sale and 50 percent in the next month.

**7–21.  Budgeted Balance Sheet.** The balance sheet for Griffith Stores, Inc. at December 31, 2007, is:

| Assets: | | Liabilities and Equity: | |
|---------|---|------------------------|---|
| Cash | $ 82,000 | Accounts payable | $ 62,000 |
| Accounts receivable | 112,000 | | |
| Inventory | 136,000 | Capital stock | 300,000 |
| Building and fixtures, net | 358,000 | Retained earnings | 326,000 |
| Total assets | $688,000 | Total liabilities & equity | $688,000 |

Cash receipts for the year are collections on accounts receivable amounting to $846,000. Cash payments are budgeted at $838,000. Included in those payments is $126,000 for various expenses that do not flow through accounts payable. Credits to accounts payable for the year are estimated at $715,000, all merchandise purchases. All cash payments are for expenses or purchases. Depreciation expense is $75,000. Net sales are estimated at $930,000. The inventory of merchandise is expected to increase to $147,000 by the end of the year.

**Required:**

From the information given, prepare a budgeted balance sheet at December 31, 2008. Prove the retained earnings balance by computing the net income. Income tax is estimated at 40 percent and will be paid after December 31, 2008.

**7–22.** **Managerial Behavior and Budget Ethics.** Puidokas Corporation has seen a new revision of the budget system each year for the past five years. Bonuses followed strong budget performances. The following are changes made during the past few years:

**Change 1:** One year top management felt that, since wages were 60 percent of total expenses, the budget should simply focus on keeping next year's headcounts equal to or below the current year's level. Most managers did this by shifting work to outside contractors.

**Change 2:** Concern over customer service caused top management to budget the number of back orders issued because an item was not available from existing inventory. A trip to Tahiti was given to managers with zero actual back orders.

**Change 3:** Because corporate expenses were viewed as being too high, the president decided to allocate all home office expenses to the nine divisions. Each division head budgeted down to "net income" and was evaluated on the comparison of actual to planned "net income."

**Change 4:** Also, at the final budget approval stage for the last several years, the president forced each division to reduce its total expenses by an even five percent across the board. This year, the president increased the across-the-board cuts to 10 percent.

**Required:**

Comment on Puidokas Corporation's approach to budgeting and the possible impacts each change might have on the budget process and managers' behavior.

**7–23.** **Ethical Budget Issues.** Don Bjorn, a salesperson with Great Lakes Steel, is working on his next year's sales budget. Don is paid on a half-salary and half-commission basis for a target salary of $90,000. Based on his approved sales budget, Don would receive commissions equivalent to one-third of his target salary if he achieves the sales budget. By exceeding his sales budget he could and has earned 50 percent above his target salary in a good year. This year he will sell 8,000 tons of all grades of steel. This was a little over the prior year's actual total and well above his current sales budget of 6,000 tons. He did well.

So far Don has filled in the preliminary sales forecast forms. This is a first estimate of sales on a product-by-product estimate. Don's total adds up to 5,200 tons. His sales manager has sent the forms back for a redo, since he obviously missed some sales someplace. His second version showed 5,400 tons. The third round requested a customer-by-customer breakdown in addition to the product estimates. A memo from the vice-president of marketing asks that each salesperson be as accurate as possible in estimating sales. Don has just mailed his estimates. They call for 5,600 tons.

The process from this point, as Don describes it, is that he will receive a call from his manager telling him to redo the latest estimate and make sure it is 10 percent above the current year's budgeted number. Don will "hem and haw" on the phone, redo the form, and send it in showing 6,600 tons, exactly a 10 percent increase. Don says everyone will be happy, particularly him. Don says he has one last hurdle to jump—a visit to corporate and a conference with the vice-president and sales manager. Under great protest, Don will agree to a 6,750 ton target. Next year's budget is approved.

Don, an effective salesperson in all respects, has done it again. He checks his early order book for next year and his penciled notes, adds up the first-quarter early bookings, sees orders adding up to nearly 3,200 tons, and smiles. "Ah, yes!  It should be a great year. Maybe this is the year for that 38-foot sailboat!"

**Required:**
Evaluate Great Lakes Steel's sales budgeting and incentive systems. Comment on Don's approach to the process. How could it be strengthened?

# PROBLEMS

Service

**7–24.**   **Evaluation of a Responsibility Report.** Acosta Bank Security Services prepared the following responsibility report for its armored car cost center:

| Budget Report for the Week Ended April 14, 2007 | | | |
| --- | --- | --- | --- |
| Supervisor responsible: | Kelli Tunnell | | |
| | Cheryl Broadway | | |
| **Fav/(Unfav)** | **Budget** | **Actual** | **Variance** |
| Cost driver–personnel hours | 800 | 850 | (50) U |
| Variable costs: | | | |
| Delivery personnel | $16,000 | $16,500 | $(500) U |
| Departmental fixed costs: | | | |
| Equipment maintenance | 30,000 | 29,250 | 750 F |
| Supervisor salaries | 10,000 | 10,610 | (610) U |
| Administrative overhead— | | | |
| allocated by payroll | 8,000 | 9,000 | (1,000) U |
| Total costs | $64,000 | $65,360 | $(1,360) |

**Required:**
Given the concepts of responsibility accounting, evaluate the appropriateness of this report. If necessary, revise the report.

**7–25.**   **Responsibility Accounting and Roll-up Reporting.** Pampa Packaging Corporation has two plants, one in Illinois and one in Singapore. Each plant has a forming and a packing department. Production for the forming department of the Illinois Plant is estimated at 1,600 tons for June. The budgeted costs per ton are as follows:

| | |
| --- | --- |
| Direct materials | $8 |
| Direct labor | 15 |
| Factory overhead | |
| (half fixed and half variable) | 10 |
| Total per ton | $33 |

Total budgeted production costs for the packing department are $33,000 for June. Budgeted costs for the plant manager's office are $57,000.

Budgeted costs for the Singapore plant total $67,000. The vice-president of production is responsible for both plants and has $54,000 of budgeted expenses. Budgeted expenses for the company's vice-president of marketing's office are $112,600. The president's office budget is $60,000.

In June, 1,500 tons were produced; and actual expenses were as follows:

| | | | |
|---|---|---|---|
| President's office. | $ 62,300 | Illinois plant: | |
| Vice-president of marketing | 109,800 | Plant manager's office. | $ 58,300 |
| Vice-president of production. | 55,500 | Packing department. | 34,900 |
| Singapore plant—total costs. | 70,100 | Forming department: | |
| | | Direct materials. | 10,600 |
| | | Direct labor. | 23,400 |
| | | Overhead. | 13,200 |

**Required:**

Prepare responsibility reports showing the appropriate budget, actual expenses, and variances from budget for each of the following:

**(a)** Forming department in Illinois plant.

**(b)** Plant manager for the Illinois plant.

**(c)** Vice-president of production.

**(d)** President of the company.

**7–26. Budget Constraints.** Rollin Parts, Inc. has the capacity to manufacture 400,000 units of a certain product line each year. Each unit of product requires 2 pounds of a metal that is difficult to obtain. The sales department estimates that 300,000 units of product can be sold next year. The purchasing department states that 30,000 pounds of the metal are on hand at the beginning of the year and that only 290,000 pounds can be purchased on the market next year. The purchasing department has found a company that is willing to produce 100,000 units of product on a contract basis. That company has enough of the required metal on hand to make the 100,000 units.

**Required:**

**1.** What is the limiting factor in budgeting next year? Why?

**2.** How many units of the product can be produced internally and sold next year?

**3.** What is the maximum forecast sales possible for next year?

**7–27. Responsibility Reporting.** The following accounts and amounts (with 000s omitted) for Giacomazza Company were taken from the accounting and budgeting records for June:

| Acct. No. | Account Name | June Actual | June Budget | Year-to-Date Actual | Year-to-Date Budget |
|---|---|---|---|---|---|
| 5110 | Advertising | $ 125 | $ 135 | $ 833 | $ 810 |
| 5120 | Bad Debt Expense | 37 | 36 | 218 | 216 |
| 5130 | Sales Commissions | 109 | 111 | 754 | 670 |
| 6100 | Direct Materials | 1,319 | 1,388 | 8,178 | 8,328 |
| 6200 | Direct Labor | 749 | 751 | 4,599 | 4,506 |
| 6310 | Depreciation—Factory Machinery | 45 | 45 | 275 | 280 |
| 6320 | Factory Rent | 244 | 244 | 1,464 | 1,464 |
| 6330 | Factory Utilities | 34 | 33 | 237 | 218 |
| 6340 | Indirect Labor | 176 | 174 | 1,056 | 1,044 |
| 6350 | Property Taxes—Factory Machinery | 19 | 21 | 114 | 126 |
| 6360 | Repairs and Maintenance—Factory | 47 | 50 | 351 | 320 |
| 7120 | Property Taxes—Office Equipment | 7 | 8 | 42 | 48 |
| 7130 | Salaries of Administrative Personnel | 1,687 | 1,601 | 9,122 | 9,606 |

**Required:**

Prepare a responsibility performance report for manufacturing operations. Use a format you think will best show budget performance.

**7–28.    Cash Forecasting.** John Iannotti is preparing his budgets. He has written the following on a pad of legal paper:

| Forecast Sales | | Actual December 31 Balance Sheet Data | |
|---|---|---|---|
| January | $70,000 | Cash | $8,000 |
| February | 90,000 | Accounts Receivable | 20,000 |
| March | 80,000 | Inventory | 40,000 |
| April | 60,000 | Accounts Payable | 45,000 |

Other data are as follows:

**(a)** Sales are on credit with 40 percent collected in the month of sale and 60 percent in the next month.

**(b)** Cost of sales is 60 percent of sales.

**(c)** Other variable costs are 10 percent of sales, paid in the month incurred.

**(d)** Inventories are to be 80 percent of next month's budgeted sales requirements.

**(e)** Purchases are paid in the month after purchase.

**(f)** Fixed expenses are $3,000 per month; all are paid in the month incurred.

**Required:**

**1.** Prepare a cash budget for February.

**2.** Comment on which assumptions may be the most tenuous and which may be the most certain.

**7–29.    Budgeted Income Statement for a Service Organization.** The Ole Route 66 Motel is a low-priced motel in Winslow, Arizona, along Interstate 40. It has 50 rooms, each with two double beds. The rates are $18 for one person, $10 for the second person, and $3 each for the third and fourth persons. Rollaway beds are available for $2 per night.

During April, the motel manager expects an 80 percent occupancy rate. Past experience suggests that 20 percent of the rooms rented will be to only 1 person, 20 percent to 2 persons, 30 percent to 3 persons, and 20 percent to 4 persons. Ten percent will have 5 persons and use rollaway beds.

Laundry costs average $1.00 per person per night. Cleaning workers earn $6.00 per hour, and it takes 30 minutes to clean each room. Other variable operating costs (utilities, for example) are $4 per occupied room per night. Maintenance and grounds personnel costs are about $1,500 per month. Two clerks each have a salary of $1,200 per month. Depreciation is $2,000 per month. Other cash fixed expenses are $3,500 per month.

**Required:**

**1.** Prepare a budgeted income statement for April.

**2.** Suggest an average occupancy percentage needed to break even if the average number of people staying in a room is three.

**7–30.    Labor Cost Budget.** Budget plans of Baxter Medical Services are being revised for the last two quarters of this year. Two main procedures are provided to patients referred by area physicians. Under the revised plan, the forecast volume of procedures is estimated as follows:

| | Procedure 1 | Procedure 2 |
|---|---|---|
| Third quarter | 1,200 | 1,500 |
| Fourth quarter | 1,600 | 1,800 |

Personnel schedules indicate that 15 minutes are required for Procedure 1 and 20 minutes for Procedure 2. Technicians labor rate per hour is $15 during the third quarter. On October 1, a $1.00 per hour raise contained in the Baxter labor contract with its union will go into effect.

In preparation of the budget, provision is to be made for fringe benefit costs such as pensions and medical health insurance. The total fringe benefit cost is estimated to be 55 percent of the hourly labor cost for the third quarter. Health insurance cost will increase the fringe cost to 60 percent of the hourly labor cost for the fourth quarter.

**Required:**

1. Prepare a budget showing the direct labor cost per procedure and in total dollars for each quarter.

2. Add a section to the direct labor cost schedule showing the estimated fringe benefit cost and total labor cost for each quarter. Comment on the increase in costs and its possible implications.

**7–31.  Production and Inventories.** Handorf Company has irregular sales volume during the year, and management is planning to produce at a uniform rate with inventories increasing or decreasing throughout the year. A sales budget in product units is forecast for the first six months of 2006 as follows:

| Months | Units | Months | Units |
|--------|-------|--------|-------|
| January | 40,000 | April | 25,000 |
| February | 25,000 | May | 40,000 |
| March | 20,000 | June | 50,000 |

The production cycle is short, and work in process inventories are insignificant. An inventory of 10,000 units was on hand at January 1, and 20,000 units of inventory are planned for June 30.

**Required:**

Prepare a production schedule that will have level production each month while showing the expected inventories at the end of each month. Comment on the problems this approach creates. Why is it attractive?

Service

**7–32.  Supplies and Labor Cost.** The Greenberg Health Clinic serves as an outpatient clinic for citizens in Brant City. Medicines, drugs, and various medical supplies must be purchased; and cost estimates must be made for each month. In addition to physicians who are available on a contract basis at a cost of $50,000 a month, nurses salary costs are $40,000 a month. Other employees are engaged on a part-time basis at a cost of $12.00 per hour. Past experience shows that one part-time person is required for every 50 patients served in a month. The typical part-time employee works 100 hours in a month.

The costs of medicines and various supplies average $5 per patient served plus a fixed cost of $15,000 each month. A forecast of patients to be served in the last quarter is:

| | Number of Patients |
|---|---|
| October | 900 |
| November | 1,100 |
| December | 1,200 |

**Required:**

1. Prepare a schedule showing the costs of the medicines and other supplies for each month.

2. According to the estimates, how many part-time people will be needed each month, and at what cost?

3. Prepare a budget schedule showing the costs of contract services, salaries, medicines and other supplies, and part-time labor cost for each month.

Service

**7–33.** **Project Management.** In the Osann Corporation, an advertising project is forecast to cost $100,000, generate $200,000 in additional variable contribution margin, and take 6 months to complete.

It is now 4 months into the project, and $60,000 has been spent. Osann estimates that it is one-third done and that it will take another 8 months and $100,000 to complete the project. Current estimates now show that the forecast additional variable contribution margin will be $160,000. Osann is at a "go" or "no go" point on this project.

**Required:**
1. How does Osann report the project relative to the budget?
2. How does Osann report this project in its "plan of action," if approved for continuation?
3. Should the project be "canned" or continued at this "go" or "no go" point? Explain.

**7–34.** **Probabilistic Budgeting.** Anderson Manufacturing Company is in the process of preparing its operating budget for next year. Bill McCarthy, controller, wants to include in the budget documents a budgeted income statement based on probabilities. In visiting with selling, production, and administrative personnel, McCarthy has obtained estimates and probabilities for each area.

Unit sales estimates, with associated selling prices and probabilities, are:

| Units | Selling | Price Probability |
|---|---|---|
| 800,000 | $25 | .20 |
| 700,000 | 28 | .30 |
| 600,000 | 32 | .40 |
| 500,000 | 36 | .10 |

Variable manufacturing costs will either be $8 per unit, with a probability of 80 percent, or $10 per unit, with a probability of 20 percent. Fixed manufacturing costs have a 90 percent chance of being $4,000,000 and a 10 percent chance of being $5,000,000. Variable selling and administrative expenses are estimated at $2, $3, or $4, with probabilities of 20 percent, 70 percent, and 10 percent, respectively. Fixed selling and administrative expenses have a 60 percent chance of amounting to $5,000,000 and a 40 percent chance of being $6,000,000.

**Required:** Prepare a budgeted income statement based on expected values.

**7–35.** **Expected Cash Flow.** Knevil Equipment Company is planning to expand beyond the industrial market of its materials handling equipment to produce trailers for the sports and recreation markets. The president, Spike Knevil, estimates that the company must invest $1,800,000 in new equipment up front. He wants to know how much cash flow can be provided by operations next year to apply toward acquiring the equipment and how much of the cost will have to be financed.

His sales staff estimates revenue next year at $8,500,000. However, if economic conditions deteriorate, sales revenue may be only $6,500,000.

Cost of goods sold has historically been 70 percent of revenue. A possibility exists that the company will have to absorb cost increases that cannot be passed along to customers. In this case, the cost of goods sold will be 80 percent of revenue. With sales down to $6,500,000, the cost of goods sold will definitely be 80 percent of revenue. Probabilities of occurrence have been estimated for each of three alternatives as follows:

| Revenues and Cost of Goods Sold | Operating Expenses | Probabilities |
|---|---|---|
| Sales at $8,500,000, cost of goods sold at 70 percent | $1,050,000 | 30 % |
| Sales at $8,500,000, cost of goods sold at 80 percent | 1,200,000 | 50 % |
| Sales at $6,500,000, cost of goods sold at 80 percent | 1,100,000 | 20 % |

Depreciation of $280,000 is included in operating expenses under each alternative, and depreciation of $350,000 is included in cost of goods sold for each alternative. Income taxes are estimated at 40 percent of income before income taxes.

In making the transition, equipment will be sold for $600,000, net of income taxes. A payment of $350,000 must be made on long-term notes payable. Spike wants dividends of $300,000 to be paid under each alternative.

**Required:**

1. What is the "worst case" cash-flow scenario that Spike could face?
2. Prepare a statement to show the forecast cash flow provided by operations under each assumption and the expected value of cash flows.
3. Continue the forecast statement to show how much additional cash will be needed to finance the new project after considering the information given. Show the impact of all three assumptions on expected cash flows.

Service

**7–36.  Expenses and Cash Disbursements.** Danell Andersen, the treasurer of Danish Ancient Studies Association, is planning an expense budget in Danish krone. Rent for the office is expected to amount to DKr6,000 for the year and will be paid in a lump sum during January. Insurance costing DKr840 for the year is to be prepaid in January for the entire year. Salaries for the employees have been budgeted at DKr72,000 for the year and are evenly distributed throughout the year.

An outside service has been engaged to obtain speakers and to schedule visits to archaeological digs during the year. The entire cost for the year, estimated at DKr36,000, must be paid during September. It is estimated that the services will be distributed throughout the year as follows:

| | |
|---|---|
| First quarter. | DKr3,000 |
| Second quarter | 12,000 |
| Third quarter. | 15,000 |
| Fourth quarter | 6,000 |

Telephone and postage have been budgeted at DKr600 each quarter with payment being made during the quarter. Travel expenses for the year of DKr6,000 will be paid during the second quarter with the cost being equally divided between the second and third quarters of the year.

Depreciation on office furniture and various implements has been estimated at DKr600 for the year. Supplies costing DKr300 are to be used each quarter with payment for the entire year being budgeted for February.

**Required:**

1. Prepare an accrual expense budget for Danell Andersen by quarters.
2. Convert the expense budget into a cash payments budget by quarters.

**7–37.  Budgeted Cost of Goods Manufactured.** Saleem Plastic Products had inventories of 75,000 pounds of raw materials and 25,000 units of finished product on January 1. Sales forecasts for the first six months are as follows:

| | | | |
|---|---|---|---|
| January. | 40,000 units | April | 70,000 units |
| February. | 55,000 | May | 60,000 |
| March. | 50,000 | June | 70,000 |

Saleem maintains a finished goods inventory equal to 40 percent of the forecast sales of the next month and a raw materials inventory equal to 30 percent of the next month's production requirements. Each unit of product requires 3 pounds of raw materials at $5 per pound.

The budgeted direct labor cost is $8 per hour, and each finished unit requires 30 minutes. Variable factory overhead is 40 percent of raw materials costs. Fixed factory overhead, including depreciation of $10,000, totals $90,000 per month and is applied using units. Normal volume is 60,000 units per month.

**Required (Use of spreadsheet software is recommended.):**
1. Prepare a budgeted cost of goods manufactured schedule. Include supporting schedules needed to calculate product cost components and unit costs.
2. Analyze the overhead flexible budget and amounts applied.
3. Comment on the following:
   (a) "What if" beginning inventory of raw materials was only 15,000 pounds?
   (b) "What if" finished goods inventory level is only 20 percent of next month's sales?
   (c) "What if" normal capacity is 50,000 units per month?

**7–38.    Forecasting Income and Cash.** Last December, Newton Company negotiated a $100,000 bank loan from the 3rd National Bank of Cincinnati. As part of the loan agreement, the bank requires a cash-flow forecast for the current year to help determine whether Newton can repay the loan. These December 31 data are available:

| *Assets:* | | *Liabilities & Equities:* | |
|---|---|---|---|
| Cash. | $15,000 | Accounts payable. | $s56,000 |
| Accounts receivable. | 110,000 | Wages payable | 15,000 |
| Inventory | 100,000 | Bank loan | 100,000 |
| Equipment | 600,000 | Capital stock | 250,000 |
| Accumulated depreciation. | (250,000) | Retained earnings | 154,000 |
| Total assets. | $575,000 | Total liabilities & equities | $575,000 |

Other data relating to next year include:
(a) Sales are expected to be $1,000,000. Accounts receivable at yearend is expected to be $140,000.
(b) Cost of goods sold is expected to be $400,000, and yearend inventory is expected to be $150,000.
(c) Accounts payable is expected to increase by $15,000.
(d) Wages payable is expected to be $22,000 at yearend, and the wages expense is expected to be $230,000.
(e) Depreciation expense will be $50,000.
(f) Other expenses, all paid in cash, are expected to be $95,000, including interest on the loan.
(g) Cash expenditures for plant and equipment are expected to be $160,000.
(h) Newton expects to pay a dividend of $40,000.

**Required:**
1. Calculate the forecast net income for next year.
2. What is the anticipated cash provided by operations in the coming year?  Is this cash flow adequate to meet the bank's expectation of loan repayment?  Comment.

**7–39.    Cash Flows and "What If."** M. W. Cope, a member of the board of directors of Bryja Markets, Inc., is concerned about the ability of the company to repay a loan in the amount of $250,000 that matures on June 30, 2008. In addition to the principal of the loan, the company must pay interest of $50,000.

The cash balance at January 1, 2008, is $82,000. Sales for December 2007 through June 2008 are budgeted as follows:

|  | Net Sales |  | Net Sales |
|---|---|---|---|
| December 2007 | $236,000 | April | $170,000 |
| January 2008 | 137,000 | May | 156,000 |
| February | 142,000 | June | 148,000 |
| March | 182,000 | | |

Cash sales each month are equal to approximately 30 percent of net sales. Collections on accounts receivable are expected as follows:

60 percent collected during the month of sale

40 percent collected in the following month

Total cash disbursements are estimated at $115,000 each month.

**Required (Use of spreadsheet software is recommended.):**

1. Prepare a cash budget for each month and in total for the six months of 2008.
2. Will the company be able to pay the loan with interest and still maintain a cash balance of no less than $60,000 on June 30? Explain.
3. If actual sales are 10 percent lower than the forecast each month while cash expenses drop by only $5,000 per month, what will happen to Bryja's ability to pay off the loan and keep the cash balance at the desired level?
4. If the sales and expenses fall as in Part (3) and collections patterns change to 40 percent collected in the current month and 60 percent in the following month, what will happen to the Bryja's cash situation?

Service

**7–40.** **Interpreting Overhead Budget Data.** The following data come from an office overhead section of a master budget for Tyson Services:

| Office Overhead Flexible Budget: | Quarterly Activity in Hours | | |
|---|---|---|---|
|  | 6,500 | 7,000 | 7,500 |
| Variable overhead expenses ($1.50 per hour) | $9,750 | $10,500 | $11,250 |
| Fixed overhead expenses ($10,500 per quarter) | $10,500 | $10,500 | $10,500 |
| Total flexible overhead budget. | $20,250 | $21,000 | $21,750 |
| Variable overhead rate per hour |  | $1.50 | |
| Fixed overhead rate per hour. |  | | 1.50 |
| Office overhead rate per hour |  | $3.00 | |

| Office Overhead Spending Budget by Quarter: | | | | | |
|---|---|---|---|---|---|
|  | Q–1 | Q–2 | Q–3 | Q–4 | Total |
| Budgeted volume (hours) | 6,800 | 6,500 | 6,900 | 7,400 | 27,600 |
| Budgeted office spending: | | | | | |
| Variable overhead expenses. | $10,200 | $9,750 | $10,350 | $11,100 | $41,400 |
| Fixed overhead expenses | 10,500 | 10,500 | 10,500 | 10,500 | 42,000 |
| Total overhead expenses | $20,700 | $20,250 | $20,850 | $21,600 | $83,400 |
| Budgeted applied overhead: | | | | | |
| Variable overhead applied | $10,200 | $ 9,750 | $10,350 | $11,100 | $41,400 |
| Fixed overhead applied. | 10,200 | 9,750 | 10,350 | 11,100 | 41,400 |
| Total overhead applied. | $20,400 | $19,500 | $20,700 | $22,200 | $82,800 |
| Overapplied or (underapplied) | $(300) | $(750) | $(150) | $600 | $ (600) |

**Required:**

1. What was the apparent annual normal volume in hours? Explain how you know this.
2. Explain the overapplied or (underapplied) overhead variance for each quarter and for the year. Why is it underapplied for the year?
3. Based on the data and your knowledge of flexible budgeting, what is Tyson Services expected to spend on office overhead for the year?

**7–41.   Product Cost Budget.** The management of Ingham Glass Products is aware of increased competition in the industry and has taken steps to improve cost control. Product costs on a per unit basis for last year are as follows:

|  | Product Lines | | |
|---|---|---|---|
|  | Red | White | Blue |
| Direct materials | $6 | $3 | $5 |
| Direct labor | 3 | 2 | 3 |
| Applied factory overhead | 3 | 2 | 3 |
| Total unit cost | $12 | $7 | $11 |
| Units produced last year | 300,000 | 240,000 | 340,000 |

The direct materials are manufactured by another division of the company which agreed to lower its price by 10 percent for this year. Direct labor cost will increase from $12 to $15 an hour, but increased productivity is planned. The revision of the production process will make it possible to manufacture 6 units of Red per hour, 8 units of White, or 10 units of Blue. Fixed overhead cost will, however, increase by $100,000 a year.

This year's planned volumes are the same as last year's actual output. Last year the company operated at a normal activity level set at 200,000 direct labor hours with budgeted and actual factory overhead costs of $2,400,000. This year, normal activity is to be reset at 150,000 direct labor hours with factory overhead amounting to $2,100,000 (including the fixed overhead increase).

**Required:**

1. Determine the cost of production this year in total and on a per unit basis.
2. Compute the expected cost savings in total. Comment on the impact of the changes.

**7–42.   Estimated Cash Flow.** The controller of Vardallas Services, Inc. observes that accounts receivable are expected to decrease by $47,000 from March 31 to June 30. In preparation for increased activity in the summer months, however, inventory of materials and supplies will increase by $62,000. Also, accounts payable will likely increase by $38,000.

Early in July, short-term loans of $150,000 must be paid along with the regular quarterly dividend of $0.40 per share on 60,000 outstanding shares of stock. Plans have been made to acquire new office equipment at a cost of $38,000, with payment to be made by mid-July. The cash balance on March 31 was $142,000. An estimated income statement for the second quarter is:

| *Estimated Income Statement for the Quarter Ended June 30* | |
|---|---|
| Service revenue | $528,000 |
| Cost of materials and supplies used. | $136,000 |
| Operating expenses (including depreciation of $81,000) | 177,000 |
| Interest expense | 23,000 |
| Total deductions from revenue | $336,000 |
| Income before income taxes | $192,000 |
| Income taxes | 78,000 |
| Net income | $114,000 |

**Required:**

Without considering the results of operations in early July, does it appear that operations in the quarter ended June 30 can supply sufficient cash to meet payment obligations in early July, while maintaining a cash balance of at least $120,000? Prepare a forecast cash-flow schedule to support your position.

**7–43. Forecast Balance Sheet.** Adelberg Electronics, Inc. designs and assembles electronic systems used by a variety of organizations. Its principal products are medical measurement systems and instrumentation systems for chemical analyses.

As a member of the budgeting team, your assignment is to prepare the budgeted balance sheet, based on information provided by other team members. The latest actual balance sheet shows:

**Beginning Balance Sheet, December 31 (in millions)**

| Current assets: | | | Current liabilities: | | |
|---|---|---|---|---|---|
| Cash | $479 | | Accounts payable | $249 | |
| Accounts receivable | 590 | | Accrued income taxes | 132 | |
| Inventories | 511 | | Other liabilities | 280 | $661 |
| Prepaid expenses | 30 | | Long-term debt | | 143 |
| Total current assets | | $1,610 | Total liabilities | | $804 |
| Plant and equipment | $1,397 | | Shareholders' equity: | | |
| Less: depreciation | 462 | | Common stock | $356 | |
| | | | Retained earnings | 1,385 | 1,741 |
| Net plant and equipment | | 935 | Total liabilities & equity | | $2,545 |
| Total assets | | $2,545 | | | |

Joe Silk, another member of the team, has given you the following budgeted income statement for the coming year:

**Forecast Income Statement (in millions)**

| | | |
|---|---|---|
| Sales revenue | | $3,253 |
| Cost of goods sold | | 1,583 |
| Gross profit | | $1,670 |
| Operating expenses: | | |
| Marketing | $590 | |
| General and administrative | 358 | |
| Research and development | 343 | 1,291 |
| Net income before taxes. | | $379 |
| Provision for income taxes | | 134 |
| Net income after taxes | | $245 |

The controller has also furnished you with a number of assumptions, policies, and other information as follows:

1. The company has made arrangements to acquire plant and equipment during the year for $339 million. Long-term debt will finance $18 million, and cash will be used for the remainder.
2. All sales are on credit. Collections on credit sales for the year are scheduled to be $3,218 million.
3. Changes in several account balances are planned.
   (a) Inventories will decrease by $15 million.
   (b) Other accrued liabilities will increase by $70 million.
   (c) Prepaid expenses will increase by $10 million.
4. Depreciation expense in the forecast income statement totals $105 million.
5. Payments of accounts payable will total $2,682 million and on accrued income taxes will be $179 million.

**6.** Common stock will be sold to employees in a special stock purchase plan for $34 million.

**7.** Dividends of $29 million will be declared and paid during the year.

**Required:**

**1.** Prepare a forecast yearend balance sheet.

**2.** Does the proposed financing of new plant and equipment strain the cash position? Explain.

**3.** Identify several danger areas in the forecast that might cause the asset acquisition to be difficult to finance. What other sources of cash might exist?

**7–44. Budgeted Savings—Materials and Labor.** Paul Horton is concerned about losses of materials in production, especially since the prices of materials may increase. Data with respect to materials for one product line are:

| | Quantity Per Unit In Final Product | Materials Price Per Pound |
|---|---|---|
| Materials A | 24 pounds | $0.12 |
| Materials B | 12 pounds | 0.08 |
| Materials C | 12 pounds | 0.08 |

The product weight yield is 75 percent of the input for all three materials.

The labor rate is $14.40 an hour, and 12 finished units are made each hour. Variable overhead is $2 per unit of product. Fixed overhead is budgeted at $2,700,000 for the next quarter. The company includes only variable costs as product costs.

Horton believes that the yield from materials should be increased to 80 percent of materials inputs. Also, with some changes in production methods, 15 finished units could be made each hour. During the next quarter, the company plans to produce and sell 1,800,000 finished units at a price of $14 per unit.

**Required (Use of spreadsheet software is recommended.):**

**1.** Prepare a budgeted income statement for the manufacturing operation under present conditions without savings in materials or labor time.

**2.** Comment on the following:

   **(a)** "What if" Horton achieves the planned savings in materials yield?

   **(b)** "What if" Horton implements the planned labor saving changes?

   **(c)** "What if" Horton achieves the planned savings in materials yield and the planned labor saving changes?

**7–45.    Ethical Use of Modeling.** Jeff McNish, a personal financial planning consultant, uses a "personal wealth builder" financial model to help evaluate his clients' current financial positions and desired retirement and estate goals. Most clients are relatively naive about financial matters. He represents a national life insurance company, a set of mutual fund companies, and other investment programs such as real estate and energy partnerships, precious metals, and annuities. He is properly licensed to provide counsel and to sell these products. He derives the majority of his income from insurance and mutual fund sales. He also does personal advising on a fee-only basis, a minor part of his business.

Jeff's model has numerous assumptions built in to allow quick evaluation of a person's wealth potential given that person's current investment program and income levels. Jeff knows about these assumptions, many of which he can change given the client situation and need. Much data must be provided by the client, mostly current and historical data and some forecast or desired future needs and goals. From the model comes a set of suggestions for financial planning. These suggestions identify (1) serious gaps in current financial protection, such as disability insurance and accidental death coverage; (2) changes in current investments to increase rates of return or safety; (3) actions needed to achieve near-term financial goals, such as paying for college tuition; (4) retirement planning to ensure adequate income and financial safety to enjoy the "golden years;" and (5) estate planning to ensure that the client's heirs receive their maximum entitlements.

### Required:

Jeff has found that the "personal wealth builder" financial model has great credibility with clients. They see it as a "black box" that provides financial answers to difficult questions. Identify possible ethical problems with using this model in Jeff's normal client contracts. Give suggestions to Jeff about how he can assure his clients of a fair evaluation.

**7–46.** **Financial Planning Model (Appendix).** For a number of years, Brugge Company of Brussels, Belgium, has had difficulty in budgeting its monthly income statement and cash flows. As an outside consultant, you have been hired by the controller to develop a rudimentary financial planning model that will lead to budgeted monthly income statement and cash receipts and cash disbursements schedules. Upon investigation, you find the following relationships:

**(a)** Sales revenue is growing at 0.5 percent per month.

**(b)** Sixty percent of each month's sales are for cash; the remaining 40 percent are credit sales.

**(c)** Credit sales are collected at 50 percent in the month of sale, 45 percent in the month after the sale, and 5 percent in the second month after the sale.

**(d)** Cost of goods sold averages 75 percent of sales.

**(e)** Purchases in units each month equal the forecast sales units for the next month.

**(f)** Seventy percent of purchases are paid in the month of purchase, with half of these qualifying for a 2 percent cash discount. The remaining 30 percent is paid in the following month.

**(g)** The monthly operating expenses are 1 percent of monthly sales revenue plus fixed costs in euros of €20,000, of which €2,000 is depreciation. These expenses are paid in the month incurred.

**(h)** Income taxes are ignored on a monthly basis.

### Required:

Prepare a series of equations, based on the foregoing relationships, that will allow the company to budget net income and cash flow. Define independent and dependent variables by symbols or abbreviations. Use subscripts to indicate time periods, such as $_t$ for the current month, $_{t-1}$ for the prior month, and $_{t+1}$ for the next month.

Service

**7–47.** **Financial Planning Relationships (Appendix).** Hool Contract Engineering would like to develop a financial planning model to aid in its monthly and annual financial planning. Bob Johannes, accountant, has identified the following relationships among the key planning variables for next year:

**1.** Revenues are constrained by the number of skilled computer-aided design (CAD) engineers employed by Hool. Each engineer works 2,000 hours per year and has a billing time ratio of 75 percent. All available billable time is utilized. Salaries, billing rates, and headcounts by skill levels are:

| | *Salary* | *Billing Rate* | *Number Employed* |
| --- | --- | --- | --- |
| Professional grade 1 | $90,000 | $120 per hour | 20 |
| Professional grade 2 | 60,000 | 90 per hour | 30 |
| General design engineer | 45,000 | 80 per hour | 15 |
| Administration | 70,000 | | 10 |

**2.** Customers are billed during the first week of the next month for engineering time. About 75 percent of the customers pays by the end of the billing month. The remainder pays during the following month.

3. Equipment and software lease costs are forecast to be $1,890,000 annually but are paid monthly.

4. Other annual administrative expenses include cash expenses of $500,000 plus $10,000 per employee and 10 percent of total salaries. Per employee costs are paid one month in advance (i.e., health insurance). The percentage of salaries expenses (i.e., payroll taxes) is paid in the month following the payroll expense.

5. Income taxes are 40 percent.

**Required:**

Using symbols similar to those shown in the example in the Appendix of this chapter, prepare a series of equations that can represent the following relationships:

1. Engineering revenue for the current month.
2. Costs of engineers for the current month.
3. Total payroll for the current month.
4. Cash inflow from customers for the current month (dollars).
5. Cash outflow for all nonpayroll administrative expenses for the current month.
6. Net income before taxes for the current month.
7. Income taxes for the current month.
8. Ending cash account balance for the current month.

Use subscripts of $_t$ for the current month, $_{t-1}$ for last month, $_{t+1}$ for next month, and $_{t+2}$ for two months after the current month.

Service

# CASE 7A—COSMO LEARNING SYSTEMS

Cosmo Learning Systems specializes in education and training. One responsibility center in the Professional Seminar Division is Government Contract Seminars. It is treated as a profit center for performance evaluation purposes.

Because the Department of Defense is downsizing, many companies are cutting back and sending people to fewer training seminars. Actual results and variances for the last fiscal year for Government Contract Seminars are as follows:

| | Actual | Fav/(Unfav) Budget |
|---|---|---|
| Seminar participants | 7,020 | 1,380 |
| Number of seminars given | 175 | 25 |
| Revenues | $1,404,000 | $(396,000) |
| Costs which vary with number of participants: | | |
| Food. | $ 70,200 | $10,800 |
| Workbooks and handouts | 274,890 | 85,110 |
| Costs which vary with number of seminars: | | |
| Instructors' fees. | $280,000 | 40,000 |
| Rental of sites | 21,600 | (2,630) |
| Equipment rental (overhead projectors, etc.) | 8,110 | (510) |
| Fixed costs of Government Contract Seminars: | | |
| Salaries of managers and assistants. | $124,000 | (4,000) |
| Office expenses. | 13,000 | (640) |
| Promotion of seminars. | 89,000 | 7,500 |
| Divisional overhead allocated to this profit center | $389,000 | 9,000 |
| Total expenses | $1,269,800 | $144,630 |
| Profits. | $134,200 | $(251,370) |

Seminars are for one, two, and three days. The budget expected the average class days per seminar to be 2.5 days; the actual average was 2 days. The manager's salary, included in salaries, is $60,000 and was budgeted at that level.

**Required:**

1. Since Government Contract Seminars is a profit center, the presumption is that the manager controls revenues. The factors influencing revenues are the number of seminar participants and the number and length of seminars. Does the manager really control these factors? Explain.

2. In general, are the variances in this report controllable by the manager of the profit center? Which costs and related variances are not controllable by the manager?

3. Suggest improvements in the report. Prepare a performance report which you believe better describes the manager's performance than the preceding report.

# CASE 7B—BRIDGES & BRIDGES

Service

Bridges & Bridges is a regional food distribution company. Ms. Bridges, CEO, has asked your assistance in preparing cash-flow information for the last three months of this year. Selected accounts from an interim balance sheet dated September 30, have the following balances:

| Cash | $142,100 | Accounts payable | $354,155 |
|------|----------|------------------|----------|
| Marketable securities | 200,000 | Other payables | 53,200 |
| Accounts receivable | 1,012,500 | | |
| Inventories | 150,388 | | |

Mr. Bridges, CFO, provides you with the following information based on experience and management policy. All sales are credit sales and are billed the last day of the month of sale. Customers paying within 10 days of the billing date may take a 2 percent cash discount. Forty percent of the sales is paid within the discount period in the month following billing. An additional 25 percent pays in the same month but does not receive the cash discount. Thirty percent is collected in the second month after billing; the remainder is uncollectible. Additional cash of $24,000 is expected in October from renting unused warehouse space.

Sixty percent of all purchases, selling and administrative expenses, and advertising expenses is paid in the month incurred. The remainder is paid in the following month. Ending inventory is set at 25 percent of the next month's budgeted cost of goods sold. The company's gross profit averages 30 percent of sales for the month. Selling and administrative expenses follow the formula of 5 percent of the current month's sales plus $75,000, which includes depreciation of $5,000. Advertising expenses are budgeted at 3 percent of sales.

Actual and budgeted sales information is as follows:

| **Actual:** | | **Budgeted:** | |
|-------------|---|---------------|---|
| August | $750,000 | October | $826,800 |
| September | 787,500 | November | 868,200 |
| | | December | 911,600 |
| | | January | 930,000 |

The company will acquire equipment costing $250,000 cash in November. Dividends of $45,000 will be paid in December.

The company would like to maintain a minimum cash balance at the end of each month of $120,000. Any excess amounts go first to repayment of short-term borrowings and then to investment in marketable securities. When cash is needed to reach the minimum balance, the company policy is to sell marketable securities before borrowing.

**Required (Use of spreadsheet software is recommended):**

1. Prepare a cash budget for each month of the fourth quarter and for the quarter in total. Prepare supporting schedules as needed. (Round all budget schedule amounts to the nearest dollar.)

2. You meet with the two Bridges to present your findings and happen to bring along your PC with the budget model software. They are worried about your findings in Part 1. They have obviously been arguing over certain assumptions you were given.

    (a) Mr. Bridges thinks that the gross margin may shrink to 27.5 percent because of higher purchase prices. He is concerned about what impact this will have on borrowings. Comment.

    (b) Ms. Bridges thinks that "stock outs" occur too frequently and wants to see the impact of increasing inventory levels to 30 and 40 percent of next quarter's sales on their total investment. Comment on these changes.

    (c) Mr. Bridges wants to discontinue the cash discount for prompt payment. He thinks that maybe collections of an additional 20 percent of sales will be delayed from the month of billing to the next month. Ms. Bridges says "That's ridiculous! We should increase the discount to 3 percent. Twenty percent more would be collected in the current month to get the higher discount." Comment on the cash-flow impacts.

# COST CONTROL THROUGH STANDARD COSTS

## LEARNING OBJECTIVES

1. Explain the significance of profit analysis for an organization.
2. Describe the major characteristics and conditions of a standard cost system.
3. Compute materials price and usage variances, and identify potential causes of such variances.
4. Compute labor rate and efficiency variances, and identify potential causes of such variances.
5. Describe the interrelationships that exist among materials and labor variances.
6. Explain the major considerations that are the basis of standard costs for overhead.
7. Distinguish between a budget variance and a capacity variance for overhead.
8. Explain why the capacity variance is related only to fixed overhead costs.
9. Explain how standard costs can be used in a process cost system.

---

### Where Do I Start With Standard Costs?

*Jean-Claude Recca, President of Rue de Pierre, a chain of fast food restaurants in central France, just returned from a reunion of his INSEAD graduating class. During the day of activities in the Riviera, he talked with several of his classmates who have become extremely successful in various businesses. One of those classmates suggested to Jean-Claude that adoption of a standard cost system eliminated most of her firm's unacceptable scrap and spoilage, caused an examination of non-value-added activities, and substantially reduced several inefficient operations.*

*Jean-Claude did not know whether his restaurant chain would really benefit from a standard cost system. If he did make the change, which costs should be put on standards? How does he set up standards? When do variances mean something? Isn't a standard cost system expensive to use? Isn't it a pain in the derriere? Wouldn't a tight budget do the same thing?*

*These questions were more than Jean-Claude could deal with. He decided to bounce the idea of standard costs off his controller.*

---

IN MEASURING SUCCESS in any undertaking, a comparison is usually made between actual performance and expected performance. Any difference is a variance. A manager is then left with the responsibility to explain the what, why, and how of the variance. In doing so, the manager must understand the influence of key variables on the actual results, focus on areas that deserve more detailed investigation, and determine changes that must be made in future planning and control. This chapter introduces the concept of profit analysis and then concentrates on variances associated with a standard cost system for direct materials, direct labor, and factory overhead. The next chapter extends these concepts to analyzing revenues and operating expenses.

## PROFIT ANALYSIS

Profit is an overall measure of how well an organization is doing. A profit variance then is the difference between the actual net income and the planned net income for the same period. The causes of such a variance are related to the various elements that make up net income: revenues, cost of goods sold, and operating expenses. The following table shows a disaggregation of the profit variance into more detailed elements.

|  | Actual | Budget | Variance |  |
| --- | --- | --- | --- | --- |
| Revenues | $385,000 | $365,000 | $20,000 | Favorable |
| Cost of goods sold | 282,500 | 227,250 | 55,250 | Unfavorable |
| Gross margin | $102,500 | $137,750 | $35,250 | Unfavorable |
| Operating expenses | 81,250 | 90,000 | 8,750 | Favorable |
| Net income | $ 21,250 | $ 47,750 | $26,500 | Unfavorable |

To have a variance, a baseline with which to compare actual results is necessary. Common baselines are results of a prior month or year, a budget, a flexible budget, or a standard. The analysis of a profit variance necessarily looks at each significant area in the income statement, and each area has a baseline that management feels is appropriate for the circumstances. The analysis then looks at causes of variation from the baseline.

The cost of goods sold, comprised of the cost of materials, labor, and factory overhead, is generally the most significant cost in the income statement. Consequently, companies expend great effort to manage and control these costs. Managers can easily cite examples of how small savings on a unit basis or on a single operation or task performed add many dollars to profit. Analysis of cost variances helps managers to find cost savings.

Besides cost control, cost variances are also used to evaluate the performance of managers who are responsible for particular costs. For example, a plant manager might examine materials, labor, and overhead cost variances in the grinding department to evaluate the performance of the grinding department manager.

Cost variances are often based on comparisons between actual and standard costs.

# THE USE OF STANDARDS

Standard costs are appropriate where an organization has standard products, services, or repetitive operations, and where management controls the factors comprising a standard cost.

## Definition of Standard Costs

A **standard cost** for a product consists of a **price standard** (a generic term indicating price for materials, rate for labor, and rate for factory overhead) and a **quantity standard** (a generic term indicating quantity for materials, time for labor, and activity or volume for factory overhead). Setting standards for price and quantity involves management judgments, industrial engineering studies, work measurement studies, vendor analyses, union bargaining, as well as a number of other techniques.

Standards are generally stated on a per unit basis: per unit of quantity, per unit of time, per unit of activity, or per unit of product. Once set, these standards remain unchanged as long as no changes occur in operating methods, in factors that influence quantities, or in unit prices of materials, labor, and factory overhead.

## Advantages of Standards

A standard cost system presents many advantages to an organization. Although the primary purpose has always been cost control, properly set standards have many other advantages. This section covers five major advantages of standard costs.

**Cost Control.** Cost control is comparing actual performance with the standard performance, analyzing variances to identify controllable causes, and taking action to correct or adjust future planning and control. As discussed later in this chapter and the next chapter, costs can change for at least four reasons: (1) changes in levels of prices or rates, (2) changes in efficiency, (3) changes in activity or volume, and (4) changes in the product mix. Variance analysis must identify these changes as well as the managers responsible for these differences so that adjustments can be made to the standards or that good performance can be rewarded.

Standard cost accounting follows the principle of **management by exception**. Actual results that correspond with the standards require little attention. The exceptions, however, are emphasized. Management by exception can be desirable because it highlights only those weak areas that require management's attention. However, a behavioral effect can occur when management by exception is applied to people. If a worker is ignored when operating according to the standard and is noticed only when something is wrong, the worker may become resentful and perform less satisfactorily. While it may be argued that the worker is being paid to operate at standard, the human factor cannot be ignored. Without recognition, the worker becomes discontented; and this discontentment may spread throughout the organization with a loss of both morale and productivity.

**Cost Management.** Cost management is related to cost control, but here the emphasis is on establishing the level of costs that becomes the benchmark for measuring performance. It can be as simple as decreasing the costs of operations through improved methods and procedures, using better selection of resources (human, materials, and facilities), or eliminating unnecessary (nonvalue-added) activities. As standards are set and periodically reviewed, operations can be analyzed to identify waste and inefficiency and to eliminate their sources. These reviews can also highlight better than expected performance; appreciation will motivate employees to continue looking for better ways to operate. A standard cost system creates an environment in which people become cost conscious, always looking for continuous improvements in the process.

**Decision Making.** If standards are set at currently attainable levels (a concept discussed later in the "Quality of Standards" section), the standard costs are useful in making many types of decisions. For example, some common decisions involve regular, special order, or transfer pricing; sell or process further; make or buy; and cash planning. When an analysis is used as the basis for setting the standard costs, managers need not perform a new analysis for each decision.

**Recordkeeping Costs.** A standard cost system saves recordkeeping costs, not during the initial start-up, but in the long-run operation of the system. When using actual costs, each item of materials issued from a storeroom has its cost that came from a specific purchase order. The cost transferred to work in process inventory is calculated using an inventory flow method: specific identification, FIFO, LIFO, moving average, or weighted average. For companies with thousands of different materials categories in stock, identifying costs to move to work in process inventory can be an enormous task. When standard costs are in place, each item in the same materials classification has the same standard cost. Therefore, costs transferred to work in process inventory are the standard cost per unit times the number of units issued. This same process applies to work in process inventory transfers to finished goods. All inventories have their standard costs, and balances are always stated at standard.

**Inventory Valuation.** A standard cost system records the same costs for physically identical units of materials and products; an actual cost system can record different costs for physically identical units. Differences between the two costs tend to be waste, inefficiency, and nonvalue-added activities. Such items, if incurred at all, are period costs and excluded from inventory amounts. They should not be capitalized and deferred in inventory values. Therefore, standards provide a more rational cost in valuing inventories.

Occasionally, differences between actual and standard costs show positive efficiencies. Performance has been better than expected. If this situation will continue, the standards are revised. Otherwise, the current standards still provide a rational basis for costing products.

## The Quality of Standards

The term "standard" has no meaning unless we know on what the standard is based. A standard may be very strict at one extreme or very loose at the other extreme. We broadly classify standards as strict or tight standards, attainable standards, and loose or lax standards.

No easy solution exists as to how standards should be set. The objective, of course, is to obtain the best possible results at the lowest possible cost. Often human behavior becomes the dominant concern in setting standards. A very rigorous standard may motivate some employees to produce exceptional results. On the other hand, a standard that is too strict and cannot be reached may discourage employees and produce only modest results. In setting a level of standards, management must consider the employees, their abilities, their aspirations, and their degree of control over the results of operations.

**Strict standards** are set at a maximum level of efficiency, representing conditions that can seldom, if ever, be attained. They ignore normal materials spoilage and idle labor time due to such factors as machine breakdowns. These standards appear to represent perfection, something few employees will achieve. Although a standard should challenge people, a standard that is virtually unattainable will not motivate most employees to do their best. An employee is more likely to put forth increased effort when feeling successful. In other words, a person's aspirations increase with success and decrease with failure.

In addition, variances from strict standards have little significance for control purposes. There will never be a favorable variance, only zero or unfavorable variances. In fact, most variances will be large and unfavorable. The question is: "What does such a variance measure?"

**Loose standards** tend to be based on past performance and represent an average of prior costs. They include all inefficiency and waste in past operations. Such standards are not likely to motivate employees to high performance. The very nature of loose standards means less than efficient performance. As a result, variances from loose standards are almost always favorable and provide little useful information for cost control. Again, the question is: "What does such a variance measure?"

**Attainable standards** can be achieved with reasonable effort. Perhaps the standards should be somewhat lower than what can be achieved by earnest effort. With success, the employees gain confidence and tend to be more productive. For a more experienced group of workers, an exacting standard may serve as a challenge that motivates an employee to higher levels of performance. With less experienced workers, standards may have to be set at a lower level at first. As learning takes place, the standards may be raised. Increases in standards should be made with caution and should be accepted by the employees as being fair.

Managers should expect to see favorable and unfavorable variances with an attainable standard. Some employees will meet and exceed the standard with reasonable effort, while others will not meet the standard because of poor performance.

## Revising the Standards

Standard costs should be reviewed periodically to see if revisions are necessary to maintain a selected level of quality. Although many factors may combine that determine the best time to review standard costs, they should be reviewed at least once a year. Otherwise, they may not be current. This does not mean waiting until the end of the year. Companies with thousands of items on standards will have a department dedicated to reviewing standards throughout the year.

A key for reviewing standards is to identify changes taking place that outdate existing standards. Changes that typically call for a revision to one or more standard costs include:

1. Increases or decreases in the price levels of specific materials and supplies.
2. Changes in personnel payment plans or wage schedules.
3. Modifications of materials type or specifications.
4. Acquisitions of new equipment or dispositions of old equipment.
5. Modifications of operations or procedures.
6. Additions or deletions of product lines.
7. Expansions or contractions of facilities.
8. Changes in management policies that affect the amount of costs and the way costs are accumulated and identified with activities, operations, and products.
9. Increased experience of employees.

Management policies can have a significant impact on standard costs. Examples of the most common policy areas are the definition of capacity, the classification of fringe benefits, depreciation methods, and capitalization and expense policies. Capacity definitions influence the level of waste and inefficiency that management will tolerate and the amount of fixed costs applied to individual units of an operation, task, or product. A redefinition of capacity can be due to changes in the number of shifts, in hours of operation with given shift schedules, or in demand for the product or service. Fringe benefits can appear in several ways, any of which can influence a product cost significantly. Management can classify any element of fringe benefit cost as a direct cost of the product, an indirect cost through a labor-related cost pool, an indirect cost through a factory overhead cost pool, or a period cost through a general and administrative cost pool. Management determines which depreciation methods are in use. One common policy is to change from a declining balance method for existing equipment to a straight-line method at about the mid-life point of the asset life. Occasionally, management will change the method applied to new equipment purchased. The criteria for capitalization and expense decisions determine which costs are capitalized as assets and charged to operations through depreciation and amortization and which costs are charged immediately upon incurrence. Any change in the criteria alters the treatment of those costs affected.

Throughout the chapter, we assume that standards are entered into the formal accounting system. As such, product costing is determined through a standard cost system. Many companies do not follow this practice. Instead, they use standards as a part of statistical supplements in arriving at information for control purposes. Revision of standards is much more critical if the standards are the basis for product costing.

## STANDARD COST SHEET

Once standards have been set for each cost component, the costs are summarized in a **standard cost sheet**. Here the cost of each category of direct materials used, the cost of each direct labor operation employed, and the cost of all overhead tasks, operations, processes, and support functions applied to a unit of final product are itemized. Standard cost sheets can be extremely lengthy or very simple depending on the product and manufacturing process.

Suppose that Zaner Restaurants, Inc., owner of over 200 Steakout Restaurant franchises, uses a standard cost system in accounting for its daily dinner special, the "Goliath Feast." The standards currently are as follows:

| Component | Total Cost of Component | Unit Cost |
|---|---|---|
| Materials | 3 lbs. at $4.00 per pound | $12.00 |
| Direct labor | .5 hour at $7.00 per hour | 3.50 |
| Variable overhead | .5 hour at $6.00 per hour | 3.00 |
| Fixed overhead | .5 hour at $9.00 per hour | 4.50 |
| Total cost per meal | | $23.00 |

This standard cost sheet gives the total unit cost of each meal produced. For each completed meal, three pounds of direct materials at a total cost of $12 is taken from materials inventory and charged to work in process. Also, $3.50 is charged for direct labor; and a total of $7.50 in overhead costs is applied. Nothing is noted here about the actual costs incurred because all production is carried only at standard cost. Thus, when completed meals are transferred from work in process to finished goods and later to cost of goods sold, the cost is $23 per meal. The standard cost sheet becomes the basis for all accounting entries related to the cost of the meal.

To explain standards for materials, direct labor, and overhead, we need to know the volume of output and the materials quantities allowed for that volume in order to calculate certain variances. The standard cost sheet lists the allowed amounts. The volume of output will be expressed as units of product or equivalent units, depending on the circumstances in production.

## STANDARDS FOR MATERIALS

Standards are established for the cost of obtaining materials and for the quantities to be used in production. Managers then compare actual costs against these standards to ascertain variances. Basically, two types of variances exist: price and usage. Different variances may be developed for specialized purposes, but they can always be classified as variations in the price of materials or in the quantities used, or as a combination of price and usage. If the actual cost is greater than the standard cost, the variance is an **unfavorable variance**; if actual cost is less than the standard cost, the variance is a **favorable variance**.

### Materials Price Variance

A **materials price variance** measures the difference between the prices at which materials are acquired and the prices established in the standards. What is in the standard, how a variance is calculated, and what are potential causes of variances are now explained.

**Setting the Price Standard.** A standard price is set for each item of materials the company expects to use. The cost elements that make up the standard are a matter of management policy. Although the purchase price is the dominant element, other costs may also be included, such as the cost of insurance for materials in transit, the cost of transporting materials, various cash and trade discounts, and costs of receiving and inspecting materials at the receiving dock. Once management decides on the elements, the next step is assessing prices. The estimation techniques are not discussed here, but common approaches to determining amounts include:

1. Statistical forecasting.
2. Knowledge and experience in the particular type of business.
3. Weighted average of prices in most recent purchases.
4. Prices agreed upon in long-term contracts or purchase commitments.

**Accounting for a Price Variance.** A materials price variance is isolated at the time of purchase. The actual quantity of materials purchased is entered in the materials inventory at standard prices. The liability to the supplier is recorded at actual quantities and actual prices. Any difference between the two amounts is recorded as a price variance.

To illustrate, assume that Zaner Restaurants bought 40,000 pounds of materials for $159,200, which is $3.98 per pound. To make the example easier to follow, we will use the following symbols:

$$AQP = \text{Actual quantity purchased}$$
$$AP = \text{Actual price}$$
$$SP = \text{Standard price}$$
$$MPV = \text{Materials price variance}$$

The cost flow of actual and standard costs would appear in T-account form as follows:

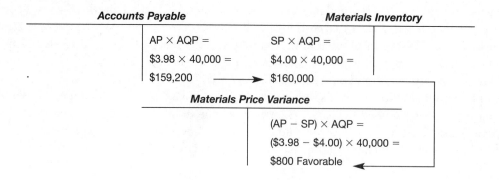

To calculate the variance without thinking in terms of accounts, the information from the T-accounts can be summarized into convenient formulas.

$$AP \times AQP = \$3.98 \times 40,000 = \$159,200$$
$$SP \times AQP = \$4.00 \times 40,000 = \$160,000$$
$$MPV = (AP - SP) \times AQP = -\$0.02 \times 40,000 = \$800 \text{ Favorable}$$

Note that the actual quantity is used in all calculations. Only the prices differ. A materials price variance can be either favorable or unfavorable when actual costs are compared with standard costs. In this illustration, the materials price variance is favorable because the materials were purchased at a cost below the standard.

**Causes of the Price Variance.** A variance occurs for any number of reasons. If the variance is significant, we must identify causes. If performance is deemed good, the responsible people should be praised and, where appropriate, rewarded. If the investigation finds out-of-control situations, corrections can be made so variations are eliminated in the future. In some cases, outdated standards are being used and need to be adjusted.

Although many causes for variances pertain to any given situation, a list of the common sources is as follows:

1. Random fluctuations in market prices.
2. Materials substitutions.
3. Market shortages or excesses.
4. Purchases from vendors other than those offering the terms used in the standard.
5. Purchases of higher or lower quality materials.
6. Purchases in nonstandard or uneconomical quantities.
7. Changes in the mode of transportation.
8. Changes in the production schedule that result in rush orders or additional materials.
9. Unexpected price increases or decreases.
10. Fortunate buys.
11. Failure to take cash discounts.

**Responsibility for the Price Variance.** The purchasing department is usually charged with the responsibility for price variances. If the purchasing function is carried out properly, the standard price should be attainable. When lower prices are paid, a favorable materials price variance is recorded, indicating that the department's purchases were below the standard cost. Higher prices are reflected in an unfavorable materials price variance. In some circumstances price variances really should be charged to a production department instead of to the purchasing department. As examples, a rush order is caused by last minute production changes; or production people request a specific brand name for materials rather than allowing the purchasing department to buy by specifications.

Periodic reports show how actual prices compare with standard prices for the various types of materials purchased. Reports on price variances may be made as frequently as daily but will generally be weekly and monthly. They reveal which materials, if any, are responsible for a large part of any total price variation and can help the purchasing department in its search for more economical vendors.

## Materials Usage Variance

Materials are put into production, but the actual quantity used may be more or less than specified by the standards. The variation in the quantity of materials is called a **materials usage variance**. Other names for the variance are materials quantity variance, materials use variance, and materials efficiency variance.

**Setting the Quantity Factor.** The quantity factor in a materials standard is based on engineering specifications, blueprints and designs, bills of materials, and routings. Combined, these items specify the quality, size, thickness, weight, and any other factors necessary for a good unit of final product. Also included in the quantity factor are any desired allowances for normal acceptable waste, scrap, shrinkage, and spoilage that may occur during the manufacturing process.

**Accounting for a Usage Variance.** As materials are used, the work in process account is increased by the standard quantity used multiplied by the standard price. The materials inventory account is decreased by the actual quantity used multiplied by the standard price. Returning to Zaner Restaurants, assume that 31,000 pounds of materials are withdrawn from Materials Inventory for making 10,000 meals. Because the standard cost sheet indicates only three pounds should be used for each meal, the standard quantity of materials that should have been used is 30,000 pounds (3 pounds × 10,000 meals).

For our example, we will use the following symbols:

$$SP = \text{Standard price}$$
$$AQU = \text{Actual quantity used}$$
$$SQ = \text{Standard quantity allowed}$$
$$MUV = \text{Materials usage variance}$$

The cost flow of actual and standard costs would appear in T-account form as follows:

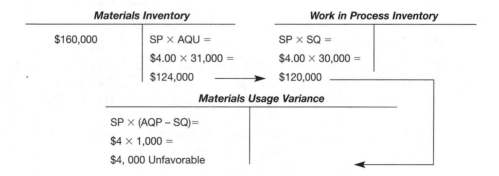

To calculate the variance without thinking in terms of accounts, the above information can be summarized into convenient formulas.

$$SP \times AQU = \$4.00 \times 31,000 = \$124,000$$
$$SP \times SQ = \$4.00 \times 30,000 = \$120,000$$
$$MUV = SP \times (AQU - SQ) = \$4.00 \times 1,000 = \$4,000 \text{ Unfavorable}$$

In the first two equations, the standard unit price is used; but the quantities differ. In one case, the actual quantities issued from the storeroom are used. In the other, the standard materials quantity allowed for each meal is used. Because only quantities can differ in the equations, any variation is a usage variance. The variance for Zaner Restaurants is unfavorable because the amount of materials used is greater than the amount called for by the standard.

**Causes of the Usage Variance.** What causes a materials usage variance? To answer this question, we look at the elements that make up the quantity standard and the specific situation. Examples of common causes include:

1. Changes in product specifications.
2. Materials substitutions.
3. Breakage during the handling of materials in movement and processing.
4. Improper use of materials by workers.
5. Machine settings operating at nonstandard levels.
6. Waste.
7. Pilferage.

**Responsibility for the Usage Variance.** Ordinarily, materials usage variances are chargeable to production departments. They often arise as a result of wasteful practices in working with materials, or they arise because of products that must be scrapped through faulty production.

Reports on the quantities of materials used are given to the responsible production department supervisor. A production supervisor, for example, may receive daily or weekly summaries showing how the quantities used in the department compare with the standards. At the operating level, managers can directly control the use of materials. Often, reports on variations from standard are for physical quantities only. Managers may not need immediate feedback from a cost report. Daily or weekly cost reports simply tell managers the financial magnitude of variations and serve as a reminder that corrections should be made before losses become too great.

Summary reports of actual and standard materials consumption given in dollars, with variances and variance percentages, also go to the plant superintendent at least monthly. If the variances in any department are too large, the superintendent can take steps to reduce them. During the month, of course, the operating managers will watch materials usage; and, if they have been doing their jobs properly, the accumulated variances for the month should be relatively small.

## Interrelationships of Price and Usage Variances

We have treated the materials price and usage variances as though they are independent and unrelated. In many cases, the event that causes one variance also causes the other. For example, assume the purchasing department buys lower grade materials at a substantially reduced price. This generates a favorable price variance for purchasing. When those materials reach production, they result in a higher than normal waste. This gives the operating supervisors unfavorable usage variances. Keeping the two variances in isolation makes the purchasing agent look good, while the operating supervisors turn in poor performances. In reality, both variances are the responsibility of the purchasing department. If the variances net out favorable, the purchasing decision has benefited the company. On the other hand, a net unfavorable variance is a loss to the company.

The operating people can also influence the price variance. If improperly adjusted machines, for instance, generate a higher than usual waste, more materials may be needed from the storeroom. When a production supervisor requisitions the materials and the storeroom manager realizes sufficient quantities are not available, a request is made to the purchasing department to order more. To keep the production schedule current, a rush order is issued. The higher prices paid for a rush order will result in an unfavorable price variance.

The warning of these situations is simple: Investigation of variances must not be done in isolation.

## STANDARDS FOR LABOR

We can set standards for direct labor and measure variances from the standards in much the same way as we did for materials. The price factor is called rate; the quantity factor is time. When referring to variations in time, we use the term efficiency. The **labor rate variance** measures the portion of the total labor cost variance caused by the difference between the actual wage rate paid and the standard wage rate. The **labor efficiency variance** measures the portion of the total labor cost variance caused by the difference between the actual hours worked and the standard hours required for production.

When discussing standards for labor, we assume direct labor only. Indirect labor consists of the costs for people working in the production departments but not directly on products, and for the time of direct laborers classified as training time, break time, overtime premium, and idle time. These costs are often distributed from payroll to overhead and become part of overhead standards. Therefore, indirect labor is discussed later as part of overhead.

### Setting Rate Standards

Standard cost systems rely on individual labor rates by skill-level classification for better control and accuracy. However, in some cases, standard rates can be set for entire cost centers or departments. Regardless of how it is structured, the underlying wage or salary rate used as the standard rate will be either established through contract negotiations or by the prevailing rates in the location where the work is performed. The details for selecting wage-level classifications cover training, education, experience, special physical abilities, and set of task skills.

When setting the standard rates, management must decide whether to use a basic labor rate or a "loaded" labor rate as the standard. A "loaded" labor rate includes labor-related costs such as overtime premiums, shift premiums, bonuses and incentives, payroll taxes, and fringe benefits. Those factors not included in the labor rate standard will be included in overhead. Therefore, management will look at the advantages of treating these cost factors as direct costs or as indirect costs. For example, if the company is performing contracted work for the federal government, the company would typically recover more of its costs through the "loaded" standard labor rate.

### Setting Time Standards

Time standards are more difficult to establish than materials quantity standards. People's productivity is the basis for setting time standards; and people tend to differ in behavior from one time to the next. Setting time standards involves answering two questions: (1) What operations are performed? and (2) How much time should be spent on each operation for the product or service? The answer to the first question is determined by reviewing operations and procedures, process charts, and routing lists. The answer to the second question will be determined from one or more of the following ways:

1. Operation and body movement analysis. (This involves dividing each operation into the elementary body movements such as reaching, pushing, turning over, etc. Published tables of standard times are available for each movement. These standard times are applied to the individual movements and added together for the total standard time per operation.)

2. Time and motion studies conducted by industrial engineers.

3. Averages of past performance, adjusted for anticipated changes.

4. Test runs through the production process for which standards are to be set.

## Accounting for the Rate and Efficiency Variances

Unlike materials, labor cannot be purchased and stored until needed. We purchase and use labor at the same time. Therefore, accounting for both variances is combined.

Zaner Restaurants shows a payroll for its direct workers of $38,584 and 5,200 hours. That gives an actual rate of $7.42 per hour. The standard cost sheet shows that each completed meal requires one-half hour of direct labor time. Since 10,000 meals were produced, 5,000 hours should have been worked (.5 hour × 10,000 meals).

For our example, we will use the following symbols:

$$AR = \text{Actual rate}$$
$$SR = \text{Standard rate}$$
$$AH = \text{Actual hours}$$
$$SH = \text{Standard hours allowed}$$
$$LRV = \text{Labor rate variance}$$
$$LEV = \text{Labor efficiency variance}$$

The cost flow of actual and standard costs would appear in T-account form as follows:

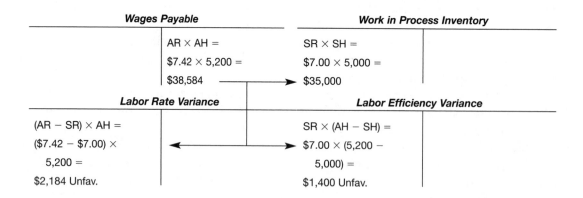

The labor rate variance is commonly calculated first. It results whenever the actual rate paid to a worker differs from the standard rate. Calculating a labor rate variance requires holding the actual hours constant while comparing the difference in rates, as follows:

$$AR \times AH = \$7.42 \times 5,200 = \$38,584$$
$$SR \times AH = \$7.00 \times 5,200 = \$36,400$$
$$LRV = (AR - SR) \times AH = \$0.42 \times 5,200 = \$2,184 \text{ Unfavorable}$$

The variance is unfavorable because the actual rate exceeds the standard rate.

The labor efficiency variance (also called quantity, time, or usage variance) results when employees' total actual hours worked differ from the standard. We calculate the variance by holding the rate constant while comparing the difference in hours. The following summarizes this procedure:

$$SR \times AH = \$7.00 \times 5,200 = \$36,400$$

$$SR \times SH = \$7.00 \times 5,000 = \$35,000$$

$$LEV = SR \times (AH - SH) = \$7.00 \times 200 = \$1,400 \text{ Unfavorable}$$

The variance is unfavorable because the actual hours worked are more than the standard hours allowed for the 10,000 meals produced.

Because the hours are purchased and used at the same time, an alternate approach to calculating the variances can be used:

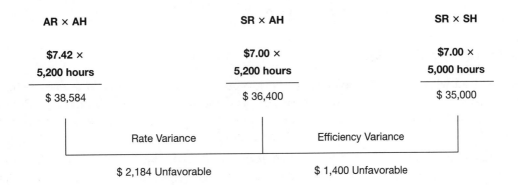

| AR × AH | SR × AH | SR × SH |
|---|---|---|
| $7.42 × 5,200 hours | $7.00 × 5,200 hours | $7.00 × 5,000 hours |
| $ 38,584 | $ 36,400 | $ 35,000 |

Rate Variance — $ 2,184 Unfavorable

Efficiency Variance — $ 1,400 Unfavorable

## Causes of Labor Variances

Labor rates are usually set by contract, negotiations, management, or federal laws or regulations. So, why would a labor rate variance occur? Two basic reasons exist. First, labor rates often represent an average for a task, operation, or work center. If a departmental manager shifts workers' assignments because of sudden changes in personnel requirements or a shortage of personnel, the average rate can easily change depending on how the shift relates to higher paid or lower paid workers. A second reason is that standard labor rates may include cost elements beyond the basic labor rate. Any changes in overtime worked, shift differentials, payroll taxes, or fringe benefits will show up in a labor variance if these elements are part of the standard rate.

Labor efficiency relates to how many units are completed per actual hour for each task, operation, or process. Many reasons exist for why productivity varies from the level assumed in the standard time. Some of the common causes of a labor efficiency variance include:

1. Use of lower skilled or higher skilled workers.
2. Effects of a learning curve.
3. Use of lower quality or higher quality materials.
4. Changes in production methods.
5. Changes in production scheduling.
6. Installation of new equipment.

**7.** Poorly maintained equipment or machine malfunction.

**8.** Delays in routing work, materials, tools, or instructions.

**9.** Insufficient training, incorrect instructions, or worker dissatisfaction.

## Responsibility for Labor Variances

Labor rate and efficiency variances are charged to the department managers who have control over the use of workers. Labor rate variances are often the responsibility of personnel managers who manage hiring, union contracts, and perhaps labor scheduling. Although a labor rate variance is important to understand and control, managers tend to concentrate more on the labor efficiency variance because it has a greater impact on capacity utilization and the department's ability to meet production schedules. Labor efficiency is compared by department and by job with established standards. Daily or weekly reports to department managers and the plant superintendent help to locate and solve difficulties on a particular job or in a department. Differences between standard costs and actual costs incurred by a job or department may show that a job cannot be handled at the standard labor cost or that a department is not managed properly.

## Interrelationships of Variances

As discussed with materials, variances should not be analyzed in isolation from one another. The event that causes one variance can easily be the cause for one or more other variances. Future cost planning and control can be improved when interrelationships among labor variances and between materials and labor variances are identified and understood.

**Labor Rate and Efficiency Variances.** People perform the productive effort; thus, the rate of pay and the time required are related. Because so many relationships can exist between the two factors, only a few examples are cited to aid in identifying what to look for in a specific operation.

Assume a number of employees are in various military reserve units that have been called to active duty. As a short-term solution, a manager has two options: (1) employ temporary workers or (2) shift other workers internally and add overtime. Using temporary workers may be cheaper or more expensive depending on the situation. They are not as experienced with the equipment, procedures, and processes. They may take more time than the standard allows. Therefore, hiring temporary workers can result in both rate and efficiency variances. The second option is to shift existing workers and use overtime. The move will put differently skilled workers on new jobs. The move can create either a favorable or an unfavorable rate variance depending on the mix of workers. Their experience levels may be higher or lower than the specific job requires and can result in an efficiency variance. Adding overtime could affect a rate variance, depending on how the company treats the overtime premium. Efficiency should not be an issue of overtime unless the workers become less productive through fatigue.

In another case, suppose an employee is having difficulties working on a particular machine. The worker is taking more time than standard to complete good units. The manager, trying to keep production on schedule and not lose capacity to inefficiency, shifts a more skilled, higher paid worker to the job. The higher paid worker will yield an unfavorable rate variance but can reduce the unfavorable efficiency variance or create a favorable one.

**Materials and Labor Variances.** Materials and labor variances can also be related to the same source. Assume, for instance, that a purchasing agent made a fortunate buy on a lower quality grade of materials. The "good buy" yields a favorable materials price variance for purchasing. However, when the materials are used in production, they crumble and create more waste than anticipated. More materials are needed, and an unfavorable materials usage variance arises. A department manager, desiring to minimize the lost time, moves higher skilled people to the operation where the higher waste occurs. This action leads to a labor rate variance and may influence the magnitude or the direction of a labor efficiency variance.

In another case, a worker starts the shift fatigued and stressed. Lack of concentration results in higher waste which takes more materials and time. This results in unfavorable materials usage and labor efficiency variances. Because more materials are need, the manager requisitions additional materials from the storeroom. The storekeeper finds fewer materials available than are now required. Purchasing is asked to place a rush order so that production can proceed with minimum delay. The rush order increases the purchasing costs, causing an unfavorable materials price variance.

## The Influence of Automation

We are seeing a trend where many companies are automating various aspects or even all aspects of their production. The purpose of this movement is to increase productivity and quality while keeping unit costs low. With automatic equipment, the need for high-skill levels of direct labor is substantially reduced. Direct labor in such an environment becomes such an insignificant element of cost that variances have little meaning.

In some industries, automation may not go beyond a certain point; in which case, direct labor will remain a smaller but significant cost element. However, with a great deal of automation, direct labor time becomes more dependent on the speed of a machine operation than on the speed of individual workers. Hence, labor efficiency is more related to machine efficiency than to employee efficiency. Therefore, a labor efficiency variance will carry little meaningful information.

# STANDARDS FOR OVERHEAD

The factory overhead costs consist of all manufacturing costs that are not classified as direct materials and direct labor. Examples of factory overhead costs include indirect materials and supplies, indirect labor, maintenance and repairs, lubrication, power, factory property taxes and insurance, and depreciation. Service organizations will have similar overhead costs related to providing services.

In a standard cost system, we use a standard overhead rate to apply these costs to products and services. We accumulate the actual overhead costs and compare them to the applied amounts to determine whether the standards were met. Variances from the standard help to direct management's attention to situations where costs should be controlled more closely, where managers should be praised and rewarded for good performance, or where the standards should be revised.

## Development of Overhead Rates

Standard costs for overhead have price and quantity factors, just like direct materials and direct labor. Price is reflected in one or more overhead rates; quantity is the measure of activity. Price and quantity in this case are closely linked. In developing standard overhead rates, five major considerations must be evaluated.

First, which cost elements are included in overhead? We need to identify the individual costs which compose overhead. When certain variances occur, these items will be examined for specific changes.

The second consideration is the measure of activity for relating overhead costs to products. A **measure of activity** for this purpose represents the factor that best expresses how costs change as volume increases or decreases. As noted in earlier chapters, we refer to the measure of activity as an allocation base or cost driver. Although many factors can influence costs, we select a dominant cost driver. The common ones are direct labor hours or costs, machine hours, and units of products. In Chapter 6, we examined activity-based costing and identified other cost drivers that cause costs to be incurred. Our use of the measure of activity is the same as a primary-stage cost driver in those discussions. For standard costs, the appropriate measure must be selected if variances are to provide any meaningful information.

Third, and closely related to the measure of activity, is the concept of capacity and the anticipated volume level for the current period. We discussed several capacity concepts in Chapter 4. The capacity or volume concept selected and the determination of the current period level significantly influence overhead rates because of the presence of fixed costs.

A fourth consideration is cost behavior. The behavior of each cost within overhead is important because management plans and controls variable costs differently than it plans and controls fixed costs. Consequently, distinguishing variable from fixed overhead costs aids in analyzing variances for cause and responsibility. Standard cost systems often use dual overhead rates for variable overhead costs and for fixed overhead costs. In separating the variable and fixed cost rates, different cost drivers may be used for each cost behavior.

The fifth consideration is the level at which overhead rates should be set: by task, by machine or labor operation, by activity center, by department, by facility, or overall. For a single product operation, overall rates for variable and fixed costs are sufficient. The greater the product and operation diversity, the more likely it is that rates are set for smaller groupings of costs. For our illustration with Zaner Restaurants, we assume an overall rate merely to illustrate the concepts. The same considerations will apply should a company compute rates by task, activity center, and so forth.

## Flexible Overhead Budgets

As we have noted in previous chapters, a **flexible overhead budget** is based on a formula that expresses the budgeted overhead at any point within the relevant range. The formula recognizes that some costs are variable and some are fixed. The following schedule shows the flexible overhead budget formula for Zaner Restaurants. We assume here that the measure of activity is direct labor hours.

| Cost Item | Fixed Cost | Variable Cost Per Direct Labor Hour |
|---|---|---|
| Indirect materials | — | $1.90 |
| Hourly indirect labor | — | 1.27 |
| Supervision | $21,000 | — |
| Repair and maintenance | 3,600 | 1.11 |
| Utilities and occupancy | 10,580 | 1.00 |
| Depreciation | 13,800 | — |
| Miscellaneous costs | 520 | 0.72 |
| Totals | $49,500 | $6.00 |

The flexible budget cost function is: $49,500 + ($6.00 × number of hours). Since we know that the hours are related to meals prepared in terms of two per hour, we can restate the formula as: $49,500 + ($3.00 × meals prepared). Typically, we would have multiple products using different amounts of direct labor which would require the use of the basic formula.

As a sidelight, the overhead rates are also available from these numbers, if we assume a volume of 5,500 direct labor hours or 11,000 meals prepared. For variable costs, the rate is $6.00 per hour or $3.00 per unit (.5 hour × $6.00). The fixed costs are $9.00 per hour ($49,500 ÷ 5,500 hours) or $4.50 per unit (.5 hour × $9.00).

The significance of the flexible overhead budget becomes apparent in the next section where we identify variances for overhead costs.

## Framework for Two-Way Overhead Variance Analysis

Because different factors give rise to underapplied or overapplied overhead, we need a framework to identify the areas of potential causes of variations. In our framework, we compare actual overhead costs with a flexible budget and with the applied overhead to arrive at two possible variances: budget variance and capacity variance.

To begin, we need to know the actual overhead costs and the applied overhead costs. We have already seen for Zaner Restaurants that the company produced 10,000 meals during the month. Actual overhead costs for the month are $31,500 variable and $50,000 fixed. The overhead accounts would then show the following information:

| | | |
|---|---|---|
| Actual costs: | | |
| Variable | $31,500 | |
| Fixed | 50,000 | $81,500 |
| Applied costs: | | |
| Variable ($3.00 × 10,000 meals) | $30,000 | |
| Fixed ($4.50 × 10,000 meals) | 45,000 | 75,000 |
| Underapplied | | $ 6,500 |

Remember, the cost per unit for variable and fixed overhead is calculated in advance and appears on the standard cost sheet for individual products. Therefore, the rates used in the example are applied directly to actual units or equivalent units of product.

The next step is to compare the actual costs and applied costs with the flexible budget for 10,000 meals produced. Figure 8.1 summarizes this information. Note that the two-way overhead variance analysis actually produces three variances: variable and fixed overhead budget variances plus the fixed overhead capacity variance.

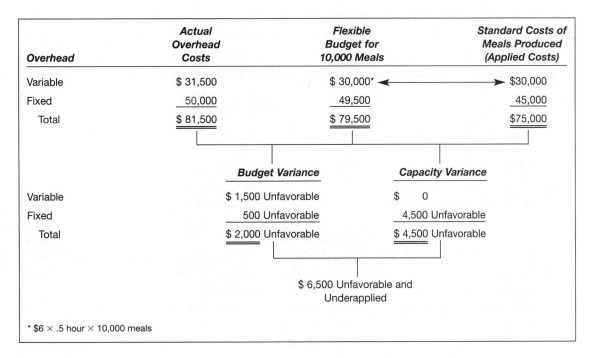

**FIGURE 8.1**

Overhead Variances for Zaner Restaurants

**Budget Variance.** A **budget variance** is the difference between actual overhead costs and the flexible budget for actual units produced. It is also called a **controllable variance**. This variance is deemed controllable by the appropriate operating departments. In the foregoing example, the variance is unfavorable; more dollars were spent than were budgeted for 10,000 meals. A more detailed examination of the variance is necessary to identify areas where managers need to take action. One approach for providing greater detail is to show the budget variance by individual cost item with the use of the flexible overhead cost function, as shown in the following table:

| Cost Item | Actual Overhead | Flexible Budget for 10,000 units | Budget Variance | |
|---|---|---|---|---|
| Indirect materials | $ 10,250 | $ 9,500 | $ 750 | U |
| Hourly indirect labor | 6,250 | 6,350 | 100 | F |
| Supervision | 21,400 | 21,000 | 400 | U |
| Repair and maintenance | 9,050 | 9,150 | 100 | F |
| Utilities and occupancy | 15,930 | 15,580 | 350 | U |
| Depreciation | 13,800 | 13,800 | 0 | |
| Miscellaneous costs | 4,820 | 4,120 | 700 | U |
| Totals | $ 81,500 | $ 79,500 | $ 2,000 | U |

A number of causes may exist for either a favorable or an unfavorable budget variance. The common causes will fall into one of four categories:

1. Price changes in individual cost components comprising overhead costs.
2. Quantity changes in individual items within overhead cost components, probably in the variable overhead area.
3. Estimation errors in segregating variable and fixed costs.
4. Any overhead costs that are incurred or saved because of inefficient or efficient use of the underlying activity measure (machine hours or labor hours, for example).

The estimation errors come in two varieties: (1) the inaccuracies in predicting what will occur in the future and (2) the reliability of approximations made in separating overhead costs into variable and fixed categories. The inefficient or efficient use of activity relates to the fact that in an activity (labor worked, for example) overhead costs are incurred to support that activity. If the activity is inefficient, overhead costs support inefficiency. On the other hand, if less activity occurs, lower total overhead costs are incurred to support it. Therefore, efficient resource use also saves overhead costs.

**Capacity Variance.** The **capacity variance** (also called a volume variance) is the difference between the flexible budget for the actual units produced and the amounts applied to work in process inventory. In Figure 8.1, because the variable overhead costs are the same in each column, the capacity variance is the difference between the budgeted fixed overhead and the applied fixed overhead. Therefore, the capacity variance is the amount of budgeted fixed overhead not applied (unfavorable) or the amount applied in excess of the budgeted fixed costs (favorable). A capacity variance, then, occurs when actual production differs from the capacity level used to calculate the standard fixed overhead rate.

Continuing with the example, we know that fixed overhead for the month was budgeted at $49,500; and we presume that 5,500 direct labor hours or 11,000 meals constitute a normal level of operation. We first compute the hourly overhead rate:

$$\frac{\$49,500 \text{ (Budgeted fixed overhead)}}{5,500 \text{ (Hours of direct labor)}} = \$9.00 \text{ per hour}$$

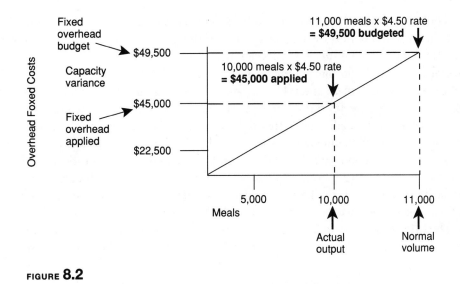

**FIGURE 8.2**

Analysis of Capacity Variance

We then convert the hourly rate to a rate per meal with the following computation:

$$0.5 \text{ hour per unit} \times \$9.00 = \$4.50 \text{ per meal}$$

We see that the standard overhead rate for costing meals is computed at the normal volume, so in this case it is $4.50 per meal. During the month, Zaner Restaurants produced 10,000 meals. Fixed overhead is costed to the meals by multiplying the standard rate of $4.50 per meal by the 10,000 meals.

$$\$4.50 \times 10,000 \text{ meals} = \$45,000 \text{ applied}$$

| | |
|---|---|
| Fixed overhead budget | $49,500 |
| Fixed overhead applied | 45,000 |
| Capacity variance (unfavorable) | $ 4,500 |

Figure 8.2 illustrates a graphical approach to the capacity variance concept. The diagonal line on the graph represents the amount of fixed overhead applied for various meal volumes. It rises at the rate of $4.50 per meal and reaches the $49,500 budgeted fixed overhead level at the normal volume of 11,000 meals. However, the company only produced 10,000 meals. With the rate of $4.50 per meal, only $45,000 of the budgeted fixed overhead was applied. The difference between the budgeted fixed overhead and the fixed overhead applied is the capacity variance, as designated on the vertical scale.

Earlier we presented the budget variance for individual categories of overhead costs. We could extend the idea to the capacity variance, but we do not gain additional information from further detail. The capacity variance is an overall issue and has little to do with individual costs.

## CAPACITY AND CONTROL

In general, we consider the capacity variance as an item that production departments do not control. The plant produces what marketing identifies as the sales requirements. Therefore, the production departments cannot be held responsible if the sales demand exceeds or falls below production at a normal level of plant operation. Other factors, however, may contribute to producing below capacity. Some of these factors are controllable (or somewhat controllable) by production departments. Excessive machine downtime (due to poor maintenance, for example) or inefficient production scheduling could be problems traceable to production managers. Lack of rapidity in completing tasks due to unskilled workers is a factor that is expected to some degree, but an excess of this condition may also be traceable to one or more production managers.

For Zaner Restaurants, normal volume was defined at 5,500 direct labor hours or 11,000 meals. Normal volume, as defined in Chapter 4, represents the average level of actual operation over several years. Practical capacity, on the other hand, is the level at which all facilities are used to full extent. Some allowance is made under this definition for expected delays because of changes in machine setups, necessary maintenance time, and other interruptions. Hence, practical capacity is less than theoretical maximum capacity which could be obtained only under ideal conditions.

A comparison of the actual output with the output for practical capacity broadly measures the failure of the facility to operate at the level for which it was designed. Assume, for example, that Zaner Restaurants can reasonably be expected to produce 15,000 meals a month. Yet only 10,000 meals were produced. The **idle capacity** is defined as the difference between the practical capacity and the actual production for a given month. The idle capacity for Zaner Restaurants is determined as follows:

| | |
|---|---|
| Practical capacity | 15,000 meals |
| Actual production | 10,000 |
| Total idle capacity | 5,000 meals |

The idle capacity can be analyzed further to determine why facility capacity was not used as intended. Assume that the sales budget shows that 12,000 meals were expected to be sold during the month but that orders for only 11,500 meals were received. The differences between practical capacity, sales budget, orders received, and actual production are illustrated as follows:

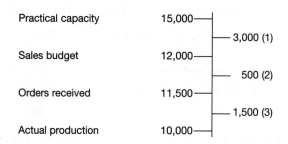

1. **Practical capacity minus sales budget.** The difference between the practical capacity and the sales budget for the month requires further investigation. Perhaps the company was overly optimistic and provided too much capacity. Or the Marketing Department may not be obtaining potential available customers. Additional analysis may reveal the nature of the problem and provide a foundation for improvements.

2. **Sales budget minus orders received.** The difference between the sales budget for the month and the orders received is a measurement of the inability of the Marketing Department to meet the budget quota. Perhaps the quota was too high, or the Marketing Department was not sufficiently aggressive.

3. **Orders received minus actual production.** The difference between the orders received and actual production reflects a mixture of idle time and inefficiency. Suppose that Zaner Restaurants used 5,200 hours to produce 10,000 meals and 5,000 hours were allowed. The 200 hours of inefficiency, in this case, consumed time that could have been used for production of an additional 400 meals (200 hours ÷ .5 hour per unit). The difference between the orders received and the expected production for the time used (11,500 − 10,400 = 1,100 meals) is a measurement of idle time.

## Contemporary Practice 8.2
### Survey on Variance Reporting

*A survey of 51 U.S. service organizations revealed the following distribution of cost variance reporting frequencies:*

| | |
|---|---|
| Monthly | 77 |
| Quarterly | 4 |
| Not done | 7 |
| | 100% |

| Frequency | Percentage |
|---|---|
| Daily | 2% |
| Weekly | 10 |

*Source: Martinson, O. B., Cost Accounting in the Service Industry, Institute of Management Accountants, Montvale, NJ: 1994, p. 40.*

# VARIANCE INVESTIGATION

When cost variances occur, managers need to know what caused them. Knowing the amount of variance does not disclose the cause(s); rather, investigation is required. However, managers must decide whether the benefits of investigation and corrective action exceed the related costs. Obviously, a $10 unfavorable materials usage variance from a standard cost of $50,000 would not be worth investigating. But where should the line be drawn?

Ideally, if the costs and benefits of investigating and correcting can be estimated, these costs and benefits should be compared in deciding whether to investigate. In practice, however, this is extremely difficult. Instead, many companies use simple decision rules based on prescribed dollar limits, such as "investigate any variance over $500." The main problem with this method is that $500 may be significant when the standard cost is $2,000 but may be insignificant when the standard cost is $20,000. Therefore, many companies use a percentage rule, such as "investigate any variance of 10 percent or more." Some companies use more sophisticated statistical approaches that set limits based on standard deviations from the standard cost. As Contemporary Practice 8.3 illustrates, however, most companies do not seem to have formal decision rules; rather, managers are instructed to use "judgment."

## Contemporary Practice 8.3
### Survey on Variance Investigation

*A survey of controllers from 115 U.S. manufacturing firms reported the following distribution of policies used regarding the investigation of direct labor cost variances:*

| | |
|---|---|
| Investigate variances over prescribed percentage limits | 14.1 |
| Statistical procedures | 0.9 |
| Variances never investigated | 0.9 |
| Judgment (no formal rule) | 47.8 |
| | 100.0% |

| Policy | Percentage |
|---|---|
| Investigate all variances | 5.3% |
| Investigate variances over prescribed dollar limits | 31.0 |

*Source: Gaumnitz, B.R., and F.P. Kollaritsch, "Manufacturing Variances: Current Practices and Trends," Journal of Cost Management, Volume 5, No. 1, Spring 1991, pp. 58–64.*

## SUMMARY OF STANDARD COST VARIANCES

We have completed a number of variance computations for the cost elements of production. Figure 8.3 contains a summary of all variances and the methods of calculating them. It also emphasizes that the costs charged to units produced are the standard costs. Therefore, work in process inventory and all

**ACTUAL COSTS INCURRED**
(Resource Inputs)

**STANDARD COSTS OF UNITS PRODUCED**
(Costs Charged to Production)

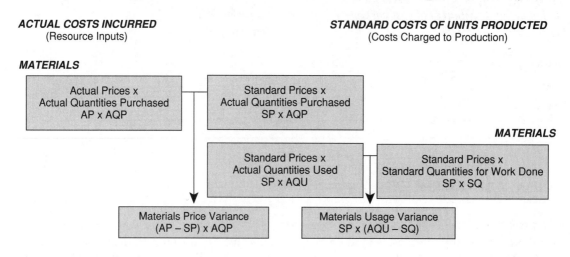

**MATERIALS**

| Actual Prices x Actual Quantities Purchased AP x AQP | Standard Prices x Actual Quantities Purchased SP x AQP |

**MATERIALS**

| Standard Prices x Actual Quantities Used SP x AQU | Standard Prices x Standard Quantities for Work Done SP x SQ |

| Materials Price Variance (AP – SP) x AQP | Materials Usage Variance SP x (AQU – SQ) |

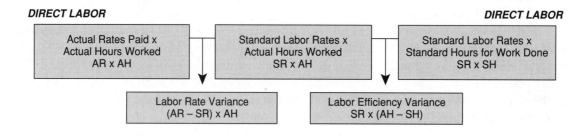

**DIRECT LABOR**                                                    **DIRECT LABOR**

| Actual Rates Paid x Actual Hours Worked AR x AH | Standard Labor Rates x Actual Hours Worked SR x AH | Standard Labor Rates x Standard Hours for Work Done SR x SH |

| Labor Rate Variance (AR – SR) x AH | Labor Efficiency Variance SR x (AH – SH) |

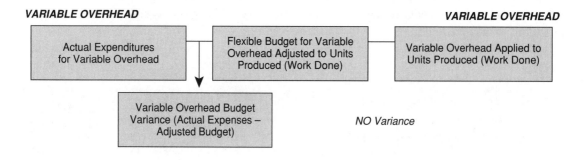

**VARIABLE OVERHEAD**                                          **VARIABLE OVERHEAD**

| Actual Expenditures for Variable Overhead | Flexible Budget for Variable Overhead Adjusted to Units Produced (Work Done) | Variable Overhead Applied to Units Produced (Work Done) |

| Variable Overhead Budget Variance (Actual Expenses – Adjusted Budget) |    *NO Variance* |

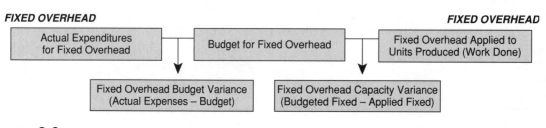

**FIXED OVERHEAD**                                               **FIXED OVERHEAD**

| Actual Expenditures for Fixed Overhead | Budget for Fixed Overhead | Fixed Overhead Applied to Units Produced (Work Done) |

| Fixed Overhead Budget Variance (Actual Expenses – Budget) | Fixed Overhead Capacity Variance (Budgeted Fixed – Applied Fixed) |

**FIGURE 8.3**

Summary of Standard Cost Variances

subsequent accounts containing product costs will be stated at standard. Notice that costs on the far left side are all actual costs, while costs on the far right side are standard costs. If dollar amounts become smaller as we move from left to right, we experience unfavorable variances. If amounts become larger, we experience favorable variances.

## DISPOSITION OF VARIANCES

In our discussion of materials and labor variances, we set up separate variance accounts. Overhead variances, although identified separately in worksheet analysis, are combined in the underapplied or overapplied amounts. At the end of each period, variance accounts must be closed. Where do these variances go? As a practical matter, all standard cost variances eventually go to cost of goods sold. The most common practice is to close the variance accounts directly to cost of goods sold, thus, treating them as period costs. Occasionally, if the variances are significant in amount, they will be prorated to cost of goods sold and to the appropriate materials, work in process, and finished goods inventories. We assume here that variances are closed to the cost of goods sold account.

## THE LEARNING CURVE

In many industries, labor is a substantial part of the cost of production. Management applies quantitative methods in attempting to calculate how much labor time should be used in carrying out certain functions. Time and motion studies, that take into account human limitations, can help to determine how much labor time is required for an operation.

Management can obtain additional profit from increased productivity. With more units produced in a given time period, a greater gross margin occurs even after sharing the benefits of increased productivity with the employees. Management is constantly trying to upgrade the skills of employees and to increase their efficiency through education and motivation.

We call the rate of learning a new task a **learning curve**. The curve shows that the average time to produce a unit will decrease as workers gain experience with a task. The initial or start-up phase is called the **learning phase**. Assume, for example, that the first batch of 100 units to be produced takes 500 labor hours. After this experience, the workers can produce the next 100-unit batch in less time. Perhaps the second 100-unit batch can be produced in 300 hours. An additional batch of 200 units may be produced with an additional 480 hours. When an optimum point is reached, no further increases in productivity can be expected; and productivity is said to be at the **static phase**. Many, however, would argue that further improvement is always possible.

The foregoing example illustrates an 80 percent learning curve. This rate of learning means that when production doubles, the cumulative average time per unit decreases to 80 percent of the previous cumulative average time. The following table shows this relationship.

| Units Per Batch | Cumulative Number of Units | Hours Per Batch | Cumulative Hours | Cumulative Average Hours Per Unit* |
|---|---|---|---|---|
| 100 | 100 | 500 | 500 | 5.0 |
| 100 | 200 | 300 | 800 | 4.0* |
| 200 | 400 | 480 | 1,280 | 3.2* |

* Cumulative average is 80 percent of previous cumulative average.

The learning rate may be such that when the production is doubled, the cumulative average time per unit is 70 percent, 60 percent, or any other percentage of the previous cumulative average

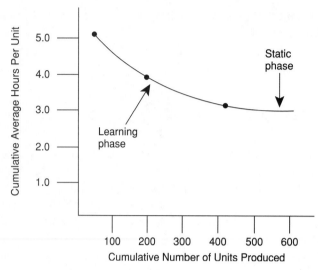

**FIGURE 8.4**

An 80 Percent Learning Curve

time per unit. At some point, the learning stage is completed; and further increases in productivity may not be expected. Experience with the learning rates for certain types of functions may be used in predicting expected results. Figure 8.4 shows the data for the 80 percent learning curve plotted on a graph.

## STANDARD COSTS IN SERVICE ORGANIZATIONS

Standard costs are applicable to service organizations, as we have shown with Zaner Restaurants. As with manufacturing companies, the more routine the service organization's activities, the easier it is to set standards. Generally, though, a service organization's activities are less routine than those of a manufacturing company. The following list contains examples of service organization activities for which standard costing would be appropriate:

1. Filling prescriptions in a pharmacy.
2. Picking orders in a warehouse.
3. Preparing food in a restaurant.
4. Answering telephones in travel agencies, airline offices, customer service departments, and computer technical hotlines.
5. Processing orders in a mail-order house.
6. Calling on customers (by phone or door-to-door).
7. Processing computer center transactions from a modem.

Standard costing in a service setting will tend to emphasize labor and overhead, since materials are usually not a significant item. Notable exceptions, however, would be restaurants and auto repair shops, where food ingredients and car parts, respectively, are sizable cost elements. Calculating standard costs and variances for service organizations is similar to manufacturing companies. The main difference is that in determining standard quantities, the output of a service organization is often not

*For hospitals, cost variance analysis requires explicit assumptions about expected membership levels, inpatient and outpatient use rates (i.e., admissions and visits per member), patient mix, and costs per case or per outpatient visit. "Budgeting membership levels and use rates is a new activity for many financial managers.*

*In addition, collecting and analyzing meaningful outpatient data continue to be major challenges for hospitals."*

Source: Miller, T.R., and J.B. Ryan, "Analyzing Cost Variance in Capitated Contracts," Healthcare Financial Management, February 1995.

as clear as for a manufacturing company. The following list contains examples of output measures that might be chosen in various service settings:

1. Number of claims processed in an insurance company.
2. Number of loan applications processed at a bank.
3. Number of deliveries made by a delivery service.
4. Number of patients treated in a particular department of a hospital.
5. Number of passengers transported by an airline.

## STANDARD COSTS IN A PROCESS COST SYSTEM

Standard costs are appropriate for job cost systems or process cost systems. Where we have a process cost system, the equivalent units are calculated using the FIFO method discussed in Chapter 5. Remember that equivalent units can be different for materials, labor, and overhead.

One convenience realized in a standard cost system is the availability of unit costs without the computations we did in Chapter 5. Since standard costs are predetermined, we simply multiply the equivalent units by the appropriate standard costs to determine costs of goods completed and costs of the ending inventory. Except for the use of equivalent units, variance analysis in a process cost system does not differ from the analysis used in a job cost system.

*Mitsubishi Kasei Corporation, a large chemical company in Japan, decided not to use a standard cost system because of large unavoidable variances that it would have generated for two main reasons. "First, the changes in price of raw materials (such as oil) and fluctuations in exchange rates would have caused the raw material price variances to be large. Second, the yield would decrease for a couple of months after each production process' annual over-*

*haul until the process was brought back under control. This reduction in yield could not be estimated with any accuracy. Therefore, for the two months after the overhaul, the material usage variances would be large because the performance forecasts were too inaccurate to be useful."*

Source: Harvard Business School, "Mitsubishi Kasei Corporation: Product Line Cost System," Case No. 195–066, 1994.

## Standard Costs in JIT/CIM Environments

In JIT and computer-integrated manufacturing (CIM) environments, standard cost systems face greater challenges. These environments are often characterized by rapid technological changes in production processes and products produced, which make it very difficult to set standards. Furthermore, the prevalence of short production runs and the need for real-time information require variance reporting on a much more timely basis than the typical monthly or even weekly basis.

Companies with JIT/CIM environments are increasingly turning to a philosophy of continuous improvement. With this approach, the focus is more on trends of variances rather than their magnitudes.

Generally, fewer types of cost variances are computed in JIT/CIM environments. Since JIT/CIM companies tend to be highly automated, direct labor variances are of little or no relevance. Also, materials price variances have little relevance because JIT companies usually have long-term contracts with a small number of suppliers.

In many companies with JIT/CIM processes, cost variances are being supplemented or, in some cases, replaced by nonfinancial measures of performance. We discuss these types of measures in Chapter 14.

## Target Costing and Kaizen Cost Targets

Recognizing that most costs of production are determined when products are developed and designed, many companies are turning to a technique developed by Japanese companies known as **target costing**. After a target selling price and a target profit are established, an allowable cost consistent with these targets is obtained for the product. The company then designs the product and sets cost standards based on the allowable (target) cost. To promote continuous improvement, these cost targets, known as **kaizen cost targets**, are reduced in each successive period. Target costing and kaizen cost targets are discussed more fully in Chapter 14.

## Ethical Considerations

Because cost variances are used to evaluate performance of cost center managers, there may be temptation to compromise ethics. This might happen in the standard setting process or in reporting actual costs. A manager who has input in setting standards might deliberately provide inaccurate information in an attempt to produce loose standards. Likewise, a manager who plays a role in gathering or reporting actual costs might intentionally distort actual data. Top management should be aware that performance evaluation based on cost variances can produce these behaviors. Cost center managers must guard against compromising their integrity for a possible short-term gain.

A more subtle form of unethical behavior results when managers avoid doing their best for fear of causing the standards to be tightened. A manager might believe that cost decreases in the current period are unlikely to be replicated due to some unique conditions. In that case, the manager should prepare a convincing argument to upper management not to revise standards significantly. Upper management can alleviate these types of problems by not automatically adjusting the cost standard by the full amount of cost reduction. For instance, if the production manager knows that any cost reduction will cause next period's cost standards to decrease by only 50 percent of the cost reduction, the manager would tend to put more effort into cutting costs than if the standards were to be adjusted by the full cost reduction.

# SUMMARY

When actual performance varies from expectations, explanations for the differences are sought. Once causes of variations are identified, changes can be made through the planning process or control mechanisms. One aid to the analysis is the use of a standard cost system for costs that ultimately flow into cost of goods sold. Standard cost systems operate effectively in situations where standardized products or standardized operations exist. Although the primary advantage of such a system is cost control, several other advantages can also be achieved: cost management, improved decision making, savings in recordkeeping costs, and more rational inventory valuation.

A standard cost consists of a price factor and a quantity factor. The quality of a standard is expressed as strict, attainable, or loose. The preferred standard for all purposes is one that is current and attainable. A standard cost sheet is a basic element of the standard cost system. Here the standard quantities and prices are stated for direct materials, direct labor, and all overhead. The standard cost sheet gives the total unit cost that is attached to a completed unit of a given product.

Materials standards are set after considering the purchase price and other dollar amounts to be included and after determining the quantities needed for the intended operations. A materials price variance occurs anytime the actual price differs from the standard price. The variance is calculated as the actual quantity purchased times the difference between the actual price and the standard price. A materials usage variance is caused by using more or less materials than set by the standard. This variance is calculated as the standard price times the difference between the actual quantity used and the standard quantity allowed. Price variances are generally the responsibility of the purchasing department while usage variances are generally the responsibility of production department managers.

In establishing labor standards, management looks at what operations are performed, how much time should be spent in each operation, what labor skills are needed to perform the operations, and what rate should be paid. The standard labor rate is the base rate of pay plus any other costs associated with labor that management chooses to include. A labor rate variance occurs any time the actual rate differs from the standard rate. The variance is the actual hours worked times the difference between the actual rate and the standard rate. A labor efficiency variance is caused by using more or less time than the standard specifies. This variance is calculated as standard rate times the difference between actual hours worked and the standard hours allowed. Both variances generally are the responsibility of production department managers.

Standards for overhead are set after considering five important factors: the cost elements to include in the standards, the measure of activity that best relates the costs to the work done, the capacity concept for the selected measure of activity, the cost behavior of each element of overhead cost, and the rate structure, whether by task, operation, process, department, or overall. During any period, the actual overhead cost can differ from the overhead applied to products. To understand the significance of the underapplied or overapplied amounts, we calculate a budget variance and a capacity variance. A budget variance is the difference between actual overhead costs incurred and the flexible budget for the actual number of units produced. It represents those overhead cost elements over which department managers have control. The capacity variance is the difference between the flexible budget for the actual units produced and the amounts applied to products. This variance consists only of fixed overhead costs and represents the amount by which actual production differs from planned capacity.

## PROBLEM FOR REVIEW

Shoen Lawn Service chemically treats residential lawns with spraying machines. The standard cost per lawn is as follows:

| | | |
|---|---|---|
| Direct materials: | 5 gallons of chemicals × $2 standard price | $10 |
| Direct labor: | 0.5 hour × $6 standard labor rate | 3 |
| Overhead: | 0.25 machine hours × $8 standard overhead rate | 2 |
| Standard cost per lawn | | $15 |

The total overhead at normal operating volume has been budgeted at $40,000; and 5,000 machine hours or 20,000 lawns have been budgeted as normal volume. The overhead rate per machine hour is $8.

Summary transactions and cost data pertaining to the year are as follows:

1. Materials purchases were 100,000 gallons at a cost of $2.04 per gallon.
2. Direct materials used were 93,000 gallons.
3. The payroll totaled $59,500, of which indirect labor was $10,000.
4. Actual direct labor hours and rates were 7,500 hours at $6 and 500 hours at $9.
5. The overhead other than indirect labor was:

| | |
|---|---|
| Indirect materials | $7,500 |
| Reduction of prepaid insurance | 2,000 |
| Accrued expenses | 9,000 |
| Depreciation | 8,000 |

Variable overhead costs totaled $8,500. Fixed costs were $28,000. These amounts include indirect labor and the previously listed costs.

6. Actual machine hours totaled 4,500 hours.
7. The number lawns serviced during the year totaled 18,000.
8. A portion of the flexible overhead budget in summary form is as follows:

| | Percentage of Normal Operating Volume | | |
|---|---|---|---|
| | 80% | 90% | 100% |
| Standard output (number of lawns) | 16,000 | 18,000 | 20,000 |
| Budgeted machine hours | 4,000 | 4,500 | 5,000 |
| Variable overhead | $8,000 | $9,000 | $10,000 |
| Fixed overhead | 30,000 | 30,000 | 30,000 |
| Total overhead | $38,000 | $39,000 | $40,000 |

**Required:**
Compute the following standard cost variances:
1. Materials price variance and materials usage variance.
2. Labor rate variance and labor efficiency variance.
3. Overhead variances: budget variance and capacity variance. Show what portions of the variances are variable and fixed.

**Solution:**

**1.** Materials price variance and materials usage variance:

   **(a)** Materials price variance:

$$AP \times AQP = \$2.04 \times 100{,}000 = \$204{,}000$$
$$SP \times AQP = \$2.00 \times 100{,}000 = \$200{,}000$$
$$MPV = (AP - SP) \times AQP = \$0.04 \times 100{,}000 = \$4{,}000 \text{ Unfavorable}$$

   **(b)** Materials usage variance:

$$SP \times AQU = \$2.00 \times 93{,}000 = \$186{,}000$$
$$SP \times SQ = \$2.00 \times 90{,}000 = \$180{,}000$$
$$MUV = SP \times (AQU - SQ) = \$2.00 \times 3{,}000 = \$6{,}000 \text{ Unfavorable}$$

**2.** Labor rate variance and labor efficiency variance:

   **(a)** Labor rate variance:

$$AR \times AH = \$49{,}500^{*}$$
$$SR \times AH = \$6.00 \times 8{,}000 = \$48{,}000$$
$$LRV = (AR - SR) \times AH = \$ 1{,}500 \text{ Unfavorable}$$

   * 7,500 hours at $6.00 + 500 hours at $9.00

(The actual labor rate is not necessary to calculate the labor rate variance. However, the actual rate is required if the formula $LRV = (AR - SR) \times AH$ is used. The actual rate is found by dividing actual cost of $49,500 by 8,000 actual hours. The rate is $6.1875.)

   **(b)** Labor efficiency variance:

$$SR \times AH = \$6.00 \times 8{,}000 = \$48{,}000$$
$$SR \times SH = \$6.00 \times 9{,}000 = \$54{,}000$$
$$LEV = SR \times (AH - SH) = \$6.00 \times (1{,}000) = \$6{,}000 \text{ Favorable}$$

**3.** Overhead variances:

   **(a)** Underapplied or overapplied overhead:

| | | |
|---|---:|---:|
| Actual overhead costs: | | |
| Indirect labor | $10,000 | |
| Indirect materials | 7,500 | |
| Reduction of prepaid insurance | 2,000 | |
| Accrued expenses | 9,000 | |
| Depreciation | 8,000 | $36,500 |
| *Applied costs:* | | |
| $2.00 × 18,000 units | | 36,000 |
| Underapplied | | $ 500 |

   **(b)** Budget variance:

| | | |
|---|---:|---:|
| Actual overhead costs | | $36,500 |
| Budgeted overhead costs at 18,000 units: | | |
| Variable | $9,000 | |
| Fixed | 30,000 | 39,000 |
| Budget variance—favorable | | $ 2,500 |

**(c)** Capacity variance:

| | | |
|---|---|---|
| Budgeted overhead costs at 18,000 units: | | |
| Variable | $9,000 | |
| Fixed | 30,000 | $39,000 |
| Applied overhead | | 36,000 |
| Capacity variance—unfavorable | | $ 3,000 |

**(d)** Summary of overhead variances:

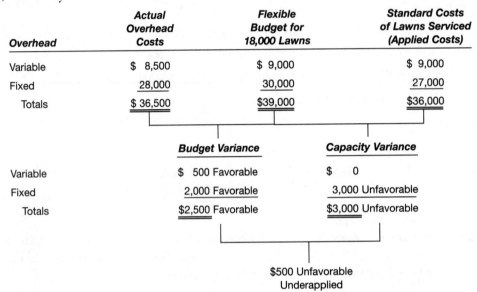

| Overhead | Actual Overhead Costs | Flexible Budget for 18,000 Lawns | Standard Costs of Lawns Serviced (Applied Costs) |
|---|---|---|---|
| Variable | $ 8,500 | $ 9,000 | $ 9,000 |
| Fixed | 28,000 | 30,000 | 27,000 |
| Totals | $ 36,500 | $39,000 | $36,000 |

| | Budget Variance | Capacity Variance |
|---|---|---|
| Variable | $ 500 Favorable | $ 0 |
| Fixed | 2,000 Favorable | 3,000 Unfavorable |
| Totals | $2,500 Favorable | $3,000 Unfavorable |

$500 Unfavorable
Underapplied

# APPENDIX

## THREE-VARIANCE METHOD FOR OVERHEAD

In many business situations, management needs more information about overhead costs to investigate variances and make appropriate adjustments. For example, measuring efficiency through comparing input activity bases with output activity bases provides a particularly helpful expansion to the variance analysis in certain situations where overhead cost behavior parallels resource input activity more closely than production output volumes. Consequently, we move from the two-variance approach discussed in the chapter to a three-variance method. The information is available also to expand to four variances.

## FRAMEWORK FOR THREE-WAY OVERHEAD VARIANCE ANALYSIS

The difference between the two-way and the three-way variance analysis is the treatment of the budget or controllable variance. The budget variance is divided into a spending variance and an efficiency variance. The capacity variance is the same in both approaches.

To show how the variances fit together, remember that overhead costs for Zaner Restaurants are related to direct labor hours. The actual direct labor hours worked were 5,200. Since Zaner Restaurants produced 10,000 meals, it was allowed 5,000 (.5 hour × 10,000 meals) direct labor hours. Based on the variable and fixed costs we have shown in the chapter and the underapplied overhead of $6,500, we adapt Figure 8.1 to obtain Figure 8.5.

### Spending Variance

A **spending variance** is the difference between the actual overhead cost and the flexible overhead budget for the actual activity base (hours of operation in our example). The variance assumes that the best measure of the amount spent on overhead is based on the actual activity base. Therefore, the actual overhead for the preceding data is the cost of 5,200 direct labor hours; and this amount is compared with the budget for those hours.

A spending variance is similar to the combination of the price (or rate) variances and the usage (or efficiency) variances in direct materials and direct labor. It shows that either the prices paid for overhead goods or services and/or the quantity used were not in agreement with the budget. A separate price or usage variance could be calculated.

The causes of spending variances include three of those categories presented for the budget variance:

1. Price changes in the individual cost components comprising overhead costs.
2. Quantity changes in individual items within overhead cost components.
3. Estimation errors in segregating variable and fixed costs.

### Efficiency Variance

The **efficiency variance** is the difference between the flexible budget for the actual activity base and the flexible budget for the standard activity base allowed for actual units of product produced. Because fixed overhead costs are identical in both budgets, the efficiency variance consists only of differences

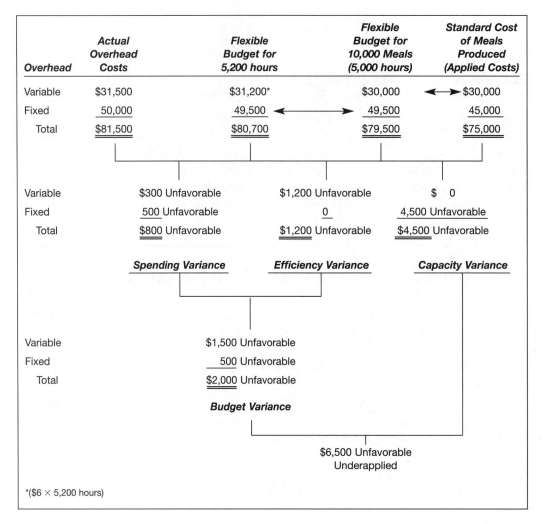

| Overhead | Actual Overhead Costs | Flexible Budget for 5,200 hours | Flexible Budget for 10,000 Meals (5,000 hours) | Standard Cost of Meals Produced (Applied Costs) |
|---|---|---|---|---|
| Variable | $31,500 | $31,200* | $30,000 | $30,000 |
| Fixed | 50,000 | 49,500 | 49,500 | 45,000 |
| Total | $81,500 | $80,700 | $79,500 | $75,000 |

| | Variable | | Efficiency | | Capacity |
|---|---|---|---|---|---|
| Variable | $300 Unfavorable | | $1,200 Unfavorable | | $ 0 |
| Fixed | 500 Unfavorable | | 0 | | 4,500 Unfavorable |
| Total | $800 Unfavorable | | $1,200 Unfavorable | | $4,500 Unfavorable |

**Spending Variance**          **Efficiency Variance**          **Capacity Variance**

| Variable | $1,500 Unfavorable |
|---|---|
| Fixed | 500 Unfavorable |
| Total | $2,000 Unfavorable |

**Budget Variance**

$6,500 Unfavorable
Underapplied

*($6 × 5,200 hours)

**FIGURE 8.5**

Three-Way and Four-Way Overhead Variance Analyses

in variable overhead costs. Therefore, we have an alternate means of calculating the variance. The formula is similar to that used for materials usage and labor efficiency variances: standard variable overhead rate per hour times the difference between the actual activity base and the standard activity base allowed. For Zaner Restaurants, the efficiency variance is unfavorable because the workers used more than the standard hours allowed to complete the 10,000 meals.

The term "efficiency" is in some sense a misnomer because it does not measure the efficient or inefficient use of individual overhead items. These are included in the spending variance. The efficiency variance measures the additional overhead costs incurred or saved as a result of inefficient or efficient use of the overhead activity base. That is, overhead must be incurred to support the cost driver. If the cost driver is inefficient, overhead costs are incurred to support inefficiency.

When direct labor hours are the measure of activity, a relationship exists between the labor efficiency variance and the overhead efficiency variance—they move in the same direction. If labor hours are inefficiently used, the labor efficiency variance measures the labor costs incurred for that inefficiency; and the overhead efficiency variance is the additional overhead cost incurred to support the inefficient labor. A favorable labor efficiency variance indicates the overhead efficiency variance must be favorable also. Consequently, to find the causes of an overhead efficiency variance for a direct labor activity base, look for the causes of inefficient or efficient labor.

## Four-Way Analysis

Some managers prefer an additional level of detail. We already know that an efficiency variance involves variable cost only and a capacity variance involves fixed cost only. Since the spending variance can be split into variable and fixed components, we have four variances: variable overhead spending, variable overhead efficiency, fixed overhead spending, and fixed overhead capacity. These variances are also shown in Figure 8.5.

## TERMINOLOGY REVIEW

| | |
|---|---|
| Attainable standards (325) | Loose standards (325) |
| Budget variance (338) | Management by exception (323) |
| Capacity variance (338) | Materials price variance (327) |
| Controllable variance (338) | Materials usage variance (327) |
| Cost control (323) | Measure of activity (335) |
| Efficiency variance (351) | Price standard (323) |
| Favorable variance (327) | Quantity standard (323) |
| Flexible overhead budget (336) | Spending variance (351) |
| Idle capacity (340) | Standard cost (323) |
| Kaizen cost targets (346) | Standard cost sheet (326) |
| Labor efficiency variance (331) | Static phase (343) |
| Labor rate variance (331) | Strict standards (324) |
| Learning curve (343) | Target costing (346) |
| Learning phase (343) | Unfavorable variance (327) |

## QUESTIONS FOR REVIEW AND DISCUSSION

1. Explain the significance of profit analysis for an organization.

2. Under what conditions will a standard cost system work best?

3. Define a standard cost. Explain what constitutes the components of a standard cost.

4. What are the five major categories of advantages for a standard cost system? Why are they important?

5. Point out advantages and disadvantages of following the principle of management by exception.

6. What are some of the aspects of human behavior that must be considered in setting standards? Relate these to the quality of standards.

7. Which level of standard (tight, attainable, or loose) will give the lowest standard cost per unit? Explain.

8. Standards should be reviewed from time to time and examined for possible revision. What events would call for a review of standards?

9. A standard cost sheet is a key component of a standard cost system. Describe a standard cost sheet and explain why it is significant.

10. Define a materials price variance. What determines whether it is favorable or unfavorable?

11. In purchasing materials, what amounts are recorded in Accounts Payable and what amounts in Materials Inventory? What happens to the difference?

12. Describe five potential causes of a materials price variance.

13. Define a materials usage variance.

14. As materials are issued from the storeroom, what amounts are credited to Materials Inventory and what amounts are charged to Work in Process? What happens to the differences?

15. List and explain five potential causes of materials usage variances.

16. Who is responsible for a materials price variance? For a materials usage variance?

17. Explain how the purchase of materials at less than the standard price may have an adverse effect on other production variances.

18. How are labor rate variances and labor efficiency variances computed?

19. The departmental supervisor assigned three people with a labor rate per person of $10 an hour to a project with a standard labor rate of $9 an hour. Each person spent 70 hours on this project. What effect will this have on the labor rate variance?

20. List five causes of a labor rate variance.

21. List five causes of a labor efficiency variance.

22. Give an example of how a labor rate variance and a labor efficiency variance are related.

23. Give an example of how labor variances and materials variances are related.

24. Discuss the major considerations in the development of overhead rates.

25. Explain briefly how underapplied or overapplied overhead can be analyzed into a budget variance and a capacity variance.

26. Define a budget variance and list the major causes of a budget variance.

27. Define a capacity variance and explain why it consists solely of fixed overhead costs.

28. Can a capacity variance be controlled? Explain.

29. What is the primary difference between using standard costs in a job cost system and a process cost system?

# EXERCISES

8–1.  **Standard Cost Sheet.** Arnovitz Enterprises manufactures special electronic equipment and parts. It has adopted a standard cost system with separate standards for each part. A special electronic "black box" has standards set with the following components. Materials include both iron and copper. Each "black box" requires six sheets of iron which cost $7 per sheet and four spools of copper at $3.50 per spool. Four hours of direct labor are needed for producing each box and the standard rate per hour is $6. Overhead costs are charged to products on the basis of direct labor time. The variable overhead rate is $3 per hour and the fixed overhead rate is $2 per hour.

**Required:**
Prepare a standard cost sheet that shows the standard cost per unit for each "black box."

Service

8–2.  **Materials Variances and T-accounts.** Mickey Stanley's Car Wash uses one packet of soap per wash. The standard cost is $3 per packet. Last year, the company purchased 150,000 packets of soap at a cost of $2.91 per packet and 30,000 packets at a cost of $3.15 each. The company used 180,000 packets to wash 178,500 cars.

**Required:**
1. Determine the materials price variance.
2. Determine the materials usage variance.
3. Using T-accounts, show the accounts and amounts involved in purchasing of the soap and in its usage. Use a Completed Jobs account rather than Work in Process.

**8–3.  Labor Variances.** Marvin & Singer TV Repair Shop fixed 550 television sets during the year using 1,447 direct labor hours. Standards state that television sets, on average, should take 2.5 hours to repair. The standard direct labor rate is $19 per hour, while the actual rate averaged $18.60 per hour.

Service

**Required:**
Compute the labor rate variance and the labor efficiency variance.

**8–4.  Materials Variances—Missing Information.** In May, Liu Equipment Company, of Shanghai, China, purchased 50,000 parts at a total cost (in yuan) of Y600,000. During the month, 46,000 parts having a standard unit cost of Y11 were used in production. The materials usage variance for the month was unfavorable by Y33,000. According to the standards, five parts should be used for each unit of product.

**Required:**
1. Calculate the materials price variance.
2. How many units of product were made?
3. How many units of parts should have been used in production?
4. What amount should be charged to Work in Process for materials requisitioned?

**8–5.  Materials Variances.** Selwyn Enterprises installs shingle roofs on single-family residential houses in Atlanta. The standard materials cost for one house is $1,260 based on 1,000 shingles at a cost of $1.26 each. During July, the company installed roofs on 20 houses, using 23,000 shingles at a cost of $1.21 each.

**Required:**
Compute the materials price variance and the materials usage variance.

**8–6.  Materials Variances and T-accounts.** Joyce Melvin & Company has the following data for the month of November:

| | |
|---|---|
| Materials purchased, 2,600 kilograms | $8,580 |
| Materials used in production | 1,320 kilograms |
| Units of product manufactured | 17,000 |
| Materials usage variance | $   384 Unfavorable |
| Standard price per kilogram | $      3.20 |

**Required:**
1. Find the standard quantity of materials allowed for the units of product manufactured.
2. Determine the materials price variance.
3. Trace the materials costs and variances through T-accounts with Work in Process Inventory as the final account.

**8–7.  Labor Standards.** Four employees each work 38 hours a week in an assembly operation at Goozh Company. Standard production for the week was established at 2,280 assemblies, or at a rate of production of 15 assemblies per labor hour. A time study person, Keith Baker, has observed that it is possible to make 20 assemblies an hour, and this rate has been set as the new standard. Production data for one week under the new standard are as follows:

| Employee | Hours Worked | Units Assembled |
|---|---|---|
| 1 | 38 | 660 |
| 2 | 38 | 590 |
| 3 | 38 | 630 |
| 4 | 38 | 620 |

The standard labor rate per hour is $12. During this week, an unfavorable materials usage variance due solely to above normal scrap and waste was $2,500. Also, 500 units that had been fully assembled were rejected by Bruce Yovits, an inspector.

**Required:**
1. What was the standard labor cost per assembly under the old standard of 15 assemblies per hour?
2. What was the anticipated labor cost per assembly under the new standard of 20 assemblies per hour?
3. What was the actual labor cost per assembly during the week (after deducting the rejected units)?
4. Comment on the new labor standard and possible reasons for the losses.

8–8.  **Labor Variances and T-accounts.** Hellman Industries manufactures sports equipment and uses a standard cost system. The general manager of the U. S. Division, Mike Moses, reports the following direct labor standards for the production of one boxing glove:

| | |
|---|---|
| Standard hours | 2 |
| Standard cost | $24 |

During April, 1,400 direct labor hours were worked to produce 675 boxing gloves. The cost of labor time averaged $13 per hour.

**Required:**
Using T-accounts, show the amounts recorded in the Wages Payable account, the variance accounts, and the Work in Process account.

8–9.  **Labor Efficiency Variance and Ethics.** Gold Burgers is a large fast-food restaurant located in downtown Silver Spring and managed by Randi Menashe. Standards indicate that each hamburger cook should make 100 burgers per hour and that the labor rate is $10 per hour. This month, 263,000 burgers were cooked in 2,150 hours.

**Required:**
1. What was the labor efficiency variance this month?
2. Why might the restaurant manager be tempted to report to top management a smaller variance than actually occurred?

8–10.  **Labor Variances and T-accounts.** The payroll for Tate Medical Claims Processors for the year was $516,000. Income taxes of $105,000 and FICA taxes of $42,000 were withheld, and employee voluntary withholdings totaled $4,000. The net amount paid to employees was $365,000. Included in the total payroll was indirect labor of $141,000 (not on an hourly basis).

The standard labor rate of $5.00 per hour was paid for 60,000 hours, and $7.50 per hour was paid for 10,000 hours. The company processed 550,000 claims during the year. Standards show that eight claims should be processed each hour.

**Required:**
1. Calculate the labor rate variance.
2. Calculate the labor efficiency variance.
3. Using T-accounts, show how much direct labor cost was charged to Work in Process, to the various payroll-related accounts, and to the appropriate variance accounts.

**8–11.** **Labor Variances—Incomplete Data.** Lipis & Glinsky, a consulting firm, reports the following data related to its labor cost:

| | |
|---|---|
| Labor efficiency variance | $7,000 favorable |
| Total labor cost variance | $13,000 unfavorable |
| Actual wage rate paid | $120 per hour |
| Standard wage rate | $110 per hour |

**Required:**
Determine the actual hours worked.

**8–12.** **Overhead Variances.** Shapiro's Delivery Service hires drivers to deliver packages in St. Louis. An average standard time to make a delivery has been established as one hour. The office is centrally located, and it takes about as much time to deliver to one location as it does to another. Fixed costs have been budgeted at $240,000 for the year. Under normal conditions, the company expects to make 60,000 deliveries a year. The variable cost has been budgeted at $12 per hour. Last year, the company made 63,000 deliveries in 59,000 hours and incurred total costs of $988,000, including fixed costs.

**Required:**
1. Compute the standard cost of making a delivery.
2. How much overhead costs were charged to deliveries in total during the year?
3. Determine the budget variance.
4. Determine the capacity variance.

**8–13.** **Overhead Variance Analysis.** A flexible budget for Mark Fisher's Tire Service is given in summary form as follows:

| Machine hours | 60,000 | 70,000 | 80,000 | 90,000 |
|---|---|---|---|---|
| Variable overhead | $240,000 | $280,000 | $320,000 | $360,000 |
| Fixed overhead | 480,000 | 480,000 | 480,000 | 480,000 |
| Total overhead | $720,000 | $760,000 | $800,000 | $840,000 |

The standard rate of production is six jobs per machine hour, and normal volume has been defined at 80,000 machine hours. The company performed 420,000 jobs in 70,000 machine hours. Actual variable overhead was $287,000, and the fixed overhead was $475,000.

**Required:**
1. Compute the amount of underapplied or overapplied overhead.
2. Compute the budget variance.
3. Explain the major causes of a budget variance.
4. Compute the capacity variance.
5. Cite three possible reasons for the existence of this capacity variance.

**8–14.** **Materials Price Variance and Finding Unknowns.** The BJ Youth Baseball League has 3,000 baseballs in inventory, which were purchased by the director, Jack Williams, for a total of $6,600. Each baseball game should require a standard usage of five baseballs. During July, 330 baseball games were played. The total standard cost allowed for the baseballs amounted to $3,762. There was an unfavorable materials usage variance of $800.

**Required:**
1. Compute the standard price for one baseball.
2. How many baseballs were used in July? (Round to nearest whole number.)
3. Compute the price variance for the baseballs used in July.

**8–15.** **Fixed Overhead Relationships.** Czinn University Medical Center has a radiology department that operated at 50,000 standard hours last year. The standard calls for five patients per hour, and the department actually handled 9,000 patients. Fixed overhead data are as follows:

| | |
|---|---|
| Fixed overhead charged to patients | $630,000 |
| Unfavorable capacity variance | 350,000 |

**Required:**
1. What was the fixed overhead budget last year?
2. What was the fixed overhead rate per patient?
3. How many patients were considered to be normal volume?
4. Would the capacity variance have been smaller or larger if the radiology department had processed 12,000 patients? Explain.

**8–16.** **Learning Curve.** Frankel Brothers & Company is planning to submit a bid on equipment to be used in space exploration. Experience on similar contracts indicates that a 70 percent learning curve may be appropriate in estimating labor hours and costs. The first 500 units of this equipment will require an estimated 10,000 labor hours. The next 500 units should be completed in 4,000 hours. Another 1,000 units should follow the 70 percent learning curve, after which the learning process will be completed. The labor rate per hour is $20.

**Required:**
1. What will be the cumulative average hours per unit after production of the third batch (1,000-unit batch)? (Assume a 70 percent learning curve.)
2. Estimate the labor cost per unit after the completion of the learning process.

**8–17.** **Learning Curve and Profitability Analysis.** A potential customer approaches J. Levin, Inc. with a proposal to buy seven complex agricultural pumps for a total of $2,000. The pump is a new product, and only one unit has been produced at the request of another customer. The following cost data are available on the first pump:

| | |
|---|---|
| Direct materials (15 pounds at $2 per pound) | $ 30 |
| Direct labor (50 hours at $10 per hour) | 500 |
| Variable overhead ($2 per direct labor hour) | 100 |
| Fixed overhead ($1 per direct labor hour) | 50 |
| Total cost | $680 |

The engineering department head, Mark Brooks, believes an 80 percent learning curve exists for this situation. Also, if the bid is accepted, the company will be eligible for a 3 percent quantity discount on direct materials.

**Required:**
Estimate the incremental profit or loss J. Levin, Inc. would realize if it accepted the proposal for the seven pumps.

**8–18.** **Three-way Overhead Analysis (Appendix).** The manufacturing overhead costs for Marley's Bobsled Factory of Kingston, Jamaica, are on a standard cost system. The flexible overhead budget formula (in Jamaican dollars) is:

| | |
|---|---|
| Fixed costs: | J$100,000 per period |
| Variable costs: | J$10 per bobsled |

Each bobsled requires two hours of machine time. Normal production is 25,000 bobsleds per month. During the most recent period, 42,000 hours of work produced 20,000 bobsleds. The actual manufacturing overhead costs totaled J$350,000, of which J$120,000 was fixed cost.

**Required:**
1. Calculate the underapplied or overapplied manufacturing overhead.
2. How much of the total overhead variance is fixed cost and how much is variable cost?
3. Compute the spending and efficiency variances.
4. Compute the capacity variance.
5. Prove that the spending, efficiency, and capacity variances account for the total overhead variance.

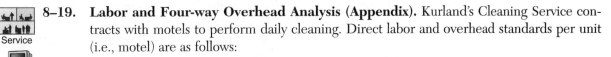

**8–19.** **Labor and Four-way Overhead Analysis (Appendix).** Kurland's Cleaning Service contracts with motels to perform daily cleaning. Direct labor and overhead standards per unit (i.e., motel) are as follows:

| | |
|---|---|
| Direct labor: | 10 hours at $5.00 per hour |
| Variable overhead: | 10 hours at $2.00 per hour |
| Fixed overhead: | 10 hours at $3.00 per hour |

Budgeted fixed overhead costs per month are $150,000. During March, 5,000 units were cleaned. Direct labor costs were $234,000 (52,000 hours). Actual variable overhead costs were $103,000, and actual fixed overhead costs were $147,000.

**Required:**
1. Determine the rate and efficiency variances for direct labor for March.
2. Compute the underapplied or overapplied overhead for the month.
3. Calculate the spending, efficiency, and capacity variances for the month.
4. Explain how the labor efficiency and overhead efficiency variances are related.
5. Split the spending variance into its variable and fixed components.

# PROBLEMS

**8–20.** **Standard Cost Sheet—Materials and Labor.** An industrial solvent with the brand name Velocidad is produced by Proveedor Chemical Company in Caracas, Venezuela, and sold in 25-liter drums. Data with respect to materials and labor are as follows:
1. A batch of 1,500 liters of Velocidad is made from an input of 1,500 liters each of Destino and Promesa. In the boiling operation, 50 percent of the volume of both Destino and Promesa is lost through evaporation.
2. At the end of the boiling operation, 2 kilograms of Bono are added to each 1,500-liter batch. (This has no measurable effect on volume.)
3. A worker can process one 25-liter drum in 20 minutes.
4. At the final inspection, two 25-liter drums are rejected out of every ten drums received from the production line.
5. Standard materials prices and the labor rate (in bolivars) are as follows:

| | |
|---|---|
| Destino | B 200 per liter |
| Promesa | B 150 per liter |
| Bono | B 600 per kilogram |
| Labor rate | B 1,200 per hour |

**Required:**
Prepare a standard cost sheet that shows the standard materials and labor costs for each 25-liter drum of completed product.

**8–21.** **Standard Cost Sheet—All Cost Elements.** Glusman Office Furniture is a well-known supplier of quality office furniture. It is currently setting up a standard cost system for its products. One product is the Home Office Workstation for those who operate a business in their homes. The production process for this workstation involves four departments: Cutting, Assembly, Staining, and Finishing. Materials, labor, and overhead costs are accumulated by department.

Raw materials include lumber, stain, drawer handles and fixtures, screws, dowels, and glue. Each workstation requires 64 feet of lumber at $1.60 per foot. Drawer handles and other drawer fixtures are $16.80 per workstation. Stain required is 0.8 gallons at $16.70 per gallon. Screws, dowels, and glue are included in the overhead costs of the Assembly Department. Lumber enters the process in the Cutting Department; drawer handles and other drawer fixtures in the Assembly Department; and stain in the Staining Department.

Direct labor occurs in Cutting, Assembly, and Finishing. Cutting requires 30 minutes per workstation with labor cost at $9.50 per hour. Assembly requires two hours per workstation with a labor cost of $11.60 per hour. Finishing requires 20 minutes with a labor cost of $7.80 per hour. Staining is an automated department and has no direct labor.

Factory overhead is applied to workstations by department on the basis of direct labor hours in the three departments with direct labor. Cutting is $10 per hour; Assembly is $9.50 per hour; and Finishing is $9 per hour. The Staining Department overhead is applied on the basis of machine time, and the rate is $18 per machine hour. Each workstation requires one-fourth of an hour of machine time.

**Required:**

Prepare a standard cost sheet that shows all of the elements of cost for a completed workstation. For convenience, identify the cost elements by department.

**8–22.** **Materials Price and Usage Variances: Two Plants.** Levene Coatings Company manufactures a roof coating and sealant product in 5-gallon pails in both the Gurvey plant and the Oliker plant. Materials cost is a large part of the total costs and varies from month to month. Standard quantities of materials used to manufacture each 5-gallon pail and the standard prices are as follows:

|  | Standard Quantities | Standard Prices |
|---|---|---|
| Oil | 5 gallons | $3.00 per gallon |
| Metal | 2 pounds | 2.50 per pound |
| Sealer | 10 ounces | 0.10 per ounce |

Production and cost data for the two plants for both June and July are as follows:

|  | Gurvey Plant | Oliker Plant |
|---|---|---|
| Product units manufactured: |  |  |
| June | 80,000 | 50,000 |
| July | 85,000 | 60,000 |
| Quantity of materials used: |  |  |
| June: |  |  |
| Oil | 416,000 gals. | 252,000 gals. |
| Metal | 163,000 lbs. | 102,000 lbs. |
| Sealer | 800,000 oz. | 502,000 oz. |
| July: |  |  |
| Oil | 427,000 gals. | 320,000 gals. |
| Metal | 170,000 lbs. | 126,000 lbs. |
| Sealer | 855,000 oz. | 604,000 oz. |

All materials purchased were used in production. The actual prices for the materials purchased and used were the same for both plants. Actual prices are as follows:

| | Actual Unit Prices | |
|---|---|---|
| | June | July |
| Oil | $3.40 | $3.45 |
| Metal | 2.30 | 2.40 |
| Sealer | 0.12 | 0.13 |

**Required:**
1. Compute the total materials price variance by ingredient for both June and July.
2. Compute the materials usage variance by ingredient for each plant for each month.
3. Which plant had the larger usage variance in June? Which had the larger usage variance in July?

8–23. **Labor Variances and T-accounts.** Danburke Corporation manufactures a popular breakfast cereal. The company adopted a standard cost system that has the following labor standards for 1,000 cartons of cereal:

| Department | Rate | Hours | Standard Cost |
|---|---|---|---|
| Crushing | $20 | 100 | $2,000 |
| Baking | 12 | 40 | 480 |
| Mixing | 16 | 20 | 320 |
| Packaging | 12 | 40 | 480 |
| Total | | 200 | $3,280 |
| Labor cost per carton | | | $ 3.28 |

During September, the company produced 83,000 cartons and had the following actual costs and hours:

| Department | Cost | Hours Worked |
|---|---|---|
| Crushing | $159,358 | 8,400 |
| Baking | 52,752 | 3,820 |
| Mixing | 29,172 | 1,410 |
| Packaging | 29,368 | 2,653 |
| Total | $270,650 | 16,283 |

**Required:**
1. Calculate the labor rate variance for each of the four departments.
2. Calculate the labor efficiency variance for each of the four departments.
3. Using T-accounts, show the amounts recorded in the Wages Payable account, the variance accounts, and the Work in Process account.

8–24. **Standard Costs of Materials and Labor.** Lisa Galanti, vice-president of production at Hal's Fabrics, Inc., believes that a net savings in production cost can be realized by using stronger and more expensive yarn in production. In her opinion, far too much labor time is wasted in working with poor grade yarn that breaks or gets jammed in the knitting machines.

At the present time, 20,000 product units are made with a total of 200,000 yards of yarn costing $0.12 cents a yard. With a better grade of yarn costing $0.25 cents a yard, the same number of units could be made with 160,000 yards of yarn.

The standard labor rate is $8.50 per hour, and the standard time to make 20,000 units with the cheaper yarn is 20,000 hours. Galanti estimates that with the better yarn, only 16,000 hours will be needed for 20,000 product units.

**Required:**
1. Calculate the standard costs of yarn and labor when using the cheaper yarn.
2. Calculate the standard costs of yarn and labor when using the more expensive yarn.
3. Does a net cost savings exist with the better yarn?
4. Besides the factors previously mentioned relating to current cost savings, give other reasons why better yarn might be favored.

**8–25. Reconstructing Actual Inputs.** T. Senior Company manufactures a number of different products. Its most profitable product comes from a division in northern Mexico, which has the following standard cost sheet (all monetary amounts are in pesos):

| | |
|---|---|
| Materials (2 kilograms at M$8.50 per kilogram) | M$17 |
| Labor (.5 hour at M$12 per hour) | 6 |
| Overhead (M$18 per labor hour) | 9 |
| Total product cost | M$32 |

Income statements are prepared for each product line on a monthly basis. At the end of a recent month, the following income statement information was available for the product:

| | | |
|---|---|---|
| Sales (M$45 × 92,000 units) | | M$4,140,000 |
| Cost goods sold at standard (M$32 × 92,000 units) | | 2,944,000 |
| Gross profit at standard | | M$1,196,000 |
| Manufacturing cost variances: | | |
| Materials price | M$7,500 F | |
| Materials usage | 8,500 U | |
| Labor rate | 5,900 U | |
| Labor efficiency | 12,000 F | 5,100 |
| Adjusted gross profit | | M$1,201,100 |

Materials purchases for the month were 300,000 kilograms. The division produced 120,000 units, with no work in process inventories at the beginning or end of the month. All variances are closed to the Cost of Goods Sold account at the end of each month.

**Required:**
1. Calculate the actual materials price per kilogram.
2. Calculate the number of kilograms of materials actually used in production.
3. Calculate the actual number of labor hours worked.

Service

**8–26. Interrelationship of Materials and Labor Variances.** Vicki Kayser, purchasing agent for the western region of Knockout Nail Salons, was pleased to report that she bought 50,000 units (i.e., nails) for $15,000, which was lower than the $22,500 cost at its standard price. The nails also were a lower grade than called for by the standard. According to rather obvious standards here, five nails should be used for each hand.

When these nails were used on customers, breakage was higher than normal. To keep the abnormal breakage to a minimum, the operating manager, Sydney Rubin, shifted more skilled workers into the salons where breakage occurred. The standard labor rate was $8 per hour. One half hour is the standard time for putting nails on one hand.

Last month, the salons used 42,000 units and 3,300 hours in doing 6,000 hands. The labor cost was $31,750.

**Required:**
1. Compute materials price and materials usage variances.
2. Compute labor rate and labor efficiency variances.
3. Combine the four variances to obtain the net effect. Did the purchasing agent save the company money in buying the nonstandard nails?
4. Which variance amounts would be assigned to the purchasing agent and which would be assigned to the operating manager? Comment on the interrelationships among the variances here.

Service

**8–27.  Materials Variances.** The current year budget for Ed Lynn's Courier Service estimated 153,000 miles to be driven by its couriers based on a forecast of 17,000 deliveries. The standard price of gasoline was set at $1.20 per gallon, and the company expected to drive an average of 22 miles per gallon for its deliveries. During the year, 18,480 deliveries were actually made, 165,600 miles were driven, the average price per gallon of gasoline purchased was $1.16, and an average of 24 miles per gallon was achieved for the company's deliveries.

**Required:**
Compute the materials price variance and the materials usage variance for the current year.

Service

**8–28.  Materials and Labor—Missing Information.** You have been asked to provide your supervisor with cost information about operations in the South Euclid Dog Kennel. Unfortunately, you are furnished with only partial information; you must calculate much of what is needed. The information you have to work with is as follows:
1. The kennel purchased 350,000 pounds of materials (dog food) during the year. The standard price is $3.10.
2. Materials on hand at the beginning of the year at the standard price cost $52,700. The standard price has not changed during the past two years.
3. Materials on hand at the end of the year at the standard price cost $108,500.
4. The materials price variance was unfavorable by $175,000.
5. The materials usage variance was unfavorable by $21,700.
6. Actual direct labor cost was $320,000, but the labor rate variance was unfavorable by $10,000.
7. Actual direct labor hours were 32,000.
8. The kennel's output was 65,000 dog-days (a dog-day means one dog housed for one day).
9. The labor efficiency variance was favorable by $15,000.

**Required:**
Using the data above, furnish the following information:
(a) Actual quantity of materials used at the standard price.
(b) Actual cost of materials purchased.
(c) Number of pounds of materials needed for each dog-day according to the standard.
(d) Standard direct materials cost for the year.
(e) Standard direct labor cost for the year.
(f) Standard direct labor rate per hour.
(g) Standard direct labor hours per dog-day.

**8–29.  Overhead in an Automated Operation.** Barbara James observes, "The nature of costs has changed since Oak Grove Windings Company installed more automated equipment. At one time, direct labor was an important factor. With automation, direct labor is essentially a fixed cost with workers monitoring the operation on television screens. Variable overhead cost is lower and is related to hours of machine operation. On the other hand, fixed cost is much higher than it was in a labor-oriented operation. However, the production line can only move so fast. If it is stepped up, too many pieces are broken."

Jan Spector, the production manager, says, "We may not obtain much more savings from increases in productivity. Additional savings will have to come by holding down fixed costs and receiving a large volume of orders."

Data from last year are as follows:

| | |
|---|---:|
| Variable cost per machine hour | $4 |
| Number of standard units of product per machine hour | 100 |
| Fixed overhead budget | $6,000,000 |
| Normal number of product units produced in a year | 60,000,000 |
| Actual hours of operation | 500,000 |
| Actual product units produced | 58,000,000 |
| Actual overhead cost: | |
|    Variable overhead | $1,935,000 |
|    Fixed overhead | $6,030,000 |

**Required:**

1. What was the standard variable overhead cost per product unit and the standard fixed overhead cost per product unit?
2. How much overhead was applied to production for the year?
3. Determine the following variances:
   (a) Overhead budget variance.
   (b) Overhead capacity variance.
4. Prepare a graph that shows how a capacity variance arises in this case.

8–30. **Complete Variance Analysis and Cost Flow.** Palay & Brown Machine Company operates with a standard cost accounting system and uses cost variances as a means of detecting costs that may require more control. A standard cost sheet for a component that is manufactured exclusively in one plant is as follows:

| | |
|---|---:|
| Direct materials (6 units @ $4) | $24.00 |
| Direct labor (0.7 hour @ $8) | 5.60 |
| Variable overhead (0.75 machine hour @ $4) | 3.00 |
| Fixed overhead (0.75 machine hour @ $20) | 15.00 |
| Standard unit cost | $47.60 |

Data from the past year are as follows:

1. Purchased 2,000,000 units of materials at a cost of $7,540,000.
2. Manufactured 300,000 units of product.
3. Budgeted $6,400,000 for fixed overhead for the year.
4. Used 1,812,000 units of materials in production.
5. Used 200,000 direct labor hours.
6. Spent $1,610,000 for direct labor.
7. Spent $880,000 for variable overhead.
8. Spent $6,321,000 for fixed overhead.
9. Completed 300,000 units and sold 250,000 units.

**Required:**

1. Determine the following variances:
   (a) Materials price variance.
   (b) Materials usage variance.
   (c) Labor rate variance.
   (d) Labor efficiency variance.
   (e) Overhead budget variance.
   (f) Overhead capacity variance.
2. Which is the largest unfavorable variance that may be controllable by production management? Explain.
3. If the capacity variance is unfavorable by a large amount, what steps may be taken in the future to correct it?
4. Using T-accounts, trace all costs through the accounts and close all variances to Cost of Goods Sold. Show the ending balances in the following accounts:
   (a) Materials Inventory.
   (b) Work in Process Inventory.
   (c) Finished Goods Inventory.
   (d) Cost of Goods Sold.

**8–31.** **Overhead Budget and Capacity Variances.** Grinzaid Finance, Inc. specializes in home equity loans. It bases its overhead on the flexible budget cost function of:

$$\$33,000 + (\$2.40 \times \text{labor hours})$$

Normal volume is based on 12,000 labor hours. Standards call for two labor hours per loan processed.

For the current period, the operating results were as follows:

| | |
|---|---|
| Actual labor hours worked | 11,400 |
| Loans processed | 5,800 |
| Actual variable overhead costs | $28,460 |
| Actual fixed overhead costs | $31,950 |

**Required:**

1. Calculate the rates for variable and fixed overhead that would be used to apply overhead to loans.
2. Calculate the underapplied or overapplied overhead for the period.
3. Determine the following variances:
   (a) Overhead budget variance.
   (b) Overhead capacity variance.
4. How much of the budget variance is due to variable costs and how much to fixed costs?

**8–32.** **Materials and Labor Variances with Incomplete Data.** Andy Lewis, the cost accountant for New Brittany Zoo, has provided you with actual and standard cost data for feeding elephants during the year:

| | *Materials* | *Labor* |
|---|---|---|
| Purchased and used at actual cost, 38,000 pounds | $104,500 | |
| Actual direct labor payroll | | $63,000 |
| Standard materials (lbs. per feeding) | 2 | |
| Standard labor time per feeding | | 20 minutes |
| Standard price per pound of materials | $  2.50 | |
| Standard labor rate per hour | | $10 |
| Labor rate variance (unfavorable) | | $6,000 |

During the year, there were 18,000 feedings for the elephants.

**Required:**

1. Determine the materials price variance.
2. What was the standard cost of the standard pounds of materials used?
3. Compute the materials usage variance.
4. How many labor hours were used during the year?
5. Compute the labor efficiency variance.
6. What was the total standard cost of labor?

**8–33. Comprehensive Variance Analysis.** Shenk Company uses a standard cost system and isolates the following six variances for the appropriate departments:

| | |
|---|---|
| Materials price variance | Labor efficiency variance |
| Materials usage variance | Overhead budget variance |
| Labor rate variance | Overhead capacity variance |

The company uses direct labor as the measure of activity for each of the producing departments.

**Required:**

For each of the following *independent* events, indicate which variances would be affected. Briefly explain why they would be affected, and indicate whether the effect is favorable or unfavorable. If more than one variance is influenced in a given situation, limit your discussion to the two or three most important variances for that situation.

(a) Demand exceeded expectation, and the number of units produced during the year was much greater than the number planned.

(b) Because of an improperly adjusted machine, more materials were wasted than anticipated. When the department supervisor requisitioned more materials from the storeroom, no materials were there. A rush order for more materials was placed, and the materials arrived by special delivery before the end of the day.

(c) A purchasing agent bought substandard materials at a large savings. Because of the lower quality of the materials, more scrap was produced; and an additional employee was hired to assist in the cutting operation.

(d) Several customer rush orders were accepted and placed into production. The orders were completed within the standard time allotted; however, overtime was required to meet the customers' delivery schedules.

(e) A new union contract at the beginning of the year required an increase in labor rates. Adjustments to the standard wage rates were made as required at the beginning of the year. During the year, the rate of inflation in the economy was lower than what was predicted for the contract wage rates.

(f) Due to food poisoning in the plant cafeteria, several highly skilled employees from one department were sick for two days. The department supervisor hired temporary, unskilled production-line workers to substitute for the skilled workers. The wages for the temporary help were less than standard; and the output was also less than standard.

(g) Because of more than usual machine breakdowns, repair and maintenance personnel used more supplies than called for in the overhead budgets.

(h) A brownout caused by the overload of extra power usage in the city resulted in the inability to run machines at full power for four hours during a second shift.

(i) A forklift driver inadvertently ran into a large machine, dumping his load and stopping the machine. Several direct labor workers and the machine operator helped clean up the mess and got the machine going again.

**(j)** A new quality control inspector was less strict than policy standards required; and units that should have been reworked were passed over, released to the finished goods warehouse, and sold to customers.

Service

**8–34.    Labor Variances.** Ruth Corporation is an Ohio marketing firm that services a large number of consumer products manufacturing companies in the midwest. Ruth Corporation receives product coupons from these manufacturers and puts together packets containing a variety of the coupons. Then, Ruth Corporation sends out mass mailings of these packets to the general public throughout the country. The company president, Sam Baker, has provided the following information for the month of July:

| | |
|---|---|
| Standard labor rate | $10.25 per hour |
| Budgeted number of packets | 3,100 |
| Budgeted labor hours | 9,300 |
| Actual number of packets | 3,175 |
| Actual labor hours worked | 9,700 |
| Actual direct labor cost | $90,000 |

**Required:** Compute the labor rate variance and the labor efficiency variance for July.

Service

**8–35.    Budget Variance for Individual Costs.** Elaine Alexander, administrator of Peyton Dialysis Clinic, has estimated overhead costs for the year at an expected operating level of 6,000 dialyzer machine hours. Past experience indicates a rate of cost variability per hour as follows:

| | |
|---|---|
| Lubrication | $.75 |
| Supplies | .30 |
| Power | .25 |
| Repairs | .50 |
| Maintenance | .80 |

Costs that are fixed are budgeted as follows:

| | |
|---|---|
| Supervision | $ 4,500 |
| Indirect labor | 11,500 |
| Heat and light | 3,200 |
| Taxes and insurance | 1,600 |
| Depreciation | 1,800 |

During the year, the clinic incurred 5,500 dialyzer machine hours and treated the number of patients that should have been treated in 5,000 dialyzer machine hours. The clinic incurred the following overhead costs:

| | |
|---|---|
| Lubrication | $  3,900 |
| Supplies | 1,700 |
| Power | 1,500 |
| Repairs | 2,800 |
| Maintenance | 4,300 |
| Supervision | 4,000 |
| Indirect labor | 12,000 |
| Heat and light | 3,200 |
| Taxes and insurance | 1,400 |
| Depreciation | 1,600 |
| Total | $ 36,400 |

**Required:**

1. Prepare a budget of overhead costs for 5,000 dialyzer machine hours.
2. Compare the actual overhead costs with the budget for 5,000 dialyzer machine hours. Show budget variances for each item.
3. Explain what factors could cause the budget variance to arise.

Service

**8–36. Learning Curves and CVP Analysis.** Emmer Nursing Home is considering accepting a new type of patient for a charge of $1,700 per month. The Accounting Department has studied the projected costs and arrived at the following estimates:

1. Labor will follow an 80 percent learning curve.
2. The first new patient will require 100 labor hours.
3. The labor rate is $10 per hour.
4. Variable overhead is $4 per direct labor hour.
5. Fixed overhead will increase $5,000 per month as a result of this new type of patient.
6. Materials will cost $100 per patient.

**Required:**

1. Assuming there is no constraint on the available labor time during the month, how many new patients would be needed in order to break even?
2. Assuming that maximum labor time available is 300 hours during the month, how many new patients can be admitted? Will the nursing home break even within that constraint? Explain.
3. Returning to Part 1, if the nursing home could improve its learning rate to 75 percent, how many more patients could be handled at the break-even point than for an 80 percent learning curve?

**8–37. Learning Curves and Estimating Costs.** Sobel Space Systems, Inc. is developing a new but complex part for a sophisticated missile. In making the first unit, the company used 500 direct labor hours at a cost of $8,000. The Engineering Department head, Randy Gold, is trying to estimate a learning curve but has not yet decided whether it is 80 percent or 90 percent.

**Required:**

1. Determine the cumulate average work-hours per unit under an 80 percent and a 90 percent learning curve for a total of:
   (a) 2 units.
   (b) 4 units.
   (c) 8 units.
   (d) 16 units.
2. After completing the first unit, a prime contractor has ordered 15 additional units. What is the estimated direct labor cost for this order:
   (a) for an 80 percent learning curve?
   (b) for a 90 percent learning curve?
3. Suppose the actual learning curve realized in producing the additional 15 units was 85 percent, what is the additional cost or savings on the order as compared to an 80 percent and a 90 percent learning curve?

**8–38. Efficiency or Capacity Variance (Appendix).** Argentina Metals Company produces a magnetic instrument at its Buenos Aires plant. A standard cost accounting system is used. When operating at a normal volume of 300,000 machine hours, the plant should produce 1,200,000 units of this instrument. In the past few years, the company has been able to sell only 800,000 units of this product line each year. Management is aware of the relatively high fixed overhead costs budgeted at 4,800,000 pesos for the year and of the need to operate as closely to normal volume as possible.

The company has two categories of variable overhead: one varies at the rate of 3 pesos per unit of product; the other, which is based on machine hours, varies at 2 pesos per unit of product. Therefore, a total of 5 pesos is charged to each product for variable overhead.

Last year the plant operated at 250,000 machine hours and produced 800,000 units of the magnetic instrument. The standard variable overhead cost is 8 pesos per machine hour, and the company incurred 2,050,000 pesos of actual variable overhead. It incurred 4,800,000 pesos in fixed overhead.

One of the production supervisors, Ernesto Valdez, has stated that some improvement has been made in operating more closely to normal volume. "By operating at 250,000 machine hours, the plant is up to 5/6 of normal volume. If the plant had operated at only 200,000 hours, as it did the year before last, we would have absorbed only 2/3 of the fixed overhead. This year the unfavorable capacity variance is only 800,000 pesos. The year before that, the unfavorable capacity variance was 1,600,000 pesos."

The supervisor of another department, Julio Diaz, disagreed and replied, "You can't eliminate a capacity variance by using more hours. Ernesto, you are confusing the concept of a capacity variance with an efficiency variance."

Valdez answered by saying, "An efficiency variance involves only the variable overhead and has nothing to do with what we are discussing, the absorption of fixed overhead."

**Required:**
1. Calculate both the overhead efficiency variance and the capacity variance for both years.
2. Explain what the efficiency variance measures as compared to what the capacity variance measures.
3. Which of the two supervisors is correct? Explain.

8–39.   **Multiple Products and Overhead Analysis (Appendix).** Tiby Electrical Instruments manufactures three product lines used by the military: electronic support devices (SD), electronic counter measure devices (CMD), and electronic counter counter measure devices (CCD). The company has one large production facility in University Heights, Ohio. Most of the components are manufactured by various divisions, although a few components are purchased from outside vendors. The Assembly Department is responsible for the final assembly of all three products.

Assembly operations are labor intensive and operate under a standard cost system. Because overhead costs are driven by direct labor hours, overhead is applied to each product on that basis. The standard overhead costs for Assembly on each of the three products are as follows:

|     | Hours | Variable | Fixed | Total | Per Unit |
| --- | --- | --- | --- | --- | --- |
| SD  | 3.0 | $10.00 | $7.50 | $17.50 | $52.50 |
| CMD | 4.0 | 10.00 | 7.50 | 17.50 | 70.00 |
| CCD | 5.0 | 10.00 | 7.50 | 17.50 | 87.50 |

Normal volume for Assembly is 36,000 direct labor hours per month. During January, the Assembly Department had the following production performance:

|     | Units | Hours Worked |
| --- | --- | --- |
| SD  | 3,800 | 10,900 |
| CMD | 2,700 | 10,400 |
| CCD | 2,200 | 11,500 |

Actual variable overhead amounted to $326,540 for the month. Actual fixed overhead totaled $271,000. No in-process inventories existed at the beginning or the end of the month.

**Required:**
1. How many standard direct labor hours were allowed for actual production in Assembly during the month?
2. Calculate the underapplied or overapplied overhead for the month.
3. Calculate the following overhead variances:
   (a) Variable spending variance.
   (b) Variable efficiency variance.
   (c) Fixed spending variance.
   (d) Fixed capacity variance.
4. Explain how the variable efficiency variance is related to direct labor.
5. Explain how the variable efficiency variance and the fixed capacity variance are related.

**8–40. Three-Way Overhead Variance Analysis (Appendix).** Edinburgh Sport & Entertainment Services has four operating divisions in Scotland. The controller, Pat Brittain, wants monthly reports on the operations for each division and for the total company. Data for each of the divisions are as follows: (All figures are in thousands.)

| | Divisions | | | |
| --- | --- | --- | --- | --- |
| | **1** | **2** | **3** | **4** |
| Budgeted variable overhead at normal volume | £40 | £60 | £100 | £400 |
| Budgeted fixed overhead | £60 | £90 | £150 | £100 |
| Normal volume — labor hours | 20 | 10 | 20 | 50 |

Operating data for the months of August, September, and October are as follows: (All figures are in thousands.)

| | Divisions | | | |
| --- | --- | --- | --- | --- |
| | **1** | **2** | **3** | **4** |
| **August:** | | | | |
| Actual overhead | £92 | £155 | £240 | £487 |
| Actual labor hours | 14 | 10 | 19 | 48 |
| Standard labor hours for work done | 15 | 8 | 20 | 45 |
| **September:** | | | | |
| Actual overhead | £83 | £188 | £226 | £498 |
| Actual labor hours | 12 | 15 | 16 | 50 |
| Standard labor hours for work done | 14 | 12 | 12 | 50 |
| **October:** | | | | |
| Actual overhead | £76 | £197 | £233 | £475 |
| Actual labor hours | 9 | 16 | 18 | 47 |
| Standard labor hours for work done | 10 | 15 | 16 | 50 |

**Required:**
1. Prepare monthly reports for each division and for the company as a whole for August, September, and October. Show the following variances:
   (a) Overhead spending variance.
   (b) Overhead efficiency variance.
   (c) Overhead capacity variance.

**2.** Identify the division(s) with the worst spending variance, the worst efficiency variance, and the worst capacity variance for each of the three months.

**3.** If the economy were to turn downward, which division would be most likely to run into problems first? Explain.

# CASE 8A—STROLL'S BICYCLES, INC.

Stroll's Bicycles, Inc. is a large manufacturer located in Denver. Its usual production of bicycles is 10,000 units per year. The company has been a leader in the 21-speed bike industry for several years. However, with increasing competition and a higher public emphasis on quality, the company has been searching for ways to maintain quality and cut costs. Art Saul, production planner, suggested that starting at the beginning of 2009 the company invest in higher quality materials and hire more experienced workers at a slightly higher pay rate.

The company has used a standard cost system for the past five years. The current standard costs for one bicycle, based on production of 10,000 units, are as follows:

| | |
|---|---:|
| Materials | $ 60 |
| Direct labor (4 hours at $10) | 40 |
| Variable overhead (based on labor) | 20 |
| Fixed overhead (based on labor) | 8 |
| Standard cost per bicycle | $128 |

David Weissmann, president, is skeptical about decreasing costs by increasing materials and labor costs. However, after much debate, he agrees to try the changes for one year beginning with January 2009. Because the exact costs of changes were not known at the beginning of 2009, the existing standard costs were retained. Therefore, the changes will be in the variances from standard costs.

During 2009, the company produced only 9,500 bicycles because the marketplace showed a decreasing demand. The following data show the actual results for 2009:

**1.** Materials costing $617,500 were purchased and used. No usage variance existed, so any differences were due solely to price changes.

**2.** Direct labor was $249,375 for 23,750 direct labor hours.

**3.** Actual variable overhead totaled $163,000.

**4.** Actual fixed overhead totaled $80,000.

Mr. Weissmann was pleased with the results. Even though production was down by 500 bicycles, the difference in costs was significant. He would like to know why.

**Required:**
**1.** Compute all appropriate variances for the following categories:
 **(a)** Materials.
 **(b)** Labor.
 **(c)** Overhead.
**2.** Explain how any of the variances interrelate (have the same basic cause).
**3.** Explain which of the variances are controllable.
**4.** Assuming that the actual cost results for 2009 represent the new standard performance, calculate the new standard cost per bicycle, showing separately the materials, labor, and overhead components. (Normal production is still based on 10,000 bicycles.)

Service

# CASE 8B—DUWELL CASINOS

Duwell Casinos owns and operates thirty casinos throughout Nevada. The following flexible budget information has been prepared by Duwell's controller, Danny Frank, for one of its casinos located just twelve miles south of Reno:

| | |
|---|---:|
| Direct labor hours at normal capacity | 5,000 |
| **Variable overhead:** | |
| Indirect labor | $ 3,500 |
| Supplies | 2,500 |
| Repairs and maintenance | 1,000 |
| Electricity, other than lighting | 5,000 |
| Total variable overhead | $12,000 |
| **Fixed overhead:** | |
| Supervision | 3,000 |
| Supplies | 1,700 |
| Repairs and maintenance | 3,000 |
| Depreciation on machinery | 6,500 |
| Insurance | 1,800 |
| Property taxes | 1,000 |
| Heating | 600 |
| Lighting | 400 |
| Total fixed overhead | $18,000 |

The overhead costs are allocated on the basis of direct labor hours. The standard calls for the servicing of ten patrons per hour.

During May, 4,650 direct labor hours were actually worked; and 48,530 patrons were serviced in the casino. The following actual overhead costs were incurred:

| | |
|---|---:|
| **Variable overhead:** | |
| Indirect labor | $ 3,400 |
| Supplies | 2,200 |
| Repairs and maintenance | 960 |
| Electricity, other than lighting | 4,740 |
| Total variable overhead | $11,300 |
| **Fixed overhead:** | |
| Supervision | $ 2,800 |
| Supplies | 1,570 |
| Repairs and maintenance | 3,380 |
| Depreciation on machinery | 6,500 |
| Insurance | 1,900 |
| Property taxes | 1,100 |
| Heating | 845 |
| Lighting | 405 |
| Total fixed overhead | $18,500 |

**Required:**

1. Prepare a report that shows each category of overhead cost with individual budget variances.

2. What are the major potential causes of the budget variances?

3. Calculate an overall capacity variance.

# PROFIT ANALYSIS: VARIANCES AND VARIABLE COSTING

## LEARNING OBJECTIVES

1. Identify the differences between planned and actual net income.

2. Calculate these sales variances: sales price, sales quantity, and sales mix.

3. Calculate these cost variances: cost performance, cost quantity, and cost mix.

4. Explain why actual contribution margin or gross margin differs from budget.

5. Recast absorption costing income statements into variable costing income statements.

6. Reconcile the differences between absorption costing net income and variable costing net income.

7. Understand arguments supporting both variable costing and absorption costing.

## A Credit Union's Interest Margin: Where're the Earnings?

*Joyce Clouse, president of Roaring Spring Community Credit Union, has just received the first quarter financial statements from her vice-president and controller, Hal Hoover. She immediately sees that net income is up, return on assets is now 1.2 percent, and total assets have grown to $125 million. From the income statement, she notes that interest margin (interest income minus interest and dividends expense) is up by $150,000 over the same quarter last year. It's also $50,000 ahead of this quarter's financial plan. Pondering, she asks, "What'd we do? Yes, we're bigger, and interest rates jumped more than we expected." She calls Hal and asks, "Have we run the interest margin variance report for last quarter?" Hal responds, "No, but I'll have it in half an hour."*

*Like clockwork, Hal knocks on the president's door, enters, and hands Joyce the one-page report. "Ah yes, of that $50,000 interest margin variance, we earned $60,000 on the asset side and only lost $10,000 to budget in higher dividends on member deposits," Joyce says with a smile. She also notes that the $50,000 was split almost equally among higher rates, more deposits than expected, and a higher earning mix of loans. "You know," Joyce tells Hal, "we can't take much credit for higher interest rates and getting more deposits, but all that work we put into shifting our loan mix really did pay off. Our variable-rate loan yield shifted right with the rates."*

*While in financial institutions this analysis is called interest margin variance analysis, it is the same tool used by other firms to analyze changes in gross margin and contribution margin. It is a powerful tool for both planning and control if used and interpreted carefully by managers.*

I N MANY SITUATIONS, managerial performance focuses on how actual net income compares to budgeted net income. When differences occur, management is interested in where and why. To answer these questions, the income statement is divided into sections and then dissected into individual variances that can highlight the major causes.

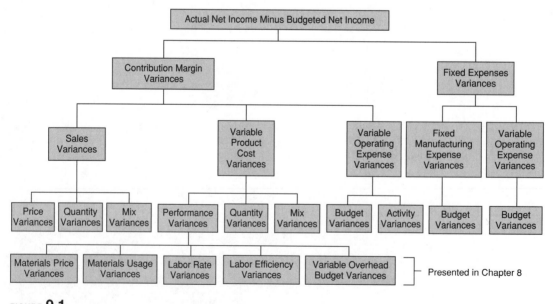

**FIGURE 9.1**

Net Income Variance Analysis–Contribution Margin Approach

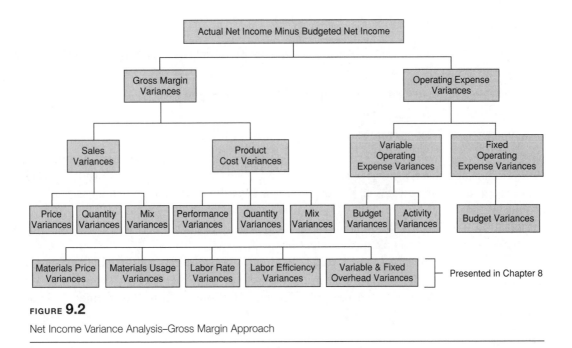

**FIGURE 9.2**

Net Income Variance Analysis–Gross Margin Approach

In Chapter 7, flexible budgeting helped analyze variable cost budget variances. Chapter 8 discussed standard costs and how actual product costs are compared to a performance standard. Product cost variances are important, but they explain only a portion of why net income varies from budget. Figure 9.1 provides a framework for analyzing the total income statement. **Contribution margin variance analysis** focuses on measuring revenue and product variable cost variances. Figure 9.2 shows the same structure using **gross margin variance analysis**. The difference between the two methods rests with how fixed costs are handled. Later in the chapter, we discuss fixed costs within variable and absorption costing.

To explain the net income variance in Figure 9.1, revenues, variable production costs, variable operating expenses, and fixed production and operating expenses are analyzed separately. Revenues and variable production costs are part of contribution margin variance analysis. Then variances for variable operating expenses and finally fixed manufacturing and operating expenses are discussed.

These analyses can be used to make a number of comparisons such as:

- Actual results for this period to budget.
- Actual results for this period to actual results for a prior period.
- A "what if" plan to a base plan.

The period may be a day, week, month, or year, depending on the needed timeframe.

## CONTRIBUTION MARGIN ANALYSIS

Using Figure 9.1 as a discussion base, product contribution margin is revenue minus variable product costs. Then, after subtracting variable operating expenses, we have variable contribution margin. A product contribution margin analysis framework views sales and product cost variances as a symmetric picture—price, quantity, and mix on both sides.

## Product Contribution Margin Analysis

Product contribution margin analysis can be used in a wide variety of situations. But certain conditions should be met. These include:

- Product lines where individual products are similar in price and type.
- Products that are complementary or substitutes.
- Product mixes that can vary as total quantity increases or decreases.

While products are emphasized, services also fit the analysis well. For instance, margin analysis applies to financial institutions where certain types of assets and liabilities are viewed as products. Cases where products are diverse, such as paper clips and washing machines, are not easily adaptable to this tool.

As an illustration, Vistavia Wholesalers in Figure 9.3 includes budget and actual units and dollars per unit data for four products from its product line.

Important variables are total quantity of units, sales mix, and price and variable cost per unit. Quantity is total units of all products. Sales mix is the percentage that each product represents of total sales. The task is to explain why contribution margin dropped from the planned $54,000 to $52,350. Notice that Products A and B have high contribution margins per unit, while the more popular products, C and D, have rather low margins.

Figure 9.4 presents the sales, costs, and contribution margin variances. Actual results are at the left with variances from budget presented in sequence as calculated. Budgeted amounts are on the right. Favorable variances are indicated with a *F*, and unfavorable variances are indicated with a *U*.

## Sales Variance Analysis

In any sales analysis, only three changes can cause actual and budgeted sales to differ. These are:

**1.** Prices can be higher or lower than expected.

**2.** The quantity of total units sold can be higher or lower than expected.

**3.** The mix of products sold can be different from the planned mix of sales.

| Products | *Budgeted* | | | | *Actual* | | | |
|---|---|---|---|---|---|---|---|---|
| | Units | Mix | Price | Cost | Units | Mix | Price | Cost |
| A | 1,000 | 10.0% | $30 | $18 | 1,200 | 11.76% | $28 | $17.50 |
| B | 2,000 | 20.0 | 20 | 10 | 1,500 | 14.71 | 25 | 11.00 |
| C | 3,000 | 30.0 | 10 | 8 | 3,000 | 29.41 | 11 | 8.50 |
| D | 4,000 | 40.0 | 15 | 11 | 4,500 | 44.12 | 14 | 11.50 |
| Total quantity | 10,000 | 100.0% | | | 10,200 | 100.00% | | |

| Products | Budgeted Contribution Margin | Actual Contribution Margin |
|---|---|---|
| A | 1,000 × ($30 − $18) = $12,000 | 1,200 × ($28 − $17.50) = $12,600 |
| B | 2,000 × ($20 − $10) =  20,000 | 1,500 × ($25 − $11.00) =  21,000 |
| C | 3,000 × ($10 − $ 8) =   6,000 | 3,000 × ($11 − $ 8.50) =   7,500 |
| D | 4,000 × ($15 − $11) =  16,000 | 4,500 × ($14 − $11.50) = $11,250 |
| Total margin | $54,000 | $52,350 |

**FIGURE 9.3**

Product Line Quantity, Price, and Variable Cost Data

**Sales Variances:**

| Product | Actual Sales | Price Variances | Adjusted Sales $M_a \times Q_a \times P_b$ | Quantity Variances | Adjusted Sales $M_a \times Q_b \times P_b$ | Mix Variances | Budgeted Revenue |
|---------|-------------|-----------------|-------------------------------------------|--------------------|-------------------------------------------|---------------|------------------|
| A | $ 33,600 | $ 2,400 U | $ 36,000 | $ 706 F | $ 35,294 | $5,294 F | $ 30,000 |
| B | 37,500 | 7,500 F | 30,000 | 588 F | 29,412 | 10,588 U | 40,000 |
| C | 33,000 | 3,000 F | 30,000 | 588 F | 29,412 | 588 U | 30,000 |
| D | 63,000 | 4,500 U | 67,500 | 1,324 F | 66,176 | 6,176 F | 60,000 |
| Totals | $167,100 | $ 3,600 F | $163,500 | $3,206 F | $160,294 | $ 294 F | $160,000 |

**Cost Variances:**

| Product | Actual Costs | Purchase Price Variances | Adjusted Costs $M_a \times Q_a \times C_b$ | Quantity Variances | Adjusted Costs $M_a \times Q_b \times C_b$ | Mix Variances | Budgeted Costs |
|---------|-------------|--------------------------|-------------------------------------------|--------------------|-------------------------------------------|---------------|----------------|
| A | $ 21,000 | $ 600 F | $ 21,600 | $ 424 U | $ 21,176 | $3,176 U | $ 18,000 |
| B | 16,500 | 1,500 U | 15,000 | 294 U | 14,706 | 5,294 F | 20,000 |
| C | 25,500 | 1,500 U | 24,000 | 471 U | 23,529 | 471 F | 24,000 |
| D | 51,750 | 2,250 U | 49,500 | 971 U | 48,529 | 4,529 U | 44,000 |
| Totals | $114,750 | $4,650 U | $110,100 | $2,160 U | $107,940 | $1,940 U | $106,000 |

**Contribution Margin Variances:**

| Product | Actual Contribution Margin | Price Variances | Adjusted Margin $M_a \times Q_a \times (P_b - C_b)$ | Quantity Variances | Adjusted Margin $M_a \times Q_b \times (P_b - C_b)$ | Mix Variances | Budgeted Contribution Margin |
|---------|---------------------------|-----------------|----------------------------------------------------|--------------------|----------------------------------------------------|---------------|------------------------------|
| A | $ 12,600 | $ 1,800 U | $ 14,400 | 282 F | $ 14,118 | $ 2,118 F | $ 12,000 |
| B | 21,000 | 6,000 F | 15,000 | 294 F | 14,706 | 5,294 U | 20,000 |
| C | 7,500 | 1,500 F | 6,000 | 117 F | 5,883 | 117 U | 6,000 |
| D | 11,250 | 6,750 U | 18,000 | 353 F | 17,647 | 1,647 F | 16,000 |
| Totals | $ 52,350 | $ 1,050 U | $ 53,400 | $ 1,046 F | $ 52,354 | $ 1,646 U | $ 54,000 |

**FIGURE 9.4**

Contribution Margin Variance Analysis–An Example

The analytical task separates the single difference in sales into three variances—price, quantity, and mix. Figure 9.5 presents the framework for calculating these variances. Actual sales is an array of product prices (P) times the total quantity of units (Q) times an array of mix percentages (M).

As shown in Figure 9.5, each variance is the difference found by changing one variable at a time from actual to budget. The subscripts indicate actual ($_a$) or budget ($_b$). Typically, the analysis runs from actual back to budget. One variance is found at each step. Any sequence of variance calculations could be used, but the most common is price, quantity, and finally mix. Remember that price is the first variance calculated in standard costing in Chapter 8.

| | | | |
|---|---|---|---|
| Actual: | Actual sales | $P_a \times Q_a \times M_a$ | Sales price variances |
| Step 1: | Use budgeted prices | $P_b \times Q_a \times M_a$ | Sales quantity variances |
| Step 2: | Use budgeted Quantity | $P_b \times Q_b \times M_a$ | Sales mix variances |
| Step 3: | Use budgeted sales | $P_b \times Q_b \times M_b$ | |

**FIGURE 9.5**

Matrix for Calculating Sales Price, Quantity, and Mix Variances

Let us follow Product A through the calculation sequence. Actual sales are $33,600 from selling 1,200 units (11.76 percent of total unit quantity of 10,200 units) at $28 per unit. A price cut apparently generated more volume.

**Sales Price Variances.** The **sales price variance** is the difference between actual and budgeted sales caused by price changes. From Step 1 in Figure 9.5, the sales price variance is computed as: $(P_a - P_b) \times Q_a \times M_a$. For all products, an additional $3,600 in sales was earned from price differences. For Product A, sales dollars decreased by $2,400 [($28 - $30) \times 10,200 \times (1,200 \div 310,200) = $2,400]. The variance is the difference between the actual and the budgeted price per unit, using actual total quantity and mix percentages.

**Sales Quantity Variance.** The **sales quantity variance** is important for the total product line but not very meaningful for individual products. The impact of total quantity increases or decreases is analyzed by the quantity variance. The variance is the difference between actual and budgeted total units, using budgeted prices and actual mix percentages. From Step 2 of Figure 9.5, the formula is: $P_b \times (Q_a - Q_b) \times M_a$. Broken down for Product A, it is: $30 \times (10,200 – 10,000) \times (1,200 10,200) = $706. The total sales quantity variance for all four products is $3,206, which is the weighted-average revenue per unit (apparently $16.03) multiplied by the sale of an additional 200 units (10,200 – 10,000).

**Sales Mix Variances.** The **sales mix variance** measures the change in each product's portion of total sales. The mix variance measures the impacts of fast and slow selling products. The variance is the difference between the actual and budgeted mix percentages, using budgeted prices and total quantity. Using Step 3 of Figure 9.5, the formula is: $P_b \times Q_b \times (M_a - M_b)$. From Figure 9.3, the sales mix variance for Product A is calculated as follows: $30 \times 10,000 \times [(1,200 \div 10,200) - (1,000 \div 10,000)] = $5,294. This is Product A's increased portion of total unit sales. Notice that some products increased and others decreased, a normal situation. Did high-priced products increase or decrease relative to lower-priced products? The small positive sales mix variance of $294 implies that a slight shift to higher-priced products occurred.

The three sales variances must be viewed together. A drawback is the fact that one product's changes can impact the others' variances. A large sales jump for Product A will cause quantity and mix variances for the other products. Thus, quantity and mix variances must be interpreted carefully.

**Single Product Variances.** In single product situations, the mix variance disappears; and only sales price and quantity variances are calculated. The same formulation in Figure 9.5 is used but without the mix component.

## Product Cost Variance Analysis

In any product cost analysis, only three changes can cause actual product variable cost of sales to differ from budgeted costs. These are:

1. Variable product costs can be higher or lower than expected.
2. The quantity of total units sold can be higher or lower than expected.
3. The mix of products sold can be different from the planned mix of sales.

The causes of product cost and sales variances are similar. In fact, sales and cost quantity and mix variances will have the same direction and magnitude. The sales price and cost performance or purchase price variances are independent. Figure 9.6 shows that the sequence of calculation is cost performance variances, to total quantity variance, and finally to product mix variance. The data are from Figure 9.3, and the variances are shown in Figure 9.4. Let us follow Product A through the calculation sequence.

| | | |
|---|---|---|
| Actual: Actual product costs | $C_a \times Q_a \times M_a$ | Cost purchase price variances or |
| Step 1: Use budgeted unit costs | $C_b \times Q_a \times M_a$ | Cost performance variances |
| Step 2: Use budgeted quantity | $C_b \times Q_b \times M_a$ | Cost quantity variances |
| Step 3: Use budgeted product costs | $C_b \times Q_b \times M_b$ | Cost mix variances |

FIGURE **9.6**

Matrix for Calculating Cost Performance, Quantity, and Mix Variances

**Cost Performance or Purchase Price Variances.** The **cost performance variances** here are the same variable standard cost variances discussed in Chapter 8. This variance could also be a **purchase price variance** if the firm purchases its products, as does Vistavia Wholesalers in this example. The difference between the budgeted, or standard, unit cost of $18 for Product A and the actual unit cost of $17.50 is $0.50 per unit. In manufacturing, the $0.50 per unit variance is the sum of the materials, direct labor, and variable overhead variances. From Step 1 in Figure 9.6, the purchase price variance is computed as: $(C_a - C_b) \times Q_a \times M_a$. For all products, additional costs of $4,650 were incurred from unit cost differences. For Product A, costs decreased by $600 [($18 − $17.50) × 10,200 × (1,200 ÷ 10,200) = $600].

If the firm is a manufacturer and has a standard costing system, cost performance variances are identified and recorded in the factory. Products are inventoried at standard costs, and no cost performance variances will appear here.

Also, remember cost variances are based on units produced, while contribution margin variances are based on units sold. Changes in inventory levels will require adjustments to equate the two sets of variances.

**Cost Quantity Variance.** The **cost quantity variance** is a mirror image of the sales quantity variance. While the total quantity variance is important, variances for specific products are of little significance. The variance is the difference between actual and budgeted total quantity, using budgeted unit costs and actual mix percentages. From Step 2 of Figure 9.6, the formula is: $C_b \times (Q_a - Q_b) \times M_a$. Broken down for Product A, it is: $18 × (10,200 − 10,000) × (1,200 ÷ 10,200) = $424. The total cost quantity variance for all four products is $2,160.

**Cost Mix Variances.** The **cost mix variances** are also mirror images of the sales mix variances. The cost mix variance measures the impacts of faster and slower selling products on total variable costs. The variance is the difference between the actual and budgeted mix percentages, using budgeted unit costs and total quantity. Using Step 3 of Figure 9.6, the formula is: $C_b \times Q_b \times (M_a - M_b)$. From Figure 9.3, the cost mix variance for Product A is calculated as follows: $18 × 10,000 × [(1,200 ÷ 10,200) − (1,000 ÷ 10,000)] = $3,176.

The three product cost variances sum to the difference between total actual and total budgeted costs. As with the sales variances, product cost variances must be analyzed individually and together and with the sales variances.

## Contribution Margin Variances—Bringing Together Sales and Product Costs

By combining the sales and cost variances, changes in contribution margin can be seen. Figure 9.4 concludes with the summed sales and cost variances.

Many interrelationships can be examined. For Product A, Vistavia Wholesalers apparently reduced the price to increase volume. Combined with a cost per unit reduction, contribution margin increased by $600. Similar impacts arose from the opposite actions with Product B—higher price, lower volume, and higher cost per unit. Product B's actions earned a $1,000 higher contribution margin. Product C's higher price had a no impact on volume. But Product D experienced a serious drop in contribution margin per unit, from $4 to $2.50 per unit, because of price and cost changes. The positive changes in Products A, B, and C were overwhelmed by the contribution margin loss from Product D.

## Calculation Issues

In any multiple-variance situation, the calculation order issue arises. We have used the price, quantity, and mix sequence. Other sequences produce different variances, but the magnitude (large or small) and the direction (positive or negative) rarely change. It is worthwhile to note that these analyses focus on magnitude and direction and not on precision.

Moving from actual to budget, or vice versa, and having the three variances add to 100 percent of the total variance are intuitively appealing. Other approaches are occasionally used in the real world. For example, the Security and Exchange Commission requires financial institutions to file an interest margin variance report that uses the base period (last year) as the starting point for calculating each variance. The sum of the individual variances does not equal the total variance. Any residual is allocated to the other variances, but that's government regulation.

## Variable Operating Expense Variances

From Figure 9.1, the next step is to evaluate performance of variable operating expenses. Since these expenses vary with sales activities, their expense budgets are based on expected activity levels. A flexible budget is the best approach to build the budget and to evaluate performance. The discussion of flexible budgeting in Chapter 7 focused on determining the relationships among activities, resource use, and costs—the cost function.

Any variable operating expenses that can be traced to specific products should be analyzed as part of the product cost variance analyses discussed previously. ABC techniques can identify these direct relationships. Differences between actual and budgeted expense levels would appear in the cost performance variance section as spending variances. An example of these expenses might be commissions paid as a percentage of revenue or of contribution margin.

In comparing actual performance to budget, variable expenses are adjusted to the actual activity level. As an example, a cost function for Leff's Package Transfer Service is $4 per delivery.

## Contemporary Practice 9.1
### Menu Engineering: Restaurant Contribution Margins

A restaurant's revenues can be viewed as a sales mix of individual menu items, categories of offerings (e.g., appetizers, entrees), and meal periods or categories (e.g., breakfast, banquets). Variable costs of foods and other direct expenses can be subtracted to find contribution margin per item. A contribution margin per seat per hour could be determined. High and low performers can be identified to help decide which items should be dropped, added, repriced, or reconfigured. A 1992 survey of over 100 restaurants showed that 72 percent broke down their costs into variable and fixed. And, 55 percent used a direct cost approach for menu items, which is the basis for contribution margin analysis.

Source: Bayou, M. E., and L. E. Bennett, "Profitability Analysis for Table-Service Restaurants," Cornell Hotel and Restaurant Administration Quarterly, April 1992, pp. 49–55.

If expected activity were 4,000 transfers, the variable expense budget would be $16,000. But if 4,200 transfers were performed and $17,000 were spent, variances could be identified as follows:

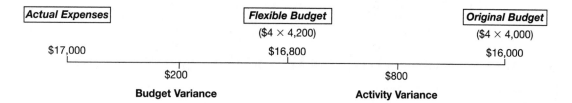

The budget variance is unfavorable. The activity variance reflects the difference between planned and actual activity, in this case an actual higher spending level—viewed as unfavorable. The responsible manager is allowed to spend $800 more than the original budget because of the higher activity, but that amount plus an additional $200 were spent.

In certain situations, the budget variance can be separated into price and usage variances. A brief example illustrates this concept. Wooly Jumbuck Department Store operates a gift wrapping department. The departmental variable operating expense budget is developed around an estimate of parcels wrapped, which is forecast based on total sales quantity of the store. Two variable expense items are wrapping materials and wages of associates (employees).

| | Actual Results | Flexible Budget | Original Budget | Price Variance | Usage Variance | Budget Variance | Activity Variance |
|---|---|---|---|---|---|---|---|
| Parcels wrapped | 1,020 | 1,020 | 1,000 | | | | |
| Hours worked<br>Budget: 10 parcels per hour | 110 | 102 | 100 | | | | |
| Yards of wrapping paper<br>Budget: 1 yard per parcel | 980 | 1,020 | 1,000 | | | | |
| Associates wages<br>Budget: $8 per hour worked | $ 850 | $ 816 | $ 800 | $30 F | $64 U | $34 U | $16 U |
| Cost of wrapping paper used.<br>Budget: $1 per parcel | $1,010 | $1,020 | $1,000 | $30 U | $40 F | $10 F | $20 U |

Associates wage price variance is calculated as: ($8 × 110) − $850 = $30 favorable. The usage variance is: $880 − $816 = $64 unfavorable. The associates worked slower than expected (used more labor), but the average wage is lower than budgeted. The wrapping paper variances are found similarly. The paper price variance is: ($1 × 980) − $1,010 = $30 unfavorable. The paper usage variance is: (1,020 − 980) × $1 = $40 favorable. Wrapping paper costs are higher than budgeted, but they used less paper than expected.

## GROSS MARGIN VARIANCES

In Figure 9.2, gross margin variances appear in place of contribution margin variances. The main difference is where product fixed overhead costs are analyzed. If Vistavia Wholesalers manufactured its products and used the gross margin approach, fixed manufacturing product costs would be included in the product cost variances. Thus, performance cost variances include the fixed overhead budget and volume variances in addition to materials, labor, and variable overhead variances. Calculations based on Figure 9.3 data and outlined in Figures 9.5 and 9.6 are the same under both versions.

In many sales organizations, the terms contribution margin and gross margin are used interchangeably. In manufacturing, the two approaches differ because of fixed overhead. In sales organizations, other variable operating expenses may be included in contribution margin analysis.

## USES AND LIMITS OF CONTRIBUTION MARGIN AND GROSS MARGIN VARIANCE ANALYSIS

Margin variance analyses identify reasons for change in performance. They are predominately sales tools. Sales managers are typically responsible for increases or decreases in sales quantities and shifts in sales mix. Uses of variance analysis include:

- Planning pricing strategies to set optimal prices and volume forecasts.
- Planning interrelationships among products to find complementary effects (Higher sales of one product generates higher sales of another product.) and substitution effects (Higher sales of one product causes lower sales of another product.).
- After-the-fact analysis of actual results for comparison to budgets.
- Analysis of changes from period to period.

Linking contribution margin variances and standard costing variances developed in Chapter 8 gives managers powerful tools for analyzing market and manufacturing environments.

Unfortunately, these analyses identify variances, but answers must be assembled from the parts presented. In the real world, a skilled manager can review a profit margin variance report in a few minutes and be prepared to ask penetrating questions about results and operations.

One problem with quantity and mix variances is the impacts a change in one product's volume has on other products' variances. For example, if one product's sales units double, the other unchanged products will show unfavorable mix and favorable quantity variances, as did Product C in the Vistavia Wholesalers example.

## FIXED COST VARIANCE ANALYSES–MANUFACTURING AND OPERATING EXPENSES

Because of the nature of fixed costs, variance analysis is often an actual versus budget comparison. Under flexible budgeting, fixed costs remain constant. Fixed is fixed. Therefore, the analysis merely identifies a variance from budget. Many fixed costs are planned using a **static budget**, which is oblivious to volume or activity changes. The budgeted amount is the expected spending level. Any variation from that amount is a budget variance.

In prior chapters, we discussed creating cost functions, applying fixed costs to products, budgeting fixed product costs, and analyzing fixed overhead variances. We linked a cost's behavior, activities, and resource use. Fixed operating expenses include fixed costs of engineering, administration, distribution, marketing, and many staff functions.

Managing fixed cost budget variances can be challenging. If a cost is fixed, why did we spend more than budgeted? Many fixed costs are fixed only over a narrow relevant range, are largely fixed but contain a small variable element, or are a variety of expenses that together appear fixed but have numerous cost behavior patterns. Fixed cost budget variances may require careful followup analyses.

## Activity-Based Cost Analysis

Planning and controlling fixed expenses are related to management activities in each responsibility center. Variances are primarily spending, but activity factors come into play because of the diversity involved. In ABC applications, all variances are activity based or spending based. Thus, fixed costs in a product output sense may really be variable if linked to other activity bases.

If activity-based costing is applied to nonproduction areas, certain fixed costs may also become variable, linked to their respective activity bases. For example, many data processing operations collect activity data, particularly for certain on-line applications such as inventory systems and customer databases. In fact, data processing costs are often "billed" to users to reassign costs to departments using the data processing resources. These "transfer prices" are based on planned volumes and costs. A comparison of costs transferred to actual costs is one measure of operating performance. Such systems are also used for maintenance, training, and multimedia departments.

By relating costs to activities in staff and support service areas, cost management is exercised. Detailed costs can highlight expensive activities and processes that add little or no value. Improvement goals can be linked to cost functions from ABC. Process reengineering can change the way work is done and improve cost efficiency and productivity measures.

## Use of Benchmarking

Many nonproducing areas need a basis for evaluation. World-class manufacturing comparisons can be paralleled in nonmanufacturing units. This is called **benchmarking**. In accounting areas, the cost of processing a payment to a vendor can be measured by activity-based costing. That cost can be compared to other units within the company or, more likely, to world-class operators. Networks of companies willing to share benchmarking data are growing rapidly.

Benchmarking in many areas has been going on for years through trade and industry association work. Sharing operating data along with financial statement information can help firms create a "peer group" for comparing operating methods, expenses, and improvement factors. Peers should be selected carefully to represent high-quality performances and challenges for improvement.

As an example, Rousso Enterprises, an internet service provider, is attempting to get better control over customer inquiries. The firm uses an ABC system to find the cost of servicing customer

## Contemporary Practice 9.2
### Benchmarking at a Leasing and Fleet Management Company

"A leasing and fleet management company made site visits to Federal Express, an emergency (911) operation, a travel agent, an bank, a mortgage company, and a brokerage firm to get a sense of where they stacked up against these wildly disparate organizations in such areas as vendor partnering, interactive remote order entry, electronic data interchange (EDI), payment of production, electronic funds transfer (EFT), and knowledge-based systems/client-server systems."

Source: Walther, T., Johansson, H., Dunleavy, J., and Hjelm, E., Reinventing the CFO, McGraw Hill: New York, 1997, p. 109.

calls. Through an information sharing arrangement, monthly cost data from three other firms are compared to Rousso data over several years as follows:

| | 2003 Costs | 2004 Costs | 2005 Actual Costs | 2005 Budgeted Costs | Peer Firm A | Peer Firm B | Peer Firm C |
|---|---|---|---|---|---|---|---|
| Inquiries per month | 1,120 | 1,322 | 1,954 | 1,800 | 5,000 | 1,200 | 7,500 |
| Customer inquiry costs | $6,455 | $6,835 | $10,004 | $9,000 | $16,400 | $5,300 | $29,500 |
| Cost per inquiry | $5.76 | $5.17 | $5.12 | $5.00 | $3.28 | $4.42 | $3.93 |

"World-class performers" are ahead of Rousso Enterprises. Care must be taken to have comparable work requirements, cost pools, and activities. Growth in activity levels may be causing Rousso Enterprises' inability to meet the budgeted cost per inquiry goal in 2005. Yet, the peer data indicate that potential for significant cost reductions exists.

# VARIABLE COSTING

**Variable costing** (also known as **direct costing**) is an approach to product costing that assigns only variable manufacturing costs (direct materials, direct labor, and variable factory overhead) to items produced. Thus, inventoriable costs are limited to the variable manufacturing costs; and period costs include all fixed costs and variable nonmanufacturing costs. **Absorption costing**, the method typically used for external income statement reporting, allocates all manufacturing costs (variable and fixed) to products. This section compares these two costing methods.

Variable costing, like absorption costing, can be used in conjunction with actual, normal, or standard costing systems. For simplicity, we will restrict our discussion in this chapter to situations in which actual costing is used.

## Characteristics of Variable Costing

The two costing methods vary as to the cost elements for product costs, the difference in inventory values, and the difference in profits. These differences all result from one basic item–the treatment of fixed manufacturing costs. Absorption costing includes these costs in product costs while variable costing considers them as period costs to be included with the operating expenses. The following summary contrasts the two costing approaches:

| Cost Category | Variable Costing | Absorption Costing |
|---|---|---|
| Direct materials | Product | Product |
| Direct labor | Product | Product |
| Variable factory overhead | Product | Product |
| Fixed factory overhead | Period | Product |
| Marketing expenses | Period | Period |
| Administrative expenses | Period | Period |

Variable costing typically uses a contribution margin approach as a reporting format. Variable marketing and administrative costs are included in the computation of the contribution margin. However, variable marketing and administrative costs are not product costs.

Selecting variable costing or absorption costing has an impact on inventory values and profits because of the variation in the treatment of fixed factory overhead. Although the profit can differ between the two costing methods, profit under variable costing is not always higher or lower than absorption costing. The difference between profits under the two methods is determined by the relationship of production to sales. Assuming that the fixed manufacturing costs per unit remain the same from one period to the next, we have three possibilities, as follows:

|  | Net Income |
| --- | --- |
| Production units equal sales units | AC = VC |
| Production units greater than sales units (building inventory) | AC > VC |
| Production units less than sales units (liquidating inventory) | AC < VC |
| AC = Absorption costing | VC = Variable costing |

The magnitude of any difference in profits is a function of the fixed manufacturing costs per unit and the changes in inventory levels, as we shall discuss later.

## Comparing Variable Costing and Absorption Costing

Let's assume that Morris the Florist sells one type of floral arrangement. In its first year, 2007, Morris the Florist produced 100,000 arrangements and sold 75,000 at $25 each. The costs for the year are:

| Production costs (per unit): | |
| --- | --- |
| Materials | $3.00 |
| Labor | 8.00 |
| Variable overhead | 5.00 |
| Fixed overhead ($200,000/100,000 units) | 2.00 |
| Marketing and administrative costs: | |
| Variable | $1.00 per unit sold |
| Fixed | $150,000 |

The absorption costing income statement that reflects these results is as follows:

### Absorption Costing Income Statement
### For the Year Ended December 31, 2007

| | | |
| --- | --- | --- |
| Sales revenue ($25 × 75,000) | | $1,875,000 |
| Cost of sales: | | |
| Variable ($16 × 75,000) | $1,200,000 | |
| Fixed ($2 × 75,000) | 150,000 | 1,350,000 |
| Gross profit | | $ 525,000 |
| Marketing and administrative expenses: | | |
| Variable ($1 × 75,000) | $ 75,000 | |
| Fixed | 150,000 | 225,000 |
| Net profit | | $ 300,000 |

A variable costing income statement would be as follows:

|  | | |
|---|---|---|
| *Variable Costing Income Statement* | | |
| *For the Year Ended December 31, 2007* | | |
| Sales revenue ($25 × 75,000) | | $1,875,000 |
| Variable costs: | | |
| Production ($16 × 75,000) | $1,200,000 | |
| Marketing and administrative ($1 × 75,000) | 75,000 | 1,275,000 |
| Contribution margin | | $  600,000 |
| Fixed costs: | | |
| Production | | $  200,000 |
| Marketing and administrative | 150,000 | 350,000 |
| Net profit | | $  250,000 |

Notice that the variable costing profit is lower than the profit from absorption costing. Why does this happen? The next section answers this question.

## Reconciliation of Variable and Absorption Costing

The difference in net profit figures between absorption costing and variable costing is due solely to the treatment of fixed production costs. Absorption costing includes those costs in the inventory costs; variable costing treats them as expenses to be charged to the period incurred. During any given time period, the amount of fixed costs in inventory will increase or decrease as production differs from sales. If production is greater than sales (as is the case with Morris the Florist in 2007), fixed costs in the ending inventory are deferred to future periods under absorption costing. Alternatively, all fixed costs are expensed under variable costing. Therefore, absorption costing will show a higher net profit. Conversely, if sales are greater than production, fixed costs in the beginning inventory are expensed in the current period and added to the fixed costs incurred during the current period. Therefore, fixed costs in the income statement under absorption costing are higher than under variable costing; and the result is a lower net profit for absorption costing.

In the simplified case in which fixed overhead costs per unit are the same in beginning and ending inventories, the difference in net profits is exactly equal to the change in inventory units times the fixed overhead rate per unit. For Morris the Florist, the change in inventory is:

| Units produced | 100,000 |
|---|---|
| Units sold | 75,000 |
| Increase in inventory | 25,000 |

Using a fixed overhead rate of $2 per unit, the difference in net profits is: $2 × 25,000 units = $50,000. Let's check this result:

| Absorption costing net profit | $ 300,000 |
|---|---|
| Variable costing net profit | 250,000 |
| Difference | $  50,000 |

When the fixed overhead rates are different in beginning and ending inventories, the reconciliation of net profit figures is performed as follows:

|   | Absorption costing net profit |
|---|---|
| + | Fixed overhead in beginning inventory |
| − | Fixed overhead in ending inventory |
| = | Variable costing net profit |

To illustrate, suppose that in 2008, Morris the Florist produces 80,000 floral arrangements and sells 100,000. We will presume the same total fixed costs, unit variable costs, and selling price as in 2007. Morris the Florist uses a FIFO cost flow. As a result, the fixed overhead per unit produced during 2008 is $2.50 ($200,000/80,000).

The 2008 absorption costing income statement would be as follows:

*Absorption Costing Income Statement*
*For the Year Ended December 31, 2008*

| | | |
|---|---:|---:|
| Sales revenue ($25 × 100,000) | | $2,500,000 |
| Cost of sales: | | |
| Variable ($16 × 100,000) | $1,600,000 | |
| Fixed [($2 × 25,000) + ($2.50 × 75,000)] | 237,500 | 1,837,500 |
| Gross profit | | $ 662,500 |
| Marketing and administrative expenses: | | |
| Variable ($1 × 100,000) | $ 100,000 | |
| Fixed | 150,000 | 250,000 |
| Net profit | | $ 412,500 |

Note that the fixed portion of cost of sales is consistent with the FIFO cost flow assumption. The first 25,000 units come from 2007 production, which had a unit cost of $2 for fixed overhead; the remaining 75,000 units come from 2008 production, which had a unit cost of $2.50 for fixed overhead.

The 2008 variable costing income statement would be as follows:

*Variable Costing Income Statement*
*For the Year Ended December 31, 2008*

| | | |
|---|---:|---:|
| Sales revenue ($25 × 100,000) | | $2,500,000 |
| Variable costs: | | |
| Production ($16 × 100,000) | $1,600,000 | |
| Marketing and administrative ($1 × 100,000) | 100,000 | 1,700,000 |
| Contribution margin | | $ 800,000 |
| Fixed costs: | | |
| Manufacturing | $ 200,000 | |
| Marketing and administrative | 150,000 | 350,000 |
| Net profit | | $ 450,000 |

We reconcile the 2008 net profits as follows:

| | | |
|---|---|---:|
| | Absorption costing net profit | $412,500 |
| + | Fixed overhead in beginning inventory ($2 × 25,000) | 50,000 |
| − | Fixed overhead in ending inventory ($2.50 × 5,000) | (12,500) |
| = | Variable costing net profit | $450,000 |

The reconciliation of net profits between the two costing methods is independent of inventory cost flow assumptions. A company can use FIFO, LIFO, or some average cost method; and the reconciliation of net profits follows the same procedures.

Another observation about the difference between the two methods relates to the profit patterns over time with respect to production and sales strategies. Let's consider the case of a constant production schedule over time while sales fluctuate each period. The absorption costing net income will fluctuate up and down with sales, but the constant production will have a leveling effect on the swings. The peaks will not be as high nor as low as the corresponding sales changes. Variable costing net income, on the other hand, will have swings that match those of sales, in both direction and relative magnitude. For the situation where production fluctuates while sales remain rather constant, a different picture appears. Absorption costing net income will fluctuate with production, in both direction and relative magnitude. Variable costing net income will remain constant, corresponding with sales levels.

While absorption and variable costing methods yield different profit figures during periods when units sold do not equal units produced, these are timing differences. If over the course of several time periods, aggregate production equals aggregate sales, then the aggregate profits will be the same for both costing methods despite differences in profits during specific periods.

## Arguments for Either Costing Method

Neither variable costing nor absorption costing is correct or incorrect. Their usefulness correlates with management's attitudes and with philosophies of organizational behavior. Some companies will find variable costing extremely useful, while other companies will find it less meaningful. Any manager can make a valid case for either variable or absorption costing. The primary arguments, for and against, are discussed next.

**Short Term Versus Long Term**. Those who favor variable costing (We call them the "variable costers.") believe it focuses on the short-term consequences of accounting and is more realistic of the way managers make decisions. Those who favor absorption costing (We call them the "absorption costers.") assume that long-run performance is more important and that absorption costing more appropriately reflects long-term consequences.

**Unethical Behavior By Managers**. Variable costers assume that managers can easily adapt to a new accounting method with little additional cost. They further argue that managers will be rewarded for playing games with absorption costing reports. They specifically refer to a manager's ability to manipulate net profit by increasing or decreasing inventory levels that are valued under

---

### Contemporary Practice 9.3
### *Earnings Manipulation with Absorption Costing*

*An experiment with individuals in graduate and executive education managerial accounting classes, who averaged about six years of full-time work experience, tested whether they would manipulate earnings in an absorption costing setting. Specifically, unit costs could be lowered by merely producing unneeded units. This would lower cost of goods sold, and in turn, increase the*

*reported profit. The study estimated that about 51 percent of the participants would intentionally overproduce in order to meet a targeted pretax income figure.*

*Source: Schneider, A., "Ethical Decision Making on Various Managerial Accounting Issues,"* Journal of Applied Management Accounting Research, *Summer 2004, pp. 29–39.*

## Contemporary Practice 9.4
### Income Reporting at Northern Telecom

Northern Telecom uses a variable costing P&L (i.e., income statement) for internal purposes, while reporting on an absorption basis for statutory and regulatory purposes. To reconcile the two, Northern Telecom created a new line item at the bottom of its variable costing P&L, known as the "Balance Sheet Adjustment." This became the repository for all reconciling accounting adjustments between the absorption costing P&L and the variable costing P&L. "Through this mechanism, Northern Telecom was able to satisfy the needs of both the outside world and its managers."

Source: Sharman, P., "Time to Re-examine the P&L," CMA Magazine, September 1991, p. 25.

absorption costing. The absorption costers admit that occasional short-term decisions (e.g., amount of ending inventory to hold) will be made incorrectly. However, over the long term, the mistakes will be more obvious, and the "games" will be discovered by competent superiors. Absorption costers might assert that unethical managers cannot be suddenly rehabilitated by a change in accounting methods.

**Variable Versus Fixed Costs.** Variable costers believe that costs can be easily and meaningfully divided into variable and fixed categories and that using a contribution margin is much more useful for planning and decision making and for control and performance evaluation. Since absorption costing is primarily for external reporting purposes, absorption costers do not see this distinction as meaningful for reports. They will also argue that managers can still make the cost behavior distinctions for internal purposes. They also point out that the variable/fixed split is not easily made in practice.

**External Versus Internal Reports.** Financial statement reporting using generally accepted accounting principles, as well as tax reporting for the Internal Revenue Service, require absorption costing. Variable costers argue that allowing external reporting requirements to dominate how useful and meaningful information should be reported is not a valid philosophy for competent management. Since information should be geared to the needs of management, external requirements should not drive the internal accounting system. Absorption costers argue that to have one set of requirements for external reporting and another set for internal reporting gives managers conflicting and inconsistent information. It also forges an image that the company is hiding something in the two approaches.

## Effects of New Manufacturing Environments

Since the major variation between the two methods is the treatment of fixed costs as product or period costs, the difference in net profits disappears when little or no inventory of work in process or finished goods exists. For companies implementing JIT production procedures, inventories will be eliminated or substantially reduced. Hence, the particular costing method chosen loses significance in this environment. Also, this controversy is irrelevant to service organizations which do not carry inventories.

In automated production environments, whether JIT or not, the bulk of labor and factory overhead costs is fixed. Variable costs represent a low percentage of total manufacturing costs. In these environments, therefore, variable costing loses much of its appeal because the product cost will be a small fraction of the total manufacturing cost.

## SUMMARY

The analyses of income statement variances can identify the sources of the difference between planned net income and actual net income. This difference can be broken into sales, product cost, and variable and fixed operating variances. Each of these variances can be subdivided into more detailed variances to point to causes. The sales variance is the sum of the sales price, quantity, and mix variances. In a parallel analysis, the product cost variance is the sum of cost performance or purchase price, quantity, and mix variances. Together the sales and product cost variances explain the variation in contribution margin or gross margin. Similar analyses compare plan and actual for operating expenses.

Variable costing includes only variable manufacturing costs as an element of product cost. The traditional method of income statement preparation is called absorption costing. It includes fixed manufacturing costs as an element of product cost. As a result of this difference, net profit under the two methods will not necessarily be the same. Anytime production exceeds sales, absorption costing yields a higher net profit; when sales exceeds production, variable costing yields a higher net profit. The arguments for and against using either costing method apply to individual situations and management philosophy. Neither method is inherently correct or incorrect.

## PROBLEMS FOR REVIEW

### Review Problem A

The Safe Bank provided the following information about its 2007 and 2008 earning assets and interest-paying liabilities:

| ($ millions) | 2007 Results Average Balance | 2007 Results Mix Percentage | 2007 Results Interest Amount | 2007 Results Interest Rate | 2008 Results Average Balance | 2008 Results Mix Percentage | 2008 Results Interest Amount | 2008 Results Interest Rate |
|---|---|---|---|---|---|---|---|---|
| Assets: | | | | | | | | |
| Short-term investments | $ 1,000 | 10.0% | $ 40 | 4.0% | $ 1,500 | 12.5% | $ 51 | 3.4% |
| Long-term investments | 2,000 | 20.0 | 100 | 5.0 | 1,800 | 15.0 | 81 | 4.5 |
| Commercial loans | 4,000 | 40.0 | 400 | 10.0 | 4,500 | 37.5 | 414 | 9.2 |
| Consumer loans | 3,000 | 30.0 | 240 | 8.0 | 4,200 | 35.0 | 315 | 7.5 |
| Total | $10,000 | 100.0% | $780 | 7.8% | $12,000 | 100.0% | $861 | 7.2% |
| Liabilities: | | | | | | | | |
| Demand deposits | $ 4,000 | 40.0% | $120 | 3.0% | $ 6,000 | 50.0% | $210 | 3.5% |
| Certificates | 6,000 | 60.0 | 300 | 5.0 | 6,000 | 50.0 | 288 | 4.8 |
| Total | $10,000 | 100.0% | $420 | 4.2% | $12,000 | 100.0% | $498 | 4.2% |
| Interest margin | | | $360 | 3.6% | | | $363 | 3.0% |

**Required:**

Lisa Belinky, president, is depressed about the lack of growth in interest margin in spite of a 20 percent growth in assets. She asks you for an analysis of 2008's interest margin relative to 2007's.

**Solution:**

Among the first steps in the analysis will be to perform an interest margin variance analysis. The format and variances are as follows:

| ($ millions) | 2008 Interest Margin | Rate Variance | Quantity Variance | Mix Variance | 2007 Interest Margin |
|---|---|---|---|---|---|
| Interest income: | | | | | |
| Short-term investments | $ 51 | $ 9 U | $ 10 F | $10 F | $ 40 |
| Long-term investments | 81 | 9 U | 15 F | 25 U | 100 |
| Commercial loans | 414 | 36 U | 75 F | 25 U | 400 |
| Consumer loans | 315 | 21 U | 56 F | 40 F | 240 |
| Total | $861 | $75 U | $156 F | $ 0 | $780 |
| Interest expense: | | | | | |
| Demand deposits | $210 | $30 U | $ 30 U | $30 U | $120 |
| Certificates | 288 | 12 F | 50 U | 50 F | 300 |
| Total | $498 | $18 U | $ 80 U | $20 F | $420 |
| Interest margin | $363 | $93 U | $ 76 F | $20 F | $360 |

As an example of the calculations, short-term investment variances are found as follows (all dollars in millions):

| | | |
|---|---|---|
| Rate variance: | $(0.04 - 0.034) \times (\$12{,}000 \times 0.125)$ | $= \$ 9$ unfavorable |
| Quantity variance: | $0.04 \times (\$10{,}000 - \$12{,}000) \times 0.125$ | $= \$10$ favorable |
| Mix variance: | $0.04 \times \$10{,}000 \times (0.10 - 0.125)$ | $= \$10$ favorable |

The analysis shows that interest rates declined in general. The interest margin line shows that $93 million was lost due to rate changes. Most came from lower earnings on assets. But a big problem was the higher rate paid on demand deposits, a management decision. This drew in an additional $2 billion in deposits, but the bank paid 0.5 percent more in 2008 than in 2007. The bank grew in total in interest margin and earned a net $76 million more from that growth. It did shift its mix of liabilities to a lower cost source of funds (demand deposits) and saved $20 million.

Also, if interest rates are falling in general, the bank may want to be less dependent on certificates of deposit that appear to be longer term. Also, certificates showed a very small decline in interest rates from 5 to 4.8 percent while loans appear to be either variable rate or short term because their rates dropped much more. These are policy and decision questions that Belinky must review.

## Review Problem B

Rita Pollack, the sales manager of Meadowbrook Machine Company, Inc., objects to the accounting procedure in costing the manufactured products. She states that sales were lost from a failure to grant price concessions to customers. By including fixed overhead as a part of product cost, the costs are, of course, higher than they would be under variable costing. As a result, the president is reluctant to authorize sales below the full cost. But at any price above the unit variable cost, Ms. Pollack states that the company can earn additional profits. Furthermore, she believes that the income statements give a false picture by shifting fixed costs from one year to another as a part of inventory cost.

Joe Pearl, the chief financial officer, defends the accounting policy. The objective, he says, is to maintain prices and gain a reputation for quality products at an established price. Too many companies, he continues, have been shortsighted and have spoiled their markets at an established price by granting price concessions merely to increase volume. Profits are not earned until after all costs are covered, and each unit of product should bear a share of the fixed overhead.

The following cost and sales data are given for the past three years:

| Year | Units Produced | Units Sold |
|------|----------------|------------|
| 2007 | 20,000 | 16,000 |
| 2008 | 25,000 | 22,000 |
| 2009 | 25,000 | 30,000 |

No inventories were on hand at the beginning of 2007. The company increased inventories over the three years in anticipation of growth in sales volume. Variable manufacturing cost per unit was constant throughout the three years and appears as:

| | |
|---|---|
| Materials | $140 |
| Labor | 80 |
| Variable overhead | 40 |
| Variable manufacturing cost per unit | $260 |

The fixed factory overhead was $8,750,000 each year. The administrative expenses have averaged $40 per unit sold for variable costs and a total of $750,000 per year for fixed costs. The selling price remained the same throughout the three years at $720 per unit. The company uses a FIFO cost flow.

**Required:**
1. Prepare income statements using absorption costing for each of the three years.
2. Prepare income statements using variable costing for each of the three years.
3. Reconcile the difference in profits between the two statements for each of the three years.

## SOLUTION:

1. Income statements with absorption costing:

### ABSORPTION COSTING INCOME STATEMENT
### FOR THE YEARS 2007, 2008, AND 2009

| | 2007 | 2008 | 2009 |
|---|---|---|---|
| Units sold | 16,000 | 22,000 | 30,000 |
| Units produced | 20,000 | 25,000 | 25,000 |
| Sales | $11,520,000 | $15,840,000 | $21,600,000 |
| Cost of goods sold: | | | |
| Inventory, beginning | $ 0 | $ 2,790,00 | $ 4,270,000 |
| Current production | 13,950,000 | 15,250,000 | 15,250,000 |
| | $13,950,000 | $18,040,000 | $19,520,000 |
| Inventory, ending | 2,790,000 | 4,270,000 | 1,220,000 |
| Cost of goods sold | $11,160,000 | $13,770,000 | $18,300,000 |
| Gross profit | $360,000 | $ 2,070,000 | $ 3,300,000 |
| Administrative expenses: | | | |
| Variable | $ 640,000 | $   880,000 | $ 1,200,000 |
| Fixed | 750,000 | 750,000 | 750,000 |
| Total administrative expenses | $ 1,390,000 | $ 1,630,000 | $ 1,950,000 |
| Net profit (loss) | $ (1,030,000) | $   440,000 | $ 1,350,000 |

**2.** Income statements with variable costing:

### Variable Costing Income Statement
### For the Years 2007, 2008, and 2009

|  | 2007 | 2008 | 2009 |
|---|---|---|---|
| Units sold | 16,000 | 22,000 | 30,000 |
| Units produced | 20,000 | 25,000 | 25,000 |
| Sales | $11,520,000 | $15,840,000 | $21,600,000 |
| Variable cost of goods sold: | | | |
| inventory, beginning | $        0 | $ 1,040,000 | $ 1,820,000 |
| Current production | 5,200,000 | 6,500,000 | 6,500,000 |
|  | $ 5,200,000 | $ 7,540,000 | $ 8,320,000 |
| Inventory, ending | 1,040,000 | 1,820,000 | 520,000 |
| Variable cost of goods sold | $ 4,160,000 | $ 5,720,000 | $ 7,800,000 |
| Administrative expenses: | | | |
| Variable | 640,000 | 880,000 | 1,200,000 |
| Total variable costs | $ 4,800,000 | $ 6,600,000 | $ 9,000,000 |
| Contribution margin | $ 6,720,000 | $ 9,240,000 | $12,600,000 |
| Fixed costs: | | | |
| Manufacturing | $ 8,750,000 | $ 8,750,000 | $ 8,750,000 |
| Administrative | 750,000 | 750,000 | 750,000 |
| Total fixed costs | $ 9,500,000 | $ 9,500,000 | $ 9,500,000 |
| Net profit (loss) | $(2,780,000) | $  (260,000) | $ 3,100,000 |

**3.** Reconciliation of net profits between the two costing methods:

|  | 2007 | 2008 | 2009 |
|---|---|---|---|
| Net profit — absorption costing | $(1,030,000) | $  440,000 | $1,350,000 |
| Add: Fixed costs in beginning inventory | 0 | 1,750,000 | 2,450,000 |
|  | $(1,030,000) | $2,190,000 | $3,800,000 |
| Less: Fixed costs in ending inventory | 1,750,000 | 2,450,000 | 700,000 |
| Net profit — variable costing | $(2,780,000) | $ (260,000) | $3,100,000 |

## TERMINOLOGY REVIEW

**Absorption costing (384)**
**Benchmarking (383)**
**Contribution margin variance analysis (375)**
**Cost mix variance (379)**
**Cost performance variance (379)**
**Cost quantity variance (379)**
**Direct costing (384)**

**Gross margin variance analysis (375)**
**Purchase price variance (379)**
**Sales mix variance (378)**
**Sales price variance (378)**
**Sales quantity variance (378)**
**Static budget (382)**
**Variable costing (384)**

## QUESTIONS FOR REVIEW AND DISCUSSION

1. What are the major causes of actual net income differing from budgeted net income?
2. Using contribution margin analysis in an appliance store:
   (a) What changes could cause February's revenue to be greater than January's revenue?
   (b) What changes could cause February's cost of sales to be greater than January's cost of sales?

3. If a firm has only one product, what changes would contribution margin analysis identify?

4. What are the differences between gross margin and contribution margin analyses?

5. Explain the difference between purchase price variances and cost performance variances.

6. Why would a manager be interested in the variances generated by a contribution margin or gross margin analysis?

7. Explain how a change in mix:
   (a) Can result from price changes.
   (b) Can cause profits to drop even if the same total quantity is sold.
   (c) Will have similar impacts on both the revenues and product costs.

8. Under what conditions can a spending variance be divided into price and quantity variances?

9. Does it matter in what sequence the mix, quantity, and price variances are calculated? Is there a traditional sequence? Will the sequence change the importance of specific variances? Explain.

10. In nonproductive areas, how can benchmarking be used to measure expense control performance?

11. Differentiate between variable costing and absorption costing.

12. Explain whether variable costing or absorption costing will have the higher net profit under each of the following conditions:
    (a) Production equals sales.
    (b) Production exceeds sales.
    (c) Production is less than sales.

13. How is it possible to increase net profit using absorption costing when sales are not increasing?

14. Identify the four major areas of argument for and against variable costing or absorption costing.

15. A company had a highly labor-intensive manufacturing process. Recently it implemented robotics and a number of other technological changes that made the process capital intensive. What impact would this change make on the inventory valuations for variable costing and for absorption costing?

16. How is it possible to show zero profit at a break-even point using variable costing but show a profit using absorption costing?

## EXERCISES

9–1.  **Variance Analysis With A Single Product.** Information for May from the Natalie Corporation controller, Michael Ross, is as follows:

|  | Budget | Actual |
|---|---|---|
| Sales units | 2,500 | 3,000 |
| Sales | $20,000 | $22,500 |
| Cost of sales | 15,000 | 19,500 |
| Gross margin | $ 5,000 | $ 3,000 |

**Required:**
Explain why gross margin declined by $2,000 from the budgeted level.

**9–2. Contribution Margin and Expenses With a Single Product.** Yuma Lamps has a subsidiary in Mexicali, Mexico. The subsidiary is operating under the following approved profit plan for June (in pesos):

| | | |
|---|---|---|
| Sales revenue (24,000 lamps) | | M$528,000 |
| Variable costs: | | |
| Cost of goods | M$312,000 | |
| Variable operating expenses | 24,000 | 336,000 |
| Contribution margin | | M$192,000 |
| Direct fixed costs | | 46,000 |
| Product net profit | | M$146,000 |

Actual operations produced and sold 25,000 units at an average selling price of M$20 per unit. Actual cost of goods equaled M$12.50 per unit, and variable operating expenses were M$28,000. Actual fixed costs were M$50,000.

**Required:**
1. Prepare an income statement that compares budget and actual results.
2. Prepare an analysis that explains the variance in contribution margin. Include the variable operating expenses as part of the variance analysis.
3. Explain why the actual product net profit is not M$146,000.

Service

**9–3. Revenue and Variable Cost Variances.** Emmanuel Ilan is a Las Vegas clergyman who, as an individual contractor, performs two types of wedding services—Bland and Grand. He has provided the following data for the past year:

| | Budgeted Results | | Actual Results | |
|---|---|---|---|---|
| | Bland | Grand | Bland | Grand |
| Number of weddings | 25 | 13 | 24 | 15 |
| Prices | $500 | $390 | $490 | $420 |
| Variablecosts | $125 | $130 | $135 | $165 |

**Required:**
1. Compute the revenue variances for each type of wedding service.
2. Compute the variable cost variances for each type of wedding service.

**9–4. Analysis of Operating Expenses.** Richman Company has marketing and administrative expenses that follow a cost function of $15,000 plus 6 percent of sales. Sales were budgeted at $150,000 for the month. Actual sales were $160,000, and marketing and administrative expenses were $24,000.

**Required:**
Identify all variances possible from the data provided. Which variances are the marketing manager's responsibility? Why?

Service

**9–5. Contribution Margin Analysis.** Falk Auto Cleaners has two services that it provides to its customers. The vice president of operations, Jed Linsider, has provided data from 2007 and 2008, which show the following:

| | 2007 Results | | 2008 Results | |
|---|---|---|---|---|
| | Partial | Complete | Partial | Complete |
| Services provided | 200,000 | 300,000 | 120,000 | 380,000 |
| Sales price per service | $5.00 | $6.00 | $5.50 | $5.90 |
| Variable cost per service | $3.00 | $3.20 | $3.10 | $3.18 |

**Required:**

1. Determine the change in contribution margin between the two years.
2. Analyze the revenue, variable cost, and contribution margin changes.
3. Comment on the changes from 2007 to 2008.

Service

**9–6.    Analysis of Budget versus Actual Results.** Jerry's Wine Garden, a wholesale distributor, sells two items, Cheap and Expensive. Dick Peppy is pleased that the June contribution margin is above budget, but he believes something strange happened as he sold less and made more money. The data are as follows:

|  | Budgeted Results | | | Actual Results | | |
|---|---|---|---|---|---|---|
|  | Cheap | Expensive | Total | Cheap | Expensive | Total |
| Sales units | 240,000 | 120,000 | 360,000 | 250,000 | 100,000 | 350,000 |
| Revenues | $2,400,000 | $2,160,000 | $4,560,000 | $2,750,000 | $1,800,000 | $4,550,000 |
| Variable costs | 1,200,000 | 930,000 | 2,130,000 | 1,350,000 | 750,000 | 2,100,000 |
| Contribution margin | $1,200,000 | $1,230,000 | $2,430,000 | $1,400,000 | $1,050,000 | $2,450,000 |

**Required:**

1. Prepare an analysis of revenues, variable costs, and contribution margin.
2. Explain to Dick Peppy how he could sell less and make more.

Service

**9–7.    Analysis of Performance.** Hampshire Dry Cleaners has an operating expense function of $200,000 plus $1 per garment processed and expects to handle 100,000 garments. Units is the cost driver. Actual fixed costs were $203,000, actual variable costs were $101,000, and 102,000 garments were handled.

**Required:**

How did Hampshire Dry Cleaners perform? Show all variances from budget.

Service

**9–8.    Sales Variances.** Toco Hills Publishing sells four reference books through local bookstores. Salespersons have authority to match competitors' prices and are encouraged to maximize revenues. Following are sales figures for the third quarter of this year and last year.

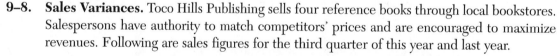

| Reference Books | 3rd Quarter Sales–Last Year | | 3rd Quarter Sales–This Year | |
|---|---|---|---|---|
|  | Units | Price | Units | Price |
| Medical dictionary | 12,000 | $41 | 10,000 | $43 |
| Bible concordance | 20,000 | 20 | 18,000 | 19 |
| Thesaurus | 8,000 | 26 | 9,000 | 25 |
| Global dictionary | 35,000 | 44 | 43,000 | 41 |
| Total quantity | 75,000 | | 80,000 | |

**Required:** Compare last year's revenue to this year's results, and explain the differences.

**9–9.    Comparing Net Incomes.** Joe Carmela & Company started business in 2006 and had the following sales and production experiences:

|  | 2006 | 2007 | 2008 | 2009 | 2010 |
|---|---|---|---|---|---|
| Sales (units) | 1,000 | 1,000 | 1,100 | 1,100 | 1,300 |
| Production (units) | 1,000 | 1,500 | 900 | 1,100 | 1,000 |

Selling price was $2 per unit. Product costs were $1 per unit for all variable costs plus $1,000 for fixed costs. Fixed overhead was applied using 1,000 units as the expected production level each year ($1 per unit). Operating expenses were the same in each year.

**Required:**
Comment on each of the following:
- (a) Net income under variable costing is the same for 2008 and 2009.
- (b) Net income in 2006 is the same for both absorption costing and variable costing.
- (c) The total five-year net income for absorption costing will be greater than the five-year net income for variable costing.
- (d) Under absorption costing, which year will show the highest profit? Why?
- (e) Under variable costing, which year will show the highest profit? Why?
- (f) Why is net income for the two methods different in 2008? Explain in dollars.

Service

**9–10.  Variable and Absorption Costing Unit Costs.** Yu, Li & Goh Bakeries operates several retail bakeries in Kaohsiung, Taiwan. During December, Cheng produced 24,000 breads. Costs incurred by Yu, Li & Goh during December were (in New Taiwanese dollars):

| | |
|---|---:|
| Direct materials | NT$44,000 |
| Direct labor | 17,000 |
| Variable production overhead | 8,000 |
| Variable selling and general | 1,000 |
| Fixed production overhead | 15,000 |
| Fixed selling and general | 19,000 |
| Total | NT$104,000 |

**Required:**
1. Compute the cost of each bread under absorption costing.
2. Compute the cost of each bread under variable costing.

**9–11.  Inventory and Cost of Goods Sold.** Karchava Industries is headquartered in Tbilisi, Republic of Georgia, and has three manufacturing plants near the Black Sea. Nino Aladashvili, the company's cost accountant, reports the following data for October:

| Units: | Beginning inventory | 135,000 |
|---|---|---:|
| | Production | ? |
| | Sales | 250,000 |
| | Ending inventory | 142,000 |
| Costs (in lari): | Beginning inventory | 7,000,000 |
| | Variable manufacturing costs | 19,000,000 |
| | Fixed manufacturing costs | 8,000,000 |
| | Variable selling & administrative costs | 9,000,000 |

**Required:**
1. Compute the unit cost of the inventory produced during October using variable costing.
2. Compute the unit cost of the inventory produced during October using absorption costing.
3. If the company uses absorption costing and assumes a FIFO cost flow, what is the cost of goods sold for October?

**9–12.** **Variable and Absorption Costing Income Statements.** Springhill Lake Products, Inc. started producing and selling a new product. Selected operating results for this new product line for its first year of operations are as follows:

| | |
|---|---:|
| Units: | |
| Produced | 16,000 |
| Sold | 14,500 |
| Sales price per unit | $   12 |
| Variable costs: | |
| Direct materials | $44,000 |
| Direct labor | 36,000 |
| Factory overhead | 16,000 |
| Marketing and administration | 12,000 |
| Fixed costs: | |
| Factory overhead | $40,000 |
| Marketing and administration | 20,000 |

**Required:**
1. Prepare an income statement for the year using the variable costing method.
2. Prepare an income statement for the year using the absorption costing method.
3. Prepare a reconciliation of net profits resulting from the two methods. Comment on the difference in profits.

**9–13.** **Variable Costing.** Nahmias Bee Hives produces honey for sale to various food manufacturers. The income statement for last year, prepared on an absorption costing basis, is as follows:

| | |
|---|---:|
| Number of containers produced and sold | 250,000 |
| Sales revenue | $2,000,000 |
| Cost of goods sold | 1,500,000 |
| Gross profit | $  500,000 |
| Operating expenses (includes variable costs of $125,000) | 225,000 |
| Profit before income taxes | $  275,000 |
| Income taxes | 110,000 |
| Profit after income taxes | $  165,000 |

The fixed production cost per container of honey was $3.00.

**Required:**
Revise the income statement on a variable costing basis.

**9–14.** **Variable Costing and Inventory Increase.** Helfand Logging Company cuts trees and sells the logs to furniture manufacturers. In 2009, the company plans to operate at normal capacity and produce 400,000 logs, as in 2008. Sales for 2009 have been estimated at 350,000 logs with a total revenue of $17,500,000. The cost of the 20,000 logs in the finished goods inventory on January 1, 2009, was $600,000. Included in this amount was $400,000 in fixed production overhead. No changes in fixed production costs are expected in 2009, and the variable cost per log will also remain unchanged.

**Required:**
1. Prepare an estimated income statement for 2009 under absorption costing.
2. Prepare an estimated income statement for 2009 under variable costing.
3. Explain why the income is higher under absorption costing than under variable costing. Your explanation should identify the fixed costs in beginning inventory and in ending inventory.

**9–15.** **Variable Costing and Inventory Decrease.** Gershon Memory Chips reduced its finished goods inventory in 2009 from 80,000 units at the beginning of the year to 50,000 units at the end of the year. Fixed manufacturing overhead of $1,360,000 was incurred, and 170,000 units were produced during the year. The fixed overhead cost per unit was the same as in 2008. Variable manufacturing cost per unit was $9. Each unit of product was sold for $20.

**Required:**

1. Prepare an income statement for the manufacturing operation in 2009 using absorption costing.
2. Prepare an income statement for the manufacturing operation in 2009 using variable costing.
3. Provide a reconciliation for the difference in profit between the two methods. Comment.

## PROBLEMS

Service

**9–16.** **Salespersons Behavior.** Rick Halpern, controller of Kittredge Retail Outlet, has an ear-to-ear smile. He tosses an analysis of last year's gross margin on President Lenny Habif's desk and says a soft "I told you so." Lenny looks up and says, "I hope this is good news; volume is way down from the first half."

Salespersons had been paid 5 percent of sales. At midyear, Rick convinced Lenny to change the commission payment to 10 percent of gross margin. The analysis Rick gave Lenny showed an average budget month, an average month from the first half of last year, and an average month from the second half of last year. All costs are purchase prices. He used the following data:

| | **Budget Month** | | | **Average Month – 1st Half** | | | **Average Month – 2nd Half** | | |
| Products | Price | Cost | Quantity | Price | Cost | Quantity | Price | Cost | Quantity |
| --- | --- | --- | --- | --- | --- | --- | --- | --- | --- |
| Able | $20 | $10 | 10,000 | $18 | $10 | 12,000 | $22 | $10 | 9,000 |
| Baker | 30 | 15 | 10,000 | 25 | 15 | 14,000 | 29 | 15 | 11,000 |
| Charlie | 40 | 20 | 10,000 | 38 | 20 | 11,000 | 43 | 20 | 10,000 |

**Required:**

1. Prepare an analysis similar to the one that Rick probably just gave Lenny, comparing an average actual month from both halves to an average budget month using gross margin variance analysis.
2. Compare the salespersons' commission results for the two time periods relative to the budget.
3. Should Lenny and Rick both be smiling? Comment on the salespersons' behavior.

**9–17.** **Analyzing Results.** J. Pepper Walkie-Talkie markets two models of its main product line. Budgeted and actual results for the year are as follows:

| | **Budget** | **Actual** |
| --- | --- | --- |
| Sales revenue | $1,080,000 | $1,120,850 |
| Cost of sales | 756,000 | 829,445 |
| Gross margin | $ 324,000 | $ 291,405 |
| Operating expenses | 174,000 | 198,000 |
| Net profit | $ 150,000 | $ 93,405 |

| | Budget | | Actual | |
|---|---|---|---|---|
| | NearBy | FarAway | NearBy | FarAway |
| Units sold | 3,000 | 6,000 | 3,200 | 6,300 |
| Selling price per unit | $166.00 | $97.00 | $162.25 | $95.50 |
| Cost of sales per unit | $116.20 | $67.90 | $120.07 | $70.67 |

Operating expenses follow a budget formula of $10 per unit sold plus $84,000.

**Required:**

1. Analyze the change in gross margin.
2. Analyze the change in operating expenses.
3. Identify and comment on the three main reasons for the decline in net profit.

Service

**9–18. Interest Margin Analysis.** Friendly Bank, the friendliest in the East, had a profit plan that showed a $34.8 million interest margin for the year. Results are in. The president, Ann Friendly, called the CFO, Jim Friendly, and asked how the bank could have earned so much more interest margin than expected. She recalls that some rates went up but others went down. She knows growth was higher than expected. Operating expenses were right on target. She plans to share the good news with all the other Friendlys working at the bank (43 at last count); but she needs some answers. Jim hands you the following data and a calculator.

| | Budgeted Results | | | | Actual Results | | | |
|---|---|---|---|---|---|---|---|---|
| | | | Interest | | | | Interest | |
| ($ millions) | Average Balance | Mix Percentage | Amount | Rate | Average Balance | Mix Percentage | Amount | Rate |
| Assets: | | | | | | | | |
| Investments | $300 | 33.3% | $12.0 | 4.0% | $250 | 26.9% | $10.5 | 4.2% |
| Short-term loans | 300 | 33.3 | 27.0 | 9.0 | 400 | 43.0 | 35.6 | 8.9 |
| Long-term loans | 300 | 33.3 | 30.0 | 10.0 | 280 | 30.1 | 26.6 | 9.5 |
| Total | $900 | 100.0% | $69.0 | 7.7% | $930 | 100.0% | $72.7 | 7.8% |
| Liabilities: | | | | | | | | |
| Deposits | $900 | 100.0% | $34.2 | 3.8% | $930 | 100.0% | $37.2 | 4.0% |
| Interest margin | | | $34.8 | 3.9% | | | $35.5 | 3.8% |

**Required:**

Explain how the bank earned $0.7 million more in interest margin than planned. How much of this comes from having more assets than expected?

Service

**9–19. Analyzing Variable Operating Expenses.** Irish Melodies, owned by Pat Flaherty, prepares embroidered sayings and limericks of the customer's choice for mail orders to the U. S. The length of the verses varies, but Pat has decided to charge the same price for verses up to 50 letters. She uses very expensive lace ribbon to do the embroidery. She is analyzing her costs to determine if pricing changes should be made for next year. She hired several aunts and cousins to do the stitchery. Her data show:

| | Actual Results | Original Budget |
|---|---|---|
| Embroidered verses | 250 | 200 |
| Letters embroidered | 8,250 | 6,000 |
| Inches of lace used (budgeted at 8 inches per letter) | 67,650 | 48,000 |
| Cost of lace used (in euros) | 16,024 | 12,000 |

**Required:**

Given the data available, prepare an analysis, in as much detail as possible, to explain the 4,024 euro difference in lace cost. Use variance names that would be appropriate, such as "letter variance."

**9–20.**  **Revenue and Cost Variances.** Hedy Silber Tours arranges and conducts travel tours for retirees in eastern Pennsylvania. Three basic tours are most popular: New York City, Cape Cod, and Williamsburg. Prices and variable costs per person for each tour are:

|  | Prices | Variable Cost |
|---|---|---|
| New York City | $400 | $250 |
| Cape Cod | 350 | 175 |
| Williamsburg | 540 | 360 |

The fixed costs, such as managers' and tour guides' salaries and office rent, have been estimated at $800,000 per year and are allocated to each tour based on the estimated number of customers served. A forecast income statement shows:

|  | New York City | Cape Cod | Williamsburg | Total |
|---|---|---|---|---|
| Number of customers | 6,000 | 1,500 | 2,500 | 10,000 |
| Revenues | $2,400,000 | $525,000 | $1,350,000 | $4,275,000 |
| Total costs | 1,980,000 | 382,500 | 1,100,000 | 3,462,500 |
| Estimated income | $ 420,000 | $142,500 | $ 250,000 | $ 812,500 |

Actual results for the year include $810,000 for fixed costs and are as follows:

|  | New York City | Cape Cod | Williamsburg |
|---|---|---|---|
| Number of customers | 7,000 | 1,000 | 4,000 |
| Price realized | $390 | $330 | $500 |
| Variable cost incurred | $255 | $175 | $350 |

**Required:**

1. Develop comparative income statements on a contribution margin basis for forecast and actual.
2. Explain the variation in contribution margin through variance analysis.
3. Comment on the major reasons for the change in net income for the year.

**9–21.**  **Comprehensive Operating Expense Variance Analysis.** Bauman Computer Programmers provides contract programming services to major corporations. It budgets around programming hours sold (worked). For the third quarter, Bauman budgeted 180,000 hours of sales. An hour is billed at $45 per hour and has a "loaded" cost of $35.50. Bauman's flexible operating expense budget formulas are:

| Administrative salaries | $90,000 | + | $0.04 per hour sold |
|---|---|---|---|
| Sales salaries | 60,000 | + | 0.06 per hour sold |
| Utilities and supplies | 11,500 | + | 0.25 per hour sold |
| Training costs | | | 2.05 per hour sold |
| Depreciation expense | 61,000 | | |
| Property | 2,000 | | |

Actual results for the third quarter showed that 195,000 hours generated revenue of $8,190,000 and programmer costs of $6,630,000. Actual operating costs were:

| | |
|---|---|
| Administrative salaries | $ 96,800 |
| Sales salaries | 73,600 |
| Utilities and supplies | 58,060 |
| Training costs | 415,250 |
| Depreciation | 61,000 |
| Property taxes | 1,850 |

**Required:**
1. Prepare income statements that show the original budget, a flexible budget based on actual hours sold, and actual results.
2. Prepare an analysis of gross margin differences.
3. What type of cost behavior appears in the operating expense spending variances?

**Service**

**9–22. Contribution Margin Analysis.** Danlauren Temps provides temporary employees for general office services. The services are classified as clerical and secretarial. Assignments can be for one day or for several months. Employees are paid based on classification and experience. Steve Berman, the owner, bills clients an average of $15 per hour for clerical time and $20 per hour for secretarial time. Berman pays clerical workers an average of $9 per hour and secretaries an average of $13 per hour. The workers are paid only for hours worked. Wages are the only variable expenses. Danlauren Temps forecasts monthly overhead costs of $35,000.

During November, Danlauren's clerical workers generated 4,400 hours and $63,500 in revenue. Secretarial workers generated 3,600 hours and $73,200 in revenue. Wages and related expenses were $43,122 for clerical workers and $44,565 for secretarial workers. Danlauren's actual November overhead was $36,400.

Danlauren's budget for November showed 4,500 hours and 3,500 hours, respectively, for clerical and secretarial work.

**Required:**
Evaluate November's contribution margin. Using variance analysis, highlight the major causes of November's difference in profits.

**9–23. Variable Costing and Two Product Lines.** Presupuesto Co. manufactures lawn rakes and shovels at its San Juan, Puerto Rico, plant. Data with respect to sales and production have been estimated by Javier Clemente, the controller, for next year as follows:

| | Rakes | Shovels |
|---|---|---|
| Estimated units to be sold | 240,000 | 160,000 |
| Unit selling price | $3.50 | $6.00 |
| Unit variable cost of manufacturing | $1.75 | $2.75 |
| Production time per unit of product | 10 min. | 30 min. |

The fixed factory overhead of the San Juan plant is apportioned to the products at the rate of $3 per production hour. Total corporate fixed overhead of $300,000 has been apportioned to the San Juan plant, but this is not apportioned to the products.

**Required:**

1. Assuming a variable costing approach, prepare an income statement that will show for each product line and in total:

   **(a)** The contribution margin.
   **(b)** The apportioned fixed factory overhead.
   **(c)** The profit for each product.
   **(d)** The final profit after recognizing apportionment of the corporate fixed overhead.

2. What is the expected total unit cost of each product line without apportioning the corporate fixed overhead?

3. Apportion corporate fixed overhead to each product on the basis of production time. Now, what is the expected total unit cost of each product line?

4. Which unit cost number would be best to use in establishing a cost-based selling price? Why?

**9–24.** **Variable and Absorption Costing and Profit at the Break-Even Point.** The president of Robbins Supply Company, Trudy Raymond, is surprised to learn that the company earned a profit in 2008 even though sales were at the break-even point (before considering non-production costs).

Service

"When we were going over the budget for 2008," she said, "I was told that we would have a poor year and could expect to break even with sales of only 206,000 units. Now, I find that we earned a modest pretax profit with sales of 206,000 units, although selling prices and costs were as budgeted. I am not complaining about a profit, mind you, but I can't understand how a profit can be made when operating at the break-even point."

Data pertaining to 2008 are as follows:

| | |
|---|---|
| Unit selling price | $35 |
| Unit variable cost | 20 |
| Unit contribution | $15 |

$$\frac{\$3,090,000 \ (\text{fixed production cost})}{\$15 \ (\text{unit contribution margin})} = 206,000 \text{ units break even}$$

Fixed production costs are applied to products at $10 per unit. The inventory of finished goods was 30,000 units on January 1, 2008, and 133,000 units on December 31, 2008. The marketing and administrative expenses were fixed in the amount of $90,000.

**Required:**

1. Prepare an income statement for 2008 using absorption costing.
2. Prepare an income statement for 2008 using variable costing.
3. Explain to the president how a profit was made when using absorption costing even though sales were at the break-even point.
4. Explain whether the absorption costing income statement or the variable costing income statement gives the more realistic results.

**9–25.** **Conversion of Absorption Costing to Variable Costing.** Yaffe Electrical Supply Company manufactures electric switches and timing devices in three operating divisions: Utility, Household, and Commercial. An income statement, showing the results for each division, is given for 2008. The company had total fixed manufacturing overhead of $8,900,000. Inventories were increased during the year in anticipation of more sales volume in 2009.

**YAFFE ELECTRICAL SUPPLY COMPANY**
**INCOME STATEMENT FOR THE YEAR 2008 (IN THOUSANDS)**

|  | Utility | Household | Commercial | Total |
|---|---|---|---|---|
| Net sales | $6,200 | $5,150 | $6,300 | $17,650 |
| Cost of goods sold: |  |  |  |  |
| Inventory, beginning | $ 540 | $ 240 | $ 150 | $ 930 |
| Production cost | 5,400 | 4,000 | 4,200 | 13,600 |
| Cost of goods available for sale | $5,940 | $4,240 | $4,350 | $14,530 |
| Less inventory, ending | 900 | 640 | 900 | 2,440 |
| Cost of goods sold | $5,040 | $3,600 | $3,450 | $12,090 |
| Manufacturing profit | $1,160 | $1,550 | $2,850 | $ 5,560 |

The plant controller, Jennifer Barry, believes that profits may be higher than they would be otherwise because of fixed costs being carried over to the next year as a part of inventory. She would like to have the statement revised to a variable costing basis and would like to know the manufacturing contribution margin for each division.

Additional analyses show the units and unit variable costs as follows. There are no partially completed units.

|  | Utility | Household | Commercial |
|---|---|---|---|
| Units in beginning inventory | 30,000 | 15,000 | 10,000 |
| Units produced | 300,000 | 250,000 | 280,000 |
| Units in ending inventory | 50,000 | 40,000 | 60,000 |
| Unit variable manufacturing cost | $6 | $6 | $5 |

**Required:**

1. Prepare an income statement on a variable costing basis that shows a contribution margin and direct profits by division and in total.
2. Prepare a reconciliation between the variable costing and absorption costing income statements. This reconciliation should show results by division and in total.
3. How much of the fixed cost was carried over to 2009 as a part of ending inventory cost for each division?

**9–26. Ethics and Creating Profits through Accounting Methods.** Sloan Mining Corporation sells its minerals to various manufacturing companies. Recently, the vice-president of sales, Allan Sadell, gave the bad news to Gerald Ruby, the vice-president of production: "Our sales volume will be 20 percent less than the 400,000 units we mined and sold last year. So, we may as well forget about year-end bonuses."

Ruby smiled and replied, "We'll just pump the inventories up by mining 500,000 units. There is plenty of storage area in the warehouse."

"We'll never get away with it. The president will see what we are doing," Sadell answered.

"No, he knows nothing about accounting. Let me handle it, and we'll still get our bonuses."

A partial income statement for last year is as follows:

| | |
|---|---|
| Net sales | $18,000,000 |
| Cost of goods sold: | |
|     Inventory, January 1 | $ 175,000 |
|     Production cost | 14,000,000 |
|     Cost of goods available for sale | $14,175,000 |
|     Less inventory, December 31 | 175,000 |
|     Cost of goods sold | $14,000,000 |
| Gross profit | $ 4,000,000 |

Product costs for last year included fixed production overhead of $20 per unit. Unit variable costs and total fixed costs are expected to remain the same next year. The company uses a FIFO cost flow.

**Required:**
1. How is Ruby planning to build up the profits?
2. Prepare an estimated income statement for the next year assuming that Sadell's estimate of sales is correct and that 500,000 units are mined. Use absorption costing.
3. Recast last year's partial income statement and the estimated statement for this year on a variable costing basis.
4. Discuss whether Gerald Ruby is behaving in an ethical manner.

**9–27.** **Comparison of Absorption and Variable Costing**. Ripans Frame Factory has just completed its first three years of operation. Gail Ripans, president, has reviewed the audited financial statements for those three years and compared them to the statements her chief accountant, Allen Shaw, prepared for internal use. She questions why the two sets of financial statements have different net income numbers. When asked about this, Shaw responded that the audited statements were prepared using absorption costing and the internal statements using variable costing. Gail still didn't understand why differences in net income would appear. She wants an analysis of the two results.

The selling price and cost data are identical for each of the three years and appear as follows:

| | |
|---|---|
| Selling price per unit | $15.00 |
| Manufacturing costs: | |
|     Direct materials cost per unit | $ 2.80 |
|     Direct labor cost per unit | 4.70 |
|     Variable factory overhead per unit | 0.50 |
|     Fixed factory overhead in total | $120,000 |
| Marketing and administrative expenses: | |
|     Variable | 25% of sales |
|     Fixed | $ 35,000 |

| | Units | |
|---|---|---|
| Year | Production | Sales |
| 2003 | 60,000 | 50,000 |
| 2004 | 60,000 | 55,000 |
| 2005 | 50,000 | 60,000 |

The company uses a FIFO cost flow.

**Required:**

1. Prepare a three-year comparative income statement using absorption costing.
2. Prepare a three-year comparative income statement using variable costing.
3. Reconcile the net income figures of absorption costing and variable costing for each of the three years.
4. Using a graph with sales units on the horizontal axis and dollars (net income) on the vertical axis, plot and connect the following points:
   (a) Net income and sales units assuming absorption costing.
   (b) Net income and sales units assuming the variable costing.
   (c) The difference in net income between the two costing methods and their related sales units.
5. What conclusions can you derive from the graph in Part (4) about the advantages of the variable costing approach?

Service

**9–28.** **Conversion of Absorption Costing to Variable Costing.** Silver Spring Pet Shops purchases a variety of household pets (mostly dogs), as well as breeds their own pets, for sale to customers. The following income statement for July 2008 was prepared by the corporate controller, Kay Nyne, using absorption costing:

| | | |
|---|---:|---:|
| Sales(200 pets) | | $22,000 |
| Cost of sales: | | |
| July 1 inventory | $ 5,000 | |
| Breeding and purchase costs | 10,000 | |
| July 31 inventory | (2,500) | 12,500 |
| Gross Margin | | $ 9,500 |
| Fixed selling and administrative expenses | | (3,700) |
| Operating income | | $ 5,800 |

During 2008, the average unit variable costs have not changed, and fixed "production" overhead has remained at $2,000 per month. During July, 160 pets were either born or purchased by the store owner, Myrna Goldman. Assume that all inventories of pets are "finished"–there is no beginning or ending "work in process."

**Required:**

1. Prepare an income statement for July using variable costing.
2. Reconcile the absorption and variable costing operating incomes.

Service

# CASE 9–MERLIS RANGES

Merlis Ranges operates a chain of pistol shooting ranges in the southwestern U. S. The company rents lanes for shooting and shooters often share lanes. They must wear protective earpieces and protective eyepieces, so Merlis rents these items to them. The following rental data are available for the past two years:

| | Lanes | Ear Muffs | Eye Goggles |
|---|---|---|---|
| 2008 prices | $11.40 | $2.45 | $1.90 |
| 2007 prices | $10.95 | $2.55 | $2.20 |
| 2008 volume | 33,100 | 29,000 | 21,700 |
| 2007 volume | 35,400 | 28,600 | 21,900 |

The company president, Jeff Prince, has just seen the 2008 rental revenue figures and is dismayed that total rental revenues have declined by $19,120 from the previous year. Prince was also concerned about the profits on ammunition ("rounds") sales. Merlis sells these rounds in boxes of 50. Prior to 2008, Jan Siegelman, the vice president of operations, purchased all ammunition from a supplier who provided good quality rounds and dependable deliveries. However, late in 2007, the purchase price of new rounds and reloads increased by 15 percent. Consequently, Prince told Siegelman to begin production of reloads at a location near corporate headquarters.

Reloads are made of a shell, primer, gunpowder, and a bullet. Merlis Ranges pays nothing for the shells, as they merely retrieve spent rounds from the shooting lane floors. Siegelman was able to find reliable suppliers for the other three reload cartridge materials.

Prince offered to give Siegelman a large cash bonus if the 2008 profits on reloads, after a $19,000 allocation of selling and administrative expenses, were over five percent of total reload sales. Siegelman, however, had trouble keeping the cost of reloads as low as he had hoped. Hence, late in 2008, he drastically stepped up production, spreading costs over a greater number of reloads. While 31,500 boxes of reloads were produced in 2008, only 25,900 of those had been sold by year-end at $22.95 per box.

Cost information for the 31,500 boxes produced in 2008 is as follows:

| Materials: | 1,590,000 rounds @ $0.19 per round | = $302,100 |
| Labor: | 21,240 hours @ $10.60 per hour | = $225,144 |
| Variable Overhead: | 20% of total labor cost | = $ 45,029 |
| Fixed Overhead: | 40% of total labor cost | = $ 90,058 |

The 31,500 boxes should have required only 1,575,000 (31,500 x 50) rounds of materials. Materials for an extra 15,000 rounds were purchased and used due to ineffective handling.

At the end of 2008, Siegelman wanted to analyze the materials and labor costs more carefully. The company controller, Steve Zuckerman, provided him with the following standards:

| | | |
|---|---|---|
| Materials price per reload | $0.16 | |
| Materials quantity per reload | 1 | (This represents one "unit" containing primer, gunpowder, and a bullet.) |
| Wage rate | $10.30 | |
| Hours per box | 0.7 | |

## Required:

1. Prepare a sales variance analysis to explain the decrease in rental revenue and compute price (rate) and usage (efficiency) variances for the materials and labor costs. Discuss these variances.
2. Compute the profits for reloads using absorption costing and variable costing. Reconcile the difference between these two amounts.
3. Discuss the ethics of Siegelman's production decision late in 2008.
4. How will Siegelman's actions impact company profits after 2008?

# four

# DECISION-MAKING FRAMEWORK

# MANAGERIAL DECISIONS: ANALYSIS OF RELEVANT INFORMATION

## LEARNING OBJECTIVES

After studying Chapter 10, you will be able to:

1. Understand the use of differential analysis in making basic decisions.

2. Identify and use relevant costs and revenues in decision making.

3. Recognize the decision type; know the basic decision rule and guidelines; identify major constraints, assumptions, and underlying concerns; format the problem data for analysis; and apply the decision logic to similar real-life problems.

4. Evaluate make or buy, special sales pricing, scarce resource, process further, and add or delete a segment decisions.

5. Explain the role of market and cost information in pricing decisions.

## *Decisions, Decisions, Decisions*

*Kelley Rich operates a chain of take-out ribs and sandwich shops, called Rich Ribs, in the city's suburbs. Before leaving on vacation, Kelley asked her controller, Nick Schunck to prepare cost analyses of several decisions she has been considering. She met with Nick to outline each decision.*

*__Decision 1:__ A major employer in the area called Kelley and asked whether a deal could be arranged to serve Rich Ribs at a company picnic and later perhaps regularly in its cafeteria, depending on the employees' reaction. Kelley's company name may or may not be identified. The company's offering price is roughly 60 percent of Rich's a la carte menu price.*

*__Decision 2:__ The Riverwood shop has been showing a monthly net operating loss for the last six months. The shop's lease expires at yearend. Also, a new mini shopping mall is opening in a growing part of the city not presently served by Kelley's shops. Kelley could close the Riverwood shop and shift the manager to the new mall shop.*

*__Decision 3:__ A local bakery with an excellent reputation in the area has offered to sell bread sticks to Kelley. Rich Ribs includes a serving of bread sticks with every take-out dinner order. Now Kelley bakes her own bread sticks in her kitchen every day and is proud of their quality, but the bakery price offer seems very low.*

*__Decision 4:__ Kelley is thinking of adding pizza to her menu, but the kitchen's oven capacity would be stretched severely if she keeps all other menu items. She wants to use her kitchen capacity in the most profitable way.*

*Kelley has a "common sense feel" about the answers to these decisions, but she needs economic proof. She looks to Nick to assemble, analyze, and present the relevant information for each issue. She must then weigh all the quantitative and qualitative factors and decide.*

YES, "DECISIONS, DECISIONS, decisions" is a common lament. But, decision making creates action. It is the exciting part of management. Managers' experiences and skills are applied to specific problems. The decision may be significant, such as when and where to build a new $1 billion manufacturing facility. Or it may be mundane, such as sending a customer contract by first-class mail or overnight by Federal Express. In either case, consciously or subconsciously, managers follow a process: define the problem, consider choices, collect and analyze relevant data, make a decision, and act.

This chapter examines groups of decisions that require particular decision rules, relevant data, and formats. These decision types occur commonly in all business activities and even in our personal lives. These groups are:

1. **Make or buy**—where to get resource inputs.
2. **Special sales pricing**—where and at what price to sell.
3. **Use scarce resources**—how to get the most out of limited resources.
4. **Sell or process further**—when to sell.
5. **Add or delete a segment**—which to do.

Other decision groups, such as replacing equipment and expanding capacity, are explored in Chapters 11 and 12.

Decisions discussed here are necessarily simplified. The real world offers much more complexity. Decisions are about the future, where much uncertainty exists. The printed page implies a certainty about the future that actual decision makers strangely do not enjoy. In textbook problems, we consider only a few variables that impact decision results. In reality, literally hundreds of variables are moving in different directions at the same time. Therefore, an organized approach helps managers establish a process, select relevant variables, and add format to their analysis.

# THE DECISION-MAKING PROCESS

Every managerial decision is made with the mission and the strategic goals of the organization in mind. Organizing to make decisions implies structure and methodology, but not arbitrariness or rigidity. In Chapter 1, an eight-step process was outlined:

1. Define the decision issue.

2. Specify the decision objective and decision rule.

3. Identify the choices or alternatives.

4. Collect relevant data on the choices.

5. Format and analyze information about each choice.

6. Make the decision.

7. Implement the decision.

8. Evaluate the results of the decision.

This chapter focuses on certain steps. For Step 2, we outline a decision rule and guidelines. For Step 4, we define relevant data. For Step 5, we present formats for analyses. In addition to quantitative analysis, major qualitative issues that influence decisions are raised. And for Step 6, we apply differential analysis to select the preferred choice, given the facts.

An important element underlying these processes is the empowerment of managers throughout the firm to make decisions. Decisions are based on a clear understanding of organizational goals, training in decision analysis, sharing decision-making information, the authority to act, and an evaluation process.

# DIFFERENTIAL ANALYSIS

**Differential analysis** uses relevant revenues and costs to make decisions. It is the result of defining a decision rule and quantifying and formatting relevant information.

## The Basic Decision Rule

The basic differential analysis decision rule is:

*Select the choice that yields the greatest incremental profit.*

**Incremental profit** is the difference between the relevant revenues and the relevant costs of each choice. **Relevant revenues and costs** are defined as the current and future values that differ among the choices considered. In most cases, the term "incremental" is used as a substitute for "relevant." In choosing among choices, all past and committed costs (often referred to as **sunk costs**) and all costs that remain the same across all choices are irrelevant and are ignored.

A decision is frequently a choice of:

**Do it**, or **don't do it**. *or* **Do A**, or **do B**, or **do C**, or **etc**.

In the first case, "don't do it" is the status quo; and "do it" has incremental revenues and costs attached. In the second case, incremental revenues and costs for each choice are measured. In either case, the decision is based on which choice generates the highest incremental profit—incremental revenues minus incremental costs.

Relevant revenues are often assumed to be cash inflows, and relevant costs are cash outflows. **Out-of-pocket costs** refer to costs that are cash outflows. If cash flow and accrual numbers differ, the managerial emphasis is often on cash.

In many cases, capacity impacts decisions. Capacity costs are frequently fixed and are irrelevant to most short-term decisions. A relevant factor is the **opportunity cost** of using capacity.

If excess capacity exists and no alternative uses are apparent, the opportunity cost is zero–the unused capacity has no next-best use. If capacity is fully used, earnings from its alternative uses and costs of acquiring additional capacity are weighed.

## Incremental Analysis Versus Total Analysis

Differential analysis contrasts choices by comparing incremental contribution margins. Two commonly used approaches are applicable to all decision types—the incremental analysis approach and the total analysis approach. The **incremental analysis approach** includes only incremental revenues and costs of each choice. The **total analysis approach** shows the results for the total entity, including the alternative and then excluding the alternative. To evaluate adding a new product, the format is:

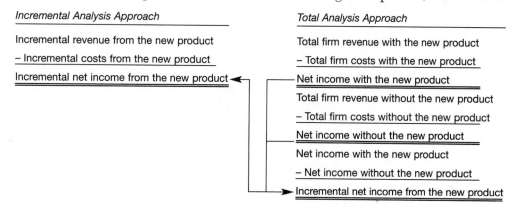

| Incremental Analysis Approach | Total Analysis Approach |
|---|---|
| Incremental revenue from the new product | Total firm revenue with the new product |
| − Incremental costs from the new product | − Total firm costs with the new product |
| Incremental net income from the new product | Net income with the new product |
| | Total firm revenue without the new product |
| | − Total firm costs without the new product |
| | Net income without the new product |
| | Net income with the new product |
| | − Net income without the new product |
| | Incremental net income from the new product |

Clearly, the two approaches yield the same incremental net income. The incremental analysis approach has the advantage of showing only relevant amounts. All sunk and nonchanging amounts are ignored. The total analysis approach reports the firm's gross results, with and without the decision's impacts.

## An Example of Differential Analysis

MaineLine (ML) Caps is located in Augusta, Maine with a factory in South Carolina. Bill O'Connell, CEO, recently purchased this small manufacturer of baseball-type hats. It produces several styles in a variety of materials, but all caps are essentially the same. The caps are marketed under the name ML Caps. Bill has just finished an initial budget for 2008, including this income statement:

| | | |
|---|---|---|
| Sales (100,000 units at $10 per unit) | | $1,000,000 |
| Less production costs: | | |
|   Variable production costs ($3 per unit) | $300,000 | |
|   Fixed factory costs | 300,000 | − 600,000 |
| Gross profit | | $ 400,000 |
| Less operating expenses: | | |
|   Selling expenses (15 percent of sales) | $150,000 | |
|   Administrative expenses | 150,000 | − 300,000 |
| Net income | | $ 100,000 |

Bill's factory operates at 80 percent of capacity. He is currently weighing several alternatives to increase capacity utilization and profits. His analysis shows the choices as:

1. Maintain the status quo.

2. Expand sales of ML Caps to 125,000 by lowering the selling price from $10 to $9 per unit.

3. Use the remaining capacity to make an insulated cap for cold weather runners, called CoolHat. He estimates a sales price of $8 per unit, selling expenses of 15 percent of sales, variable costs of $4 per unit, and no change in fixed costs.

The three choices are compared in Figure 10.1 using a total analysis approach. Choice 2 increases net income to $131,250, a differential increase of $31,250. With Choice 3, the CoolHat, net income increases by $70,000.

| | Choice 1 | Choice 2 | Choice 3 ML Caps | Choice 3 CoolHats | Total |
|---|---|---|---|---|---|
| Units of sales | 100,000 | 125,000 | 100,000 | 25,000 | |
| Sales price | $   10.00 | $    9.00 | $   10.00 | $    8.00 | |
| Variable costs: | | | | | |
| Production costs | $    3.00 | $    3.00 | $    3.00 | $    4.00 | |
| Selling costs | 1.50 | 1.35 | 1.50 | 1.20 | |
| Total variable costs | $    4.50 | $    4.35 | $    4.50 | $    5.20 | |
| Contribution margin per unit | $    5.50 | $    4.65 | $    5.50 | $    2.80 | |
| Sales | $1,000,000 | $1,125,000 | $1,000,000 | $200,000 | $1,200,000 |
| Variable costs: | | | | | |
| Production costs | $  300,000 | $  375,000 | $  300,000 | $100,000 | $  400,000 |
| Selling costs | 150,000 | 168,750 | 150,000 | 30,000 | 180,000 |
| Total variable costs | $  450,000 | $  543,750 | $  450,000 | $130,000 | $  580,000 |
| Variable contribution margin | $  550,000 | $  581,250 | $  550,000 | $ 70,000 | $  620,000 |
| Fixed costs: | | | | | |
| Fixed factory costs | $  300,000 | $  300,000 | | | $  300,000 |
| Administrative costs | 150,000 | 150,000 | | | 150,000 |
| Total fixed costs | $  450,000 | $  450,000 | | | $  450,000 |
| Net income | $  100,000 | $  131,250 | | | $  170,000 |

**FIGURE 10.1**

Total Analysis Approach to Differential Analysis

The incremental analysis approach is shown in Figure 10.2. No mention is made of the original sales of 100,000 units or fixed costs which do not change. All choices are incremental to Choice 1, the status quo. Therefore, while Choice 1 is not shown in Figure 10.2, the other choices show the contribution margin differential to Choice 1's $100,000 of net income.

Based on quantitative facts, O'Connell will select Choice 3. But before the decision is made, long-term considerations should be evaluated. Is the CoolHat consistent with the firm's product plans? Will it take resources from Bill's primary market—ML Caps? Because Bill is an avid runner, are his personal biases confusing his thinking? Are additional equipment or worker skills needed? Although supposedly a short-term decision, these policy issues concern Bill.

| | Choice 2 | Choice 3 |
|---|---|---|
| Incremental sales of ML Caps ($9 × 25,000) | $225,000 | |
| Incremental production costs of BT Caps ($3 × 25,000) | (75,000) | |
| Lost revenue from price reduction [($9 – $10) × 100,000] | (100,000) | |
| Sales of Coolhats ($8 × 25,000) | | $200,000 |
| Incremental production costs of Coolhats ($4 × 25,000) | | (100,000) |
| Incremental sales commissions (15% × increased revenue) | (18,750) | (30,000) |
| Incremental contribution margin | $ 31,250 | $ 70,000 |

**FIGURE 10.2**

Incremental Analysis Approach to Differential Analysis

## Policy Issues Affecting Relevant Costing Decisions

As with all real-world issues, the decision-making path is more complex than the basic rules imply. The differential analysis model is so simple and appealing that we can easily be lulled into a false sense of objectivity.

### ABC and Relevant Costs

Companies with well-developed activity-based cost systems are in more knowledgeable positions to make relevant costing decisions. With carefully selected cost drivers and cost functions, changes in costs from a change in activity can be seen more clearly.

### The Timeframe

Certain assumptions are made in differential analysis. A short-term horizon is assumed; variable costs are relevant; and most fixed costs are irrelevant. However, managers must recognize that all important decisions have both short-term and long-term impacts. In many cases, investments must be made that last longer than the immediate timeframe. Decisions made today often are not easily reversed tomorrow. Also, decisions made on a one-time basis or made for an immediate gain may change the options available in the long run. By selecting Choice 3 in our above example Bill has committed all unused capacity. If ML Caps sales grow, he must somehow expand capacity or lose sales.

### Strategic Planning Issues

A firm's strategic plan looks at product offerings, pricing strategies, competitive positions, and financial performance goals. "Long haul" policies are implemented in the short run by tactics and decision guidelines. By overaggressive use of marginal costing principles, managers may be letting the "tail wag the dog." Incremental decisions are often just minor additions at the margin. The major pricing, production, and marketing decisions must follow long-term strategies that have been carefully thought through.

Often decisions are masked as an incremental decision, when they are really policy-making, long-term decisions. For example:

- A one-time sale at a low price becomes repeat business.
- Regular customers seek price breaks to compete with off-brand look-a-likes.
- Purchasing cheaper lower-quality parts eventually hurts a firm's image as a high-quality producer. This same outsourcing may undermine harmony that the company and its labor union have worked hard to develop.
- Stopping and starting production of a temporarily unprofitable product may cause losses of market share for an entire product line and of skilled employees who make the product.

While relevant costing is a powerful analytical tool, no decision can be made in isolation.

## MAKE OR BUY DECISIONS

The decision questions are:

*Should we make an item or perform the service ourselves, or should we purchase the item or service from a vendor?*

| The "Make" Alternative | The "Buy" Alternative |
|---|---|
| Make the component part in our factory in Indiana. | Buy it from a nearby supplier, a nonunion vendor in another state, Taiwanese producer, or another division of our own company. |
| Operate our fleet of delivery trucks. | Hire various freight companies. |
| Run our printing shop. | Contract with local printers. |
| Employ our own cleaning staff. | Hire a cleaning service. |
| Manage our data processing operation. | Hire a facilities management company. |
| Cook for ourselves. | Eat in the dorm cafeteria. |

Nearly all products and services offered on the market today result from basic make or buy decisions. A sample of these decisions includes:

Managers consider make or buy decisions for various reasons, including to:

- Reduce costs.
- Use or to free up capacity.
- Improve quality or delivery performance.
- Encourage greater productivity from internal operations by forcing competition with outsiders.
- Get new technology.
- Free scarce investment funds for other uses.

## Key Decision Rule and Guidelines

The key decision rule is:

> *Buy it if the out-of-pocket costs of buying the product or service are less than the out-of-pocket costs of making the product or service; otherwise make it.*

Out-of-pocket costs are the relevant costs in this decision. The decision rule is still to earn the highest profit. But since make or buy decisions generally deal only with costs, the decision rule minimizes cost. If we buy from a vendor, we **outsource**. We are **in-house sourcing** if we make the item ourselves.

**Relevant make costs** are the direct costs of producing an item plus any opportunity costs. Direct costs include variable materials, direct labor, and variable factory overhead costs. Included also are any incremental fixed costs caused by the make decision plus any traceable costs, such as unique tooling costs. These are called avoidable costs if the decision is to buy.

**Relevant buy costs** are the item's purchase price, shipping and handling costs, and any costs incurred to get the purchased item into usable form. Inspection and testing costs are examples. Another relevant cost issue is alternative uses of space vacated, if the part is now purchased. The space could be rented at some market rate, used by another department or used to make other parts.

## Data Analysis Format

The make or buy analysis format lists the relevant costs to make and the relevant costs to buy in a two-column format, shown as follows:

| Make Costs | | Buy Costs | |
|---|---|---|---|
| Materials and direct labor | $ | Purchase cost plus handling costs | $ |
| Variable overhead costs | $ | | |
| Avoidable fixed overhead costs | $ | | |
| Other avoidable or incremental costs | $ | | |

| Opportunity costs of additional resources needed | $ | **or** | Incremental revenue or earnings from use of released resources | ($) |
|---|---|---|---|---|
| Total make cost | $ | | Total buy cost | $ |

Any costs that do not change are ignored, since they are irrelevant. Direct product costs and purchase costs are easily listed. Items can be either an additional cost on one side or a negative cost on the other. For example, if, by outsourcing, office space is no longer needed and can be leased for $5,000, the revenue reduces the buy costs. Or, it can be viewed as an additional make cost, since by performing the service ourselves we incur a $5,000 opportunity cost. Either way works. The bottom line is the comparison of the incremental make cost and the incremental buy cost. Select the alternative with the lower cost.

## An Example

Sharp Corporation has bids from several suppliers for a control device, a unit used in several models of its Hibeam Line of lighting fixtures. Sharp made these devices for the past several years and needs 30,000 units for 2008 production requirements. Walker Wiring returned the most attractive bid at $3 per unit delivered. Quality control inspections of purchased units would cost Sharp $3,000. Sharp's costs for 25,000 units made in 2007 were:

| | Per Unit | Total Costs |
|---|---|---|
| Materials | $1.25 | $31,250 |
| Direct labor | .60 | 15,000 |
| Variable overhead | .50 | 12,500 |
| Fixed overhead applied | 1.00 | 25,000 |
| Total | $3.35 | $83,750 |

All costs are direct costs, except fixed factory overhead. The only direct and avoidable fixed factory overhead is $6,000, the cost of leasing specialized equipment required to make the control device. If the device is purchased, Sharp could return the specialized equipment, void the lease, and use the space for storage. Renting storage space would cost $4,000 next year.

The relevant make and buy costs are:

| Make Costs | | Buy Costs | |
|---|---|---|---|
| Materials ($1.25 × 30,000) | $37,500 | Purchase cost ($3 × 30,000) | $90,000 |
| Direct labor ($0.60 × 30,000) | 18,000 | Quality control costs | 3,000 |
| Variable overhead ($0.50 × 30,000) | 15,000 | Rent savings | (4,000) |
| Equipment lease cost | 6,000 | | |
| Total make costs | $76,500 | Total buy costs | $89,000 |
| Net make advantage | $12,500 | | |

We can make several observations:

- The variable costs on both sides are relevant.
- The $6,000 cost of leasing the equipment is relevant because the equipment lease payment is avoided under the buy choice. The remaining fixed factory overhead is unavoidable and irrelevant to the decision.
- The $4,000 rent savings is relevant because it occurs only in the buy choice.

## Contemporary Practice 10.1
### Outsourcing Government Services—Pretty Controversial, but Necessary

*In periods of tight budgets, many governments are under pressure to do "more with less." One way to reduce costs is to outsource services to private firms, non-profit organizations, or other governments—to provide services more efficiently and perhaps at higher quality level. In some cases, outsourcing can result in significant cost savings over the long run. But, in other cases outsourcing may actually end up increasing a government's total costs.*

*Two key points warrant emphasis: (1) a make-versus-buy cost analysis should use a differential cost perspective and (2) the analysis should have a multi-year timeframe (and include discounting future cash flows to their present value—a topic introduced in Chapter 11). A potential mistake in a make-versus-buy cost analysis is the inclusion of sunk costs. Another important concept is opportunity cost. Opportunity cost is the lost opportunity of using an asset or resource in a way other than the chosen alternative. For example, if a suburban government sells a public swimming pool to a private company to own and operate, the opportunity*

*cost would include the admittance fee revenue that would have been collected if the pool remained a public asset. Likewise, the opportunity cost of not selling the pool would be the revenue from the sale of the pool.*

*Non-financial issues are very important: service quality and control, including safety and reliability; ability to control who receives service; ability of the government unit to change to improve its own performance; and risk of contractual nonperformance. Other issues include: management quality on both sides, public access to information, ability to create competition in service delivery, impacts on outstanding debt and grant eligibility, impact on stakeholders including employees and taxpayers, and statutory and regulatory issues including federal and state requirements, and liability.*

Source: Michel, R. Gregory, "Make or Buy? Using Cost Analysis to Decide Whether to Outsource Public Services," Government Finance Review, *August 2004, pp. 15–21.*

- The relevant volume is 30,000 units (the 2008 expected volume).
- Comparing the 2007 make full cost of $3.35 per unit to the buy cost of $3 hides important cost behavior patterns.

The recommendation is to continue to make the unit and save $12,500.

## Strategic and Qualitative Factors

The make or buy decision is a least cost choice. But many subtleties surround the decision. In the prior example, only quantitative monetary facts were considered. Quality, delivery, labor force, and investment implications are frequently key issues.

Often, product and service quality is the highest ranking factor and could support either the make or buy side. By making the product, we can control quality in all aspects of production. On the other hand, a particular task may require specialized knowledge. We may not have this expertise. Whereas, an outside specialist may be faster and produce higher quality output. Quality can be so important that cost differentials are ignored.

Delivery capability in just-in-time systems is critical. Again, perhaps in-house sourcing has an advantage since our production planners can schedule production on an "as needed" basis. Or the outside supplier may use delivery capability as a key competitive issue and be better able to meet complex requirements. Vendor certification programs have allowed buying firms to set benchmarks for performance and to narrow possible suppliers to a group known for high achievement.

Labor stability is another major make or buy consideration. For the United Auto Workers Union (UAW) and American auto producers, outsourcing is a major area of contention in labor negotiations. The auto companies have historically been vertically integrated. These companies, to be competitive with foreign producers and to increase internal productivity, are searching for the most efficient suppliers. Many suppliers are "lean and mean," more so than the auto makers' own captive divisions. The UAW, concerned about member job losses, is demanding labor contract provisions that guarantee in-house production. Also, a sense of community responsibility affects how managers decide where work and, therefore, jobs are located.

Global business transactions expand the decision beyond whether to make or buy. Now, if we make, where do we make? If we buy, where do we buy? Brazil, Mexico, China, Korea, and eastern or western Europe are possible sources. Also, many multinational firms have facilities in several countries and can shift production depending on costs, quality, materials proximity, and product demand.

## SPECIAL SALES PRICING DECISIONS

The decision question is:

> **Will we benefit from special sales generally made at prices lower than those charged to our regular customers?**

This decision evaluates added sales opportunities using contribution margin analysis. Often, one company's make or buy problem is another company's special sales pricing problem. Examples of special pricing decisions include:

- Generating discount-priced sales to use excess production capacity.
- Accepting sales that cover only out-of-pocket costs to keep a workforce employed during a recession.
- Making a one-time sale to move stale merchandise.
- Responding to a request for a special feature from a regular customer.
- Pricing to enter a new competitive marketplace.

Clearly, knowledge of cost behavior, volumes, and capacities is a major influence on pricing and marketing.

### Key Decision Rule and Guidelines

The key decision rule is:

> **Subject to the following specific guidelines, make the special sale if we earn a positive contribution margin from the special sale.**

The guidelines or assumptions necessary to allow the basic rule to work are:

- Excess capacity exists, with no alternative use of the capacity. The opportunity cost of using the capacity is zero or at least very low.
- Special sales should not interfere with regular sales.
- The special sale is a one-time order and will not become repeat business.

If all of these guidelines are not met, the analysis will have additional relevant revenues and costs to consider.

The minimum price must cover out-of-pocket costs plus any opportunity cost of making the sale (lost profits from regular sales or lost production). The economic rule is to produce and sell until the marginal revenue equals marginal cost—until a zero incremental profit is reached.

## Contemporary Practice 10.2

### *Fill the Seat, Get the Marginal Dollar*

*Near the Christmas season, Delta Airlines tried to fill its excess capacity anticipated on December 25th by offering round-trip fares of $79 for flights of 500 miles or less. Passengers would have to depart and return on Christmas day. This was expected to fill otherwise empty seats without significantly affecting flights before and after Christmas.*

Source: Thurston, S., "Delta Reduces Prices on Some Holiday Flights," Atlanta Constitution, December 23, 1993, p. F1.

## Data Analysis Format

The format of relevant data for special sales decisions appears as follows:

| | |
|---|---|
| Incremental revenue | $ |
| Less incremental costs: | |
|    Additional variable costs | ($) |
|    Additional direct fixed costs | ($) |
| Incremental profits | $ |

Only relevant revenues and costs are shown. Variable costs are often taken from the variable costs of regular business adjusted for any changes in features, such as different formulas for baby foods, heavy-duty shock absorbers for police cars, and overtime police wages for a special concert on campus. Any additional supervision, preparation time, shipping, and packaging are relevant. Generally, variable costs are relevant; and fixed costs remain unchanged and are irrelevant unless otherwise indicated.

## An Example

Assume that North Comm's capacity is 90,000 units of a cellular phone receiver, including 15,000 units made on overtime. North Comm is currently producing and selling 80,000 units per year at $8 per unit. Variable production costs are $3 per unit, and annual fixed factory overhead costs are $200,000. Variable shipping costs are $0.50 per unit; all administrative expenses are $120,000 and fixed. The profit calculation is as follows:

| | | |
|---|---|---|
| Sales (80,000 units × $8) | | $640,000 |
| Less factory and shipping costs: | | |
|    Variable (80,000 units × $3.50) | $280,000 | |
|    Fixed overhead | 200,000 | −480,000 |
| Gross profit | | $160,000 |
| Less administrative expenses | | −120,000 |
|    Net income | | $ 40,000 |

An Argentine communications company approaches North Comm with an offer to buy 10,000 receivers at $6 each. Sales in Argentina should not affect North Comm's regular sales. The special units would require minor modifications and force more overtime, adding $0.80 per unit to variable costs. Additional supervision would cost $3,000. The entire lot would be packed and shipped to Argentina for $2,000. The analysis shows:

| | |
|---|---:|
| Incremental sales | $60,000 |
| Less incremental costs: | |
| Incremental variable factory costs (10,000 × $3) | −30,000 |
| Additional variable factory costs (10,000 × $0.80) | −8,000 |
| Additional fixed supervision costs | −3,000 |
| Additional shipping costs | −2,000 |
| Incremental profit (loss) | $17,000 |

Incremental profits of $17,000 are added to the net income from regular sales to create a forecast of $57,000 for net income. The special sale adds to North Comm's total profit even though the $6 price is $1.50 below the average cost of $7.50 (total product and administrative expenses of $600,000 divided by 80,000 units). The decision rule and the criteria are met. Do it.

## Nonsegmented Markets

Accepting special prices is a sound policy only if the special market can be kept separate from the regular market. For example, in the preceding illustration, assume that the international market begins to affect the domestic market to the extent that the domestic price drops from $8 per unit to $7.60 per unit (a 5 percent drop). In this case, the firm's profit calculation for the next period would appear as follows:

| | |
|---|---:|
| Incremental profits from the Argentine sale | $ 17,000 |
| Less lost revenue from price reduction (80,000 units × $0.40) | −32,000 |
| Incremental profit (loss) | $(15,000) |

If the special market price influences the domestic market, profits decrease from $40,000 to $25,000–a loss of $15,000. Don't do it.

## No Excess Capacity

Assume that North Comm's capacity was only 85,000 units instead of 90,000 units and that the Argentine sale is all or nothing. By accepting the order, 5,000 units of regular business must be given up. The calculations are as follows:

| | |
|---|---:|
| Incremental profits from Argentine sale | $ 17,000 |
| Less contribution margin on lost regular sales (5,000 × $4.50) | −22,500 |
| Incremental profit (loss) | $ (5,500) |

Losing 5,000 units of regular sales to accommodate the 10,000 unit Argentine sale will cost North Comm profits. Don't do it.

## Not a One-Time Sale

This may be a sample order, with an unknown probability of larger future contracts. If repeat sales are expected, North Comm must be very careful not to commit itself to a lowmargin business.

## Strategic and Qualitative Factors

Product pricing is a key market positioning tool. Capacity use is a resource management decision. Lowpriced special sales can preempt strategic plans. The first question: How does the sale fit into our long-term marketing goals? Tied to this is a second question: Is using capacity for this sale consistent with the strategic use of production capabilities? The decision guidelines previously presented (excess capacity, segmented markets, and one-time sale) are tactical rules to help prevent subtle economic errors. If we want a premium product and price image, discount deals may tarnish it. Our dealers probably depend on our pricing and product image stability.

Accepting one more one-time sale is an easy path to follow. More of our capacity becomes allocated to low-profit business on a routine basis. If the market segmentation guideline does not hold, regular business begins to shrink; and special sales expand. Fewer and fewer customers are paying prices that cover all costs, while more sales at special prices pay only a portion of the firm's operating costs.

## USE OF SCARCE RESOURCES DECISIONS

The decision question is:

> *When a productive resource is limited, how do we allocate the use of the scarce resource?*

The scarce or limited resource decision is an extension of the special sales pricing decision except that no excess capacity exists. Some constraint exists. Several examples are shown in Figure 10.3.

All of these examples use **contribution margin per unit of scarce resource**, which is contribution margin per unit divided by the amount of scarce resource used by each unit. For example, assume that Product 28 has a $10 per unit contribution margin and needs 30 minutes on a polishing machine that is a major factory bottleneck. Then, $20 per hour ($10 ÷ 0.5 hours) is the contribution margin per hour of polishing machine time when producing Product 28. Expressed differently, what price should be charged for a product or service that uses a given amount of the scarce resource?

## Key Decision Rule and Guidelines

The scarce resource decision rule is:

> *Optimize profits from a scarce resource by selecting the products or services with the highest contribution margin per unit of the scarce resource.*

This rule yields the product mix that maximizes total profits. Products are ranked by their ability to generate the highest contribution margin per unit of scarce resource used. The scarce resource

| Scarce Resource | Issue |
|---|---|
| • Specialized machine time | What are the most profitable products per machine hour to produce? |
| • Shelf space in a grocery store | What mix of products earns the most profit per shelf foot? |
| • Salesperson time during sales calls | Which products should they attempt to sell during the limited time allowed them? |
| • A seat in a popular restaurant | Which menu items generate the most profit per seat per dinner hour? |
| • A fixed advertising budget | Which media expense generates more sales and profits? |
| • Your study time | How should you allocate available study hours to earn the highest average grade? |

**FIGURE 10.3**

Scarce Resource Examples

constraint is often a temporary situation. Over time, we can train more skilled workers, buy more equipment, or rent more space to eliminate the constraint.

Guidelines for selecting the most profitable set of products or services are:

- We must know the amount of scarce resource needed (input) to produce a unit of output.
- The product with the highest contribution margin per unit of scarce resource is selected, then the second highest, and so on until the scarce resource is used.
- Normally, the analysis uses variable contribution margin.
- Allocated, common, or indirect fixed costs are irrelevant to the decision.

When incremental direct fixed costs exist, we should also incorporate these costs into the analysis.

## Data Analysis Format and an Example

The data analysis format uses the contribution margin per unit of output and the scarce resource needed to produce that unit. The result is a profit ranking of all products based on a contribution margin per unit of scarce resource.

As an example, the Museum Repro Company (MRC) markets reproductions of well-known sculptures. Finish work is done by four highly skilled artists. MRC cannot find additional artists to meet the sales demand. Data on four MRC's pieces are:

|  | Roman | Greek | Aztec | Egyptian |
|---|---|---|---|---|
| Sales demand (units) | 1,000 units | 200 units | 500 units | 500 units |
| Hours of work per unit | 2 | 5 | 6 | 10 |
| Indirect fixed costs per unit | $ 50 | $110 | $120 | $ 200 |
| Sales price per unit | $250 | $350 | $600 | $1,000 |
| Variable costs per unit | 150 | 150 | 240 | 550 |
| Contribution margin per unit | $100 | $200 | $360 | $ 450 |
| Divided by hours of detail work per unit | ÷2 | ÷5 | ÷6 | ÷10 |
| Contribution margin per hour of work | $ 50 | $ 40 | $ 60 | $ 45 |
| Priority ranking | 2nd | 4th | 1st | 3rd |

Assume that the four artists each work about 2,000 hours per year. MRC will use the 8,000 hours available as follows:

| Priority | Piece | Hours Per Unit | | Units | | Hours Required | Remaining Available Hours | Contribution Margin Per Hour | Contribution Margin |
|---|---|---|---|---|---|---|---|---|---|
|  |  |  |  |  |  |  | 8,000 |  |  |
| 1st | Aztec | 6 | × | 500 | = | 3,000 | 5,000 | $ 60 | $ 180,000 |
| 2nd | Roman | 2 | × | 1,000 | = | 2,000 | 3,000 | $ 50 | 100,000 |
| 3rd | Egyptian | 10 | × | 300 | = | 3,000 | 0 | $ 45 | 135,000 |
| Total contribution margin generated | | | | | | | | | $ 415,000 |

Sales demand not met:

Egyptian    200 units

Greek    200 units

If MRC produces all of the needed Aztec and Roman units and only 300 Egyptian units, the detail artists' 8,000 hours are entirely used. This product mix generates the highest contribution margin

*Andre was disappointed with profits from his hairstyling business. He worked at controlling costs and advertised to increase his client base. Revenues increased, but profits lagged. A consultant analyzing his operations suggested increasing the contribution margin per hour of stylists' time. This meant converting fixed stylist salaries to*

*a commission basis to get stylists to work more efficiently, changing prices to reflect higher costs of certain services, and advertising discounts during slack periods. Bingo! More profits.*

*Source: Sprohge, H., and J. Talbott, "How Contribution Margin Analysis Helped Andre's Salon," Journal of Accountancy, August 1990, pp. 110–117.*

given the artists' available time. Note that indirect fixed costs are ignored in the analysis, since these costs will not change regardless of the production mix.

## Qualitative and Strategic Factors

The qualitative issues in the scarce resource analysis are questions of price and product offerings. Why is MRC's capacity limited? Is the marketplace demand driven? Prices should be set based on competition and customer demand. Scarce resource analysis can highlight possible poor pricing. In the MRC example, Egyptian and Greek prices might be raised to improve the contribution margin per hour of artist time to match or exceed Aztec's contribution margin. Also, the basic analysis ignores the complementary aspect of various items in a product line. To compete in a market may require a complete product offering or a full menu.

Also of concern is the use of the scarce resource itself. Can steps be taken to conserve capacity, to substitute less critical resources, or to buy additional capacity? MRC can get an estimate of the value of additional capacity. In the MRC example, another employee working 2,000 hours per year would produce the following additional contribution margin:

| | Hours Per Unit | | Units | | Hours Required | | Contribution Margin Per Hour | | Additional Contribution Margin |
|---|---|---|---|---|---|---|---|---|---|
| Egyptian | 10 | × | 200 | = | 2,000 | × | $ 45 | = | $90,000 |

The added contribution margin is $90,000, which is after the variable labor costs have been deducted. At that price, should MRC train another detail artist? Probably yes.

## SELL OR PROCESS FURTHER DECISIONS

The decision questions are:

> *Should the product be sold as is, or should it be processed further and then sold?*

A common sell or process further decision deals with a product that can be sold now or processed further and sold later as another product. In other cases, processing further can spawn multiple products from a common input. These are called **joint products**, and the further processing becomes a **decision point** or **split-off point**. Until this point, the common input is a single product. An example of a decision point in a refining process is where the decision to process crude oil into joint products of gasoline, heating oil, and motor oil is made. The decision is to sell the crude oil or to refine and sell the joint products.

## Key Decision Rule and Guidelines

The key decision rule is:

> ***Process further if the incremental revenue from processing further is greater than the incremental costs of processing further***.

The basic guidelines are:

- All relevant additional processing costs are assumed to be incremental.
- Costs incurred prior to the decision point are common to both sell and process further choices and are irrelevant to the process further decision.
- The decision is independent of product costing. Product costing attaches all product costs to units, including common and past costs. In process further decisions, only present and future revenues and costs are relevant.
- The decision assumes that products are *either* sold as is *or* processed further. If capacity allows, we could do *both* if both generate a positive contribution margins.

The decision task is to always look forward and never look backward. We are standing here today with something of value and looking into the future. We can sell it now. Or, we can do additional work, spend more money, and sell in the future. Past costs cannot be changed and are common to both choices.

While common or **joint costs** may be irrelevant in process further decisions, they are real costs, must be incurred, and should be attached to products as they flow through production processes. The appendix to this chapter discusses product cost procedures when products are produced from common processes.

## Data Analysis Format and Examples

Assume, for example, that unfinished hardwood desks for home offices sell for $180, with a manufacturing cost of $100. The company can stain the desks at an additional cost of $30 each, yielding a desk that sells for $225. Due to market demand, the company could only sell 500 stained desks. The data format shows:

| | |
|---|---:|
| Revenue from sale of stained desks (500 units × $225) | $112,500 |
| Less revenue from sale of unstained desks (500 units × $180) | −90,000 |
| Incremental revenue | $22,500 |
| Less cost of staining (500 units × $30) | −15,000 |
| Incremental contribution margin from processing further | $ 7,500 |

The decision is obvious: Stain and sell 500 desks.

Four important assumptions were made. First, the desk's manufacturing cost is assumed to be irrelevant, because the cost of desks is the same for unstained or stained desks. Second, the company is assumed to have capacity to process desks further without losing sales of other products. Third, the process further costs are assumed to be avoidable costs. And fourth, if the desks are not processed further, they can be sold unstained.

## Joint Products—Process All or None

Assume that we produce an industrial wax with a sales value of $4 per gallon. The manufactured cost is $3.25 per gallon. We can convert 60,000 gallons of industrial wax through a process that yields equal amounts of three high-quality auto waxes: Super Gloss, Shiner, and Deep Glow. Costs of converting industrial wax into the three products are $40,000. The market values of the three waxes are $6, $5, and $4.80 per gallon, respectively. Should we process further?

|  | Quantity |  | Price |  | Revenue |
|---|---|---|---|---|---|
| Super Gloss | 20,000 gallons | × | $6.00 | = | $120,000 |
| Shiner | 20,000 | × | 5.00 | = | 100,000 |
| Deep Glow | 20,000 | × | 4.80 | = | 96,000 |
| Total revenue after processing |  |  |  |  | $316,000 |
| Less revenue lost from industrial wax ($4 × 60,000 gallons) |  |  |  |  | −240,000 |
| Incremental revenue from processing further |  |  |  |  | $ 76,000 |
| Less cost of processing further |  |  |  |  | −40,000 |
| Incremental contribution margin |  |  |  |  | $ 36,000 |

The decision is to process further. Notice that the industrial wax production cost is not included since it is a sunk cost.

## Joint Products—Which Products Should Be Processed Further?

If processing costs are variable and if each auto wax can be produced independently, what should be done? Assume that variable costs per gallon were $1, $1.25 and $0.40, respectively. The analysis on a per gallon basis is:

| | Process Further Price | | Industrial Wax Price | | Additional Revenue | | Additional Processing Costs | | Additional Contribution Margin | Process Further Decision |
|---|---|---|---|---|---|---|---|---|---|---|
| Super Gloss | $6.00 | − | $4 | = | $2.00 | − | $1.00 | = | $1.00 | Yes |
| Shiner | 5.00 | − | 4 | = | 1.00 | − | 1.25 | = | (0.25) | No |
| Deep Glow | 4.80 | − | 4 | = | 0.80 | − | 0.40 | = | 0.40 | Yes |

Super Gloss and Deep Glow should be produced, but Shiner has a negative incremental contribution margin and should not be made. If we have a limited supply of industrial wax, we should make Super Gloss first and then Deep Glow.

## Qualitative and Strategic Factors

The short-term version of this decision assumes further processing stages can be shut down or started up with few impacts. Rarely is this the case. Fixed costs will continue; skilled labor may be difficult to keep available; and product market shares may be difficult to maintain. Thus, the best short-run quantitative choice may not achieve the planned results, or the long-run damages may overwhelm the short-run benefits.

In many processing operations, significant capacity costs exist. In real life, metals commodity prices often determine whether copper, zinc, and gold mines operate or temporarily suspend production. In beef cattle, pork, and poultry operations, prices of retail, wholesale, and "on the hoof" products and processing costs are constantly monitored and forecast at each stage to make optimal sell versus process further decisions.

## ADD OR DELETE A SEGMENT DECISIONS

The decision question is:

**Is the firm more profitable with or without the segment?**

Examples of this decision include:

- Opening or closing a retail branch store.
- Adding or eliminating a product or an entire product line.
- Adding or eliminating a specialized service in a hospital.
- Combining purchasing departments in two plants into one unit.

In each of these examples, the answer depends on whether the firm is better off with or without the particular segment and hinges on the direct or segment contribution margin, which excludes allocated common costs. The analysis must resist the temptation to focus on net income of the segment. Also, the decision must consider the strategic value of the segment to the firm's long-term success.

### Key Decision Rules and Guidelines

The key decision rules are:

**Add the segment if the firm's profits are higher after adding it. Delete the segment if the firm's profits are higher after eliminating it.**

These rules assume that the following guidelines are in place:

- Segment evaluations use direct contribution margin.
- Segment eliminations focus on lost revenue and avoidable costs.
- Segment additions focus on incremental revenues and costs.

Figure 10.4 shows two income statements for Narasimhan Clothiers and its three departments. One format shows net income for each department, after allocating common indirect expenses

| | Net Income Approach | | | | Contribution Margin Approach | | | |
|---|---|---|---|---|---|---|---|---|
| | Dept. A | Dept. B | Dept. C | Totals | Dept.A | Dept.B | Dept. C | Totals |
| Sales | $400 | $500 | $100 | $1,000 | $400 | $500 | $100 | $1,000 |
| Cost of sales | 200 | 320 | 60 | 580 | $200 | $320 | $ 60 | $ 580 |
| Variable sales commissions* | | | | | 40 | 50 | 10 | 100 |
| Total variable costs | | | | | $240 | $370 | $ 70 | $ 680 |
| Gross margin | $200 | $180 | $ 40 | $ 420 | | | | |
| Variable contribution margin | | | | | $160 | $130 | $ 30 | $ 320 |
| Direct expenses* | $ 80 | $ 90 | $ 20 | $ 190 | | | | |
| Direct fixed expenses* | | | | | 40 | 40 | 10 | 90 |
| Direct contribution margin | | | | | $120 | $ 90 | $ 20 | $ 230 |
| Common indirect expenses | 50 | 50 | 50 | 150 | | | | 150 |
| Total operating expenses | $130 | $140 | $ 70 | $ 340 | | | | |
| Net income | $ 70 | $ 40 | $(30) | $ 80 | | | | $ 80 |

* Each department pays sales commissions of 10 percent on all sales. The variable sales commissions are part of each department's direct expenses. Other direct expenses are fixed costs.

**FIGURE 10.4**

Department Performance for Narasimhan Clothiers—A Merchandiser

equally to the three departments. The other shows direct contribution margin for the three departments. Amounts are in thousands.

Department C appears to be losing $30,000 under the net income format. Using this format, the firm is attempting to evaluate its segment's performance based on its net income. But is Department C a loser? By reorganizing the data into a contribution margin format, Department C shows a $20,000 contribution to common expenses and profits. This difference results from the fact that no indirect costs are eliminated if Department C is deleted.

The net income format often hides the expense behavior (variable and fixed) and traceability (direct and indirect). The contribution margin format generally presents a clearer story.

## Data Analysis Format and an Example

Narasimhan's president sees the net loss for Department C and considers eliminating the department. Assume that deleting Department C has no impact on Departments A and B or on indirect expenses. An incremental analysis in thousands shows:

| | |
|---|---|
| Department C revenue lost | $(100) |
| Department C cost of sales avoided | 60 |
| Department C variable selling expenses avoided | 10 |
| Department C direct fixed expenses avoided | 10 |
| Lost direct contribution margin from Department C | $ (20) |

Narasimhan would lose $20,000 in profits if Department C is dropped. Department C should be kept unless a higher earning alternative exists.

## Strategic and Qualitative Factors

This decision is tied to the scarce resource decision. To drop or add a segment is rarely an isolated decision. What will replace the dropped segment? What does the new segment replace? The opportunity cost is generally not zero, must be quantified, and is then compared to the incremental change in contribution margin. In the previous example, a Department D and its incremental revenues and expenses could replace Department C, or Departments A and B could expand.

While complementary and substitution effects have been shown already, the subtle impacts on other products and departments are often difficult to measure. While direct contribution margin is used, certain direct costs may be neither entirely avoidable nor controllable by the decision maker.

Many companies are "downsizing," which includes a variety of strategies. Simple cost reduction should mean eliminating expenses which are contributing least to organizational goals. Seeking out waste, nonvalue-adding activities, should be part of normal budgeting and cost control systems. Major organizational restructuring may include the elimination of product lines, entire factories, or a layer of management. Each of these is a version of the delete a segment decision. The same analytical process applies.

# EQUIPMENT REPLACEMENT DECISIONS

The basic question asks:

*Is greater benefit received from acquiring new equipment or continuing to use the old equipment over the life of the equipment?*

To answer this question, expenses incurred or revenues earned from using the old and the new equipment must be known. New equipment has two relevant measures: the incremental investment in new equipment and the increased contribution margin earned from the new equipment. Decision rules that include multiyear investment analyses are discussed in Chapter 11. For illustration purposes here, we assume new equipment is rented and not purchased.

For example, a computer center has reached an activity level that requires two Model 310 mainframe units. These machines have a total annual rental cost of $500,000. Operating costs add another $100,000 per machine. A larger and faster Model 420 would have more capacity than two Model 310s. A Model 420 rents for $480,000 per year and has an operating cost of $150,000 per year. With this simplified data, the analysis is:

| | |
|---|---:|
| Rent of two Model 310s avoided | $500,000 |
| Operating costs of two Model 310s avoided | 200,000 |
| Rent of Model 420 incurred | −480,000 |
| Operating costs of Model 420 incurred | −150,000 |
| Savings from renting Model 420 | $ 70,000 |

The quantitative analysis says rent Model 420. We also get more capacity, which actually is another quantifiable benefit.

While renting or leasing equipment is a common financing alternative, purchasing is the basic method of acquiring new assets. An investment is made today, and benefits are earned over the asset's life. Evaluating all aspects of these decisions is a Chapter 11 task.

## ETHICAL CONSIDERATIONS

The fundamental ethical issue in incremental decision making is validity of estimates of future revenues and costs. "Show me a proposal, and I can make it look good or bad" epitomizes the ethical problem facing many managerial accountants. The objective approach, reflected in another quote of "just give me the facts," is often easier said than done. Facts are often estimates of the future. Biases, known or unrealized, can easily influence these estimates. What does the boss want the analysis to show? How can I make this project look good enough to get approved? These are pressures and influences that can destroy the basic "level playing field" decision-making process. Steps can be taken to reduce the likelihood that decision analyses are not subverted by biases, intentional or unintentional, and include:

- In-depth management reviews of assumptions and supporting data before a decision is made to ensure management's conspicuous attention to objectivity.
- Development of managerial attitudes that support critical evaluations and avoid "kill the messenger bearing bad news" attitudes.
- Creation of known criteria that emphasize the importance of validating relevant revenue and cost data estimates.
- Post-decision audits to validate past estimates of future results.

In many cases, managerial attitudes toward objective assessments begin at the top of the organization and "trickle down" to the lowest management levels.

## COSTS AND PRICING DECISIONS

One of the most difficult and critical decisions facing a manager is pricing. A firm's pricing policy is a major part of its overall strategic positioning. A great pricing debate centers on whether prices are based on market conditions (supply and demand) or on production costs (recovery of costs). Certain environments tend to emphasize one or the other as shown in Figure 10.5.

| Market-Driven Prices— Common Conditions and Products: | Cost-Based Prices— Common Conditions and Products: |
|---|---|
| Consumer products | Industrial and durable goods |
| Service activities | Capital intensive industries |
| Highly competitive markets | Regulated industries |
| Few distribution layers | Many distribution layers |
| Primarily direct costs | Many indirect costs |
| Adaptable capacity | Government contracting (low bidder) |
| New products | Intermediate products |
| Commodities | Entrenched industries |

**FIGURE 10.5**

Characteristics That Encourage Certain Pricing Behaviors

In spite of the characteristics shown in Figure 10.5, market prices are still strongly influenced by cost functions. For example, competitive copy center pricing near college campuses pushes the per copy price close to actual cost, given volume and cost behavior. And, conditions do change. The long-distance telephone industry has moved from a regulated industry to a highly price-competitive situation, while becoming even more capital intensive.

Global competitiveness has introduced market price as a starting point in product design and costing—a target market price minus a desired markup equals an allowable product cost.

In cost-based pricing, **markup pricing methods** are widely used. To arrive at the price, a cost is computed; and a **markup** stated as a percentage of cost is added. The purposes of the markup is to cover nonproduct costs and generate a profit. The term "cost" as used in this method is ambiguous until carefully defined.

## Full Cost Pricing

The most widely used markup pricing approach is full cost. **Full cost pricing** is a price commonly based on total manufacturing costs, including fixed and variable product costs. Proper treatment of fixed cost presents a problem in full cost pricing. As volume increases, the fixed cost and full cost per unit decrease. If price follows cost, price goes down, which further spurs demand. Unfortunately, volume decreases create serious distress. Per unit full costs increase, forcing up prices. Demand falls more, costs go up again, and so on. Full cost pricing does have the following potential problems:

- A full cost per unit is accurate at only one level of volume.
- Seldom does a full cost reflect incremental costs when volume changes.
- To calculate a full cost, often arbitrary cost allocations are made.
- Given a market framework in which price is set where marginal cost equals marginal revenue, full cost pricing almost guarantees a "wrong" price.

However, full costing does offer some countering benefits:

- Using full costs causes all products to bear a "fair share" of all common costs that must be covered.
- Full cost pricing includes long-term cost patterns in pricing strategies.
- For certain ranges of activity (perhaps the relevant range), the per unit full cost may change very little as volume increases or decreases.
- Being the long-term, low-cost provider is a very effective competitive strategy, particularly when cost includes both product and nonproduct costs.

## Variable Cost Pricing

Another pricing approach uses variable cost as the cost base. One advantage is that difficulties with allocating indirect and fixed costs are avoided. Also, if reasonably accurate estimates of demand given various prices exist, it may be possible to find a price that maximizes profits in a classic supply-demand economic sense.

If variable cost is used, any added markup must be large enough to cover all fixed costs and to provide a profit. A danger always exists that variable cost may be thought of as full cost. Prices that cover only a portion of total costs will, in the long run, lead to serious financial problems.

## Market-Based Pricing

If prices are market driven, the debate over full or variable costs does not disappear. Market price minus cost yields a profit measure: (1) using full cost, a gross margin or a net profit and (2) using variable cost, a version of contribution margin. These margins can be linked to return on investment in evaluating the performance of existing investments (more in Chapter 13) and in making new investments (more in Chapters 11 and 12). Prices are nearly always part of return-on-investment analyses. Thus, even when prices are not cost based, costs influence how managers view product profitability, attack market segments, and decide whether to enter or exit markets.

## SUMMARY

Managers in any organization make decisions; some are short run, while others have long-run implications. This chapter creates a structured approach to make and implement decisions involving costs and revenues.

Differential analysis can be applied to a wide variety of decisions. The basic rule is to select the choice that gives the greatest incremental profit. Incremental profit is the difference between the relevant revenues and the relevant costs of each choice. Relevant revenues and costs are defined as the current and future values that differ among the choices considered.

The decision groups examined are make or buy, special sales pricing, scarce resource, sell or process further, and delete or add a segment. For each decision group, a key decision rule and guidelines are stated; and a format for analyzing relevant data is developed. While the basic decision assumes a short-term timeframe, the real-world applications often include long-term elements. Qualitative issues affect every decision, with strategic and policy concerns looming in the background.

Cost information is relevant to pricing analyses regardless of whether prices are market driven or cost based. Finally, full cost and variable cost pricing approaches give a different base for determining a markup for cost-based prices.

## PROBLEMS FOR REVIEW

### Review Problem A—Special Sale

Calderone Company, of Milano, Italy, sells a consumer electronics product called Teris at a price of €35(euros) per unit. Teris costs per unit are:

| | | |
|---|---|---|
| Prime costs | €15 | |
| Overhead | 15 | (60 percent of which is fixed) |
| Total costs | €30 | |

A special order for 20,000 units was received from Chou Distributors, an import/export firm in Beijing, PRC, a new market area for the company. Additional shipping costs on this sale are €4 per unit.

**Required:**
1. If Calderone is operating at full capacity, what is the minimum price per unit that should be set for the Beijing order? Comment.
2. If Calderone has excess capacity, what is the minimum price? Comment.

**Solution:**
This is a special pricing problem. Calderone must determine whether:
1. Excess capacity exists—"no" for Part 1 and "yes" for Part 2.
2. The order will not interfere with regular business—probably will not since the order is from an importer in Beijing and the firm has no other business in the PRC.
3. A positive contribution margin exists—will depend on the price selected.

For Part 1, Calderone must take sales from regular customers and, thus, must earn at least the same contribution margin from Beijing sales as from regular sales. Since the Beijing sale will cost €4 per unit more in shipping costs, the selling price should be at least €39 per unit.

For Part 2, the price should cover only incremental costs of the additional units: €15 for prime costs, €6 for variable overhead (0.40 × €15), and €4 for shipping costs. The minimum price must, therefore, be greater than €25 to earn a positive contribution margin.

## REVIEW PROBLEM B—SELL OR PROCESS FURTHER

The Lanier Corporation creates Products A, B, and C from a joint process costing $60,000. This cost is divided equally among A, B, and C. Each product can be sold at the split-off point or processed further. Additional processing costs are $1 per gallon. Available data are:

| Product | Gallons From Joint Process | Sales Price Per Gallon at Split-Off | Sales Price Per Gallon if Processed Further |
|---------|---------------------------|-------------------------------------|---------------------------------------------|
| A | 10,000 | $3 | $6 |
| B | 5,000 | 4 | 8 |
| C | 20,000 | 7 | 9 |

**Required:**
If Lanier has only $12,000 available for further processing, which product should be processed further to earn the highest incremental contribution margin? Why?

**Solution:**
First, find the incremental profit per gallon of processing further:

| Product | Sales Price if Processed Further | | Sales Price at Split-Off | | Incremental Revenue | | Incremental Cost | | Incremental Profit | Priority Rank |
|---------|----------------------------------|---|--------------------------|---|---------------------|---|------------------|---|--------------------|---------------|
| A | $6 | − | $3 | = | $3 | − | $1 | = | $2 | 2nd |
| B | 8 | − | 4 | = | 4 | − | 1 | = | 3 | 1st |
| C | 9 | − | 7 | = | 2 | − | 1 | = | 1 | 3rd |

Lanier can process 12,000 gallons ($12,000 ÷ $1). Using the priorities, processing Product B costs $5,000, leaving $7,000 to process Product A. Even though a positive contribution margin could be earned from processing more A and then C, no funds remain to do so. Lamier's incremental contribution margin is $29,000 as follows:

| Product B: ($4 × 5,000 gallons) − ($1 × 5,000 gallons) | = | $15,000 |
| Product A: ($3 × 7,000 gallons) − ($1 × 7,000 gallons) | = | 14,000 |
| Incremental contribution margin | | $29,000 |

Note that the joint costs of $60,000 already spent do not impact the decision.

## TERMINOLOGY REVIEW

| | |
|---|---|
| **Contribution margin per unit of scarce resource (422)** | **Markup pricing methods (430)** |
| **Decision point (424)** | **Opportunity cost (412)** |
| **Differential analysis (412)** | **Outsource (416)** |
| **Full cost pricing (430)** | **Out-of-pocket costs (412)** |
| **Incremental analysis approach (413)** | **Relevant buy costs (416)** |
| **Incremental profit (412)** | **Relevant make costs (416)** |
| **In-house sourcing (416)** | **Relevant revenues and costs (412)** |
| **Joint costs (425)** | **Scrap (453)** |
| **Joint products (424)** | **Split-off point (424)** |
| **Markup (430)** | **Sunk costs (412)** |
| | **Total analysis approach (413)** |

## QUESTIONS FOR REVIEW AND DISCUSSION

1. What is the basic decision rule in differential analysis? Explain each noun in the rule.

2. Refer to the decision steps defined in Chapter 1. In which steps does the managerial accountant play major roles?

3. Remembering the discussions in chapter 2, what are the three reasons that an amount of money would be irrelevant to a decision? And, what are the two reasons that an amount would be relevant?

4. Why is identifying decision alternatives one of the most important steps in the decision-making process?

5. Lisa Forrest, owner of several small local businesses, said recently, "The general rule I follow in making short-run decisions is that variable costs are almost always relevant and fixed cost are almost always irrelevant." Do you agree? Why or why not?

6. Distinguish between:
   (a) The incremental analysis approach and the total analysis approach.
   (b) An out-of-pocket cost and an opportunity cost.

7. Why is the timeframe—short term or long term—important in decision making?

8. "Accounting is common sense! Any rational person should be able to look at the relevant dollars and cents and make a decision." Do you agree or disagree? Why?

9. The president of Bethany Company said, "Accounting data are useful for predicting the results of various choices; but, in my company, the final decision often depends on other factors." Explain this statement.

10. For each of the five major decision types discussed, give an example that has not been mentioned in the text.

11. Identify the guidelines that should be met for a special sales pricing decision. Explain why they are important. What happens when each is violated?

12. What is the decision rule in a make or buy decision? Define relevant costs on both sides.

13. If capacity is scarce, how can opportunity costs be used to decide whether a product should be sold now (an intermediate product) or finished and sold as a completed product?

14. Nehlsen Company prepares tax returns and charges $100 for simple returns and $500 for more complicated returns. Nehlsen's receptionist is making customer appointments for the second weekend of April. Write the receptionist a memo as a guide to which customers should be scheduled and which should be told to go elsewhere. Before you write the memo, list the assumptions you are making.

15. Explain how a special sales decision in one firm might be a make or buy decision in another firm.

16. Why might a company produce a subassembly at a higher cost, rather than buy the same subassembly from an outside supplier?

17. If a restaurant owner considers adding a new main course and deleting another for profitability purposes, what decision rule should be applied? What type of decision is this?

18. Joe French of Quick Supplies says he prefers the incremental analysis method because it eliminates all unnecessary data. Jan Dutch of Office Managers, Inc. prefers the total analysis approach because she can see the "big picture." Comment.

19. Although a firm has unused capacity and a special order would contribute $75,000 to profits, a manager rejected the order. Why might the manager do this?

20. In markup pricing, what elements must be covered by the markup when full costs are used? When variable costs are used?

21. The marketing vice-president of Janelle Fabrics says that product prices should always be set by supply and demand in the marketplace to ensure high sales levels. The controller says that product prices should always be based on cost to ensure profitability. Who's right? Explain.

## EXERCISES

Service

**10–1. Incremental vs. Total Analysis Approaches.** Kramer Company currently handles 8,000 information requests per month. Financial data for last month are:

| | |
|---|---|
| Sales | $240,000 |
| Variable costs | 144,000 |
| Fixed costs | 60,000 |

The company needs to expand its operations to serve 9,000 requests per month. Fixed costs would increase $15,000 because of the expansion.

**Required:**
Prepare both a total analysis approach and an incremental analysis approach to evaluate the decision. Compare the results.

**10–2. Special Sales.** Trembath Company sells Product A for $30 per unit. Trembath's per unit cost on the full capacity of 200,000 units is:

| | |
|---|---|
| Direct materials | $10 |
| Direct labor | 5 |
| Overhead | 12 |
| Manufacturing costs | $27 |

The overhead is one-third variable and two-thirds fixed.

A Japanese firm has offered to buy 20,000 units. Additional shipping costs of this order would be $3 per unit. Trembath has sufficient existing capacity to manufacture the additional units. The Trembath sales manager wants to earn an incremental profit of $50,000 from this sale.

**Required:** What is the minimum price per unit Trembath should charge?

**10–3. Make or Buy Analysis.** Stace Company needs 20,000 units of a certain part to use in its production cycle. If Stace buys the part from Vaz Company instead of making it, Stace could rent the released facilities as storage to another manufacturing firm for $10,000. Sixty percent of the fixed overhead applied will continue to be incurred regardless of what decision is made. The following information is available:

| | |
|---|---:|
| Cost to Stace to make the part: | |
| Direct materials | $4 |
| Direct labor | 16 |
| Variable overhead | 8 |
| Fixed overhead applied | 10 |
| | $38 |
| | |
| Cost to buy the part from the | |
| Vaz Company | $36 |

**Required:**
1. Which alternative is more desirable for Stace and what amount?
2. What assumptions about cost behavior might be troublesome by either buying or making?

**10–4. Additional Processing.** Puidokas Company produces a vitamin supplement from a common mixture at a cost of $50 per pound. Puidokas sells this mixture as HiEnergy for $80 per pound. Or any one or all of three new products (called GoGetEm, ReallyGo, and SuperGo) can be made from the mixture. Puidokas can sell all HiEnergy it produces.

| | Additional Production Costs Per Pound | Sales Value Per Pound |
|---|:---:|:---:|
| HiEnergy | | $80 |
| GoGetEm | $15 | 100 |
| ReallyGo | 35 | 110 |
| SuperGo | 40 | 130 |

**Required:**
1. What should the firm do, given the facts above?
2. What should the firm do, if the market for HiEnergy is limited?

**10–5. Sell or Process.** Zelenski produces three products: X, Y, and Z in a single process that costs $30,000. They can each be sold as is or processed further into another product. Quantities, market values, and additional costs are:

| Products | Gallons | Market Value Now | Additional Costs | Market Value After |
|---|:---:|:---:|:---:|:---:|
| X | 10,000 | $1.00 per gallon | $10,000 | $3.20 per gallon |
| Y | 10,000 | 2.00 per gallon | 20,000 | 3.75 per gallon |
| Z | 10,000 | 3.00 per gallon | 15,000 | 5.00 per gallon |

**Required:** What should Zelenski do? Identify several assumptions you made.

**10–6. Sales Priorities.** The Martinez Cooperative employees highly skilled Native American artists to produce sand paintings for sale in craft stores. The artists make large, medium, and small paintings. The sales and production data are:

|  | Large | Medium | Small |
|---|---|---|---|
| Sales price | $80 | $50 | $25 |
| Materials and artists' time costs | 38 | 25 | 16 |
| Hours per piece | 1 | 0.5 | 0.2 |

**Required:** If artists' time is scarce, what size priorities should be set by the cooperative?

**10–7. Make or Buy.** Li Lieu, owner of Emperor of Xi'an Restaurant in Xi'an, PRC, uses 5,000 fancy dumplings per month. Current costs in Chinese yuan are:

Service

| Ingredients costs | Y2 |
|---|---|
| Labor and other variable expenses | Y1 |

Wang Cao offers to sell Mr. Li dumplings at Y3 each. If Mr. Li buys dumplings, he can eliminate Y4,000 per month in fixed making costs. He thinks he can also earn an additional Y3,000 per month in contribution margin by adding three tables where the dumplings had been made.

**Required:** Should Mr. Li make or buy? Comment on concerns you might have.

**10–8. Incremental Sales.** Clouse Dairy produces and sells 10,000 gallons of Joyce's Sweet Cream, a premium ice cream, per month. Capacity is 12,000 gallons. A supermarket in another city has offered to buy 3,000 gallons of ice cream for $1 per gallon. Clouse would give up some regular sales to fill the new order. Costs and revenues per unit are:

| Ingredients and labor | $.60 |
|---|---|
| Variable overhead | .20 |
| Fixed overhead | .30 |
| Cost per gallon | $1.10 |
| Sales price | $1.30 |

**Required:**
1. Using only quantitative facts, should Clouse sell to the supermarket? Explain your reasoning.
2. Comment on strategic and qualitative issues that might concern Clouse.

**10–9. Department Profits.** Plesz Sales runs several small department stores. The Toledo store showed the following "poor" results:

Service

|  | Dept 1 | Dept 2 | Dept 3 | Dept 4 | Totals |
|---|---|---|---|---|---|
| Sales | $700 | $1,000 | $ 800 | $1,500 | $4,000 |
| Cost of goods sold | (350) | (500) | (450) | (800) | (2,100) |
| Gross margin | $350 | $ 500 | $ 350 | $700 | $1,900 |
| Direct expenses | (100) | (400) | (400) | (300) | (1,200) |
| Common expenses | (100) | (300) | (100) | (300) | (800) |
| Net income | $150 | $ (200) | $(150) | $100 | $(100) |

**Required:** Comment on the impact of each of the following actions.
**(a)** Delete Department 2.
**(b)** Delete Department 3.
**(c)** Delete Departments 2 and 3.
**(d)** Replace Departments 2 and 3 with a new Department 5 that would earn a positive direct contribution margin of $25.
**(e)** Reallocate the common expenses.

**10–10. Markup Pricing.** The following cost analysis has been performed for a specific customer order for Lila Products, Inc. The president, Lila Ganong, is experimenting with different pricing strategies. She thinks 100,000 units can be sold. Fixed costs have been allocated using various activity bases.

|  | Per Unit | Total |
|---|---|---|
| Variable manufacturing costs | $4.25 | $425,000 |
| Direct fixed manufacturing costs | 1.50 | 150,000 |
| Indirect fixed manufacturing costs | 3.75 | 375,000 |
| Total manufacturing costs | $9.50 | $950,000 |
| Variable selling expenses | $1.80 | $180,000 |
| Indirect fixed selling expenses | 1.45 | 145,000 |
| Total selling expenses | $3.25 | $325,000 |

**Required:**
What markup percentage is required to earn $120,000 if the price is set:
**1.** Assuming that the order is a one-time sale?
**2.** Assuming that the order will become part of Lila's regular product line?

**10–11. Special Hat Sales.** A. J. Inc. can make 10,000 caps per year. A. J. can sell 9,000 caps per year to NASCAR racing fans for $10 per hat. His cost per hat based on making 10,000 caps is:

| | | |
|---|---|---|
| Prime costs | $5.00 | |
| Overhead costs | 3.00 | (Overhead is two-thirds fixed at that volume.) |

Sugar Ray Hinsky offers to buy 1,000 hats with special boxing insignias for $7 per hat. Attaching special insignias will cost A. J. $200.

**Required:** What should A. J. do? Explain.

**10–12. Sell Now or Later.** Ballou Corporation uses a joint process to produce products A, B, and C. Each product may be sold at its split-off point or processed further. Additional processing costs are entirely variable and are traceable to the respective products. Annual joint production costs were $50,000 and are allocated equally to A, B, and C.

| | | | If Processed Further | |
|---|---|---|---|---|
| Product | Units Produced | Sales Value at Split-Off | Sales Value | Additional Costs |
| A | 20,000 | $45,000 | $60,000 | $20,000 |
| B | 15,000 | 75,000 | 98,000 | 20,000 |
| C | 15,000 | 30,000 | 62,000 | 18,000 |
| | | $150,000 | | |

**Required:** To maximize profits, which products should Ballou process further?

Service

**10–13. Incremental Pricing.** Diliberti Copies arranges for the preparation of course packets used in many courses. Prof. Sollenberger has asked for a price for his managerial accounting course packet. Danielle, the owner, really wants this business. She calculates her average costs to be $5 per copy for 400 packets and $4 per copy for 600 packets. Also, she generally adds $1 to each packet to help cover her common fixed overhead and earn a profit. All costs are either fixed or variable. Sollenberger also needs 30 complimentary copies for his teaching assistants. Enrollment estimates are for 600 students, of which 80 percent buys the packets.

**Required:** What is the lowest price she can offer and cover incremental costs?

Service

**10–14. Studying—A Student Dilemma.** Ryan is concerned about grades in 4 courses he is taking this semester. Between now and his final exams, he has a maximum of 40 hours of study time. He can also sleep, watch TV, or "goof off." The grade system uses 4.0, 3.5, 3.0, 2.5, 2.0, 1.5, 1.0, and 0.0, where 4.0 is an A. If he does not study for a course, he thinks he can keep his current grade. Ryan thinks that a higher can be earned only if it is earned completely—5 hours of additional study in Course 1 will earn a 2.5 grade. His grades now and effort needed to get a 0.5 higher grade are:

| | Grade Now | Study Hours Required to Earn an Additional 0.5 Grade |
|---|---|---|
| Course 1 | 2.0 | 5 hours |
| Course 2 | 3.0 | 4 hours |
| Course 3 | 1.0 | 6 hours |
| Course 4 | 1.0 | 8 hours |

**Required:** Prioritize his study time to earn the highest grade average.

**10–15. Equipment Replacement.** Merle Murphy, owner of Murphy Farms, is considering plans to rent a new sprinkler system for his navy bean business. He currently uses a system that rents for $25,000 per year and has annual operating costs of $20,000 plus $100 per acre. The new system will rent for $10,000 per year and have annual operating costs of $30,000 plus $40 per acre. Both systems will perform the same function. He will plant 200 acres of beans. The contribution margin next year from beans is estimated to be $125,000.

**Required:** Should Murphy change to the new system? Explain your conclusion.

Service

**10–16. Scarce Resource Decision.** The DeClercq Company performs three different services: Able, Baker, and Charlie. Because of unusual demand, all service requests cannot be filled. Fixed cost allocations are based on service hours. DeClercq has 2,000 hours of available service time.

| | Able | Baker | Charlie |
|---|---|---|---|
| Sales price | $50 | $40 | $30 |
| Variable costs | 30 | 25 | 20 |
| Allocated fixed costs | 10 | 10 | 10 |
| Service time per request | 0.8 hour | 0.5 hour | 0.2 hour |

**Required:**
1. Assume that DeClercq must meet at least 500 requests for each type of service for regular customers. What quantities of each service should be performed to meet regular customer needs while maximizing profits?
2. Assume that DeClercq can generate 3,000 service requests for each type of service. What priorities should Soma set to maximize profits?

**10–17. Make or Buy.** Gramlich Corporation operates its own cafeteria for employees. The cafeteria prices are only 75 percent of the full costs of preparation. Management feels this is an important employee benefit. ASF, Inc. is offering to operate the cafeteria and promising to increase the quality of menu items, reduce prices, and reduce the needed subsidy. ASF would use Gramlich's existing facilities and even transfer some of the current cafeteria employees to its staff. ASF submitted a formal bid based on comparable services. As Gramlich's controller, you have summarized the next year's budget for cafeteria operations and ASF's numbers from its proposal as follows:

|  | Internally Managed | ASF, Inc. Managed |
|---|---|---|
| Food costs | $ 500,000 | $450,000 |
| Preparation costs | 200,000 | 180,000 |
| Administrative overhead | 300,000 | |
| Management fee | | 200,000 |
| Total cafeteria costs | $1,000,000 | $830,000 |
| Cafeteria revenue | 800,000 | 750,000 |
| Operating subsidy | $ 200,000 | $ 80,000 |

**Required:**

Comment on the numbers. Outline key issues that are of concern to you. What data will you need to collect and analyze to resolve the issues?

**10–18. Process Further Decision.** Silver Bullet Refining produces naphtha, kerosene, and other distillates from a joint process costing $120,000 for a certain volume of crude oil. From this process, 1,000 barrels of naphtha can be produced and are allocated $35,000 of joint costs. This can be sold at the split-off point for $60 per barrel or further processed into other products and sold for $85 per barrel. The processing cost for further refining 1,000 barrels of naphtha is $20,000.

The other distillates can be sold now for $80,000 or processed further for $40,000 and sold for $110,000. Kerosene can be sold for $60,000 at the split-off point. Kerosene is also allocated $35,000 of the joint costs. Other distillates are allocated the remaining joint costs.

**Required:**

**1.** Which products should be sold at the split-off point or processed further?

**2.** What is the most Silver Bullet can pay for crude oil and not lose money on the refining process?

**10–19. Eliminating a Department.** ABCDE Department Store has five departments—A, B, C, D, and E. Department E's future is being evaluated using the data below:

|  | All Others | Department E | Total |
|---|---|---|---|
| Sales | $4,500,000 | $500,000 | $5,000,000 |
| Cost of sales | 2,200,000 | 300,000 | 2,500,000 |
| Gross margin | $2,300,000 | $200,000 | $2,500,000 |
| Rent and services | $800,000 | $200,000 | $1,000,000 |
| Direct salaries | 450,000 | 50,000 | 500,000 |
| Advertising expenses | 450,000 /2 = 225 | 50,000 /2 = 25 | 500,000 /2 = 250 |
| Total expenses | $1,700,000 | $300,000 | $2,000,000 |
| Net profit (loss) | $600,000 | $(100,000) | $500,000 |

*Fixed* (handwritten annotation next to "Rent and services")

Rent and services are corporate committed fixed expenses and are allocated evenly to the five departments. Half of the advertising expenses varies with sales; the other half will not change regardless of the decision and is allocated using sales dollars.

**Required:**
Comment on the following statements:
**(a)** Department E is earning $150,000 in variable contribution margin for ABCDE.
**(b)** Department E is earning $100,000 in direct contribution margin for ABCDE.
**(c)** The company's overall profitability without Department E would be $600,000.

**10–20. Make or Buy Indifference Point.** Stephen Wegener contacted a Malaysian manufacturer that will charge $40 per unit plus $200,000 for special equipment and dies for a lens assembly for an overhead projector. But he thinks he can make it himself for the following costs:

| | |
|---|---|
| Prime costs | $21 |
| Other variable costs | 3 |
| Total variable costs | $24 |

Steve knows that incremental salaries, equipment rentals, and other fixed costs to make the assembly will run $360,000 per year. Common costs of manufacturing are applied to products at 60 percent of prime costs. Steve plans to sell these projectors for $150 per unit.

**Required:**
Find sales volume in units where Wegener would be indifferent between making the lens assembly or buying it.

**10–21. Product Combination Decision.** Data concerning four product lines are as follows:

| | Product Line | | | |
|---|---|---|---|---|
| | **A** | **B** | **C** | **D** |
| Selling price per unit | $300 | $250 | $130 | $70 |
| Variable cost per unit | 250 | 80 | 50 | 40 |
| Hours required for each unit | 5 | 10 | 4 | 2 |
| Maximum market potential (units) | No limit | 6,000 | 8,000 | 4,000 |
| Total fixed costs | $100,000 | | | |
| Total hours available | 96,000 hours | | | |

**Required:**
1. Based on these data, choose the best product combination.
2. How would the answer change if the company were required to deliver 2,000 units of each product line to a major distributor? The maximum market potential includes the distributor's units.

**10–22. Process or Sell Decision.** The Smokey Meat Company produces a meat product which can be sold after the slaughtering process, or it can be smoked and then sold. For next month the company has scheduled production of 40,000 pounds which, if sold unsmoked, would bring a selling price of $2.30 per pound. Costs associated with producing the unsmoked product are $1.20 per pound plus fixed facilities costs of $30,000 for the month. If 40,000 pounds are produced, the entire slaughtering capacity will be used.

If the 40,000 pounds are smoked, smoking capacity, which would otherwise be idle, will be used entirely also. The additional variable costs, mainly for heat and smoking ingredients, are estimated to be $0.40 per pound; and the selling price of the smoked product is $3.30

per pound. The monthly committed fixed costs on the portion of the facility used for smoking the meat amount to $8,000, and avoidable fixed costs are $5,000.

**Required:**
Prepare an analysis to help the manager, Cristina, decide whether the 40,000 pounds should be smoked or should not be smoked.

Service

**10–23. Buying Legal Services.** Jon Jenkins, a local attorney, was contacted by a doctors' professional corporation to represent it in a series of legal matters. After a negotiating conference, Jon offers to provide up to 400 hours of legal services during the next year if the corporation will pay a retainer of $3,000 per month plus direct expenses. After 400 hours, his rate is $100 per hour. Or he could charge the corporation $130 for each billable hour plus direct expenses. Dr. Beall, chief administrator for the doctors' group, thinks that a competent attorney could be hired full time for $90,000 per year including direct support costs. He knows that the firm has used about 15 hours of legal services per month for the past two years. He sees a 50 percent probability that this trend will continue for the coming year, a 20 percent chance that 20 hours per month will be needed, and a 20 percent chance that 40 hours per month will be needed. A 10 percent like-lihood exists that one particular case may force the firm to need 100 hours per month.

**Required:**
Recommend an approach to analyzing Dr. Beall's purchase of legal services. What decision does your approach suggest?

**10–24. Equipment Replacement.** Last week Souza Enterprises purchased a new irrigation system called Spray costing $60,000. Its annual cash operating costs are estimated to be $35,000. It has a four-year useful life and no residual value. Today, a salesman has offered Souza a new system called Sprinkle that will cost $60,000 and will also have a four-year useful life with no residual value. The Spray equipment can be used as a trade-in for a $10,000 allowance. The annual cash operating costs of Sprinkle are estimated to be $20,000. Sales of $400,000 and other operating expenses of $180,000 per year will be the same under either alternative.

**Required:**
Ignoring the time value of money to be discussed in Chapter 11, should Souza purchase the Sprinkle system? Explain.

**10–25. Sell or Process Further.** Harrell Company produces Green Awfully Sticky Stuff (GASS) at a cost of $30,000 per batch. A batch of GASS can be sold as is for $50,000 or processed through Department A where Products A and AA are made. Or the GASS batch can be processed through Department B where Products B and BB are made. Costs and revenues of processing further in Departments A and B are:

|  | *Incremental Costs* | *Products* | *Market Value* |
| --- | --- | --- | --- |
| Department A | $ 20,000 | A | $ 13,000 |
|  |  | AA | $ 72,000 |
| Department B | $150,000 | B | $100,000 |
|  |  | BB | $ 95,000 |

**Required:**
1. What should be done with a batch of GASS that Harrell has on hand? Show calculations to support your decision.
2. If the cost to produce a batch of GASS increased to $60,000, would you decide to continue to produce GASS?

**10–26. Decisions, Decisions, Decisions.** In the following vignettes, make a recommendation to your boss—the person described in each situation. And, suggest any other issues your boss should consider beyond the data provided.

**A.** Darichuk Corp. incurs the following annual costs in making one part for its products:

|  | Total Costs for 20,000 Units |
|---|---|
| Prime costs | $200,000 |
| Variable factory overhead | 200,000 |
| Fixed factory overhead | 300,000 |

Hubbard Co. offers the same part for $25 per unit. If the parts are purchased from Hubbard, plant space currently used by Darichuk for making the parts can be rented for $30,000 a year. Also, $100,000 of fixed factory overhead could be avoided if the part is purchased. Make or buy?

**B.** Misty Pleiness is thinking of making a key part for her main product. She forecasts 40,000 units as being required. Kelley Corp. offers to make this part for $5 per unit. Her make costs are shown below. Make or buy?

| | |
|---|---|
| Purchased materials costs | $60,000 |
| Variable labor and overhead | 40,000 |
| Common fixed overhead | 70,000 |
| Avoidable direct fixed overhead | 50,000 |
| Unavoidable direct fixed overhead | 30,000 |

**C.** Nate Ferguson is considering an outside cleaning service for his office building. He knows that Fischer's Maidens will clean for a contract price of $25 per hour with hours estimated to be 2,000 per year plus supplies of $5,000. Ferguson knows his current annual costs are $40,000 for a full time cleaner, $12,000 for equipment rental and supplies used, and $10,000 for allocated corporate common expenses based on square feet used by the cleaning department. Make or buy?

Service

**10–27. Changing Product Lines.** Dale Kim, president of Kim's Department Store, thinks that the Paint Department should be dropped. He wants to add a Peanut Butter Boutique in the same space. Data for next year in thousands are:

| | Paint | All Other Departments | Store Total | Proposed Peanut Butter Boutique |
|---|---|---|---|---|
| Sales | $10,000 | $90,000 | $100,000 | $20,000 |
| Cost of sales | −6,000 | −54,000 | −60,000 | −15,000 |
| Gross margin | $ 4,000 | $36,000 | $ 40,000 | $ 5,000 |
| Direct expenses | −1,000 | −14,000 | −15,000 | −3,000 |
| Allocated expenses | −4,000 | −16,000 | −20,000 | −1,000 |
| Net income | −$1,000 | $ 6,000 | $ 5,000 | $ 1,000 |

Allocated expenses are common costs and are assigned by a mathematical formula.

**Required:**

Ignoring your attitude toward peanut butter, what should he do to maximize profits? Explain.

**10–28. Special Sales Pricing.** Chung Company, in Hong Kong, is selling 80,000 pairs of jade earrings at HK$10 per pair. The variable cost is HK$6 per pair, and the annual fixed cost is

HK$120,000. A U.S.A. discount house has offered to buy 10,000 additional pairs of the product which would be slightly modified for the U.S. market, but the modifications would not affect production costs. The discount house will pay HK$7 per pair.

**Required:**

1. If the two markets can be distinguished, should the order be accepted (assuming capacity exists and has no other use)? Explain.
2. The manager feels that the two markets might not be distinguished and that the lower price would cause regular sales to fall by 5,000 pairs. Should Chung accept the discount house offer? Explain.
3. If the discount house offer is raised to HK$9 per pair and competition resulting from the special sale causes the regular price to drop to HK$9.50 to maintain the same regular sales volume, should Chung accept the discount house offer? Explain.

**10–29. Make or Buy.** Slowik, Inc. makes steel blades for lawn mowers that it heat treats, assembles, and sells. The cost accounting system gives the following data:

| | |
|---|---|
| Prime costs | $80,000 |
| Variable factory overhead | 60,000 |
| Fixed factory overhead | 90,000 |
| Units produced | 100,000  units |

Slowik has an opportunity to purchase its 100,000 blades from an outside supplier at a cost of $2.20 per blade. Inspection of the purchased blades will cost an additional $5,000 in the quality assurance department. Certain leased equipment, which costs $30,000 and is included in fixed overhead, can be avoided if the blades are purchased. The released space could be used to make a part that is now purchased, which would net Slowik a savings of $46,000.

**Required:**

1. In quantitative terms, should Slowik buy the blades from the outside supplier? Explain your decision.
2. What major factors might change the decision?

**10–30. Segment Profit Performance Analysis.** Blaufuss Sausages has a central processing plant and three stores. Recently, profits have been declining. The projected income statement for the three stores is as follows:

| | Main Street | King Street | Queen Street | Total |
|---|---|---|---|---|
| Sales | $200 | $175 | $190 | $565 |
| Product cost of sausages | −120 | −100 | −110 | −330 |
| Gross margin | $ 80 | $ 75 | $ 80 | $235 |
| Direct store expenses | −60 | −85 | −35 | −180 |
| Allocated administrative expenses | −25 | −15 | −20 | −60 |
| Net income | $ (5) | $(25) | $ 25 | $ (5) |

**Required:** What will each of the following actions do to Blaufuss' profits?

**(a)** Eliminate Main Street store.
**(b)** Eliminate King Street store.
**(c)** Eliminate Main and King Street stores.
**(d)** Close all stores.
**(e)** Open a fourth store and divide allocated administrative expenses among four stores. (Assume that the new store will have a zero net income.)

**10–31. Ethics of Product Pricing.** Vine Resources (VR) provides office equipment systems development and maintenance services. Its customers are a wide array of businesses. Maintenance services are provided through an annual contract with a fixed annual fee plus additional charges for "emergency calls" on an as needed basis. VR won a competitive bid with the City of Dermit to maintain a large number of office work stations. The contract is for three years and calls for routine maintenance checks to be done quarterly as part of the annual fee, emergency calls to be billed at the "full" cost per hour of service representatives, and parts to be replaced for free except for major hardware components. The per hour rate will be updated annually.

It is now a year and a half into the contract. The city controller is concerned with the growing cost of machine maintenance. After examining the situation, the controller has found:

1. Emergency calls have doubled in the past six months and are growing.
2. The "full" cost service rate has gone from $25 per hour last year to $32 per hour this year.
3. Office workers are complaining about too much downtime.

A meeting with the VR representative found that all routine maintenance has been performed on schedule. Also, while some personnel costs have increased, the main reason for the jump in service rate was a change made in how certain fringe benefit costs were assigned to service personnel. The VR rep also mentioned the aging nature of the equipment and the need to upgrade the entire system.

**Required:** Comment on possible implications of each of the controller's findings.

**10–32. Cost Analysis and Pricing.** Sales in the Jackson office of Fast Print Company for the past year were $475,000. Costs were:

| | |
|---|---|
| Materials and variable supplies expenses | $ 200,000 |
| Direct labor expenses | 100,000 |
| Occupancy and other fixed operating expenses | 100,000 |
| Total expenses | $ 400,000 |

For most printing jobs, a cost-plus pricing policy is used. To find a job's cost, estimated labor costs are doubled to cover labor and overhead and then added to estimated materials costs. The total job costs are then multiplied by 120 percent to calculate customer price.

The advertising manager for a regional supermarket has proposed a deal. She has a weekly advertising piece which will be mailed to local residents. The printing job would require $200 of materials and supplies and $100 of direct labor time. She is willing to pay $420 per week and would like a one-year contract. The Jackson office manager rejects the offer since it violates his pricing strategy.

**Required:**
1. Would the supermarket business be profitable for Fast Print:
   (a) On a one-time basis?
   (b) On a regular (annual) basis?
2. What qualitative issues might impact your answer?

# PROBLEMS

**10–33. Costing a Service.** Up-and-Away Airlines, a regional commuter airline, flies routes among mid-sized cities in the midwest. The firm owns six airplanes, which can hold 150 passengers each. All routes are about the same distance, and all fares are $55 one way. The line operates 200 flights per month. Each flight costs $2,000 for gasoline, crew salaries, and so forth.

Variable costs per passenger are $5, to cover meals and head taxes levied for each passenger departure at each airport. Other fixed costs are $60,000 per month.

**Required:**

1. How many passengers must the airline carry on 200 flights to earn a $30,000 per month profit? What percentage of capacity does this number represent?
2. What impact does a $1 increase in airfare have on the capacity percentage needed to break even?
3. Comment on the cost behavior of each cost element.

**10–34. Dropping a Product.** Bob Leverenz, an old prospector, runs a side business. He buys rattlesnakes from "snake hunters" in west Texas, paying an average of $10 per snake. Each snake comes complete. He produces canned snake meat, cures hides, and makes souvenir rattles. At the end of a recent season, Bob is evaluating his financial results:

|  | Meat | Hides | Rattles | Total |
|---|---|---|---|---|
| Sales | $30,000 | $8,000 | $2,000 | $40,000 |
| Cost of snakes | 18,000 | 4,800 | 1,200 | 24,000 |
| Gross profit | $12,000 | $3,200 | $800 | $16,000 |
| Processing expenses | $6,000 | $900 | $600 | $7,500 |
| Common expenses | 4,000 | 600 | 400 | 5,000 |
| Operating expenses | $10,000 | $1,500 | $1,000 | $12,500 |
| Income (loss) | $2,000 | $1,700 | $(200) | $3,500 |

Cost of snakes assigned to each product is based on a ratio of cost to revenue. Processing expenses are direct costs. Common expenses are allocated on the basis of direct processing expenses and are Bob's basic living expenses. Bob has a philosophy of "every tub on its own bottom" and is determined to cut his losses on rattles.

**Required:**

1. Is he really "losing" money on rattles? Explain.
2. An old miner has offered to buy every rattle "as is," without processing, for $0.50 per rattle. Will this eliminate the "loss" problem and improve Bob's profitability?

**10–35. Elimination of a Department.** The Halverson's Old General Store is currently divided into three departments. Over the past several months, sales and profit have declined, although the situation is now considered stable. Department 2 has begun to show a loss; and the owner, Joan Halverson, is thinking of discontinuing it. The space could be rented to a chain shoe store which would pay a flat fee of $12,000 a month.

Below is last month's income statement, considered to be typical. Sales salaries are fixed but traceable to each department and could be avoided if the department were eliminated. Total fixed administrative costs (allocated equally to all departments) are common costs.

|  | Department 1 | Department 2 | Department 3 | Total |
|---|---|---|---|---|
| Sales | $185,000 | $80,000 | $135,000 | $400,000 |
| Costs: |  |  |  |  |
| Cost of goods sold | $96,000 | $44,000 | $ 70,000 | $210,000 |
| Sales salaries | 28,000 | 8,000 | 24,000 | 60,000 |
| Administrative expenses | 30,000 | 30,000 | 30,000 | 90,000 |
| Total costs | $154,000 | $82,000 | $124,000 | $360,000 |
| Net income before taxes | $31,000 | $(2,000) | $ 11,000 | $ 40,000 |

**Required:**
Prepare an analysis to show Halverson whether Department 2 should be discontinued and the space rented.

**10–36. Make or Buy Decision.** Ling Automotive Systems developed a new windshield cleaning system for the original-equipment auto market. The system requires an electronic motor that the firm does not currently produce but is available from suppliers. The best bid is from Fiero Electronics, an Italian firm, at $23 per unit for any volume within the firm's relevant range.

Ling's production manager believes that the motor can be made in-house, although additional space and machinery would be required. The firm now leases, for $80,000 per year, space that could be used to make the new motors. However, another subsystem is now assembled in this space. Ling would have to lease additional space which rents for $175,000 per year in an adjacent building for the assembly process. It is suitable for assembly work but not for motor production. Additional equipment needed would rent for $200,000 per year.

The controller has developed the following unit costs based on the expected demand of 100,000 units per year:

| | |
|---|---|
| Prime costs | $ 14.00 |
| Rent for space | .80 |
| Machinery rental | 2.00 |
| Variable overhead | 4.00 |
| Allocated fixed overhead | 6.00 |
| Total costs | $ 26.80 |

**Required:** Should Ling make or buy the motors? What assumptions are you making?

**10–37. Process Further Situations.** In the following cases, what decisions would maximize profits for each firm?

**Situation # 1:** Sarah Baker purchased the champion cow at the county 4-H Fair. The city government has demanded that she get rid of it and stop violating the city's noise and odor ordinance because of the mooing. It cost $2,000 and weighed a ton! Her best options are shown below. What is her best alternative use for the cow? (Ignore vegetarian preferences!)

Option A: Sell the whole cow to the Carl's Meat Market for $2,500.
Option B: Make hamburger. Processing costs of $200, revenue of $2,600.
Option C: Fatten cow, make Kobe beef (a Japanese delicacy). Processing costs of $3,900, revenue of $5,800.
Option D: Feed cow (Cost $1,000, including fines.), take cow to football games—no revenue, but a lot of fun.

**Situation # 2:** The Vehlewald Juice Company presses Michigan cherries producing raw cherry juice. The cost of producing a "batch" of cherry juice is $10,000 including the cost of the cherries. From one batch comes 10,000 gallons of juice. This can be sold on the cherry juice market for $15,000. The owner is considering various "all natural" products that would give alternative uses for the juice. Estimated revenues, costs, and volumes for each option are:

| Option | Additional Costs | Product Outputs | Quantities | Market Value |
|--------|------------------|-----------------|------------|--------------|
| A: | $4,000 | Cough medicine | 2,000 gallons | $6 per gallon |
| | | Coffee substitute | 1,000 gallons | $4 per gallon |
| | | Cherry drink powder | 500 pounds | $10 per pound |
| B: | $15,000 | Frozen concentrate | 14,000 cans | $2 per can |
| C: | $20,000 | Muscle ointment | 2,000 cases | $15 per case |
| | | Hair growth grease | 1 pound | $500 per ounce |

As the financial advisor, how would you rank the four alternatives?  Show dollars?

**10–38. Special Sales Pricing.** Aoi Company manufactures study lamps in Osaka, Japan. Next year's budget estimates sales to be 500,000 lamps at ¥1,700 each. Variable costs are ¥900 per lamp, and fixed costs are budgeted at ¥300 million or ¥600 per lamp. Recently, a purchasing agent from Nationwide Superstores in the U.S.A. offered to buy 100,000 lamps at a price of ¥1,350 each. By working overtime and adding extra shifts, Aoi would have sufficient capacity. Additional overtime premiums would be ¥7.5 million. Additional supervision costs are ¥2 million. Total selling and administrative expenses will not change if the order is accepted.

Aoi's finance manager argues, "With the extra volume, the full cost of regular sales would be reduced from ¥1,500 per unit to ¥1,400. At this level Aoi would make an extra ¥100 per unit on all regular sales but still lose money on the special sales because of overtime costs and the lower price." He thinks that the 'economics of the deal' are too risky and that it violates the firm's strategic pricing policies that have helped Aoi create a reputation for quality.

**Required:**

**1.** Is the finance manager's quantitative analysis sound? Explain your decision.

**2.** What does the finance manager mean by "too risky?"

**3.** Why might this be a violation of the firm's pricing policies?

**10–39. Evaluating a Segment.** The Yablanka family has developed an extensive bakery business in Chicago and now has 90 shops. Annually, several new outlets are opened, and old ones are closed. Fred, the controller, reviews the performance of each location and of all store managers. He is currently evaluating Store 54, operated by a relatively experienced manager. Business statistics for the company and Store 54 data are:

| | Average Store Percentages | Store 54 |
|--|---------------------------|----------|
| Sales | 100 % | $400,000 |
| Expenses: | | |
| Cost of baked goodies | 35 % | $150,000 |
| Store salaries and wages | 20 | 110,000 |
| Store occupancy costs | 30 | 120,000 |
| Home office expenses | 10 | 50,000 |
| Total expenses | 95 % | $430,000 |
| Net income | 5 % | $(30,000) |

The store's lease is a three-year commitment for $30,000 per year. If Store 54 is closed, a nearby Yablanka store would attract $50,000 of Store 54's lost gross margin. Store 54's manager has a five-year personal services contract for $30,000 per year and could be transferred to a new store. All other salaries and occupancy costs can be eliminated. Home office expenses are allocated evenly among the 90 stores.

**Required:**

1. Should Store 54 be closed now? Why or why not?
2. If Store 54 gets a 6-month reprieve, in which areas should the manager attempt to improve?

**10–40. Evaluating a Special Order.** Huang Automotive in Taiwan is presently operating at 75 percent of practical capacity and producing annually about 200,000 units of a power steering system component. Huang recently received an offer from a Korean truck manufacturer to purchase 40,000 components at NT$225 (new Taiwanese dollars) per unit. Flexible budgets for production of 200,000 and 250,0000 units are:

|  | 200,000 Units | 250,000 Units |
|---|---|---|
| Direct materials | NT$18,000,000 | NT$22,500,000 |
| Direct labor | 6,000,000 | 7,500,000 |
| Factory overhead | 24,000,000 | 27,000,000 |
| Total costs. | NT$48,000,000 | NT$57,000,000 |
| Cost per unit. | NT$240 | NT$228 |

Peter Wu, vice-president of sales, thinks accepting the order will get the company's "foot in the door" of an expanding international market, even if the company loses a little on this order.

T. J. Chan, vice-president of engineering, feels that any new market should first show its profitability and that this offer is below last year's cost per unit of NT$240. "This guarantees a loss on the order," he says.

Lili Zhang, treasurer, has made a quick computation which indicates that accepting the order will actually increase dollars of gross margin.

**Required:**

1. Estimate Huang's variable cost per unit.
2. Show how Mr. Chan and Ms. Zhang are analyzing the situation. Using the given facts, what does the incremental analysis of the Korean sale show?
3. What major nonquantitative factors might affect the decision to accept or reject the special order?

**10–41. Scarce Resources with Other Constraints.** Data for four products are given below:

|  | Product A | Product B | Product C | Product D |
|---|---|---|---|---|
| Selling price per unit | $13 | $20 | $5 | $25 |
| Variable cost per unit | 5 | 7 | 2 | 16 |
| Allocated costs per unit | 4 | 8 | 1 | 3 |
| Units produced per hour | 4 units | 2 units | 10 units | 3 units |
| Maximum sales limit | 5,000 units | 5,000 units | 10,000 units | No limit |
| Minimum requirements | 1,000 units | None | 2,000 units | 1,200 units |

Total capacity is 6,000 hours. Minimum requirements meet existing sales commitments. Marketing has provided a "best estimate" of maximum sales expected for each product.

**Required:** Based on the above data, choose the best product combination.

**10–42. Alternative Uses of Capacity.** Harris Equipment built a new facility five years ago but is using only 60 percent of its capacity to produce several machining equipment product lines.

Management would like to use the excess capacity and has three possibilities. Only one of the three can be selected.

**(a)** Harris could produce an additional 600 units per year of its most popular machine and focus marketing efforts on European metal parts producers. Management estimates that additional freight costs would amount to $550 per machine and fixed factory overhead would increase by $150,000. To cover the additional cost, the selling price per machine on European sales would be increased by $800 per machine. Incremental international selling costs would be about $200,000 per year. Harris has earned a contribution margin of $1,800 on each unit in the past.

**(b)** Harris could produce and market a smaller model of an existing laser lathe. The capacity could be used to produce 200 units per year that would sell for $15,500 each. Management has estimated the following unit variable costs.

| | |
|---|---:|
| Prime costs | $ 4,500 |
| Variable overhead | 2,000 |
| Variable selling. | 500 |
| Total costs | $ 7,000 |

The new lathe would add fixed costs of $700,000 to fixed overhead expenses and $250,000 to fixed selling expenses.

**(c)** Olson Testing Company has offered to lease the facilities at $30,000 per month plus 2 percent of the net revenues generated from the facilities by Olson. Net revenues are estimated at $15,000,000 per year.

**Required:**

1. Which of the three alternatives should management select? Show calculations to substantiate your decision. Comment on the relative riskiness.
2. What is the opportunity cost of this decision?

**10–43. Use of Capacity.** Bucien Specialty Compounds manufactures chemical compounds for industrial use. Department 23 produces related products—Pre and Post. Pre can be sold for $3 per pound or processed further and sold as Post. Pre can also be bought at a market price of $3 per pound plus $0.25 per pound for hauling. One pound of Pre is used to produce one pound of Post. Post has been selling for $7.20 for several years but has recently fallen to $6.80 per pound. Production could be Pre only, Pre and Post, or Post only.

Department 23's available capacity is 1,500 ton hours. (Processing one ton for one hour is a ton hour.) It takes three hours to process 10 pounds of Pre and Post—one hour for Pre and two for Post.

Marcia Bailey, marketing vice-president, has analyzed the markets and costs. She thinks that Post production should be halted when its price falls below $6.55 per pound. At that point, the profit from a pound of Post would be less than two times the profit from a pound of Pre. She says this is important since Post uses twice as much production time as Pre. She cites the following data:

| **Department 23 Analysis of Pre:** | | |
|---|---:|---:|
| Selling price, net of any selling costs | | $3.00 |
| Direct materials and labor. | $1.95 | |
| Manufacturing overhead. | .60 | 2.55 |
| Operating profit per pound. | | $.45 |

**Department 23 Analysis of Post:**

| | | |
|---|---:|---:|
| Selling price, net of any selling costs | | $ 6.80 |
| Cost of 1 pound of Pre (from above) | $ 2.55 | |
| Additional direct materials and labor | 1.90 | |
| Manufacturing overhead. | 1.20 | 5.65 |
| Operating profit per pound | | $ 1.15 |

Direct materials and labor costs are variable. Manufacturing overhead is fixed and is allocated to products by budgeting the total overhead for the coming year and dividing it by the total ton hours of capacity available.

**Required:**

1. Is Ms. Bailey correct? Why or why not?
2. Recommend a production plan given current prices.
3. Suggest a market price decision rule to guide production.

**10–44. Contribution Margins.** Zehnder Company, a Swiss firm, sells three products. Financial data for a typical month are (in thousands of Swiss francs):

| | Products | | | |
|---|---|---|---|---|
| | **J** | **K** | **L** | **Total** |
| Sales | SFr300 | SFr500 | SFr800 | SFr1,600 |
| Variable costs | 90 | 200 | 400 | 690 |
| Contribution margin | SFr210 | SFr300 | SFr400 | SFr 910 |
| Fixed costs: | | | | |
| Separable and avoidable | SFr 90 | SFr100 | SFr120 | SFr 310 |
| Joint, allocated on sales dollar basis | 60 | 100 | 160 | 320 |
| Total fixed costs | SFr150 | SFr200 | SFr280 | SFr 630 |
| Profit | SFr 60 | SFr100 | SFr120 | SFr 280 |

**Required:**

1. The firm is considering the introduction of a new Product M to replace Product J. Product M sells for SFr12 per unit, has variable costs of SFr5 per unit, and has separable fixed costs of SFr104,000. How many units of Product M must be sold to maintain the existing income of SFr280,000?
2. Revenues of Product K could increase by 20 percent by reducing variable contribution margin to 45 percent and increasing separable and avoidable fixed costs by SFr40,000. Should Zehnder do this? Show your logic.
3. Rank each product by total sales, variable contribution margin percentage, direct contribution margin percentage, and net profit percentage. Comment on how Zehnder might use each ranking.

**10–45. "Lose a little on each one, and make it up on volume."** Adams Company currently sells three products whose quantities, selling prices, and variable costs are:

| Product | Quantity | Selling Price | Variable Cost |
|---|---|---|---|
| 110 | 10,000 | $22 | $14 |
| 111 | 15,000 | 12 | 7 |
| 112 | 25,000 | 27 | 16 |

The plant is currently operating at capacity. Each unit requires the same production time. Fixed operating costs are $350,000 and are applied using units as the cost driver. An analysis shows that Product 111 is not profitable:

| | | |
|---|---|---|
| Selling price per unit | | $12 |
| Less: Variable cost per unit | $7 | |
| Fixed cost per unit | 7 | 14 |
| Profit (loss) per unit | | $(2) |

**Part A:** The sales manager argues that Product 111 should be dropped, stating that it is difficult to make profits on volume when every unit loses money.

**Required:**
1. Under what conditions should Product 111 be dropped? Should not be dropped?
2. If Product 111 is dropped, comment on profits per unit of Product 110.
3. If Product 111 is dropped, how many more units of Product 112 need to be sold to maintain current profit levels?

**Part B:** The sales manager finds another product, 113, to replace Product 111. No additional sales of Product 110 or Product 112 will occur. Product 113 can be sold for $8 and has a variable cost of $6. But, it uses only half of the production time per unit that Product 111 uses. Sufficient sales can be generated to use all of Product 111's current capacity.

The sales manager, arguing that Product 113 should be added and Product 111 should be dropped, says "It is true that the contribution margin of Product 113 is only $2 per unit; but since more units of Product 113 can be produced, the fixed cost per unit will go down. Look, the fixed cost per unit on all units will drop by $1.62—from $7 to $5.38 ($350,000 divided by 65,000)—if we switch to Product 113. It'll increase profits on Products 110 and 112, too."

**Required:**
1. Is the sales manager right? Explain.
2. What price must Adams charge for Product 113 for profits to equal current profits with Product 111?

Service

**10–46. Department Profitability.** White's Grocery Store is a small-town operation being threatened by a national discount store outlet being built nearby. Mickey White, the owner, is studying the addition of a department to sell either garden supplies or beer and wine. He has talked to several other owners of similar stores and has reached the following conclusions:

1. A garden supplies department would generate sales of $40,000 per year with a gross profit of 60 percent. No other variable costs would be added. Additional fixed costs would be $12,000. Grocery sales would increase by 5 percent because of increased traffic through the store.
2. A beer and wine department would generate sales of $60,000 per year with a gross profit of 40 percent. No other variable costs would be added, but fixed costs would increase by $18,000. Grocery sales would increase by 8 percent.

The income statement for a typical year for grocery sales alone is as follows:

| | |
|---|---|
| Sales | $ 600,000 |
| Cost of goods sold (variable) | 240,000 |
| Gross profit | $ 360,000 |
| Other variable costs | 120,000 |
| Contribution margin | $ 240,000 |
| Fixed costs | 140,000 |
| Net income | $ 100,000 |

**Required:**

**1.** Recompute the effects on income of adding each department.

**2.** Which department should be added? What qualitative issues appear important?

**10–47. Make or Buy Decision.** Hillman Company produces iron and steel building products. The product lines include numerous subassemblies and parts. Many of these parts can be either produced in Department 8 or outsourced. Four parts are listed below with their related cost and production data, including normal batch sizes and estimated setup costs:

|  | Iron Frames # 10 | Steel Frames # 11 | Steel Housing # 12 | Assembly Unit # 13 |
|---|---|---|---|---|
| Materials cost | $5.00 | $6.00 | $18.00 | $8.00 |
| Variable labor cost | 1.50 | 1.00 | 5.00 | 3.00 |
| Overhead cost (excluding setup costs) | 4.50 | 3.00 | 15.00 | 9.00 |
| Time required per unit | 1 hour | 4 hours | 5 hours | 2 hours |
| Units required | 80,000 | 40,000 | 15,000 | 100,000 |
| Batch size (in units) | 10,000 | 10,000 | 3,000 | 5,000 |
| Estimated setup costs per batch | $4,000 | $3,000 | $3,000 | $2,000 |
| Outsourcing prices | $10.00 | $11.00 | $32.00 | $18.00 |

Department 8's facilities are flexible in that these parts can be produced in any combination. Department 8's capacity is 300,000 machine hours. Materials and labor costs are considered variable. Batch sizes and setup costs are estimated based on past experience. Overhead costs, except for setup costs, are fixed. Total overhead is assigned to products at the rate of 300 percent of direct labor cost, established after preparing the factory overhead budget.

**Required:**

Write a memo presenting your recommendation and describing your decision logic for producing and outsourcing.

**10–48. Purchasing Ethical Dilemmas.** Over the years, Don Dremmen has been "on the road" selling a variety of industrial goods for several different distributors. He keeps a small diary of "problems" he has encountered over the years that concern him. Among these are:

**(a)** A competing salesperson, selling a high-quality product at a high price, would routinely give purchasing agents of certain large customers tickets to Bulls' basketball games.

**(b)** A close friend, also a salesperson, died recently of serious health problems that Don thinks was caused by excessive entertaining of potential clients over many years.

**(c)** When he was selling certain heavy equipment, he had difficulty competing with a rival salesperson who actually moved a service representative into his territory to be close to several large construction firms headquartered there. The service rep visited with their service personnel almost every week and even taught maintenance courses for free.

**(d)** One particular customer worked out a schedule to have him and several other sales representatives bring in donuts for the office staff on Fridays. His turn was always the third Friday of the month.

**(e)** Another current customer called him last week and said, "You know that fastener we buy from you? I just got a quote from a Singapore supplier at $23.50 a thousand. You gotta meet it, or I drop ya. Well?"

**Required:** Comment on whether these are a typical salesperson's laments or ethical issues?

## CASE 10A—KAHN PRODUCTS

Bernie Steer, the production vice-president at Kahn Products, located in Amsterdam, complains that the quality of a part used in manufacturing is poor. He states that this part costs €23 per unit (in euros) but that 10 percent of the parts break in the assembly process. This part is now purchased from a supplier that uses a lighter gauge of steel. As a result of bending operations in assembly, it can snap at a stress point. The supplier has been willing to split the cost of replacement parts with Kahn. Breakage of this part during assembly has caused rework and **scrap** costing Kahn about €150,000 in addition to the cost of broken parts. Also, the engineering and customer service staffs estimate that about 25 percent of the firm's warranty claims of €660,000 last year was related to in-service failures of this part.

The best alternative supplier using the higher gauge of steel has quoted a price of €28. Any price increase to cover the higher costs would cause serious competitive problems for Kahn's salespersons.

Sue Svatik, the controller, states that idle plant capacity exists and suggests that Kahn makes its own higher quality parts. Svatik believes that the suppliers are unwilling to reduce their profits and are cheapening their products instead of absorbing higher metal costs.

The company needs 50,000 of these parts each year. A study reveals that if Kahn produced the parts, the following additional costs would be incurred:

| | |
|---|---|
| Direct materials (including higher gauge of steel) | €1,050,000 |
| Direct labor (15,000 labor hours) | 225,000 |
| Variable overhead (30,000 machine hours) | 180,000 |

Engineering believes that failure rates will become negligible.

Steer is not convinced that the components can be made at a lower cost than the purchase cost. The plant's substantial fixed overhead must be absorbed at a €10 per machine hour rate. In Steer's opinion, use of any idle capacity should cover at least this fixed overhead.

### Required:
1. Based on the quantitative data given, how should the part be sourced? Show computations.
2. Evaluate Steer's argument. Does he make a valid point?
3. Discuss the possible long-term ramifications of this decision on the factory, on sales, on customers, and on profits.

Service

## CASE 10B—LITTLE BEARS' HOUSE

Little Bears' House is a day-care center/preschool which operates as a partnership of Linda Rivera and Bei Dong. The center is in a city that has a large base of two-income families who have a need for quality day care. The two women started the center this year. Dong contributed $40,000 to get the business started—to purchase equipment and to operate through the early months. Rivera, who previously managed another center, is the director of the center and draws $2,000 per month for her services. Partnership profits and losses, after Rivera's salary, are split 75 percent for Dong and 25 percent for Rivera.

Little Bears' House operates from 6 a.m. to 6 p.m., Monday through Friday, is in a single building, which has a capacity limit of 120 children, and meets city and state regulations. At present, the center has six classes, all at maximum sizes, structured as follows:

| Age | Number of Classes | Children Per Class | Total Children | Monthly Tuition Per Child |
|-----|-------------------|--------------------|----------------|---------------------------|
| 2 to 3 | 2 | 10 | 20 | $320 |
| 3 to 4 | 1 | 15 | 15 | 280 |
| 4 to 5 | 1 | 15 | 15 | 280 |
| 5 to 6 | 2 | 15 | 30 | 260 |

Class sizes are determined by state law which sets a limit on the number of children per instructor. The center uses one instructor per classroom.

Tuition is charged monthly. Minor adjustments are made on an individual basis. In October, the most recent month with data available, revenues were $21,500 ($22,600 less $1,100 adjustments). Monthly revenues should be rather stable since classes are full most of the time. Expenses for October were:

| | | |
|---|---|---|
| Salaries for instructors. | | $9,600 |
| Salary of director. | 2,000 | |
| Salary of part-time cook. | | 900 |
| Food expenses | 2,200 | |
| Staff benefits expenses | | 2,450 |
| Supplies expenses | | 600 |
| Occupancy and other administrative expenses | | 3,250 |
| Total expenses. | | $21,000 |

Fixed expenses are the salary of the part-time cook and occupancy and other administrative expenses. The salary of the director is fixed; but, as a partnership, this is in reality a distribution of profits but is included in expenses for comparative purposes.

Food is $1.25 per student per day. Staff benefits are 10 percent of salaries plus $200 per person for benefit programs for instructors and the part-time cook. Variable supplies are $1 per student per month. Step costs are salaries for instructors, averaging $1,600 per instructor per class.

Rivera wants to increase the quality of service by decreasing class sizes and also expanding student enrollments. These alternatives are interrelated. Rivera thinks that class sizes are too large and that children are not getting the individual attention they require. Rivera surveyed parents of all 80 students to measure their support for a tuition increase tied to a reduction in class size. For children ages 2 to 5, most parents would support a 25 percent tuition increase, and nearly 50 percent would support a 50 percent increase. Of the 5-to-6 age group parents, nearly three-fourths did not want any increase. The remainder said they would support a 25 percent increase but no more.

Proper class size is very subjective. However, Rivera feels that she could achieve a child/instructor ratio of 6 to 1 for the 2-to-3 age group; an 8 to 1 ratio for the 3-to-4 and 4-to-5 age groups; and a 10 to 1 ratio for the 5-to-6 age group.

The center has easily maintained the 80 student level, with each class full. Rivera keeps in touch with waiting-list parents to make certain each is still interested. This list provides children when someone leaves the center. The current waiting list is as follows:

| Age Group | Number of Children | Age Group | Number of Children |
|-----------|--------------------|-----------|--------------------|
| 2 to 3 | 5 | 4 to 5 | 4 |
| 3 to 4 | 7 | 5 to 6 | 11 |

Rivera does not start a new class unless more students are on the waiting list than are required per class. Obviously, enough students are on the 5-to-6 age group waiting list to start a new class. Lately, however, she has wondered if the center could make a profit by starting classes with fewer than the requisite number, taking the chance that new students would appear and could be added immediately.

Information from her various inquiries implies that a potential market for quality infant care (0 to 24 months) exists. Rivera doesn't think this expansion would be profitable. However, she has never done an analysis of the situation and has not thought about an appropriate tuition. She believes that the infant/instructor ratio in her center should be no higher than 5 infants to one instructor. The center would have no food costs for the infants.

Dong will only agree to Rivera's suggested changes if the center will continue to operate at or above the current profit level.

**Required:**

1. Look at each decision separately, as incremental to the current situation, and evaluate the marginal profit:

   **(a)** If class size is decreased (keeping the same 80 students), what increase in tuition is necessary to keep the current monthly profit level?

   **(b)** Without regard to (a), is it profitable to create the new class from the waiting list? Explain.

   **(c)** Use the new fee structure as found in (a). Is it profitable to move to smaller class sizes, if new full classes are created and filled to their new maximums using the waiting list? Show calculations.

   **(d)** Is a class for infant care profitable if tuition is the same as the proposed class tuition for the 2-to-3 age group?

2. Write a brief memo to Rivera and Dong highlighting any concerns that underlie the analyses you have performed in Part 1.

# CAPITAL INVESTMENT DECISIONS

## LEARNING OBJECTIVES

After studying Chapter 11, you will be able to:

1. Explain the nature and importance of capital investment decisions.

2. Identify the relevant cash inflows and outflows in an investment proposal.

3. Know how to format the relevant cash flows data in an investment proposal.

4. Understand how to apply present value evaluation methods to capital investment decisions.

5. Understand how to apply payback period and accounting rate of return methods to capital investment decisions.

6. Compare strengths and weaknesses of capital investment evaluation methods.

7. Comprehend how income taxes impact the cash flows of capital investments.

## Capital Investment Alternatives

*Chloe White, president of Fine Tone Instruments, grabbed her briefcase and headed for the airport. After clearing security, running to her gate, and just making her flight, Chloe settled into her coach seat, in front of two screaming kids and behind two salespersons who apparently just made the deal of the century. She opened her briefcase and found the Capital Spending Proposals file. The deadline for submitting proposals to her was yesterday. She plans to review these on her cross-country flight. The variety surprises her:*

- *Engineering is pushing to integrate a newly announced semiconductor into an aging product. The new technology will push Fine Tone into new markets with great sales potential but against stiff competition.*

- *Adding space to the corporate headquarters will bring three administrative departments together, increase efficiency, and reduce operating expenses.*

- *Her production planning manager proposes rearranging several work centers to improve production efficiency for a family of current products.*

- *Another project adds capacity to a specialized assembly operation.*

- *The plant manager requests funding for an air purification system, which must be installed by yearend to meet new state air quality requirements.*

- *An information systems proposal would automate several manual operations, save personnel, and slice inventory by an estimated 10 percent.*

- *Her finance manager is negotiating for controlling interest in a firm with technical expertise that Fine Tone needs for new product development.*

- *Marketing has proposed a major jump in advertising spending for a product line that has not been meeting sales targets.*

*    Chloe clearly wants to get the "biggest bang for the bucks" from Fine Tone's limited capital investment budget. But, a quick calculation shows her that this year's investment dollars will fund about half of these proposals. Some proposals are risky, while others have predictable outcomes. Some are straightforward, but many include many extraneous issues. Also, financial data are overstated for some proposals and understated for others. Some generate immediate returns; others promise big cash flows years from now.*

THIS CHAPTER EXTENDS the study of incremental analysis begun in Chapter 10 into multiperiod decisions, which are called **capital investment decisions**. Chapters 11 and 12 discuss:

1. Identification of relevant cash fows in capital investments.
2. Techniques and methods for analyzing project data.

These issues depend on an understanding of the time value of money. For those who are unfamiliar with the time value of money or have not applied present values in financial accounting or other courses, the Appendix to this chapter explains the concept. Present value tables necessary for **discounting** future cash flows are located inside the back cover of the book.

Relevant revenues and operating costs for multiperiod decisions are defined as cash inflows and cash outflows. Since these decisions extend over a period of years, opportunity costs and timing of these cash flows are major factors. For short timeframes, opportunity costs are small and may be ignored. But when days become years, the time value of money becomes an important decision factor.

Capital investment analysis is a planning task and is directly linked to budgeting as discussed in Chapter 7. **Capital budgeting** is the process of evaluating specific projects, estimating benefits and costs of the projects, and selecting which projects to fund.

## THE IMPORTANCE OF CAPITAL INVESTMENT DECISIONS

**Capital investment** is the acquisition of assets with an expected life greater than a year. These decisions attract managers' interest for good reasons:

1. **Long-term commitments.** Capital decisions often lock the firm into assets for many years.
2. **Large amounts of dollars.** Capital projects often have big price tags. From Ford Motor Company with an annual investment budget of $7 billion to a small firm buying a $50,000 truck, large relative dollar amounts get attention.
3. **Key areas of the firm.** New products, new production technology, and research efforts are crucial to a firm's ongoing competitiveness.
4. **Source of future earnings.** Investing with foresight is the key to the firm's future profits and financial performance.
5. **Scarce capital dollars.** In most firms, more demands exist for capital funds than the firm can generate. Only the best opportunities should be funded.

Excellent analyses and decisions increase the firm's capacity, technology, efficiency, and cash generating power. Poor decisions waste resources, lose opportunities, and impact profits for many years.

## THE CAPITAL INVESTMENT DECISION

Capital investments generally include a cash outflow, which is the investment, and cash inflows, which are the returns on the investment. The decision maker expects cash inflows to exceed cash outflows. The typical investment project has cash outflows at the beginning and cash inflows over the life of the project.

### Cash Flows

Cash flows are the key data inputs in capital investment analyses. Cash has an opportunity cost, since it could be used to buy a productive or financial asset with earning power. Cash is a basic asset. Prices, costs, and values can all be expressed in cash amounts. If the decision impacts several time periods, cash-flow timing becomes a relevant factor.

Cash outflows commonly include:

1. The cash cost of the initial investment plus any startup costs.
2. Incremental cash operating costs incurred over the project's life.
3. Incremental working capital such as inventories and accounts receivable.
4. Additional outlays needed to overhaul, expand, or update the asset during the project's life.
5. Additional taxes owed on incremental taxable income.

Cash inflows include:

1. Incremental cash revenues received over the project's life.
2. Reduced operating expenses received over the project's life.
3. Cash received from selling old assets being replaced in the new project, net of any tax impacts.
4. Released working capital, perhaps at the project's end.
5. Salvage value realized from asset disposition at the project's end.

These relevant cash flows occur after the "go" decision is made to proceed with the project. Therefore, we estimate future cash flows. Certain cash flows are estimated based on current prices and known technology; whereas others are estimates based on vague facts and unproven methods. Often, cost savings and project benefits are not easily quantified. Much time and expense are spent to develop supporting forecast data. It is important to understand that the *same cash-flow estimates* are used regardless of the project evaluation method used.

## Decision Criteria

Winning projects generally have the highest rates of return on investment. Decisions are either:

**Accept or reject**    *or*    **Select A or B or C or etc.**

In the first type, we decide whether the return is acceptable or unacceptable. This is a screening decision. Is the return "good enough?" The second type is a preference or ranking decision—select the best choice from a set of mutually exclusive projects. By picking A, we reject B, C, and any other choices. A possible choice is to do nothing—the status quo.

Generally, projects are ranked on a scale of high to low returns. The highest ranking projects are selected, until the capital investment budget is spent. Often, funds are limited; and many acceptable projects will go unfunded. The firm's goal is to select projects with the highest returns. As in Chapter 10, pertinent nonquantitative factors may sway a decision and cause lower ranked projects to be selected.

## Time Perspectives

In the real world, every conceivable combination of cash-flow timing can exist. But, we assume a simplified timeline. The present point in time is today, Year 0. This is when we assume investments are made—new assets acquired, old assets sold, and any tax consequences of these changes felt. In real life, several years of cash outflows may precede the start of a project's operation.

Generally, annual time periods are used. Using shorter time periods is possible, such as one-month periods for monthly lease payments. Annual flows of cash are assumed to occur at year end. In the inside front covers, Tables 1 and 2, show "end of period" present value factors. Other tables exist that can reflect smooth cash flows within a time period. But this fine tuning is probably necessary only in specialized situations.

## An Example—Equipment Replacement and Capacity Expansion

As an illustration, Quartz Timepieces, a Seattle firm, is considering a device costing $100,000 to replace an obsolete production device:

1. The new device's expected life is five years and can probably be sold at the end of Year 5 for $10,000.
2. The vendor recommends an updating in Year 3 at a cost of $20,000.
3. Capacity will increase by 1,000 units per year. Each unit sells for $55 and has $30 of variable costs.
4. Additional inventory of $3,000 is needed and will be released at the project's end.

| Cash Flows: | Today | Life of the Project | | | | |
| --- | --- | --- | --- | --- | --- | --- |
| | | Year 1 | Year 2 | Year 3 | Year 4 | Year 5 |
| New device | $(100,000) | | | | | |
| Salvage value | | | | | | $10,000 |
| Sale of old device | 8,000 | | | | | |
| Added inventory | (3,000) | | | | | 3,000 |
| Added contribution margin | | $25,000 | $25,000 | $25,000 | $25,000 | 25,000 |
| Operating cost savings | | 15,000 | 15,000 | 15,000 | 15,000 | 15,000 |
| Updating costs | | | | (20,000) | | |
| Net cash investment | $ (95,000) | | | | | |
| Net cash inflows | | $40,000 | $40,000 | $20,000 | $40,000 | $53,000 |

FIGURE **11.1**

Format for Relevant Capital Investment Data—Quartz Timepieces

5. Operating costs will be reduced by $15,000 per year.

6. The old device can be sold for $8,000 now, which is its book value. But, it could be used for five more years with no salvage or book value at that time.

Remember that any cash revenue or cost that does not change is irrelevant and can be ignored. Any cash flow that differs among decision choices is relevant. Additional taxes or tax savings on incremental income or expenses are also relevant cash flows. But, until income tax issues are discussed, taxation implications are ignored.

## Formatting the Relevant Data

As in Chapter 10, adopting a uniform format for analysis of capital investments helps to organize data and to present it in a logical pattern. Using data from the previous example, the timeframe format shown in Figure 11.1 is used throughout our capital investment discussions.

Cash outflows are negative numbers, and inflows are positive numbers. Project years begins now, Year 0 or today, and are shown as columns. Specific cash-flow items are shown as rows. The investments of $100,000 in equipment and $3,000 in inventory costs are reduced by the sale of old equipment for $8,000. The **net initial investment** is $95,000. The additional 1,000 units of sales generate incremental contribution margin of $25,000, using a $55 sales price less a $30 variable cost per unit.

Remember that volumes of analytical support may be developed to backup each number in Figure 11.1. The $100,000 device cost would result from evaluations of many devices and negotiations with vendors. Estimates of additional revenues and variable costs come from marketing studies and capacity use. Cost savings come from production, industrial engineering, and cost accounting analyses. Each dollar amount is the best estimate that Quartz personnel can provide.

## THE EVALUATION METHODS

The evaluation methods discussed here are:

1. Present value methods (also called discounted cash-flow methods).
   (a) Net present value method (NPV).
   (b) Internal rate of return method (IRR).

**2.** Payback period method.

**3.** Accounting rate of return method.

Nearly all managerial accountants agree that methods using **present values** (Methods 1a and 1b) give the best assessment of long-term investments. Methods that do not involve the time value of money (Methods 2 and 3) have serious flaws; but, since they are commonly used for investment evaluation, their strengths and weaknesses are discussed.

## Net Present Value Method

The **net present value (NPV) method** includes the time value of money by using an interest rate that represents the desired rate of return or, at least, sets a minimum acceptable rate of return. The decision rule is:

If the present value of incremental net cash inflows is greater than the incremental investment net cash outflow, approve the project.

Using Tables 1 and 2 found on the inside front covers, the net cash flows for each year are brought back to Year 0 and summed for all years. An interest rate must be specified. This rate is often viewed as the cost of funds needed to finance the project and is the minimum acceptable rate of return. Note that the present value of cash flows in the Today column is the amount itself–no discounting is needed. In Figure 11.2, the net cash investment ($95,000) is subtracted from the sum of cash-inflow present values ($137,331).When the residual is positive, the project's rate of return (ROR) is greater than the minimum acceptable ROR. If:

Present value of incremental net cash inflows ≥ Incremental investment cash outflows

then:

Project's ROR ≥ Minimum acceptable ROR

If net present value is zero or positive, the project is acceptable. When the sum is negative, the project's ROR is less than the discount rate. If:

Present value of incremental net cash inflows < Incremental investment cash outflows

then:

Project's ROR < Minimum acceptable ROR

If net present value is negative, the project should be rejected.

| | Today | | Life of the Project | | | |
| --- | --- | --- | --- | --- | --- | --- |
| | | Year 1 | Year 2 | Year 3 | Year 4 | Year 5 |
| Net cash flows (Figure 11.1) | $(95,000) | $40,000 | $40,000 | $20,000 | $40,000 | $53,000 |
| Present value factors at 12% | x 1.000 | x .893 | x .797 | x .712 | x .636 | x .567 |
| Present values at 12% | $(95,000) | $35,720 | $31,880 | $14,240 | $25,440 | $30,051 |
| Sum of PVs for Years 1 to 5 | 137,331 ◄ | | | | | |
| Net present value | $42,331 | | | | | |

**FIGURE 11.2**

Net Present Value of Capital Investment Cash Flows

**The Interest Rate.** What interest rate should be used for discounting the cash flows? This rate has many names that help explain its source and use. Among them are:

1. **Cost of capital**—a weighted-average cost of long-term funds. Only projects that can earn at least what the firm pays for funds should be accepted. Later, we illustrate a calculation of cost of capital.

2. **Minimum acceptable rate of return**—a particular rate that is considered to be the lowest ROR that management will accept.

3. **Desired rate of return, target rate of return,** or **required rate of return**—a rate that reflects management ROR expectations.

4. **Hurdle rate**—a threshold that a project's ROR must "jump over" or exceed.

5. **Cutoff rate**—the rate at which projects with a higher ROR are accepted and those with a lower ROR are rejected; often the rate where all available capital investment funds are committed.

A firm will use one or more of these terms as its **discount rate**. While these terms sometimes produce different rates in the real world, we use these terms interchangeably here. Generally, if a project's ROR is below this percentage, it is rejected; above this rate, the project is acceptable. Still, whether it is funded depends on the availability of capital funds.

In the Quartz Timepieces example, we assume that management has decided that 12 percent is the minimum acceptable rate of return. Calculations needed to obtain a net present value are shown in Figure 11.2. The net present value is a positive $42,331; therefore, the project earns more than a 12 percent ROR. The net present value method does not give the project's exact ROR.

If other discount rates had been selected, we would find the following net present values:

| Percentage | Present Value of Net Cash Inflows | – | Investment | = | Net Present Value |
|---|---|---|---|---|---|
| 16 % | $124,328 | | $95,000 | | $29,328 |
| 20 | 113,246 | | 95,000 | | 18,246 |
| 24 | 103,713 | | 95,000 | | 8,713 |
| 28 | 95,523 | | 95,000 | | 523 |
| 30 | 91,797 | | 95,000 | | (3,203) |

Notice that, as the interest rate increases, the present values of the future cash flows decrease. At 30 percent per year, the project's net present value is negative, and the project is unacceptable. The project's rate of return must be between 28 and 30 percent.

**Project Ranking.** Even though a project has a positive net present value, too many attractive projects may exist, given the investment dollars available. A ranking system is needed. We can rank projects by the amount of net present value each generates, but this ignores the relative size of the initial investments. An extension of the net present value method is the **profitability index**. It is found by dividing the present value of a project's *net cash inflows* by its *net initial investment*. The resulting ratio is cash in to cash out. The higher the ratio is, the more attractive the investment becomes. Notice that an acceptable project should have a profitability index of at least 1. The following projects are ranked by the profitability index.

| Project | Present Value of Net Cash Inflows | Initial Investment | Net Present Value | Profitability Index | Ranking |
|---|---|---|---|---|---|
| A | $235,000 | $200,000 | $35,000 | 1.18 | 5 |
| B | 170,000 | 140,000 | 30,000 | 1.21 | 4 |
| C | 80,000 | 60,000 | 20,000 | 1.33 | 1 |
| D | 98,000 | 80,000 | 18,000 | 1.23 | 3 |
| E | 52,000 | 40,000 | 12,000 | 1.30 | 2 |

We would typically accept projects with the highest profitability index until we exhaust the capital budget or the list of acceptable projects.

## Internal Rate of Return (IRR) Method

The **internal rate of return** is the project's ROR and is the rate where the:

Net initial investment cash outflow = Present value of the incremental net cash inflows

Without calculator or computer assistance, the specific ROR is found by trial and error. We search for the rate that yields a zero net present value.

In the Quartz Timepieces example, the internal rate of return was found to be between 28 and 30 percent. The net present value at 28 percent is positive and at 30 percent is negative. By interpolation, we can approximate a "more accurate" rate as follows:

| Rate of Return | Net Present Value | | Calculations | | |
|---|---|---|---|---|---|
| 28% | $  523 | | Base rate | = | 28.00% |
| 30 | (3,202) | | ($523 ÷ $3,725) × 2% | = | 0.28% |
| 2% difference | $ 3,725 | absolute difference | Internal rate or return | | 28.28% |

In most cases, however, knowing that the rate is between 28 and 30 percent is adequate. Also, calculators and software do this automatically.

**Estimating the Internal Rate of Return.** By using Table 2 and knowing certain project variables, we can estimate other unknown variables including a project's internal rate of return. This estimate requires that the annual net cash inflows be an annuity. The variables and a sample set of data are:

| Variable | Example Data |
|---|---|
| A = Initial investment cash outflow | $37,910 |
| B = Life of project | 5 years |
| C = Annual net cash inflow | $10,000 per year |
| D = Internal rate of return | 10 percent |
| E = Present value factor at 10 percent (Table 2) | 3.791 |

If we know any three of A, B, C, or D, we can find E and the missing variable. A variety of questions can be answered:

1. **What is the internal rate of return of the project?** If A, B, and C are known, we can calculate E and find D as follows:

$$E = A \div C \quad \$37,910 \div \$10,000 = 3.791$$

On Table 2, we go to the 5-period (year) row and move across until we find 3.791 (E) in the 10 percent column (D). At 10 percent, the cash outflow ($37,910) equals the present value of the net cash inflows (3.791 × $10,000). The internal rate of return is 10 percent.

2. **What annual cash inflow will yield a 10 percent IRR from the project?** If A, B, and D are known, we can find E and calculate C. E is found in Table 2 by using five years and 10 percent ROR. The annual cash inflow is found as follows:

$$C = A \div E \quad \$37,910 \div 3.791 = \$10,000 \text{ per year}$$

We need $10,000 per year in cash inflow to earn a 10 percent IRR.

3. **What can we afford to invest if the project earns $10,000 each year for five years and we want a 10 percent IRR?** If we know B, C, and D, we can find E and then calculate A. The investment is found by using the annual net cash inflow and 3.791 (E) as follows:

$$A = C \times E \quad \$10,000 \times 3.791 = \$37,910$$

We can pay no more than $37,910 and still earn at least a 10 percent return.

4. **How long must the project last to earn at least a 10 percent IRR?** If we know A, C, and D, we calculate E and find B as follows:

$$E = A \div C \quad \$37,910 \div \$10,000 = 3.791$$

For a 10 percent IRR, 3.791 (E) is on the 5-period row (B) of Table 2. The project's life must be at least five years.

Most business calculators and spreadsheet software have built-in functions to find the internal rate of return. This simplifies the calculation burden that has limited its use in the past.

**Project Ranking.** Since each project has a specific rate of return, ranking projects under the IRR method is relatively simple. All projects are listed according to their rates of return from high to low. The cost of capital or a cutoff rate can establish a minimum acceptable rate of return. Then, projects are selected by moving down the list until the budget is exhausted or the cutoff rate is reached.

**Reinvestment Assumption.** The internal rate of return method assumes that cash flows are reinvested at the project's internal rate of return. While this assumption may be realistic for cost of capital rates, it may be wishful thinking for projects with high internal rates of return. This issue, however, is best left to finance texts and courses.

**High Discount Rates.** A concern exists about the use of high discount rates in present value methods. Any project with significant long-term payoffs will not appear strong because the long-term payoffs will be discounted so severely. Even huge cash inflows due ten years or more into the future appear to be less valuable than minor cost savings earned in the first year of another project. High discount rates may encourage managers to think only short term, to ignore research, market innovations, and creative product development projects, and to ignore long-term environmental effects. Thus, positive or negative impacts can result from the wise or unwise use of accounting tools and policies.

## The Payback Period Method

The **payback period method** is a "quick and dirty" evaluation of capital investment projects. It is likely that no major firm makes investment decisions based solely on the payback period, but many ask for the payback period as part of their analyses. The payback period method asks:

**How fast do we get our initial cash investment back?**

No ROR is given, only a time period. If annual cash flows are equal, the **payback period** is found as follows:

Net initial investment ÷ Annual net cash inflow = Payback period

If the investment is $120,000 and annual net cash inflow is $48,000, the payback period is 2.5 years. We do not know how long the project will last nor what cash flows exist after the 2.5 years. It might last 20 years or 20 days beyond the payback point.

If annual cash flows are uneven, the payback period is found by recovering the investment cost year by year. In the Quartz Timepieces example:

| Year | Cash Flows | Unrecovered Investment |
|------|-----------|------------------------|
| 0 | $(95,000) | $95,000 |
| 1 | 40,000 | 55,000 |
| 2 | 40,000 | 15,000 |
| 3 | 20,000 | 0 |

In Year 3, the cost is totally recovered, using only $15,000 of Year 3's $20,000 (75 percent). The payback period is 2.75 years.

The payback method is viewed as a "bail-out" risk measure. How long do we need to stick with the project just to get our initial investment money back? It is used frequently in short-term projects where the impact of present values is not great. Such projects as efficiency improvements, cost reductions, and personnel savings are examples. Several major companies set an arbitrary payback period, such as six months, for certain types of cost-saving projects.

**Using the Payback Reciprocal to Estimate the IRR.** The payback period can be used to estimate a project's IRR, assuming a fairly high ROR (over 20 percent) and project life that is more than twice the payback period. For example, if a $40,000 investment earns $10,000 per year and could last 12 years, the payback period is four years. The reciprocal of the payback period is 1 divided by 4 and gives an IRR estimate of 25 percent. From Table 2 for 12 years, the present value factor (payback period) of 4 indicates a rate of return of between 22 and 24 percent. The payback reciprocal will always overstate the IRR somewhat. If the project's life is very long, say 50 years, the **payback reciprocal** is an almost perfect estimator. (See the present value factor of 4.000 for 25 percent and 50 periods on Table 2.)

**Ranking Projects.** When the payback period is used to rank projects, the shortest payback period is best. Thus, all projects are listed from low to high. A firm's policy may say that no project with a payback period of over four years will be considered. This acts like a cutoff point. Then, projects would be selected until capital funds are exhausted. The major complaints about the payback period method are that it ignores:

1. The time value of money.
2. The cash flows beyond the payback point.

These are serious deficiencies, but the method is easily applied and can be a rough gauge of potential success.

## Accounting Rate of Return (ARR) Method

This method:

1. Ignores the time value of money.
2. Presumes uniform flows of income over the project's life.
3. Includes depreciation expense and other accounting accruals in the calculation of project income, losing the purity of cash flows.

In fact, we only discuss this approach because many internal corporate performance reporting systems use accrual accounting data. Many companies use discounted cash flows for investment decisions but report actual results using accrual income and expense measures.

The **accounting rate of return method** attempts to measure *accrual net income* from the project. The ARR subtracts depreciation expense on the incremental investment from the annual net cash inflows. Other accrual adjustments may also be made. The general formula is:

$$\frac{\text{Annual operating cash in flow} - \text{Annual depreciation expense on incremental investment}}{\text{Average investment}} = \text{Accounting rate of return}$$

The average investment, the denominator, is the average of the net initial investment and the ending investment base ($0 if no salvage value exists). This is the average book value of the investment over its life. Some analysts prefer to use the original cost of the investment or replacement cost as the denominator. The numerator is the incremental accrual net income from the project. To illustrate, assume the following:

| | | | |
|---|---|---|---|
| Initial investment | $110,000 | Salvage value | $10,000 |
| Annual cash inflow | 35,000 | Project life | 5 years |
| Depreciation expense | 20,000 | | |

ARR calculations are:

$$\frac{\$35,000 - \$20,000}{(\$110,000 + \$10,000) / 2} = \frac{\$15,000}{\$60,000} = 25 \text{ percent}$$

The 25 percent must be viewed relative to other projects' ARR and cannot be compared to present value rates of return. For ranking purposes, projects are ranked from high to low. An arbitrary percentage may be set as a minimum rate, similar to an accrual return on equity.

Another problem with the ARR is the impression it gives of an increasing ROR on an annual basis as an asset grows older. A manager would see this project's performance on annual investment center responsibility reports as follows:

| | Average Investment (Book Value) | Project Net Income | Annual ARR |
|---|---|---|---|
| Year 1 | $100,000 | $15,000 | 15.0% |
| Year 2 | 80,000 | 15,000 | 18.8 |
| Year 3 | 60,000 | 15,000 | 25.0 |
| Year 4 | 40,000 | 15,000 | 37.5 |
| Year 5 | 20,000 | 15,000 | 75.0 |

The average annual book value declines each year; and net income is assumed to remain constant. As the asset gets older, the ARR increases. It is tempting for managers to reject any proposal that will make their performance reports look less favorable. This is particularly true when their bonuses are tied to accrual accounting performance numbers. Managers will be biased toward sticking with older assets with higher accounting rates of return. They forego new investments that offer new technology, lower operating costs, and greater productivity.

## Capital Budgeting in Major Lodging Chains

In a recent study, major lodging chains were surveyed about their capital budgeting methods. The reported frequencies of use of each method for making four types of investment decisions were:

When compared to an earlier study, IRR tripled in its popularity, NPV nearly doubled, and payback declined slightly. Notice that more than one method was used since the sum of the four methods exceeds 100 percent. Payback was often used as supporting information but not as the major decision variable.

| | ARR | Payback | NPV | IRR |
|---|---|---|---|---|
| Asset replacement | 13% | 46% | 19% | 35% |
| Facility renovation | 17 | 35 | 28 | 44 |
| Facility expansion | 20 | 39 | 37 | 57 |
| Property acquisition | 15 | 37 | 46 | 57 |

Source: Schmidgall, R. S., and J. Damitio, "Current Capital Budgeting Practices of Major Lodging Chains," Real Estate Review, Fall 1990, pp. 40–45.

## ETHICAL ISSUES AND PRESSURES ON MANAGEMENT

In many corporate situations, managers are under pressure to earn high rates of return in the short run. All capital investment analyses depend on the credibility of future cash-flow estimates. Unlike past facts which are measured very objectively, future values are based on predictions, opinions, judgments, and perhaps wishful thinking. The quality of decision making rests on a premise that future estimates are made objectively and in good faith. A manager trying to get a needed project approved may develop estimates that are too optimistic because of the manager's enthusiastic support of the idea.

Company policies compound the problem by setting very high hurdle or cutoff rates that encourage proposal developers to overestimate future revenues and underestimate investment costs. Managers have been heard to say, "Show me the hurdle, and I'll make the project jump over it." In fact, a vicious cycle may develop—higher hurdles, more bias in estimates; higher hurdles, and so on.

To control these problems, many firms have special analysts who evaluate proposals independent of the sponsoring managers. Others perform post-audits (discussed in Chapter 12) to compare actual results to the estimates. Tying responsibility for the project's promises to the manager's future evaluations may help solve some of these problems.

The second issue is the severe pressure on managers to show growth in immediate earnings. Key investment analysts and shareholders watch quarterly earnings announcements and other short-term information about the company to make almost daily buy and sell decisions. Capital investment proposals include a mix of short-term and long-term projects. Short-term projects often emphasize cost savings, which may be worthwhile but not strategically important. Long-term projects include research and development and new technology. Unfortunately, these projects often have long payback periods but with very significant future potential. If hurdle rates are high, long-term projects will rarely rank as high as short-term projects. The long-run competitiveness and success of a firm may be damaged severely if its managers are biased toward short-term rewards.

Japanese firms, for a number of reasons, are said to have a much longer term investment horizon. They are less concerned about the immediate profitability of new products and markets. Market penetration and market share are more important. This allows managers to develop a strategic plan that emphasizes the long-run success of the firm.

## Contemporary Practice 11.2
### *Political Risk in International Capital Investments*

*In a recent interview survey, managers indicate that political events and changes in political relationships between countries are important risks in evaluating capital investments in other countries. But they also report that the evaluation is subjective rather than formal. Little use is made of external consultants. And these decisions are often made without determining if the expected ROR is high enough to compensate for the higher international risk.*

Source: Goddard, S. "Political Risk in International Capital budgeting," Managerial Finance, Vol. 16, Issue 2, 1990, pp. 7–12.

## TAXES AND DEPRECIATION

The illustrations have thus far ignored income taxes. Also, depreciation expense, being noncash, was used only in the accounting rate of return method. These factors impact capital budgeting significantly.

### Income Taxes and Capital Investments

Except for nonprofit organizations, the real world is a tax-paying world; and capital investment analysis must consider taxes. Taxation rules are complex and impact many cash flows. Taxable income and gains include:

1. Incremental revenues minus incremental expenses.
2. Incremental operating expense savings.
3. Gains on sales of old assets now and of new assets at the project's end.

   Incremental expenses and losses reduce taxes and include:

1. Incremental operating expenses.
2. Losses on sales of assets now and at the end of a project's life.

   The tax rate should be the expected **marginal tax rate** for the future year being analyzed. The marginal tax rate is the tax rate applied to any incremental taxable income. While the corporate federal income tax maximum rate is currently 35 percent, many companies also pay state and local income taxes. For simplicity,we assume that the marginal income tax rate is 40 percent for all income tax-related issues. Clearly, income taxes reduce the ROR on capital projects by reducing net cash inflows.

### Depreciation Expense

The only role that depreciation expense plays in cash-flow-based capital investment analysis is as a deduction in calculating income taxes. If taxes are ignored or are not applicable, as in nonprofit organizations, depreciation expense is also ignored.

The Internal Revenue Code uses the terms **Accelerated Cost Recovery System (ACRS)** and the **Modified Accelerated Cost Recovery System (MACRS)** to depreciate tangible assets for tax

| Cash Flows: | Today | Life of the Project | | | | |
|---|---|---|---|---|---|---|
| | | Year 1 | Year 2 | Year 3 | Year 4 | Year 5 |
| Net investment cash flows | $(95,000) | | | | | $13,000 |
| Annual cash inflows (taxable) | | $40,000 | $40,000 | $20,000 | $40,000 | $40,000 |
| Taxes on taxable income (40%) | | (16,000) | (16,000) | (8,000) | (16,000) | (16,000) |
| Aftertax cash inflows | | $24,000 | $24,000 | $12,000 | $24,000 | $24,000 |
| Net annual cash flows | $(95,000) | $24,000 | $24,000 | $12,000 | $24,000 | $37,000 |
| Present value factors at 12% | × 1.000 | × .893 | × .797 | × .712 | × .636 | × .567 |
| Present values at 12% | $(95,000) | $21,432 | $19,128 | $ 8,544 | $15,264 | $20,979 |
| Sum of PVs for Years 1 to 5 | 85,347 ◄ | | | | | |
| Net present value | $ (9,653) | | | | | |

**FIGURE 11.3**

Net Present Value Analysis With Taxes But Without Depreciation

purposes. ACRS, MACRS, and their impacts are discussed in Chapter 12. To simplify our depreciation expense and taxation discussions, we assume that: *(1) straight-line depreciation is used; (2) depreciation expense calculations ignore salvage values; and (3) salvage values are net of tax consequences.*

To understand the tax and depreciation expense impacts, let us look again at the Quartz Timepieces example in Figure 11.2 and now apply a tax rate of 40 percent to the incremental operating cash flows. For now, we ignore the effects of depreciation. This is shown in Figure 11.3.

As Figure 11.3 shows, suddenly a very profitable project (just under 30 percent ROR on a no-tax basis) now has a negative net present value using a 12 percent discount rate. We assume that the overhaul in Year 3 is a deductible expense, salvage value is net of taxes, and inventory recovery has no tax effects.

## The Tax Shield

Depreciation expense is a noncash expense, is a legitimate deduction for tax purposes, and creates a tax shield. By reducing taxable income, cash paid for taxes is reduced. Depreciation saves cash by reducing tax payments. Thus, if depreciation expense increases, tax payments decrease. Cash outflow is reduced. A reduced outflow has the same effect as an increased inflow. Remember, cash was paid out when the asset was originally purchased.

| Cash Flows: | Today | Life of the Project | | | | |
|---|---|---|---|---|---|---|
| | | Year 1 | Year 2 | Year 3 | Year 4 | Year 5 |
| Net investment cash flows | $(95,000) | | | | | $13,000 |
| Annual cash inflows (taxable) | | $40,000 | $40,000 | $20,000 | $40,000 | $40,000 |
| Incremental income taxes | | (8,640) | (8,640) | (640) | (8,640) | (8,640) |
| After tax cash inflows | | $31,360 | $31,360 | $19,360 | $31,360 | $31,360 |
| Net annual cash flows | $(95,000) | $31,360 | $31,360 | $19,360 | $31,360 | $44,360 |
| Present value factors at 12% | × 1.000 | × .893 | × .797 | × .712 | × .636 | × .567 |
| Present values at 12% | $(95,000) | $28,004 | $24,994 | $13,784 | $19,945 | $25,152 |
| Sum of PVs for Years 1 to 5 | 111,879 ◄ | | | | | |
| Net present value | $ 16,879 | | | | | |

**FIGURE 11.4**

Net Present Value Analysis With Depreciation and Taxes

The depreciation impact is seen in the Quartz example. The increase in depreciable assets is $92,000 ($100,000 – $8,000) and is spread over five years. Currently, salvage value is ignored in most IRS depreciation calculations. Assuming traight-line depreciation, the *incremental* depreciation expense is $18,400 per year. Aftertax cash flows are:

|  | **Year 1** |
|---|---|
| Incremental revenues | $55,000* |
| – Incremental cost of sales | – 30,000* |
| + Operating cost savings | 15,000* |
| Incremental cash inflow | $ 40,000 |
| – Depreciation expense | – 18,400 |
| Taxable income | $ 21,600 |
| – Incremental taxes (40 percent) | – 8,640* |
| Aftertax project net income | $ 12,960 |
| + Add back depreciation expense | 18,400 |
| Aftertax cash inflow | $ 31,360 |

\* Cash flows

The project's Year 1 aftertax profit, $12,960, and the incremental depreciation expense, $18,400, are summed to find the Year 1 aftertax cash flow. Tax cash outflows for the entire project are added to the Figure 11.4 analysis. The increased tax deduction for depreciation moves the net present value of the project from a negative $9,653 to a positive $16,879, a $26,532 change. This is the present value of the depreciation expense tax savings.

| Depreciation Expense | | Tax Rate | | Present Value Factor (for 5 years at 12 percent) | | Present Value of Tax Shield |
|---|---|---|---|---|---|---|
| $18,400 | × | 0.40 | × | 3.605 | = | $26,533 |

**Accelerated Depreciation Benefits.** The cash saving power of depreciation can be increased by using **accelerated depreciation** to deduct more depreciation earlier in a project's life. Deferring taxes has a time value of money. By merely changing depreciation methods, the net present value can increase or decrease. This is strictly from speeding up or slowing the depreciation expense deductions and the time value of the tax deferrals. Chapter 12 will discuss further the advantages of accelerated depreciation and shorter tax lives for assets.

# COST OF CAPITAL

Throughout our discussions, cost of capital is mentioned frequently. Long-term money has a cost, either a real cost, as in interest paid on bonds payable, or an opportunity cost, as in the use of earnings retained in the business. A basic approach is explained here to show the source of this rate.

A **weighted-average cost of capital** pools a firm's long-term funds and is used because the relative amount of each funds source affects the average cost. Debt generally is less costly than equity since the creditor assumes less risk and interest is deductible for tax purposes. If a firm has a pretax debt cost of 10 percent and a 40 percent tax rate, the after tax cost is 6 percent. Dividends, on the other hand, are not deductible for tax purposes and are profit distributions to owners, not a business expense.

Assume that a firm has the following long-term funds structure and cost of funds:

| | Book Value | Mix Percentage | Pretax Cost | Aftertax Cost | Weighted Average |
|---|---|---|---|---|---|
| Bonds payable | $10,000,000 | 25% | 10% | 6% | 1.5% |
| Preferred stock | 4,000,000 | 10 | 12 | 12 | 1.2 |
| Common stock | 14,000,000 | 35 | 18 | 18 | 6.3 |
| Retained earnings | 12,000,000 | 30 | 18 | 18 | 5.4 |
| Total long-term funds | $40,000,000 | 100% | | | 14.4% |

The pretax cost percentages come from financial markets calculations. The weighted-average cost of capital is 14.4 percent. Often financially strong companies have low cost of funds. High risk, financially unstable, or new firms often have high funds costs.

# SUMMARY

Capital investment decisions are critical to the firm's long-term success. The relevant data for making investment decisions are incremental cash flows, using criteria established in Chapter 10. Capital investments generally have multiperiod cash flows, requiring the use of the time value of money. The opportunity cost of cash to be received in the future can be a significant variable in measuring returns.

Four methods are discussed to evaluate the cash flows. Two methods use present values for all cash flows:

1. Net present value, where a rate of return is set and decisions are made based on whether the net present value is positive or negative.

2. Internal rate of return, where the rate of return is found by setting the initial investment equal to the present value of future net cash inflows.

Two other methods discussed that do not use the time value of money are the payback period and the accounting rate of return methods.

Rarely are funds available to finance all attractive projects. Projects are selected based on rankings of their relative attractiveness. Taxes on profits from capital investments must be calculated and do affect the ROR of projects. The cost of capital is often used to develop a minimum acceptable rate of return.

# PROBLEM FOR REVIEW

Baxter Insurance is evaluating a new processor to prepare personalized reports for insurance clients. Baxter will serve 200,000 clients per year for the foreseeable future. The report is currently prepared on a three-year old machine that could be used for another five years. The machine cost $160,000 new and was to last eight years. It is now worth $85,000 net of taxes, or it will have a $15,000 salvage value net of taxes in five years.

The new machine will have a useful life of five years, cost $275,000, and have a $25,000 salvage value net of taxes. Comparative cash operating expenses are:

| | Old Machine | New Machine |
|---|---|---|
| Variable cost | $2.00 per client | $1.70 per client |
| Fixed cost | $100,000 | $80,000 |

Assume straight-line depreciation, a 40 percent tax rate, and a 14 percent cost of capital.

**Required:**
1. Find the relevant cash flows for the machine replacement decision.
2. Using the NPV method, should the new machine be acquired?
3. Find the IRR, the payback period, and the ARR.

**Solution:**

1. The differential cash flows are:

| Cash flows: | Today | Year 1 | Year 2 | Year 3 | Year 4 | Year 5 |
|---|---|---|---|---|---|---|
| | | | | Life of the Project | | |
| New machine | ($275,000) | | | | | |
| Sale of old machine | 85,000 | | | | | |
| Incremental salvage value | | | | | | $10,000[1] |
| Variable cost savings | | $60,000[2] | $60,000 | $60,000 | $60,000 | 60,000 |
| Fixed cost savings | | 20,000[3] | 20,000 | 20,000 | 20,000 | 20,000 |
| Incremental income taxes | | −18,000[4] | −18,000 | −18,000 | −18,000 | −18,000 |
| Net cash flows | $190,000 | $62,000 | $62,000 | $62,000 | $62,000 | $72,000 |

[1] Salvage value of the new machine minus the salvage value of the old machine.
[2] Variable cost savings are $0.30 per unit on 200,000 units, $60,000 per year.
[3] Fixed cost savings are $20,000 per year ($100,000 – $ 80,000).
[4] Incremental tax payment is based on:

| | | | |
|---|---|---|---|
| Variable cost savings | $60,000 | Annual depreciation expense: | |
| Add fixed cost savings | 20,000 | Old machine ($160,000 ÷ 8) | $20,000 |
| Less incremental depreciation | −35,000 | New machine ($275,000 ÷ 5) | 55,000 |
| Incremental taxable income | $45,000 | Incremental depreciation | $35,000 |
| Incremental cash taxes (40%) | $18,000 | | |

2. Using the Part 1 cash flows, the net present value method shows:

| Cash flows: | Today | Year 1 | Year 2 | Year 3 | Year 4 | Year 5 |
|---|---|---|---|---|---|---|
| | | | | Life of the Project | | |
| Net cash flows | $(190,000) | $62,000 | $62,000 | $62,000 | $62,000 | $72,000 |
| Present value factors at 14% | × 1.000 | × 0.877 | × 0.769 | × 0.675 | × 0.592 | × 0.519 |
| Present value of cash flows | $(190,000) | $54,374 | $47,678 | $41,850 | $36,704 | $37,368 |
| Sum of PVs for Years 1 to 5 | 217,974 | | | | | |
| Net present value | $27,974 | | | | | |

The investment earns a positive net present value. If a 14 percent rate of return or better is the goal, we should approve the investment.

**3.** To find the **internal rate of return**, we use the trial and error method. Using various discount rates, a negative net present value is found at 20 percent:

|  | **18%** | **20%** |
|---|---|---|
| Net present value | $8,244 | $(538) |

The rate of return is between 18 and 20 percent, actually nearer to 20 percent. Using a business calculator, the rate is 19.88 percent.

The **payback period** is: $190,000 ÷ $ 62,000 = 3.06 years

The **accounting rate of return** is:

$$\frac{(\$60,000 + \$20,000 - \$35,000 - \$18,000)}{[(\$190,000 + \$10,000) \div 2]} = 27.0 \text{ percent}$$

# APPENDIX

## THE TIME VALUE OF MONEY

Dollars promised in the future are not equal to dollars received now. When given a choice, we all prefer getting $100 today versus $100 two years from now. Dollars due in different time periods should be valued on a uniform scale that recognizes the **time value of money**. **Present value** converts future dollars into current dollar equivalents. **Future value** converts all dollars into equivalent dollars as of some future date. To find these values, we need an interest rate and the number of time periods between today and the future cash flows.

Money has earning power. Dollars today grow to larger sums through earning interest on the principal plus earning interest on interest. The investment principal plus **compound interest** is the future value (FV). The future value of $100 in two years, with interest compounded at the rate of 10 percent annually, is $121. The formula for the future value of $1 is:

$$FV = (1 + i)^n \qquad \text{where} \qquad i = \text{interest rate}$$
$$n = \text{number of years}$$

In the example, the future value is computed as follows:

$$\text{FV of } \$1 = (1.10)^2 = \$1.21$$

$$\text{FV of } \$100 = \$100 \times \$1.21 \text{ or } \$121$$

An investor who is happy with a 10 percent ROR looks at the receipt of $121 in two years as equivalent to $100 today, assuming certainty. This investor is indifferent between the $100 today or $121 in two years.

The interest rate influences the values. If a decision maker has a choice of investments, the preferred choice is the investment with the highest ROR. The reason, of course, is that the investment with the highest ROR will yield the largest future amount or require the smallest current investment. For example, an alternative investment will earn a 15 percent ROR. Assuming certainty, the future value in two years of the $100 at 15 percent is:

$$\$100 \times (1.15)^2 = \$100 \times 1.3225 = \$132.25$$

Since $132.25 is larger than $121, the project earning 15 percent is preferred to the 10 percent project.

### Present Value of Money

Because decisions are made today and because future cash flows come in many different patterns and time periods, present values of future dollars are more useful and easier to analyze. It is conventional to use present value analysis.

How much money must we invest today to earn a given dollar amount in the future? Or, given an investment, how much will be earned in the future? Or, given an investment and a set of future cash inflows, what is the ROR? Answers to these questions can be found by computing the present value of the future cash flows and comparing it with the amount invested.

The **present value** (PV) of a future value can be computed by multiplying the future value by the present value of $1. The present value of $1 is:

$$\text{PV of } \$1 = 1 \div (1 + i)^n$$

Assume, for example, that $121 is needed in two years; and the rate of interest is 10 percent. How much must be invested today to have $121 after two years? We first determine the present value of $1 due in two years with interest compounded annually at 10 percent:

PV of $1 for 2 years at 10 percent = $1 \div (1.10)^2 = 0.826$

Next, we multiply by the future value:

PV of $121 for 2 years at 10 percent = $121 \times 0.826 = $100$ (rounded)

The computation can be viewed as:

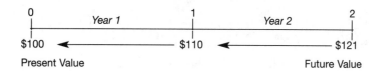

$121 \div 1.10 = $110$ is the value at the end of Year 1.

$110 \div 1.10 = $100$ is the investment at the start of Year 1, or today.

This is summarized as follows:

$121 \div (1.10)^2 \quad \textbf{or} \quad [1 \div (1.10)^2] \times $121 = $100$

The process of reducing a future amount to a present value is called **discounting**. The present value is sometimes called the **discounted value**. The rate of interest is the **discount rate**. The 0.826 is called the **present value factor** or **discount factor**.

It is seldom necessary to calculate either future values or present values as done here. Calculators and spreadsheet software easily perform these functions. Tables 1 and 2, found on the inside front covers, give present value factors for various discount (interest) rates for various time periods expressed in years. Table 1 gives the present value of $1 to be received at the end of the various time periods at interest or discount rates shown across the top row of the table. Thus, it is a tabulation of the factor $1 \div (1 + i)^n$, where ***n*** is the number of years and ***i*** is the discount rate. The factor for two years at 10 percent is 0.826, and the present value (PV) of $121 to be received in two years is calculated as follows:

PV = $121 \times 0.826 = $100$ (rounded)

The discount factors appearing in Tables 1 and 2 are rounded to the third digit, which is sufficient precision for most capital investment problems.

## The Present Value of a Series of Future Cash Flows

Often, a series of future cash inflows are earned from an investment instead of one cash inflow. As an example, a machine costing $3,500 today is forecast to generate cash inflows of $1,000 each year for five years. The time interval for most decisions is annual, but any time interval (a day, week, month, quarter, etc.) can be used as long as the interest rate (***i***) is adjusted to correspond to the time period.

Calculating present values depends on whether the cash flows series are equal or unequal amounts. An **annuity** refers to a series of equal cash flows. In either case, however, the underlying concepts are the same. The present value of a series is the sum of the present values of the individual amounts. The present value of five annual receipts of $1,000 using a 10 percent discount rate is computed as follows:

| Year | Computation | | Explanation |
|---|---|---|---|
| 1 | $1,000 \times (1 \div 1.10)$ | = | $909 PV of $1,000 received at the end of Year 1 |
| 2 | $1,000 \times [1 \div (1.10)^2]$ | = | 826 PV of $1,000 received at the end of Year 2 |
| 3 | $1,000 \times [1 \div (1.10)^3]$ | = | 751 PV of $1,000 received at the end of Year 3 |
| 4 | $1,000 \times [1 \div (1.10)^4]$ | = | 683 PV of $1,000 received at the end of Year 4 |
| 5 | $1,000 \times [1 \div (1.10)^5]$ | = | 621 PV of $1,000 received at the end of Year 5 |
| | | | $3,790 PV of an annuity of $1,000 for 5 years |

The present value can also be computed as follows:

$$\$1,000 \times \left[ \frac{1}{1.10} + \frac{1}{(1.10)^2} + \frac{1}{(1.10)^3} + \frac{1}{(1.10)^4} + \frac{1}{(1.10)^5} \right] = \$3,790$$

The decimal equivalents of the fractions can be found in Table 1 and applied to the annual cash inflow:

$$(0.909 + 0.826 + 0.751 + 0.683 + 0.621) = 3.790$$
$$\$1,000 \times 3.790 = \$3,790$$

Note that the factor, 3.791, can be found on Table 2 using the 10 percent column and the 5-period row. The factors in Table 2 are the sums of the present value factors in Table 1. The difference between 3.790 and 3.791 is due to rounding. The following calculations using interest rates of 8 percent, 10 percent, and 12 percent for five years illustrate this point.

| | 8 % | | 10 % | | 12 % | |
|---|---|---|---|---|---|---|
| Years | Table 1 | Table 2 | Table 1 | Table 2 | Table 1 | Table 2 |
| 1 | 0.926 | | 0.909 | | 0.893 | |
| 2 | 0.857 | | 0.826 | | 0.797 | |
| 3 | 0.794 | | 0.751 | | 0.712 | |
| 4 | 0.735 | | 0.683 | | 0.636 | |
| 5 | 0.681 | | 0.621 | | 0.567 | |
| Total | 3.993 | 3.993 | 3.790* | 3.791* | 3.605 | 3.605 |

* Difference due to rounding.

When calculating, it is easier to add the annual factors and make one computation. Thus, Table 2 is more convenient for evaluating equal cash flows. If the annual cash-flow amounts are not equal, it is necessary to use Table 1.

## Present Value Analysis Applied

Assume that we sell machinery and offer financing to our customers using long-term notes payable. When a contract is signed, the customer makes two promises:

**1.** To pay the principal amount (the **face value** of the note) at maturity.

**2.** To pay interest periodically at the rate stated in the contract.

We can either hold the note (earning interest and collecting the principal at the end of the contract) or sell the contract to an investor to get the cash for the sale now. The contract's market value depends on several factors, including the **market rate of interest** for similar contracts. The sum of the present values of the two promises is the contract's market price. As the market rate of interest rises, the contract's value declines, and vice versa.

To illustrate, assume that we sell a $100,000 machine. The buyer signs a ten-year $100,000 contract with an interest rate of 10 percent, paid annually. This contract specifies the following cash payments:

| Year | Interest at 10 Percent | Payment of Principal | Total Cash Outflow |
|------|------------------------|----------------------|--------------------|
| 1    | $10,000                |                      | $10,000            |
| 2    | 10,000                 |                      | 10,000             |
| 9    | 10,000                 |                      | 10,000             |
| 10   | 10,000                 | $100,000             | 110,000            |

Suppose that the current market rate of interest is 12 percent. In this case, investors are not willing to buy the contract at face value, because they could earn 12 percent elsewhere. To sell the contract, we must price the contract below face value. Selling at a price below face allows the investor to increase the rate of return by paying less for the two promises.

| | | |
|---|---|---|
| Promise 1: | $100,000 × 0.322 (10 periods at 12 percent from Table 1) | $32,200 |
| Promise 2: | $ 10,000 × 5.650 (10 payments at 12 percent from Table 2) | 56,500 |
| | Proceeds from sale of the contract | $88,700 |
| | Discount | $11,300 |

The investor who purchases the contract from us at $88,700 (with a **discount** of $11,300) will earn 12 percent interest on the $88,700 invested. The 12 percent earned is usually called the **yield** or the effective rate of interest. An **effective interest rate** or **yield to maturity** is the rate of interest earned regardless of the compounding period or the stated interest rate.

Likewise, if the current market rate of interest is 8 percent, an investor will pay a **premium** for a contract with a 10 percent interest rate. The selling price and premium are determined as follows:

| | | |
|---|---|---|
| Promise 1: | $100,000 × 0.463 (10 periods at 8 percent from Table 1) | $ 46,300 |
| Promise 2: | $ 10,000 × 6.710 (10 payments at 8 percent from Table 2) | 67,100 |
| | Proceeds from sale of the contract | $113,400 |
| | Premium | $ 13,400 |

# TERMINOLOGY REVIEW

**Accelerated Cost Recovery System (ACRS) (468)**
**Accelerated depreciation (470)**
**Accounting rate of return  method (ARR) (466)**
**Annuity (475)**
**Capital budgeting (458)**
**Capital investment (458)**
**Capital investment decisions (457)**

**Compound interest (474)**
**Cost of capital (462)**
**Cutoff rate (462)**
**Desired rate of return (462)**
**Discount (477)**
**Discount factor (475)**
**Discount rate (462)**

Discounted value (475)

Discounting (475)

Effective interest rate (477)

Face value (476)

Future value (474)

Hurdle rate (462)

Internal rate of return method (IRR) (463)

Marginal tax rate (468)

Market rate of interest (476)

Minimum acceptable rate of return (462)

Modified Accelerated Cost Recovery System (MACRS) (468)

Net present value (NPV) method (461)

Net initial investment (460)

Payback period (464)

Payback period method (464)

Payback reciprocal (465)

Premium (477)

Present value (474)

Present value factor (475)

Profitability index (462)

Project ranking (462)

Required rate of return (462)

Target rate of return (462)

Tax shield (485)

Time value of money (474)

Weighted-average cost of capital (470)

Yield to maturity (477)

## Questions for Review and Discussion

1. Why is timing important in a capital investment decision? What is meant by the time value of money?

2. What is meant by "net initial investment" in a capital investment decision?

3. Could the net present value method and the internal rate of return use the same interest rate? Explain.

4. The formula used to derive the numbers in Table 1 is:

$$P = \frac{1}{(1+i)^n}$$

Where:  P = Present value factor

i = Interest rate

n = Number of periods

Explain the math in words.

5. Are the returns from an investment the same as the accounting profit? Explain.

6. What are the advantages and disadvantages of the payback method?

7. What are the advantages and disadvantages of the accounting rate of return method?

8. John Bassey, a sales representative for a machine tool company, used the following phrase over and over with his customers: "Buy this thing; depreciate it; and watch the cash come rolling in from Uncle Sam!" What does he mean?

9. Explain the difference between the internal rate of return method and the net present value method.

10. The net present value of a certain investment is zero. Does this mean the investment earns no profit? Explain the significance of a zero net present value.

11. How can project rankings using the internal rate of return and the profitability index differ?

12. Why can the terms cutoff rate, hurdle rate, minimum acceptable rate of return, target rate of return, and desired rate of return be used interchangeably?

13. Explain the tax shield. Tie this explanation to the comment: "Depreciation is a source of cash."

14. How would you estimate the internal rate of return if you know the life of the project? How would you estimate the project's life if you know its internal rate of return?

15. Are definitions of relevant costs and revenues different for capital investment analysis than the definitions used in Chapter 10? Explain.

**16.** Doris Suntag is buying a car for $12,000. After a down payment of $3,000, she finances the remainder at 12 percent annual interest with monthly payments. If she signs a 50-month financing contract, what will be her monthly payment?

**17.** What is the advantage of accelerated depreciation over straight-line depreciation in a capital investment decision?

**18.** Cash, accounts receivable, and inventory are classified as current assets. How can they be considered part of a long-term capital investment?

**19.** Knowing the cost of capital is a necessary part of present value analysis. What does it represent? Explain one way to measure it.

## EXERCISES

**11–1. Time Value of Money.** Walt Zarnoch has won second prize in THE BIG Lottery. Friends who he never knew have offered him several "opportunities of a lifetime." He would like a 14 percent annual return. The lottery prize was a check for $300,000. Among the "opportunities" were:

**(1)** $50,000 per year for ten years.
**(2)** $400,000 on the same date in the next U. S. presidential election year.
**(3)** $20,000 per year for the rest of his life (about 50 years).
**(4)** A penniless friend told Zarnoch that he wrote him a check for $1,000,000 and has put it "in the mail" several years ago and asks whether he received it, yet.
**(5)** $500,000 to be paid on this same date five years from now.

**Required:**
After judging uncertainty, which should he select? Explain.

 **11–2. Determining the Life of an Investment.** Edward's Electronics is considering expanding its business by adding one more store in Amsterdam. The building and its operating contents will cost 1 million euros and generate about €200,000 in cash inflows each year after taxes. The manager feels the investment should not be made unless the store realizes a 10 percent rate of return on the cash invested.

**Required:**
For how many years must the store operate to earn a 10 percent return?

**11–3. Four Methods.** Crandall Company purchased a farm tractor for $100,000. The cash inflow from using the tractor is expected to be $30,000 per year for eight years. Crandall uses a 15 percent cutoff rate.

**Required:**
Use straight-line depreciation where needed, and ignore taxes. What is the payback period, the estimated IRR, the NPV, and the ARR?

 **11–4. Investment in Another Company.** The management of Musser Enterprises, in Cologne, Germany, is considering a €10,000,000 investment to acquire the assets of Ener-Tec Company, a small company that has developed a more economical means of using electrical energy. Last year, Ener-Tec reported net sales of €20,000,000 and operating expenses of €18,000,000. Included in the operating expenses is depreciation of assets in the amount of €800,000. This level of earnings is expected to continue for five years, after which the technology will be outdated, and the assets will have no value.

**Required:**

Ignoring income taxes and using present value, what is the approximate rate of return earned by the investment?

**11–5. Payback Method.** Bakker Company purchased a machine for $125,000 and will depreciate it on a straight-line basis over a 5-year period with an aftertax salvage value of $15,000. The related cash operating savings, before income taxes, is expected to be $50,000 a year.

**Required:**
1. Find the payback period ignoring taxes.
2. Assume that Bakker's effective income tax rate is 40 percent and that salvage value is ignored when calculating depreciation. What is the payback period?

**11–6. Different Capital Investment Methods.** Chen Center Company plans to acquire equipment costing $600,000. Depreciation on the new equipment would be $100,000 each year for six years. The annual cash inflow before income tax from this equipment has been estimated at $210,000. The tax rate is 40 percent.

**Required:**
1. Find the payback period.
2. Find the ARR using the average investment.
3. Find the NPV if Chen's minimum acceptable rate of return is 16 percent.
4. Estimate the IRR from Table 2 (e.g., between 10 and 12 percent).

**11–7. Cash Flows and NPV.** Woods wants to expand his current operations. Additional equipment will cost $100,000, last 10 years, have no salvage value, and be depreciated using the straight-line method. Sales will increase by $80,000 per year. Variable contribution margin is 40%, and additional cash fixed costs incurred will be $6,000. The tax rate is 40%. Woods knows that the short-term bank-borrowing rate is 10%, that the firm's outstanding long-term debt pays 12%, that the firm's weighted average cost of capital is 14%, and that stockholders want a return on common equity of 16%.

**Required:**
1. What is the annual net cash flow from this project for each year?
2. What is the net present value from this project?

**11–8. Determining the Required Investment.** The Tuntland Company would like to initiate an advertising campaign to increase its annual sales volume. Data show that the proposed advertising will add $80,000 to the annual cash flow for each of the next two years and $30,000 in the third year.

**Required:**

What is the maximum amount that Tuntland would invest in this campaign if the company sets a minimum rate-of-return objective of 18 percent?

**11–9. Investments With Uneven Cash Flows.** Icon Consolidated has data on two $100,000 investment opportunities. With only $100,000 in cash available, the owners must decide which is the better opportunity. The controller has gathered the following data:

**Investment 1:** $30,000 of cash inflow for each of the first three years and $90,000 for each of the last three years.

**Investment 2:** $80,000 of cash inflow in the first year, $60,000 in the next four years, and $40,000 in the sixth year.

**Required:**

If 14 percent ROR is needed, which investment will be preferred? Why?

**11–10. Comparing Alternatives.** The Mohr Company is considering a new popper for one of its portable caramel popcorn stands. The analysis is narrowed to the "Bang" or the "Pow." Information on the two devices is:

|  | Bang | Pow |
|---|---|---|
| Purchase price | $90,000 | $60,000 |
| Annual cash inflows | 34,000 | 24,000 |
| Salvage value in 5 years | 8,000 | 5,000 |
| Useful life. | 5 years | 5 years |

Either device will do the job equally as well. Mohr uses a 16 percent cost of capital. Ignore taxes.

**Required:**
1. Which machine has the higher NPV? Is this a proper basis for making this investment decision?
2. Using the profitability index, which machine is more attractive?
3. If Mohr has $180,000 to invest in popping machines, what should it do? Why?

**11–11. Equipment Replacement.** By replacing an old refrigeration unit, Rachel Simon of Simon's Produce in Liverpool, U. K., thinks that sales from the greater capacity will increase by £100,000 per year and that cash operating costs will decline by £60,000 per year. The new refrigerator will cost £350,000. Her variable contribution margin is 40 percent. The old equipment is fully depreciated but can be sold for £8,000. The new refrigerator will use straight-line depreciation, has a 5-year life, and is expected to have a salvage value of £40,000. Ignore taxes.

**Required:**
Format the cash flows for the refrigeration unit proposal.

**11–12. Multiple Projects.** Ryan Darichuk manages a temporary hiring service and is considering several investments for his business. He expects a 16 percent ROR. Ignore taxes. The basic facts about three opportunities are.
A. More office space. The space will cost $400,000, earn a net cast inflow of $120,000 per year after taxes, last 5 years, have no salvage value, and be depreciated using straight-line. What is the net present value?
B. An opportunity to run a training program. The project will earn $50,000 per year and have a life of 5 years. What is the most he should pay for up-front preparations and still meet his ROR expectations?
C. New computer equipment. He thinks the cost of the equipment needed is $60,000. The expected cash inflow per year is $12,000. How long must the equipment last (in years) to meet his ROR expectations?

**Required:**
Answer the question related to each opportunity.

**11–13. Net Returns and Discounted Rate of Return.** The LaLonde Company is considering new word processing equipment that can reduce personnel costs by an estimated $60,000 a year. The new equipment is also expected to generate annual intangible customer service benefits of $70,000. The new equipment will cost $400,000 and will be depreciated on a straight-line basis for tax purposes. The asset will have no residual value at the end of ten years, the estimated life of the equipment. Income tax is estimated at 40 percent.

**Required:**
1. Determine the annual net cash inflow from the proposed investment.
2. Will the investment earn an 18 percent aftertax rate of return?
3. Comment on the NPV.

Service

**11–14. Sales Offer as Investment.** Katie Williams, owner of a self-storage business, has just received an offer that is worth $600,000 after taxes for the storage buildings. She is interested in another investment opportunity that can probably yield an annual discounted return of 15 percent after taxes. The storage business is expected to continue to yield an annual cash inflow, before taxes, of $170,000 for a period of 15 years. The book value of the storage buildings is $660,000, and straight-line depreciation is used for tax purposes. Zero salvage value is predicted. A 40 percent tax rate applies.

**Required:**
Should the offer to sell the storage business be accepted? Explain.

**11–15. Different Investment Goals.** Three projects are being evaluated. All have the same initial investment and expected life. Data from the projects are:

| | Net Present Value (Using 16%) | Payback | Accounting Rate of Return |
|---|---|---|---|
| Project A | $22,000 | 2.8 years | 18% |
| Project B | 23,000 | 2.7 | 16 |
| Project C | 21,000 | 2.6 | 17 |

**Required:**
1. If present value and profitability are important, rank the projects.
2. If we want the project that will make us look best in accrual accounting reports, rank the projects.
3. If avoiding risk and getting our cash investment back quickly are key factors, rank the projects.

**11–16. Uneven Cash Flows.** The following projects each require an $80,000 investment:

| | Project | | | | |
|---|---|---|---|---|---|
| Cash inflows: | 98-A4 | 98-G3 | 98-K1 | 98-P6 | 98-S4 |
| Year 1 | $20,000 | $10,000 | $40,000 | | $60,000 |
| Year 2 | 20,000 | 10,000 | | | 30,000 |
| Year 3 | 20,000 | 15,000 | 40,000 | | 10,000 |
| Year 4 | 20,000 | 15,000 | | $160,000 | (60,000) |
| Year 5 | 20,000 | 25,000 | 40,000 | | |
| Year 6 | 20,000 | 25,000 | | | 40,000 |
| Year 7 | 20,000 | 30,000 | 40,000 | | |
| Year 8 | 20,000 | 30,000 | | | 80,000 |

**Required:**
1. For each project, find the payback period.
2. For each project, find the ARR.
3. For each project, find the NPV (using a 15 percent discount rate).

**11-17. Expanding Business.** Mohnke Company sells packaged donut mix for home bakers in the Detroit area. The firm could create a similar firm in Chicago that will sell about 200,000 packages annually. To operate the firm, Mohnke would have to hire a nutrition specialist who will cost $100,000 annually. Machinery will cost $500,000. The machinery should last 5 years, have no salvage value, and be depreciated on a straight-line basis. Inventories of $30,000 will need to be maintained. A one-time tax incentive (with no other tax consequences) to invest in a new business in Chicago could be received by Mohnke during the first year of operation and would be worth $20,000.

Other data are as follows:
**(a)** Variable costs are $0.80 per package.
**(b)** Selling price is $3 per package.
**(c)** Annual cash costs of operating the Chicago business are $120,000.
**(d)** Tax rate is 40 percent.
**(e)** Cost of his capital is 16 percent.

**Required:**
On the basis of this information and a 5-year time horizon, is the investment opportunity worth undertaking?

**11-18. New Business.** Litowich Co. purchased a new machine for $50,000 to expand capacity. Sales are expected to increase by 20 percent. The only additional fixed expense is the depreciation on the new machine (straight-line over five years with no salvage value). The income statement for the past year is:

| | |
|---|---|
| Sales | $300,000 |
| Variable expenses | (180,000) |
| Fixed expenses | (100,000) |
| Net income before taxes | $ 20,000 |
| Taxes (40%) | (8,000) |
| Net income after taxes | $ 12,000 |

**Required:**
**1.** What is the expected annual aftertax cash inflow from the new machine?
**2.** Find the NPV using a hurdle rate of 15 percent and the payback period.

**11-19. Basic Replacement Decision.** You are given the following data:

| Existing machine: | | Replacement machine: | |
|---|---|---|---|
| Cost | $70,000 | Cost | $180,000 |
| Current value (net of taxes) | 32,000 | Salvage value (net of taxes) | 20,000 |
| Salvage value (end of life) | 0 | Annual cash operating costs | 8,000 |
| Annual depreciation | 5,000 | Useful life | 6 years |
| Annual cash operating costs | 50,000 | | |
| Remaining life | 6 years | | |

The income tax rate is 40 percent. The target rate of return is 14 percent. Straight-line depreciation is used. Assume that salvage value is ignored in calculating depreciation expense.

**Required:**
Determine the NPV of the replacement decision.

**11-20. Equipment Replacement.** By replacing present equipment with more efficient equipment, Sitaram Company estimates that cash operating costs can be reduced by $65,000 a year. In addition, increased sales volume can result in a larger contribution margin of $25,000 a year without considering the efficiency savings. Depreciation of $50,000 per year will be taken on new equipment. Depreciation on present equipment is $10,000 per year. The income tax rate is 40 percent.

**Required:**
What is the estimated incremental annual aftertax cash inflow on this investment?

Service

**11-21. Capital Budgeting Ethics.** Tadd and Todd manage similar stores of Tough Tires. They met at a recent managers' conference and discussed their need for new car lifts at their stores. At the meeting, the company's controller made a presentation on next year's capital investment budget. Funds are scarce, proposals will be studied carefully; the cutoff rate will be raised, and fewer proposals approved. Tadd and Todd return to their stores and prepare competing proposals for the lifts. Tough Tires assumes a 40 percent tax rate. Their data show the following:

|  | Tadd's Proposal | Todd's Proposal |
|---|---|---|
| Cost of equipment | $100,000 in Year 0 | $100,000 in Year 0 |
| Installation costs | 15,000 in Year 0 | 5,000 in Year 0 |
| Sale of old equipment net of taxes | 5,000 in Year 0 | 10,000 in Year 0 |
| Incremental depreciation expense each year | 11,500 per year | 7,000 per year |
| Reduced operating expenses per year | 20,000 per year | 25,000 per year |
| Increased contribution margin per year | 15,000 per year | 25,000 per year |
| Salvage value of new machine net of taxes | 10,000 in Year 10 | 30,000 in Year 15 |
| Life of equipment | 10 years | 15 years |

**Required:**
1. Develop a rough estimate of the IRR for the two proposals.
2. Why would the two sets of estimates differ so much?
3. How might the Tough Tires controller test the managers' estimates?

**11-22. Find the Missing Values.** For these projects, provide the missing values:

|  | Initial Investment | Life of the Project | Annual Net Cash Inflow | Internal Rate of Return | |
|---|---|---|---|---|---|
|  |  |  |  | Percentage | Present Value Factor (Table 2) |
| Project 1 | $118,932 | 6 years | $34,000 | ? % | ? |
| Project 2 | ? | 5 years | 12,000 | ? % | 3.605 |
| Project 3 | 68,000 | 15 years | ? | 16 % | ? |
| Project 4 | 84,750 | ? years | 15,000 | 12 % | ? |
| Project 5 | ? | ? years | 20,000 | 20 % | 2.991 |
| Project 6 | 11,925 | 20 years | ? | 8 % | ? |

**11-23. Ranking Projects.** The following projects have been evaluated using four capital budgeting techniques.

|  | Project A | Project B | Project C | Project D |
|---|---|---|---|---|
| Net present value (Using 14%) | $3,440 | $8,550 | $300 | $(2,000) |
| Internal rate of return | 18% | 16% | 20% | 12% |
| Payback period | 3 Years | 2 Years | 4 Years | 5 Years |
| Accounting rate of return | 25% | 18% | 22% | 20% |

**Required:**

1. Based only on the information provided, rank the projects for each of the capital investment methods shown.
2. What additional information is needed to make better rankings? Discuss what might cause the differences in the rankings.

**11–24. Tax Shield.** Your boss is considering a new parking lot for employees that will cost $200,000. The company is in the 40 percent tax bracket. Your boss says, "It will only cost us $120,000 after taxes to put in the lot." The firm has a 14 percent cost of capital and would depreciate the lot over eight years using the straight-line method.

**Required:**

Tell your boss what the net cost, in present value terms, will be to build the new parking lot. Comment on the absence of "benefits."

# PROBLEMS

**11–25. Payback and Discounted Returns.** Ignore tax impacts. Carol Towel, manager of Timber Ridge Investments, uses the payback method in selecting investment alternatives. She states that, "If I can recover the investment in three years, I'm virtually in the same position as another investor who earns an 18 percent internal rate of return on a 5-year investment." In her business, investments produce uniform returns over a 5-year period and have no salvage value. Three investment choices are outlined as follows:

|  | Choice 1 | Choice 2 | Choice 3 |
|---|---|---|---|
| Investment | $90,000 | $24,000 | $44,000 |
| Annual return for each of 5 years | 30,000 | 9,000 | 12,500 |

**Required:**

1. Which, if any, of the investment choices meet the 3-year payback criterion?
2. Evaluate the three choices by the NPV method with a minimum rate of return of 18 percent, and compare the results with those found in Part 1.
3. Comment on her statement.

**11–26. Relevant Costs.** Aussie Auto Wash Company has just installed a special machine for washing cars in its Perth outlet. The machine cost A$20,000. Its operating costs, based on a yearly volume of 100,000 cars, total A$15,000, exclusive of depreciation. After the machine has been used one day, a salesperson offers a different machine that promises to do the same job at a yearly operating cost of A$9,000, exclusive of depreciation. The new machine will cost A$24,000, installed. The "old" machine is unique and can be sold outright for only A$8,000, less A$2,000 removal cost. The old and new machines will have a 4-year useful life and no residual value. Sales, all in cash, will be A$150,000 per year; and other cash expenses will be A$110,000 annually, regardless of this decision.

**Required:**

1. Ignore taxes. Calculate net income for each of the four years assuming that the new machine is not purchased and then assuming that it is purchased. Sum the net incomes for the four years for each alternative. What should be done?
2. Ignore taxes, and consider the time value of money. If a 15 percent return on investment is desired, what should be done?

**11–27. Incremental Costs and Revenues.** The Sopariwala Company has the opportunity to market a new product. The sales manager believes that the firm could sell 5,000 units per year at $14 per unit for five years. The production manager has determined that machinery costing $60,000 and having a 5-year life and no salvage value would be required. The machinery will have annual fixed cash operating costs of $4,000. Variable costs per unit will be $8. Straight-line depreciation is to be used for both book and tax purposes. The tax rate is 40 percent, and the firm's cost of capital is 14 percent.

**Required:**
1. Determine the NPV of the investment if taxes are ignored.
2. Determine the NPV of the investment if taxes are paid but no depreciation is taken.
3. Determine the NPV of the investment if taxes and depreciation are included.
4. Comment on the differences in net present values.

**11–28. Improving Investment Returns.** For many years Emilio Perez has been successful in the retail garment industry in Nogales, Mexico. Recently he has learned of an opportunity to purchase a two-story modern building for M$750,000. He believes that he can operate successfully by using only one of the two floors. At the present time, his business is operating in an older building where he uses three floors. This has sales and production constraints, he admits.

With uncertainties about inflation and interest rates, he would hesitate to invest unless he could obtain a discounted rate of return of at least 15 percent. Yet, he estimates that the annual returns from his business after income tax would probably increase by M$150,000 for each of the next ten years if he moved. This investment opportunity does not appear that good to him, and he is inclined to continue the current arrangements.

His daughter, who has recently graduated from medical school, disagrees with his position: "You forget that this area is growing. We have no professional building; and I know of several doctors, dentists, and attorneys who would be happy to have offices on the second floor if you did some remodeling. I already have estimates and find that you can have the second floor remodeled for M$100,000. The offices should yield annual aftertax rental income of M$40,000."

**Required:**
1. From the data given, what is the approximate IRR on the building itself?
2. What is the approximate IRR on the building and the remodeling investment together?
3. Comment on the worthiness of the incremental investment.

**11–29. Finding Unknowns.** Fill in the blanks for the following independent cases. The investments have a life of ten years and no salvage value. Ignore taxes.

| | Annual Cash Inflow | Investment | Cost of Capital | Internal Rate of Return | Net Present Value |
|---|---|---|---|---|---|
| Case 1. | $ 45,000 | $188,640 | 14% | ? | $    ? |
| Case 2. | $ 80,000 | $    ? | 12% | 18% | $    ? |
| Case 3. | $    ? | $300,000 | ? | 16% | $ 81,440 |
| Case 4. | $    ? | $450,000 | 12% | ? | $115,000 |
| Case 5. | $100,000 | $    ? | ? | 14% | $(38,300) |

**11–30. Investment Returns and Sales Volume.** D. D. Ward, whose uncle whispered "plastics" into his ear soon after he graduated from college years ago, founded Plastic Opportunities, Inc. Ward is considering an investment of $2,000,000 in a new product line. Depreciation of $200,000 is to be deducted in each of the next ten years. Salvage value is estimated at zero. A selling price of $50 per unit is decided upon; unit variable cost is $30. The sales division believes that a sales estimate of 50,000 units per year is realistic. His controller states that a solid market exists for only 20,000 units a year. Projects must meet a minimum rate-of-return requirement of 15 percent. Income tax is estimated at 40 percent of income before tax.

**Required:**
1. Evaluate the project using each of the sales volume estimates. Use the NPV method.
2. At what volume will the project earn exactly a 15 percent return?

**11–31. Management Ethics and Cost Savings.** Lueders Company operates several factories, one of which was built some 70 years ago and is in poor condition. The factory has a fire insurance policy covering machinery, inventory, and the building itself. Premiums on the policy are $40,000 per year. The president has refused to approve several proposals for modernizing the fire safety system.

Recently, a fire inspector from the insurance company has recommended that the premium be increased to $80,000 per year because the older factory's fire protection has been diminished. The existing sprinkler system has stopped functioning and cannot be repaired at a reasonable cost. The plant manager was told by the inspector that a new system, costing $200,000 with a 10-year life and no salvage value, is needed to continue the policy at the current premium level.

The system would be depreciated on a straight-line basis. The tax rate is 40 percent, and Lueders' cost of capital is 12 percent. The manager resubmitted the fire safety system proposal with the new insurance data.

**Required:**
1. In a quantitative sense, should the sprinkler system be installed? Explain.
2. Discuss other issues that should be considered in making this decision.
3. How can sound capital budgeting decisions be made while still considering human issues?

Service

**11–32. Alternative Uses.** The Edo Building Company owns an office building in the business center of Tokyo. The building has a large unused lobby area. The facilities manager for the firm, Koji Seguchi, is planning to get a greater financial return from the unused space and believes that a convenience shop should be placed in the lobby. He talked to managers of several other office buildings and projected the following annual operating results if the company establishes the shop:

| | |
|---|---|
| Sales | ¥8,500,000 |
| Cost of sales | 4,000,000 |
| Salaries and benefits of clerks | 2,400,000 |
| Licenses and permits. | 100,000 |
| Share of utilities on the building. | 200,000 |
| Share of building depreciation. | 100,000 |
| Advertising for the shop. | 100,000 |
| Allocation of Edo administrative expense. | 150,000 |

The investment required would be ¥5,000,000, all for equipment that would be worthless in ten years. Before presenting the plan to the executive manager, Koji learned that the space could be leased to an outside firm that would operate a convenience shop. The lease firm would pay a commission of ¥500,000 per year for ten years. Because the lobby is heated and lighted anyway, Edo would supply utilities at a minimal added cost. Edo's cost of capital is 12 percent. Ignore taxes.

**Required:**

1. Determine the best course of action for Edo Building Company.
2. Determine how much annual rent Edo would have to receive to equalize the attractiveness of the options.

**11–33. Value of a Business.** Jawbreaker, Ltd., a Hong Kong firm, makes and sells candy in large lots for other firms that package and sell the candy under various brand names. The firm could acquire a small candy exporting firm that has sold about 800,000 kilograms of candy annually to Korea and Japan. To operate the firm, Jawbreaker would have to hire a specialized salesperson for HK$1,200,000 annually, including travel and entertainment expenses. Additional packaging machinery costing HK$1,600,000 must be acquired. The machinery would last five years, have no salvage value, and be depreciated on a straight-line basis.

Other data are as follows:

**(a)** Variable costs are HK$0.80 per kilogram.
**(b)** Selling price on the export business is HK$4 per kilogram.
**(c)** Annual cash costs of operating the new machinery are HK$320,000.
**(d)** Tax rate is 40 percent. (Assume that Hong Kong and U. S. tax rules are the same.)
**(e)** Cost of capital is 16 percent.

**Required:**

On the basis of this information and a 5-year time horizon, what is the most Jawbreaker should pay for this investment opportunity?

**11–34. Expanding a Product Line.** Ghafari Brothers Company makes office equipment, such as tables, desks, computer equipment consoles, and work tables. The sales manager is trying to decide whether to expand the relatively new computer equipment console product line. The average console will sell for $300 and has a variable cost of $140 per unit. Volume is expected to be 4,000 units per year for five years. To make the desks, the firm will have to buy additional machinery that will cost $900,000, has a 5-year life, and has a $100,000 salvage value net of taxes. Straight-line depreciation is used, and salvage value is ignored in depreciation calculations. Additional fixed cash operating costs will be $200,000 per year. Ghafari has a 40 percent tax rate, and its cost of capital is 16 percent.

**Required:**

1. Using NPV, determine whether the computer console line should be expanded.
2. Compute the payback period.
3. Determine the approximate IRR that the firm expects to earn on the investment. Ignore salvage value.

Service

**11–35. Changes in the Economic Environment.** Four years ago, Curell Properties, Inc. invested $10,000,000 in a venture in an economic development zone in another country. The investment was estimated to have a 10-year life and was expected to produce a cash inflow of $2,500,000 each year before income taxes.

It did exactly this for four years. Conditions are less favorable now, and the revised estimate indicates that the annual cash inflow will be only $1,300,000 but will last for eight more years. Because of its foreign investment classification, it has a special tax status and is not subject to normal income taxes. The investment can now be sold for $5,400,000. At present, an investment can be justified only if the IRR is expected to be at least 18 percent.

**Required:**

Should the investment be sold for $5,400,000 or be continued? Show computations using the NPV method. Comment on the changed estimates.

**11–36. Equipment Replacement Concerns.** The molding department of Rayon, Inc. has been investigating the acquisition of new equipment costing $100,000. Cash savings before income taxes from the use of this equipment are estimated to be $40,000 per year for ten years. At the end of five years, the new equipment must be overhauled at a cost of $35,000. The new equipment will have no salvage value after ten years. The new machine would replace an old machine that would need a $30,000 overhaul now and again in five years, if it is not replaced. The old machine is fully depreciated but can still function. To remove the old machine, environmental precautions (mainly an asbestos problem) will cost the firm $40,000. The rate used in evaluating investments is 10 percent. The income tax rate is 40 percent. Rayon uses straight-line depreciation.

**Required:**

1. Calculate the NPV. Make a recommendation.
2. If the asbestos will need to be removed within two years anyway, how does this impact your answer to Part 1? Comment.

**11–37. Break-Even Volume and Investment.** For several years, Grabski Company has used a combination of its own equipment and rental equipment to handle materials. The company has its own equipment to handle routine work but must rent equipment to handle particularly bulky materials. The cost to rent equipment has been estimated to average $4,000 a year.

An evaluation of cash operating expenses indicates that the company can save $0.15 per cubic yard of materials by buying its own equipment instead of renting equipment. An equipment manufacturer offers the necessary additional equipment at a cost of $80,000. The equipment will probably have a useful life of six years with no salvage value.

Uncertainty exists with respect to how much work will be required from the new equipment if it is purchased. Estimates of the number of cubic yards that might possibly be handled in each of the six years are 80,000 cubic yards, 100,000 cubic yards, or 120,000 cubic yards. On this type of investment, a 15 percent discounted return is considered to be appropriate. Ignore taxes.

**Required:**

1. Can the investment meet the minimum rate-of-return requirement if 80,000 cubic yards are handled? 100,000 cubic yards? 120,000 cubic yards?
2. Determine the break-even volume, that is, the number of cubic yards at which the investment can just meet the 15 percent return requirement. Round all amounts to the nearest dollar.

**11–38. Ranking Investment Alternatives.** Mazzeo Industries has designated $1.2 million for capital investment expenditures during the upcoming year. Its cost of capital is 14 percent. Any unused funds will earn the cost of capital rate. The following investment opportunities along with their required investment and estimated net present values have been identified:

| Project | Net Investment | NPV | Project | Net Investment | NPV |
|---------|---------------|------|---------|---------------|------|
| A | $200,000 | $22,000 | F | $250,000 | $30,000 |
| B | 275,000 | 21,000 | G | 100,000 | 7,000 |
| C | 150,000 | 6,000 | H | 200,000 | 18,000 |
| D | 190,000 | (19,000) | I | 210,000 | 4,000 |
| E | 500,000 | 40,000 | J | 250,000 | 35,000 |

**Required:**

1. Rank the projects using the profitability index. Considering the limit on funds available, which projects should be accepted?
2. Using the NPV, which projects should be accepted, considering the limit on funds available?
3. If the available investment funds are reduced to only $1,000,000:
   (a) Does the list of accepted projects change from Part 2?
   (b) What is the opportunity cost of the eliminated $200,000?

**11–39. Proposal Preparation.** Yoder Instruments Company manufactures a variety of products. The sales manager of Yoder, Dave Shockley, has stated repeatedly that he could sell more units of one of the firm's products if they were available. To prove his claim, the sales manager conducted a market research study last year at a cost of $60,000 to determine potential demand for this product. The study indicated that Yoder could sell 25,000 units annually for the next five years. A unit sells for $20 per unit.

The machinery currently used has capacity to product 15,000 units annually. This machinery has a book value of $80,000 and a remaining useful life of five years. The salvage value of the machinery is negligible now and will be zero in five years. The variable production costs using this equipment are $12 per unit.

New machinery could produce 30,000 units annually. The new machinery costs $250,000 and has an estimated useful life of five years with no salvage value at the end of the five years. Yoder's production manager, Jean Smith, has estimated that the new equipment would provide increased production efficiencies, reducing the variable production costs to $10 per unit. She also explains that the machine's higher capacity would cause factory administrative overheads to be reallocated. She thought a charge of $4 per unit for the additional 10,000 units produced would be the amount calculated by the cost accounting department.

The Shockley felt so strongly about the additional capacity that he prepared an economic justification for the equipment. His analysis, which follows, excited him because it covered all expenses including the bank's 9 percent prime interest rate and "still returned a small sum to the bottom line." He was last seen on his way to the president's office to schedule a meeting with the executive finance committee. A quick peek at his analysis shows:

*Initial investment:*

| | | |
|---|---:|---:|
| Purchase price of new machinery. | | $250,000 |
| Disposal of present equipment: | | |
|    Loss on disposal | $80,000 | |
|    Less benefit of tax loss (40%) | 32,000 | 48,000 |
| Market research study costs | | 60,000 |
|    Total new investment needed | | $358,000 |

*Additional annual profit:*

| | | |
|---|---:|---:|
| Contribution margin from product: | | |
|    New machinery output—30,000 × [$20 – ($10 + 4)] | | $180,000 |
|    Existing machinery output—15,000 × [$20 – ($12 + 4)] | | 60,000 |
|    Added contribution margin | | $120,000 |
| Less depreciation on new machinery | | 50,000 |
| Increase in taxable income | | $ 70,000 |
| Income tax (40%) | | 28,000 |
| Increase in income | | $ 42,000 |
| Cost of borrowed funds—0.09 × $358,000 | | 32,220 |
| Net annual return on the new machinery | | $  9,780 |

**Required:**

Dave Shockley's executive secretary, who has kept him out of "hot water" in the past, is worried about his numbers. She asks you to evaluate his project numbers and see if he has his "gear together." You recall that the firm's cost of capital has been 16 percent and that the tax rate is 40 percent. Straight-line depreciation is used. Revise the numbers as you feel necessary.

# CASE 11A—GRANTHAM MACHINING

Grantham Machining purchased a new grinding machine one year ago at a cost of $68,000. The machine has been working very satisfactorily, but the shop manager, Liz Shimak, has just received information on an electronically controlled grinder that is vastly superior to the machine that she now uses. While both machines can meet all required existing quality standards and tolerances, the new machine's quality potential can far exceed the old machine's capabilities. Comparative data on the two machines follow:

|  | Present Machine | Proposed New Machine |
|---|---|---|
| Purchase cost new (including installation costs) | $70,000 | $ 90,000 |
| Salvage value today | 35,000 | |
| Salvage value at end of life | 5,000 | 10,000 |
| Annual costs to operate | 95,000 | 75,000 |
| Estimated useful life when new | 7 years | 6 years |

Liz makes a few quick computations and exclaims, "Wow! We need that machine and its capabilities. But, no way can I sell it upstairs. When the boss sees the loss on the old machine, he'll have kittens." She's looking at this:

| | |
|---|---|
| Remaining book value of the old machine. | $60,000 |
| Salvage value now of the old machine | 35,000 |
| Net loss from disposal (before tax deduction of the loss). | $25,000 |

Grantham uses straight-line depreciation and ignores salvage value in its depreciation calculations. Sales from the grinding operation are expected to remain unchanged at $300,000 per year indefinitely. Other cash costs of the grinding operation total $80,000 annually. The corporate tax rate is 40 percent.

**Required:**

1. Prepare summary income statements covering the next six years for the grinding operation, assuming that:
   **(a)** the new machine is not purchased.
   **(b)** the new machine is purchased.
2. What do you recommend? Show any needed additional analysis.
3. Comment on the reality of the $25,000 loss Liz has calculated. Can or should this be ignored?
4. Comment on why introducing new technology is difficult to justify to management.
5. Develop a policy that would encourage investment in new technology and yet would avoid wasting scarce capital investment money.

## CASE 11B—HILL HOSES

The production manager of Hill Hoses is considering a project to modernize its equipment. The company produces assorted rubber and metal hoses and pipes needed by a variety of automotive and appliance manufacturers. One of Hill's major customers is Kim Appliances which purchases specialized hoses. Hill has negotiated an annual contract with Kim in each of the past eight years. In the past, requirements have averaged about 800,000 hoses per year.

The present arrangement of the factory includes four hose forming machines currently devoted to the Kim business. Each machine is operated by a skilled worker. The management is considering replacing these manual machines with an automatic forming, pressing, and testing machine, capable of performing all operations necessary for making hoses. This machine would produce hoses at a rate equal to five existing machines.

The four existing manual machines are four years old. Each can produce 200,000 hoses on a 2-shift, 5-day per week basis. Their total cost new was $570,000. The remaining useful life of these machines is estimated to be eight years. The salvage value at the end of their useful life is estimated to be $5,000 each net of taxes and was ignored in depreciation calculations. Depreciation totalling $190,000 has been accumulated on the four machines. Cash for the purchase of these machines was partially supplied by a 10-year, 14 percent, unsecured bank loan, of which $250,000 is still outstanding. The best estimate of the current selling price of the four machines in their present condition is $200,000, after removal costs. A write-off of the loss on disposal will net an immediate tax savings of $72,000.

The automatic machine needs only one highly skilled operator to feed raw rubber and metal sleeves, observe its functioning, and make necessary adjustments. It would have an output from two shifts of 1,000,000 hoses annually. No present use exists for the extra capacity. The machine's cost is estimated to be $900,000, delivered and installed. The useful life is estimated to be ten years. No reliable estimate of its salvage value can be made. An educated guess is that the residual value would equal its book value at any time in its life. No salvage value is used in depreciation calculations.

From a study prepared by the cost accountant, the following information has been compiled. The direct labor rate for machine operators is $15 per hour. The new machine would use less floor space, which would save $16,000 annually on the allocated charges for square footage of space used, although the layout of the plant is such that the freed space would not be used for other purposes. Miscellaneous cash expenses for supplies and power would be $20,000 less per year if the automatic machine is used. Assume that all depreciation calculations will use straight-line depreciation

If purchased, the new machine would be financed by a 12 percent secured bank loan, that would include paying off the loan on the old machines. Outstanding notes payable are at 9 percent. The company treasurer assumes that the weighted-average cost of equity and debt is about 16 percent. The company desires a rate of return of 20 percent on new investments.

**Required:**
1. Summarize the net investment and net cash flows for the proposed project.
2. Evaluate the project using the capital investment methods you have studied.
3. Comment on the important qualitative factors in evaluating this project.
4. What decision would you recommend? Why?

# CAPITAL INVESTMENT DECISIONS: ADDITIONAL ISSUES

## LEARNING OBJECTIVES

Based on your understanding of Chapter 11, studying the Chapter 12 material will enable you to:

1. Analyze several issues that complicate calculations in capital investment decisions.

2. Evaluate the financing decision independent of the acquisition decision.

3. Understand the significance of accelerated depreciation and MACRS.

4. Understand the use of life-cycle costing in capital budgeting.

5. Use sensitivity analysis and expected values to help assess risk in capital investment decisions.

6. See the importance of a post-audit of capital investment decisions in improving control and in evaluating future capital investments.

7. Integrate the evaluation of social costs of capital investments into the quantitative analysis.

## More Complexities in Capital Investments

*At the beginning of Chapter 11, Chloe White, President of Fine Tone Instruments, is reviewing investment proposals. She is amazed by the complexity of making the decisions. Few projects are straightforward cash out and cash in propositions. Inflation is a worry. Alternatives may have different lives, initial investments, and promised RORs. Also, why purchase equipment when it could be leased? Then, there are taxes. Depreciation appears to make certain capital investments more attractive. But should White make investment choices based on tax advantages? Comparisons often appear to be between apples and oranges.*

*In making capital investment decisions, she thinks it's important to include all relevant money over the entire life of a project, including any environmental impacts. In a few years, she would like to look at the proposals again, then with the wisdom of hindsight. Can differences in key variables be reduced to a manageable level? She knows that the success of certain projects depends heavily on one or two key variables. If estimates for these key variables are off by a small amount, the feasibility of the entire project may be in doubt. White shakes her head and digs into the stack of proposals.*

BASED ON CHAPTER 11 discussions about capital investment decisions, Chapter 12 contains a set of more complex issues and extensions of basic analyses. While certain topics in Chapter 12 are relevant to undergraduate managerial accounting courses, the majority of topics are more appropriate for extending capital investment discussions in graduate settings.

Since capital investment projects vary widely and depend heavily on estimates of the future, additional issues and levels of complexity often need to be considered. Among these are calculation issues, financing alternatives, taxation and depreciation concerns, and risk analysis. Finally, the planning and control cycle is closed with a post-audit of the investments' results.

## CALCULATION ISSUES

The variety of issues surrounding capital investment decisions are sufficient that entire textbooks have been written about them. Here, we introduce a few of the more significant complexities.

### Inflation and Future Cash Flows

**Inflation** is a common economic problem. Over the past 20 years in the United States, annual inflation rates have ranged from a high of over 12 percent to a low of under 2 percent. These levels are moderate compared to rates in many other countries. Yet, capital investment decisions should consider inflationary impacts on future cash flows.

While several approaches could be used to incorporate inflation into the analysis, the approach we suggest is to build the impacts of inflation into the expected future cash flows. This allows the use of specific inflation rates for each cash-flow component. Also, rates can be changed for each future period. The discount rate will be the noninflated desired rate of return times one plus the expected general inflation rate.

To illustrate inflation impacts on estimates of future cash flows, assume that Fischer Motors plans to expand its engine diagnostic business. Equipment will cost about $120,000 and should last about three years. After three years, it is thought that greater on-board computer use will require more powerful testing technology. Annual revenues are expected to be $150,000; personnel costs are $60,000; and other support costs would be about $30,000. Fischer uses a 10 percent desired rate of return.

Economic forecasts indicate that inflation will be 6 percent per year for the next few years. But Fisher feels that, at best, prices could be raised no more than 4 percent per year. Personnel costs will probably increase at a 10 percent rate, primarily because of benefits costs. Other costs will increase at an average of 6 percent annually. The equipment, which has no salvage value, will be depreciated on a straight-line basis. Assume a 40 percent tax rate. Cash flows related to the equipment are as follows:

| Cash Flows: | Investment Year 0 | Life of the Project Year 1 | Year 2 | Year 3 |
|---|---|---|---|---|
| Initial investment | $(120,000) | | | |
| Revenues | $ 150,000 | $ 156,000 | $ 162,240 | |
| Personnel costs | | (60,000) | (66,000) | (72,600) |
| Other costs | | (30,000) | (31,800) | (33,708) |
| Incremental taxes* | | (8,000) | (7,280) | (6,373) |
| Net cash flows | $(120,000) | $  52,000 | $ 50,920 | $ 49,559 |

| * Taxes in Year 1: | ($150,000 – 60,000 – 30,000 – 40,000) × 0.4 = $8,000 |
|---|---|
| Taxes in Year 2: | ($156,000 – 66,000 – 31,800 – 40,000) × 0.4 = $7,280 |
| Taxes in Year 3: | ($162,240 – 72,600 – 33,708 – 40,000) × 0.4 = $6,373 |

Notice that depreciation, being based on the historical cost of the investment, is still $40,000 in each year. While all other revenues and costs have inflation built into them, the tax law requires that the depreciation expense is always expressed in historical-cost dollars from the year of acquisition. Using historical cost-based depreciation in tax calculations often leads to higher tax payments since profits grow from inflated revenues. The discount rate would be [(1 + 0.10) × (1 + 0.06)] – 1 or 16.6 percent. This includes the compounding impacts of inflation.

It is dangerous to ignore inflation. To do so, assumes that all inflation effects sum to zero, which is rarely the case. Certain cost areas, such as health care, have had unusually high increases in recent years. Forecasting these costs should include estimated inflationary impacts to make cash-flow estimates credible.

## Working Capital

When expansion occurs, inventories and receivables often grow. Financing **working capital** growth is an integral part of a project's total investment. Unlike depreciable equipment and fixed assets, working capital is committed and can probably be recovered at the end of the project. Often, working capital requirements grow slowly over time as sales increase. Incremental inventories and accounts receivable net of incremental accounts payable can easily be overlooked and omitted from a project's analysis. In contrast, JIT projects often release working capital by reducing inventories, which can help finance the project itself.

Assume that Athletic Champs operates a chain of sporting goods stores in shopping malls. Opening a new store requires layout, equipment, and fixtures costing about $450,000. In addition, about $200,000 of inventory is needed to stock a new store. Experience shows that inventory and other working capital needs will grow at about $20,000 per year for the first five years. If Athletic Champs uses an eight-year timeframe for evaluating a store location, assumptions will be needed about the equipment salvage value and the recovery of the working capital investment. The fixed assets' salvage values are estimated to be $50,000 net of taxes, and the entire working capital investment (now $300,000) is thought to be recovered. The cash flows would look like:

|  | Life of the Project | | | | |
| --- | --- | --- | --- | --- | --- |
| Cash flows: | Today | Year 1 | Year 2 | Year 5 | Year 8 |
| Initial construction | $(450,000) | | | | $ 50,000 |
| Working capital needs | (200,000) | $(20,000) | $(20,000) | $(20,000) | 300,000 |

Working capital recovery is not automatic. Inventory may be obsolete, and receivables might not be collectable. A going-concern assumption can generally be made if the business is expected to continue past the timeframe cutoff.

## Uneven Project Lives

When comparing projects, lives of each project may not match. How can a 3-year solution to a problem be compared to a five-year or a eight-year solution? The decision must be viewed from the timeframe of the job to be done. Do we want a solution for three, five, or eight years? How long can the physical asset last? Often, technology changes make an asset's economic life shorter than its physical life. A three-year solution may be sought, while an asset's physical life might well be twice that long.

If the time period is based on the needs of the problem, the task is to find salvage or market values for assets at the end of the defined time period. If the time period is based on the physical lives of the proposed assets, different useful lives of the proposed solutions must be somehow matched. One approach is to use a shorter-lived project as the comparison time period. This requires finding salvage or market values for assets at midpoints in their lives. While no specific rule exists, the investment's timeframe as defined by management seems to be the better choice. Management's intent and common sense, rather than the physical lives of assets, should govern the time period choice.

## Evaluation of Projects With Different Initial Investments

Up to this point, most of the illustrations have assumed that a single investment alternative existed. The firm had to decide whether to invest in that project. Actually, a firm may have several alternatives but still have to select only one. In such a case, care must be exercised in using the internal rate of return method, because the project with the highest internal rate of return may not be the most desirable. This can happen in those cases where the dollar investment is not the same. The dollar amount of the return from a larger investment, in many cases, will exceed the dollar return from a smaller investment having a better internal rate of return.

Assume that Vista Transit Company must choose between two delivery vans. Each has an estimated life of five years with annual returns as follows:

|  | Van I | Van II |
| --- | --- | --- |
| Net investment | $75,000 | $100,000 |
| Net cash inflow for each of 5 years | 26,000 | 33,000 |

Investments are expected to earn a desired rate of return of at least 12 percent. Van II requires an investment of an additional $25,000 versus Van I. The approximate internal rate of return is computed for each alternative and for the incremental investment as follows:

|  | Van I | Van II | Incremental (II – I) |
|---|---|---|---|
| Net investment | $(75,000) | $(100,000) | $(25,000) |
| Annual return | 26,000 | 33,000 | 7,000 |
| Payback period | 2.885 | 3.030 | 3.571 |
| Nearest PV factor on Table 2 for 5 periods | 2.864 | 2.991 | 3.605 |
| Nearest IRR given on Table 2 | 22% | 20% | 12% |

It appears that Van I should be selected because the internal rate of return is higher. The additional $25,000 investment needed by Van II yields a much lower rate of return—12 percent. But, if the rate of return on the incremental investment is greater than the hurdle rate of return, the larger investment could still be made. In this example, an additional $7,000 per year is returned on an additional investment of $25,000. The rate of return on the incremental investment barely meets the 12 percent desired rate of return.

In another situation, Van I could be a Phase I of a pair of sequential jobs, and Van II could be Phases I and II combined. Phase I may be executed without Phase II but not vice versa. Advocates of Phase II would clearly argue that both phases be approved at one time. However, as we have seen, Phase II has an IRR of about 12 percent. If the cutoff rate is 15 percent, Phase I and the combined phases are acceptable. But Phase II by itself is unacceptable. Breaking down projects into their subcomponents can give useful insight into the yields on incremental investments.

## Gains and Losses on Asset Disposals

If assets are sold at more or less than their book values, gains or losses appear with tax implications. The book value is an asset's original cost minus its accumulated depreciation. In the real world, accounting book values and tax cost bases often differ. In our discussions here, unless specifically mentioned, these two amounts are assumed to be the same. If the sale is for more than the book value, a gain occurs; and if for less, a loss occurs.

### Contemporary Practice 12.1
### *Coke Improves Profits by Picking High Earning Capital Projects*

*Coca Cola depends on new investments to generate future profits. In its* **2001 Annual Report**, *the company clearly states its intent and approaches.*

"*New investments must directly enhance our existing operations and must be expected to provide cash returns that exceed our long-term, after-tax, weighted-average cost of capital, currently estimated at between 10 and 11 percent. . . . In highly developed markets, our expenditures focus primarily on marketing our company's brands. In emerging and developing markets, our objective is* to increase the penetration of our products. In these markets, we allocate most of our investments to enhancing our brands and infrastructure such as production facilities, distribution networks, sales equipment, and technology. We make these investments by forming strategic business alliances with local bottlers and by matching local expertise with our experience, resources, and focus.*"

*Source:* The Coca-Cola Company 2001 Annual Report, *p. 41.*

Gains and losses on disposals and their impacts on cash flows arise at two points in the capital investment decision:

1. Old assets may be sold as part of investing in a new asset.
2. New assets may be sold at the end of the project's expected life.

Sales and trade-ins are handled differently for tax purposes. In trade-ins, the market value of the old asset reduces the cash paid to acquire the new asset. For tax purposes, the old book value is added to the cash cost of the new asset to create the new asset's book value. For example, assume that a new asset is purchased for $20,000 cash plus the trade-in of an old asset having a book value of $5,000. Also, assume that the new asset will have a five-year life and no salvage value. Straight-line depreciation over five years will be $5,000 per year [($20,000 + $5,000) ÷ 5]. No gain or loss is recognized.

When old assets are sold and new assets are purchased in separate transactions, a gain or loss on the old asset is recognized; and the new asset's cost is depreciated. Tax-related issues surrounding gains and losses on sales depend on current legislation applicable to capital gains and losses. Most issues related to taxation of gains and deductibility of losses are beyond the scope of this text. The concern here is to recognize cash inflows from asset sales and to identify the basic tax impacts of the gains and losses. It is assumed here that gains and losses are capital gains and losses and that the firm's tax liability is increased or reduced by a percentage of the gain or loss as specified in the problem.

## FINANCING VERSUS INVESTMENT DECISIONS

Many capital investments are directly tied to how the investment outlay will be financed. Often debt is issued; existing cash is used; bank borrowing is arranged; or **leases** are signed. The acquisition question and the financing question are clearly separate and are answered sequentially:

1. Make the capital investment decision without regard to the method of financing by assuming a cash purchase.
2. Then, make the financing decision.

The general rule says that the "go" or "no go" decision should be dependent on the project's basic cash flows. Financing choices may increase or decrease the firm's financing costs but should not change the inherent quality of the project.

A common situation is the choice of using the firm's own cash reserves or leasing the asset. The timing of cash flows and the interest costs of these alternatives can differ dramatically.

Leases have an interest rate embedded in the lease payment. Aside from tax issues, the financing decision can depend on whether the embedded lease interest rate is higher or lower than either the firm's borrowing or investment rate. Using either a short-term borrowing rate or the cost of capital rate may be a function of the length of the lease. A 24-month auto lease might be compared to the firm's bank borrowing rate, while a building lease for ten years would use the cost of capital rate.

Assume a copying machine can be leased for $10,000 per year for five years with payments due at the beginning of the year. The alternative is to buy the machine for $43,120 cash. The **embedded interest rate** is found as follows:

Cash price – Initial cash payment = Present value of future cash flows

Present value of future cash flows ÷ Annual cash payment = Present value factor

$43,120 – $10,000 = $33,120 present value

$33,120 ÷ $10,000 = 3.312 present value factor

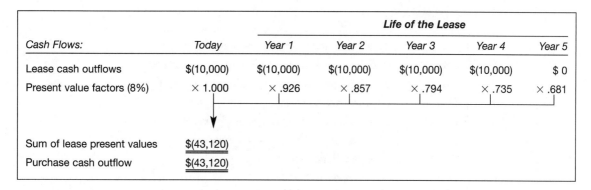

| Cash Flows: | Today | Life of the Lease | | | | |
| --- | --- | --- | --- | --- | --- | --- |
| | | Year 1 | Year 2 | Year 3 | Year 4 | Year 5 |
| Lease cash outflows | $(10,000) | $(10,000) | $(10,000) | $(10,000) | $(10,000) | $ 0 |
| Present value factors (8%) | × 1.000 | × .926 | × .857 | × .794 | × .735 | × .681 |
| Sum of lease present values | $(43,120) | | | | | |
| Purchase cash outflow | $(43,120) | | | | | |

**FIGURE 12.1**

Financing Cash Flows for a Lease and a Purchase

We use Table 2 and the 4-period row because the first payment is made immediately. We are paying the copying equipment firm 8 percent interest for financing. The cash flows are shown in Figure 12.1.

If the lease's embedded rate is lower than the cost of funds rate, often the advantage is often to lease. This commonly occurs in two situations. First, some businesses use an artificially low interest rate for leases either to give them a competitive advantage or to encourage customers to lease instead of to buy. It is through promotional efforts such as this that the "tail (the financing decision) might wag the dog (the acquisition decision)." In these cases, the cash purchase cost would be the present value (using the cost of capital) of the annual lease payments. The vendor's lease present value would be below its cash purchase price. See the Contemporary Practice 12.1 example.

Second, the financial condition of some firms is so poor that they may have exhausted both debt and equity sources of additional funds. Leasing may be their only way to acquire needed new assets, regardless of the embedded interest rate. Yet, lessors generally perform credit checks on lessees for credit worthiness.

## ACCELERATED DEPRECIATION, MACRS, AND THE TAX SHIELD

Historically, cumbersome and complex rules developed around depreciation deductions. In the 1980s, as part of a series of "tax reform" laws, a new depreciation system was introduced—the **Accelerated Cost Recovery System (ACRS)**. Currently, **Modified Accelerated Cost Recovery**

### Contemporary Practice 12.2
### *Yes, I can drive a Cadillac!*

*Recently, television and newspaper ads announced a special Cadillac leasing opportunity called 24-Month SmartLease Plus. Pay $12,405 at the signing date, and drive off in a Seville SLS. Or you can pay $2,200 plus $499 per month for 24 months under a regular 24-Month SmartLease. Ads say you save $1,771, the difference between the sums of the two cash payment streams. Are present values involved? Yes, that's how the monthly payments are set,*

*considering residual values and special fees. But GMAC, the lessor, also changed the embedded lease interest rate from 4.0 percent to 2.5 percent for this promotion. The car's MSRP is $43,143, and leases include numerous conditions. Present values impact this deal in many ways, but you have to analyze your options, and the fine print, yourself.*

*Source: General Motors Acceptance Corporation personnel.*

| Class | Type of Assets |
|---|---|
| 3 Year | Certain tools and assets of specialized industries |
| 5 Year | Autos and trucks, research equipment, and computers |
| 7 Year | Office equipment and most production equipment |
| 10 Year | Machinery and equipment in selected industries |
| 15 Year | Certain utility facilities and land improvements |
| 20 Year | Certain agricultural buildings and utility equipment |
| 27½ Year | Residential rental property |
| 31½ Year | Nonresidential real property |

**FIGURE 12.2**

MACRS Classes by Life and Type

**System** or **MACRS** is applicable to assets acquired since 1987. Figure 12.2 lists eight classes of depreciable assets.

## MACRS Classes and Deduction Percentages

For each class, specific percentages of cost are deducted annually. The percentages for 3-, 5-, 7-, and 10- year classes are shown in Figure 12.3. MACRS uses the declining-balance depreciation method as the base for determining the annual percentages. The deduction percentage declines each year and eventually falls below the annual straight-line percentage deduction for the asset's remaining life. In that year, the MACRS method assumes a switch to straight-line depreciation for the rest of the asset's life. A series of accounting conventions such as the half-year deduction are used. The half-year

| Recovery Year | Property Class | | | |
|---|---|---|---|---|
| | 3-Year | 5-Year | 7-Year | 10-Year |
| 1 | 33.33 | 20.00 | 14.29 | 10.00 |
| 2 | 44.45 | 32.00 | 24.49 | 18.00 |
| 3 | 14.81 | 19.20 | 17.49 | 14.40 |
| 4 | 7.41 | 11.52* | 12.49 | 11.52 |
| 5 | | 11.52 | 8.93* | 9.22 |
| 6 | | 5.76 | 8.92 | 7.37 |
| 7 | | | 8.93 | 6.55* |
| 8 | | | 4.46 | 6.55 |
| 9 | | | | 6.56 |
| 10 | | | | 6.55 |
| 11 | | | | 3.28 |

*\* Year of switch to straight-line to maximize depreciation.*

**FIGURE 12.3**

MACRS Accelerated Depreciation Percentages

convention says that only one half of the first year's depreciation can be taken in the first tax year. The remaining half of the first year's depreciation is taken in the second tax year, along with half of the second year's depreciation. This explains the transition from normal declining-balance percentages to MACRS percentages.

The advantage of MACRS, the current form of tax-law accelerated depreciation, is the present value of greater depreciation deductions earlier in a project's life. In total dollars, no more depreciation is taken; and no fewer tax dollars are paid. The key is when the tax dollars are paid.

## An Example of MACRS

Assume that a company is considering the purchase of computer equipment costing $100,000, with an estimated useful life of six years. The income tax rate is 40 percent, and the firm's minimum acceptable rate of return on investments is 16 percent. The tax savings and present values of the savings are shown in Figure 12.4. The equipment falls into the 5-year class with no salvage value. The half-year convention is also used for both straight-line and MACRS depreciation. The comparative advantage of the MACRS method can be seen.

The advantage of using MACRS depreciation over straight-line depreciation is $2,625 using a 16 percent discount rate. Incrementally, this is a significant addition to the net present value. Thus, the early deductions of depreciation can be an important macroeconomic policy tool. Unfortunately, the legislative process often prevents quick implementation of changes to promote investment when economic stimuli are needed.

## Immediate Expensing of Assets for Small Businesses

Another feature of tax law is to allow an immediate tax deduction for up to $10,000 of new assets. Firms purchasing new depreciable assets over $210,000 lose this option. Companies immediately expensing any amount must deduct that amount from the basis of the asset to determine the asset's depreciable base. This provision is to assist small firms.

| | Today | Life of the Project | | | | | |
|---|---|---|---|---|---|---|---|
| | | Year 1 | Year 2 | Year 3 | Year 4 | Year 5 | Year 6 |
| **MACRS depreciation:** | | | | | | | |
| Tax depreciation expense | | $20,000 | $32,000 | $19,200 | $11,500 | $11,500 | $ 5,800 |
| Tax savings (40%) | | $ 8,000 | $12,800 | $ 7,680 | $ 4,600 | $ 4,600 | $ 2,320 |
| **Straight-line depreciation:** | | | | | | | |
| Tax depreciation expense | | $10,000 | $20,000 | $20,000 | $20,000 | $20,000 | $10,000 |
| Tax savings (40%) | | $ 4,000 | $ 8,000 | $ 8,000 | $ 8,000 | $ 8,000 | $ 4,000 |
| **Advantage of MACRS over Straight-Line (S-L):** | | | | | | | |
| MACRS over S-L depreciation | | $10,000 | $12,000 | $ (800) | $(8,500) | $(8,500) | $(4,200) |
| MACRS over S-L tax savings | | $ 4,000 | $ 4,800 | $ (320) | $(3,400) | $(3,400) | $(1,680) |
| Present value factors at 16% | | × .862 | × .743 | × .641 | × .552 | × .476 | × .410 |
| Present values at 16% | | $ 3,448 | $ 3,566 | $ (205) | $(1,877) | $(1,618) | $ (689) |
| MACRS advantage over S-L | $2,625 | | | | | | |

**FIGURE 12.4**

Comparing Tax Impacts of MACRS and Straight-Line Depreciation Methods

## LIFE-CYCLE COSTING AND INVESTMENT ANALYSIS

A concept that has increased in managerial importance in recent years is **life-cycle costing**, which tracks and accumulates costs and revenues over the entire life span of a product. As innovative products appear, flourish, and disappear with increasing frequency, the need to measure the total results becomes more important than year-to-year accrual accounting profit measurements. **Product life cycles** have been plotted for many years and typically include four phases: development, introduction and growth, maturation, and decline. Life-cycle analysis affects managerial accounting in several areas:

1.  Budget revenues and costs for the entire project or product life.
2.  Account for performance on a cumulative basis rather than on annual slices.
3.  Develop a pricing strategy for each phase of the product's life cycle to maximize market penetration and total product profits.
4.  Report on projects that have significant timing mismatches of cash inflows and outflows.
5.  Recognize and include hidden or ignored costs such as environmental impacts.

While many patterns exist, Figure 12.5 illustrates the cash flows over the phases of a product's life cycle. Without details, observe the unit sales patterns, the pricing strategy, and the drop in unit costs over the product's life. These estimates require involvement of research, marketing, and production personnel very early in the project's life. An integrative team approach to planning and development is becoming more critical to successful project planning.

Year-by-year product income statements could be very misleading. In Figure 12.5, of the 6-year life, only three years show a profit; and only in the fifth year does the cumulative cash flow turn positive. By the fifth year, the initial research and introduction costs were recorded and perhaps forgotten. Product responsibility may have shifted managers several times, from research to market research to sales and production. The ability to measure life-cycle revenues and costs may be dissipated throughout the accounting system. Coding of revenues and costs is needed to continue monitoring the actual cash flows similar to the estimated patterns shown in Figure 12.5.

In the trucking industry, it is common to track vehicle costs during the life of a vehicle to assist in replacement decisions. Many use computer models to track mileage, repairs, overhauls, and operating costs. Thus, life-cycle costs are estimated in the acquisition decision, monitored during operation for operations management, and evaluated for disposal purposes. By being included in the initial analysis, lifetime financial consequences of asset ownership can be assessed under a variety of assumptions.

## Contemporary Practice 12.3
### Contemporary? Not Quite! But Still Apropos.

Shakespeare's Merchant of Venice *is a classic application of this "new idea" in management literature, life-cycle investment analysis. How did the merchant operate? This man, with considerable wealth, commissioned a sailing captain, contracted to build a ship, hired a crew, filled the ship with merchandise, sent the ship off to the Orient, and waited for* its return. Upon its arrival, he sold the commodities and treasures, compensated the captain and crew, sold the ship, and accounted for the venture. With the profits, he made more investments. If he experienced losses, Shylock was always nearby.

Source: William Shakespeare, The Merchant of Venice.

| | Life of the Project | | | | | |
|---|---|---|---|---|---|---|
| | Year 1 | Year 2 | Year 3 | Year 4 | Year 5 | Year 6 |
| Life-Cycle Phases: | Develop & Design | | Introduce & Grow | | Mature | Decline |
| **Product data:** | | | | | | |
| Units produced and sold | | | 5,000 | 15,000 | 20,000 | 10,000 |
| Price per unit | | | $ 80 | $ 60 | $ 45 | $ 30 |
| Production cost per unit | | | 30 | 20 | 18 | 16 |
| Cash revenues | | | $ 400,000 | $ 900,000 | $900,000 | $300,000 |
| **Cash expenses:** | | | | | | |
| Research & design expenses | $ 100,000 | $ 300,000 | $ 100,000 | $ 10,000 | | |
| Production preparation | | 80,000 | 100,000 | 50,000 | | |
| Marketing expenses | | | 150,000 | 150,000 | $100,000 | $ 20,000 |
| Production costs | | | 150,000 | 300,000 | 360,000 | 160,000 |
| Total expenses | $ 100,000 | $ 380,000 | $ 500,000 | $ 510,000 | $460,000 | $180,000 |
| Net cash flow | $(100,000) | $(380,000) | $(100,000) | $ 390,000 | $440,000 | $120,000 |
| Cumulative cash flows | $(100,000) | $(480,000) | $(580,000) | $(190,000) | $250,000 | $370,000 |
| Present value (12%) | $ (89,300) | $(302,860) | $ (71,200) | $ 248,040 | $249,480 | $ 60,840 |
| Cumulative present value | $ (89,300) | $(392,160) | $(463,360) | (215,320) | $ 34,160 | $ 95,000 |

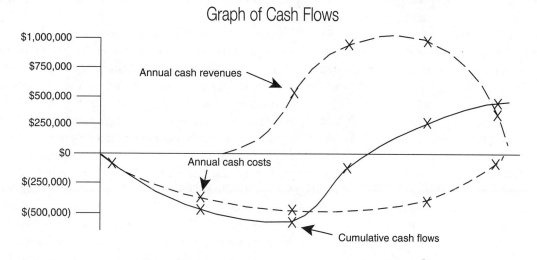

### Graph of Cash Flows

**FIGURE 12.5**

Product Life-Cycle Cash-Flow Patterns

## Combining the NPV and Payback Methods–Break-even Time

Pressure to reduce the time needed to introduce new products has brought an interesting twist to the financial analysis of product life cycles. Product developers want to know if a project's life will have a positive return. Figure 12.5 shows a positive cumulative cash flow. We could estimate the payback period for this project in terms of years. But since the payback method ignores the time value of money, this measure is less useful than a discounted approach. By building in a discount rate (12 percent in Figure 12.5), we can find a discounted payback period. This is called the **break-even time**. In the example, the changeover from a negative cumulative net present value to a positive position occurs near the end of Year 5. Thus the breakeven time using a 12 percent ROR is 4.87 years, found by interpolation.

## Environmental Costs

Of particular importance to life-cycle costing advocates is the inclusion of environmental costs in the initial project evaluation. If reforestation, land reclamation, pollution prevention safeguards, environmental impact studies, and asset disposals are involved, costs of these activities are relevant to the projects' ROR analyses. The advantage is that these costs are recognized and considered when the decision to incur them is made.

# MONITORING AND POST-COMPLETION AUDITING OF CAPITAL INVESTMENTS

Many capital investments are one-time undertakings. In many firms, managing projects is more difficult than managing repetitive tasks. Having strong project managerial tools and controls is necessary to avoid cost overruns, missed timetables, lost benefits, and disruption of normal business activities.

Once an investment proposal is approved, controls over expenditures and a reporting system to keep managers apprised of the project's status are needed. An essential key is a project control system. All expenditures should be traced to the project. Oversight should be applied to ensure that expenditures are consistent with the approved investment proposal. Systematic status reporting of each project allows those persons who manage projects and those who approved the investment to track project progress and compare it to the original plan.

After equipment is acquired or after a project is completed, performance should be monitored. Results, both from technical and economic points of view, need to be audited or evaluated at the end of a "shakedown period." During this period, it may be found that certain corrections or changes have to be made if the project is to realize its promised potential. Also as noted in Chapter 11, managers may make exaggerated promises to get initial project approval. Knowledge that these claims must be verified is in itself a control. A postcompletion audit or evaluation shows whether the forecast benefits are being achieved and may indicate ways in which operations can be improved.

The audit referred to is not an audit in a financial accounting sense. In reality, it is a management review and, like the original evaluation, may have estimation problems. Quantification of intangible benefits after-the-fact may be just as difficult as when the original investment proposal was evaluated. The review may also be limited by the available accounting information. For a special project where a new segment is added, the operating results may be shown separately in the accounting records. But on an individual piece of equipment, which is part of a larger project, separate accounting data may not exist. How much additional effort should be exerted to separate relevant revenues and costs depends on the importance of the investment and the costs of data collection.

The **post-audit** is a mechanism that:

1. Compares actual operating results with forecast cash flows to improve the estimation process in future capital investment proposals.

2. Makes managers aware of a control that will evaluate their forecasts and recommendations and reflect on their ability to produce promised results.

3. Can review project management and evaluate cost and technical performance.

4. Can detect early operating problems.

The post-audit closes the planning and control cycle. Both better control and improved planning should be the long-term expectations.

# PROBLEMS OF UNCERTAINTY

The future is never certain. Capital investment analysis depends heavily on estimates of future cash flows. All estimates are risky. How can the risk be measured and incorporated into the analysis? Several steps can be taken:

1. Test the forecast data for source credibility and reasonableness.
2. Test the assumptions underlying the forecasts and the project itself.
3. Create managerial responsibility for the estimates.

The goal is to create the strongest estimates possible. Responsibility for developing the proposal and for executing the project is linked to performance. An audit trail is developed.

Basically, risk can be incorporated into capital investment analysis in three ways:

1. Adding a risk percentage factor to the cost of capital to compensate for risk and differences in risk.
2. Performing a sensitivity analysis of key project variables.
3. Incorporating expected values into the cash-flow forecasting.

## Risk Percentage Factor

Adding a **risk percentage factor** to the cost of funds is an approach used to recognize the risk of error in estimates. By adding a percentage to the cost of capital, a safety shield is created. The minimum acceptable rate of return is now higher than the cost of capital by the risk factor. This represents a cushion against the prospect that a project's costs were understated, revenues overstated, or that other key estimates were too optimistic.

A number of firms extend this idea still further to recognize differences among divisions or types of projects within a firm. Divisions with histories of strong earnings and successful capital investments might be assigned a lower desired ROR, with a smaller risk factor. New divisions or ones in high-risk areas, such as research and development, might be assigned a desired ROR with a higher risk factor. The following is an example:

| | Cost of Capital | Risk Factor | Desired Rate of Return |
|---|---|---|---|
| High risk division | 12% | 8% | 20% |
| Normal risk | 12 | 4 | 16 |
| Low risk division | 12 | 2 | 14 |

However, difficulties exist. Not all projects in a given division deserve the same risk "penalty." Also, past results may not be good indicators of future risks and returns. Yet, adding a risk factor does attempt to recognize relative **uncertainty** of certain types of future cash-flow forecasts.

## Sensitivity Analysis

All examples presented thus far assume that estimates of future revenues and costs are valid. However, the possibility always exists that forecast variables could change. **Sensitivity analysis** measures how much key variables can change and still not affect the capital investment decision. Among variables commonly tested are:

1. Sales prices and volumes.
2. Operating and product costs.
3. Life of the project.
4. Development costs.

Many firms have simulation capabilities available to test "what if" scenarios. If sales volume were to drop by 10 percent from the forecast level, what is the impact on ROR or NPV? If because of technological advances a particular machine's life is cut from six years to four years, how badly will losing Years 5 and 6 cash flows hurt the proposal?

For example, assume that the net present value of Project 52 is $80,000. Project 52 will add 10,000 units of productive capacity to our factory. We earn a $10 contribution margin per unit. The expanded capacity should last five years. Our desired rate of return is 15 percent. Thus, ignoring taxes, the value of 1 unit of sales per year for five years is $33.52 (from Table 2, 3.352 × $10). We can answer several questions:

1. **What if sales only reach 80 percent of new capacity?**

PV of the lost contribution margin:        2,000 units × $33.52 = $67,040
NPV of project if sales equal 8,000 units:        $80,000 – $67,040 = $12,960

The project still earns better than a 15 percent return.

2. **What unit sales are needed to earn at least 15 percent?**

Units of allowed lost sales:        $80,000 ÷ $33.52 = 2,386 units
Units of sales to have a 15 percent ROR:        10,000 – 2,386 = 7,614 units

This means that a 23.86 percent drop in expected new sales will cause the project to have a zero net present value—a return of 15 percent. A drop of 3,000 units would cause the project to have a negative net present value and to be rejected.

3. **What if the project lasted only four years, not five years?**

PV of Year 5 sales:        10,000 × $10 × 0.497 = $49,700
NPV of Project 52 if Year 5 is eliminated:        $80,000 – $49,700 = $30,300

The project is still acceptable.

Cutting years off the end of a project's life is a common method of reducing uncertainty. We have less confidence in estimates that are further into the future.

## Using Expected Values

Incorporating multiple estimates for key variables into the analysis has long been attempted. We suggested this approach in budgeting in Chapter 7. One method of incorporating multiple estimates uses optimistic, most likely, and pessimistic estimates of sales, costs, and lives. Another similar method assigns probabilities to various values of key variables. Weighted averages are then used to generate the cash-flow estimates called **expected values**. Using the Project 52 example from the last section, a sales forecast with probabilities could be created:

| Sales Level | Probability of Occurrence | | | |
|---|---|---|---|---|
| 10,000 units | × | 0.4 | = | 4,000 units |
| 9,000 units | × | 0.3 | = | 2,700 units |
| 8,000 units | × | 0.2 | = | 1,600 units |
| 7,000 units | × | 0.1 | = | 700 units |
| Expected value of sales volume | | | | 9,000 units |

Obviously, "what ifs" of many variable changes can be analyzed. Spreadsheet capabilities now make these simulations routine and a normal part of project evaluation.

## CAPITAL INVESTMENTS IN NONPROFIT ORGANIZATIONS

In most cases, capital investment decisions in nonprofit organizations are no different than in profit-making concerns. A notable exception is that nonprofit organizations need not consider income tax effects on each flow. The goal is to obtain the highest benefit from the money spent. For example, in choosing between two firefighting trucks with equal operating ratings, the choice is the lowest NPV of total costs. Often, the legislative and appropriation processes in governmental units may obscure the basic purposes of public spending. Solving social problems, providing public services, and operating quasi-business activities must include cost and benefit analyses to help select efficient and effective solutions.

In special cases, a project's profits and cash flows may not be the primary goals of the expenditure. In the case of a city government, an investment may be made for the general welfare of the citizens. A city will attempt to obtain the highest level of benefits for its citizens at a given cost. For example, neighborhood playgrounds may be built in various sections of the city. The benefits for the children and young people of the city are evident, but how can they be measured? Can the quality of life be quantified? What is the value of a life saved? Intangible benefits are sometimes difficult or impossible to quantify or even to estimate. But estimation of benefits and costs can often help in selecting from among alternatives. Decisions can be and are made that include public good trade-offs. In many cases, publicly elected officials make those judgments based on their assessments of citizens' preferences. Yet, the managerial accountant must collect, format, and report the quantitative facts as clearly in nonprofit situations as in all others.

## SOCIAL COSTS OF CAPITAL INVESTMENT DECISIONS

Social costs are growing in importance in the capital investment decisions of both public and private organizations. **Social costs** and **social benefits** are costs and benefits that the community shares. The community can be defined locally, nationally, or globally. Social cost concerns arise from a wide variety of sources and include the costs of:

1. Protecting the health of employees, consumers, and persons in the community.
2. Providing employment and training for workers in the community.
3. Handling substances that endanger the environment.
4. Evaluating environmental impacts prior to capital development.
5. Choosing among various benefits for employees, taxpayers, and other groups given limited resources.
6. Considering public policy, political pressures, and public opinion in allocating capital resources.

Many of these considerations have intangible costs and benefits, legal requirements, and no direct positive cash-flow possibilities for the firm. Pollution controls are often legally required. Good citizenship would expect a firm to want to prevent air and water pollution. But few "win/win" situations exist. New regulations may impose additional costs on a firm that has been experiencing marginal profitability. Capital spending on pollution equipment may mean that equipment purchases to improve the firm's technology and competitiveness must be delayed or eliminated, threatening the firm's survival.

An additional difficulty is that diverse viewpoints value social costs and benefits very differently. Nuclear power plants are classic examples of strong opinions on all sides, which have largely brought a halt to nuclear power development in the United States. Increased and changing regulations, public protests, strong "not-in-my-back-yard" reactions, and major project management problems have caused public utilities to shelve new nuclear power plant construction.

The analysis task is to incorporate the relevant impacts of social costs on the firm into the capital proposal. This means recognizing tangible costs of compliance, of solving environmental problems, and even of public relations. Converting intangibles to dollar estimates can be done easily in some cases but only with great difficulty in others. Equipment costs to achieve air particulate content compliance can be estimated. Valuing clean air, a human life, and wet lands is nearly impossible (but has been attempted), even though we know great value exists. Thus, quantitative analysis should be as complete an assessment as possible of the impacts of social costs on the firm .

The real difficulty arises in the analysis of the qualitative issues. Reducing social costs and maintaining the firm's short-term profitability are often in natural conflict. Enlightened managers have seen that a firm's single goal of profit maximization has evolved into a multipronged set of goals that includes employees', consumers', and the community's concerns.

## SUMMARY

This chapter examines additional complexities of capital investment decisions. Even after this chapter's discussion, a student of capital investment decisions can see the difficult task managers have in forecasting the future, considering relevant costs and revenues, and assessing qualitative competitive and social issues. Computational issues such as uneven lives, working capital needs, incremental investment analysis, and inflationary impacts on forecasts are examined. The discussion of tax and accelerated depreciation actually only scratches the surface of tax impacts on capital decisions.

A distinction is drawn between the acquisition and financing decisions. A project proposal must stand on its own merits. Selecting a financing alternative is another decision where relevant cash flows must be evaluated to find the low-cost alternative.

Life-cycle costing is almost assumed in capital investment analysis. But the concept is also useful in measuring the project's performance. Risk analysis, sensitivity analysis, and expected values are tools used to incorporate risk into the cash-flow analysis.

Having a post-audit of capital investment projects closes the planning and control cycle. This post-completion management review is a control tool to evaluate original proposal data, implementation, and actual performance. It is a control tool to improve the planning process for future capital spending.

Social costs and benefits are both difficult to measure and often highly controversial. Many types of social costs bring legal, political, and community pressures to managers who make capital investment decisions. The same reasons that make capital investing critical to a firm make these decisions important to employees and to local and global communities.

## PROBLEM FOR REVIEW

Amarillo Metal Works is considering the replacement of a precision cutting machine. The new machine would cost $40,000 and generate annual cost savings of about $20,000. The $20,000 estimate is the most likely cost savings (a 50 percent likelihood), but could be lower by 20 percent (20 percent likelihood) or be higher by 20 percent (30 percent likelihood). Inflation will increase the savings by five percent per year. The machine has a useful life of six years, and it qualifies as a 5-year class asset under MACRS. The current cutting machine has a book value of $18,000 and could be made to last six more years. Depreciation on this machine is straight-line. If the machine were sold now, proceeds would be $10,000. Amarillo has a cost of capital of 12 percent and has added a four percent risk factor. The company's current tax rate is 40 percent.

**Required:**

1. Calculate the net initial investment assuming the old machine is sold.
2. Calculate the aftertax annual cash flows assuming the new machine will be used for six years with tax depreciation for five years. Consider the cost savings, expected probabilities, and the estimated inflation rate.
3. Evaluate this investment using the net present value method.

**Solution:**

1. Net investment:

| | |
|---|---|
| Investment in new machine | $ (40,000) |
| Less proceeds from the sale of old machine | 10,000 |
| Less income tax reduction [.40 × ($18,000 – $10,000)] | 3,200 |
| Net investment | $ (26,800) |

2. Annual net cash flows for six years:

| *Inflation adjustment:* | | Year 1 | Year 2 | Year 3 | Year 4 | Year 5 | Year 6 |
|---|---|---|---|---|---|---|---|
| Cash cost savings | | $20,000 | $20,000 | $20,000 | $20,000 | $20,000 | $20,000 |
| Inflation factor | | × 1.0000 | × 1.0500 | × 1.1025 | × 1.1576 | × 1.2155 | × 1.2763 |
| Inflation adjusted cash savings | | $20,000 | $21,000 | $22,050 | $23,152 | $ 24,310 | $25,526 |

| *Expected cost savings:* | Probability | Year 1 | Year 2 | Year 3 | Year 4 | Year 5 | Year 6 |
|---|---|---|---|---|---|---|---|
| Optimistic ( +20%) | 30% × | $24,000 | $25,200 | $26,460 | $27,782 | $29,172 | $30,631 |
| Most likely | 50 × | 20,000 | 21,000 | 22,050 | 23,152 | 24,310 | 25,526 |
| Pessimistic (−20%) | 20 × | 16,000 | 16,800 | 17,640 | 18,522 | 19,448 | 20,421 |
| Expected value | 100% | $20,400 | $21,420 | $22,491 | $23,615 | $24,796 | $26,037 |

| *Incremental depreciation:* | Year 1 | Year 2 | Year 3 | Year 4 | Year 5 | Year 6 |
|---|---|---|---|---|---|---|
| New depreciation (MACRS): | | | | | | |
| Year 1–20.00% | $ 8,000 | | | | | |
| Year 2–32.00% | | $12,800 | | | | |
| Year 3–19.20% | | | $ 7,680 | | | |
| Year 4–11.52% | | | | $ 4,608 | | |
| Year 5–11.52% | | | | | $ 4,608 | |
| Year 6–5.76% | | | | | | $ 2,304 |
| Old depreciation (S−L) | −3,000 | −3,000 | −3,000 | −3,000 | −3,000 | −3,000 |
| Incremental depreciation | $5,000 | $9,800 | $4,680 | $1,608 | $1,608 | $(696) |

| *Calculation of annual cash inflows:* | Year 1 | Year 2 | Year 3 | Year 4 | Year 5 | Year 6 |
|---|---|---|---|---|---|---|
| Cash cost savings | $20,400 | $21,420 | $22,491 | $23,616 | $24,795 | $26,037 |
| Less incremental depreciation | −5,000 | −9,800 | −4,680 | −1,608 | −1,608 | 696 |
| Taxable income | $15,400 | $11,620 | $17,811 | $22,008 | $23,187 | $26,733 |
| Incremental tax (40%) | −6,160 | −4,648 | −7,124 | −8,803 | −9,275 | −10,693 |
| Aftertax cash flow | $14,240 | $16,772 | $15,367 | $14,813 | $15,520 | $15,344 |

**3.** Net present value method:

|  | Year 0 | Year 1 | Year 2 | Year 3 | Year 4 | Year 5 | Year 6 |
|---|---|---|---|---|---|---|---|
| Calculations: |  |  |  |  |  |  |  |
| Net investment | $ (26,800) |  |  |  |  |  |  |
| Net cash inflow |  | $ 14,240 | $ 16,772 | $ 15,367 | $ 14,810 | $ 15,517 | $ 15,351 |
| PV factors (16%) | × 1.000 | × 0.862 | × 0.743 | × 0.641 | × 0.552 | × 0.476 | × 0.410 |
| Present values | $ (26,800) | $ 12,275 | $ 12,462 | $ 9,850 | $ 8,175 | $ 7,386 | $ 6,294 |
| Total PV of inflows | 56,442 |  |  |  |  |  |  |
| Net present value | $ 29,642 |  |  |  |  |  |  |

## TERMINOLOGY REVIEW

**Accelerated Cost Recovery
   System (ACRS) (499)**
**Break-even time (503)**
**Embedded interest rate (498)**
**Expected values (506)**
**Inflation (494)**
**Leases (498)**
**Life-cycle costing (502)**
**Modified Accelerated Cost Recovery
   System MACRS (499)**

**Post-audit (504)**
**Product life cycles (502)**
**Risk percentage factor (505)**
**Sensitivity analysis (505)**
**Social benefits (507)**
**Social costs (507)**
**Uncertainty (505)**
**Working capital (495)**

## QUESTIONS FOR REVIEW AND DISCUSSION

**1.** Why is an initial investment in additional inventory different than an investment in machinery? Explain the difference in cash flows.

**2.** How can inflation can be incorporated into capital investment analysis?

**3.** What problem arises if alternative investments have different useful lives? Identify at least one solution.

**4.** By incorporating inflation into the discount rate, what assumptions are made?

**5.** A project can be divided into Phase I and Phase II. Phase II is a continuation of Phase I, cannot be developed by itself, and may or may not be developed. Phase I looks like a sure "winner," but Phase II is questionable. Capital investment analyses are done on Phase I and on Phases I and II together. What might be learned from each of the analyses? What extension might you suggest?

**6.** What is meant by financing decisions and investing decisions? Why should they be analyzed separately?

**7.** Why would the annual cost of leasing differ from the annual cost of buying? Identify factors on both sides.

**8.** How are the ideas of social costs, environmental costs, and intangible benefits linked to lifecycle costing in capital investment analysis?

**9.** What depreciation methods are built into most of the annual MACRS depreciation percentages?

10. If capital investment analysis depends so heavily on estimates of future cash flows, what controls exist to prevent over optimistic estimates from inflating a given project's rate of return?

11. **(a)** ABC Company uses a 14 percent hurdle rate. XYZ Company uses a 20 percent hurdle rate. What could cause this difference in rates?

   **(b)** In DEF Corporation, Division G uses a 12 percent hurdle rate; Division H uses a 14 percent hurdle rate; and Division I uses a 16 percent hurdle rate. What could cause these differences in rates?

12. What information does sensitivity analysis provide that net present value analysis does not?

13. What does the term "expected value" mean? Is it real? How can it replace a specific estimate of a key variable?

14. How can intangible benefits and costs be incorporated into capital investment analysis?

15. A business analyst recently said, "Social costs of many decisions often far outweigh the business dollars and cents amounts." Why might this be true?

16. A local not-for-profit organization's director was heard to say, "Capital investment analysis works for profit-making organizations but not for us. We're trying to maximize benefits to the people whom our organization serves and not trying maximize profits." Comment on the pros and cons of the quote.

17. Suggest several advantages of using life-cycle costing for capital project analysis.


# EXERCISES

**12–1. Gains and Losses on Disposal.** Pierce company is considering the purchase of a new machine for $200,000 which would have a 5-year life. The company would sell for $50,000 its old machine which cost $180,000 and has a book value of $20,000. Gains, losses, and profits have a tax rate of 40 percent. The new machine will require about $30,000 less in raw materials inventory to operate.

**Required:**
What is the net cash outflow for the investment?

**12–2. Mutually Exclusive Alternatives.** The Jason Company has $50,000 to invest in either of two alternatives. Investment I yields $12,000 a year in aftertax annual cash flows for ten years. Investment II yields a one-time, aftertax return of $180,000 at the end of ten years.

**Required:**
1. Using Tables 1 and 2 found immediately after the Index at the back cover of this book, find the PV for all interest columns from 4 percent through 25 percent, using the 10-year row for each investment.
2. Which investment is preferred over what ranges of minimum RORs?
3. At approximately what ROR would you reject Investment I and Investment II?

**12–3. Unequal Lives.** Having given the matter some thought, you decide that you would be equally happy buying and driving any of the following cars:
   **(a)** A Supreme Deluxe and trading every sixth year.
   **(b)** A Premium Fairmont and trading every third year.
   **(c)** An Economy Delight and trading every second year.

You have decided to base your decision on the present value of the expected future costs. You have predicted your costs as follows:

|  | Supreme<br>Deluxe | Premium<br>Fairmont | Economy<br>Delight |
|---|---|---|---|
| Original cost. | $ 30,000 | $ 20,000 | $ 15,000 |
| Market value at trade-in time. | 8,000 | 8,000 | 8,000 |
| Annual cash operating costs. | 2,400 | 2,000 | 1,500 |
| Overhaul, fourth year. | 2,000 | 0 | 0 |
| Overhaul, second year. | 0 | 1,000 | 0 |

You believe that you will stick with this approach for at least six years. Your minimum desired rate of return is 10 percent. Ignore taxes.

**Required:**
Select the alternative that promises the greatest financial advantage.

12–4. **Net Investment.** The management of Westport Metal Fabricators plans to replace a forming machine that was acquired several years ago at a cost of $45,000. The machine has been depreciated to its salvage value of $5,000. A new machine can be purchased for $80,000. The dealer will grant a trade-in allowance of $6,000 on the old machine. If a new machine is not purchased, the company will spend $20,000 to repair the old machine. Gains and losses on trade-in transactions are not subject to income tax. The cost to repair the old machine can be deducted in the first year for computing income tax. Income tax is estimated at 40 percent of the income subject to tax.

**Required:** Show the net investment in the new machine for decision-making purposes.

12–5. **Working Capital.** Kim Andrews sells a very successful line of skin protection creams to Scottish golfers. She can spend £$100,000 now on additional inventory. The added inventory will increase earnings after taxes by £40,000 per year. She is looking at a 6-year time horizon. She expects to recover the £100,000 inventory investment at the end of the six years. She must earn a 16 percent ROR.

**Required:**
What is the NPV of this decision? Is this a wise use of funds? Why?

12–6. **Incremental Investment and Discounted Rate of Return.** A manufacturer of equipment quotes a price of ¥1,300,000 for a unit of equipment that is being considered by Wiescinski Products, Inc. This equipment should be able to produce net returns of ¥400,000 each year for five years. Another equipment manufacturer offers a similar unit at a price of ¥1,800,000. This unit of equipment is expected to yield ¥550,000 in net returns each year for five years. These are mutually exclusive investment alternatives. An investment of this type is expected to yield a discounted ROR of no less than 16 percent. Ignore taxes.

**Required:**
1. Which investment alternative is more attractive if a minimum acceptable ROR of 16 percent is expected? Show computations.
2. What is the approximate IRR for each project?
3. What is the approximate IRR for the incremental investment?
4. Comment on the differences between solutions to Part (1) and Parts (2) and (3).

12–7. **MACRS Depreciation.** The Buccalo Company will buy tooling equipment for research purposes for $800,000. No salvage value is expected at the end of the 5-year life. The equipment qualifies as a 3-year class asset for MACRS depreciation. Annual net cash inflow before taxes is $300,000. The tax rate is 40 percent. Buccalo wants at least a 16 percent ROR.

**Required:**
Find the NPV, the ARR, the payback period, and the approximate IRR.

**12–8. Basic MACRS Application.** Sizemore Company is considering an investment opportunity involving a cash outlay of $120,000 for new office building machinery that would last about ten years and have no estimated residual value. The machinery would reduce annual cash operating costs by $25,000. The firm's tax rate is 40 percent, and its cost of capital is 14 percent. The company considers this asset to be a 7-year asset for MACRS purposes.

**Required**: Find the NPV, the payback period, and the approximate IRR.

**12–9. Environmental Costs and Ethical Issues.** Mark Johnson, controller of St. Johns Hospital, is reviewing capital proposals for next year's capital budget. The proposals have been put together by the managers responsible for their respective areas. He is concerned that the figures in several proposals do not seem to reflect some sensitive factors. The proposals include:

**Building Expansion:** A new wing will use a site that included a vacant gasoline station. Mark is aware of problems at other similar sites with underground contamination from leaking storage tanks. Cleanup costs have ranged from several thousand to nearly half a million dollars at other sites. The only cost shown in the proposal is demolition costs to remove the building.

**Equipment Acquisition:** A new diagnostic machine is being requested by the Endocrinology Department. The machine uses radioactive isotopes. The proposal includes costs of handling these radioactive wastes as part of the hazardous materials management policies. Mark, however, knows that this machine will significantly increase the hospital's involvement with these materials and will change its status for handling and storage. He does not know what these additional requirements are. These costs are not mentioned.

**Parking Lot Improvement:** Expansion of the parking area will include removal of several older homes, owned by the hospital and rented to low-income families. Several community organizations have voiced concerns about losing more quality housing in the area. One group threatens to protest the loss of housing. No mention of this is given in the proposal.

**Required:**
1. Mark has asked you for suggestions as to how the issues he has raised regarding these proposals might be incorporated into the decision-making process.
2. He is also interested in preventing these omissions in the future. Prepare an addition to the capital investment policy manual that would ensure specific consideration of such issues.

**12–10. Net Investment and Discounted Rate of Return.** A unit of equipment used in research and development can be acquired from a manufacturer at a $200,000 cost. If this equipment is acquired, an old unit of equipment that is fully depreciated will be sold for $20,000. Annual savings from using the new equipment, before deducting depreciation or taxes, have been estimated at $80,000. The new equipment is a 3-year class asset for MACRS depreciation purposes, should have a 5-year life, and will have no salvage value. Income tax rate is 40 percent for all taxation items.

**Required:**
1. Determine the net investment in the new equipment.
2. Will this investment be acceptable if the minimum ROR has been established at 16 percent? Explain.

**12–11. Ethics of Financing.** Jane Outslay, a community activist, has just opened the first community development credit union in the Overton section of Metro City. Its goal is to provide credit to low-income persons living in Overton, the poorest area of Metro City. For several years, no financial institution has operated in this square-mile area. Jane has made many presentations to community groups and needs illustrations of how the credit union can help low-income people establish credit to buy furnishings, remodel homes, and buy autos. She has these facts:

**Buying living room furniture:** Sam's Rent-to-Own offers a low-quality living room set, table, lamps, and entertainment center for $2,000 cash or a monthly payment of $75 per month, with nothing down and 48 months to pay. The monthly payment includes simple interest of 18 percent for 48 months plus a small monthly service charge of $3.33, common terms in the area.

Somewhat better quality furniture at a reputable store some distance away would cost $1,500. Jane's credit union could provide credit to a working person for 48 months at a 9 percent interest rate. A 10 percent downpayment is required.

**Buying a car:** Joe's Deal and Drive will sell and finance a $10,000 new car. The monthly payment includes 15 percent simple interest on the $10,000 for four years, a required $1,800 per year insurance policy, a credit-checking fee of $500, and a required $5 per month credit life policy.

Mike's Autos will lease the same car on a 24-month lease with a 12 percent imbedded interest rate. The lease on the $9,000 car includes a residual value for the car of $3,000 at the end of the lease period. Insurance from an independent agent will cost $100 per month. A $500 up-front lease contract fee is required.

Jane's credit union will lend 90 percent of the car's cost of $9,000. A 48-month loan can be made at 9 percent. Insurance is again $100 per month.

**Required:**

Prepare a comparative analysis for each situation for Jane to use in community talks. Assume that all monthly payments on loans or leases are at the end of all periods. Insurance and fees are assumed to be paid in advance. Highlight qualitative advantages and disadvantages of each financing choice in each situation.

**12–12. MACRS and the Replacement Decision.** You are given the following data:

| Existing machine: | | Replacement machine: | |
|---|---|---|---|
| Cost | $70,000 | Cost. | $180,000 |
| Book value | 30,000 | Estimated salvage value | 10,000 |
| Salvage value. | 0 | Annual cash operating costs | 8,000 |
| Annual depreciation. | 5,000 | MACRS depreciation method | 5 years |
| Annual cash operating costs | 50,000 | Useful life | 6 years |
| Present sales value. | 50,000 | | |
| Remaining life | 6 years | | |

**Required:**

Determine the NPV of the replacement decision assuming a desired ROR of 16 percent and a 40 percent income tax rate.

**12–13. Lease Versus Purchase.** Zalka and Daughters, a Finnish publisher, is considering the purchase of a photocopy machine. The dealer has offered a sale or a lease contract. Maintenance and supplies costs are the same under either arrangement. The cash purchase price in euros is €45,000. The lease arrangement is monthly payments of €2,000 for 24 months. Zalka's annual cost of funds is approximately 12 percent (or 1 percent per month). Assume that the machine will have a technological life of two years. Ignore taxes.

**Required:**

Which is the more appealing financial arrangement? Explain.

**12–14. Inflation and Investment Analysis.** Sittin'-in-the-Sun Health Spas is evaluating an expansion of its existing facilities this fall. The proposal calls for a 6-year building rental contract at $10,000 a year. Equipment purchases and facility improvements are expected to cost $60,000. Straight-line depreciation ignoring the half-year convention is used. Other cash operating expenses are estimated at $25,000 annually. Based on past experience, the company thinks new revenues should be $50,000 annually. Sittin'-in-the-Sun will not expand unless the project covers its 14 percent cost of capital. The company's effective tax rate is 40 percent.

Inflation is a concern. The controller thinks that revenues and cash expenses will inflate by 5 percent per year. Round the discount rate to the next highest rate available in Table 2 found immediately after the Index at the back cover of this book.

**Required:** Using NPV, suggest whether the expansion project should be adopted.

**12–15. Community Service.** Jon Jensen, president of Jensen Groceries, is evaluating several marketing and community charitable activities. The activities include:

**Jensen's 10K Run for Food:** This popular event gets 400 participants, raises about $10,000 for the local food bank, and costs Jensen about $5,000 in support costs. Jensen does worry about legal liability for race accidents.

**United Way Contribution:** Jensen matches all contributions made by his employees to the local United Way. Jensen's contribution was $15,000 last year. The company receives a plaque and newspaper coverage.

**Gourmet Cooking Classes:** Jensen hires a local cooking expert to teach a series of ethnic foods classes. The classes cost about $6,000 per year and have helped give the store a reputation as a connoisseur's food center.

**Jensen's Helpers:** The company encourages employees to give volunteer time to community organizations. If an employee gives forty hours to predetermined charities, Jensen gives the person two days of paid vacation time. Last year this cost Jensen $8,000 in vacation time and overtime for replacements.

**Required:**
Suggest how Jensen can evaluate these "investments" in the community.

**12–16. Lease Versus Purchase Alternatives.** Al Williams in Freeport, Bahamas, is evaluating two similar machines. Both machines do the same tasks and generate the same revenues. Cash operating costs, however, differ and are as follows:

|         | Alternative A | Alternative B |
|---------|---------------|---------------|
| Year 1. | B$125,000     | B$ 80,000     |
| Year 2. | 100,000       | 80,000        |
| Year 3. | 80,000        | 120,000       |
| Year 4. | 80,000        | 100,000       |
| Year 5. | 60,000        | 100,000       |
| Year 6. | 40,000        | 100,000       |

Both alternatives can be leased under a 6-year contract for B$50,000 per year or purchased for B$200,000. Al's long-term funds have a cost of 14 percent. Borrowing against his bank line of credit costs him 10 percent.

**Required:**
1. Which alternative is the better operating decision?
2. Which financing alternative is better?
3. What should be done? Explain this decision.

**12–17. Lease Financing.** Vehicle A can be leased under a 4-year contract for $16,000 per year or purchased with cash for $54,400. Vehicle B can be leased on a 6-year contract for $15,000 per year or purchased with cash for $74,900. Assume cash funds at a cost of 10 percent. The first payment is due today on both vehicles. Ignore taxes.

**Required:**

**1.** What is the embedded interest rate in each vehicle's contract?

**2.** If we want both vehicles, which should be purchased or leased?

**12–18. Net Present Value and Expected Values.** Two competing investment alternatives are being considered by the Corden Company. One alternative costs $130,000. The other alternative costs $160,000. An investment of this type is expected to earn a discounted ROR of at least 14 percent. The two projects are each expected to last five years. Ignore taxes. Probabilities of annual revenues from each project differ as follows:

**Annual Revenue Probabilities**

| $130,000 Investment | | $160,000 Investment | |
| --- | --- | --- | --- |
| 10% | $10,000 | 10% | $20,000 |
| 10% | 20,000 | 20% | 40,000 |
| 15% | 30,000 | 40% | 60,000 |
| 20% | 40,000 | 20% | 80,000 |
| 25% | 50,000 | 10% | 100,000 |
| 10% | 60,000 | | |
| 10% | 90,000 | | |

**Required:**

Determine the more desirable alternative by the NPV method.

**12–19. Sensitivity Analysis of Future Estimates.** Frear Industries estimated the following figures on a bid for a 10-year government contract:

| | |
| --- | --- |
| Investment in machinery | $ 800,000 |
| Additional inventory (funds to be released when contract ends) | 100,000 |
| Cost of equipment overhaul at the end of sixth year | 120,000 |
| Machinery salvage value at the end of contract (10 years) | 80,000 |
| Annual revenue from the contract | 200,000 |
| Cost of capital | 14 % |

**Required:**

Ignoring taxes, what impacts (amount and percentage change) will the following mistakes in estimation have on the NPV of this contract?

**(a)** An understatement of $20,000 in the investment in machinery.

**(b)** An understatement of $20,000 in the inventory needed.

**(c)** An understatement of $30,000 in the cost of the overhaul.

**(d)** An overstatement of $50,000 in the salvage value at the end of the contract.

**(e)** An overstatement of $4,000 in the annual revenue from the contract.

**12–20. Value of MACRS.** Huffman Company plans to buy a piece of equipment that will cost $120,000 and have a useful life of ten years with no salvage value. The expected incremental annual cash inflows from using the new machine are $32,000, and the expected incremental annual cash outflows are $6,000. The tax rate is 40 percent. The company uses a 12 percent cutoff rate.

**Required:**
1. Using straight-line depreciation and ignoring the half-year rule, what is the net annual aftertax cash benefit? Find the NPV.
2. Assuming that the 5-year MACRS asset class is used, what is the net annual aftertax benefit? Find the NPV, and compare it to your answer to Part 1.

# PROBLEMS

 **12–21. Incremental Investment.** Welton Company is introducing a product that will sell for $10 per unit. Annual volume for the next four years should be about 200,000 units. The company can use either of two machines to make the product. Data are as follows:

|  | Machine X | Machine Y |
| --- | --- | --- |
| Per unit variable cost | $     4 | $     2 |
| Annual cash fixed costs | 725,000 | 850,000 |
| Cost of machine | 800,000 | 1,400,000 |

Both machines have 4-year lives and no anticipated salvage value. The firm uses straight-line depreciation, has a 40 percent income tax rate, and has a 14 percent cost of capital.

**Required:**
1. Determine which machine has the higher approximate IRR.
2. What is the approximate IRR on the incremental investment needed for Machine Y beyond Machine X's investment?

**12–22. Comparing Unequals.** Data relating to three possible investments are as follows:

|  | X | Y | Z |
| --- | --- | --- | --- |
| Cost | $ 34,000 | $ 25,000 | $ 75,000 |
| Annual cash savings | 8,111 | 7,458 | 14,011 |
| Useful life—years | 10 | 5 | 20 |

**Required:**
1. Ignoring taxes, rank the investments according to their desirability using the payback period, IRR, NPV with a discount rate of 12 percent, and the profitability index.
2. Comment on the impact that the unequal lives have on the rankings.
3. Comment on the impact that the unequal investments have on the rankings.

**12–23. Sell or Use Equipment.** An offer of $130,000 has been received for equipment that Herrera Products has been using to make certain parts. The equipment is fully depreciated but can be used for five more years. After five years, it is expected to have little, if any, value.

The variable cost of producing the parts is $10 per unit. A total of 10,000 units are needed each year. If the parts are not manufactured, the company must buy them from an outside supplier at a cost of $15 per unit. Also, if the parts are not produced, the space occupied by the equipment can be rented for $12,000 per year. Income tax is estimated at 40 percent of the income before tax. The company uses a 12 percent hurdle rate on this type of investment.

**Required:**
Prepare a recommendation for Herrera's president on the proposed equipment sale.

**12–24. Sensitivity of Key Variables.** The Richmond Company owns a machine that cost $50,000 five years ago, has a book value of $20,000, and has a current market value of $14,000. The machine costs $25,000 per year after tax effects to operate and will have no market value at the end of five more years.

The firm has an opportunity to buy a new machine that costs $60,000, will last five years, have no salvage value, and costs $10,000 per year after tax effects to operate. It will perform the same functions as the machine currently owned. The firm has a cost of capital of 12 percent. Ignore income taxes.

**Required:**

1. Determine the approximate ROR that the firm would earn on the investment.
2. Suppose that the production manager is not sure of the cost savings. By what percentage could the cost savings change and still allow the company to earn a 12 percent return?
3. Suppose that the estimate of annual cash flows is considered reliable but that the useful life of the new machine is in question. How many years must the new machine last for the firm to earn a 12 percent return?

**12–25. Required Investment in Current Assets.** An interesting project is being considered by Deer Creek, Inc. The project will require an investment of $300,000 in equipment that is expected to have a useful life of eight years with no salvage value. Initially, additional cash, accounts receivable, and inventory will be required in the amount of $100,000. This working capital will be released at the end of eight years. Annual cash inflows from this project before income tax have been estimated at $100,000.

Depreciation is to be deducted by the MACRS method assuming a 7-year MACRS class. Income tax is estimated at 40 percent of income before income tax. The minimum desired ROR is 14 percent.

**Required:** Does the investment meet the ROR objective? Explain.

**12–26. Equipment Replacement.** Guarantee Insurance Company has been operating a cafeteria for its employees at its headquarters, but it is considering a conversion to a completely automated set of coin vending machines. The old equipment would be sold, and the vending machines would be purchased immediately for cash. A reputable catering firm would take complete responsibility for servicing the vending machines and would simply pay Guarantee a contracted percentage of the gross vending receipts. The following data are available:

| | |
|---|---:|
| Current cafeteria: | |
|   Cash revenues per year. | $240,000 |
|   Cash expenses per year. | 265,000 |
| | |
| Equipment (6-year remaining life): | |
|   Net book value. | $ 60,000 |
|   Annual depreciation expense | 10,000 |
|   Disposal value now. | 10,000 |
|   Disposal value in six years | 0 |
| | |
| New vending machines: | |
|   Purchase price. | $120,000 |
|   Forecast disposal value | 20,000 |
|   Expected annual gross receipts. | 180,000 |
|   Estimated useful life | 6 years |
|   Guarantee's percentage receipts | 10 % |

Guarantee uses straight-line depreciation without the half-year rule and has a tax rate of 40 percent.

**Required:**
1. Evaluate the financial aspects of the change in Guarantee's approach to the cafeteria problem by measuring:
   (a) Expected change in net annual operating cash flow.
   (b) Payback period.
   (c) Approximate IRR.
2. Prepare a report highlighting your findings in Part 1 and any nonquantitative variables that you see impacting this decision. Comment on whether and how the nonquantitative variables can be quantified.

**12–27. Equipment Replacement.** Dodd Company owns a specialty truck with the following attributes:

| | |
|---|---:|
| Book value. | $ 55,000 |
| Current market value. | 40,000 |
| Expected salvage value (after 5-year remaining useful life) | 0 |
| Annual depreciation expense, straight-line method | 11,000 |
| Annual cash operating costs | 18,000 |

The firm's cost of capital is 14 percent, and a 40 percent tax rate is applicable to all taxation items.

The firm plans to replace the truck with one costing $80,000 and having an expected salvage value net of taxes of $5,000, annual cash operating costs of $3,000, and a useful life of five years. Straight-line depreciation of $16,000 per year would be taken on the new truck. Additionally, because the new truck is more dependable, the firm could reduce its repair parts inventory by $15,000.

**Required:**
Determine whether the new truck should be bought. Use whatever capital investment methods you believe will best present the facts to Dodd's management.

**12–28. Life-Cycle Budgeting.** Steve Poulios, product development director of MS Labs, is meeting with the research, marketing, and finance directors tomorrow. His staff has brought together pieces of a financial puzzle on a potential new product. The research lab has spent $100,000 last year (2006) and $300,000 this year (2007) on a project that looks promising. The product, apparently environmentally safe, would cause ground moles to pack their bags and move on. Steve's projections show a huge market and strong profits if final testing and production problems can be solved. The research lab forecasts continuing development costs of $500,000 next year (2008) and $300,000 in 2009. Production engineering costs will start in 2008 at $200,000 and continue in 2009 at $400,000. Equipment costs for production would be $2,000,000, incurred at the end of 2008, and would be depreciated over the next five years using straight-line depreciation.

The product will be introduced in 2009 with annual sales projected at $800,000, $3,000,000, $5,000,000, $4,000,000, and $3,000,000 through 2013, respectively. Cash production costs as a percentage of sales are expected to be 60, 55, 50, 40, and 40 percent through 2013, respectively. After an initial advertising campaign of $300,000 per year in 2009 and 2010, advertising expenses should be $200,000 per year. Steve's reports show possible international licensing arrangements. Licensing fees would be 5 percent of international sales. Steve thinks international sales will parallel U. S. domestic sales but will lag by one year and cease in 2013. Assume all cash flows occur at yearend. The tax rate is 40 percent.

**Required:**

1. Comment on the role of 2006 and 2007 expenditures in the project's analysis.
2. Prepare a product life-cycle project analysis showing cumulative expected cash flows through 2013.
3. Evaluate the project for capital investment purposes if MS Labs uses a 15 percent hurdle rate.
4. Comment on the impact of the discount rate on this project.

**12–29. Acquisition of Equipment Using Expected Values.** A new product line is being considered by the Vehlwald Company. Special equipment will be required for the manufacturing process. To handle the expected volume, Ingram may need to purchase multiple machines if the project is to be accepted. Data with respect to the production of this product are:

| Number of Equipment Units | Product Unit Capacity |
|---|---|
| 1 | 60,000 units |
| 2 | 120,000 units |
| 3 | 160,000 units |
| 4 | 200,000 units |
| 5 | 240,000 units |

The new product line will increase out-of-pocket annual fixed costs (excluding depreciation) by $140,000. It is estimated that this increase can be expected regardless of the number of machines purchased. The variable cost of producing a unit has been estimated at $6, and the selling price has been estimated at $10. The company has the physical space to install up to five units of equipment. Each machine sells for $300,000 per unit, and the useful life is estimated at six years with no salvage value.

A survey has been made to estimate the potential demand for this product. Probabilities of the estimated demand are as follows:

| Sales Probability | Units of Sales |
|---|---|
| 10% | 40,000 units |
| 20% | 80,000 units |
| 30% | 120,000 units |
| 20% | 160,000 units |
| 10% | 200,000 units |
| 10% | 240,000 units |

**Required:**

Using straight-line depreciation, a 40 percent tax rate, and a 16 percent discount rate, determine how many machines, if any, should be purchased.

**12–30. Purchase vs. Lease Decision.** Helsel Brothers Farms is considering replacing a technologically obsolete and fully depreciated tractor currently used in farming operations. The tractor is in good working order and will last, physically, for at least six years. However, the proposed tractor is so much more efficient that Helsel Brothers Farms predicts cost savings of $25,000 a year. The tractor's delivered cost is $80,000. Its technological useful life is six years, although the physical useful life is 15 years. The salvage value of the tractor is $10,000 in six years and zero in 15 years. The 5-year class MACRS depreciation will be used on the new tractor. If the new tractor is acquired, Helsel Brothers Farms can sell the old tractor at a capital gain of $5,000.

Helsel Brothers Farms requires a minimum of a 14 percent aftertax return on all investments. The income tax rate is 40 percent. If Helsel Brothers Farms decides to acquire the new tractor, it has the option of purchasing or leasing the tractor. The distributor will sell the tractor outright for $80,000 delivered cost or will lease the tractor at $24,000 per year for six years. Under the lease, the first payment of $24,000 is due now; and, at the end of six years, the tractor reverts to the distributor.

**Required:**
1. Should Helsel Brothers Farms acquire the new tractor? Explain.
2. If Helsel Brothers Farms should acquire the new tractor, would the company prefer an outright purchase or a lease? Why?

**12–31. Financing Alternatives.** Chizuk Surveying Company is a regional geographic consulting firm. The CEO has approved the acquisition of new plotting equipment. Because of the size of the dollar commitment, the Chizuk board of directors must approve the expenditure. Financing choices must be evaluated along with the decision to acquire the equipment itself The equipment will cost $1,000,000, have a life of five years (assume straight-line depreciation), and have no salvage value. Three financing choices have been suggested.

    **Finance internally:** Chizuk will pay the vendor from its cash balance on the date the machine is certified as ready for operations.

    **Finance with a bank loan:** Chizuk would obtain a bank loan to finance 90 percent of the equipment cost at 10 percent annual interest. Five annual payments of $237,418 each would be due at the end of each year, beginning one year from the certification date. Chizuk will pay the remaining $100,000 from its cash balance at certification date.

    **Lease from a lessor:** EcoDevLease, a local economic development organization, could lease the equipment to Chizuk for an initial $50,000 payment and five annual payments of $220,000 each starting one year from the certification date. At the lessee's option, the equipment can be purchased at the fair market value at the lease's termination. (The lessor is currently estimating a 30 percent residual value.) At this time, however, Chizuk does not plan to buy the machine.

    Chizuk has a bank borrowing rate of 10 percent, a corporate hurdle rate of 12 percent, and a 40 percent income tax rate.

**Required:**
1. Prepare a PV analysis as of the certification date of the expected aftertax cash flows for the three financing choices.
   (a) Identify the discount rate(s) you used and explain why you selected it.
   (b) Recommend the preferred financing choice.
2. Discuss the qualitative factors Chizuk should consider before a final financing decision is made.

**12–32. Inflation Impacts.** Goslin Company designs and makes lighting fixtures. The sales manager is deciding whether to introduce a new line of lights. The lights will sell for $100 and have variable costs of $40. Volume is expected to be 2,000 units per year for five years. Additional fixed cash operating costs will be $50,000 per year. Additional machinery costing $200,000 is needed. The new machinery will have a five year life and have no salvage value. Goslin uses straight-line depreciation. Goslin's tax rate is 40 percent, and the company uses a hurdle rate of 15 percent.

    The sales manager sees a serious threat to the project's profitability—inflation. He knows competition will allow only small increases in prices, perhaps 4 percent per year. But he knows labor and materials cost pressures could cause variable costs to increase by double that rate, probably 8 percent per year. Fixed costs are likely to increase by $2,000 per year. The general inflation rate is forecast to be 6 percent.

**Required:**

1. Evaluate the NPV of the project, assuming that inflation is included in the hurdle rate.
2. By adjusting each cost and revenue element by its estimated inflation factor, evaluate the project using NPV. Round the discount rate to the nearest whole percent.
3. Comment on the impact of inflation on the NPV of the project.

**12–33. Sensitivity Analysis.** Coles Corporation wants to expand a production facility because of increasing demand for its specialty line of cycling shorts. The following information is available for management's consideration in this decision:

| Investment: | |
|---|---|
| Increase in fixed assets | $ 125,000 |
| Increase in working capital. | $  45,000 |
| Recovery at the end of five years: | |
|     Fixed assets | $  25,000 |
|     Working capital. | $  45,000 |
|     Project life | 5 years |
| | |
| Annual operations: | |
| Volume in units. | 10,000 |
| Selling price per unit | $      28 |
| Variable cost per unit | 15 |
| Fixed cost, exclusive of depreciation. | $  24,000 |

Straight-line depreciation is used for tax purposes. Ignore salvage value and the half-year convention. The company's tax rate is 40 percent. On investments of this nature, the company uses a 15 percent aftertax ROR cutoff.

**Required:**

1. Determine the NPV of this investment proposal.
2. If variable costs are underestimated, by how much can the estimates be off and the investment still return 15 percent?
3. Holding costs and prices constant, by how much can unit volume fall and still have the firm earn 15 percent?
4. Given the original data, by how much can fixed costs increase (exclusive of depreciation on the new investment) and still have the project earn a 15 percent return?

# CASE 12A—Plastic Productions, Inc.

On Monday morning, Megan Messana, major shareholder and president of Plastic Productions, Inc. (PPI), sits in her office pondering the acquisition of a new machine for the company. PPI is in need of an additional plastic injection molding press. A former coworker, who now works at a large plastics firm on the East Coast, mentioned at a recent trade show that his firm was leasing new injection molding presses. In fact, Messana maintains a favorable relationship with Fourth Sixth Bank so that PPI can borrow needed cash for capital investments. Realizing she lacks knowledge about leasing, Messana somewhat reluctantly calls in Clyde Ringer, her controller.

"Claudia," says Messana, "I wonder if it's possible for us to lease that press. Trouble is, I don't know the first thing about leasing. And to tell you the truth, I've always liked owning my equipment. But, I want you to show me whether my negative gut feeling on leasing is right or wrong."

"No problem," replies Ringer. "Consider it done."

PPI is a small, closely-held firm that employs 50 people. As a job-shop plastics molder, PPI offers a full-service approach to its customers. The process starts when PPI receives an order from a buyer, typically a large original equipment manufacturer. An order is the design specifications for a mold. Once PPI's tooling engineers finish the mold, a product prototype is made and shipped to the buyer for inspection. When the prototype is approved, it is returned to PPI; and production begins.

Driving the decision to acquire the additional injection molding press is a major strategic decision based on two significant factors. First, the technical experience at PPI has grown greatly over the past several years to the point where the engineering staff and the production personnel feel that PPI is ready to tackle specialty low-volume, high-margin jobs that require considerably more technical and production expertise.

The second factor is the increasing control high-volume customers exercise over PPI. These customers are typically large original equipment manufacturers that face increasingly stiff foreign competition. To stay competitive, these customers employ just-in-time techniques. Basically, PPI has been forced to incur higher costs since it produces the entire contract amount in one run but only ships when the customer calls. Realizing that these JIT techniques will only become more prevalent with the high-volume customers, PPI wishes to increase its flexibility.

The sales rep at the molding machine company quotes Ringer a price of $25,000 for the press. The company is willing to lease the press to PPI at $6,000 annually for six years, with the first payment due upon the arrival of the equipment at PPI. If the press is leased, maintenance is included at no cost. If purchased, PPI could enter into a series of one-year maintenance contracts with the molding machine company at the cost of $900 annually. The first annual maintenance payment would be due when the machine is delivered to PPI.

The bank officer at Fourth Sixth Bank tells Ringer that the bank would make a loan to PPI for $25,000. The terms would be four years at a 10 percent annual rate. Equal annual payments are due at the end of each year.

Ringer determines that the press will have a useful life of six years, with no salvage value, and will have to be replaced due to heavy use in spite of strong maintenance. He notes that the equipment is eligible for the MACRS 5-year class life. PPI's current marginal tax rate is 40 percent.

**Required:**
Prepare a memo to Ms. Messana from Mr. Ringer evaluating the purchase or lease of the press and the financing alternatives. Provide spreadsheets that will support your analyses.

## CASE 12B—DIVISIONAL PERFORMANCE IN THE LANSING COMPANY

Lansing Company has four business units, each in a different industry. Alpha Division does repair and modifications on stamping machine dies. Its management is preparing its capital investment requests for next year. Six projects have about the same degree of risk and are being reviewed for inclusion in Alpha's capital budget request sent to Lansing headquarters. The unit manager must select which to forward. The six projects and their data are as follows:

|  | Project A | Project B | Project C | Project D | Project E | Project F |
|---|---|---|---|---|---|---|
| Economic life | 6 years | 8 years | 5 years | 8 years | 6 years | 8 years |
| Initial investment | $106,000 | $200,000 | $140,000 | $160,000 | $144,000 | $130,000 |
| PV of cash inflows (12%) | 175,683 | 223,773 | (10,228) | 234,374 | 150,027 | 199,513 |
| IRR | 35% | 15% | 9% | 22% | 14% | 26% |
| Payback period | 2.2 years | 4.5 years | 3.9 years | 4.3 years | 2.9 years | 3.3 years |

Projects A and D use the same excess capacity; therefore, both could not be accepted. Lansing has set its hurdle rate at 12 percent. The same hurdle rate is used for all four divisions.

**Required:**

1. If Alpha has no budget restrictions for capital investments and has been told to maximize its value to the Company, which projects should be recommended to Lansing? Explain your recommendation.

2. If Alpha will be restricted to $450,000 for capital investments and has been told to maximize its value to the Company, which projects should be recommended? Assume that any unused funds will be invested at the hurdle rate. Explain your recommendation.

3. Discuss the propriety of using the same hurdle rate for all four divisions.

# ANALYSIS OF DECENTRALIZED OPERATIONS

## LEARNING OBJECTIVES

1. Define the components of division net income, division direct profit, division controllable profit, and division contribution margin.

2. Describe the problems of selecting an investment base for evaluating performance.

3. Evaluate a division manager's performance using return on investment, residual income, and the economic value added approach.

4. Identify the criteria for developing and evaluating transfer pricing policies.

5. Discuss the advantages and disadvantages of alternative transfer pricing methods.

6. Explain how the importance of intracompany dealings, the existence of external markets, the relative power positions of the divisions, the intent of managers, and other factors affect transfer pricing and divisional evaluations.

7. Understand transfer pricing issues in the international arena.

## Dividing the Profit Pie: Whose Is Whose?

*Shagari Petroleum Company is a large Nigerian oil company headquartered in Lagos. The company has five operating divisions: Exploration & Production, Trading & Supply, Gas Processing, Refining, and Marketing & Distribution. Each division is responsible for generating a profit and for managing its investment in assets. Debates have raged among division managers about who earned what profits since, in many cases, "Your revenues are my costs."*

*The Exploration & Production Division has the task of finding, developing, and producing oil and gas reserves. Oil produced is sold to the Trading & Supply Division or to outside customers, depending on who offers the best prices. Gas produced is sold to the Gas Processing Division, petrochemical companies, or pipeline companies.*

*The Trading & Supply Division is responsible for meeting the crude oil needs of the Refining Division. It purchases crude oil from the Exploration & Production Division and the open market. Crude oil not sold to Refining is marketed overseas. Consequently, the division engages in speculative buying and selling as a major means of generating profits.*

*Although the Gas Processing Division may purchase gas from other companies, 90 percent of its gas needs are met by the Exploration & Production Division. Processing results in liquid petroleum gas products such as ethane, propane, and butane. These products are sold to the Marketing & Distribution Division and to petrochemical companies.*

*The Refining Division has refineries in Kano, on the Niger River, and in Ibadan. The refineries have the capability to produce a full range of petroleum products. Finished products are sold either to the Marketing & Distribution Division or to an overseas wholesale market.*

*Marketing & Distribution sells to utilities and international resellers, plus industrial, governmental, commercial, and residential customers. It buys its products from the Refining and Gas Processing Divisions. If shortages occur, it may purchase from overseas wholesale markets. The division sells a wide range of products. It owns a barge fleet, tanker trucks, and some pipeline facilities for transporting the products. Other product shipments are contracted with shipping companies.*

*Since the divisions each generate profits and have tremendous investments in assets, Shagari Petroleum wants to develop an appropriate measure for evaluating the financial performance of the divisions and their managers. Also, a transfer price policy should value intracompany deals fairly.*

O NE OF THE most striking characteristics of organizations over the past thirty years has been top management's desire to grow and yet retain the advantages of smallness. Companies have decentralized operations to retain this element of smallness, to build "entrepreneurial spirit," and to motivate division managers to act as the heads of their "own" companies.

In general, a **decentralized company** is one in which operating subunits (usually called divisions) are created with definite organizational boundaries and in which managers have decision-making authority. Thus, responsibility for portions of the company's profits can be traced to specific division managers. Even though the amount of authority granted to these managers varies among companies, the spirit of decentralization is clear—to divide a company into relatively self-contained divisions and allow them to operate in an autonomous fashion.

This chapter discusses two problem areas common to evaluating divisional performance. Evaluation measures and how these measures can be used are covered first. Then we discuss criteria, approaches, and problems associated with transfer prices for goods and services moving among divisions.

# REVIEW OF RESPONSIBILITY CENTERS

Before discussing decentralization and performance measures, it is essential to review the types of responsibility centers first introduced in Chapter 7. A **responsibility center** is any organizational unit where control exists over costs or revenues. Managers of **cost centers** have control over the incurrence of cost but not over revenues. Cost centers are usually found at lower levels of an organization but may include entire plants or even entire parts of an organization, such as manufacturing or the controller's office. In contrast, managers of **profit centers** have control over both costs and revenues. These managers are responsible for generating revenues and for the costs incurred in generating those revenues.

In **investment centers**, managers control costs, revenues, and assets used in operations. The investment represents plant and equipment, receivables, inventories, and, in some cases, payables traceable to the investment center's operations. Companies or subsidiaries could be investment centers or profit centers, depending on whether the corporate headquarters gives investment responsibility to these levels. Investment responsibility is defined as authority to buy, sell, and use assets.

Top management's intent often determines the type of responsibility center. In a large company, a data processing center could be a cost center, either absorbing its own costs or allocating its costs to users of the firm's computer operations. As a profit center, it would be allowed to charge a rate for data processing services it provides to internal users and be expected to earn a profit on its operations. To create an investment center, the manager would be given responsibility to acquire equipment and update services from funds generated by its charges for services provided. Often, organizational structures create natural cost, profit, or investment centers. But managerial intent is perhaps the most important factor in determining how a decentralized unit will be viewed and managed.

# ADVANTAGES OF DECENTRALIZATION

**Decentralization** is the delegation of decision-making authority to lower management levels in an organization. The degree of decentralization depends on the amount of decision-making authority top management delegates to successively lower managerial levels. Advantages of decentralizing include:

1. **Motivated managers.** Managers who actively participate in decision making are more committed to working for the success of their divisions and are more willing to accept the consequences of their actions, whether positive or negative.

2. **Faster decisions.** In a decentralized organization, managers who are close to the decision point and familiar with the problems and situations are allowed to make the decisions. Consequently, decisions can be made faster without moving data up the organization and having a decision made by a manager far removed from the action.

3. **Enhanced specialization.** Delegating authority permits the various levels of management to do those things each does best. For example, top management can concentrate on strategic planning and policy development; middle management on tactical decisions and management control; and lower management on operating decisions.

4. **Defined span of control.** As an organization increases in size, top management has more difficulty controlling the organization. Decentralizing the authority defines more narrowly the span of control for each manager and thus makes the control system more manageable.

5. **Training.** Experience in decision making at low management levels results in trained managers who can assume higher levels of responsibility when needed.

To realize the full benefits of these advantages, top management must resolve the following issues:

1. **Competent people.** Without competent people, the best policies break down; and a lack of control reduces the efficiency and effectiveness of operations.

2. **Measurement system.** The same measurement system should be used for all divisions. Top management must develop policies that provide consistency in reporting periods, methods of reporting, and methods of data collection.

3. **Suboptimization.** Left to themselves, division managers may work for their own interests without consideration of benefits to the entire organization. Top management needs to focus all managers' efforts on corporate goals through planning and incentive systems.

Formulating the best method for controlling and evaluating divisions is usually more complex than any other single control activity within a company. Motivation, control, and managerial behavior are broad topics and are far beyond the scope of this book.

## MEASUREMENT OF FINANCIAL PERFORMANCE

In previous chapters, planning and control methods were discussed. We apply these to cost, profit, and investment center evaluations. Cost controls used in cost centers are also relevant for profit and investment centers. Revenue and profit measurements used in profit centers are also applied to investment centers. Thus, we can build the following planning and control structure:

|  | Cost Center | Profit Center | Investment Center |
|---|:---:|:---:|:---:|
| Expense budgeting | X | X | X |
| Flexible budgets | X | X | X |
| Plan versus actual expense comparisons | X | X | X |
| Standard cost variances | X | X | X |
| Revenue and profit budgeting |  | X | X |
| Plan versus actual controllable contribution margin |  | X | X |
| Plan versus actual direct contribution margin |  | X | X |
| Asset utilization and rate of return target setting |  |  | X |
| Plan versus actual asset utilization comparisons |  |  | X |
| Plan versus actual rates of return comparisons |  |  | X |

It is rare that financial measures alone can evaluate the performance of a responsibility center. Product or service quality, delivery reliability, market share, and responsiveness to customers are all nonfinancial measures critical to the overall success of a firm. Both financial and nonfinancial goals are often part of a manager's business plan. We discuss in detail nonfinancial performance measures in the next chapter.

For profit and investment centers, selecting proper financial performance measures is not an easy task. The financial measures chosen:

- Send messages to all managers about what is important to the firm's executive managers.
- Are often the basis for calculating incentive compensation, personnel evaluations, and promotion decisions.
- Influence the allocation of new capital and personnel resources.

Rate of return on investment is widely accepted as the primary measure of performance for investment centers.

## Return on Investment

**Return on investment (ROI)** is defined as a ratio:

$$\text{Return on investment} = \text{Profit} \div \text{Investment}$$

We can decompose this ratio into two elements for better control and evaluation:

$$\text{Return on investment} = (\text{Profit} \div \text{Sales}) \times (\text{Sales} \div \text{Investment})$$

The first term is **return on sales (ROS)** (sometimes called the profit margin). It measures the percentage of each sales dollar that is turned into profit. The second term is **asset turnover** which measures the ability to generate sales from the assets a division employs.

Implementing the ROI concept raises a number of issues. Problems exist in defining the profit numerator, investment denominator, and the ratio itself. Even then, divisions within a company may be dissimilar, creating "apples and oranges" comparisons.

**The Numerator—Division Profit.** The choice of the profit figure is not simple. The first problem is how the profit number will be used. Will it be used to evaluate the division as an economic unit or to evaluate the division manager's performance? A different profit is appropriate for each. Once the purpose is decided, the next problem is how to construct the best measure from several profit concepts commonly available. Assume that a division of Taratoot Financial Consulting reports the following profit and loss data (all numbers in thousands):

| | |
|---|---:|
| Division revenues | $1,000 |
| Direct division costs: | |
|     Variable operating costs | 700 |
|     Fixed division overhead—controllable at the division level | 100 |
|     Fixed division overhead—noncontrollable at the division level | 50 |
| Indirect division costs: | |
|     Allocated (fixed) home office overhead | 60 |

Four alternative income statements organize the data for different purposes. (The profit titles are also consistent with those used in Chapter 2.)

| | Division Variable Contribution Margin | Division Controllable Contribution Margin | Division Direct Contribution Margin | Division Net Profit |
|---|---:|---:|---:|---:|
| Revenue | $1,000 | $1,000 | $1,000 | $1,000 |
| Direct cost: | | | | |
|     Variable costs | 700 | 700 | 700 | 700 |
| | $ 300 | | | |
|     Fixed controllable costs | | 100 | 100 | 100 |
| | | $ 200 | | |
|     Fixed noncontrollable costs | | | 50 | 50 |
| | | | $ 150 | |
| Indirect cost: | | | | |
|     Allocated home office overhead | | | | 60 |
| | | | | $ 90 |

*Division Net Profit.* The best profit measure for division performance may appear to be **division net profit**. However, the net profit calculation includes allocated home office overhead. An example of this cost would be the cost of operating the president's office. Although each division benefits from these costs, they are not controllable at the division level nor traceable to specific divisions. Generally, net profit is a poor indicator of a division's performance. The main arguments for using net profit are that the division manager is made aware of the entire firm's operating costs and that these costs must be covered by the divisions' earnings. Another argument is that the allocated home office costs stimulate division managers to pressure corporate managers to control their costs.

Home office expenses that are traceable to specific divisions should be assigned directly to those divisions. Allocated home office expenses are likely to be arbitrary and open to question by the division managers. Often, division managers spend much time attempting to reduce their costs by getting top management to change the allocation procedure.

*Division Direct Contribution Margin.* **Division direct contribution margin** is defined as total division revenue less direct costs of the division. This concept avoids the main difficulty of division net profit since common costs of the firm are excluded. The direct contribution margin is the most useful profit measure for comparing divisions' performances, for resource allocation decisions, and for corporate planning purposes. All revenues and costs traceable to the divisions are included.

Often, corporate-level decision makers use the direct contribution margin to indicate where additional investments should be made to generate the greatest incremental returns. Certainly, specific projects must justify themselves as Chapters 11 and 12 demonstrate. But more attention will be paid to high performing divisions.

*Division Controllable Contribution Margin.* **Division controllable contribution margin** is defined as total division revenue less all costs that are directly traceable to the division and that are controllable by the division manager. This calculation is best for managerial performance measurement, because it reflects the division manager's ability to execute assigned responsibilities. Any variances between actual and plan can be explained in terms of factors over which the division manager has control.

Sometimes direct costs are traceable to a division but cannot be controlled at that level. For instance, a division head's salary is controllable only at a higher management level. Also, some division costs, such as long-term leases and depreciation, are from past investment decisions that may have been made by higher level managers or previous division managers. These direct but noncontrollable costs should be excluded from the profit calculation for managerial evaluations. If this is not done, the division profit used for performance evaluation may be affected by actions outside the division or of prior managers.

Some factors in the division controllable contribution margin may be difficult for the division manager to influence; for example, the materials prices may increase. Even though the price cannot be changed, perhaps alternate materials can be used; or alternate sources of supply can be found. Problems of this nature may be difficult to solve, but they are part of the division management's responsibility. Failure to solve such problems is different from being unable to take action due to lack of authority.

*Division Variable Contribution Margin.* The **division variable contribution margin** is defined as total revenue less variable costs. Although variable contribution margin is useful in decision making, for performance evaluation its defect is obvious; namely, direct and controllable fixed costs are excluded from the calculation. Variable costs do have an important role in intracompany pricing policies and decisions, which are discussed later in this chapter.

**The Denominator—Investment.** If divisions are to be evaluated by ROI, it is necessary to measure the investment base. The **investment base** may be total direct assets, net direct assets, or net direct assets managed. Net direct assets would be traceable assets minus any traceable liabilities. Again, the distinction between direct and controllability is important. Certain assets may be traced to a division but not be in service or usable by the division manager.

Since ROI is a measure for a period of time, which date during that period should be chosen to measure the amount of assets? Usually, a simple average of the beginning and ending amounts is used.

*Asset Identification.* The first task is to decide which assets to assign to each division. Many assets can be traced directly to a division. For example, much of a firm's physical property can be traced to a particular division. A division may handle its own receivables and inventory and may even have jurisdiction over its own cash. But sometimes, these traceable assets are centrally administered and controlled. By proper account coding, it is possible to trace receivables and inventories to specific divisions. Cash, as a corporate asset, is rarely traceable to specific divisions.

For assets that are common to several divisions, no amount of coding, sorting, or classifying will enable tracing them to the divisions. An example of a common asset would be the administrative offices used by two product divisions. Any basis of allocation would be arbitrary. As with home office expenses, avoiding these arbitrary allocations generally improves the analysis.

*Asset Valuation.* Once the assets have been identified with the divisions, the value of the assets must be determined. It may seem that the assets should be stated at some current value (e.g., replacement cost, original cost adjusted for price-level changes) rather than on a historical-cost basis. The obvious difficulty is measurement. How can replacement costs be determined? If a common-dollar base is desirable, which price-level index should be used? It is easier to raise questions than to give answers.

**Preferred Relationships.** Matching an income measure and an investment base is the next step. If the purpose is to evaluate the division itself, direct contribution margin would be the natural match with net division direct assets, which are assets traceable to the specific division less traceable liabilities. To evaluate the division managers, controllable contribution margin should be matched with net direct managed assets. Managed assets include the assets controlled by the division manager having the authority to acquire, use, and dispose of these assets.

**Additional Problems with ROI.** Using the ROI concept as a means of evaluating performance raises some concerns about how effective ROI can be and about potential undesirable impacts that may arise from its use.

*Comparability Among Divisions.* One of the major concerns is that ROI comparisons should use the same definitions for the same purposes. Divisions being compared should have the same or similar accounting methods.

The same depreciation method should apply to similar classes or categories of assets. Likewise, incorrect comparisons result when one division uses FIFO for inventories and another division uses LIFO. Also, each division being compared should have the same or similar policies for capitalizing or expensing costs. For instance, one division might expense tools whenever they are purchased. Another division might capitalize the original tools plus any increments and expense replacement tools. It would be inappropriate to compare these two divisions on the basis of ROI without making appropriate adjustments.

*Motivational Impact on Managers.* From top management's point of view, division managers should be working to achieve the overall objectives of the organization. This requires strategies, policies, techniques, and incentives to act as motivators for division managers. **Goal congruence** is the term often used to link each division manager's goals with top management's goals. Individual managers may have personal and organizational goals that differ from top management's goals. When designing managerial performance criteria, senior management must carefully select measures to promote goal congruence. Thus, managers should be motivated to work for their own benefit while, at the same time, benefiting the whole organization.

ROI may sometimes promote decisions that are not goal congruent. For example, suppose that the Northern Division of Ellman's Payroll Service is currently earning 25 percent ROI. The division manager may be reluctant to make additional investments at, perhaps, 20 percent because the average return of the division would drop. However, if new investments in other divisions of the company yield only 15 percent, company management may prefer that the investment with a yield of 20 percent be accepted. The high-earning manager may still be reluctant to lower the average ROI from 25 percent even though company management has set 15 percent as the base rate for comparison. Thus, the use of ROI might restrict additional investment to the detriment of company-wide profitability.

**Improving ROI.** Since division managers are expected to improve ROI, they look to components they can control. ROI can be improved in three direct ways: by increasing sales, by decreasing expenses, and by reducing the level of investment. To see how individual changes affect the ROI calculation, consider the following data for the Sports Division of Eddington Entertainment Corporation:

| | |
|---|---|
| Sales | $2,500,000 |
| Variable costs | 1,500,000 |
| Contribution margin | $1,000,000 |
| Fixed costs | 600,000 |
| Net income | $ 400,000 |
| Investment base | $2,000,000 |
| Return on sales | 16.00% |
| Asset turnover | 1.25 times |
| ROI | 20.00% |

*Increase Sales.* Looking at ROI as a product of return on sales and asset turnover might give the impression that the sales figure is neutral, since it is the denominator in the return on sales and the numerator in asset turnover. However, suppose the Sports Division can increase ticket sales without increasing unit variable costs or fixed costs. The return on sales improves. This happens anytime the percentage increase in total expenses is less than the percentage increase in dollar sales. The increase in sales also improves the asset turnover as long as there is not a proportionate increase in assets. The objectives are to attain the highest level of net income from a given amount of sales and the highest level of sales from a given investment base.

Continuing the numerical example for the Sports Division, assume that ticket sales and total variable costs increase by 5 percent and that fixed costs and the investment base remain constant. ROI, return on sales, and asset turnover all increase, as follows:

| | |
|---|---|
| Sales (105%) | $2,625,000 |
| Variable costs (105%) | 1,575,000 |
| Contribution margin | $1,050,000 |
| Fixed costs | 600,000 |
| Net income | $ 450,000 |
| Investment base | $2,000,000 |
| Return on sales | 17.14% |
| Asset turnover | 1.31 times |
| ROI | 22.50% |

*Reduce Expenses.* Often, the easiest path to improved ROI is to implement a cost reduction program (focusing on certain expense areas or across-the-board cuts). Reducing costs is usually the first approach managers take when facing a declining return on sales. A rather typical pattern has emerged. First, review the discretionary fixed costs, either individual cost items or programs representing a package of discretionary fixed costs, and find those that can be curtailed or eliminated quickly. Second, look for ways to make employees more efficient by eliminating duplication, nonvalue-adding time, or downtime and by increasing individual workloads. Third, review costs of resource inputs for operations and seek less costly choices.

*Reduce Investment Base.* Managers have traditionally sought to control sales and expenses. Their sensitivity to asset management, however, has not always been at the same high level. Managers, whose performances are evaluated using ROI, will find that trimming any excess investment can have a significant impact on the asset turnover and, therefore, on ROI. Reducing unnecessary investment often involves selling or writing off unused or unproductive assets. Recently, many companies have reduced investment in inventories, and also lowered nonvalue-added expenses, by changing to just-in-time inventory systems. Referring to the original Sports Division data, assume that its managers are able to reduce the investment by 4 percent but still maintain the same level of sales and expenses. As a result, both the asset turnover and ROI increase:

| | |
|---|---|
| Sales | $2,500,000 |
| Variable costs | 1,500,000 |
| Contribution margin | $1,000,000 |
| Fixed costs | 600,000 |
| Net income | $  400,000 |
| Investment base (96% of original) | $1,920,000 |
| Return on sales | 16.00% |
| Asset turnover | 1.30 times |
| ROI | 20.83% |

If the eliminated investment is a depreciable asset, depreciation expense will also be reduced. This causes a compound reaction: profitability increases, return on sales increases, and ROI increases by improvement in both the return on sales and the asset turnover.

## Residual Income

The use of residual income has been proposed as an alternative to ROI. Residual income focuses attention on a dollar amount instead of a ratio. The maximization of a dollar amount will tend to be in the best interest of both the division manager and the company as a whole.

In general, **residual income** is defined as the operating profit of a division less an imputed charge for the operating capital used by the division. The same measurement and valuation problems we encountered with ROI still apply to residual income. But motivational problems should be eased.

## Contemporary Practice 13.1
### ROI and the Slammer

A study on crime and prison populations in 12 states by the National Bureau of Economic Research found that the release of a prisoner was associated with an additional 15 crimes per year, on average. The cost of these additional crimes to their victims (and hence, the benefit of preventing these crimes) is estimated to average $45,000, while the cost of imprisoning a convict is estimated to average $30,000. "So we are looking at an extremely juicy ROI . . . we have a 50 percent return," noted Daniel Seligman.

Source: Seligman, D., "Investing in Prison," Fortune, April 29, 1996, p. 211.

Assume that, for Marvin Gross Moving Company, a division's current controllable contribution margin (before any imputed capital charge) is $250,000 and the relevant investment is $1,000,000. The ROI, then, is 25 percent. Suppose top management wants division management to accept incremental investments so long as the return is greater than 15 percent. We refer to this rate as a **minimum desired rate of return**.

This minimum desired rate of return is then used to calculate an imputed charge for division investment funds. The residual income would be calculated as follows:

| | |
|---|---|
| Division controllable profit (before imputed capital charge) | $250,000 |
| Less imputed capital charge (15% × $1,000,000) | 150,000 |
| Division residual income | $100,000 |

The advantage of this evaluation measure is that the division manager is concerned with increasing a dollar amount (in this case, the $100,000) and is likely to accept incremental investments which have a yield of over 15 percent. The division manager's behavior, then, is congruent with company-wide objectives. This would less likely be true with the ROI measure, since any incremental investment earning less than 25 percent pulls down the division's current ROI.

A disadvantage with residual income arises when comparing the performance of divisions of different sizes. For example, a division with $50 million in assets should be expected to have a higher residual income than one with $2 million in assets.

The stage of growth and other risk factors influence the potential profits that a division can generate. Consequently, top management might select different minimum desired rates of return for each division to recognize the unique role each plays in the organization. For example, a startup division may be more expensive to operate than a division in the mature stage—justifying a lower initial rate of return.

## Economic Value Added

In recent years, an approach quite similar to residual income has been developed to evaluate performance. Like residual income, the **economic value added (EVA)** approach deducts a capital charge from the division's profits, as follows:

$$\text{EVA} = \text{Adjusted accounting profit} - (\text{Cost of capital} \times \text{Total capital})$$

Hence, like residual income, the EVA measure is a dollar amount. ROI, in contrast, is a pure number.

The adjusted accounting profit is an after-tax profit with some expenses, such as research and development, treated differently than is done for external reporting requirements. Managers often have incentives to reduce expenses by cutting amounts spent on items such as research and development. To counteract this short-sighted inclination, research and development can be treated as a depreciable asset rather than as an expense, which would not be allowed for external reporting. The resulting profit number better reflects the division's long-run profit potential. The total capital would also include these expenditures. Another frequent adjustment to total capital is the exclusion of current liabilities.

Whereas the capital charge in the residual income measure is based on the minimum *desired* rate of return, EVA uses the *actual* cost of capital. The EVA approach often determines the cost of capital differently than the traditional weighted average cost of capital calculation, which is a weighted average of the cost of debt and the cost of equity. EVA derives a cost of capital based on the industry and risk characteristics of the particular division.[1]

---

[1] The methodology used is the capital asset pricing model.

## Contemporary Practice 13.2
### Conflicts of Interest with ROI

An experiment with individuals in graduate and executive education managerial accounting classes, who averaged about six years of full-time work experience, investigated investment decisions where the participants would be evaluated using ROI. In one setting, the investment under consideration would benefit the company but would reduce the current ROI of the participant. The study estimated that about 51 percent of the respondents would reject the investment.

In another setting, a proposed asset replacement would benefit the company in the long-run but would lower the participant's current ROI because the book value of assets is used in the denominator of ROI. The study estimated that about 38 percent of the respondents would reject the investment.

Source: Schneider, A., "Ethical Decision Making on Various Managerial Accounting Issues," Journal of Applied Management Accounting Research, Summer 2004, pp. 29–39.

Many large companies such as Tenneco, Equifax, Coca-Cola, and AT&T have begun using the EVA approach and linking EVA to incentive compensation. EVA is viewed as the amount which is added to shareholder wealth. When divisions are making investments that earn returns higher than the cost of capital, then the company's shareholders should earn a return in excess of their expectations and the company's stock price is likely to rise.[2]

## Ethical Concerns Relating to Performance Measures

Division managers can increase short-run profits of divisions to the detriment of the company as a whole. For example, it may be possible to delay maintenance costs. Such an action will increase short-run profits but adversely affect long-run profitability of the division and the company. Expenditures that engender employee loyalty such as employee physical fitness programs may be eliminated. By reducing training costs, the division manager may not develop long-run top management personnel.

Our earlier discussion that the use of ROI may not promote goal congruent behavior has ethical implications also. A manager should consider whether it is ethical to reject an investment that would benefit the company even though it would reduce the manager's average ROI.

## PERFORMANCE EVALUATION SYSTEMS IN SERVICE ORGANIZATIONS

Service organizations, like manufacturers, also need evaluation systems. Evaluation criteria and measures can depend on whether the service organization is commercial or not-for-profit.

Profit-oriented operations have an incentive to be profitable. They may use ROI, residual income, or EVA, if an appropriate profit measure and an investment base are available. Obviously, organizations such as CPA firms, law firms, insurance agencies, and consulting firms do not have large investment bases. Personnel is their prime resource. Furthermore, they often lease equipment, space, cars, and other operating assets. Using ROI, residual income, or EVA in these situations will not give a realistic measure of performance for the divisions within the organization. Return on revenue is a better measure and a greater management motivator than are ROI, residual income, and EVA.

---

[2] For a useful website with EVA information and links, see http://evanomics.com.

Not-for-profit organizations are different because profits are not the prime interest of managers. Moreover, revenues are often unrelated to services performed; rather, they come from funding agencies. For example, a police department obtains its operating funds from the local government. The department's mandate is to provide law enforcement services within the limits imposed by the operating funds. But how does one measure the level of services performed—by the number of cases investigated? by time spent on cases? by the number of arrests? Finding criteria for evaluating performance is not an easy task in not-for-profit settings.

## INTRACOMPANY TRANSACTIONS AND TRANSFER PRICING PROBLEMS

In calculating division profit, problems arise when the divisions are not completely independent. If one division furnishes goods or services to another division, a **transfer price** must be set to determine the buying division's cost and the selling division's revenue.

The following list illustrates a variety of intracompany transactions:

1. A centralized accounting department serves all divisions of a company, and its costs are allocated to divisions based on the number of employees in each division.

2. One department provides repairs and maintenance for production departments' equipment in a factory and bills for those services at an average actual cost per hour of service.

3. A Data Processing Services Division provides computer-based information systems services to all other divisions in the company and allocates costs on the basis of predetermined prices for volumes of transactions and data handled.

4. Plant A produces components which are shipped to Plant B for assembly into an end product which is then transferred to the Sales Division for sale to outside customers. Components and products are billed at a "full cost plus a profit" basis between Plants A and B and between Plant B and the Sales Division.

5. Plant J sells strategic raw materials to a variety of customers, including Plant K in the same company. Managers negotiate a special price each year for the raw materials, depending on the supply and demand factors for each plant.

6. Division R sells an industrial product to a broad array of customers. Division S happens to need the product and buys from the sister division at the prevailing market price because of the product's high quality or the division's delivery reliability.

This continuum of accounting approaches for intracompany dealings is shown in Figure 13.1. While not representing any numerical measuring scale, this line does illustrate the range of accounting techniques for intracompany transactions. At one end is pure (arbitrary) cost allocation. At the other end is pure market-driven pricing.

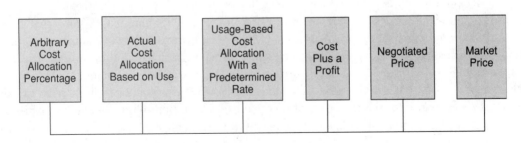

**FIGURE 13.1**

Continuum of Accounting Approaches for Intracompany Transactions

On the left side of the continuum, overhead or administrative costs are being roughly redistributed to other units using cost drivers, benefits received, or even arbitrary rules. Commonly, service departments are transferring costs to producing departments. The middle portion involves internal sales of goods and services where external markets do not exist or where company policies force the divisions to deal with each other internally. The right end of the continuum represents situations where external markets do exist and where market prices are used, in part or in total, as the exchange price. Buyers seek suppliers. Sellers seek customers. If an intracompany sale takes place, it is the best source for the buyer and a profitable sale for the seller.

## Desired Qualities of Transfer Prices and Policies

No one transfer pricing method will be best for all situations. A manager who has spent years supervising internal sales and purchases for a major company has said: "Perhaps the optimal policy is one that will produce the least amount of dysfunctional behavior or, at best, an amount that we can tolerate." Hopefully, policies encourage positive behavior. But dysfunctional behavior, actions which hurt the firm's results, can be frequent by-products.

Let us first outline the criteria for creating a transfer pricing system; second, discuss alternative transfer prices; and third, identify the ability of each price to meet the criteria. Criteria for a transfer price can be reduced to four main elements:

1. **Goal congruence.** Will the transfer price encourage each manager to make decisions that will maximize profits for the firm as a whole? In decentralized organizations, perhaps one of the most difficult tasks is to get everyone to pull toward the common goal—the financial success of the whole firm. Success of each division will not guarantee the optimal success for the whole firm.

2. **Performance evaluation.** Will the transfer price allow corporate-level managers to measure the financial performance of division managers in a fair manner? How will power positions that certain divisions have over other divisions be neutralized? For instance, if one division sells its entire output to another division, the buyer can demand concessions from the seller that can cause the seller to appear unprofitable. If the two divisions are to remain independent, the pricing policy must allow the seller to get a reasonable price for its output.

3. **Autonomy.** Will the transfer price policy allow division managers to operate their divisions as if they were operating independent businesses? If a division manager must ask for approval from some higher level, the firm's policies have diluted the autonomy of its managers. If autonomy is restricted greatly, the objectives of decentralization are defeated.

4. **Administrative cost.** Is the transfer pricing system easy and inexpensive to operate? As with all accounting costs, an incremental cost should generate a positive contribution margin. Where internal transaction volume is large and complex, a more extensive internal pricing system is justified. Administrative costs also include waiting for decisions, hours spent haggling, and internal divisiveness.

These four criteria should be prioritized when forming transfer pricing policies. Different situations will demand different transfer pricing policies.

## Transfer Prices

The most common transfer prices are:

1. Market price.
2. Cost-based prices including:
   (a) Actual full cost.
   (b) Target or predetermined full cost.

**Contemporary Practice 13.3**
*Transfer Pricing in the Canadian Government*

*Transfer prices are charged for goods and services exchanged between Canadian federal government departments and agencies. For instance, auditing services are provided on an optional basis to all departments and agencies through the Audit Services Bureau (ASB) of Supply and Services Canada. Private sector companies compete with*

*ASB. "Although pricing in ASB is based on direct salary costs plus allocated indirect and overhead costs, some flexibility is provided to cope with private sector rates in particular situations.*

*Source: Johri, H., P. Charko, and G. Headley, "Transfer Pricing in the Federal Government," CMA Magazine, July/August 1990, pp. 12–16.*

    **(c)** Cost plus a profit.
    **(d)** Variable cost.
**3.** Negotiated price.
**4.** Dual prices.

We now examine each method with comparison to the transfer pricing criteria.

**Market Price. Market price** is a price set between independent buyers and sellers. Two contrasting conditions are typical:

**1.** A market price exists, and both buyer and seller have access to other sellers and buyers for the same products.

**2.** A market price is not readily available, but a pseudo-price is created either by using similar products or by getting outside bids for the same item.

Market price meets more of the transfer pricing criteria than any other method. But finding a market price may be difficult since one may not exist. Examples include intermediate components, industrial supplies, and "make or buy" jobs. The buyer's purchasing department may request bids from outside suppliers. If, because of company policy, the outside bidders are rarely considered seriously, the outside bidders will not play this game for long. Bidding is an expensive process. Some companies have a policy of considering outside vendors seriously and committing a certain percentage of business to these bidders to help keep the system viable.

Even if a market price exists, it may not be appropriate. For instance, catalog prices may only vaguely relate to actual sales prices. Market prices may change often. Also, internal selling costs may be less than would be incurred if the products were sold to outsiders.

Despite the problems of finding a valid market price, managers generally agree that market prices are best for most transfer pricing situations. A market transfer price parallels the actual market conditions under which these divisions would operate if they were independent companies.

*Goal Congruence.* When excess capacity exists, market prices may not lead to goal congruence. For instance, Division A, which has excess capacity and a mixture of fixed and variable product costs ($50 per unit and $100 per unit, respectively), could benefit greatly from additional production volume. Division A sells its output on the market for $200 per unit. Division B is looking for a supplier for a part that Division A can easily provide. Division B asks for bids from a variety of suppliers. Company C, an unrelated firm, may be selected because it has bid $160 per unit. This price is well above Division A's variable cost but below A's market-price bid. Managers in A and B are making the best decisions for their respective divisions as they see it, but total company profit is hurt. The firm as a whole would be better off by $60 per unit ($160 − $100) if Division B purchased from Division A.

But Division B would need to pay Division A a \$40 higher price (\$200 – \$160), or Division A would have to accept a lower contribution margin (\$160 – \$100 = \$60) than its regular business generates (\$200 – \$100 = \$100).

Many believe that this is a small cost to incur if the individual division managers act in an aggressive, competitive style. What is lost from suboptimization is gained in greater profits from highly motivated quasi-entrepreneurs. Depending on results in specific firms, this trade-off may or may not be justified.

*Performance Evaluation and Autonomy.* Market prices form an excellent performance indicator because they cannot be manipulated by the individuals who have an interest in profit calculations. A market price eliminates negotiations and squabbling over costs and definitions of fairness. If market power positions exist, they also exist in the general marketplace.

Where market prices are less clear and are either created or massaged, the pure advantage of market prices declines. In fact, as we move away from a true market price, the price becomes a negotiated price, which is discussed later.

*Administrative Cost.* As part of normal buying and selling, the transfer price is determined almost costlessly. As we move away from a clear market price, costs increase. Negotiations are expensive in terms of consuming executive time, getting outside bids, and creating support data for negotiating positions.

**Cost-Based Prices.** Unless market price is readily available, most transfer prices are based on production costs. Three issues stand out in **cost-based transfer pricing**:

1. Actual cost versus a target cost, such as standard or budgeted cost.
2. Cost versus cost plus a profit.
3. Full cost versus variable cost.

*Actual Cost Versus a Target Cost.* A primary problem with an actual **full-cost transfer price** is that it gives the selling division no incentive to control costs. All product costs are transferred to the buying division, "reimbursed" as revenue to the selling division. This can create a serious competitive problem for the vertically integrated firm that passes parts through numerous divisions before selling a product in a competitive market. Historically, this has been a problem for General Motors Corporation.

Moving to a target cost helps promote cost control but is not a perfect solution. If a budget or standard cost is used for cost control and also for transfer pricing, profit pressures may well subvert the cost system and damage its usefulness as a cost control device. Furthermore, who sets the standard? Is it a tight or lax standard?

*Cost Versus Cost Plus a Profit.* If cost only is used as a transfer price, the selling unit cannot earn a profit. Full cost plus a profit percentage is a popular solution. Adding a percentage to cost for a profit creates a question: "What percentage?" Somehow 10 percent seems attractive and common. This is, however, an arbitrary choice. Perhaps a markup percentage can be calculated that will cover operating expenses and provide a target return on sales or assets. Even here, these prices fail to produce the kind of competitive environment that decentralization promotes.

*Full Cost Versus Variable Cost.* Another version of cost-based transfer pricing is variable cost. With **variable-cost transfer prices**, only variable production costs are transferred. These costs are generally materials, direct labor, and variable overhead. Variable cost has the major advantage of encouraging maximum profits for the entire firm when excess capacity exists. This will be illustrated later. The obvious problem is that the selling division must absorb all of its fixed costs. That division is now a loss division, nowhere near a profit center.

With these issues in mind, how well do cost-based transfer prices match with the evaluation criteria?

*Goal Congruence.* Full-cost transfer prices generally produce suboptimal profits for the firm as a whole. Variable-cost transfer prices generate an optimal firm-wide profit when the selling division

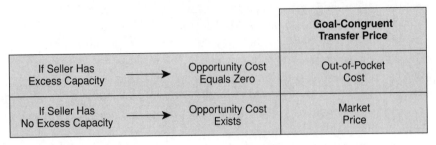

**FIGURE 13.2**

Goal-Congruent Transfer Prices

has excess capacity. Otherwise, market prices yield optimal firm-wide profits. In general, the definition of the most goal-congruent transfer price is out-of-pocket costs plus any opportunity cost of transferring to the next division. Usually, out-of-pocket costs are the variable costs. The opportunity cost is the contribution margin earned from best alternative use of the seller's capacity. When there is no excess capacity, the out-of-pocket cost plus opportunity cost equals the market price. These relationships are summarized in Figure 13.2.

The following example highlights these concepts. Assume that Division A sells to Division B. The output of Division A is Product A, which can be sold to an outside market or to Division B to be processed further and sold as Product B. One unit of Product B uses one unit of Product A. In Division A, variable costs are $100 per unit; and Product A sells for $175. In Division B, additional variable costs are $200 per unit; and Product B sells for $350. This scenario is diagramed in Figure 13.3. Arrows indicate costs flowing out of the divisions and revenues flowing into them.

Suppose Division A has excess capacity. Thus, there is no opportunity cost of transferring to Division B; and the company would receive a contribution of $50 per unit ($350 − $200 − $100), assuming that these units do not increase total fixed costs. A full-cost transfer price, however, might not promote a transfer. If the fixed costs per unit for Products A and B totaled more than $50, Division B would not accept a transfer since its costs would be more than $350 per unit. Consequently, the full-cost

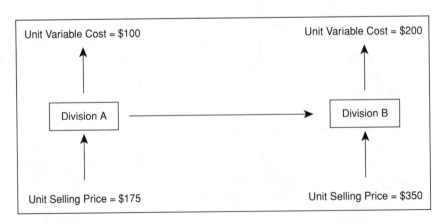

**FIGURE 13.3**

Diagram of Example Transaction Possibilities

transfer price is not goal congruent. Using a variable-cost transfer price, Division B would accept the units since now its total cost of $300 per unit is less than $350. The variable-cost transfer price is, therefore, goal congruent.

Now suppose that Division A has no excess capacity—all units produced can be sold to the outside market for $175. By selling outside instead of transferring to Division B, the company would receive a contribution of $75 per unit ($175 − $100) rather than just $50 ($350 − $200 − $100). A variable-cost transfer price, however, would not achieve this higher profit because Division B would readily accept transfers to earn $50 per unit. In contrast, a market price would be goal congruent. With a transfer price of $175, Division B's costs would total $25 more than its revenue ($350 − $200 − $175), so it would not take any units from Division A.

We summarize these analyses using the preceding decision rule:

**Excess capacity:**
$$\text{Goal congruent transfer price} = \text{Out-of-pocket cost} + \text{Opportunity cost}$$
$$= \$100 + \$0 = \$100$$

**No excess capacity:**
$$\text{Goal congruent transfer price} = \text{Out-of-pocket cost} + \text{Opportunity cost}$$
$$= \$100 + (\$175 - \$100) = \$175$$

*Performance Evaluation and Autonomy.* Clearly, a variable-cost transfer price provides little help in performance evaluation if the division is considered to be a profit center. Autonomy is also violated since close working relationships and much exchange of data are expected. When using full-cost transfer prices, an added profit percentage is necessary to get the seller to a profit position. It is difficult to support any cost-based approach as a strong performance evaluation method for profit centers. Cost-based transfer prices are best suited to cost centers.

*Administrative Cost.* Cost-based transfer prices are easy to obtain since they are outputs of the cost accounting system. Perhaps this is why, in spite of its weaknesses, cost-based transfer pricing is the most widely used transfer pricing approach.

**Negotiated Price.** The use of **negotiated transfer prices** is often suggested as a compromise between market-based and cost-based transfer prices. Real advantages may exist in allowing two division managers to arrive at the transfer price through arm's-length bargaining. The self-interests of the division managers may serve the company objectives. Negotiated prices are helpful when:

1. Cost savings occur from selling and buying internally.
2. Additional internal sales fill previously unused capacity allowing the buyer and seller to share any incremental profit.

As long as the negotiators have relatively equal power positions, negotiations can create a quasi-free market. Friction and bad feelings that may arise from centrally controlled transfer prices may be eliminated.

*Goal Congruence.* Often, the company as a whole benefits from the buying and selling divisions negotiating a price that is agreeable to both parties. Fairness is an issue that must be weighed. The firm as a whole will win if the divisions elect to enter negotiations freely.

*Performance Evaluation and Autonomy.* A negotiated price may be a suitable surrogate for a market price. A market atmosphere is created if buyers and sellers are free to go outside and if neither division has an unfair power position—such as a monopoly position for purchases or sales.

Negotiations can be between buyer and seller alone or involve the corporate office. If negotiations lead to arbitration by the corporate office or if corporate policies interfere with free negotiations, autonomy suffers. The corporate office has the delicate problem of keeping hands off and yet monitoring divisional dealings to prevent significant noncongruent behavior.

*Administrative Cost.* Negotiations are often expensive, consume time of key executives, and may cause an internal unit to be created to handle these relationships. If intracompany sales are important to a division, its managers must put a high priority on these negotiations. Its sales and profit levels are at stake. In highly integrated companies, negotiation costs can be a major operating expense.

**Dual Transfer Prices.** A **dual transfer pricing system** allows the selling division to "sell" at a real or synthetic market price (such as full cost plus a profit percentage). The transfer price to the buying division is usually the variable cost (plus perhaps identifiable opportunity costs). Use of dual transfer prices has been suggested as a way of creating a profit, and thus a positive motivation, in both the selling and buying divisions. Such a system, however, does expand the corporate office accounting task. Intracompany sales and duplicate profits have to be eliminated before total company profits can be determined.

*Goal Congruence and Performance Evaluation.* The advantages of a dual transfer price system rest on being able to evaluate performance of both units as profit centers and to encourage behavior that will benefit the firm as a whole. Thus, the dual system provides the buying division with incremental cost information and at the same time allows the selling division to show a profit. Such a system encourages the congruence of divisional goals with company-wide goals.

If the selling division has substantial fixed costs to cover, a danger does exist that the buying division will sell at cut-rate prices and fail to cover all fixed costs. Here active corporate-level monitoring may be needed.

*Autonomy and Administrative Cost.* Costs and corporate interference are the practical considerations and the major obstacles to the use of dual transfer pricing systems. From an accounting point of view, each division records its own transactions; and the central office must monitor, record, and track intracompany dealings, a clear violation of autonomy. In financial statements for the combined company, accounts representing intracompany transactions are eliminated. For example, a selling division will record a sale and establish a receivable; a buying division will record a purchase and set up a payable. In eliminating the intracompany accounts, any intracompany profits in the buying division's inventory will be adjusted out. The home office must have a special accounting system to track all transactions of a dual pricing system. These extra costs must be outweighed by the benefits of better performance evaluation and goal congruence.

Commonly, the dual transfer pricing system is an academic approach to solving transfer pricing conflicts. But occasionally, a real world firm will put a dual pricing system in place. Given the right circumstances and intent of management, a dual system can generate the desired combination of benefits.

## Grading Transfer Pricing Methods According to the Criteria

Having discussed the transfer pricing criteria and the methods commonly used, an assessment of the relative strengths and weaknesses is as follows:

| | Goal Congruence | Performance Evaluation | Autonomy | Administrative Cost |
|---|---|---|---|---|
| Market prices | Strong | Very Strong | Very Strong | Low, if available |
| Cost-based prices: | | | | |
|   Actual cost | Poor | Poor | Poor | Very Low |
|   Full cost plus profit | Poor | Average | Average | Low |
|   Variable cost | Strong | Very Poor | Poor | Often Low |
| Negotiated prices | Strong | Strong | Strong to Poor | High |
| Dual prices | Strong | Strong | Poor | High |
| | (Variable Cost) | (Market Price) | | |

Remember that specific cases can produce very different answers in each area. Clearly, no one transfer price serves all purposes. Managers must rank their priorities and select transfer pricing policies that fit the situation. Perhaps the goal really is to select a transfer pricing policy that creates the least disruption or adverse managerial behavior.

# MAXIMIZING INTERNATIONAL PROFITS: THE ROLE OF TRANSFER PRICES

"Buy low, and sell high" is the proverbial route to profits. However, other factors determine how much profit is kept and how much is taxed or restricted in global business. Income taxes, import duties, and limits on repatriation of profits are major components in creating complex international financial management problems. In a truly global world, goods and cash should flow across borders without restriction and without tariffs being imposed. Also, tax rates would be the same in all countries with little inflation and minimal changes in currency exchange rates. Absent these ideals, the company's controller must develop strategies to minimize financial risks and to maximize profits and cash flow. Historically, transfer pricing has been used to manipulate profit levels internationally.

Because a transfer between subunits of a firm does not occur at arm's length, manipulation of the transfer price can occur. Cost-based transfer prices can include, at management's discretion, more or fewer costs. Transfer prices for a multinational company are more complex because conditions differ in each country in which the company does business. Governments are concerned because transfer prices affect tax revenues. Companies are concerned because transfer prices affect direct cash flows for payments of goods, taxes, prices, and management performance evaluations.

Naturally, we want managers to make decisions that enhance company goal congruence. However, international transfer pricing goes beyond domestic needs to include:

- Minimization of world-wide income taxes and import duties.
- Avoidance of financial restrictions, including the movement of cash.
- Approvals from the host country.

Assume that Firm A in Country A and Firm B in Country B are subsidiaries of the same holding company, International Pearls. The following cases could exist:

1. If income tax rates are high in Country A and low in Country B, use a low transfer price for sales from Firm A to Firm B. More profits will be shifted to Firm B, lowering total tax payments.

2. If import duties are high for imports into Country B, use a low transfer price for sales from Firm A to Firm B. Low duties are paid; profits are higher.

3. If Country B restricts cash withdrawals from the country or imposes a tax on dividends paid to the holding company, use a high transfer price on sales from Firm A to Firm B. This allows a greater cash outflow from Country B through payments for purchases.

When these simple cases are fused and more issues are added, situations quickly become complex, particularly when revenue-hungry governments are involved.

## Minimization of World-Wide Taxes

Manipulation opportunities in the transfer price setting process mean taxable profits can be shifted from a country with high income tax rates to a country with lower taxes. For example, assume that the tax rate in Brazil is 50 percent, while the tax rate in the U.S. is 35 percent. A U. S. subsidiary of a multinational company sells a product to its sister subsidiary in Brazil. If we assume that a normal transfer price is $16 per unit but that the transfer price for units going into Brazil is set at $20 per unit, the U. S. subsidiary's profit will be higher by $4 per unit ($20 – $16) which is taxed at 35 percent. When the Brazilian subsidiary sells the units, its cost of goods is higher and profits are lower by $4 per unit. Therefore, $4 per unit is taxed at 35 percent, not 50 percent.

## Contemporary Practice 13.4
### *Transfer Pricing Methods of Multinational Companies*

A recent survey of U.S. multinational companies revealed the following transfer pricing methods used for domestic and international transfers:

| | Domestic Transfers (%) | International Transfers (%) |
|---|---|---|
| Cost-based methods: | | |
| Actual or standard variable production cost | 3.6% | 1.2% |
| Actual full production cost | 9.0 | 3.8 |
| Standard full production cost | 15.2 | 7.0 |
| Actual variable production cost plus a lump-sum subsidy | 0.9 | 1.3 |
| Full production cost (actual or standard) plus a markup | 16.6 | 26.8 |
| Other | 0.9 | 1.3 |
| Subtotal for cost-based methods | 46.2% | 41.4% |
| Market-based methods: | | |
| Market price | 25.1% | 26.1% |
| Market price less selling expenses | 7.6 | 12.1 |
| Other | 4.0 | 7.7 |
| Subtotal for market-based methods | 36.7% | 45.9% |
| Negotiated price | 16.6% | 12.7% |
| Other methods | 0.5% | 0% |
| Total—all methods | 100.0% | 100.0% |

*Source: Tang, R. Y. W., "Transfer Pricing in the 1990's,"* Management Accounting, *February 1992, p. 24.*

**International taxation** occurs when a domestic government imposes taxes on income or wealth generated within its boundaries by a company based in a foreign country. Also, taxes are levied on income earned by a domestic company from activities in foreign countries. A company is taxed in the foreign country and in the multinational's home-base country. For example, Pharmacia & Upjohn is a U.S.-based pharmaceutical firm with extensive global operations. It must comply with U.S. tax laws and tax laws of each country in which it does business.

International taxation has dramatic impacts on management decisions, such as where a company should invest; what form of business organization is used; what products are produced where; how prices and transfer prices are set; which currency should be used to denominate transactions, and what financing should be used. A firm must have professional expertise on its staff or available to review its tax status and the impacts that changes in tax treaties, agreements, laws, and regulations will have.

Governments and taxpayers are equally aware of tax minimization strategies. Tax laws in each country reduce the management accountant's flexibility. Even if we assume that they have a desire to be inherently fair, governments want to generate revenue, plug tax and cash-flow loopholes, get at least their share of tax revenues, promote specific types of economic growth, and perhaps build in subtle biases in favor of domestic firms.

The European Community (EC), General Agreement on Tariffs and Trade (GATT), North American Free Trade Agreement (NAFTA), and other bilateral and multilateral agreements have as their main themes encouraging free trade. While "free" means loosening many barriers, reducing or eliminating import duties and other cross-border taxes and fees is of major importance.

## Contemporary Practice 13.5
### Transfer Pricing—A Central Issue for Multinationals

"Two-thirds of the multinationals surveyed recently regard transfer pricing as the most important tax issue they face. Despite new transfer pricing guidelines from the Organization for Economic Cooperation and Development, half the 200-plus companies surveyed say they are currently involved in audits where transfer pricing is the central issue. Canada, Australia, and the UK are most likely to demand transfer pricing data that is difficult and costly to collect."

Source: Ernst & Young, "Going Global I: Beware Transfer Pricing Trap," Executive Upside, December 1996, p. 2.

### Avoidance of Financial Restrictions

Foreign governments often place financial restrictions on international subsidiaries operating within their boundaries. Government restrictions are placed on the amount of cash that may leave the country and for management fees charged by the parent company. Thus, moving profits and, therefore, "stuck" cash by high transfer prices can reduce those restricted profits and increase firm-wide liquidity and financial mobility.

### Gaining Host Country Approval

Governments are not naive. They are becoming sophisticated and aware of the results of using high or low transfer prices. Prices are compared to arms-length sales prices elsewhere. Products are analyzed for content. Price controls may be based on the transferred-in cost. For example, price increases may be limited by government regulators to cost increases. In the long run, companies find that transfer pricing policies which satisfy foreign authorities may be in the best interest of the company when compared to the greater profits that might be sacrificed. A foreign government's requirements about domestic ownership, percentage of locally produced content, and approval for government sales can be significant factors in determining how an international market is entered and how a company will operate there.

## SUMMARY

Many companies have sought to increase their financial performance by organizing themselves into an array of profit or investment centers. Decentralizing a company involves defining boundaries for organizational units, called responsibility centers, and delegating decision-making authority to the managers of these centers. Such a structure motivates managers to work for the benefit of the company, provides for front-line decision making by those nearest the action, enhances specialization by letting managers do what they do best, and reduces the span of control for management.

A control system is necessary if management wants to motivate its division managers and to evaluate performance. Measurements of expected performance level and of actual performance are the two essential ingredients for a control system. Since decentralized companies frequently place investment authority at the divisional level, performance measures should relate profitability to the amount of investment. Return on investment, residual income, and economic value added are approaches to divisional financial performance evaluation. Problems exist in defining both profit and investment.

Possible profit definitions include direct and controllable contribution margins. Possible investment definitions include net direct assets and managed assets.

Divisions within a company do not operate in isolation from one another; rather, they frequently do business as buyer and seller. Any time intracompany transactions occur, a transfer price must be attached to the transaction. Criteria of goal congruence, performance evaluation, autonomy, and administrative cost are developed to measure the strengths and weaknesses of each type of transfer price. Transfer prices can be market based, cost based, negotiated, or dual. No one method meets all criteria. Each has strengths and weaknesses depending on the importance of intracompany dealings and the priorities of management. Transfer pricing of goods and services moving among units of the same company and across borders takes on a meaning different from that of domestic transfer pricing.

## PROBLEMS FOR REVIEW

### Review Problem A

A division of Bakin's Office Rentals follows a pricing policy whereby normal activity is used as a basis for pricing. That is, prices are set on the basis of long-run annual volume predictions and market conditions. They are then rarely changed, except for notable changes in wage rates or supplies prices. The division controller, Shelley Greenberg, has provided the following data:

| | |
|---|---|
| Supplies, wages, and other variable costs | $ 5,000 per unit per year |
| Fixed overhead | $30,000,000 per year |
| Desired rate of return on invested capital | 20 % |
| Normal annual rental volume | 40,000 units |
| Invested capital | $90,000,000 |

**Required:**

1. What net income percentage based on revenues is needed to attain the desired rate of return?
2. What rate of return on invested capital will be earned at a rental volume of 35,000 units?
3. If rentals were to drop to 35,000 units, by what percentage must each of the following variables change from the normal level of 40,000 units to achieve the 20 percent rate of return?
   (a) Rental price.
   (b) Fixed overhead.
   (c) Return on revenues percentage.
   (d) Invested capital.

**Solution:**

1. Net income = Investment base × Return on investment
          = $90,000,000 × 20%
          = $18,000,000

To solve for the net income percentage, first find revenues necessary to earn the $18,000,000 net income:

| | |
|---|---|
| Net income | $ 18,000,000 |
| Plus: | |
| Variable cost (40,000 × $5,000) | 200,000,000 |
| Fixed cost | 30,000,000 |
| Revenues | $248,000,000 |

**Note:** The rental price is $6,200 per unit ($248,000,000 ÷ 40,000 units). This value is needed later in the solution.

$$\text{Net income percentage} = \text{Net income} \div \text{Revenues}$$
$$= \$18,000,000 \div \$248,000,000$$
$$= \underline{7.26\%}$$

2. Sales volume drops to 35,000 units:

| | |
|---|---:|
| Revenues (35,000 × $6,200) | $217,000,000 |
| Less: Variable cost (35,000 × $5,000) | −175,000,000 |
| Contribution margin | 42,000,000 |
| Less: Fixed cost | −30,000,000 |
| Net income | $12,000,000 |

$$\text{Return on investment} = \text{Net income} \div \text{Investment base}$$
$$= \$12,000,000 \div \$90,000,000$$
$$= \underline{13.33\%}$$

3. First, format the income statement for the normal volume of 40,000 units, with dollars and percentages:

| | | |
|---|---:|---:|
| Revenues (40,000 × $6,200) | $248,000,000 | 100.00% |
| Less: Variable cost (40,000 × $5,000) | −200,000,000 | 80.65% |
| Contribution margin | $ 48,000,000 | 19.35% |
| Less: Fixed cost | −30,000,000 | 12.10% |
| Net income | $ 18,000,000 | 7.25% |

Remember that this net income provides a 20 percent rate of return.

**Assume drop in volume to 35,000 units:**
**(a)** Change in rental price:

| | |
|---|---:|
| Net income | $ 18,000,000 |
| Plus: | |
| Variable cost (35,000 × $5,000) | 175,000,000 |
| Fixed cost | 30,000,000 |
| Revenues | $223,000,000 |
| Divided by volume in units | ÷ 35,000 |
| New rental price per unit | $6,372 |

This represents an increase of 2.77 percent over the original rental price of $6,200 per unit.
**(b)** Change in fixed overhead:

| | |
|---|---:|
| Revenues (35,000 × $6,200) | $217,000,000 |
| Less: Variable cost (35,000 × $5,000) | −175,000,000 |
| Contribution margin | $ 42,000,000 |
| Less net income | −18,000,000 |
| New fixed overhead | $ 24,000,000 |

This represents a decrease in fixed overhead of 20 percent over the original fixed overhead of $30,000,000.

(c) Change in return on revenues percentage:

Dividing the revenues figure of $223,000,000, from Part (a), into the net income figure of $18,000,000 gives a return on revenues percentage of 8.07. This represents an increase of 11.16 percent over the original return on revenues percentage of 7.26 ($18,000,000 ÷ $248,000,000).

(d) Change in invested capital:

$$\text{New investment base} = \text{Net income (from Part 2)} \div \text{ROI}$$
$$= \$12,000,000 \div .20$$
$$= \underline{\underline{\$60,000,000}}$$

This represents a decrease in investment base of 33.33 percent over the original investment base of $90,000,000.

## Review Problem B

The Broadway Company has several divisions. Division S produces (among other products) a metal container which is sold to customers who use it for shipping liquid chemicals. The main material used in manufacturing these containers is a metal which can be purchased from Division M, one of the other divisions of the company, or from several outside sources. Division S has received a customer order for 100 containers at $500 each. It will require two tons of materials to produce the 100 containers. The manager of Division S, Ed Bloom, requests bids for the materials required from Division M and from two outside companies. Division M, using a transfer price based on full cost, bids a price of $8,000 per ton on the materials order. Division M's variable cost is only $4,500 per ton, and it has excess capacity. However, Division M regularly bases price bids on full cost, whether the order is from another division or from an outside customer.

The two outside companies bid $6,000 and $6,500 per ton. However, the Gilmer Company, which bid $6,500, would buy the manufacturing supplies necessary to produce the materials from Division P, another division of the Broadway Company. The supplies would amount to $1,500 per ton of materials required. Division P's variable cost is about $800 per ton with a $200 freight charge for the total shipment.

**Required:**

1. What would you expect Division S to do? Explain.
2. Will Division S accept the right outside bid? Explain.
3. Should Division M's transfer pricing policy be changed? If so, how?

**Solution:**

1. Division S has a $50,000 order for containers. The manager is seeking the cheapest source of the required two tons of materials. Faced with bids of $16,000 (2 × $8,000) from Division M, $12,000 (2 × $6,000) from one outside company, and $13,000 (2 × $6,500) from the Gilmer Company, the manager will most likely accept the $12,000 bid.
2. No. The best bid is that of the Gilmer Company. The net cost to the whole company is the bid price of $13,000 minus the profit that will accrue to Division P of $1,200:

| | | |
|---|---|---|
| Revenue (2 tons × $1,500) | | $3,000 |
| Variable cost (2 tons × $800) | $1,600 | |
| Fixed cost | 200 | 1,800 |
| Profit | | $1,200 |

This means the net bid from the Gilmer Company is actually $11,800 ($13,000 − $1,200). This is $200 lower than the bid from the other outside company of $12,000.

3. If transfer prices were based on variable cost, Division S would receive an improved set of signals for decision purposes. The variable cost of two tons is $9,000 (2 tons × $4,500), which is lower than either outside bid; and excess capacity exists in Division M. Some motivational reason may exist for Division M not to use variable cost; but in the absence of such a reason, a transfer price based on variable cost, variable cost plus opportunity cost, or a profit-sharing factor would be an improvement.

## TERMINOLOGY REVIEW

Asset turnover (529)

Cost-based transfer pricing (539)

Cost centers (527)

Decentralization (527)

Decentralized company (526)

Division controllable contribution
  margin (530)

Division direct contribution margin (530)

Division net profit (530)

Division variable contribution
  margin (530)

Dual transfer pricing system (542)

Economic value added (EVA) (534)

Full-cost transfer price (539)

Goal congruence (531)

International taxation (544)

Investment base (530)

Investment centers (527)

Market price (538)

Minimum desired rate of return (534)

Negotiated transfer prices (541)

Profit centers (527)

Residual income (533)

Responsibility center (527)

Return on investment (ROI) (529)

Return on sales (ROS) (529)

Transfer price (536)

Variable-cost transfer prices (539)

## QUESTIONS FOR REVIEW AND DISCUSSION

1. What are the advantages of decentralization? What are the primary problems of decentralization?

2. Distinguish among a cost center, a profit center, and an investment center.

3. How is performance generally measured in a cost center? In a profit center? In an investment center?

4. Why is a cost budget not a good control measure in evaluating a division manager who has decision power on prices and marketing products?

5. What are some problems in using division profit as an evaluation measure?

6. Explain the difference between division controllable profit and division direct profit.

7. Identify and explain allocation problems involved in determining a profit measure and the investment base for calculating ROI.

8. When comparing various divisions, why is it important that the divisions have the same or similar accounting methods? Cite three examples of accounting methods that could cause divisions' profits to differ.

9. List the components of the ROI equation, tell how they are related, and identify an action a manager can take regarding each component to improve ROI.

10. How is residual income defined? What is the major advantage of using residual income versus ROI in performance evaluation?

11. Identify the major factors necessary in conceptually defining profit centers for promoting decentralization in an organization.

12. What is a transfer price? Under what conditions are transfer prices necessary?

13. Identify four criteria that are useful in evaluating transfer prices for intracompany transactions.

14. Using the criteria for evaluating transfer prices, evaluate each of the following transfer prices:
    (a) Market price.
    (b) Actual cost.
    (c) Standard full cost.
    (d) Cost plus a profit percentage.
    (e) Variable cost.
    (f) Negotiated price.

15. Explain and comment on the following paragraph from a recent publication:

    A pseudo-profit center is one that is artificially carved out of an organization by management, such as making the maintenance department in a factory a profit center. The primary advantage of a pseudo-profit center is that it captures the motivational advantages of real profit centers. But an analysis of pseudo-profit centers shows that the transfer pricing techniques used to create them can cause motivational disadvantages that completely overshadow any perceived advantages. Frequently, pseudo-profit centers will motivate managers to act in a dysfunctional manner.

16. If a market-based transfer price can be determined, why is such a price usually considered the best one to use?

17. Briefly describe a dual transfer price. What are the advantages and disadvantages of implementing such a pricing system?

18. If the intermediate market is perfectly competitive, will a market-based transfer price ever lead to suboptimal profits in the producing division? Explain.

19. What is the disadvantage of negotiated transfer prices when no intermediate market exists for the producing division?

20. If a full-cost transfer price does not produce an optimal profit for the firm, why is it so popular?

21. Why is an international transfer price often not the result of an arm's-length transaction?

22. How might product costs be changed to produce higher or lower costs per unit?

23. Give an example of how transfer prices could be used to minimize world-wide taxation.

# EXERCISES

Service

**13–1. Profit Measures.** The following data are from the Personal Injury Division of a law firm, Ezor & Associates:

| | |
|---|---|
| Revenues | $95,000 |
| Division variable cost | 48,000 |
| Allocated home office overhead | 7,000 |
| Fixed overhead traceable to division ($5,000 is controllable, and $15,000 is not controllable) | 20,000 |

**Required:**
Calculate division variable contribution margin, division controllable contribution margin, division direct contribution margin, and division net profit.

**13–2. Comparison of ROI and Residual Income.** The Electricity Division of North Shore Utilities reported operating income of $2,400,000 per year based on an investment of $12,000,000. The company is considering the use of ROI or residual income as an evaluation measure. At the present time, the division manager, Julie Evanamy, is faced with a decision on an incremental investment of $4,000,000 which will increase annual operating income by $700,000 per year.

**Required:**

Provide calculations showing the difference between the two performance measures, and explain the possible advantage of using residual income assuming that a 15 percent ROI is considered minimally acceptable.

**13–3. Valuing Assets.** Stanley Hoffman, the president of Rivchew Carpet Cleaners, has returned from an executive management seminar in Los Angeles. He sees you in the office coffee lounge and says, "As I read and hear more and more on valuing assets, I am increasingly bewildered by the 'language of accounting.' Yes, I understand historical cost and its problems. But you accountants also mix and match terms like market value, replacement value, economic value, present value, opportunity value, disposal value, entry value, and more values! You seem to have extra time since I see you here in the lounge a lot. Maybe you could help clear up this confusion for me by writing a memo that lays out how these terms can help us to make decisions about divisional performance and about keeping or selling these assets and to inform our shareholders about our performance."

**Required:** Respond to the president's request.

**13–4. ROI and Residual Income.** Provide the missing data for the following divisions of La Societe du Quebec, a company that owns hotels, taverns, and skating rinks (monetary amounts are in Canadian dollars):

|  | Divisions | | | |
| --- | --- | --- | --- | --- |
|  | **Un** | **Deux** | **Trois** | **Quatre** |
| Net income | ? | C$500,000 | ? | C$ 300,000 |
| Investment base | C$1,500,000 | ? | C$2,000,000 | C$3,000,000 |
| ROI | ? | 20% | 12.5% | ? |
| Imputed rate | 6% | 18% | ? | ? |
| Residual income | C$ 15,000 | C$ ? | C$ (50,000) | C$ 0 |

**13–5. ROI and Residual Income.** Puffino Life & Casualty is a large insurance company headquartered in Milan, Italy and has 14 divisions. The company has a 15 percent minimum desired rate of return. Its Residential Insurance Division has an investment base of 700,000 euros. During the current year, this division earned a residual income of 90,000 euros and had a return on sales of 8 percent.

**Required:**
**1.** Compute the division's ROI for the current year.
**2.** Compute the division's asset turnover for the current year.

**13–6. Investment Decision and Ethics.** Minsk Brothers is a securities brokerage firm with four autonomous divisions. ROI is used to evaluate each division. Cash bonuses are given to division managers who have the highest ROI figures at year end. The firm's minimum desired rate of return is 15 percent. The Southeast Division's projected operating results for this year are as follows:

| | |
|---|---:|
| Revenues | $5,000,000 |
| Variable expenses | 3,000,000 |
| Variable contribution margin | 2,000,000 |
| Direct fixed expenses | 1,600,000 |
| Direct contribution margin | $ 400,000 |

The Southeast Division has $1,200,000 of total direct assets. Early this year, Donald Malcolm, the manager of the Southeast Division, was presented with the following investment proposal:

| | |
|---|---:|
| Additional direct assets required | $ 500,000 |
| Additional revenues anticipated | $1,000,000 |
| Additional variable expenses | 60% of revenues |
| Additional fixed expenses | $ 300,000 |

**Required:**

1. Would Donald Malcolm be likely to accept the proposed investment? Explain with supporting computations.
2. Discuss the ethical issues that Donald Malcolm would face.

Service

**13–7. ROI and Divisional Charges.** The following three charges are found on the monthly report of a division of Ed Leader Enterprises. This division provides financial services primarily to outside companies. Division performance is evaluated using ROI.

(a) A charge for general corporation administration at 10 percent of division revenues.
(b) A charge for the use of the corporate computer facility. The charge is determined by taking actual annual computer department costs and allocating an amount to each user based on the ratio of divisional hours used to total corporate hours used.
(c) A charge for services provided by another division. The charge is based on a competitive market price for similar services.

**Required:**

Are any of these charges consistent with responsibility accounting and managerial performance evaluation? Explain.

Service

**13–8. ROI and Residual Income.** Iacullo Podiatry Clinic ("Time wounds all heels") provides the following information:

| | |
|---|---:|
| Cost of assets | $800,000 |
| Annual profit before depreciation expense | $480,000 |
| Desired rate of return | 14% |
| Annual depreciation expense | $ 40,000 |

For purposes of determining ROI and residual income, the clinic uses the book value of assets at the beginning of a year.

**Required:**

1. Compute ROI for the third year.
2. Compute residual income for the seventh year.

Service

**13–9. Economic Value Added.** Bill Robbins & Associates is an engineering firm with four divisions, each of which has a cost of capital of 15 percent. One of its divisions, Civil Engineering, had an EVA of $5 million in 2007. This division had total capital of $20 million, which included an addition of $2 million in research and development costs.

**Required:** Determine the adjusted accounting profit for the Civil Engineering Division.

**13–10. Selecting a Transfer Price.** The following information is available for Division X of Accortt Enterprises:

| | |
|---|---|
| Selling price to outside customers | $    74 |
| Variable cost per unit | $    60 |
| Total fixed costs | $330,000 |
| Capacity in units | 29,000 |

Division Y would like to purchase internally from Division X. Division Y now purchases 4,400 units each year from other companies at $71 per unit. Division X has enough excess capacity to handle all of Division Y's needs.

**Required:**
From the perspective of the Division X manager, what is the lowest price that should be accepted for units transferred to Division Y? Explain.

**13–11. Decision Based on a Transfer Price.** The following information is available for Division A of Copeland Corporation:

| | |
|---|---|
| Selling price to outside customers | $ 31 |
| Variable cost per unit | $ 20 |
| Fixed cost per unit (based on capacity) | $4.25 |
| Capacity in units | 17,000 |

Division B would like to purchase 5,000 units each year from Division A. Division A has enough excess capacity to handle all of Division B's needs. Division B now purchases from an outside supplier at a price of $28 and insists that it should be charged that same price by Division A.

**Required:**
If Division A refuses to accept the $28 price for transfers to Division B, what effect would this have on the annual profit of Copeland Corporation?

**13–12. Transfer Price Based on Full Cost.** The Shomovic Company has a division which produces a single product that sells for $26 per unit in the external market. The full cost of the product is $18, calculated as follows:

| | |
|---|---|
| Variable materials and labor cost per unit | $14 |
| Fixed cost per unit | 4* |
| Total cost per unit | $18 |

* Total fixed cost of $400,000 divided by current production and sales of 100,000 units.

Another division has offered to buy 20,000 units at the full cost of $18. The producing division has excess capacity, and the 20,000 units can be produced without interfering with the current external sales volume of 100,000 units. The total fixed costs of the producing division will not change as a result of the order. The producing division manager, Eugene Friedman, is inclined to reject the order, feeling that the division's profit position will not improve.

**Required:**
Explain to the producing division manager, supported by calculations, the impact of transferring 20,000 units at the full cost of $18 per unit.

**13–13. Transfer Prices and Decision Making.** Division 1 of Joel Marks & Company produces 100,000 units of a product with a variable cost of $5 per unit and a fixed cost of $3 (based on $300,000 allocated to 100,000 units). These units can be sold in an intermediate market for $1,000,000 ($10 per unit) or transferred to Division 2 for additional processing and sold in a finished market. The selling price of the fully processed units is $14, and the additional processing cost in Division 2 is $1.50 per unit. The fixed costs in Division 2 total $100,000. At this time, excess capacity exists in Division 2 if the units are not transferred.

**Required:**

Should the 100,000 units be sold by Division 1 or processed further and sold by Division 2? Would a transfer price based on either market price or variable cost be likely to lead to the right decision? Explain.

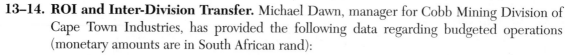

Service

**13–14. ROI and Inter-Division Transfer.** Michael Dawn, manager for Cobb Mining Division of Cape Town Industries, has provided the following data regarding budgeted operations (monetary amounts are in South African rand):

| | | |
|---|---|---|
| Average direct assets: | | |
| | Receivables | R100,000 |
| | Inventories | 300,000 |
| | Plant and equipment, net | 200,000 |
| | Total | R600,000 |
| Fixed overhead | | R200,000 |
| Variable costs | | R1.00 per gram of ore |
| Desired ROI on average direct assets | | 20% |
| Expected volume | | 100,000 grams of ore |

**Required:**

1. What average sales price per gram is needed to obtain the desired rate of return on average direct assets?

2. Assume that 30 percent of the 100,000 grams is sold to another division of the same company. The other division manager has balked at a tentative selling price of R4.00. He has offered R2.25, claiming that he can obtain the ore elsewhere for that price. The manager of Cobb Mining Division has examined his data. He has decided that he could eliminate R40,000 of inventories, R60,000 of plant and equipment, and R20,000 of fixed overhead if he did not sell to the other division. Should he sell for R2.25? Show computations to support your answer and briefly explain your reasoning.

**13–15. Transfer Pricing Problem.** Grey Company has a production division which is currently manufacturing 120,000 units but has a capacity of 180,000 units. The variable cost of the product is $22 per unit, and the total fixed cost is $720,000 or $6 per unit based on current production.

The Sales Division of the Grey Company offers to buy 40,000 units from the Production Division at $21 per unit. The Production Division manager, Debby Green, refuses the order because the price is below variable cost. The Sales Division manager, Verna Black, argues that the order should be accepted since by taking the order the Production Division manager can lower the fixed cost per unit from $6 to $4.50. (Output will increase to 160,000 units.) This decrease of $1.50 in fixed cost per unit will more than offset the $1 difference between the variable cost and the transfer price.

**Required:**

1. If you were the Production Division manager, would you accept the Sales Division manager's argument? Why or why not? (Assume that the 120,000 units currently being produced sell for $30 per unit in the external market.)
2. From the viewpoint of Grey Company, should the order be accepted if the manager of the Sales Division intends to sell each unit to the outside market for $27 after incurring an additional processing cost of $2.25 per unit? Explain.

Service

**13–16. Profit Centers and Transfer Prices.** Dave Silverman Automobile Dealership is installing a responsibility accounting system with three profit centers: Parts and Service, New Vehicles, and Used Vehicles. The department managers were told to run their shops as if they were in business for themselves. However, interdepartmental dealings frequently occur. For example:

**(a)** The Parts and Service Department prepares new cars for final delivery and repairs used cars prior to resale.

**(b)** The Used Vehicle Department's major source of inventory is cars traded in as partial payment for new cars.

**Required:**

The owner of the dealership, Dave Silverman, has asked you to outline criteria for a company policy statement on transfer pricing, together with specific rules to be applied to the common examples cited. He has told you that clarity is of paramount importance because your criteria will be relied on for settling transfer-pricing disputes.

**13–17. Decentralization and Transfer Pricing Policy Implications.** Assume you are concerned about managing corporate profitability as well as divisional decentralization and autonomy. Comment on each of these:

**(a)** From the viewpoint of the corporation, does any general transfer-pricing rule lead to the maximization of corporate profits?

**(b)** Why might a division manager reject a cost reduction proposal with a positive net present value, preferring instead to retain an inefficient old asset?

**(c)** Many firms use cost-plus or negotiated transfer prices even though they do not lead to optimal results for individual products. Why?

**(d)** Competitive market prices are often thought to be ideal transfer prices. Is this true? Explain your answer.

**(e)** Why might it be said that the goal of a divisional manager performance evaluation system should be to "create the least amount of dysfunctional behavior" by the individual manager?

Service

**13–18. Evaluating Transfer Prices.** Princeton Enterprises runs a chain of drive-in hamburger stands in Philadelphia during the summer season. Each stand's manager is told to act as if the stand will be judged on its own profit performance. Princeton has set up a separate business to rent a soft ice cream machine for the summer and to supply its burger stands with ice cream for their frappes. Rent for the machine is $1,000. Princeton is not allowed to sell ice cream to other dealers because it cannot obtain appropriate licenses. The manager of the ice cream business, Willie Green, charges the stands $3 per gallon. Operating figures for the machine for the summer are as follows:

| | | |
|---|---:|---:|
| Sales to the stands (10,000 gallons × $3) | | $ 30,000 |
| Variable costs, $1.60 per gallon | $ 16,000 | |
| Fixed costs: | | |
| Rental of machine | 1,000 | |
| Other fixed costs | 4,000 | 21,000 |
| Operating margin | | $  9,000 |

The manager of Clam Bar, one of the Princeton drive-ins, is seeking permission to sign a contract to buy ice cream from an outside supplier at $2.40 a gallon. The Clam Bar uses 2,000 gallons of soft ice cream during the summer. Adele Herman, controller of Princeton Enterprises, refers this request to you. You determine that other fixed costs of operating the machine will decrease by $500 if Clam Bar purchases from an outside supplier. Herman wants an analysis of the request in terms of overall company objectives and an explanation of your conclusion.

**Required:** Evaluate these transfer prices: $3.00, $2.40, $2.10, and $1.60. Recommend a price. Explain.

**13–19. Transfer Prices and Income Statements.** Weissman Company has two divisions, M and S. Division M manufactures a product, and Division S sells it. The intermediate market is competitive. But the product can be processed further and sold or stored for later processing and sale. Once the product is manufactured, some of it is sold by Division M; and some is transferred to Division S which decides whether to hold or to process and sell the product. The following information pertains to the current year:

| | |
|---|---:|
| Division M manufacturing cost for 1,200,000 units | $7,200,000 |
| Of the 1,200,000 units produced: | |
|    Sold by M in intermediate market—600,000 units | 6,000,000 |
|    Held by S for later sale—200,000 units (no additional | |
|       processing work done on these units in Division S) | 2,000,000 |
|    Processed by S and sold—400,000 units | 7,200,000 |
| Intermediate market value of 600,000 units when transferred to S | 6,000,000 |
|    Total additional processing costs of S | 1,300,000 |

Assume no beginning inventories.

**Required:**
1. Prepare an income statement for the whole firm.
2. Prepare a separate income statement for each division using a cost-based transfer price.
3. Prepare a separate income statement for each division using a market-value transfer price.

**13–20. Profit Impact of Various Transfer Prices.** Porath Oil Company has just decentralized its Refining and Marketing divisions. Refining is allowed to sell to outside wholesalers, while Marketing is permitted to buy from other refiners. Porath Oil produces only unleaded gasoline at a variable refinery cost of $0.30 per gallon and a fixed refining cost of $160,000 per month for a capacity of 400,000 gallons. The market price in the intermediate market is $1.00 per gallon. Marketing sells the fuel to independent service stations at $1.20 per gallon and incurs transportation costs of $0.10 per gallon.

**Required:**
Assuming all refined gallons are sold to Marketing, show the impacts on profits for Refining, Marketing, and Porath Oil Company as a whole when using each of the following transfer prices: (a) variable cost, (b) market price, and (c) full cost. What conclusion can you draw?

Service

**13–21. Transfer Pricing Problem.** The tailor shop in Sons of the Desert, a men's clothing store, is set up as an autonomous unit. The transfer price for tailoring services is based on variable cost which is estimated at $12 per hour. The store manager, Howard Newman, feels that the Suit and Sport Coat Department is currently using too much tailor time and that this department could cut down on hours used by taking more care in fitting the garments. Newman has decided to double the hourly tailor rate even though this new rate will be no reflection of the real variable cost. The idea is simply to provide an incentive to the Suit and Sport Coat Department to conserve on tailor time.

**Required:**

2. What possible disadvantages do you see in the store manager's action? Do you agree or disagree with this means of stressing the need to conserve tailor time? Why?

3. Would it make any difference if the various selling departments were not required to use the tailor shop and were allowed to take their work to some outside tailor shop? Explain.

Service

**13–22. Allocation of Cost or Transfer Price.** Adler Furniture Leasing has several operating divisions which are largely autonomous as far as decision making is concerned. The central corporate office consists mainly of the president and immediate staff. The annual cost is $1,000,000, and this cost is fixed. In calculating division profit, this cost is allocated to divisions on the basis of sales. The current allocation rate is $0.04 per sales dollar based on the company-wide normal sales volume of $25,000,000 per year. David Stuart, the company controller, does not consider this to be a transfer price because he feels that the divisions are not really buying anything. In Stuart's view, the charge is a method of allocating cost which should be absorbed by the divisions when they calculate their annual net income.

**Required:**

Do you agree with Mr. Stuart? In what sense is the charge a transfer price? Could the charge affect the decision of a division manager considering a new product with a variable cost of $5.50 and a selling price of $8? Explain.

Service

**13–23. Transfer Pricing.** Koch Enterprises is an import company which purchases men's shirts in the Far East and sells them in the U.S. The company's Acquisition Division sells to over 200 retail and wholesale establishments. In addition, Koch supplies its own Wholesale Division, which also purchases merchandise from other vendors. The following July data pertains to Koch's Acquisition Division:

| | |
|---|---|
| Selling price to outside retailers and wholesalers | $ 12 |
| Variable cost per shirt | $ 5 |
| Total fixed costs | $7,000 |
| Capacity (number of shirts) | 16,000 |

Currently, the Acquisition Division is selling all it can purchase to outside retailers and wholesalers. If it sells to the Wholesale Division, $0.75 can be avoided in variable cost per shirt. The Wholesale Division is currently purchasing from an outside supplier at $11.50 per shirt.

**Required:**

1. From the point of view of the Acquisition Division, any sales to the Wholesale Division should have a price of at least how much?

2. Use the same facts as in Part (1) except that the Acquisition Division can sell only 10,000 shirts to outside retailers and wholesalers. How would your answer to Part (1) change?

**13–24. International Transfer Pricing Problem.** Volkswerke is a Swiss subsidiary of a German company. In a normal month, Volkswerke produces 100,000 units of product with a variable cost of SFr12 per unit and fixed costs of SFr8 per unit (based on SFr800,000 of fixed costs allocated to production). These units can be sold in Switzerland for SFr26 per unit or transferred to the German subsidiary for additional processing and sold in a processed form. The selling price processed is 34 euros. The cost to complete the additional processing is 6 euros per unit. The fixed cost of processing is 300,000 euros. The current exchange rate between francs and euros is one Swiss franc to 0.90 euros. If the product is not transferred, the German subsidiary would have excess capacity.

**Required:**

1. Should the Swiss production be transferred to the German subsidiary or sold locally? Explain your answer.
2. Explain how a transfer price could be used to move cash from Switzerland to Germany, assuming Switzerland does not like to see money leave the country.

**13–25. Goal Congruent Transfer Pricing.** The Wartell Division of Wolchan Ski Products makes and sells a single product. The annual production capacity is 35,000 units and the variable cost to make each unit is $30. Currently, the Wartell Division sells 32,000 units per year to outside customers for $42 per unit. All selling costs are fixed. The Zangwill Division would like to purchase 15,000 units a year from Wartell.

**Required:**

According to the goal congruent transfer pricing formula, what unit price should the Wartell Division charge the Zangwill Division?

# PROBLEMS

Service

**13–26. ROI and Residual Income.** Ben Hirsch Properties, Inc. has three divisions. Division managers are given bonuses based on ROI figures. Last year's operating results for the Apartment Division, which had $12,000,000 in assets, were:

| | |
|---|---:|
| Revenues | $60,000,000 |
| Less: Variable expenses | − 42,000,000 |
| Contribution margin | $18,000,000 |
| Less: Fixed expenses | − 14,000,000 |
| Operating profit | $ 4,000,000 |

The company had an overall ROI last year of 17 percent. The Apartment Division has an opportunity to add another building which would require an additional asset investment of $3,500,000. Revenues and costs relating to the new investment would be:

| | |
|---|---|
| Revenues | $11,000,000 |
| Variable expenses | 70% of revenues |
| Fixed expenses | $2,500,000 |

**Required:**

1. As manager of the Apartment Division, would you accept or reject the new investment? Explain, providing appropriate computations.
2. As president of the company, would you want the Apartment Division to accept or reject the new investment? Explain.
3. Suppose the company views an ROI of 13 percent as being the minimum that should be earned by any division, and the company evaluates performance by the residual income approach. Under these conditions, as manager of the Apartment Division, would you accept or reject the new investment? Explain, providing appropriate computations.

Service

**13–27. Capital Budgeting and ROI.** Ashburn, Inc. has a division which performs telemarketing services for clients throughout the U.S. The income statement of this division is as follows:

| | | |
|---|---:|---:|
| Revenues | | $17,000,000 |
| Less: Division costs: | | |
|     Variable cost | $12,000,000 | |
|     Fixed cost | 4,000,000 | 16,000,000 |
| Division contribution margin | | $ 1,000,000 |
| Less: Allocated central office overhead | | 500,000 |
| Net income | | $ 500,000 |
| Investment allocated to division | | $ 5,000,000 |
| ROI | | 10 percent |

The management is disturbed about the low ROI. The corporate treasurer, Doreen Burton, indicates that the company can earn at least 20 percent on investment funds from any number of other projects. Furthermore, Burton points out that the investment is actually understated because the facility carried at a cost of $5,000,000 could be disposed of for about $8,000,000.

An investigation reveals that 50 percent of the division's fixed cost of $4,000,000 cannot be eliminated even if the division is sold. The allocated central office overhead is a pro-rata share of operating the corporate offices, and sale of the division would not affect this cost either.

**Required:**

1. Assuming that an expenditure of $1,000,000 annually would maintain the facility in good operating condition for at least 10 years, should the division be sold? Explain.
2. If not, does a better way of reporting the ROI exist that would alert management to consider selling if volume begins to decline? Describe.

**13–28. Allocation of Central Office Overhead.** The Skokie Company has several departments which operate quite autonomously as far as decision making is concerned. The company allocates central office overhead to these operating departments based on the total labor dollars incurred by each. The central office overhead budget and the allocation rate are as follows:

| | |
|---|---:|
| Executive offices | $ 200,000 |
| Legal | 70,000 |
| Advertising | 60,000 |
| Personnel | 100,000 |
| Accounting | 70,000 |
| Total | $ 500,000 |
| Total estimated payroll in operating departments | $1,000,000 |

Allocation rate: $500,000 ÷ $1,000,000 = $0.50 per labor dollar

The central office overhead of $500,000 is considered to be a fixed cost. Also, once the rate is established, it is not changed for one year.

The engineering research department conducts research on certain engineering problems related to the company's products and issues reports to clients who request this service. The manager of this department, Beverly Russell, is faced with a need to hire two more technical assistants because of an increased workload. If Russell hires through the company's personnel department, these positions can be filled at a cost of $1,500 per month for each employee. However, the usual $0.50 per dollar of payroll will also be charged against the research department's budget for central office overhead. Russell discovers that it is possible to contract for technical services from an outside engineering firm which will furnish two technical assistants for as long as they are required, and the cost will be considered a consulting cost and not part of the division's payroll. The cost will be $2,000 per month for each assistant.

**Required:**

1. Is the central office overhead charge a transfer price? Explain.
2. What is the manager of the engineering research department likely to do? Show your calculations.
3. If the Skokie Company wants to continue to allocate central office overhead, advise the president how this might be done so as not to affect the hiring decisions of the various department managers.

**13–29. Transfer Pricing and Purchasing Decisions.** Fernhoff Corporation, manufacturer of specialized trailers for over-the-road and container shipping, is decentralized, with each product line operating as a divisional profit center. Each division head is delegated full authority on all decisions involving sales of divisional output both to outsiders and to other divisions of Fernhoff. The International Shipping Division (ISD) has always purchased its requirements for a particular trailer platform subassembly from the Highway Division (HD). However, when informed that the HD was increasing its price to $300, ISD management decided to purchase the subassembly from an outside supplier.

ISD can purchase a similar subassembly from a reliable supplier for $260 per unit plus an annual die maintenance charge of $20,000. HD insists that owing to the recent installation of some highly specialized equipment, which has resulted in high depreciation charges, it would not be able to make an adequate profit on its investment unless it charged $300. In fact, the ISD business was part of the justification for buying the new equipment. HD's management appealed to Vivian Sweetwood, the company's CEO, for support in its dispute with ISD and supplied the following operating data:

| | |
|---|---|
| ISD's annual purchases of subassembly | 2,000 units |
| HD's variable costs per unit of subassembly | $220 |
| HD's fixed costs per unit of subassembly | $ 65 |

**Required:**

1. Assume that no alternative use for HD's internal facilities exists. Determine whether the company as a whole will benefit if ISD purchases the subassembly from the outside supplier.
2. Assume that HD's internal facilities would not otherwise be idle. By using the capacity needed to produce the 2,000 units for ISD for other production, HD can earn $40,000 in contribution margin. Should ISD purchase from the outsider? Explain.
3. If the outside supplier drops the price by another $20 per unit, would your answer to either Part 1 or 2 change? If so, why?

**13–30. Changing a Cost Center to a Profit Center.** Les Lee, the president of Morris Company, has just attended a seminar on the use of responsibility centers. He is very anxious to put "competitive zeal" into every part of the organization. Lee is especially interested in making some of the service centers within the company into profit centers. It is decided that the Maintenance Department will be the first to be made into a profit center, and it is hoped that the experience gained will be helpful if other service centers are converted to profit centers.

A meeting has been called to discuss setting prices to be charged by the Maintenance Department to units that it serves. The manager of the Maintenance Department, Pete Asher, suggests a cost-plus basis for pricing, with labor and materials costs plus a 10 percent markup being charged to the unit requesting maintenance services. He argues that a markup over cost is needed to allow the department to become a profit center; otherwise there is no point in changing from the current status—that of a cost center.

Some managers of operating departments argue that a fee schedule for each kind of maintenance job should be established. Some think a reasonable approach would be to survey local industrial maintenance firms and use their prices less a percentage for cost savings. Others think that the whole idea only creates an "artificial profit center" and that the maintenance budget should just be divided among the operating departments. Most do not seem to like the cost-plus idea.

**Required:**
1. Evaluate each position. Are there other choices? If so, what?
2. what recommendation can you make?

**13–31. Transfer Pricing and Bids.** The Jay Division of Cinnamon Corporation expects the following results for the coming year on sales to outsiders:

| | | |
|---|---|---|
| Sales (100,000 units) | | $600,000 |
| Variable cost of sales | $300,000 | |
| Fixed cost of sales | 200,000 | 500,000 |
| Profit | | $100,000 |

Yesterday, Dennis Goldstein, the manager of the Ray Division, requested a bid from Jay for 30,000 units. Ray would perform additional work on each unit at a cost of $4 per unit and sell the end product for $9 per unit. Jay can make only 120,000 units per year and would have to forego some regular sales if the Ray business is accepted. Ray has an outside bid of $4.50 per unit.

**Required:**
1. What is the minimum bid Jay should make to Ray, and what transfer pricing goal is being optimized?
2. What is the maximum bid Jay should make to Ray, and what transfer pricing goal is being optimized?
3. If Ray buys from the outside supplier, does Cinnamon gain or lose and by how much?

Service

**13–32. Transfer Pricing for a Computer Facility.** Baltic National Bank of Vilnius, Lithuania, has a central computer facility which is used by several operating departments for data processing and problem-solving purposes. The facility's budget (in Lithuanian litas) for the current year is as follows:

| | | |
|---|---|---|
| Rentals | 1,200,000 | litas |
| Payroll, operators | 260,000 | |
| Payroll, programmers | 180,000 | |
| Payroll, supervision and secretarial | 90,000 | |
| Miscellaneous supplies | 120,000 | |
| Utilities | 250,000 | |
| Total | 2,100,000 | litas |

It is estimated that 20,000 computer time units will be available. All of the costs shown in the budget are considered to be fixed, except for utilities and miscellaneous supplies which are variable.

During the past five years, the computer facility has not been operated at full capacity. The percentage of capacity has increased from 40 percent in the first year of operation to an estimated 70 percent for the current year.

A transfer price policy has been established which calls for the use of a full cost per unit of time. Thus, an operating department that needs one half of a time unit would be charged at the rate of 52.50 litas [1/2 × (2,100,000 litas ÷ 20,000 time units)]. All operating departments do most of their own programming. The computer staff has four programmers who are used to solve special problems as they arise in the facility.

The associate director of the facility, Iluv Telshe, has approached Dora Litvak, the director, to revise the transfer price policy to include only the variable costs. His argument is that the operating departments would thereby be encouraged to make greater use of the facility. Litvak's response is that she sees no reason why this should be so. "After all," she points out, "the operating departments need only so much time anyway; and besides, the various managers cannot buy computer time outside of the bank. So how could the transfer price affect their behavior?"

The associate director's response is that he knows of several instances where the operating departments have secured outside programming services so that the program submitted would require less running time. "In fact," he says, "I know of one case where a commercial lending manager spent 300 litas on additional programming to save an estimated two time units of running time."

Litvak's response is, "He should have—after all, it cost us 105 litas every time we run the program!"

**Required:**

1. Do you agree with the associate director or the director? Explain.
2. Was the behavior of the commercial lending manager (as described by the associate director) optimal as far as the bank is concerned? Why or why not?
3. Assuming that the additional programming effort could not have been done inside the bank, what is the maximum price that the commercial lending manager should have paid?

Service

**13–33. Transfer Pricing and Divisional Income Statements.** Blech Packing Company has two divisions. Division 1 is responsible for slaughtering and cutting the unprocessed meat. Division 2 processes meat such as hams, bacon, etc. Division 2 can buy meat from Division 1 or from outside suppliers. Division 1 can sell at the market price all the unprocessed meat that it can produce. The current year's income statement for the company is as follows:

| | | | |
|---|---|---|---|
| Sales | | | $2,600,000 |
| Cost of goods sold: | | | |
| Beginning inventory | | $      0 | |
| Plus: Processing costs: | | | |
| Livestock costs, Division 1 | | $  600,000 | |
| Labor, Division 1 | | 400,000 | |
| Overhead, Division 1 | | 500,000 | |
| Processing supplies, Division 2 | | 200,000 | |
| Labor, Division 2 | | 300,000 | |
| Overhead, Division 2 | | 100,000 | |
| Cost of goods available for sale | | $2,100,000 | |
| Less ending inventory cost: | | | |
| Division 1 | $ 0 | | |
| Division 2 | 200,000 | 200,000 | 1,900,000 |
| Gross margin | | | $ 700,000 |
| Operating expenses: | | | |
| Sales & administrative, Division 1 | | $ 120,000 | |
| Sales & administrative, Division 2 | | 100,000 | |
| Central office overhead | | 100,000 | $ 320,000 |
| Income before income tax | | | $ 380,000 |

The ending inventory of $200,000 is valued at the product cost incurred in Division 1. This inventory is as yet unprocessed. The market value unprocessed is $300,000. The sales for the year can be broken down as follows:

| | |
|---|---|
| Division 1 (to outsiders) | $ 600,000 |
| Division 2 | 2,000,000 |
| | $2,600,000 |

The market value of the unprocessed meat actually transferred from Division 1 to Division 2 (exclusive of the ending inventory) was $1,800,000.

**Required:**
1. Prepare divisional income statements that might be used to evaluate the performance of the two division managers.
2. Explain the transfer pricing policy you have used in preparing the statements.
3. Can you see any conflict in the policy you have used if this same transfer price is to be used for decision making? Explain.

Service

**13–34. Transfer Pricing and Decision Making.** Neumeier Security Services (NSS) has three operating divisions. The Central Division installs high tech security systems for corporate clients throughout the country. Two other divisions, Electronics and Communications, produce components for the various security systems. One particular system requires one unit from Electronics and one unit from Communications. Data for this security system follow:

| | |
|---|---|
| Selling price (Central Division) | $8,000 |
| Variable costs: | |
| Electronics Division | $2,000 |
| Communications Division | 1,400 |
| Central Division | 800 |
| Total variable costs | $4,200 |
| Current volume | 10,000 systems |

The Electronics and Communications Divisions charge the Central Division $2,500 and $1,800, respectively, for each unit. The Central Division has been approached by an outside supplier who has offered to sell, for $2,300 per unit, the component now produced by the Electronics Division.

**Required:**
1. Prepare partial income statements, down to contribution margin, for each of the three divisions based on current operations.
2. Determine whether the outside supplier's offer should be accepted. If the Electronics Division meets the price offered by the outside supplier, Central will continue to buy from Electronics. Answer from the point of view of what's best for NSS.
3. Suppose that Electronics can sell its entire annual output of 10,000 units at a price of $3,000 if it performs additional work on the component. The additional work will add $500 to the unit variable cost while fixed costs will be unaffected. The capacity of the Electronics Division is 10,000 units. Determine the incremental contribution margin to NSS if Central is allowed to buy from the outside supplier.

**13–35. Transfer Pricing and Fixed Cost Allocation.** Hardy & Laurel, Inc. has a producing division (Division 1) which supplies several parts to another producing division (Division 2) which produces the main product. These component parts are listed as follows with relevant cost information, including outside supplier prices:

| Component No. | Variable Cost Per Unit | Quantity Produced | Outside Price |
|---|---|---|---|
| 1 | $11 | 25,000 | $14.50 |
| 2 | 15 | 35,000 | 19.20 |
| 3 | 7 | 15,000 | 9.40 |
| 4 | 5 | 15,000 | 9.60 |

The out-of-pocket fixed costs of Division 1 amount to $270,000. These costs consist of salaries and other overhead. In addition, fixed costs which are not out-of-pocket (consisting mainly of depreciation on machinery) amount to $90,000 per period. In calculating unit cost, total fixed costs of $360,000 are allocated based on units produced to arrive at a full cost.

A full-cost transfer price is used. In Division 2, which uses the four components, the manager, Lou Abbot, has authority to buy inside the company or from an outside supplier. The outside prices vary somewhat throughout the year.

After calculating the full cost, Abbot notices that outside purchase prices of Components 1 and 3 are lower than the transfer prices and places orders with an outside supplier, Hooze Onfirst Enterprises. The Division 1 manager, Bud Costello, stops producing these two components, reallocates fixed costs to the remaining units, and adjusts the full-cost transfer prices.

**Required:**
1. Reallocate fixed costs and determine the adjusted transfer prices based on full costs of the remaining products. If no communication between the two divisions occurs, what action will the manager of Division 2 likely take?
2. Comment on the deficiencies of the full-cost transfer price system.
3. What if the items transferred to Division 2 from Division 1 are 100 percent of Division 1's business? Devise a method of assigning the fixed cost of Division 1 to Division 2 that will not cause Division 2 to buy outside when the components could be produced by Division 1.
4. what if the items transferred to Division 2 from Division 1 are 4 percent of Division 1's total business? How would your answer to Part 3 change?

 **13–36. Evaluation of Alternative Transfer Prices.** James Thumb Company has a division that manufactures shafts, which are sold to other divisions and to outside customers. This division is organized into two sections as follows:

**Section 1—Machining and Grinding:** This highly mechanized section has much heavy equipment that is used to give shape to shafts and to perform grinding operations on shafts with special requirements.

**Section 2—Cleaning and Packing:** This section consists primarily of workers who clean and pack all shafts.

The costing system used by the company charges materials, direct labor, and overhead to each order. Labor, materials, and one-third of overhead in both sections are considered to be variable. The overhead is allocated on the basis of labor cost for normal activity levels. Furthermore, the rate is a division-wide rate, not by section. This rate is developed as follows:

| | Direct Labor Payroll | Overhead |
|---|---|---|
| Section 1 (70% of capacity) | $200,000 | $ 900,000 |
| Section 2 (60% of capacity) | 600,000 | 300,000 |
| Total division | $800,000 | $1,200,000 |

Overhead rate: $1,200,000 \div $800,000 = 150$ percent of labor cost

The average wage for Section 1 is $15 per hour; for Section 2, $10 per hour. A full-cost transfer price is used for selling shafts to other producing divisions. If an order is placed by another producing division that calls for $100 of materials and 2 hours of labor time in each section, the price that is quoted would be arrived at as follows:

|  | *Hours* | *Total* |
|---|---|---|
| Labor: | | |
| Section 1 | 2 | $ 30 |
| Section 2 | 2 | 20 |
| | | $ 50 |
| Overhead (150% × $50) | | 75 |
| Materials | | 100 |
| Transfer price | | $225 |

Larry Katz, the assistant to the controller, has been considering a change in the costing system whereby an overhead rate would be developed for each section. It is believed that such a system would give a more equitable price for the work done for other divisions and would be a better basis for pricing outside sales. Since the shaft sold to outside customers is competitive, the price is determined by bid and negotiations; and the primary factor in deciding whether to accept or reject business is the order's profit. At times, the division is operating near enough to capacity that outside work must be stopped if inside work is to be done.

At the moment, two orders are being considered and are from another division that can buy either inside or outside the company. The details on the two orders are:

|  | *Order 1* | *Order 2* |
|---|---|---|
| Materials | $500 | $200 |
| Labor: | | |
| Section 1 | 3 hours | 6 hours |
| Section 2 | 3 hours | 1 hour |

**Required:**
1. Calculate the transfer prices for the two orders under the present system. Then, calculate the transfer prices under the proposed system.
2. If the market prices were $700 for Order 1 and $600 for Order 2, how might management decisions in both buying and selling divisions be affected by the overhead system?
3. Recalculate the transfer prices for the two orders based on variable cost only. Assume a sectional variable overhead rate is used in the manufacturing division.
4. Which system do you prefer? Why?

**13–37. Transfer Price Decision.** The Metropolis Subsidiary of Kryptonite Instruments, Inc. manufactures a small printed circuit board, SuperBoard, and has the capacity to make 100,000 units each year. At the present time, only 75,000 units are being made each year and are sold to an outside customer, Perry White Industries, for $7.50 a unit.

Fixed manufacturing costs are applied on the basis of an annual production of 100,000 units each year. Total fixed costs for the year are $175,000. The total unit cost of each circuit board is $6.50. The Reeves Subsidiary has been purchasing this type of circuit board from an outside supplier, Lois Lane Enterprises, at a price of $7.50 per unit. The president of Kryptonite, Clark Kent, requests that the Metropolis Subsidiary deliver 25,000 circuit boards to the Reeves Subsidiary at a price equal to the variable cost.

The superintendent of Metropolis, Jimmy Olsen, states that the division gains no advantage by selling at variable cost. No contribution is made to the recovery of the fixed costs. Furthermore, Olsen states that the company gains nothing. The fixed costs of Metropolis must be recovered, and Reeves should pay the full price of $7.50 as it would by buying outside.

**Required:**
1. Is the argument of the superintendent valid? Explain.
2. What is the variable cost of manufacturing each circuit board?
3. Describe a pricing system that should benefit the company and be acceptable to each division.

**13–38. Internal Pricing Decision.** Irene Henry is the manager of the Sterling Division of Arnold Phillips Corporation. This division manufactures spring assemblies that are sold to various outside customers at a price of $32 per unit. Recently, the division has been operating at 550,000 machine hours. Normal capacity has been defined as 700,000 machine hours and is approximately equal to the practical capacity.

Each assembly requires 15 minutes of machine time. The direct materials and direct labor cost per assembly is $16.20, and overhead varies at the rate of $8.40 per machine hour. The total fixed overhead for the year is $3,521,000.

Henry's division has just been awarded a contract for the sale of 400,000 units in another country at a unit price of $26. This contract will not interfere with the regular sales at a price of $32, and it is anticipated that this contract can be renewed in future years.

The Jessop Division of the company has started production of a product line that will require 400,000 units of the spring assembly made by the Sterling Division. The president of Arnold Phillips Corporation, Alan William, states that the assemblies should be transferred between the divisions at the variable cost to the Sterling Division. If Sterling Division does not furnish the units, the Jessop Division will be forced to purchase the assemblies on the outside market at $32 apiece. With higher costs, Jessop will have lower profits on the sale of the end products.

**Required:**
1. Determine the variable cost to produce each spring assembly.
2. Under the circumstances, should the Sterling Division supply the Jessop Division? Explain.
3. What price should be used for the internal transfer, assuming a transfer should be made?

**13–39. Transfer Price Based on Full Cost.** The Casper Division of Dessler Company produces a large metal frame which is sold to the Cody Division. Cody Division uses these frames in constructing metal lathes which are sold to machine tool manufacturers. In Casper Division, the frames are produced in a stamping process and are then run through a finishing process in which they are trimmed and polished before being shipped to the Cody Division.

The current estimate of the variable cost of materials and labor to produce a frame in the stamping process is $120 per frame. Fixed overhead associated with this process in the Casper Division is $700,000 per year. Current production is 50,000 frames, which is full capacity for both the stamping and the trimming and polishing processes.

The variable cost of labor in the trimming and polishing process is $12 per frame since labor in this process is paid on a piece-rate basis. (No additional materials are required.) The fixed overhead in this process is $300,000 per year and is largely due to equipment depreciation and related costs. The machines have almost no salvage value because of their special-purpose design.

The transfer price to the Cody Division is a full-cost transfer price and is calculated by prorating the current fixed cost in each process over the 50,000 frames being produced. The price is quoted for each process and is presented to the manager as follows:

| | | |
|---|---:|---:|
| Stamping process: | | |
| Materials and labor cost per unit | $120 | |
| Fixed overhead cost per unit ($700,000 ÷ 50,000 units) | 14 | $134 |
| Trimming and polishing process: | | |
| Labor cost per unit | $ 12 | |
| Fixed overhead cost per unit ($300,000 ÷ 50,000 units) | 6 | 18 |
| Total cost per unit | | $152 |

An outside company, Seide Industries, has offered to rent to Cody Division machinery which would perform the trimming and polishing process. The rental cost of the machinery is $200,000 per year. With the new machinery, the labor cost per frame would remain at $12. The Cody Division manager, Irving Stone, sees the possibility of obtaining the frames from the Casper Division for $134 by eliminating the $18 cost of trimming and polishing and of performing these processes in the Cody Division. An analysis is as follows:

| | |
|---|---:|
| New process: | |
| Machine rental cost per year | $200,000 |
| Labor cost ($12 × 50,000 units) | 600,000 |
| Total Cody Division trimming and polishing costs | $800,000 |
| Current process: | |
| 50,000 units at $18 per unit (portion of the Casper Division transfer price attributable to trimming and polishing process) | $900 000 |

Irving Stone has approached the vice-president of operations for approval to acquire the new machinery.

**Required:**

**1.** As the vice-president, how would you advise Irving Stone?

**2.** Could the transfer pricing system be improved and, if so, how?

**13–40. Transfer Pricing and ROI.** Olga Industries is organized into eight decentralized divisions. The divisions generally do little business with one another.

Service

The Bondi Division installs and services heating systems in commercial buildings. In 2009, Bondi Division plans to operate at full capacity of 100,000 labor hours. The Bondi Division is evaluated on the basis of ROI. Peter Blair, the division's general manager, achieved a 42 percent ROI in 2008. The Bondi Division charges a rate of $50 per hour to its regular customers. It has variable costs of $35 per hour and currently has $310,000 invested in equipment.

The Manley Division has recently experienced a declining market share in the installation of swimming pools. As a result, Manley Division is currently operating at only 70 percent of its capacity. Olga's controller has informed Helen Richard, Manley's general manager, that capacity utilization needs to improve to at least 85 percent.

In response to these mounting pressures, the Manley Division has developed a new swimming pool design that greatly reduces maintenance costs. A national health club franchise has already agreed to install the pools at five of its locations. The new pools require heating systems that are complex to install. Manley's employees do not have the necessary expertise. Helen Richard believes that the Bondi Division's quality of service would be ideal for the task.

The new pools will be priced at $44,000, but the first five ordered by the health club franchise had an agreed upon introductory price of $38,000 each. Because of this discount, Richard has asked the Bondi Division to work on the first five pools at a reduced rate of $40 per hour. Richard has prepared the following computations:

| Regular Orders | | Introductory Order |
|---|---|---|
| $44,000 | Price | $38,000 |
| 6,250 | Heating System Installation | 5,000 |
| 30,000 | Other Incremental Cost | 30,000 |
| $36,250 | Total Cost | $35,000 |
| $ 7,750 | Profit | $3,000 |

**Required:**
1. If you were Peter Blair, would you agree to Helen Richard's request to supply heating installation at $40 per hour?
2. Determine the incremental profit to Olga Industries from the introductory order.
3. Evaluate the reasonableness of the proposed transfer price of $40 per hour.
4. Suppose that Bondi was not operating at full capacity and could service Manley without affecting other revenues. How would your answer to part (3) change?
5. Discuss the use of ROI for a service-oriented division like Bondi.

13–41. **Transfer Pricing in a Multinational Company.** Zanitski Farming Company has two units: the Mexican Division produces grain, and the U. S. Division sells the grain. As soon as the grain is produced, it is placed in storage areas until sold by the U. S. Division. A transfer price is used to charge the U. S. Division and to recognize the Mexican Division as a profit center.

During the year, three grain crops of 1,900,000 bushels each were produced. All three have now been sold, although some were held in inventory for various periods of time. The market prices (in pesos) at production time were M$10 per bushel for the first crop (M$1 = $0.34), M$12 per bushel for the second (M$1 = $0.35), and M$8 per bushel for the third (M$1 = $0.33). No beginning inventories were on hand. The Mexican producer uses a transfer price equal to the market price in pesos.

The results for the period are:

| | |
|---|---|
| Total company revenues (5,700,000 bushels) | $22,300,000 |
| Costs: | |
| Producing division (M$1 = $0.33): | |
| Labor and materials | $13,200,000 |
| Division overhead | 5,610,000 |
| Selling division: | |
| Labor | 900,000 |
| Division overhead | 900,000 |

The company president, Barry Heifitz, is pleased with the total profit (stated in U. S. dollars) generated by the two divisions. He wants to determine whether the price speculation activities of the selling division are earning a profit.

**Required:**
1. Prepare divisional income statements for each division, using the currency of the country where each operates. Which division is more profitable?
2. Would you use the market price or the cost for the transfer price? Explain.

**13–42. Transfer Prices to Minimize Global Taxes and Duties.** Reisman Company operates in three countries, Countries A, B, and C. All company divisions sell to other company divisions in the other two countries. The following is known about tax rates, import duties, and sales. (All dollar amounts in millions.)

|  | Country A | Country B | Country C |
| --- | --- | --- | --- |
| Tax rates on profits earned | 60% | 20% | 40% |
| Import duties | 10% | 70% | 40% |
| In-country sales | $ 50,000 | $100,000 | $200,000 |
| In-country cost of sales | 40,000 | 80,000 | 160,000 |
| Sales: |  |  |  |
| To Country A |  | 10,000 | 9,000 |
| To Country B | 10,000 |  | 3,000 |
| To Country C | 5,000 | 28,000 |  |

A number of assumptions must be made:

1. All intercompany sales figures include a 25 percent markup over costs. Also, variable costs are 40 percent of costs of sales for all sales.
2. Costs of sales does not include import duties.
3. Import duties are applied to the transfer price for imported goods.
4. Costs of imported goods are included in the cost of sales for each country. No inventories exist.

**Required:**

The corporate controller, Michael Carter, is considering a change in intercompany sales pricing practices to minimize global taxes and duties. Assuming that Carter decides that all intercompany sales must show at least a 10 percent profit on variable costs, suggest a transfer price that will minimize global taxes and duties.

# CASE 13A—MEISELS CORPORATION

Meisels Corporation, headquartered in Cleveland, is a highly diversified company organized into autonomous divisions along product lines. The autonomy permits division managers a significant amount of authority in operating their divisions. Each manager is responsible for sales, cost of operations, acquisition of division assets, management of accounts receivable and inventories, and use of existing facilities. Cash management is centralized at the corporate home office. Divisions are permitted cash for their normal operating needs, but all excess cash is transferred to the corporate home office in Cleveland.

Division managers are responsible for presenting requests for capital expenditures (to acquire assets, expand existing facilities, or make any other long-term investment) to corporate management for approval. Once the proposals are analyzed and evaluated, corporate management decides whether to commit funds to the requests.

Meisels Corporation adopted an ROI measure several years ago. The measure uses division direct profit and an investment base composed of fixed assets employed plus accounts receivable and inventories. ROI is used to evaluate the performance of each division, and it is the primary factor in assessing salary increases each year. Also, changes in the ROI from year to year affect the amount of the annual bonus.

ROI has grown over the years for each division. However, the company's overall ROI has declined in recent years. Cash balances are increasing at the corporate level, and investments in marketable securities are growing. Idle cash and marketable securities do not earn as good a rate of return as division capital investments.

Two of Meisels Corporation divisions—the Apparel Division and the Sports Gear Division—operate retail stores throughout the U. S. The following data (with 000s omitted) show the operating results for these divisions for the last three years:

| | Apparel Division | | | Sports Gear Division | | |
|---|---|---|---|---|---|---|
| | 2007 | 2008 | 2009 | 2007 | 2008 | 2009 |
| Estimated industry sales | $10,000 | $11,000 | $12,100 | $5,000 | $6,250 | $7,500 |
| Division sales | $ 1,200 | $ 1,380 | $ 1,587 | $ 500 | $ 650 | $ 780 |
| Division direct costs: | | | | | | |
|   Variable costs | $ 360 | $ 396 | $ 467 | $ 160 | $ 182 | $ 203 |
|   Discretionary fixed costs | 480 | 490 | 500 | 180 | 210 | 240 |
|   Committed fixed costs | 250 | 300 | 375 | 150 | 215 | 260 |
|   Total division direct costs | $ 1,090 | $ 1,186 | $ 1,342 | $ 490 | $ 607 | $ 703 |
| Division net profit | $ 110 | $ 194 | $ 245 | $ 10 | $ 43 | $ 77 |
| Investment base | $ 1,100 | $ 1,200 | $ 1,300 | $ 125 | $ 195 | $ 280 |
| ROI | 10.00% | 16.17% | 18.85% | 8.00% | 22.05% | 27.50% |

The managers of both divisions were promoted to their positions in 2007. Samson Gabor had been assistant division manager of the Apparel Division for six years prior to his appointment as manager of that division. The Sports Gear Division was created in 2005. David Kiva had served as assistant manager of the Toy Division for four years prior to becoming manager of the Sports Gear Division, when the latter position suddenly became available in late 2006.

**Required:**

1. In general, is ROI an appropriate measure of performance? Explain.
2. Explain how an overemphasis on ROI can result in a declining corporate ROI and in increasing cash and marketable securities.
3. Describe specific actions that might have caused this increase in 2009 divisional ROI while the corporate ROI declined.
4. Assuming the minimum desired rate of return is 12 percent for Apparel and 15 percent for Sports Gear, compute the residual income and the residual income as a percentage of the investment base for each division for each year.
5. Which division manager (Gabor or Kiva) do you judge as the better manager? What are your reasons?

# CASE 13B—ERCULEAN ELECTRONICS

Erculean Electronics is a division of a major communications equipment supplier. It designs, manufactures, assembles, and tests a wide variety of electronic linking assemblies. The largest percentage of its business is internal, meaning that about 45 percent of its assemblies becomes part of the division's own end products. But in the past few years, sales have gone to a growing array of customers including:

1. Other sister divisions producing complementary products.
2. Other communications companies, often direct competitors, that use similar assemblies with minor engineering changes.
3. Automotive firms and automotive suppliers who are incorporating more electronic communications components into their products.

4. Appliance manufacturers who use specialized linkages in their electronic products.

5. Numerous international manufacturers in each of the above industries.

   In short, Erculean is enjoying success in a very specialized market. The keys to its success are high-quality products, an ability to adapt to a customer's needs quickly (sometimes in days), and highly dependable delivery to most customers on narrow just-in-time schedules. Another factor has been Erculean's manufacturing prowess. It has always been cost conscious and on the edge of manufacturing technology and processes.

   Manufacturing has expanded rapidly to meet the growth in demand. Also, since its original plants were in the high labor cost Midwest, it has sought relief in numerous ways. A brief description of its current manufacturing locations and capabilities introduces the problems facing Erculean managers:

1. The Jackson, Michigan, plant is older but highly automated; and its production employees work under an Automotive Workers Union contract that guarantees its members 2,000 hours per year of employment. It is within 200 miles of 40 percent of Erculean customers. The number of workers at this plant has dropped from over 800 in 1984 to about 225 today. Most of these workers are very experienced and have adapted very well to the increased automation and robotics introduced in the late 1990s. Worker classifications have been reduced in the latest contract by 75 percent. But the average cash wage is over $15 per hour, and the fully-loaded rate is nearly $30 per hour.

2. A Tulsa, Oklahoma, plant was built in the mid-1980s and is also highly automated; and, since 1998, its employees are represented by the International Electric Workers Union. The average cash wage is about two-thirds of the Jackson plant, and the fully-loaded rate is about half of the Jackson plant. Few worker classifications exist, and the definition of "direct labor" differs considerably from the Jackson definition.

3. Outside subcontractors are used for certain products and when company plants are operating at capacity. Generally, Erculean controls materials quality by buying the materials, selling them to the subcontractors, and buying back the finished products. The subcontractors are suppliers of electronic subassemblies in other industries. These suppliers have different cost functions and may do different amounts of work depending on the contract requirements.

4. Six small Mexican plants near the U. S. border also produce the same linkages. These plants have extremely low labor rates, are labor intensive with little automation, produce lower volumes, but have very high quality. The wage cost is around $2.00 per hour, depending on the location and the peso exchange rate.

5. Other international production has not yet been needed, but Erculean is already negotiating for a Malaysian facility. Potential European customers are pushing for close proximity plants for sourcing.

   In the U.S. plants, under recent labor contracts, new employees enter at lower wage rates or under a temporary status with no benefits. This adds to the already confusing labor costing situation.
   Very fundamental questions need answers:

1. Should the cost accounting system define costs the same way for all plants?

2. How should labor cost be defined?

3. What are variable production costs?

4. How should "where to produce" decisions be made?

5. On which costs should bids for new business be based?

6. What transfer pricing policies are appropriate for intracompany business?

**Required:**

1. Suggest an approach in the form of a policy on how costs might be incorporated in the bidding and pricing procedures for external business.

2. Suggest an approach in the form of a policy to price intracompany transfers between Erculean and other divisions of the communications equipment firm.

3. Suggest an approach to match cost functions, types of production, volumes, sources of business, and sales revenues that might help Erculean optimize its profits.

# EXTENSION IN MANAGERIAL ANALYSIS

# COSTS OF QUALITY AND OTHER COST MANAGEMENT ISSUES

## LEARNING OBJECTIVES

1. Identify four categories of costs of quality.
2. Explain relationships among the costs of quality categories.
3. Understand the concepts of target costing and kaizen costing.
4. Distinguish between value-added and nonvalue-added activities.
5. Describe various types of nonfinancial performance measures.
6. Comprehend the elements of a balanced scorecard.
7. Explain strategies to enhance productivity such as downsizing and business process reengineering.

## TQM and the Need to Measure Quality Costs

*Chuck Gaa, considered the ace trouble shooter for GreenCo Products, was sent to its Cleveland plant by "Big Jim" Thomas, president of GreenCo, about 15 months ago. What he found was "big trouble." The plant was losing about $400,000 per month—mostly from production waste, low productivity, and customer warranty claims. Sales were declining, and too many customers were unhappy. This was Spring 2003, long after Total Quality Management was a cliche and a norm in most firms. Yes, GreenCo had a TQM program that "Big Jim" had announced in late 1999. Signs had been posted about quality being "No. 1." A consulting firm had conducted seminars for workers; statistical control charts were maintained; and managers had increased inspection of incoming parts and outgoing products. Faster response to warranty claims had been implemented through a costly system to guarantee a 24-hour response to any customer problem.*

*Yet, productivity declined; scrap was up (reaching nearly 50 percent of output in certain weeks); and warranty costs soared. Workers saw the TQM program as a management project. And managers blamed much of the problem on the lack of union cooperation and of employee concern. No specific quality goals were set. Everyone lacked a sense of urgency. Chuck's arrival brought a sudden change: meetings with line workers quickly pointed to key production problems; warranty claims were grouped to identify failure causes; product design and production engineers were brought together to analyze failures; and certain changes were made "overnight." A goal of cutting scrap by 50 percent in three months was set.*

*At every step, the same question came up—"What's this costing us?" Chuck, knowing that this question was key at other plants, sought out DeAnn Ricketts, the plant cost accountant. DeAnn was in the middle of an ABC study and had begun to define new activity centers and cost drivers. While not an easy task, DeAnn was able to modify her system rather quickly to identify quality costs— which, where, and how much. Chuck and DeAnn became allies, promoting each other's views to managers and employees alike. Within two months, DeAnn gave Chuck a 2004 costs of quality analysis. These costs totaled a surprising 15 percent of sales. Of this, little was spent on prevention; about 30 percent was spent on appraisal; nearly 45 percent went to fixing internal failures; and the rest were external failure costs. Lost sales because of bad product weren't captured or estimated. In addition to many nonfinancial quality measures, the quality cost reports helped Chuck measure the impact of his recovery program.*

*Chuck is now gone, off to another problem plant. The Cleveland plant is now at breakeven. But the quality job is just now paying dividends. DeAnn's latest costs of quality report shows total costs still high at 12 percent of sales. But, the cost composition had changed already: 30 percent prevention, 30 percent appraisal, 25 percent internal failure, and 15 percent external failure. The target for 2006 was 10 percent of sales with percentages of 40, 40, 15, and 5, respectively. Long-term goals are 6 percent of sales and a percentage mix of 70, 20, 10, and 0, respectively. Incidentally, sales are rebounding.*

I N THE LAST decade, the competitive environment has forced a changed and improved focus on every business. Heightened customer service expectations, development of integrated systems, demands for cost reductions, advances in information technology, access to international markets, and speed of competitor reactions have all increased the demands on managerial accountants for relevant and timely data for decisions. This chapter examines a set of the more important areas of change in managerial accounting. These topics are heavily influenced by international competitors, particularly the Japanese. Product quality and process improvement have allowed

Japanese automakers, electronics firms, and other consumer goods producers to capture major shares of international markets. Disciplined and team-oriented approaches brought market and financial success. Soon others, particularly U.S. firms, began to adopt and adapt similar concepts and strategies. JIT, quality circles, and continuous improvement programs are examples.

In this chapter, we focus on several of these topics that have strong managerial accounting ramifications. Specifically, measuring and monitoring quality costs are major parts of any total quality management program. Team approaches to design, costing, production planning, and process improvement have yielded huge dividends. These approaches have focused on linking customer needs to the design process, on identifying and eliminating any activity that does not add value to the product, and on organizing planning and control activities that truly measure performance. Many more topics could be included and more pages added on a weekly basis. Old accounting tools are redesigned, some are abandoned, and new concepts are tried and tested. The pace of change is exciting.

## COSTS OF QUALITY

"Quality is free" is a favorite saying of many who argue for efforts to improve quality. It may be difficult to accept the concept that spending more on quality improvement efforts will lower costs. But the facts tell an exciting story:

- Increased training of workers will reduce scrap and rework costs.
- Higher quality products and services improve customer satisfaction and generate higher sales.
- Narrower control limits force improved processes and greater utilization of capacity.
- With reduced waste, more product can be generated with the same equipment and workers.
- "Designing in" quality prevents production problems and the need for engineering changes to create "fixes." An error of $1 in design can easily cause $10 in production problems.
- Empowering employees through quality circles and other participation techniques to give them control over quality-related production decisions increases total commitment.
- Employee satisfaction from eliminating rework, downtime, and scrap increases productivity and further commitment to improvement, particularly if the benefits are shared with the employees.

These results reduce quality costs and, therefore, product costs. Quality efforts come in many forms and names, including:

- **Total quality management (TQM)**—an integrated effort of training, process controls, incentives, employee empowerment, product engineering and design, supplier involvement, and customer satisfaction measurement to achieve quality goals.
- **Statistical quality control**—the use of statistical techniques on processes to measure, monitor, and evaluate performance based on goals, control ranges, and performance percentages.
- **Continuous improvement programs**—efforts to establish quality targets that represent improvement over current performance through worker involvement in evaluation processes.
- **Quality control through the guidance of quality experts**—specific approaches to quality management promoted by internationally recognized leaders such as Deming, Juran, Crosby, and Taguchi.

All of these focus on management commitment to bringing about a change in attitude and changes in processes.

Methods vary but include heavy management commitment to change. One Michigan firm's management, tired of customer complaints and nagging productivity problems, introduced an array

**Contemporary Practice 14.1**
**COQ Rings Loudly at Bell Labs**

*While a quality manager at Bell Labs was riding an elevator with the company chairperson, he "seized the opportunity to explain that the company's COQ was more than 30 percent of sales. This brief encounter and stunning statistic caught the chairperson's attention. Realizing that there was something to be gained from improved quality, he quickly authorized additional investment to support the program."*

Source: Carr, L.P., "Cost of Quality—Making it Work," Journal of Cost Management, *Spring 1995, p. 62.*

of techniques to impress employees and managers with the need to work toward zero defects in its output. Every work station was made responsible for approving the quality of its work before sending it to the next station. When defects were detected, the entire line was halted; horns sounded; the problem diagnosed; and responsibility for the solution identified. The initial result was that very little was shipped from that plant for nearly two weeks because of the nearly constant stoppage of the line. But within two months, productivity was above any prior period and continued to rise. The costs of the early stoppages were nearly fatal to the firm, but the payoffs are substantial both internally and to customers, many of whom are automotive related and are using vendor certification programs to promote quality, delivery, and cost goals and to eliminate nonperforming suppliers.

## Cost Categories

Four categories of costs are commonly identified. These are related and can be considered tradeoffs for each other. They, along with examples, are:

- **Prevention costs** are incurred to prevent the production of products or services that do not meet specifications. As these costs increase, failure costs should decrease. These costs, often spent prior to production, include:

| | |
|---|---|
| Job training | Quality training |
| Supplier evaluation and approvals | Preventive maintenance |
| Development of specifications and standards | Promotion of quality |
| Employee quality circle teams | New equipment to reduce waste |
| Design and process engineering | |

- **Appraisal costs** are incurred to monitor and inspect production. These costs are intended to detect products or services that do not meet specification during the production process. As these costs increase, failure costs should decrease. Included are:

| | |
|---|---|
| Inspections of materials | Quality control activities |
| Inspections during production | Production testing |
| Inspections of finished products | Statistical quality control |
| Line personnel's self-checking activities | Calibration of test equipment |
| Internal auditing activities | |

- **Internal failure costs** are incurred after defective or substandard product or service is detected but before it leaves the plant. These costs increase as the number of defective units detected increases. Included are:

| | |
|---|---|
| Rework, retesting, and rescheduling | Scrap |
| Lost production | Downtime |
| Lost contribution margin on defective units* | Increased inventory |

**Contemporary Practice 14.2**
## COQ is on Track at Union Pacific Railroad

One of the COQ accounts at Union Pacific Railroad is "the cost of cleaning up reportable, environmental spills that occur in the 'normal' course of business. Such spills happen for a number of reasons, ranging from a customer's failure to secure a valve on a 30,000 gallon tank car to a track maintenance crew's dropping of a 5 gallon can of cleaning solvent at a siding. The cleanup costs associated with these incidents vary widely depending on the nature of the spill; further, there is typically a time delay between the incident date and the receipt of the final bill for cleanup. For these reasons, each period's COQ is estimated using an average historical cost per incident . . . The managers use this account to detect the presence of patterns in the spills and to evaluate the effectiveness of the corrective action programs at specific locations."

*Source: "Union Pacific Railroad: Using Cost of Quality in Environmental Management," in Cases from Management Accounting Practice, Institute of Management Accountants: Montvale, NJ, 1997, pp. 108–9.*

- **External failure costs** are incurred when the defective product or service gets to the customer. These costs increase as customers find defective units and reject them. These costs include two important groups: costs of handling customer complaints and costs of future lost sales because of poor quality and customer dissatisfaction. Included are:

| | |
|---|---|
| Repairs | Logistics of returned units |
| Warranties (estimated and actual) | Processing recall programs |
| Contribution margin on replacement units | Lost contribution margin from damaged product reputation* |
| Liability claims | |
| Complaint departments | Lost contribution margin from price reductions* |
| Product service departments | |

*These items are measurable only by making estimates of external impacts and are rarely part of a costs of quality accounting report. They are the most subjective of all quality costs yet, perhaps, the most important in a strategic sense.

While these lists seem straightforward, much judgment goes into the typical quality cost analysis. If a person's duties are part production and part inspection, what percentage should be considered to be quality costs? Each firm must decide on its own definitions. Also, as time passes, processes change, greater understanding of quality issues evolves, and accounting systems change. One danger behind this discussion is that an impression is created that cost measurement is precise and easily done. Activity-based costing, special studies, and improved charts of accounts have certainly detailed the trail of costs.

Traditionally, these costs have been buried in other cost categories. Prevention costs are "lost" in administrative overhead. Appraisal costs are spread among the many locations. Internal failure costs show up in efficiency and quantity variances and allowances for "normal scrap." External failure costs are selling and administrative costs or not captured at all. In many firms, it takes a major effort to identify, measure, and track these costs with reasonable accuracy.

Prevention and appraisal costs are considered tradeoffs to internal and external failure costs. Thus, stronger training programs are viewed as important costs that help reduce internal and external failure costs. Also, a stronger appraisal program should reduce both internal and external failure costs. Yet, in the long run, spending on prevention costs may allow a company to reduce both failure costs and appraisal costs. Better trained employees will produce much higher quality products which require less testing and inspecting, a result of producing few if any defective units. Implicitly, failure costs fall to near zero levels.

## Diagramming Costs of Quality

Figure 14.1 illustrates the interaction of the four costs of quality categories. The horizontal or *X* axis reflects either a decreasing defect rate or an increasing quality-assurance level. As can be seen, an optimal cost level can be drawn. The presumption is that increased prevention and appraisal spending will lower failure costs (internal plus external). We must be careful not to oversimplify the relationships here. For example:

- The optimal spending level can be drawn but can rarely be measured accurately. Also, this optimal level of spending implies that we should be satisfied with this level of quality (defects).
- This static drawing of the four cost categories reflects general trends but implies that they are substitutes for each other, are equally important, and are of approximately equal size. Rarely is this the case.
- The cost curves imply that cost functions can be defined quantitatively to allow these costs to be plotted at various levels of quality assurance. While cost relationships do exist, they are difficult to quantify accurately.
- Too often, managers assume that by merely spending money on quality prevention and appraisal activities their quality goals can be achieved. Some TQM programs have been successful and sustainable; many others have achieved neither their quality nor cost reduction goals.

Any manager or managerial accountant who advocates finding the optimal spending and failure cost level and operating at that level fails to understand the interrelationships that exist. For example, prevention costs (i.e., training, education, and quality-enhancing investments) are in effect current investments in future defect reductions. More spending on training and vendor certification programs, for example, should reduce internal and external failure rates in the future. A highly trained workforce should reduce the need for inspections in the future.

As an offbeat example of this idea, compare the teenage driver accident rate in the U. S. with Japan. In the U. S., most teenagers take a short driver's training course with very limited coverage of driving laws, driver etiquette, and hands-on skill development. In Japan, compulsory driver education courses cost approximately $5,000 per person because of the amount of training required. Car accidents do

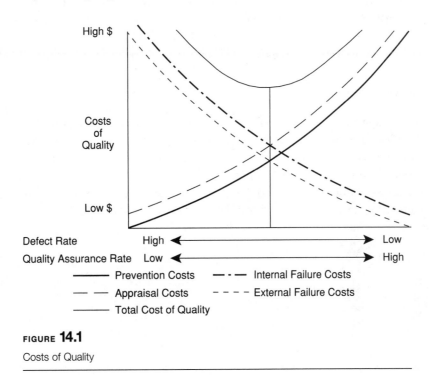

**FIGURE 14.1**

Costs of Quality

occur but at a much lower level as compared to U. S. experiences. (To test the idea, survey your current class. Odds are that well over half of your fellow students have had an auto accident before they reached 20 years of age.) Japan has traded accident costs for training costs. Other social impacts must be considered; for example, many persons might not drive because they cannot afford the $5,000.

As a numerical example of Figure 14.1, assume that 100,000 units are produced with six possible levels of spending on prevention and appraisal efforts. The contribution margin is $10 per unit. Of the defects, 60 percent is detected internally; and 40 percent is discovered externally. All defects must be reworked at a cost of $8 per unit. External failures cause a loss of future sales at a ratio of three units of lost sales for each external defect found, or $30 of lost contribution margin for each external defective unit. All dollar and unit amounts are in thousands.[1]

| | | | Rework Costs | | Lost Contribution Margin | | |
|---|---|---|---|---|---|---|---|
| Defect Rates | Prevention Costs | Appraisal Costs | Units | Costs | Units | Costs | Total Quality Costs |
| 5.00% | $100 | $100 | $8 × 5.0 | $40 | $30 × 2.0 | $60 | $300 |
| 3.50 | 120 | 80 | 8 × 3.5 | 28 | 30 × 1.4 | 42 | 270 |
| 2.25 | 140 | 65 | 8 × 2.25 | 18 | 30 × 0.9 | 27 | 250 |
| 1.25 | 160 | 55 | 8 × 1.25 | 10 | 30 × 0.5 | 15 | 240 |
| 0.50 | 190 | 50 | 8 × 0.5 | 4 | 30 × 0.2 | 6 | 250 |
| 0.10 | 240 | 48 | 8 × 0.1 | 0.80 | 30 × 0.04 | 1.20 | 290 |

To explain these numbers, the first row assumes that 5 percent of the 100,000 units produced is defective. Also, we are now spending $100,000 each on prevention and appraisal costs. It will cost $8 per unit to rework the 5,000 defective units or $40,000. Lost contribution margin is found by taking the external failures (40 percent × 5,000 units) times the contribution margin of three lost units (3 × $10)—a lost sales cost of $60,000 in contribution margin. The total costs of quality are $300,000.

Based on these numbers, the managerial accountant would recommend that the current optimal cost level is $240,000. This assumes that we can quantify the relationship between higher prevention costs and lower defective percentages. It also assumes that appraisal costs can be reduced accordingly. Internal and external discovery rates for defective units and lost sales figures are clearly estimates. Contribution margins and rework costs are reasonably solid data. This, however, is a static picture of quality costs. As time passes, these relationships will change, resulting in a new optimal spending pattern.

## Continuous Improvement

Can any firm be satisfied with a static quality level? No! Markets are demanding higher and higher quality assurance levels. Japanese auto quality levels of the 1980s well exceeded U. S. capabilities. U. S. firms now exceed those levels, but Japanese car makers have moved to still higher levels. Competition demands continuous improvement.

Prior to the implementation of a TQM program, appraisal costs and combined failure costs will likely be very high. For example, the mix of quality costs at the start of a major quality effort in a machine manufacturer was:

| | |
|---|---|
| Prevention costs | 4.5% |
| Appraisal costs | 41.7 |
| Internal failure costs | 53.4 |
| External failure costs | .4 (excluding lost sales estimates) |
| Total costs of quality | 100.0% |

---

[1] This example was adapted from an article by J. T. Godfrey and W. R. Pasewark, "Controlling Quality Costs," *Management Accounting*, March 1988, p. 72.

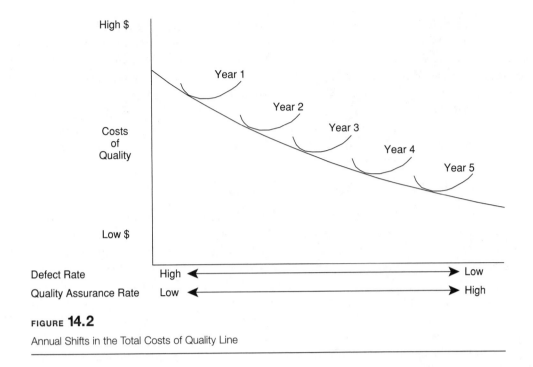

**FIGURE 14.2**

Annual Shifts in the Total Costs of Quality Line

Total costs were approximately 8 percent of total sales. As part of management efforts to get employee "buy in," figures were presented to show the impact on employee profit sharing if the percentage decreased to 6 percent.

As time passes, Figure 14.1 will be revised to reflect improvements in quality and changed cost relationships. Movement will be toward higher quality assurance and lower defect levels. Cost patterns will shift from failure to prevention. Even appraisal costs may decrease as more confidence is gained in the production processes. Figure 14.2 incorporates a sequence of Figure 14.1 diagrams and reflects this change in patterns over a series of years.

A line linking minimum cost points should always be shifting downward and to the right. Whether the company is ever at the exact optimal point each year or month is questionable. But aggressive TQM programs have produced results following this pattern. As an illustration of the shifting cost patterns, a set of summarized biannual data from a film studio appears in Figure 14.3. The data are in millions and include an approximate 10 percent increase in sales each year. Definitions of what costs belong in each category rests with company personnel.

| Cost Categories | 2002 Costs | 2002 % of Total | 2004 Costs | 2004 % of Total | 2006 Costs | 2006 % of Total | 2008 Costs | 2008 % of Total | Forecast 2010 Costs | Forecast 2010 % of Total |
|---|---|---|---|---|---|---|---|---|---|---|
| Prevention | $ 2.5 | 14.7 | $ 3.5 | 19.3 | $ 5.9 | 36.2 | $ 5.7 | 40.7 | $ 4.5 | 45.5 |
| Appraisal | 6.0 | 35.3 | 6.8 | 37.6 | 4.8 | 29.4 | 3.9 | 27.9 | 2.9 | 29.3 |
| Internal failure | 6.2 | 36.5 | 5.6 | 30.9 | 4.4 | 27.0 | 3.6 | 25.7 | 2.1 | 21.2 |
| External failure | 2.3 | 13.5 | 2.2 | 12.2 | 1.2 | 7.4 | 0.8 | 5.7 | 0.4 | 4.0 |
| Total costs | $17.0 | 100.0 | $18.1 | 100.0 | $16.3 | 100.0 | $14.0 | 100.0 | $ 9.9 | 100.0 |
| Costs as a % of sales | | 18.0% | | 15.8% | | 11.7% | | 8.3% | | 4.9% |

**FIGURE 14.3**

Shifting Patterns of Costs of Quality Over Time

Notice that, at the start of the total quality management program, internal failure is the highest percentage category; two years later, appraisal costs are the highest percentage; and finally, prevention costs become the highest percentage. Of particular note is the steadily declining percentage of quality costs to sales. While significant reductions in these percentages are rather consistent, company management feels that the TQM program training effort is approaching a steady state. The forecast for 2010 shows a further dramatic decline in the costs to sales percentage and in total quality costs. These challenges have been met in the past, but the 2010 goal is particularly rigorous. Managerial and employee efforts will determine the result.

## Sources of Costs of Quality Data—ABC and Customer Inputs

Most traditional costing systems will find it difficult if not impossible to collect the type of data needed for the preceding analyses. ABC has been a timely innovation. Activity centers that focus on quality issues (i.e., training, rework and scrap, inspections, and quality assurance program costs) can separate these activities and the resources they consume. Cost drivers can help identify relationships between failure costs and their causes. Thus, ABC increases the ability to identify quality costs, focuses attention on costly activities, and even helps recognize cause and effect linkages.

Many companies must extend even ABC data to capture more quality costs. This might include account analysis, discussed in Chapter 3. With certain costs, allocations may be needed, which introduce difficulties when measuring improvement. As improvements occur, allocations must be redone, often introducing arbitrariness.

The tough measurement is still lost sales, part of external failure. Numerous firms have made customer satisfaction surveys important and routine parts of their marketing, service, and product planning and design functions. Quality councils have included both suppliers and customers to add critical external views of internal quality levels and efforts. In the past, lost sales estimates were only vague guesses, but greater articulation of customer and potential customer inputs can push this figure toward a more valid estimate.

## Service Applications

While TQM programs are often linked to manufacturing and its quality, service organizations also find quality just as critical to customer satisfaction and to their long-term survival. The same categories of costs of quality apply to all organizations. Xerox, for example, has developed significant quality programs for its manufacturing, sales, and service activities. Training to increase service employee competence, to improve interactions with customers, and to raise the quality of services provided is similar to manufacturing tradeoffs. The focus is more heavily on customer satisfaction since providing the service, in many cases, is at the customer contact point. Lost sales, service reputation, and attributes such as "friendliness" are difficult to measure in a financial context. Yet, measuring costs of improving and sustaining quality and of eliminating service failures is critical. Hospitals, for example, have an obvious need for high levels of quality control activities. Monitoring quality costs, while important, becomes secondary to the need for assuring extremely high levels of operating quality regardless of cost. Yet, because of huge increases in health care costs, national health care policies will require measuring and analyzing operating costs including costs of quality.

## International Quality Standards and Cost Measurement

An important international force is driving many firms to establish systems to measure quality costs and to document quality levels achieved. The European Community (EC) has directed that companies doing business in its member countries have an established quality system. The International Standards Organization has created the **ISO 9000 standards** to measure firm compliance. While

## Contemporary Practice 14.3
## American Express and Total Quality Management

All American Express business units must include strategies for quality improvements as part of their annual budgets and business plans. Integrated Payment Systems (IPS) is a business unit that handles American Express Money Orders and other cash transfer services. A TQM program was instituted in 1990. This soon lead to an activity-based cost study and to implementation of a system to capture costs by customer, mission, person, expense type, cost of quality category, and cost driver. This study is known as the Functional Administrative Control Technique (FACT) and is driven by value engineering, not cost accounting. With this database, an accurate estimate of costs of quality within a particular TQM study area can be produced in a matter of hours. From these studies came restructuring plans that improved operations and yielded substantial savings. The CFO of IPS commented "In addition to hard numbers, it helped us develop an understanding for mission-related activities—what's hot and what's not." Within two months of completing the FACT, $1 million in savings was identified while several equally dramatic customer service improvements were made—a win, win situation.

*Source: Carlson, D. A., and S. M. Young, "Activity-Based Total Quality Management at American Express," Journal of Cost Management, Spring 1993, pp. 48–58.*

quality standards are beyond this text's scope, the management accountant's role is worthy of discussion. A complying firm will have access to the EC markets, be identified as a quality producer, and obtain the benefits of better quality systems. Other vendors are also indicating their intent to use ISO standards.

A complying firm must document its quality costs and their measurement processes. The ISO 9000 objectives reflect these data needs in that the organization should:

- Achieve and sustain the quality of product or service produced so as to meet the purchaser's stated or implied needs continuously.
- Give its own management confidence that the intended quality is being achieved and sustained.
- Give the purchaser confidence that the intended quality is achieved in the delivered product.

Five standards have been published and include three levels of possible registration:

**ISO 9000**   **Quality management and quality assurance standards—guidelines for selection and use.**

**ISO 9001**   **Quality systems—model for quality assurance in design/development, production, installation, and servicing.** This level of registration is for use when conformance to specified requirements is to be assured by the supplier during multiple product stages (for engineering, construction, and complete life-cycle manufacturers).

**ISO 9002**   **Quality systems—model for quality assurance in production and installation.** This level of registration is for use when conformance to specified requirements is to be assured by the supplier during production and installation (for process manufacturers).

**ISO 9003**   **Quality systems—model for quality assurance in final inspection and test.** This level of registration is for use when conformance to specified requirements is to be assured by the supplier solely at the final inspection and test (for smaller manufacturers who deliver a finished and tested product).

**ISO 9004**   **Quality management and quality system elements—guidelines.**

To meet the data requirements of these standards, management accounting systems must include the measurement and reporting of life-cycle costs, quality costs, and continuous improvement assessments. These include preproduction costs such as market research, engineering, procurement, and process planning and post-delivery costs such as technical assistance, maintenance, and disposal. Documentation and verification are keys to sustaining registration. ISO 9000 is a powerful force in quality management and is placing significant demands on accounting systems to generate evidence of quality assurance systems and costs.

## COST MANAGEMENT IN DESIGN AND PRODUCTION STAGES

Companies have traditionally emphasized cost management in the product production phase, while neglecting the design and development stages. Managers now recognize that most of the costs incurred in the production stage are, in fact, determined in the design and development stages. Accordingly, many companies are adopting target costing, a system initiated in Japan, to manage costs in the design and development stages for new (or redesigned) products. Another Japanese system known as kaizen costing is used to manage costs in the product manufacturing stage.

### Target Costing

Historically, U.S. manufacturers have set their pricing strategies by adding required profit margins to the costs of already designed products. **Target costing** reverses this process. After a target selling price and a target profit are established, an allowable cost consistent with these targets is obtained for the product. The company then designs the product based on the allowable (target) cost. Figure 14.4 compares the target costing approach to the traditional approach.

In target costing, the process begins with a general plan to produce a product based on marketing research. This marketing research also suggests a target selling price by estimating what consumers will pay for the product. The company then determines the amount of profit that would be required for this product. From this target price and target profit, a target cost is obtained:

$$\text{Target cost} = \text{Target selling price} - \text{Target profit}$$

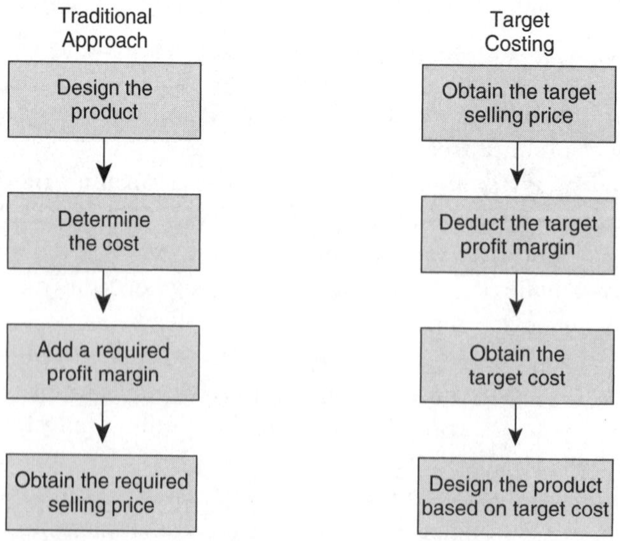

**Traditional Approach**

Design the product → Determine the cost → Add a required profit margin → Obtain the required selling price

**Target Costing**

Obtain the target selling price → Deduct the target profit margin → Obtain the target cost → Design the product based on target cost

FIGURE **14.4**

Target Costing Compared to the Traditional Approach

This overall target cost is then decomposed into specific cost elements for materials, subassemblies, direct labor, various manufacturing overhead categories, and various nonmanufacturing categories such as distribution and customer service. Finally, the design department establishes a blueprint according to the target cost for each element.

As an example of the target costing approach, suppose that Lylatove Sleepwear is considering the production of a new line of pajamas. Based on preliminary market research, management has decided that each pair of pajamas should be priced at $20. Furthermore, management believes that the profit margin should be 12 percent of sales revenue. Hence, the target profit would be $2.40 (0.12 × $20). The target cost, therefore, would be $17.60 ($20 – $2.40).

## Kaizen Costing

**Kaizen costing** is a system to support cost reduction beyond the design and development stages. "Kaizen" is a Japanese word that refers to "continuous accumulations of small betterment activities rather than innovative improvement."[2] Innovative improvements are usually introduced in the design and development stages. In kaizen costing, the actual cost for the latest period becomes the kaizen cost target for the current period. To promote continuous improvement, these kaizen cost targets must be reduced in each successive period.

These techniques have allowed many Japanese firms to overcome the effects of the increased value of the yen in international markets. Lower costs and improved products have offset less competitive yen exchange rates.

To achieve cost reduction, many companies are adopting an **activity-based management (ABM)** approach. ABM is an outgrowth of activity-based costing (ABC) that emphasizes management of activities through ABC, activity analysis, and performance measurement. We discussed ABC in Chapter 6; the latter topics are discussed in the following sections.

## ACTIVITY ANALYSIS

Companies are monitoring their activities to assess which add value to the customer, which, in turn, should add profit to the company. This technique is referred to as **activity analysis.** An emphasis on activities can help identify nonvalue-added costs and eliminate the activities that cause them. Any resource-using activity that does not add value is often called waste. Having value implies that a consumer would be willing to pay for the results of the activity. A key goal of production managers is to eliminate waste and, thereby, to have an efficient and productive operation.

Time is perhaps the most valuable resource. Study of nonvalue-added time in operations takes five forms: process time, inspection time, move time, wait time, and storage time.

**Process time** is the time during which a product is undergoing conversion activities which transform raw materials into finished products. Although most people view process time as the sum of many value-added activities, the presence of inefficiency or other nonproductive activities represents nonvalue-added time. Managers must continually review processes to catch inefficiencies that can creep in over time.

Just-in-time (JIT) production concepts are fundamental building blocks for reducing process time. Many companies have physically reorganized their factories to encourage faster process time. Figure 14.5 compares a JIT layout to a traditional factory layout. The traditional plant has large inventories, much materials movement within the plant, and a mixing of fabricating and assembly tasks. The JIT plant produces only when parts and products are needed, carries narrow safety stock

---

[2] Monden, Y. and K. Hamada, "Target Costing and Kaizen Costing in Japanese Automobile Companies," *Journal of Management Accounting Research*, Fall 1991, p. 17.

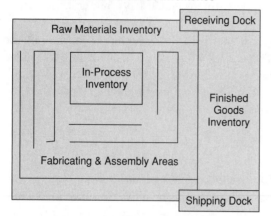

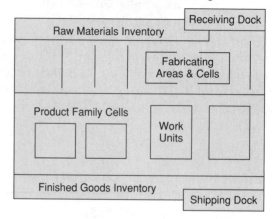

**FIGURE 14.5**

Traditional Factory Versus Just-In-Time Factory Layouts

inventories, has a north-to-south flow of production, and organizes production around product families (similar production requirements). The implication is that greater output can be achieved with the same equipment, people, and space—waste is reduced.

**Inspection time** is the amount of time spent ensuring that the product is of high quality. Typically, materials and components are inspected upon arrival. Then inspection occurs at various points during and at the conclusion of the production process. It is difficult to determine whether inspection procedures result in nonvalue-added costs without detailed knowledge of the production technology and inspection procedures. However, many companies are striving to reduce the costs of maintaining product quality and are working virtually to eliminate the costs of reworking defective products. Consequently, zero defects and total quality control programs sensitize employees to the need for eliminating spoiled and defective units. The argument is that quality is built into and not inspected into the product. Unless otherwise stated, we presume that inspection is a nonvalue-added activity.

**Move time** is the time spent moving raw materials, work in process, or finished products between operations within the plant. This includes the activities associated with receiving materials, moving them into storage, moving materials and components to the first production operation, moving partially completed products from one work center to the next, and moving the completed product to the finished goods storage area to await shipping. Many companies refer to these activities as materials-handling operations. Move time is a nonvalue-added activity. A certain amount of move time is necessary in any production process, but proper sequencing of operations and tasks and implementing automation technologies can significantly reduce move time. Figure 14.5 illustrates the importance of an efficient flow through the factory to minimize materials movement.

**Wait time** is the amount of time that materials or work in process spend waiting for the next operation. This includes the time that materials, components, and partially completed products remain in queues immediately preceding an operation and in holding areas located near each department waiting for the next production operation. Wait time potentially represents a significant nonvalue-added cost. A company's working capital is tied up in work in process, and space is unnecessarily wasted on numerous production queues and holding areas. Even in the simple diagrams in Figure 14.5, we see that space released from having inventory wait for the next production step can be used to expand production. The ultimate goal of the JIT philosophy is to eliminate wait time completely. Companies using JIT systems have proven that remarkable reductions in in-process inventories can be made. For example, a car assembly plant producing seventy cars per hour may have less than one hour's supply of car seats in the plant at any time. When a car begins its two-hour trip along an assembly line, an electronic message is received in a supplier's seating plant to trigger assembly of that car's seats. The seats are built and delivered to the car assembly line minutes before the car arrives at the seat installation point.

**Storage time** is the time during which finished products are held in stock before shipment to customers. It includes the time products spend in storage and the time spent packaging the products for shipment. Traditionally, companies have stored large inventories of finished products to avoid stockouts. Similar to waiting time, storage time ties up a company's working capital in inventories and requires large amounts of space devoted to storage activities. While not applicable to all manufacturing operations, produce-to-order is a goal—manufacture products only after a sales order is received. Improvements in order entry systems and shortened lead times in production scheduling can give the appearance of a produce-to-order operation.

The time required for an average unit to go from the beginning of the production process to completion and shipment is often referred to as **throughput time.** This time is equal to productive processing time plus nonvalue-added time. More specifically, it is the sum of all five activities previously discussed—process time, inspection time, move time, wait time, and storage time.

## Nonfinancial Performance Measures

As changes occur in the operating environment, traditional measures of performance are being re-examined. New measures are being adopted to better fit the concepts of activity-based management. In addition, accountants are measuring performance in new areas of operations, areas that have normally been outside of the accountants' domain or are new because of needs that innovative and automated environments create. This section gives a glimpse of some of the critical changes taking place.

Accountants have traditionally focused on financial measures of performance, such as variations from budgeted or standard costs. Such measures are still important, but a broader evaluation including nonfinancial measures is necessary. For example, physical measures such as throughput time, value-added labor ratio, and defective product rates are playing greater roles in helping managers achieve high quality and competitive operations. Let's look at some nonfinancial performance measures that are commonly being used.

### Measures of Manufacturing Productivity

Increasing pressure from global competition has caused many companies to focus on better measures of productivity. Traditionally, accountants have associated productivity with variances calculated for quantity, efficiency, mix, yield, and capacity. The goal was cost minimization. Other productivity measures commonly used were nothing more than quantities of output divided by quantities of input. Today, we are looking for more detailed, meaningful measures. Activity-based costing can pinpoint high-cost activities. Engineers can design for greater production efficiency and defect elimination. For example, a machine manufacturer might determine the number of machines produced per day per employee. A car assembly operation might ascertain the square footage required per day per car. An electrical generating plant might keep track of the tons of coal required to generate a thousand kilowatt hours of electricity. The measures are oriented toward specific activities and evaluate management control over these activities.

**Manufacturing cycle efficiency (MCE)** is a measure of the amount of throughput time that consists of process time. It is the following ratio:

$$\text{Manufacturing cycle efficiency} = \frac{\text{Processing time}}{\text{Throughput time}}$$

Remember that throughput time is the sum of process time, inspection time, wait time, move time, and storage time. Assuming that inspection time is nonvalue-added time, then MCE measures the portion of throughput time which is value-added time. The goal is to have MCE as high as possible. Although 100 percent is the theoretical ideal, the operations of many manufacturing companies range from the 60 to 90 percent levels; and the percentage cannot improve without major restructuring.

Another widely used productivity measure is the **first-pass yield.** This measures the percentage of nondefective items that have gone through the production process one time only (i.e., without needing any rework).

Computer-integrated manufacturing (CIM) is an attempt to optimize the entire plant's production by planning which departments will produce which parts and products, in what order, and when. Formerly, each department's efficiency was measured; and keeping all departments running at full speed was the goal. Now in CIM, certain departments may be idled until their resources are needed. This is "pull through" production and part of the JIT philosophy. Produce only what is needed immediately. Performance measures must therefore evaluate a unit based on its production assignment, not necessarily its capacity. Responsibility for productivity is now moved to higher management levels and away from the individual activity center or cost center manager.

## Productivity of Labor

The total labor expended for the benefit of a product or service is segregated into direct and indirect labor. Direct labor is all labor that can be specifically identified with a product or service in an economically feasible manner. **Value-added direct labor** is that portion of direct labor that changes raw materials into a finished product or service that is delivered to a customer. For example, value-added direct labor fabricates, assembles, and finishes products. Nonvalue-added direct labor moves, inspects, stores, examines, or otherwise handles the products without adding customer value. Indirect labor is labor that is not readily traced to a product or service. Indirect workers supervise, repair, manage, purchase, inspect, record, advise, or otherwise support the direct workers. Traditionally, indirect workers are considered nonvalue-added labor. In labor-intensive activities, one measure of performance for labor is the **value-added labor ratio** or ratio of value-added time to total time:

$$\text{Value-added labor ratio} = \frac{\text{Value-added direct labor time}}{\text{Total direct and indirect labor time}}$$

The ratio also may be computed in terms of number of employees or payroll. One goal is to reduce the number of supervisors, managers, clerical staff, accountants, engineers, inspectors, and all others that are nonvalue-added workers. This is part of empowering workers to work as teams and to assume responsibility for production.

In many operations, direct labor is being replaced by automated equipment; and indirect labor now includes technicians needed to program, set up, and maintain the equipment. Often, the distinction between direct and indirect is blurred or eliminated. Team approaches to production (work units or product family cells as shown in Figure 14.5), guaranteed wage labor contracts, and broader job classifications have further eroded the importance of direct labor as a cost group. A labor-related performance measure that does not distinguish between direct and indirect is the percentage of total labor cost in the total product cost, called the **labor content percentage:**

$$\text{Labor content percentage} = \frac{\text{Total labor cost}}{\text{Total product cost}}$$

The goals are to reduce this percentage and to increase the productivity of all labor dollars.

## Product Quality

Earlier in this chapter, we discussed financial measures of product quality. Costs of quality enable us to aggregate various aspects of quality by using a common unit of measure—dollars. Furthermore, costs of quality allow us to assess the impact of quality on the company's profits. However, knowing the costs of quality does not enable us to pinpoint specific sources of quality problems. To diagnose and correct specific problems relating to quality, we need a variety of non-financial measures of quality.

Four categories of nonfinancial measures are helpful in assessing and maintaining quality. The first, customer acceptance measures, focuses on the extent to which a company's customers perceive its product to be of high quality. It includes such measures as counts of customer complaints, warranty claims, incidence of failures at customer locations, products returned, and repeat sales.

Design quality assesses how well a product has been designed. Frequency of engineering change orders is an important measure of design quality. Other measures include the number of parts in the product and the percentage of common versus unique parts. Since simplicity is desirable, the fewer the number of parts and the higher the percentage of common parts, the better is the design quality.

In-process quality measures look at product quality during production. Rework, defects, and scrap measures are used to keep these items to a minimum. Products are also selected for testing at random or statistically sampled during the various stages of production. Defect rates are measured, and corrective actions specified.

A fourth area of quality measurement relates to purchased materials and parts. Pressure is on purchasing agents to acquire high-quality inputs to meet materials requirements at low costs and on a timely basis. Common vendor performance measures include percentage of defects in the delivery (in terms of dollars as well as number of items), percentage of orders filled, and percentage of orders delivered on time. Many companies are now computing an overall rating of suppliers based on the quality of their materials, delivery performance, and customer service. Also, waste, scrap, and defects occurring during production that are traceable to materials are identified with specific suppliers. A growing number of companies now have vendor certification programs, where managers may purchase from only those vendors who have met the company's quality standards.

## Inventory Reduction

Inventory investments, ordering costs, and carrying costs often include significant amounts of non-value-added costs. To remain price competitive, effort is necessary to reduce or eliminate inventories. The JIT philosophy focuses on keeping inventories at low or zero levels for materials and parts at every stage of production. Therefore, inventory control measures are used to minimize nonvalue-added costs. Such measures may include average inventory values, average time various categories of materials are held or inventories are standing in a production operation, and inventory turnovers (cost of goods sold divided by average inventory). Measures like manufacturing cycle efficiency also relate to inventory reduction because nonprocessing time—inspection, move, wait, and storage times—is much of the reason why inventories exist.

## Machine Maintenance

If our efforts to reduce inventories are successful, we shift our focus to the company's capability of producing goods quickly. We must keep production equipment and machinery operating. Therefore, performance measures will look at unscheduled machine downtime, equipment repair time, tooling turnaround time, engineering change time, machine availability, and adherence to maintenance schedules. Some companies even make a distinction between bottleneck and nonbottleneck machinery.

A bottleneck operation is one that limits the production capacity of the entire facility. It is vital that the machinery in bottleneck operations be available 100 percent of the time, excluding time for routine required maintenance. Managing bottleneck operations has received considerable attention in recent years and has become a central component of a management philosophy known as the **Theory of Constraints**. This philosophy emphasizes planning around constraining factors and working to relax the constraints.

## Delivery Performance

As a final point, assume that we have done a super job of reducing many nonvalue-added activities and eliminating others. Still, we are not successful until quality products are delivered on time and at the right place to the customer. This is especially important for customers that have JIT systems.

Some companies have a goal of filling 100 percent of their orders on time. Common measures of delivery performance include the percentage of orders filled, the percentage of on-time deliveries, and the average time between the receipt of a customer order and the delivery of the goods. Monitoring customer back orders also tells how many orders were not filled from stock or on time and how long a customer had to wait for an order. A desirable piece of information often impossible to measure is business lost because of delivery failure. Many managers believe that the "competitive ballgame" is won or lost with product quality and delivery performance.

In Figure 14.6, we summarize the nonfinancial performance measures previously discussed.

| *Manufacturing Productivity* | *Product Quality* |
|---|---|
| Output per day per employee | Customer acceptance: |
| Output per square foot of space |     Number of customer complaints |
| Energy required per unit of output |     Number of warranty claims |
| First-pass yield |     Incidence of failures at customer locations |
| Manufacturing cycle efficiency |     Number of returned products |
| |     Repeat sales |
| **Productivity of Labor** | |
| Value-added labor ratio | Design: |
| Labor content percentage |     Frequency of engineering change orders |
| |     Number of parts in the product |
| |     Percentage of common vs. unique parts |
| **Inventory Reduction** | |
| Average inventory values | In-process: |
| Average time inventories are held |     Amount of rework |
| Inventory turnovers |     Defect rates |
| |     Amount of scrap |
| **Machine Maintenance** | |
| Unscheduled machine downtime | Materials and parts: |
| Equipment repair time |     Percentage of defects in the delivery |
| Tooling turnaround time |     Percentage of orders filled |
| Engineering change time |     Percentage of orders received on time |
| Machine availability | |
| Adherence to maintenance schedules | |
| **Delivery Performance** | |
| Percentage of orders filled | |
| Percentage of on-time deliveries | |
| Time from customer order to delivery | |

**FIGURE 14.6**

Summary of Nonfinancial Performance Measures

# Nonfinancial Measures for the Multinational Company

Multinational companies are increasingly using nonfinancial performance measures in evaluations. Common ones for international operating units are:

1. Increasing market share and market size.
2. Relationship with host country government.
3. Quality assurance.
4. Productivity improvement.
5. Cooperation with other company units and the parent.
6. Environment compliance.
7. Employee training and development.
8. Employee safety.
9. Labor turnover.
10. Community service.

Notice that for some of these measures a company will have difficulty attaching numerical values. These measures are very important in comparing performances, particularly over time and against planned target levels.

The implication is that the corporate office is in close touch with the international operation, can assess budget and planning targets astutely, and can link successful performance in the local environment with global economic goals of the corporation.

# Balanced Scorecard

Many companies are integrating financial and nonfinancial performance measures into a tool that has become known as a **balanced scorecard.** Historically, companies' operational and management control systems have been built around short-term financial measures that have not been linked to long-term strategic objectives. A balanced scorecard attempts to overcome this deficiency by using a set of performance measures that serve to link a company's long-term strategy with its short-term actions. The scorecard communicates the long-term strategy to all levels of the organization so that both departmental and individual objectives are aligned with the company's goals.

Typically, a balanced scorecard consists of the following four categories of performance measures:

- Financial–measures that describe economic consequences and are of most interest to shareholders.
- Customer–measures that relate to the customer's perspective and to the market segment in which the company competes.
- Internal business process–measures that describe the internal processes (i.e., the means) needed to provide value for customers and shareholders.
- Learning and growth–measures that define the capabilities needed to create long-term growth and innovation.

A balanced scorecard is not simply a collection of performance measures. These measures are derived from the company's mission, strategy, and objectives and represent a balance among the four measurement perspectives. In the financial category, the strategic themes often include revenue enhancement, cost minimization, and asset utilization. Examples of these financial

| Financial | Internal Business Process |
|---|---|
| Revenue enhancement:<br>　Revenue growth from prior period<br>　Product profitability<br>Cost minimization:<br>　Product cost per unit<br>　Cost per customer<br>Asset Utilization:<br>　Residual income<br>　Economic value added | Percentage of defective units<br>Manufacturing cycle efficiency<br>First-pass yields<br>Output per square foot of space<br>Supplier ratings |
| **Customer** | **Learning and Growth** |
| Market share<br>Number of new customers<br>Percentage of returned products<br>Customer survey ratings<br>Percentage of customers paying early | Employee satisfaction ratings<br>Training hours per employee<br>Number of new brands introduced<br>Inventory of cross-functional employee skills<br>Percent of revenue from new products |

**FIGURE 14.7**

Examples of Measures in a Balanced Scorecard

measures, as well as measures for the other three categories in the balanced scorecard, can be found in Figure 14.7. Strategic themes for the customer category often include market share growth, customer retention, customer acquisition, and customer satisfaction. In the internal business process category, the strategic objectives relate to increasing the efficiency and effectiveness of operations. The objectives for the learning and growth category relate to the ability to innovate and improve.

The frequency of measurement varies depending on the type of performance measure. For instance, operating measures such as machine downtime or percentage of orders filled may be measured daily. Other operating measures such as manufacturing cycle efficiency or amount of rework may be measured weekly. Yet others such as inventory turnovers and number of warranty claims may

## Contemporary Practice 14.4
### Balanced Scorecard at Pitney Bowes

Pitney Bowes is a global provider of integrated mail and document management solutions. Three full-time staff members plus two to three part-time staff helped the director of financial planning create a balanced scorecard. After considering over 500 critical measures to assess performance of the business, various task forces narrowed this list to 55 key metrics that were rated on a six-point scale using the following criteria:

- Importance to the business;
- Electronically reportable;
- Routinely reported;
- Accurate;
- Critical to objectives.

A system was developed featuring a user-friendly, picture icon-based tool enabling instant access to the 55 metrics on the balanced scorecard plus the closing stock price and news about the company. The balanced scorecard was organized by five objectives: business results, competitiveness, quality, employees, and carriers.

*Source: Green, M., J. Garrity, A. Gumbus, and B. Lyons, "Pitney Bowes Calls for New Metrics", Strategic Finance, May 2002, p. 31.*

be measured quarterly. Some measures such as economic value added (EVA) and number of new products introduced may be measured annually. Generally, nonfinancial measures are reported more frequently than financial measures.

As a result of introducing the balanced scorecard, some companies have reduced their emphasis on short-term incentive compensation systems. Instead, they are linking bonuses to balanced scorecard measures. One particular oil company decided to base 60 percent of its executive bonuses on the achievement of targets relating to four financial factors–return on capital, profitability, cash flow, and operating cost. The remaining 40 percent is based on indicators of customer satisfaction, dealer satisfaction, employee satisfaction, and environmental responsibility.[3]

In addition to manufacturing firms, many service organizations are implementing balanced scorecards. Allstate, Sears Roebuck, AT&T, and Cigna Property & Casualty are but a few examples.

## BENCHMARKING

To improve both quality and productivity, many companies are turning to **benchmarking**. This technique identifies activities as standards ("benchmarks") by which similar activities should be judged. Simply put, it is a process of finding better practices. Benchmarking can be done with internal sources—other parts of the company—or with other companies including competitors. The external candidates are often obtained by examining lists of companies cited in trade and business journals for excellence in their business practices.

Aside from trade and business publications, performance benchmarks can be gathered from electronic data bases, professional conferences and trade conventions, commissioned studies, and site visits to companies. Benchmarking utilizes both financial and nonfinancial performance measures. But this information says nothing about the changes needed to improve quality and efficiency. Therefore, those doing the benchmarking must also obtain an understanding of these "best practices" so that they can implement them in their own organizations. Benchmarking has increased in popularity, to the point where a recent study indicates that about 95 percent of Fortune 500 companies were using benchmarking.[4]

### Contemporary Practice 14.5
### *Benchmarking in a Finance Department*

*During the course of a year, Xerox Corporation's finance department in its U.S. customer operations division conducted benchmarking studies at 24 companies including Kodak, AT&T, Digital Equipment Corporation, Abbot Laboratories, IBM, and Hewlett Packard. In addition, internal benchmarking was done with its Canadian affiliate—Xerox of Canada. Benchmarking efforts focused on* *activities such as taxes, financing businesses, financial accounting, and financial systems. Usually, three to eight people comprised the benchmarking team, including the chief financial officer, senior analysts, first-line managers, and sometimes second-line managers.*

Source: Camp, R.C., "A Bible for Benchmarking, by Xerox," Financial Executive, July/August 1993, pp. 24–25.

---

[3] Kaplan, R. S. and D. P. Norton, "Using the Balanced Scorecard as a Strategic Management System", Harvard Business Review, January–February 1996, pp. 75–85.

[4] Walther, T., Johansson, H., Dunleavy, J., and Hjelm, E., *Reinventing the CFO*, McGraw Hill: New York, 1997, p. 108.

## Ethics in Benchmarking

To promote ethical benchmarking, the International Benchmarking Clearinghouse and the Strategic Planning Institute Council on Benchmarking have adopted a common Code of Conduct. These rules of conduct cover such areas as:

- Legal matters (e.g., collusion to restrain trade).
- Integrity.
- Confidentiality.
- Proper use of information and names.
- Contacting policies.
- Preparation for benchmarking.

# STRATEGIES TO ENHANCE PRODUCTIVITY

To achieve gains in productivity, many companies have turned to various strategies in recent years. Two of these strategies are downsizing and business process reengineering.

## Downsizing

For many companies, particularly in service industries, a major portion of costs are labor-related costs. These include not only the wages and salaries of employees but also fringe benefits and overhead costs to support labor such as telephone expenses and office space. Thus, when companies look to reduce costs and improve efficiency, a prime candidate becomes the reduction of their work force. This phenomenon, sometimes referred to as **downsizing,** can involve outsourcing one or more functions, consolidating certain functions, initiating across-the-board cuts in personnel, or eliminating business segments such as product lines or geographical territories.

While downsizing may reduce costs and improve efficiency in the short run, it can harm the company's long-run competitiveness and well-being. Remaining employees sometimes become overburdened, making more mistakes and declining in productivity. Morale suffers. They fear for their jobs, and company commitment takes a back seat to personal interests. Therefore, if downsizing is deemed necessary, it must be done with extreme care.

Often, downsizing is accompanied by fundamentally changing the way a company operates. This strategy is called business process reengineering.

## Business Process Reengineering

A business process is a series of activities that are linked to perform a specific objective. Business processes include both manufacturing as well as nonmanufacturing processes such as purchasing materials or handling customer inquiries and complaints. **Business process reengineering (BPR)** refers to changes made in management, organizational structure, and work practices to achieve significant improvements in quality, cost, speed, and service. BPR is not merely a marginal changing of processes; rather, it involves major restructuring of organizational forms, management procedures, job descriptions, work flows, control systems, and organizational cultures.

One of the main principles of BPR is to organize work around processes and outcomes rather than around tasks and departments. Instead of having a specialist for each separate task, one person or group is responsible for an entire process. This has led to the replacement of functional departments like sales and production with interdisciplinary teams that focus on performing an entire process. For instance, at IBM Credit Corporation, the credit approval process formerly involved five

---

**Contemporary Practice 14.6**
## Benefits of Business Process Reengineering

*"After Citibank reengineered a credit-analysis system, its employees were able to spend 43%, instead of 9% of their time recruiting new business. Profits increased by 750% over a two-year period. When Datacard Corporation reengineered its customer-service operations, its sales* *increased sevenfold. Bell Atlantic reduced both the time (15 days to a few hours) and the costs ($88 million a year to $6 million) required to connect customers to long-distance carriers."*

Source: Romney, M., "Business Process Re-engineering," CPA Journal, October 1994, p. 30.

---

different individuals. Credit requests were forwarded to someone to check the applicant's credit, then to another person to set the interest rate, and so on. IBM Credit reengineered this process so that one individual, called a deal structurer, completely processes an application. Productivity has dramatically increased.[5]

## Ethical Considerations

Enhancing productivity via downsizing or business process reengineering can be traumatic for individuals in the organization. Therefore, management must be careful to conduct these changes in an ethical manner. A key consideration should be to communicate the changes in an honest way. Decisions as to who gets terminated and how it is done can be subject to serious abuses. Those whose job duties are changed should be properly informed about new expectations and should be trained adequately for their new roles.

Major downsizing or business process reengineering can sometimes affect entire communities. Such is often the case with plant closings. Should management consider the impact of a plant closing on the welfare of the surrounding community? Many people believe that there is an ethical responsibility to do so.

## SUMMARY

The focus on quality has caused the analysis of the costs of quality to become an important managerial task. These costs are broken into four components: prevention, appraisal, internal failure, and external failure. Often it is difficult to define these costs clearly. The goal is to reduce total quality costs. Often this is done by increasing prevention and appraisal costs to reduce or nearly eliminate failure costs. ABC systems have aided the measurement and reporting of these costs significantly. International pressures for improved quality can be typified by the EC's ISO 9000 quality standards. Quality costs and documentation are the management accountant's responsibility.

Recognizing that most costs of production are determined when products are developed and designed, many companies are turning to a technique known as target costing. After a target selling price and a target profit are established, a target cost is obtained for the product. The company then designs the product based on the target cost. To promote continuous improvement in the manufacturing stage, kaizen cost targets are reduced in each successive period.

Activity analysis involves reviewing activities and eliminating those that do not add value to the product. Throughput time is composed of process time, inspection time, move time, wait time, and

---

[5] Romney, M., "Business Process Re-engineering,"*CPA Journal*, October 1994, p. 30.

storage time. The most common place to look for nonvalue-added activities is in inspection, move, wait, and storage time.

Traditional measures of performance are being reexamined. New measures are being adopted to better fit the concepts of activity-based management. These are largely nonfinancial measures relating to manufacturing productivity, labor productivity, product quality, inventory reduction, machine maintenance, and delivery performance. Many companies are beginning to integrate nonfinancial measures with financial measures into a balanced scorecard. Companies are also benchmarking their performance against best practices from other organizations. To achieve gains in productivity, many companies have turned to strategies such as downsizing and business process reengineering.

# PROBLEMS FOR REVIEW

## Review Problem A

The following accounts were listed among the chart of accounts for Arbiser Machine Tooling:

Warranty Repairs
Supplier Training and Certification Programs
Cost Accounting Salaries
Engineering Design Reviews
Customer Returns and Allowances
Scrap
Depreciation on Machinery
Final Product Testing
Rework Time
Planned Machine Maintenance
Emergency Machine Repairs
Purchased Materials Inspection
Direct Labor

**Required:**
Classify these accounts according to the appropriate costs of quality category—prevention, appraisal, internal failure, and external failure. Not all accounts will be included.

**Solution:**
Prevention costs:
Supplier Training and Certification Programs
Engineering Design Reviews
Planned Machine Maintenance
Appraisal costs:
Final Product Testing
Purchased Materials Inspection
Internal failure costs:
Scrap
Rework Time
Emergency Machine Repairs
External failure costs:
Warranty Repairs
Customer Returns and Allowances

Cost Accounting Salaries, Depreciation on Machinery, and Direct Labor may include elements of quality costs, but they are not normally considered costs of quality accounts. If quality costs are included in these accounts, they should be segregated by creating new expense accounts to track these costs directly.

## Review Problem B

Lee & Newman, Inc. manufactured cash registers with an average throughput time of three hours during a recent quarter. Inspection time averaged 20 minutes; wait time was typically one-half hour; and move time usually totaled 15 minutes. The manufacturing cycle efficiency during this quarter averaged 50 percent. Other data were as follows:

|  | April | May | June |
|---|---|---|---|
| Average tooling turnaround time | 1/4 hr. | 1/3 hr. | 1/2 hr. |
| Cash registers produced per day per employee | 3.3 | 2.8 | 2.6 |
| First-pass yield | 78% | 85% | 88% |
| Unscheduled machine downtime | 10 hrs. | 9.5 hrs. | 8.5 hrs. |

**Required:**
1. Determine the amount of average storage time.
2. Based on the preceding data, why did the daily output of cash registers decline during the quarter?
3. What aspects of performance improved during the quarter?

**Solution:**
1. Amount of average storage time:

Manufacturing cycle efficiency = .50 = Process time ÷ 180 minutes
Process time = .50 × 180 minutes = 90 minutes

90 + 20 + 30 + 15 + Storage time = 180
Storage time = 25 minutes

2. Daily output of cash registers declined because the average tooling turnaround time increased.
3. First-pass yields and unscheduled machine downtime improved during the quarter.

## TERMINOLOGY REVIEW

Activity analysis (585)
Activity-based management (ABM) (585)
Appraisal costs (577)
Balanced scorecard (591)
Benchmarking (593)
Business process reengineering (BPR) (594)
Downsizing (594)
External failure costs (578)
First-pass yield (588)
Inspection time (586)

Internal failure costs (577)
ISO 9000 standards (582)
Kaizen costing (585)
Labor content percentage (588)
Manufacturing cycle efficiency (MCE) (587)
Move time (586)
Prevention costs (577)
Process time (585)
Storage time (587)
Target costing (584)

Theory of Constraints (590)                Value-added direct labor (588)
Throughput time (587)                      Value-added labor ratio (588)
Total quality management (TQM) (586)       Wait time (586)

## QUESTIONS FOR REVIEW AND DISCUSSION

1. Identify four categories of costs of quality. Give an example of each.

2. Production Manager Al Cohol asks Quality Manager Nick O'Teen, "Isn't a failure cost a failure cost? Why break them into two components?" Respond to Al.

3. Greg Orian, controller of Calendar Creators, sees the four categories of costs of quality as substitutions for each other. Explain why he might believe this.

4. This chapter suggests that a total quality management program may cause the portions of total quality costs to shift over time as quality efforts take hold within an organization. Explain this possible shift.

5. What important cost of quality is missing from most cost accounting systems when these costs are being monitored? Why?

6. Why might the task of measuring, reporting, and analyzing costs of quality be difficult? Can these costs be easily benchmarked across firms? Explain.

7. Discuss the possible linkage between monitoring quality by measuring quality costs and by using nonfinancial measures of quality performance. Comment on which is most important.

8. Explain why minimizing the costs of quality in one time period may not be the optimal spending level for long-run quality improvement.

9. For most firms, is it possible to eliminate failures and, therefore, failure costs? Is it possible to push total quality costs to zero? Explain.

10. Comment on the importance of costs of quality in service organizations. Among the four categories, where might the major emphasis be placed?

11. How is target costing different from the traditional approach of setting costs and prices?

12. During which stages in a product's life cycle do target costing and kaizen costing apply?

13. What is meant by the term "nonvalue-added costs?" Provide three examples.

14. List and describe the five ways that time is spent in a manufacturing process. Which of these activities are likely candidates for nonvalue-added activities? Explain.

15. Define the term "manufacturing cycle efficiency." What does it represent?

16. Explain the value-added labor ratio.

17. Why are nonfinancial measures of quality needed in addition to costs of quality?

18. Describe the four types of nonfinancial measures related to product quality.

19. Provide two examples of nonfinancial measures that assess a firm's capability to keep equipment operating and to produce goods quickly.

20. Which measure of poor delivery performance is often impossible to determine?

21. What are the common external sources for obtaining performance benchmarks?

22. What forms can downsizing take?

23. Explain business process reengineering.

# EXERCISES

**14–1. Costs of Quality Categories.** The following accounts and their costs are from Tibor Textiles.

| | |
|---|---:|
| Customer design verification | $ 5,000 |
| Machine testing after machine setup | 10,000 |
| Employee training | 40,000 |
| Raw materials testing | 12,000 |
| Scrap loss net of scrap sales | 30,000 |
| Materials reprocessing | 28,000 |
| Customer complaints and returns | 40,000 |
| Final product testing | 20,000 |
| In-process inspection | 45,000 |
| Routine machine maintenance | 25,000 |
| Nonroutine machine repairs | 50,000 |
| Discounts for missed delivery dates | 33,000 |
| Price reductions for product quality downgrades | 68,000 |
| Idle labor—downtime due to machine repairs | 37,000 |

**Required:**

1. Classify these costs by the four costs of quality categories.
2. If sales were $4,600,000, show the costs of quality as a percentage of sales for each category and in total.

**14–2. Comments on Costs of Quality.** At a recent continuing education program, Eddie Berger heard several speakers talk about measuring costs of quality. He asked questions and had good discussions with other managers. But several ideas still bothered him. He scratched some notes for further thought on his pad including:

**A.** Costs of quality are free. If we spend more to reduce failure costs than the failures cost us, how can they be free?

**B.** The second speaker said that the optimal costs of quality level can't be found in most cases. She also said that the optimal level is a moving target. If it is optimal today, isn't it optimal next year too?

**C.** Another (boring) speaker focused on how to design the chart of accounts and cost centers to better capture quality costs. That seems like a waste of time for us since we just implemented a new general ledger system last year.

**D.** The terms internal and external "benchmarking" were mentioned. What did this have to do with costs of quality?

**Required:** Eddie is back in his office. He asks your reaction to these thoughts.

Service

**14–3. Costs of Quality Trends.** Haber & Killian, an architectural firm, recently studied its costs over the past three years. The partners of the firm have been promoting total quality management programs to its clients for years. They finally decided to apply the same concepts to their own business. After much discussion, they adopted certain definitions of quality costs and began to monitor them. They did acknowledge that internal failure costs also included costs of nonvalue-added activities that were not technically failure costs. Now, three years later, they show the following data as highly summarized results of their efforts.

| | 2007 | | 2008 | | 2009 | |
|---|---|---|---|---|---|---|
| | 1st Half | 2nd Half | 1st Half | 2nd Half | 1st Half | 2nd Half |
| Prevention costs | $ 5,000 | $ 20,000 | $ 50,000 | $ 60,000 | $ 50,000 | $ 55,000 |
| Appraisal costs | 40,000 | 60,000 | 65,000 | 70,000 | 72,000 | 70,000 |
| Internal failure costs | 120,000 | 130,000 | 120,000 | 123,000 | 110,000 | 105,000 |
| External failure costs | 43,000 | 30,000 | 25,000 | 26,000 | 18,000 | 15,000 |

Client billings have gone up modestly over the three years, perhaps 20 percent in total.

**Required:** Comment on the results of the three-year effort.

Service

**14–4. Analysis of Quality Costs.** Tinter Realtors has reported the following data for 2008:

| | |
|---|---|
| Prevention costs | $374,000 |
| Appraisal costs | 615,600 |
| Internal failure costs | 651,400 |
| External failure costs | 27,100 |

**Required:**
Comment on the following thoughts:
A. Prevention and appraisal spending has eliminated nearly all customer quality problems.
B. More should be spent on prevention to even the spending among the three internal cost categories.
C. A goal of reducing costs in each category by 10 percent (or by some specific dollar amount) should be set in next year's profit plan.
D. A good job has been done if the sum of the four costs as a percentage of sales declines somewhat.

**14–5. Appraisal Costs versus Failure Costs.** In the Walle Company, a Lancaster, England firm, a production problem is being analyzed. Currently, 11,000 units of its Mark4 product are produced. All of these units could be sold. Good units sell for £100 per unit. Four production stages are required. Final inspection in Stage 4 typically finds a 10 percent failure rate. Of these, half are scrapped; and half can be reworked and sold as off-brand units to a discount house at a price equal to the normal per unit production costs. Scrap and rework costs are taken directly to cost of goods sold. Costs for the four production stages are:

| | Stage 1 | Stage 2 | Stage 3 | Stage 4 | Rework |
|---|---|---|---|---|---|
| Materials | £88,000 | £22,000 | | | £1,000 |
| Labor | 66,000 | 44,000 | £33,000 | £44,000 | 2,000 |
| Variable overhead | 66,000 | 88,000 | 99,000 | 44,000 | 2,000 |
| Cost per unit | £20 | £14 | £12 | £8 | |

Sheldon Spero, production manager, is considering adding an inspection step to each production stage. He feels that this will reduce the scrapped units to nearly zero. It will add £1 per unit to Stages 1, 2, and 3 to cover inspections, testing, and rework needed. Costs in Stage 4 would shift but remain the same in total since inspection is already being done there.

**Required:**

1. Estimate the costs of internal failure in the current process.
2. Evaluate Mr. Spero's proposal. What advantages does this approach offer aside from financial concerns?

**14–6. Quality Costs and Ethical Issues.** Janie's Dairy Products operates a network of 30 dairy processing plants across the eastern United States. A portion of the bonus system considers improvements in reducing waste and costs of quality. The payment is 5 percent of the annual improvement over the prior year. The company defines the categories of improvement as follows:

> Lost product due to operational problems (waste, production yield, or scrap)
> Product returns
> Prevention costs
> Inspection costs
> Operational efficiency savings

The results are reported as part of the overall responsibility accounting process with most of the initial transaction classification and recordkeeping done at the plant level. The data are then transferred to the corporate office for report preparation purposes. The controller, Marge Arin, is concerned about several issues:

- In several plants, the patterns of earned bonuses are erratic for certain managers—high in some years and none in others. In fact, the pattern often includes high gains in prevention and inspection cost reductions and strong efficiency savings one year, with the reverse occurring the next year.

- In another case, a frequently promoted manager (and as a result frequently transferred) has had a record of generating high bonuses for quality each year. Yet, in each case the manager who takes over a location after a transfer seems to have quality problems.

- In a recent executive staff meeting, several vice presidents mentioned problems with product yields, customer satisfaction surveys, and several small product recalls.

**Required:**

1. Comment on the bonus system and how the issues of concern to the controller might be interrelated.
2. Suggest ways the system might be improved (using both accounting and operational methods) to help resolve the issues.

Service

**14–7. Target Costing.** Janet Harris, general manager of Banks Bus Service, is considering adding a new route. Based on preliminary market research, she has decided that the fare should be $3.50.

**Required:** If the company's profit margin is 20 percent of revenues, what should the target cost be?

**14–8. Target Cost of a Product.** Professor Fruitcake has surveyed a group of companies on their needs for accounting software and the prices they are willing to pay. Based on this survey, he has developed an idea for a specialized software product which can be reasonably priced at $450. Professor Fruitcake believes that the particular product he designs and manufactures should allow him a profit of 25 percent of the product's cost.

**Required:** What is Professor Fruitcake's target cost for this new software product?

**14–9. Kaizen Costing.** In 2006, Heights High School incurred the following costs in its athletic department:

| Event | Cost per Event |
|---|---|
| Track meet | $600 |
| Swim meet | $950 |
| Soccer game | $820 |
| Water polo m.atch | $980 |

The school has recently begun a system of kaizen costing. Accordingly, the principal, Janet Orr, has asked Jim Nasium, the head of the athletic department, to reduce costs by 2 percent each year for the forseeable future.

**Required:**
Assume that Jim Nasium reduces costs according to the plans set by Janet Orr. Compute the projected kaizen cost targets in 2010 for each of the preceding events.

**14–10. Nonfinancial Performance Measurement.** Kessler Mortgage Corporation provides the following data on its loan application processing activities for the month of February:

| | |
|---|---|
| Move time | 18 hours |
| Wait time | 63 hours |
| Process time | 230 hours |
| Storage time | 15 hours |
| Inspection time | 22 hours |

**Required:** Compute the cycle efficiency for February.

**14–11. Value-Added and Nonvalue-Added Activities.** Loretta Love Clothiers manufactures denim jeans in a process that passes through three departments. The output of each department is immediately transferred to the next department to await further work. Output from the last department in the process represents the completed product, which goes to finished goods inventory to await shipping. Specifically, dyed denim cloth bales are released from the storeroom (materials inventory) and moved to the Cutting Department where the fabric is cut to patterns. The cut pieces are sorted into sets of jeans. Any miscut pieces are scrapped. The sets move to the Stitch and Form Department where the pieces are sewn together. Thread, zippers, and snaps are added during this process to make the completed jeans. The jeans are sent to the Inspection and Finishing Department. Inspection makes certain that jeans meet quality standards; spoiled and defective jeans are removed from the process. Spoiled jeans go to the scrap pile. Inspectors must determine the extent of defect in those jeans considered defective. If the defect can easily be corrected, the jeans go back into the process where the work will be done. If the defect cannot be corrected, the jeans are treated as seconds and are sold unlabeled in factory outlets and discount stores. Those jeans successfully passing inspection move to the labeling tables where brand labels are stitched on each pair of jeans. The completed jeans move to the warehouse where they become part of the finished goods inventory.

**Required:**
1. Identify the activities in the denim jeans production process that fall into process time, inspection time, move time, wait time, and storage time.
2. List the activities in the denim jeans production process that are candidates for nonvalue-added activities.

Service

**14–12. Nonvalue-Added Costs in a Doctor's Office.** Dr. Steve Rosenthal has his own medical practice. He specializes in the treatment of diabetics. His staff consists of a receptionist, two nurses, a lab technician, and a dietitian. As patients enter the outer office, they check in with the receptionist. The patient then waits until called by a nurse. When called, the patient moves from the waiting room to the inner offices. The patient must weigh in and is then assigned a room for the rest of the work and conferences. The nurse assigning the patient to a room gathers all the personal data for updating the medical records, such as insulin dosage, medication, illnesses since last visit, and so forth. The nurse also takes an initial blood sample for blood sugar testing and performs a blood pressure test. The patient then waits until the doctor comes in. After the doctor's conference, the nurse returns to take more blood samples, depending on what is ordered by the doctor. The patient then waits until the dietitian comes to review eating habits and talk about how to improve meal planning and weight control. The patient returns to the receptionist to pay for the office visit and to schedule the next visit.

**Required:**
1. Identify the activities in the doctor's office that fall into process time, inspection time, move time, wait time, and storage time.
2. List the activities in the doctor's office that are candidates for nonvalue-added activities. Explain why you classify them as nonvalue-added activities.

**14–13. Value-Added Labor.** Natasha Company produces air pumps in a small factory about 30 kilometers south of Moscow, Russia. The company employs eleven people with nine direct and two indirect laborers. The plant manager, Boris Badinov, describes the tasks of the nine direct workers as follows:
**(a)** Three fabricators who cut and grind metal parts from raw steel, aluminum, and brass.
**(b)** One parts inspector who examines and approves parts produced.
**(c)** One warehouse stocker who keeps parts in inventory and fills bins used by assembly workers.
**(d)** One molder who makes vinyl seals and plastic fittings by using an injection molder.
**(e)** Two assemblers who assemble parts into product.
**(f)** One product inspector who approves the final product.

**Required:**
1. Categorize each of the nine workers as value-added or nonvalue-added workers.
2. Compute the value-added labor ratio.

Service

**14–14. Value-Added Labor.** KATT Country is an FM radio station with the current country hits. The station manager, Jimmy Baron, has provided data on employees and wages for September, as follows:

|  | Number of Employees | Wages & Salaries | Totals |
|---|---|---|---|
| Lead disc jockeys | 8 | $2,000 | $16,000 |
| Support disc jockeys | 9 | 1,500 | 13,500 |
| News and weather staff | 3 | 1,700 | 5,100 |
| Engineering staff | 5 | 2,100 | 10,500 |
| Supervisors/managers | 5 | 2,300 | 11,500 |
| Account executives | 6 | 1,200 | 7,200 |
| Clerical/office staff | 4 | 1,100 | 4,400 |
| Totals | 40 |  | $68,200 |

**Required:**

1. Compute the ratio of value-added employees to total employees in terms of number of employees.
2. Compute the ratio of value-added employees to total employees in terms of total compensation paid.

**14–15. Nonfinancial Performance Measures.** Jagoda Hair Products manufactures a wide range of shampoos and conditioners. The company has the reputation for delivering high-quality products on time. Each month the CFO, Dan Druff, issues a production efficiency report. The data compiled on these reports for the third quarter are as follows:

|  | July | August | September |
|---|---|---|---|
| Manufacturing cycle efficiency | 94% | 96% | 92% |
| Total setup time (hours) | 62 | 60 | 58 |
| Overtime hours | 70 | 73 | 76 |
| Power consumption in kilowatt-hours (000s omitted) | 802 | 832 | 838 |
| Machine downtime (hours) | 15 | 10 | 20 |
| Number of unscheduled machine maintenance calls | 0 | 0 | 1 |
| Inventory value/Sales revenue | 4% | 4% | 5% |
| Number of defective units received in raw materials orders | 2 | 1 | 0 |
| Number of defective units—in-process | 35 | 40 | 55 |
| Number of defective units—finished goods | 18 | 12 | 24 |
| Percentage of customer orders filled | 100% | 100% | 100% |
| Percentage of on-time orders delivered | 99% | 98% | 94% |
| Number of products returned by customers | 0 | 0 | 1 |

**Required:**

Categorize each of the preceding nonfinancial performance measures as one of the following:

1. Manufacturing productivity.
2. Product quality.
3. Delivery performance.
4. Inventory control.
5. Machine maintenance.

**14–16. Measures of Delivery Performance.** Pollard Communications is an Indiana-based company that manufactures fax machines in two of its four wholly-owned subsidiaries located Kuala Lumpur, Malaysia, and Jakarta, Indonesia. Pollard wishes to compare the delivery performance between these subsidiaries. Operations managers for both subsidiaries have provided the Pollard vice-president for operations, Carol Morris, with the following data for a recent month:

|  | Malaysian Subsidiary | Indonesian Subsidiary |
| --- | --- | --- |
| Number of customer orders | 3,000 | 5,500 |
| Number of orders delivered | 2,895 | 5,250 |
| Number of orders delivered on time | 2,540 | 5,100 |
| Average time from order to delivery | 3 weeks | 4 weeks |

**Required:**

Which of the two subsidiaries is performing better delivery service? Provide support for your answer.

**14–17. Balanced Scorecard.** Nemeth's Pizza Shops ("Seven days without pizza makes one weak") operates in 55 locations throughout Pennsylvania and Maryland. The CEO, Mitchell Blass, wants to institute a performance measurement system based on a balanced scorecard. The following measures are being considered:

**a.** Percentage of pizzas delivered on time
**b.** Percentage of sales growth
**c.** Pounds of pizza scrapped
**d.** Production cost per pizza
**e.** Packaging materials cost per month
**f.** Percentage of repeating customers
**g.** Employee turnover percentages
**h.** Response time to customer inquiries

**i.** Number of customer complaints
**j.** Number of pizzas per labor hour
**k.** Hours of community volunteer work
**l.** Return on invested capital
**m.** Cost per delivery
**n.** Throughput time
**o.** Suggestions per employee
**p.** safety incident index

**Required:** Classify the performance measures into the four categories contained in a balanced scorecard.

**14–18. Downsizing, Kaizen Costing, and Ethics.** Biltmore Insurance Corporation instituted kaizen costing in 2004 for all of its divisions. During 2003, the Claims Division incurred costs of $5.6 million. Seeking to dramatically reduce costs, the manager of the Claims Division, Gail Norman, thought about cutting $200,000 in payroll costs for 2004 by eliminating all part-time claims adjuster positions. However, she soon realized that her kaizen cost target for 2005 would then be $5.4 million. Therefore, she decided to institute her reforms much more slowly and, consequently, reduced payroll costs by only $40,000 during 2004.

**Required:** Discuss the ethical dimension of Gail Norman's dilemma.

# PROBLEMS

**14–19. Trends in Quality Costs.** Kal Held Properties sells time sharing for its condominiums in Florida. Karen Bossen, the controller, has just finished a study of its quality costs. Based on recent accounting reports, quality costs for the 2001 fiscal year are as follows:

| Prevention costs | $100,000 |
|---|---|
| Appraisal costs | 300,000 |
| Internal failure costs | 400,000 |
| External failure costs (including lost sales) | 300,000 |

These costs are 11 percent of sales. The firm plans to implement a program called "TQM Victory" to reduce quality costs in total and as a percentage of sales. Sales are expected to expand by 10 percent per year. By 2003, it expects to spend $300,000 on prevention costs by substantially expanding employee training. Improved inspection efforts will add $100,000 to appraisal costs. By 2003, each failure cost category will be reduced by 10 percent.

By 2005, continued efforts will hold prevention and appraisal costs constant; but external failure costs are expected to drop to 1 percent of sales. Internal failure costs will drop 30 percent from 2003 levels.

By 2007 (the target year of the TQM effort), prevention costs should fall to $200,000; appraisal costs could be cut in half from 2003 levels. Internal failure costs should drop another 40 percent from their 2005 levels. And, external failure costs are targeted to be no higher than 0.3 percent of sales.

**Required:**
1. What are total quality costs targeted to be in 2007?
2. Can the firm get to a 4 percent of sales target by 2007? Explain.
3. Comment on at least three key assumptions you see from the data provided.

Service

**14–20. Costs of Quality.** Michael Leader Enterprises processes financial contracts for several major banks. Accuracy is essential. Errors cause inconvenience to the parties involved, legal entanglements, and embarrassment. The financial arrangements are complex and difficult to check manually. Thus, self-checking software is being considered to eliminate much of the calculation evaluation, review word processing, and check for missing items. The software purchase, modification, and installation will cost $300,000. Annual updating and routine monitoring will cost $30,000 per year. It is estimated that three clerical positions can be eliminated at a "loaded" cost of $40,000 each. Also, the rate of errors in finished documents can be cut by 80 percent. Correcting one error costs an estimated $100. A review of one sample month's work last year showed that 50 errors slipped through the review processes and had to be corrected. These errors resulted in a loss of $50,000 in costs and legal fees. This was thought to be a typical month in terms of activity and results.

**Required:**
Assuming a three-year cycle for this computer system, evaluate the costs and benefits of the new software.

**14–21. Vignettes on Costs of Quality.** Steve Fan, a quality assurance manager for Lynx Motors, has seen a lot of proposals for spending money on quality projects. He wants to "get his money's worth" from the investments he approves. He has the following on his desk now:
  **A.** Manager A recommends a $50,000 expenditure to modify equipment which will reduce the tolerances in a metal grinding operation. The equipment is expected to last another five years. Eventually, reject rates will be lowered by 50 percent.

Annually, this will save 500 units from being scrapped. The manufactured per unit cost is:

| | |
|---|---|
| Prime costs | $ 8 |
| Variable overhead | 2 |
| Fixed overhead | 8 |
| Unit cost | $18 |

Fixed overhead is common costs. Scrap revenue is $4 per unit.

**B.** Manager B wants to expand output of saleable units by 1,000 monthly. For these units, incremental costs will be $120,000. Current production capacity is 50,000 units. Typically, only 45,000 good units are produced and sold. Ten percent of the output has to be reprocessed and is sold at a price that recovers the incremental and reprocessing costs only. Steve thinks that improved training of employees would reduce the need for reprocessing by 40 percent. The training over the next year will cost $80,000.

**C.** Manager C wants to increase the number of inspectors to reduce defects leaving the plant. The plan calls for $200,000 for a testing lab and $100,000 for personnel to test every fifth item on the assembly line. Most defects are caused by adapting complex engineering designs to the production equipment. Last year, ongoing engineering changes cost $60,000 to create and another $135,000 to implement. Scrap from testing processes after each engineering change costs $36,000.

**Required:** Suggest an analysis format to evaluate each case.

**14–22. Analyzing Quality Costs Over Time.** Management of Ellin Software Services (ESS) has recently implemented a TQM program to eliminate a serious level of "program bugs" that has plagued its recent product releases. The following activities and their costs were taken from ESS's records. The data are for 2003 (the year prior to the TQM program) and 2005 (the year after the start of the TQM program).

| | 2003 | 2005 |
|---|---|---|
| Design documentation standards development | $ 0 | $100,000 |
| Documentation of customer training process | 0 | 20,000 |
| Documentation of changes to software | 5,000 | 20,000 |
| Customer training | 100,000 | 130,000 |
| Software testing—customer site | 130,000 | 80,000 |
| Software testing—prerelease | 50,000 | 140,000 |
| Telephone "on-line" customer problem support | 90,000 | 60,000 |
| Software corrections and redesign | 50,000 | 20,000 |
| Field "trouble shooting" for customer support | 140,000 | 80,000 |
| Costs of contract cancellations | 180,000 | 30,000 |
| Revenues lost due to delivery date delays | 0 | 120,000 |
| Training for systems designers/programmers | 100,000 | 250,000 |
| Training for sales staff | 10,000 | 80,000 |

**Required:**
1. Categorize the costs of quality for both years.
2. Evaluate the two years. Develop a scenario to explain the major differences in costs between the two years. In other words, what happened?

**3.** If 2003 showed an operating loss and 2005 showed a small operating profit, would this change your scenario in Part 2 or confirm it? Explain.

Service

**14–23. Classifying Costs of Quality.** Paul Miller, controller of Meta Medical, has reviewed the costs of quality records for the past year. Meta Medical provides calibration and maintenance services for sophisticated medical equipment in the midwest. Training, testing, and service calls are major costs that seem to grow each year. Miller is trying to measure possible ways of reducing the total costs of quality as part of a review of all processes and activities within the firm. He assembled the following costs.

| | |
|---|---|
| Parts warranty, including replacement labor | $ 92,000 |
| Emergency trips to service client machines | 86,000 |
| Rental of substitute equipment to cover client downtime | 43,000 |
| Training of repair technicians (time and travel) | 196,000 |
| Inspection of finished repairs | 45,000 |
| Testing and certifications of calibration equipment | 15,000 |
| Development of client testing processes and diagnostics | 31,500 |

Miller is aware of two contracts that were cancelled this past year because of client complaints about poor service response. These contracts totaled $60,000.

**Required:**

**1.** Classify these costs according to prevention, appraisal, internal failure, and external failure.

**2.** Comment on the difficulty that Paul Miller likely has in analyzing these and other costs that might be costs of quality.

Service

**14–24. Business Process Reengineering.** Fishwrap, Inc. owns a chain of 20 similar-sized newspapers. A decentralized purchasing system is used whereby each newspaper obtains its own newsprint. On average for all newspapers, 70 percent of the newsprint is delivered on time.

The following average cost data per newspaper have been obtained for the past year:

| | |
|---|---|
| Costs of newsprint | $980,000 |
| Purchasing Department salary costs | 240,000 |
| Other Purchasing Department costs | 125,000 |

Of the above newsprint, an average of $7,200 turned out to be defective.

Because of the decentralized purchasing system, Fishwrap has been unable to take advantage of quantity discounts. Therefore, the company reengineered the purchasing process by introducing a corporate Purchasing Department. Each newspaper continued to purchase its own newsprint from approved vendors. However, the corporate controller, Steve Posner, began to track the purchases of all 20 newspapers and used that data to negotiate quantity discounts and resolve problems with vendors. The on-time delivery rate improved to 85 percent. The defect rate (in terms of dollars) decreased by 60 percent. The average quantity discount amounted to 2.8 percent of newsprint cost. After reengineering, the average salary and other purchasing costs for the local departments decreased from $365,000 to $190,000. The annual costs of the centralized Purchasing Department are $1,800,000.

**Required:** Evaluate whether reengineering the purchasing process was worthwhile.

**14–25. Target Costing and Downsizing.** Blossom Enterprises manufactures mah-jongg sets that sell for $100 per set. In 2003, the following manufacturing costs were incurred to produce 12,000 sets:

| | |
|---|---|
| Direct materials | $120,000 |
| Direct labor | 210,000 |
| Energy costs—variable | 144,000 |
| Energy costs—fixed | 130,000 |
| Other fixed overhead | 175,000 |
| Other variable overhead | 96,000 |
| | $875,000 |

In addition, Blossom incurred $145,000 in marketing and administrative expenses (all fixed) during 2003.

These sales and cost figures are expected to be the same during 2004. However, to achieve a 2005 sales level of just 11,000 sets, the increasing competition from Marcy's Gaming Corporation will necessitate a price reduction from $100 to $90. To maintain the same net profit margin percentage, Blossom plans to produce 11,000 sets by downsizing the direct labor work force in 2005.

**Required:**
1. What is Blossom's target cost for 2005?
2. Compute the planned percentage reduction of the direct labor workforce for 2005.

**14–26. Nonvalue-Added Activities.** Murray's Donut Heaven manufactures donuts that are available fresh every day at several stores throughout Memphis. Donuts left over at the end of the day are packaged and sold at a reduced price as day-old donuts. Donuts not sold by the end of the second day are contributed to the local food bank. The production process consists of the following steps:

**(a)** Ingredients such as flour, sugar, and cooking oil are received, inspected, and placed in the storeroom until requisitioned by production.

**(b)** Upon requisition, the ingredients are transported from the storeroom to the production area and staged at the mixing area.

**(c)** Ingredients are blended into a dough mixture in 40-pound batches by six heavy-duty mixers.

**(d)** The dough is rolled on large boards and left to rise in a holding area.

**(e)** When the dough is ready, the boards are moved to the cutting machines; and the donuts are cut. Leftovers from each cutting are accumulated, re-rolled on another board, and processed through the cutting machine. At the end of the production day, leftovers and unprocessed dough on boards are thrown into the trash.

**(f)** The cut donuts and donut holes are placed on wire trays and taken to the cooking area, where the trays are stacked until ready for cooking.

**(g)** The cooks empty the trays into large vats of hot cooking oil where the donuts and donut holes are, in effect, fried in a sea of oil.

**(h)** The cooked products are removed from the vats and placed on drying pads which absorb the excess oil from the donuts. While the product is drying, it is inspected. Misshaped donuts are removed and set aside for disposal. What the crew doesn't eat is thrown out at the end of the production shift.

**(i)** After drying, the products are placed on large square boards and moved to the finishing area where they will be coated with glaze, icing, powdered sugar, coconut, candy chips, etc.

**(j)** After the coating settles or dries, whichever is the case, the donuts are placed in boxes of four dozen each. Donut holes are packed in boxes with 100 donut holes per box. The boxes are moved to the shipping area to await the trucks that will deliver them to the various retail outlets.

**(k)** Each morning the delivery trucks return the unsold donuts delivered the previous day. (For some reason donut holes are always sold out.) The day-old donuts are repackaged in plastic bags. Each bag contains one dozen donuts and is marked "day-old." The packages are then returned to the retail outlets. On the second day, any unsold packages are returned to the shipping area. At the end of the day, these packages are delivered to the food bank.

**Required:**

**1.** Identify the activities in the donut production process that fall into process time, inspection time, move time, wait time, and storage time.

**2.** List the activities in the donut production process that are candidates for nonvalue-added activities. Explain your rationale.

**14–27. Nonvalue-Added Activities.** McKemie Manufacturing, Inc. specializes in making products that represent the latest materials and technologies available. The company has a reputation for excellent quality and for entering the market with the best products at reasonable prices.

The Cookware Division has two product lines: Chef's Delight, a 9-piece set, and Gourmet Ease, a 20-piece set. Chef's Delight is top quality, featuring anodized solid-spun aluminum for fast, even heat conductivity and a satin finish for easy cleaning. It has bright stainless steel lids and nickel-plated cast iron handles. Stamping operations are needed for the pots, frying pans, and lids. Handles attached to all pots and pans require a molding operation. The handles for each lid are made from stainless steel rods that are bent to shape and flattened where attached to lids. In finishing and assembly, holes are drilled into each pot, pan, and lid so handles can be attached with screws. The pieces are polished, assembled, and placed in the finished goods warehouse.

The production costs for the set of Chef's Delight are as follows:

|  | Total 9 Pieces | Average Per Piece |
|---|---|---|
| Materials | $ 92.70 | $10.30 |
| Stamping and molding: |  |  |
| Direct labor | 10.80 | 1.20 |
| Overhead | 32.40 | 3.60 |
| Finishing and assembly: |  |  |
| Direct labor | 18.00 | 2.00 |
| Overhead | 27.00 | 3.00 |
| Total | $180.90 | $20.10 |

Inspection takes place at the end of each major operation. The outlines and trimmings resulting from the stamping, molding, and drilling are scrap, which is sold for the value of the materials. Pieces from the drilling operation through final assembly that do not meet quality standards are either spoilage or defective work, depending on the inspector's decision. Spoilage goes with the scrap. Defective pieces are reworked.

**Required:**
1. List the activities in the Chef's Delight production process that are probable candidates for nonvalue-added activities.
2. It is often said, "There is no free lunch." Where in the costs of the product will the costs of scrap, spoilage, and rework appear?
3. List some of the things the company might do to eliminate nonvalue-added activities.

**14–28. Cost of Breakage and Defective Customer Service.** Bangkok Trucking Co. hauls goods throughout Thailand. The company guarantees arrival at the designated place within an agreed two-hour period. Penalty for late arrival is 10 percent off the shipping rate. The penalty for being a day late is 20 percent off shipping rates. Each additional day costs an additional 20 percent. The following portion of shipments will arrive late:

| | |
|---|---|
| More than 2 hours late but less than 1 day | 3% |
| 1 day late | 2% |
| 2 days late | 1% |

Breakage of shipped goods results in additional costs related to replacing the goods, reshipping them to their destination, and the disruption of the customer's business. The company follows the policy of paying replacement costs on all broken goods, refunding shipping charges on damaged shipments, and paying a 30 percent surcharge on the replacement cost for business interruption. Approximately one percent of goods shipped (in sales value) will be damaged in shipment.

During July, Bangkok Trucking expects to make 642 shipments with total revenues (before breakage and slow service costs) amounting to 6,420,000 baht. The average shipment is expected to have an 8,000 baht replacement cost. The variable costs are 70 percent of the billed shipping rate. Fixed costs are 900,000 baht per month.

**Required:**
1. Prepare an estimate of the penalties, or revenues lost, from late shipments during July.
2. Prepare an estimate of the costs of shipments with breakage payments.
3. Assume the company can make systems changes and implement training programs that will reduce the late shipments to:

| | |
|---|---|
| More than 2 hours late but less than 1 day | 2% |
| 1 day late | 1% |
| More than one day | 0% |

The percentage of goods shipped that would be damaged would be cut in half. How much could the company afford to pay for such changes and programs?

**14–29. Value-Added Labor in Service Organizations.** Following is a listing of different business enterprises.
(a) Airline.
(b) CPA firm.

(c) Radio station.

(d) Clinic specializing in sports injuries.

(e) Rehabilitation and therapy center for accident and surgery patients.

(f) Member of a nationwide budget motel chain.

(g) Travel agency.

(h) Retail department store.

(i) Automobile garage for repairs and servicing.

(j) Funeral home.

**Required:** For each of the organizations, identify the value-added direct workers.

Service

**14–30. Productivity Measures.** Alvarez Biological Enterprises is a company located in San Jose, Costa Rica, that produces various blood products for use in hospitals throughout Central America. According to the operations manager, Ricardo Odio, the process for producing a blood coagulant used for treating hemophiliacs is as follows:

| Procedure | Average Time Required |
|---|---|
| Blood is drawn from a donor at a clinic | 20 minutes |
| Blood is tested | 30 minutes |
| Placing into proper blood group | 10 minutes |
| Blood is separated into red cell concentrate and plasma | 45 minutes |
| Waiting for delivery of plasma to fractionation plant | 2.5 hours |
| Transportation to fractionation plant | 15 minutes |
| Incoming plasma is shelved | 20 minutes |
| Plasma sits on shelf | 35 minutes |
| Plasma is taken to centrifugation center | 5 minutes |
| Plasma is pooled into batches, prepared, and centrifuged | 1.5 hours |
| Solids (cryoprecipitate) are processed further | 2 hours |
| Cryoprecipitate is frozen | 25 minutes |
| Cryoprecipitate waits for inspection | 15 minutes |
| Cryoprecipitate is inspected | 10 minutes |
| Heat treatment | 10 minutes |
| Movement to packaging center | 5 minutes |
| Packaging | 15 minutes |
| Completed coagulant is taken to storage area | 5 minutes |
| Waiting for delivery to hospital | 3 hours |

A typical batch of plasma transported to the fractionation plant weighs 80 kilograms. Of this, about half results in cryoprecipitate; the other half—a liquid residue—is transformed into other blood products. When the cryoprecipitate is inspected, about two kilograms are typically sent back to the beginning of the centrifugation procedure.

**Required:**

1. Classify the preceding activities into the five categories of throughput time.

2. Compute the manufacturing (processing) cycle efficiency for the entire process.

3. Compute the first-pass yield for the cryoprecipitate.

**14–31. Nonfinancial Measures of Product Quality.** Howard Pen Company manufactures expensive calligraphy pens in two of its Ohio plants. One plant is located in Cleveland, and the other is in Columbus. The pens produced are similar but not identical. Moe Howard, the president, wishes to evaluate the quality of production in each plant. He has asked the two plant managers, Larry Fine of Cleveland and Jerome (Curly) Howard of Columbus, to provide certain performance measures for the most recent year. After he threatened to tear out their tonsils, he received the following data from his two plant managers:

|  | Cleveland Plant | Columbus Plant |
| --- | --- | --- |
| Number of pens produced and sold | 20,000 | 20,000 |
| Number of parts in each pen | 7 | 5 |
| Number of unique parts in each pen | 3 | 1 |
| Percentage of pens returned by customers | 2% | 5% |
| Dollar amount of scrap | $ 250 | $ 370 |
| Percentage of defects in parts received | 3% | 4% |
| Dollar percentage of defects in parts received | 3.5% | 3.2% |
| Number of warranty claims | 22 | 39 |
| Amount of pens that needed rework | 950 | 1,400 |

**Required:** Provide an analysis of product quality performance for the two plants.

**14–32. Nonfinancial Performance Measures.** Robert Newman Associates manufactures transducers in one of its plants. The number produced and sold between 2002 and 2004 has remained steady. Specific performance data for these three years are provided by the plant's general manager, Cal Q. Lait, as follows:

|  | 2002 | 2003 | 2004 |
| --- | --- | --- | --- |
| Time from customer order to delivery | 3 weeks | 2.5 weeks | 2.2 weeks |
| Number of failures at customer locations | 76 | 88 | 91 |
| Transducers produced per day per employee | 25.6 | 29.1 | 30.6 |
| Number of returned transducers | 111 | 114 | 142 |
| Manufacturing cycle efficiency | 80% | 89% | 90% |
| Costs of scrap | $1,897 | $1,995 | $2,066 |
| Percentage of customer orders filled | 85% | 89% | 91% |
| Average time inventories are held | 20 days | 26 days | 28 days |
| First-pass yield | 77% | 72% | 68% |
| Unscheduled machine downtime | 10 hrs. | 9.5 hrs. | 8.5 hrs. |
| Number of engineering change orders | 5 | 3 | 2 |
| Costs of rework | $8,144 | $8,993 | $9,857 |
| Percentage of defects in delivered components | 1.5% | 1.9% | 2.2% |

**Required:**
1. Did product quality improve from 2002 to 2004? Explain.
2. Did manufacturing productivity improve from 2002 to 2004? Explain.
3. Did inventory control improve from 2002 to 2004? Explain.
4. Did delivery performance improve from 2002 to 2004? Explain.

Service

**14–33. Balanced Scorecard.** Marc Carlyn, CEO of Golden Age Nursing Homes, instituted an executive compensation plan several years ago that provides for bonuses based exclusively on return on invested capital. Each nursing home administrator is eligible for a bonus which can amount up to 35 percent of the base salary.

Doug Gray serves as the administrator for one of Golden Age's largest and most profitable nursing homes in the New England area. For each of the past three years since Gray began in this position, his nursing home has had profit increases of at least 10 percent. Last year alone, profit increased by 14 percent.

During the past year, Gray has implemented various initiatives designed to enhance the quality of service. This has resulted in the replacement and refurbishment of much of the equipment in his nursing home. As a consequence, this past year's surveys of patients and their relatives yielded the highest satisfaction indices compiled in the history of that location.

The quality initiative has also greatly improved the morale of the nurses and other health care workers at Gray's nursing home. Absenteeism declined by 28 percent from a year ago. Employee turnover, once considered a serious problem, has been minimal during the past year. Gray has also been receiving many more revenue generating and cost saving suggestions from his employees and directly attributes some of last year's profit increase to implemented improvements arising from employee suggestions.

Because executive bonuses are tied to return on invested capital, Marc Carlyn has informed Gray that his bonus for the year will be much lower than it had been in the previous two years. In a memo to Gray, Carlyn explained that while the operating income for Gray's nursing home has grown, the investment in new equipment more than offset the income growth, resulting in a return on invested capital which had declined from the prior year.

**Required:**

Compare the Golden Age Nursing Homes bonus plan to a balanced scorecard approach to incentive compensation.

Service

# CASE 14—PARE-OTT HOSPITAL

Pare-Ott Hospital, located in Oregon, is affiliated with a medical school. The hospital uses two types of physicians. Unlike in-house physicians, which are employees of Pare-Ott Hospital, the contracted physicians are independent contractors.

In 2006, Pare-Ott made quality improvement a top priority and hired Barry Kuda as Director of Quality Control. His first project was the development a cost of quality (COQ) system for the Respiratory Therapy Department. Kuda hired a COQ consultant, Anna Conda, to work with Ray Vinn, Director of Clinical Engineering, and Sal Amander, Director of Respiratory Care. Amander, a former therapist, runs the Respiratory Therapy Department and reports directly to Vinn. Conda met with Vinn and Amander several times to learn about the procedures in the Respiratory Therapy Department.

The Respiratory Therapy Department has a quality coordinator whose functions include the monitoring of clinical quality and providing training for those therapists who have been reported as being deficient. Respiratory Therapy holds monthly meetings to assess quality problems and to discuss possible remedies such as retraining.

Kuda and Conda began their work on two of the eleven treatments performed in Respiratory Therapy—intubation and bronchodilator. Intubation is the act of placing a breathing tube down the patient's nose or throat. Intubation is ordered by an emergency call and typically between six and eight doctors, nurses, and therapists respond. At the scene, one therapist examines the patient while another readies the equipment. A therapist has up to two attempts to properly insert the tube. If not successful, another therapist attempts the placement. Sometimes the wrong size tube is inserted in the patient and must be replaced. This information is recorded and delivered to Respiratory Therapy for a quality review. The bronchodilator treatment is not ordered under emergency conditions. Treatments are given every five to eight hours for four days. A written order is needed to have further treatments.

Having worked six weeks on this project, Anna Conda derived the following list of items relating to costs of quality:

**Quality Planning**—efforts to assess quality and actions for improvement; primarily performed during a monthly meeting with the Director and Assistant Director of the Respiratory Therapy Department, two Supervisors, and two Lead Therapists; also includes costs associated with activities of a Program Instructor who also serves as Respiratory Therapy's quality coordinator (approximately 10 hours per week of her time is spent on quality improvement).

**Training**—includes maintenance of manuals, educational programs, and monthly departmental awareness activities.

**Quality Audits**—whenever a therapy is ordered by a physician, a therapist must ascertain the appropriateness of the therapy (takes about 10 minutes per newly ordered therapy); also includes checking patient charts and generating quality reports.

**Write-ups**—following every procedure, the activity is written up by the therapist, which usually takes 10 minutes, except for nonroutine activities like intubation, which usually take about 15 minutes.

**Rework**—when a treatment already performed is redone for any reason.

**Malpractice Suits**—legal costs and losses resulting from malpractice lawsuits.

**Malpractice Insurance**—costs incurred for insurance premiums.

**Improper Installations**—relates to intubation procedures.

**Performance Audits**—time card reviews, where each of two Supervisors spends one hour per week reviewing time cards, and order-entry reviews, where each therapist spends one hour per week reviewing the computerized order entries.

**Forecasting and Budgeting**—a two hour task done once a month by the Director.

**Overtime**—when requirements have been underestimated for a particular period, it results in overtime cost for existing personnel.

**Patient Relations**—therapists will spend about 10 minutes explaining to the patient the need for the therapy and the procedures involved.

**Absenteeism and Turnover**—measured by the amount in excess of industry averages.

**Retraining Therapists**—resulting from unsatisfactory performance by the therapist.

**Appraisal Support**—support from two other departments: the Quality Assurance Department conducts monthly reviews of Respiratory Therapy's performance and a Quality Assurance Committee examines Respiratory Therapy's performance quarterly.

**Customer Service**—time spent handling complaints made by physicians or patients.

**Administrative Measures**—management actions resulting from poor clinical practices (approaches and guidelines may be altered; disciplinary action may be taken; additional training may be ordered).

**Required:**

1. Who are the "customers" of the Respiratory Therapy Department? Discuss the concerns and perceptions about quality for the different types of customer.

2. How would you determine the following costs for Respiratory Therapy: Quality Planning, Write-ups, and Improper Installation?

3. Categorize the list of quality costs into prevention, appraisal, internal failure and external failure.

4. Provide three additional costs of quality not found on Anna Conda's list.

# FINANCIAL PERFORMANCE ANALYSIS

## LEARNING OBJECTIVES

After studying Chapter 15, you will be able to:

1. Understand how financial statement analysis can give insight into the financial strengths and weaknesses of an organization.

2. Identify the key questions in each risk area of liquidity, capital adequacy, and asset quality and in each return area of earnings, growth, and market performance.

3. Identify and calculate specific ratios in each risk and return area.2

4. Understand how financial leverage can improve returns to owners.

5. Show how earning-power ratios can be used to improve operating profitability.

6. Know why ratio analysis has certain limitations and caveats that must be recognized.

## Why Do They All Want to Know My Business?

*Maynard Hogberg owns CAD Creations, a computer-aided engineering firm doing contract work for automotive companies and other engineering firms. His firm is now six years old. He used his own money plus venture-capital firm funds to start the company. He has just received his quarterly financial statements.*

*"It's like they have radar! As soon as these statements show up, everybody wants to see them. We're doing okay; I can pay the bills; and we're making a buck." Who are "they," and what do they want to know? Here's a sampling:*

- ***Venture capital firm and its backers.** These people own 40 percent of the stock in CAD Creations. Their primary motive is to reap large gains from an initially risky investment. They want to see the revenues and the earnings growth rates for each quarter as soon as the ink is dry.*

- ***Major Motors' procurement office.** Major Motors is negotiating a long-term contract with CAD Creations and wants a financially stable supplier.*

- ***Supplier of computer equipment.** The equipment seller wants to collect the cash from the sale. Normally, a seller will do a credit check on a prospective customer. In this case, the computer supplier is concerned about the large amount of equipment CAD Creations has purchased on credit.*

- ***Friendly banker.** Maynard has a close working relationship with a commercial lending officer at Detroit National Bank. The DNB's credit department maintains detailed files on the financial status of each borrower. The bank wants to assist Maynard in meeting his cash flow needs and yet wants to be sure that CAD Creations debt service can be paid from operating cash inflows.*

- ***Mike, Maynard's 21-year-old son.** Mike received a few shares of CAD Creations stock as a gift from his dad. Mike is planning to attend an expensive graduate school after his days at Major University. Without sounding too presumptuous, he asks if he can expect any cash dividends soon.*

*Financial statements, blessed by the firm's CPA auditor, are management's representations. Management must approve the statements, understand their contents, and communicate them to the many financial interests facing the firm.*

FINANCIAL PERFORMANCE ANALYSIS is like painting a picture. Blending colors, using different strokes, drawing certain abstractions, integrating foreground and background, and linking focal points, settings, and shapes are a few of the artist's skills which combine to bring art to life. The task of financial analysts is to utilize all the elements of their craft properly to pull the greatest understanding possible from the available data.

The primary vehicles of financial performance analysis are financial ratios. Finding the magnitude and direction of change of ratios gives the analyst insight into (a) what causes specific ratios to change; (b) how these changes are related; and (c) what impacts these changes have on the firm's financial condition. The firm's performance is evaluated relative to its financial plan, to other firms in its industry, and to the financial marketplace in general.

## USES AND USERS OF FINANCIAL PERFORMANCE ANALYSIS

Financial performance analysis interprets financial statement data and presents information in summary form to simplify users' analyses. Primary users are existing or potential investors, creditors who may extend trade credit or lend cash, and customers who are trying to determine financial stability.

Financial performance analysis can be useful for many purposes, including:

1. To set goals and targets.
2. To compare the firm's performance to others.
3. To measure financial strength for credit granting purposes.
4. To measure profitability for return-on-investment purposes.
5. To spot trends, weaknesses, and potential problem areas.
6. To evaluate alternative courses of action.
7. To understand interactions that financial changes have on a firm's financial position.

The novice analyst sees one dimension, then two, and so on. Expert financial analysts have an amazing "feel" for financial statement relationships and underlying issues and seem able to read "between the lines."

## AN EXAMPLE COMPANY—RICKMAN LIGHTING

As an illustration, a comprehensive example is used throughout the chapter. Rickman Lighting is a major distributor of electrical fixtures for commercial and retail use. It is December 31, 2007. Management has approved a profit plan for 2008. Figure 15.1 presents balance sheets for three years and a forecast for December 31, 2008. Figure 15.2 presents income statements for 2006 and 2007 and the 2008 forecast.

In addition to Figures 15.1 and 15.2, much more information is included in the annual report, such as footnotes, a ten-year summary of financial data, and the auditors' report. These are not included here for simplification.

| Balance Sheets as of December 31 (in millions) | | | | |
|---|---|---|---|---|
| | Forecast 2008 | Actual 2007 | Actual 2006 | Actual 2005 |
| Cash and marketable securities | $ 203 | $ 236 | $ 180 | $ 121 |
| Accounts receivable (net) | 363 | 345 | 300 | 284 |
| Inventories | 524 | 356 | 320 | 287 |
| Total current assets | $1,117 | $ 937 | $ 800 | $ 692 |
| Plant and equipment (net) | $ 439 | $ 396 | $ 369 | $ 370 |
| Land | 139 | 127 | 119 | 98 |
| Total noncurrent assets | $ 578 | $ 523 | $ 488 | $ 468 |
| Total assets | $1,695 | $1,460 | $1,288 | $1,160 |
| Accounts payable | $ 418 | $ 275 | $ 197 | $ 151 |
| Bonds payable—10 percent | 400 | 400 | 400 | 400 |
| Total liabilities | $ 818 | $ 675 | $ 597 | $ 551 |
| Paid-in-capital ($ 5 per share) | $ 400 | $ 400 | $ 400 | $ 400 |
| Retained earnings | 477 | 385 | 291 | 209 |
| Total equity | $ 877 | $ 785 | $ 691 | $ 609 |
| Total liabilities and equity | $1,695 | $1,460 | $1,288 | $1,160 |
| Shares outstanding (in millions) | 80 | 80 | 80 | 80 |
| Dividends paid (in millions) | $ 56 | $ 48 | $ 40 | |
| Average price per share | $17.25 | $16.75 | $15.00 | |

**FIGURE 15.1**

Forecast and Actual Balance Sheets and Other Financial Data

| Income Statements for Years Ending December 31 (in millions) | | | |
| --- | --- | --- | --- |
| | Forecast 2008 | Actual 2007 | Actual 2006 |
| Sales | $2,848 | $2,454 | $2,084 |
| Cost of goods sold | 1,721 | 1,461 | 1,210 |
| Gross margin | $1,127 | $ 993 | $ 874 |
| Operating expenses: | | | |
|   Selling and administrative expenses | $ 773 | $ 672 | $ 587 |
|   Depreciation expense | 65 | 45 | 38 |
|     Total operating expenses | $ 838 | $ 717 | $ 625 |
| Operating net income | $ 289 | $ 276 | $ 249 |
|   Interest expense | 42 | 40 | 46 |
| Net income before taxes | $ 247 | $ 236 | $ 203 |
|   Income taxes expenses (40 percent) | 99 | 94 | 81 |
| Net income after taxes | $ 148 | $ 142 | $ 122 |

**FIGURE 15.2**

Forecast and Actual Income Statements

# TYPES OF FINANCIAL STATEMENT ANALYSIS

Financial analysts examine financial statement data in every manner possible to gain insight. Traditional formats include:

**Comparative statements.** Data from two time periods are compared. Comparisons between actual and budget, two versions of a budget, and last period and this period are done routinely. As an example, the Rickman data show:

| | Forecast 2008 | Actual 2007 | Difference | Percentage Change |
| --- | --- | --- | --- | --- |
| Sales | $2,848 | $2,454 | $394 | 16.1% |
| Cost of goods sold | 1,721 | 1,461 | 260 | 17.8 |
| Gross margin | $1,127 | $ 993 | 134 | 13.5 |

The Percentage Change column is found by dividing the difference between the values for 2008 and 2007 by the 2007 base-year value.

**Percentage composition statements.** All statement values are expressed as a percentage of a base number, which is set equal to 100 percent. The base is total assets on the balance sheet and sales on the income statement. These are often called **common-sized statements** and are used for comparing multiple years of data, companies of various sizes, and one company to industry averages. A summarized presentation is:

| | Forecast 2008 | Actual 2007 | Actual 2006 | Actual 2005 |
| --- | --- | --- | --- | --- |
| Cash and marketable securities | 13.6% | 16.2% | 14.0% | 10.4% |
| Accounts receivable (net) | 21.4 | 23.6 | 23.3 | 24.5 |
| Inventories | 30.9 | 24.4 | 24.8 | 24.7 |
|   Total current assets | 65.9% | 64.2% | 62.1% | 59.7 |
| Total noncurrent assets | 34.1 | 35.8 | 37.9 | 40.3 |
|   Total assets | 100.0% | 100.0% | 100.0% | 100.0% |

If ideal mixes of assets, liabilities, and equity can be defined for an industry, percentage composition statements can quickly highlight deviations.

**Base-year comparisons.** Base-year comparisons fix a base period at 100 percent and express amounts in other periods as percentages of the base. As an example, 2006 is the base; and 2007 and 2008 figures are percentages of the base year, as follows:

| | Forecast 2008 | Actual 2007 | Actual 2006 |
|---|---|---|---|
| Sales | 136.7% | 117.8% | 100.0% |
| Cost of goods sold | 142.2 | 120.7 | 100.0 |
| Gross margin | 129.0 | 113.6 | 100.0 |

**Ratio analysis.** Ratio analysis is defined as selecting one variable as the numerator and another variable as the denominator–a ratio of two values. Ratios are expressed as a percentage (%), a ratio (X:Y), or merely a number.

In reality, all four formats are ratio based. A ratio is a numerator divided by a denominator. A few simple rules help in calculating ratios from balance sheet numbers (for a point in time) and income statement numbers (for a time period):

- When calculating a ratio using balance sheet numbers only, the numerator and denominator should be from the same balance sheet date, not from different points in time.
- When a balance sheet number and an income statement number are used in a ratio, the balance sheet number should be an average for the time period, at least an average of the beginning and ending balance sheet numbers.

## FINANCIAL PERFORMANCE ANALYSIS: RISKS AND RETURNS

Instead of merely calculating ratios, measuring financial performance requires a framework. "Why do you want to know?" and "What do you want to know?" frame an attack. Answering the "why" defines the viewpoint of the questioner: creditor, shareholder, regulator, employee, etc. The "what" question leads to specific concerns and ratios. These concerns are grouped by *risks* and *returns* as follows:

| Risks | Returns |
|---|---|
| Liquidity | Earnings |
| Capital adequacy | Growth |
| Asset quality | Market performance |

Risks areas measure the financial safety of the firm. Returns areas measure the financial success of the firm. Risks and returns are interrelated. Reducing a risk can improve a return measure, and poor financial returns can cause a more risky financial position.

Every ratio can get too high or too low. This is the "Goldilocks paradox." Remember that papa bear's porridge was too hot, momma bear's porridge was too cold, but baby bear's porridge was just right. Generally, the "just right" level is difficult to find precisely. But if a ratio is too high or too low, financial risk grows. Benchmarking, comparative financial analyses, and monitoring common stock prices can help define the optimal area.

## Contemporary Practice 15.1
### When Financial Ratios Look Really Bad

*"Cease and desist orders" carry the force of law and are issued by government regulators of banks when regulatory guidelines for safe and sound management are violated. Ratios for **C**apital adequacy, **A**sset quality, **M**anagement, **E**arnings, and **L**iquidity (**CAMEL**) are evaluated by bank regulatory auditors during bank examinations. In troublesome cases, regulators will sign an agreement with the bank's board of directors to make immediate changes. The changes often attempt to* rebuild the bank's capital, create a strategic plan and master budget to improve financial ratios, develop a plan to improve management quality, respond to specific problems, and require frequent progress reports. Failure to do so can result in fines, loss of ownership, and a possible "cease and desist order."

Source: Takser, J., "What to Do When Regulators With a Cease and Desist Order Come Knocking," Bottomline, November-December, 1991, pp. 40–42.

## Liquidity

Liquidity is the availability of cash, other near-cash assets, and assets that can be converted into cash easily. The key liquidity question is:

- What liquid assets are available or accessible to meet demands for cash from expected and unexpected sources?

Can the bills be paid on time? The answer comes from ratios that measure assets that can be converted quickly into cash for short-term needs. Traditional measures are the current and quick ratios.

**Current Ratio.** The **current ratio** indicates how many dollars of current assets are available for each dollar of current liabilities and is defined as:

$$\text{Current assets} \div \text{Current liabilities} = \text{Current ratio}$$

Current assets can be converted into cash within the operating cycle, often a one-year timeframe. From the Rickman case, yearend numbers are:

|  | Forecast 2008 | Actual 2007 | Actual 2006 | Actual 2005 |
|---|---|---|---|---|
| Current assets | $1,117 | $937 | $800 | $692 |
| Current liabilities | 418 | 275 | 197 | 151 |
| **Current ratio** | 2.7:1 | 3.4:1 | 4.1:1 | 4.6:1 |

Generally, firms want a safety cushion of more liquidity than is really needed to cover unexpected or sudden cash needs. At the end of 2007, $3.40 of current assets was available for each dollar of current liabilities. The difference between current assets and current liabilities is called **working capital**. These funds are needed to keep day-to-day operations working smoothly.

A 2:1 current ratio is often suggested as ideal but rarely is. Different industries have different needs for liquidity. Steel warehousers may need a 4:1 ratio to cover large inventories that "turn" slowly. Other firms with very predictable cash flows, few receivables, and low inventories can operate with a 1:1 ratio. Industry averages give an indication of what this ratio should be.[1]

---

[1] Sources of ratios for comparison purposes include publications of Dun & Bradstreet, Standard & Poors, and Robert Morris Associates. Many industry trade associations also publish financial data and statistics about member firms.

**Quick Ratio.** The **quick ratio**, or **acid test ratio**, tests a firm's ability to pay its bills quickly from available cash and near-cash assets and is defined as:

Cash, marketable securities, and receivables ÷ Current liabilities = Quick ratio

Inventories are excluded because they are less liquid. Receivables must still be collected, but at least cash is owed to the firm. For Rickman Lighting, the quick ratio has declined each year, from 2.7:1 to 1.4:1, a potentially serious concern.

| | Forecast 2008 | Actual 2007 | Actual 2006 | Actual 2005 |
|---|---|---|---|---|
| Cash and marketable securities | $230 | $236 | $180 | $121 |
| Accounts receivable (net) | 363 | 345 | 300 | 284 |
| Total quick assets | $593 | $581 | $480 | $405 |
| Current liabilities | 418 | 275 | 197 | 151 |
| **Quick ratio** | 1.4:1 | 2.1:1 | 2.4:1 | 2.7:1 |

**Other Liquidity Considerations.** Liquidity commonly deals with cash flows. In particular, cash from operations is the amount of cash generated from normal operations. Often, cash from operations is measured against cash needed to pay interest and principal on debt.

A missing element here is the firm's ability to borrow cash when needed, called **off-balance-sheet financing**. These liquidity sources are lines of credit, other borrowing agreements, and borrowing against inventories or other assets. Often, off-balance-sheet sources are more important than on-balance-sheet liquidity.

A firm can have too much or too little liquidity. Generally, the more liquid, the lower is the earning power—low risk, low return. One job of a corporate treasurer is to minimize idle cash.

## Capital Adequacy

Liquidity is closely tied to capital adequacy. Even if a firm has a liquidity problem, a strong capital position allows it to borrow easily. And vice versa, if a firm's capital position is weak, it should maintain more liquidity to avoid any possible cash-flow troubles. Capital is equity ownership, which is paid-in capital plus retained earnings. Two questions define capital adequacy:

- How much capital is necessary to protect creditors and shareholders against losses?
- How little capital is necessary to allow shareholders to enjoy maximum favorable returns on equity and dividends?

These are conflicting positions—more capital for protection and less capital for higher rates of return. Creditors want more; owners want less. But if capital as a portion of total assets or debt drops too low, creditors stop lending money or demand higher interest rates. If capital portions go too high, owners are disappointed by low rates of return on the large equity base. The capital adequacy ratios examined are debt to equity, capital multiplier, times interest earned, and dividend payout percentage.

**Debt to Equity.** The definition of the **debt to equity ratio** is:

Total liabilities ÷ Total equity = Debt to equity ratio

| | Forecast 2008 | Actual 2007 | Actual 2006 | Actual 2005 |
|---|---|---|---|---|
| Total liabilities | $818 | $675 | $597 | $551 |
| Total equity | 877 | 785 | 691 | 609 |
| **Debt to equity ratio** | 93.3% | 86.0% | 86.4% | 90.5% |

The debt to equity ratio is a percentage. Other ratios such as equity to total assets, debt to total assets, and equity to debt reveal similar information. Debt is often defined as long-term debt, excluding current liabilities.

**Capital Multiplier.** The **capital multiplier** indicates how much total investment can be financed from owner-provided equity and is defined as:

Total assets ÷ Total equity = Capital multiplier

|  | Forecast 2008 | Actual 2007 | Actual 2006 | Actual 2005 |
|---|---|---|---|---|
| Total assets | $1,695 | $1,460 | $1,288 | $1,160 |
| Total equity | 877 | 785 | 691 | 609 |
| **Capital multiplier** | 1.93:1 | 1.86:1 | 1.86:1 | 1.90:1 |

As the capital multiplier decreases, more equity money is used to finance assets; and more safety is assumed. A higher capital multiplier indicates an ability to lever "our" equity into more assets, using "other people's money" to finance the firm.

**Times Interest Earned.** A measure of capital adequacy is the ability of a firm to earn enough from operations to pay for the cost of debt—more debt, more interest. **Times interest earned** is defined as:

Net income before interest expense and taxes ÷ Interest expense = Times interest earned

|  | Forecast 2008 | Actual 2007 | Actual 2006 |
|---|---|---|---|
| Net income before interest expense and taxes | $289 | $276 | $249 |
| Interest expense | 42 | 40 | 46 |
| **Times interest earned** | 6.9 | 6.9 | 5.4 |

The risk is not having cash to pay the interest. A higher times interest earned number means more safety, and a lower number (particularly under 1.0) means more risk.

**Dividend Payout Percentage.** The **dividend payout percentage** shows what portion of earnings was paid in dividends to shareholders. The definition is:

Dividends paid ÷ Net income = Dividend payout percentage

|  | Forecast 2008 | Actual 2007 | Actual 2006 |
|---|---|---|---|
| Dividends paid | $56 | $48 | $40 |
| Net income after taxes | 148 | 142 | 122 |
| **Dividend payout percentage** | 37.8% | 33.8% | 32.8% |

A percentage of 30 or 40 percent is normal for a mature firm with a stable earnings record. Rapidly growing firms have lower percentages to save cash for reinvestment. If this ratio nears or exceeds 100 percent, dividend payments are using funds that the firm may need to expand or to pay bills.

**Other Capital Adequacy Considerations.** As was mentioned, capital adequacy and liquidity often offset each other. Firms with large capital bases will find borrowing much easier than heavily levered firms. Yet, liquidity has a very short-term horizon, while capital adequacy has a longer-term timeframe. Liquidity problems can arise and must be solved quickly. Except for the initial stock sales, most capital is built from earnings that may take years to accumulate.

## Asset Quality

Asset quality examines two questions dealing with balance sheet assets:

- Are assets used efficiently?
- What risk exists that the book values will not be recovered?

Measures of efficiency are plentiful and examine accounts receivable, inventories, and total assets. Often the second question must be answered using external data to ensure funding market values for assets. Increasingly, market values are being added to financial statements either through footnote disclosure or inclusion on the balance sheet itself.

**Accounts Receivable Turnover and Days Sales in Receivables. Accounts receivable turnover** and **days sales in receivables** computations are:

$$\text{Sales} \div \text{Average accounts receivable} = \text{Accounts receivable turnover}$$

$$\text{Average accounts receivable} \div (\text{Sales} \div 360 \text{ days}) = \text{Days sales in receivables}$$

Both ratios are commonly used and express the same idea. Accounts receivable turnover times days sales in receivables yields 360 days.

|  | Forecast 2008 | Actual 2007 | Actual 2006 |
|---|---|---|---|
| Sales | $2,848 | $2,454 | $2,084 |
| Average accounts receivable | 354 | 323 | 292 |
| **Accounts receivable turnover** | 8.0 | 7.6 | 7.1 |
| **Days sales in receivables** | 44.7 | 47.4 | 50.4 |

Over the past three years, the days sales in receivables have decreased. Rickman is speeding up collections. These numbers must be compared to credit terms extended to customers. Also, the portion of receivables that is past due and the bad debts expense percentage must be monitored carefully. Ratio trends and comparisons to industry leaders will help evaluate performance.

**Inventory Turnover and Days Sales in Inventory. Inventory turnover** and **days sales in inventory** are:

$$\text{Cost of goods sold} \div \text{Average inventory} = \text{Inventory turnover}$$

$$\text{Average inventory} \div (\text{Cost of goods sold} \div 360 \text{ days}) = \text{Days sales in inventory}$$

Inventory turnover ratios use cost of goods sold, not sales. Sales and accounts receivable are valued using sales prices. Cost of goods sold and inventory use purchase prices at cost (or the cost of goods manufactured).

|  | Forecast 2008 | Actual 2007 | Actual 2006 |
|---|---|---|---|
| Cost of goods sold | $1,721 | $1,461 | $1,210 |
| Average inventories | 440 | 338 | 304 |
| **Inventory turnover** | 3.9 | 4.3 | 4.0 |
| **Days sales in inventory** | 92.0 | 83.3 | 90.4 |

The 2008 forecast shows a large inventory increase with inventory turnover dropping below 4.0. A low number implies that inventory is poorly used. Perhaps too much inventory is sitting around or is out-of-date. A higher turnover indicates more sales are generated from the same amount of inventory. At high levels, frequent stock-outs occur; and sales may be lost.

**Asset Turnover.** One way to increase profits on a given set of assets is to increase the ratio of sales to total assets—assuming a constant return-on-sales percentage. The **asset turnover** is:

$$\text{Sales} \div \text{Average total assets} = \text{Asset turnover}$$

|  | Forecast 2008 | Actual 2007 | Actual 2006 |
|---|---|---|---|
| Sales | $2,848 | $2,454 | $2,084 |
| Average total assets | 1,578 | 1,374 | 1,224 |
| **Asset turnover** | 1.8 | 1.8 | 1.7 |

As assets are used more efficiently, this ratio will increase. More sales, and presumably profits, can be earned from the same dollar amount of assets.

**Other Asset Quality Considerations.** Asset quality ratios use balance sheet amounts that are assumed to be valid financial accounting amounts–not overstated. For example, it is essential that bad debts accounting is handled properly and that inventories are at cost and can be converted into sales within the normal business cycle. Often, financial analysts will automatically deduct intangible asset amounts from asset and equity totals, ignoring them in analyses.

## Earnings

The key earnings question is:

- Is net income adequate to satisfy investors' dividend and rate-of-return expectations and to support growth?

Profitability is often the focus of analysts. Announcements of financial performance emphasize quarter-to-quarter or year-to-year changes in net income. Earnings per share receives disproportionate attention. Clearly, long-term trends in earnings reflect success or difficulties in a firm's competitive markets. Rates of return are major indicators of earnings performance: return on sales, assets, and equity. Growing in importance is the cash flow per share, which indicates how much cash was generated per share from operations. Gross margin and operating expense percentages are examined for trends in operating profitability.

**Return on Sales.** The **return on sales (ROS)** is defined as:

$$\text{Net income} \div \text{Sales} = \text{Return on sales}$$

As shown in the following table, Rickman Lighting's ROS shows a continued decline into the forecast year. Internal and certain external analyses use operating net income instead of net income.

**Return on Assets.** The **return on assets (ROA)** is defined as:

$$\text{Net income} \div \text{Average total assets} = \text{Return on assets}$$

As seen in the following table, Rickman Lighting's ROA hovers around 10 percent but is forecast to drop to its lowest point in 2008. In 2008, assets appear to grow faster than net income.

Internal analyses would use **managed assets**, as discussed in Chapter 13, for the denominator to evaluate investment center managers. The numerator should be controllable or direct contribution margin—excluding allocated common costs.

**Return on Equity.** The **return on equity (ROE)** is defined as:

$$\text{Net income} \div \text{Average equity} = \text{Return on equity}$$

Because shareholders' equity finances only a portion of total assets, the ROE percentage is larger than the ROA percentage. The returns numbers for Rickman Lighting are:

|  | Forecast 2008 | Actual 2007 | Actual 2006 |
|---|---|---|---|
| Net income | $ 148 | $ 142 | $ 122 |
| Sales | 2,848 | 2,454 | 2,084 |
| **Return on sales** | 5.2 % | 5.8 % | 5.9 % |
| Average total assets | $1,578 | $1,374 | $1,224 |
| **Return on assets** | 9.4 % | 10.3 % | 10.0 % |
| Average equity | $ 831 | $ 738 | $ 650 |
| **Return on equity** | 17.8 % | 19.2 % | 18.8 % |

**Earnings Per Share. Earnings per share** is defined as:

Net income ÷ Average number of shares outstanding = Earnings per share

|  | Forecast 2008 | Actual 2007 | Actual 2006 |
|---|---|---|---|
| Net income after taxes | $ 148 | $ 142 | $ 122 |
| Average shares outstanding | 80 mill | 80 mill | 80 mill |
| **Earnings per share** | $1.85 | $1.78 | $1.53 |

Earnings per share is increasing, but slowly. Investors prefer this number to grow at a steady rate and will probably be disappointed in the 2008 forecast.

**Cash Flow Per Share.** With increased visibility, **cash flow per share** is becoming a leading indicator of the cash generating capabilities of operations. The definition is:

Cash flow from operations ÷ Average number of shares outstanding = Cash flow per share

The calculations to determine cash flow from operations are somewhat complex and not explained here in detail but convert the accrual net income into net cash flow from the operating portion of the income statement. For the Rickman Lighting, the data are:

|  | Forecast 2008 | Actual 2007 | Actual 2006 |
|---|---|---|---|
| Net income | $148 | $142 | $122 |
| + Depreciation and other amortizations | 65 | 45 | 38 |
| ± Changes in operating current assets | −186 | −81 | −49 |
| ± Changes in operating current liabilities | 143 | 78 | 46 |
| Cash flow from operations | $170 | $184 | $157 |
| Average number of shares outstanding | 80 mill | 80 mill | 80 mill |
| **Cash flow per share** | $2.13 | $2.30 | $1.96 |

The 2008 forecast growth in inventory will use cash and cause the forecast cash flow per share to decline.

**Gross Margin and Operating Expense Percentages.** The **gross margin percentage** provides information about prices (sales) relative to costs of products made or purchased (cost of goods sold) and is examined for trends. Have cost increases been passed along in price increases? Is the gross margin percentage improving or deteriorating? The **operating expense percentage** monitors the portion of revenue that the firm spends on selling, marketing, and administrative expenses. Definitions are:

$$(\text{Sales} - \text{Cost of goods sold}) \div \text{Sales} = \text{Gross margin percentage}$$

$$\text{Operating expenses} \div \text{Sales} = \text{Operating expense percentage}$$

| | Forecast 2008 | Actual 2007 | Actual 2006 |
|---|---|---|---|
| Sales | $2,848 | $2,454 | $2,084 |
| Cost of goods sold | 1,721 | 1,461 | 1,210 |
| Gross margin | $1,127 | $ 993 | $ 874 |
| **Gross margin percentage** | 39.6% | 40.5% | 41.9% |
| Operating expenses | $ 838 | $ 717 | $ 625 |
| **Operating expense percentage** | 29.4% | 29.2% | 30.0% |

Gross margin percentages are declining—a cause for serious concern. Often, very slight changes in the percentage are significant. This decline is probably the major reason that net income is not growing as fast as assets or sales and is the cause of drops in the ROS and ROA ratios. Operating expenses, however, seem to be in control.

**Other Earnings Considerations.** Strong earnings overcomes many other financial problems. But changes in earnings patterns create uncertainty. Volatile earnings bothers analysts, who like to see stable earnings percentages and growing earnings dollar amounts. Declining earnings trends are particularly upsetting. Often earnings impacts are the result of changes in other financial performance areas. Studying the impact on earnings from other financial and operating changes is an important part of analyses, particularly in financial forecasting and modeling, as discussed in Chapter 7.

## Growth

The key growth questions are:

- Is growth adequate given conditions in the firm's markets?
- Are the firm's growth patterns balanced or at least within planned growth patterns?

The first question needs external economic and market growth data and cannot be answered from financial statement data. The second question compares growth rates across a variety of balance sheet and income statement accounts. Balance implies the same relative growth rates for accounts like assets, equity, sales, and profits. The argument can be made that nearly all financial problems arise from growth imbalance.

The basic definition for all growth ratios is:

$$(\text{Year 2 balance} - \text{Year 1 balance}) \div \text{Year 1 balance} = \text{Growth rate percentage}$$

| | Forecast 2008 | Actual 2007 | Actual 2006 |
|---|---|---|---|
| Growth in assets | 16.1% | 13.4% | 11.0% |
| Growth in equity | 11.7 | 13.6 | 13.5 |
| Growth in sales | 16.1 | 17.8 | |
| Growth in operating expenses | 16.9 | 14.7 | |
| Growth in net income | 4.2 | 16.4 | |

If net income growth lags behind asset growth, equity cannot be built quickly enough to support more rapid sales and asset growth.

## Market Performance

The key market performance question is:

- How do financial markets evaluate the financial condition of the firm?

Stock prices and debt instrument prices give an assessment by investors and analysts of the firm's financial risks and returns. Ratios commonly used are the price-earnings ratio and dividend yield.

**Price-Earnings Ratio.** The definition of the **price-earnings ratio** is:

Average market price per share ÷ Earnings per share = Price-earnings ratio

|  | Forecast 2008 | Actual 2007 | Actual 2006 |
|---|---|---|---|
| Stock price (average market price per share) | $17.25 | $16.75 | $15.00 |
| Earnings per share | 1.85 | 1.78 | 1.53 |
| **Price-earnings ratio** | 9.3:1 | 9.4:1 | 9.8:1 |

The price-earnings ratio (or multiple) is monitored intensely by investors, shareholders, and the firm's management itself. Generally, the higher the ratio, the greater the investors' expectation of future growth in earnings and dividends. The lower the ratio, the less trust investors have in future earnings and dividend growth.

**Dividend Yield.** Cash dividends paid relative to share market price is the **dividend yield** and is defined as:

Cash dividends per share ÷ Average market price per share = Dividend yield

|  | Forecast 2008 | Actual 2007 | Actual 2006 |
|---|---|---|---|
| Stock price (average market price per share) | $17.25 | $16.75 | $15.00 |
| Dividends paid | $56 | $48 | $40 |
| Average number of shares outstanding | 80 mill | 80 mill | 80 mill |
| **Dividend yield** | 4.1% | 3.6% | 3.3% |

Basically, the dividend yield is the cash payout on the share price. Firms with high dividend yields are attractive to investors who need immediate cash income.

## INTERRELATIONSHIPS OF RISKS AND RETURNS

As a firm becomes more risky in one area, it compensates with safety in another area. Aggressive risk taking must be offset by strong fall-back positions and backup alternatives. Financial problems arise when this balance tilts too far.

## Ethics in Financial Analysis

Ethics come into play in many financial reporting issues and are addressed by auditors and the chief financial officer. These are of concern to management accountants because the same issues occur when evaluating business segments and their managers. Concerns in ratio analysis include:

1. Doing yearend "window dressing" to make our balance sheet look better than it normally appears to be. For example, using reserve cash balances to pay bills at yearend to increase the current ratio.

2. Failing to record all payables at yearend or shipping merchandise and recording revenue when a sale may not have occurred.

3. Defining ratios consistently from period to period and across firms.

4. Using off-balance-sheet financing to distort the picture of the underlying financial strength of the firm.

5. Over valuing assets that will directly affect the equity position of the firm.

The same issues arise in divisional performance measurement, as discussed in Chapter 13. Internally, the misstatements are ethical issues, but externally the specter of legal violations, audit fraud, and legal liability becomes involved quickly.

## Financial Leverage

**Financial leverage** uses borrowed funds to enhance the rate of return to equity owners. If only equity capital is used for long-term financing, equity owners get all profits. If owners can substitute borrowed funds, profits earned above the cost of debt funds accrue to equity owners. Less equity is needed, and the rate of return on equity should increase—perhaps dramatically. To illustrate, Common Company and Debt Company have identical operations. Condensed average balance sheets and operating results are:

|  | *Common* | *Debt* |
|---|---|---|
| Total assets | $1,000,000 | $1,000,000 |
| Liabilities and equities: |  |  |
| Current liabilities | $ 200,000 | $ 200,000 |
| Bonds payable (8%) | 0 | 400,000 |
| Equity | 800,000 | 400,000 |
| Total liabilities and equity | $1,000,000 | $1,000,000 |
| Income before interest and taxes | $ 125,000 | $ 125,000 |
| Interest on bonds payable | 0 | 32,000 |
| Income before taxes | $ 125,000 | $ 93,000 |
| Income taxes (40%) | 50,000 | 37,200 |
| Net income after taxes | $ 75,000 | $ 55,800 |
| **Return on total assets** | 7.5% | 5.6% |
| **Return on equity** | 9.4% | 14.0% |

Return on equity increases from using debt. Several observations can be made:

1. If the cost of debt is less than the return on the additional net investment, financial leverage will benefit the common equity owners.

## Contemporary Practice 15.2
### *Financial Ratios Can Foretell Hospital Closures*

*A study of open and closed hospitals shows that certain leverage, liquidity, capital adequacy, and cash-flow ratios can predict hospital closure up to two years in advance of a hospital's closure with an accuracy of nearly 75 percent. Timely detection of critical problems could prompt earlier or more aggressive development of financial, tactical, and strategic courses of action to improve a hospital's financial health.*

*Source: Lynn, M. L., and P. Wertheim, "Key Financial Ratios Can Foretell Hospital Closures,"* Healthcare Financial Management, *November 1993, pp. 66–70.*

2. If cost of debt and the preferred dividend rate are similar, debt is less expensive because interest is deductible for tax purposes and dividends are not.
3. As the proportion of debt increases, lenders will tend to increase the debt interest rate because the risk of default is greater.

Again, too much of a good thing can turn bad. Financial leverage benefits end when interest on borrowed funds exceeds the returns on investments.

## Earning-Power Model

Another extension of the ratio interrelationships and the leverage concept is the **earning-power model**, which combines return on sales, asset turnover, and capital multiplier ratios to yield return on equity. To earn a given return on equity, interrelationships among net income, sales, and asset and equity commitments can be analyzed. The basic format is presented in Figure 15-3.

Using the 2008 forecast data for Rickman Lighting:

$$\frac{\$148{,}000}{\$2{,}848{,}000} \times \frac{\$2{,}848{,}000}{\$1{,}577{,}500} \times \frac{\$1{,}577{,}500}{\$831{,}000} = 5.2\% \times 180.5\% \times 189.8\% = 17.8\%$$

To improve ROE, the following changes could be made:

1. Increase ROS by reducing expenses while holding sales constant.
2. Increase sales relative to total assets while holding ROS constant.
3. Reduce total assets while holding sales, ROS, and capital multiplier constant.
4. Replace equity with debt to increase leverage while holding asset turnover and ROS constant.

| | | | | | | | |
|---|---|---|---|---|---|---|---|
| $\frac{\text{Net income}}{\text{Sales}}$ | | | | | | = | **Return on Sales** |
| $\frac{\text{Net income}}{\text{Sales}}$ | × | $\frac{\text{Sales}}{\text{Average total assets}}$ | | | | = | **Return on Assets** |
| $\frac{\text{Net income}}{\text{Sales}}$ | × | $\frac{\text{Sales}}{\text{Average total assets}}$ | × | $\frac{\text{Average total assets}}{\text{Average equity}}$ | | = | **Return on Equity** |
| **Return on Sales** | × | **Asset Turnover** | × | **Capital Multiplier** | | = | **Return on Equity** |

FIGURE **15.3**

The Earning-Power Model

Thus, improving any of the three ratios while holding the others constant will improve ROE. These ratios are compared to those of other successful firms and to industry averages to identify problems and relative strengths and weaknesses. Leveraging net income, sales, total assets, and equity financing into high returns to owners is a major financial management task.

## Strategic Profit Model

Another approach to evaluating and testing financial ratio relationships is a very traditional model, often called the Du Pont formula. A modified version, called the strategic profit model,

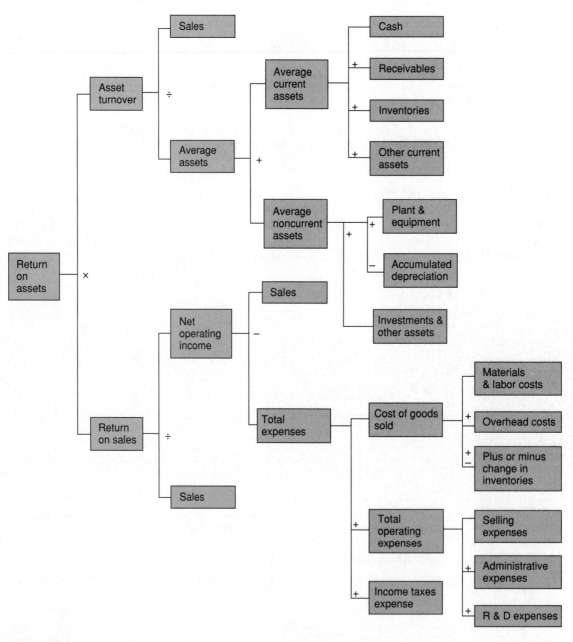

**FIGURE 15.4**

Strategic Profit Model—Return on Assets

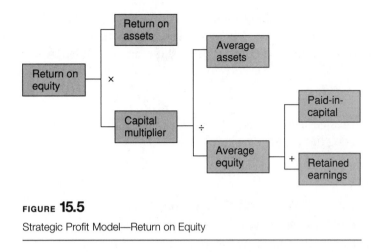

FIGURE **15.5**

Strategic Profit Model—Return on Equity

is illustrated in Figures 15.4 and 15.5. All components of ROA and ROE can be modeled. The model can:

1. Show earning-power ratios sensitivity from changes in account balances.

2. Identify financial structure and financial performance differences among firms and industries.

3. Test the impacts of proposed changes in operations, debt structure, and working capital policies and guidelines.

4. Help set long-range and near-term financial goals and targets.

Improved understanding has made this simple analytical framework popular in financial performance analysis for nearly 100 years.

Typically, the calculations on these two diagrams run right to left, resulting in the rates of return percentages. However, a rather powerful tool can be created by setting up the appropriate calculations in a spreadsheet and using a tool, such as Goal Seek in Excel, to work backwards through the spreadsheet to determine how much a certain variable must change to achieve a targeted rate of return. For example, inventories might need to decrease by $500,000 to allow a company to raise its actual ROA from 6% to a target of 10%. Many variations could be studied.

## Impact of the New Manufacturing Environment

While manufacturing and costing changes have had a dramatic impact on cost analysis and decision making, their impacts on financial performance analysis are less obvious but can still be significant. The primary changes seen in firms at the edge of manufacturing excellence are:

1. Much higher inventory turnovers as a result of just-in-time processing and the elimination of buffers and of wasted time in all stages of production and distribution.

2. Lower inventory investment that frees funds for other needed investments or debt reduction and strengthens both working capital and long-term financing positions.

3. Higher investments in fixed assets due to the substitution of capital investments for labor.

4. Shifts in expense and revenue patterns due to global sourcing, sales, and distribution. These are difficult to evaluate without more detailed analyses.

5. Product pricing and costing changes as firms use value chain advantages of low-cost production, improved quality, flexible manufacturing capabilities, and higher customer service levels to capitalize financially.

Differences in strategic approaches to sourcing, producing, and marketing can often be seen in comparative analysis of financial ratios. Major and subtle changes in financial results can be measured by astute observers. Trends can confirm these shifts and advantages.

## International Implications

While financial performance analysis is international in scope some differences do exist among countries and cultures. Among these are:

1. Japanese managers tend to focus on sales growth, market share, and return on sales as opposed to return on equity.

2. Managers in the United States tend to worry more about short-term profits and earnings per share than do most other managers.

3. European companies tend to focus on safety of the creditor rather than on the returns of the common shareholder.

4. In Germany, workers' councils are represented on boards of directors of companies. This gives labor a voice in corporate governance and a different perspective of financial reporting.

5. Different accounting principles will influence the meaning of financial ratios. Historically in Japan for example, undervalued land and intercompany investments cause asset totals and, therefore, equity to be undervalued. Debt to equity ratios may be dramatically different than in the United States.

For comparison purposes, these international differences must be recognized and incorporated into any analyses.

## CAVEATS IN USING FINANCIAL PERFORMANCE ANALYSIS

As with any tool, the strengths and usefulness of performance analyses are tempered by limits and dangers of inappropriate application. Assumptions must always be tested; underlying data must have credibility; and care must be taken in generalizing from basic ratio findings. Among the caveats are:

- **No consistently valid rules of thumb exist.** Specific industries have different acceptable ranges for certain ratios. An individual firm's strengths and weaknesses cause ratios to be case specific.

- **No one ratio can tell a story.** Sets of ratios over a series of time periods are needed to paint a firm's financial picture. Knowing one number tells little about existing interrelationships.

- **Industry averages are just that—averages.** Strong firms and weak firms are averaged. Big and little firms often have different characteristics. A group of strong peer firms (similar size, industry, competitive environment, geography, etc.) provides a more powerful comparative base.

- **Ratios must be defined uniformly and consistently.** Using multifirm ratio data is dangerous unless common definitions and accounting methods are used.

- **More ratios do not necessarily make a better analysis.** A carefully selected set of ratios should be reported routinely with internal financial reports.

- **Off-balance-sheet events and factors impact the interpretation of financial ratios.** Nonfinancial links, contracts, or business events can influence a firm's financial condition with no obvious impacts on statement numbers.

- **The goal of financial performance analysis is to diagnose the firm's financial health.** Ratio analysis is not an exercise unto itself but should measure performance.

These caveats bring ratio analysis back to reality. Care must be taken to avoid pitfalls and yet to pull maximum understanding from the firm's financial data.

## SUMMARY

Financial performance analyses should be a proactive tool–part of management's financial planning and control processes. Managers can also use ratios to capitalize on strengths and detect areas of needed improvement.

Financial performance analyses focus on the financial risks and returns areas of liquidity, capital adequacy, asset quality, earnings, growth, and market performance. Key ratios in each area are defined and illustrated.

Interrelationships among various ratios and areas of risks and returns exist. Strengths in one area can offset a weakness in another area. Financial leverage as a concept that uses debt instead of equity to finance assets is illustrated. Earning-power ratios are composed of return on sales, asset turnover, and capital multiplier ratios. A strategic profit model is presented as means of testing the sensitivity of relationships and the impacts of changes on rates of return.

Advantages of ratio analysis began the chapter. Caveats on the use of ratios ended the discussion.

## PROBLEM FOR REVIEW

Firestone Company has provided the following set of financial statements.

### Average Balance Sheets as of December 31 (in Thousands)

| Assets | 2008 | 2007 |
|---|---|---|
| Cash | $1,233 | $ 686 |
| Accounts receivable, net of allowance | 635 | 584 |
| Inventories | 1,392 | 1,705 |
| Total current assets | $3,260 | $2,975 |
| Plant and equipment, net of depreciation | 2,085 | 1,895 |
| Total assets | $5,345 | $4,870 |
| **Liabilities and Shareholders' Equity** | | |
| Accounts payable | $ 487 | $ 612 |
| Notes payable | 650 | 650 |
| Total current liabilities | $1,137 | $1,262 |
| Long-term notes payable | 450 | 315 |
| Total liabilities | $1,587 | $1,577 |
| Capital stock | $1,500 | $1,500 |
| Retained earnings | 2,258 | 1,793 |
| Total shareholders' equity | $3,758 | $3,293 |
| Total liabilities and shareholders' equity | $5,345 | $4,870 |
| Dividends declared and paid | $ 300 | $ 200 |
| Shares outstanding (in thousands) | 200 | 200 |

**Income Statements for the Years Ended December 31 (in Thousands)**

|  | 2008 | 2007 |
|---|---|---|
| Net sales | $7,100 | $6,850 |
| Cost of goods sold | 4,682 | 4,794 |
| Gross margin | $2,418 | $2,056 |
| Operating expenses | 1,047 | 1,020 |
| Operating income | $1,371 | $1,036 |
| Interest expense | 96 | 84 |
| Income before income taxes | $1,275 | $ 952 |
| Income taxes expense (40%) | 510 | 381 |
| Net income | $ 765 | $ 571 |

**Required:**

Compute the following ratios for 2007 and 2008. Comment.

(a) Return on assets

(b) Return on equity

(c) Gross margin percentage

(d) Debt to equity ratio

(e) Times interest earned

(f) Dividend payout percentage

(g) Days sales in receivables

(h) Inventory turnover

(i) Current ratio

(j) Quick ratio

**Solution:**

| Ratios | 2008 | 2007 |
|---|---|---|
| (a) Return on assets | 14.3% ($765/$5,345) | 11.7% ($571/$4,870) |
| (b) Return on total equity | 20.4% ($765/$3,758) | 17.3% ($571/$3,293) |
| (c) Gross margin percentage | 34.1% ($2,418/$7,100) | 30.0% ($2,056/$6,850) |
| (d) Debt to equity ratio | 42.2% ($1,587/$3,758) | 47.9% ($1,577/$3,293) |
| (e) Times interest earned | 14.3 times ($1,371/$96) | 12.3 times ($1,036/$84) |
| (f) Dividend payout percentage | 39.2% ($300/$765) | 35.0% ($200/$571) |
| (g) Days sales in receivables | 32 days [$635/($7,100/360)] | 31 days [$584/($6,850/360)] |
| (h) Inventory turnover | 3.4 times ($4,682/$1,392) | 2.8 times ($4,794/$1,705) |
| (i) Current ratio | 2.9:1 ($3,260/$1,137) | 2.4:1 ($2,975/$1,262) |
| (j) Quick ratio | 1.6:1 ($1,868/$1,137) | 1.0:1 ($1,270/$1,262) |

The earnings and rates of returns have all improved in 2008. Equity has grown from earnings in spite of the higher dividend payments. Debt is a small portion of the long-term financing, and interest payments have greater protection. Inventory turnover has improved greatly. We have more liquidity protection since both the current and quick ratios have improved. (This assumes that they are not getting too high.) Overall, 2008 appears to have strengthened the firm's financial position.

## TERMINOLOGY REVIEW

**Accounts receivable turnover (625)**

**Acid test ratio (623)**

**Asset turnover (626)**

**Base-year comparisons (621)**

**Capital multiplier (624)**

**Cash flow per share (627)**

Common-sized statements (620)

Comparative statements (620)

Current ratio (622)

Days sales in inventories (625)

Days sales in receivables (625)

Debt to equity ratio (623)

Dividend payout percentage (624)

Dividend yield (629)

Earning-power model (631)

Earnings per share (627)

Financial leverage (630)

Gross margin percentage (627)

Inventory turnover (625)

Managed assets (626)

Off-balance-sheet financing (623)

Operating expense percentage (628)

Percentage composition statements (620)

Price-earnings ratio (629)

Quick ratio (623)

Return on assets (ROA) (626)

Return on equity (ROE) (626)

Return on sales (ROS) (626)

Times interest earned (624)

Working capital (622)

## QUESTIONS FOR REVIEW AND DISCUSSION

1. What is asset turnover? What does a very low ratio imply? What is the danger of a very high ratio?

2. What are the risks and returns areas in financial performance analysis? How does a strong area offset a weak area? Give two examples of these tradeoffs.

3. What is the disadvantage of having more liquid assets than are needed? What is the disadvantage of having too few liquid assets?

4. What are the two conflicting questions used to assess capital adequacy? How is this conflict resolved?

5. What is the key question in assessing liquidity? What ratios are used to help answer the question? What additional off-balance-sheet data might be useful?

6. What are the primary concerns in assessing asset quality? What ratios are used to answer the concerns? What do too high and too low asset quality ratios mean?

7. What is the key question regarding earnings and profitability? Explain how short-term and long-term investor viewpoints may be in conflict.

8. What are the concerns about growth? Are these easily answered from financial statement data? Explain.

9. Why should management be concerned about how external financial markets assess the firm's financial position?

10. What is financial leverage? Explain how it works.

11. Explain the earning-power ratios. What actions can management take to increase return on equity?

12. List five caveats about financial statement analysis that limit its usefulness.

13. In general, what is being measured by the current ratio and by the quick ratio? What is the difference between the two ratios?

14. Describe the strategic profit model's structure. How can it be used to help set and achieve financial goals?

15. If return on assets is used to evaluate a manager of an operating segment, what adjustments should be made to net income and to assets? Comment.

**16.** What may be indicated by:

(a) A sharp increase in the current ratio?
(b) A return on shareholders' equity that is nearly equal to return on assets?
(c) A large increase in the dividend payout percentage?
(d) A drop in inventory turnover and an increase in days sales in inventory?
(e) A decline over several years of the gross margin percentage?
(f) An increase in the earnings per share?
(g) A decline in the price-earnings ratio?

## EXERCISES

Service

**15–1. Rate of Return.** Four Corners Stores earned $1,500,000 on net sales of $50,000,000. Beginning total assets were $10,000,000; and ending total assets were $12,000,000.

**Required:**
1. Compute the return on net sales. How could this ratio be improved?
2. Compute the return on assets. How could this ratio be improved?
3. Compute the asset turnover. How could this ratio be improved?

**15–2. Ratio Patterns.** Assets are growing at an annual rate of 10 percent, sales by 15 percent, net profit by 8 percent, and equity by 6 percent.

**Required:**
What financial problems will eventually appear for this company if these trends continue?

**15–3. Current Asset Use.** Analyze the following situations:
(a) If net credit sales for the year is $15,000,000 and average accounts receivable is $3,000,000, how many days of sales are in accounts receivable on the average? What is the receivables turnover?
(b) If the cost of goods sold is $7,200,000 and average inventory of merchandise is $600,000, how many days of sales are in inventory on the average? What is the inventory turnover?
(c) If accounts receivable should be collected in 40 days and inventory turns over six times per year, how long is the operating cycle?

**15–4. Turnovers.** The following data are taken from Jaaksi Company's accounts:

| | |
|---|---|
| Sales in 2007 | $357,000 |
| Cost of goods sold in 2007 | 216,000 |
| Accounts receivable, 1/1/07 | 220,000 |
| Accounts receivable, 12/31/07 | 242,000 |
| Inventory, 1/1/07 | 130,000 |
| Inventory, 12/31/07 | 70,000 |

**Required:**
1. Find the inventory turnover and the days sales in inventory.
2. Find the accounts receivable turnover and the days sales in receivables.
3. If industry averages for the turnover ratios are 3.0 for both inventory and accounts receivable, how is Jaaksi doing? Suggest possible causes.

**15–5. Capital Ratios.** The following data are available from the McCarthy Shipping Company. No shares were issued in 2007.

| | |
|---|---:|
| Net sales for 2007 | $6,360,000 |
| Net income for 2007 | 398,000 |
| Cash dividends—preferred | 36,000 |
| Cash dividends—common | 120,000 |
| Average market price per common share | 150 |
| Average balance amounts: | |
| Common stock—par value, $100 | 1,500,000 |
| Paid-in capital in excess of par—common | 100,000 |
| Preferred stock—par value, $100, 6 % | 600,000 |
| Retained earnings | 500,000 |

**Required:**

Five ratios with their 2006 values appear in the following list. Calculate the 2007 values and comment on the changes:

**(a)** Earnings per share of common stock ($17.60)
**(b)** Dividend yield per share of common stock (5.0 percent)
**(c)** Price-earnings ratio for common stock (13.2)
**(d)** Return on total equity (12.0 percent)
**(e)** Return on common equity (13.9 percent)

**15–6. Statements from Incomplete Data.** George Bernthal of Bernthal Company found pieces of his average balance sheet and key ratio report in his gerbil cage:

| | | | |
|---|---:|---|---:|
| Cash | $? | Gross margin percentage | 25% |
| Accounts receivable | ? | Debt to equity ratio | 0.25:1 |
| Inventory | 80 | Current ratio | 3:1 |
| Fixed assets (net) | ? | Inventory turnover | 15 times |
| Current liabilities | 100 | Days sales in receivables | 15 days |
| Common stock | 100 | (based on 360 days) | |
| Retained earnings | ? | | |

**Required:**

Add as much to his balance sheet as possible from the data provided.

**15–7. The Good News and Bad News.** A change in any financial ratio can contain good news and bad news. Bautista Financial's results of 2006 and 2007 have caused the following three ratio values to change:

| Ratio | 2006 | 2007 |
|---|---|---|
| Current ratio | 3:1 | 4:1 |
| Inventory turnover | 6 | 5 |
| Dividend payout | 30% | 40% |

**Required:**

**1.** For each ratio, what might be the good news; and what might be the bad news?
**2.** Create a scenario for the combined changes in the three ratios.

**15–8. Common-Size Statements.** Dan Schulte, president of Health Products Company, says that large dollar amounts on financial statements are confusing. However, he finds that percentage relationships are helpful. For example, he expects cost of goods sold to be 60 percent of net sales, operating expenses to be 20 percent, income taxes to be 7 percent, and a net income to be about 10 percent. Operating results for 2005 and 2006 are given as follows:

|  | 2005 | 2006 |
| --- | --- | --- |
| Net sales | $15,140,000 | $18,534,000 |
| Cost of goods sold | 9,175,000 | 11,523,000 |
| Gross profit | $5,965,000 | $7,011,000 |
| Operating expenses | 3,421,000 | 3,906,000 |
| Operating income | $2,544,000 | $3,105,000 |
| Income taxes | 1,036,000 | 1,233,000 |
| Net income | $1,508,000 | $1,872,000 |

**Required:**
1. Prepare percentage composition statements for both years.
2. Prepare a base-year comparison using 2005 as the base year.
3. What trends exist? Were the president's expectations realized? Should he worry about certain specific trends?

**15–9. Liquidity and Capital Adequacy Ratios.** X Biz and Y Biz have the following ratios:

|  | X Biz | Y Biz |
| --- | --- | --- |
| Current ratio | 4.5:1 | 1.5:1 |
| Debt to equity ratio | 0.2:1 | 1.0:1 |
| Quick ratio | 2.5:1 | 0.8:1 |
| Times interest earned | 10 times | 3 times |

**Required:**
What are the financial strengths of X Biz and of Y Biz?

**15–10. Liquidity Impacts.** Geller Company's current and quick ratios have moved as follows:

|  | 2004 | 2005 | 2006 | 2007 |
| --- | --- | --- | --- | --- |
| Current ratio | 2.0:1 | 2.5:1 | 3.0:1 | 4.0:1 |
| Quick ratio | 1.5:1 | 1.0:1 | 0.8:1 | 0.6:1 |

**Required:** Comment on the validity of the following statements:
(a) The stronger current ratio in 2007 reflects improved profitability.
(b) A large obsolete inventory may be a serious problem.
(c) The quick ratio change reflects a desire to pay bills on time.
(d) The current ratio in 2007 is clearly too high.
(e) The company is more liquid in 2007 than in 2004.

**15–11. Equity and Market Ratios.** At December 31, Richmond Company had 100,000 shares of £10 par value stock issued and outstanding. Shares outstanding during the year did not change. Total shareholders' equity was £2,800,000. Net income for the year was £400,000. During the year, Richmond paid £3 per share in dividends. The quoted market price of Richmond's stock on a London stock exchange averaged £32 during the year.

**Required:**
1. What is the price-earnings ratio at yearend?
2. What is the dividend yield at yearend?

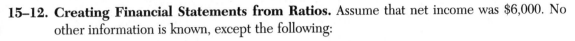

**15–12. Creating Financial Statements from Ratios.** Assume that net income was $6,000. No other information is known, except the following:

| | | | |
|---|---|---|---|
| Return on equity | 10% | Return on sales | 4% |
| Gross margin percentage | 60% | Income tax rate | 40% |
| Current ratio | 3:1 | Return on assets | 5% |
| Inventory turnover | 4 | Days sales in receivables | 90 |
| Long-term debt to equity | 2:3 | | |

**Required:**
Using the preceding ratios, construct an income statement and a balance sheet with as much detail as possible.

**15–13. Impacts on Risks and Returns Areas.** Business events impact each of these financial performance areas:
1. Liquidity
2. Capital adequacy
3. Asset quality
4. Growth
5. Earnings

**Required:**
Indicate the major impacts that the following business events have on the firm's financial performance categories. Will these impacts strengthen (S), weaken (W), or not change (NC) each area? List each event as a row and each performance category as a column. Make a brief note in each cell to explain your answer.
(a) Credit terms to customers lengthened from 30 to 60 days.
(b) Dividend declared and paid.
(c) Long-term debt issued for cash.
(d) Shares issued in trade for production equipment.

**15–14. Logical Relationships.** In each of the following situations, compute the information requested:
1. What is the return on sales if the asset turnover is 2.6 and 13 percent is earned on assets?
2. Sales for the year were $28,000,000, and the average asset investment was $8,000,000. Determine the asset turnover.
3. Assets are turned over 0.8 times in earning 15 percent on the sales dollar. What is the return on assets?
4. With an asset turnover of 2.5, what must be the return on sales if the return on assets is 15 percent?
5. If shareholders' equity is equal to 60 percent of total liabilities and shareholders' equity, what is the rate of return on shareholders' equity if 9 percent is earned on total assets invested?
6. The return on assets was 16 percent, and 8 percent was earned on net sales. What was the asset turnover?
7. The return on assets has been computed at 14 percent. The net income was $840,000, and the asset turnover was 2. Determine the amount of sales and the return on sales.
8. If the total cost of operations, excluding income tax, amounts to $2,600,000, compute sales if net income is 5 percent of sales. The income tax has been computed at $250,000.

9. The return on sales has remained at 6 percent for the past two years. The asset turnover in the first year was 2.4 and declined to 1.8 in the second year. Compute the return on assets for each of the two years.

10. Net sales for the year were $9,600,000. Assets turned over 1.2 times during the year. Cost of goods sold and operating expenses, including income tax, amounted to $8,880,000. Compute the return on net sales and on total assets.

**15–15. Financial Leverage Effects.** Deep River Brands, a Swiss company, earned net income before interest of SFr1,500,000 on sales of SFr30,000,000 and an average asset investment of SFr20,000,000. Total debt averaged SFr5,000,000 at 8 percent interest.

Valley Brands, a French competitor, also reported net income before interest of €1,500,000 on sales of €30,000,000 and an average asset investment of €20,000,000. However, total debt averaged €15,000,000 at 8 percent interest.

**Required:**
1. Compute the return on equity for Deep River Brands.
2. Compute the return on equity for Valley Brands.
3. Comment on the differences in return on equity between the two firms.

**15–16. Market Performance Ratios.** Last year Rapid Data Company reported a net income of $4,500,000 and paid a dividend of $0.90 per share on 2,000,000 shares of common stock outstanding. The market value of each share of stock averaged $45.

**Required:**
1. Compute the earnings per share, price-earnings ratio, dividend payout percentage, and dividend yield.
2. Comment on possible reasons that the market price changed (a) from $38 the previous year to $45 last year or (b) from $50 the previous year to $45 last year.

**15–17. Growth in Working Capital.** Wilhelm Company has been in operation for 20 years. Growth has been rapid in the past but is leveling off. The sales manager, who has been with the firm for 17 years, persuaded the president that the firm should carry larger inventory and grant more liberal credit terms to increase sales. The new controller believes that larger inventories and receivables are too expensive.

**Required:**
Prepare a brief statement indicating how you interpret the sales manager's arguments versus the controller's views. Include any added information you need.

**15–18. Effects of Improved Inventory Turnover.** In 2005, Achram Company earned a net income of $270,000 on an average asset investment of $3,300,000. The controller noted, however, that the inventory turnover of six represented 60 days of sales. Average inventory was $900,000 and thought to be too high. By eliminating obsolete inventory and planning target inventory levels, inventory was reduced to $600,000. Before the inventory reduction, current assets averaged $1,500,000; and current liabilities averaged $600,000. Assume that accounts payable will decrease by half of the inventory reduction and borrowings will decline by an amount equal to the other half. After the inventory reduction, 2006 operations will yield a $276,000 net income, the same as in 2005 except for interest expenses which are expected to decline by $6,000 after taxes.

**Required:**
1. Find the inventory turnover before and after the inventory reduction.
2. Find the current ratio before and after the inventory reduction.
3. What is the expected return on assets before and after the inventory investment cutback?

**15–19. Inventory Turnovers.** New management at Bosanac Supplies noted that materials inventory turned over every 18 days. Materials used during the year cost $18,000,000. The work in process inventory turnover was 24. Production costs for the year were $48,000,000.

Steps were taken to obtain more frequent deliveries from suppliers so that operations could be conducted efficiently with only a 12-day supply of inventory. In addition, bottlenecks in production were eliminated, with the result being that the production costs will be 30 times the work in process inventory.

**Required:**
1. What was the average materials inventory investment with a turnover every 18 days? Every 12 days?
2. What was the average work in process inventory investment with a turnover of 24? Of 30?
3. Explain why reducing inventory levels can improve the return on assets.

Service

**15–20. Current Asset Turnovers.** Tech Products Company is a wholesaler and has very few non-current assets. It has been growing rapidly. Operating net income increased from $130,000 in 2005 to $288,000 in 2006. Cost of goods sold and operating expenses amounted to $1,300,000 in 2005 and $4,800,000 in 2006. The average investment in current assets was $650,000 in 2005 and $1,600,000 in 2006. The company had some difficulties in meeting delivery schedules in 2006 and in making payments to creditors. Ignore taxes.

**Required:**
1. Compute the return on current assets each year.
2. Compute the current asset turnover each year, using sales as the numerator.
3. Explain why the company may be having trouble in meeting delivery schedules and in making payments to creditors.

Service

**15–21. Accounts Receivable Turnovers.** Dundee Health Services has been having difficulty paying current obligations on time and has obtained additional short-term credit from its bank. Collections on accounts receivable from health insurers have been slower than usual. Ordinarily, accounts receivable are turned over in 60 days. With the longer collection periods, the company is chronically short of cash to pay creditors promptly. Data with respect to sales and receivables are:

|  | 2006 | 2005 | 2004 |
|---|---|---|---|
| Cash patient revenues | $12,000,000 | $15,600,000 | $21,000,000 |
| Third-party insured patient revenues | 97,600,000 | 83,200,00 | 67,600,000 |
| Average accounts receivable | 28,100,000 | 15,400,000 | 8,000,000 |

**Required:**
1. Compute the accounts receivable turnover for each of the three years.
2. Compute the number of days sales in receivables.
3. From the information given, what are possible impacts on the financial condition of the center?

**15–22. International Segments.** Amity International has three international divisions: electrical wiring in Germany, flexible conduits in Korea, and fiberglass control boxes in Sweden. Each of these lines is manufactured in a separate division. Data pertaining to operations for last year are as follows:

| Divisions | Exchange Rates | Division Net Income | Average Assets |
|---|---|---|---|
| Electrical wiring | €1 per $ | €120,000 | €2,400,000 |
| Flexible conduits | W1,100 per $ | W693,000,000 | W4,620,000,000 |
| Fiberglass control boxes | SKr8 per $ | SKr816,000 | SKr6,800,000 |

The average assets given are the assets directly identifiable with the divisions. In addition, corporate assets averaged $1,080,000 and are not directly identifiable with any division. For analysis purposes, corporate assets have been allocated evenly to all divisions. Expenses (after income taxes) that are common to the total operation are $250,000 and are not deducted in computing the division net income shown above. Historically, these expenses are allocated on a 40, 40, and 20 percent basis, respectively.

**Required:**

1. Compute the direct return on assets for each division and rank the divisions.
2. Allocate the common assets and expenses. Compute return on assets and rank the divisions.
3. Comment on:
   (a) the role of common assets and expenses in the ROA analysis.
   (b) whether the analysis should be done in dollars.

**15–23. Ethics and Ratio Manipulation.** Assume that Woodhouse Enterprises has 20 divisions reporting to a corporate office. A number of services such as data processing, cash management, personnel, and legal are performed at the corporate office. Most accounting is done at the division level. Corporate evaluates the earning-power ratios to rank divisions. The corporate capital multipler is used by each division. Only traceable assets are assigned to the divisions. Corporate expenses are not allocated to the divisions.

**Required:**

Assume that Division 15 is an average performing division. Using the earning-power ratios, how might the division manager and division controller work to make the division "look good" on paper? On a short-term basis? On a long-term basis?

# PROBLEMS

Service

**15–24. Rate of Return Relationships.** Red Ball Delivery Service reported a net income of $140,000 on net sales of $2,800,000. Average investment in assets was $1,400,000. The president of the company plans to reduce the asset investment next year, observing that the company is holding some unproductive assets. Budget plans for next year show a net income of $150,000 earned on net sales of $3,000,000. The average investment in assets is to be $1,200,000.

**Required:**

1. Compute the return on net sales, the asset turnover, and the return on assets for this year.
2. Compute the return on net sales, the asset turnover, and the return on assets based on next year's budget. Comment on the impact of the asset reduction.

**15–25. Relationships.** Steinhour Company's 2006 condensed income statement and 2005 and 2006 partial balance sheets are as follows:

| | | |
|---|---:|---:|
| Sales | | $98,000 |
| Expenses: | | |
| Cost of goods sold | $56,000 | |
| Interest | 2,900 | |
| Other operating expenses | 26,000 | 84,900 |
| Net income | | $13,100 |

| Current assets: | 12/31/2006 | 12/31/2005 |
|---|---|---|
| Cash | $1,200 | $ 800 |
| Accounts receivable | 15,000 | 13,000 |
| Inventory | 23,500 | 18,000 |
| Other current assets | 1,400 | 1,600 |
| Total current assets | $41,100 | $33,400 |
| Current liabilities: | | |
| Accounts payable | $ 8,000 | $ 7,500 |
| Current portion of long-term debt | 2,000 | 2,100 |
| Total current liabilities | $10,000 | $ 9,600 |

**Required:**

1. Examine Steinhour's liquidity position for 2006. Assume that high-performing firms in this industry have a current ratio of 2.5:1 and a quick ratio of 1:1. Comment.
2. If the industry average for return on sales is 15 percent, for gross margin is 60 percent, and for times interest earned is 10, comment on Steinhour's performance.

**15–26. Financial Ratios.** The following financial statements are from Rainey Company:

| | 12/31/2006 | 12/31/2005 |
|---|---|---|
| Cash | $ 14,000 | $ 16,000 |
| Accounts receivable (net) | 22,000 | 28,000 |
| Inventories | 65,000 | 55,000 |
| Fixed assets (net) | 85,000 | 79,000 |
| Total assets | $186,000 | $178,000 |
| Accounts payable | $ 30,000 | $ 15,000 |
| Bonds payable | 60,000 | 75,000 |
| Common stock (par value $10) | 60,000 | 60,000 |
| Retained earnings | 36,000 | 28,000 |
| Total liabilities and equity | $186,000 | $178,000 |

| | 2006 |
|---|---|
| Sales | $360,000 |
| Less: | |
| Cost of goods sold | $240,000 |
| Operating expenses | 100,000 (Includes $20,000 of depreciation expense) |
| Income taxes | 8,000 |
| Income after taxes | $ 12,000 |

**Required:**

Find the following ratios for 2006:

(a) Inventory turnover.
(b) The average market price of Rainey stock, if the price-earnings ratio is 8.
(c) The earning power ratios.
(d) The current ratio by the end.
(e) Cash flow per share from operations.
(f) Gross margin percentage.

**15–27. Rate of Return on Shareholders' Investment.** Butler Products Company reported net income of $4,200,000 on net sales of $70,000,000. Selected balance sheet data follow:

| | |
|---|---|
| Average assets | $50,000,000 |
| Average liabilities | 8,000,000 |
| Average shareholders' equity | 42,000,000 |

Speier Enterprises reported net income of $6,000,000 on net sales of $100,000,000. Selected balance sheet data follow:

| | |
|---|---|
| Average assets | $50,000,000 |
| Average liabilities. | 26,000,000 |
| Average shareholders' equity | 24,000,000 |

**Required:**

1. Compare the two companies by computing the following percentages and ratios:
   **(a)** Return on sales.
   **(b)** Return on assets.
   **(c)** Asset turnover.
   **(d)** Return on shareholders' equity.
2. Identify the company that earns a better return for shareholders. Explain the factors that enhance shareholders' rate of return.
3. Which company has more risk? Why?

Service

**15–28. Percentage Composition Statements.** Park Medical Services had a good year in 2006, but its earnings fell slightly from 2005. Darrell Washington, a member of Park's board of directors, thinks that a revised presentation of income statement data would show basic relationships. Income statements for 2005 and 2006 are:

| | 2006 | 2005 |
|---|---|---|
| Revenue | $91,000,000 | $85,000,000 |
| Operating expenses: | | |
|   Materials and supplies | $ 5,920,000 | $ 5,500,000 |
|   Wages and salaries | 40,200,000 | 36,500,000 |
|   Rent | 725,000 | 725,000 |
|   Taxes and insurance | 4,200,000 | 3,400,000 |
|   Heat and light | 980,000 | 850,000 |
|   Advertising | 1,480,000 | 1,275,000 |
|   Other operating costs | 13,880,000 | 12,700,000 |
|   Interest expense | 7,250,000 | 7,350,000 |
|   Income taxes | 6,250,000 | 6,300,000 |
|   Total expenses | $80,885,000 | $74,600,000 |
| Net income | $10,115,000 | $10,400,000 |

**Required:**

1. Prepare percentage composition (common-sized) income statements for 2005 and 2006.
2. Comment on expense trends. What items might the board want to investigate further? What was the change in the return on revenue?
3. Would a base-year comparison show similar relationships? Why or why not?

**15–29. Industry Averages.** Jimmie Gilbert has recently compared his company's financial ratios to a set of average ratios for his industry that he obtained from the National Association of Financial Ratio Analysts (NAFRA). He has lined up his data, two local competitors' data, and NAFRA data as follows:

| | Gilbert | Competitor 1 | Competitor 2 | NAFRA |
|---|---|---|---|---|
| Receivables turnover | 6.3 | 4.9 | 5.6 | 5.8 |
| Inventory turnover | 4.2 | 2.6 | 3.1 | 3.1 |
| Asset turnover | 2.2 | 1.3 | 1.5 | 1.6 |
| Gross margin percentage. | 37.0 | 40.6 | 40.3 | 39.6 |
| Return on sales. | 0.3 | 7.2 | 4.9 | 9.2 |
| Return on equity | 12.2 | 11.0 | 10.6 | 17.1 |
| Current ratio | 1.6 | 2.9 | 2.1 | 1.9 |

**Required:**

1. Comment on the relative strengths and weaknesses of Gilbert as compared to the two competitors and to the national NAFRA data.
2. Using only this data, what might explain Gilbert's low return on sales?
3. Why might the three businesses in this local area have such a low return on sales when compared to the NAFRA data?

**15–30. Benefits of Financial Leverage.** A majority shareholder of Okemos Products has forced the company to hold debt to a minimum. Net income each year has been approximately $7,200,000. A summary balance sheet for a typical year is:

| | |
|---|---|
| Current assets | $ 80,000,000 |
| Plant and equipment (net) | 40,000,000 |
| Total assets | $120,000,000 |
| Current liabilities | $ 30,000,000 |
| Shareholders' equity | 90,000,000 |
| Total liabilities and shareholders' equity | $120,000,000 |

A younger member of the board, Carla Freed, is irritated with such a cautious policy. "We would be better off to liquidate and invest in government securities," she protests. She states that with new product lines and an aggressive sales stance, net income could easily grow to $15,000,000 a year. She admits that $30,000,000 in additional assets would be needed and states, "The additional assets should be financed by long-term notes." Other balance sheet relationships would remain unchanged.

**Required:**

1. Compute the typical rate of return on assets and shareholders' equity.
2. Compute the revised rate of return on assets and shareholders' equity by following the younger member's proposal.
3. Comment on the two strategies. What will be the primary arguments on both sides at the board meeting? Which do you favor?

**15–31. Rates of Return by Segments, Managerial Behavior, and Ethics.** The president of Farber Products Company is reviewing financial data and is concerned that one operating division is not doing as well as the others. The company has three separate divisions. Managers are rewarded according to divisional ROA. Current financial data are as follows:

| | Product Divisions | | |
|---|---|---|---|
| | 1 | 2 | 3 |
| Net sales | $1,700,000 | $2,000,000 | $1,800,000 |
| Cost of goods sold | $ 780,000 | $ 940,000 | $ 720,000 |
| Operating expenses | 590,000 | 860,000 | 810,000 |
| Total expenses | $1,370,000 | $1,800,000 | $1,530,000 |
| Net income | $ 330,000 | $ 200,000 | $ 270,000 |
| Direct asset investment | $1,600,000 | $2,000,000 | $1,080,000 |
| Return on assets | 21 % | 10 % | 25 % |

Closer examination reveals that certain operating expenses are common to the total operation and have been allocated to the divisions. Also, included in direct assets are amounts pertaining to the total operation but not identifiable with any particular division. The amounts allocated to divisions are as follows:

| Divisions | Allocated Expenses | Allocated Assets |
|---|---|---|
| 1 | $160,000 | $200,000 |
| 2 | 350,000 | 500,000 |
| 3 | 140,000 | 100,000 |

**Required:**

1. From the information given, recalculate the ROA for each division.
2. What type of behavior is the company trying to encourage by using divisional ROA to evaluate managers?
3. What negative or unethical behavior might result from this system? Why?

**15–32. Rates of Return and Liquidity.** Pam Ferrerio, vice-president of finance of Pacific Trade Company, is concerned that the company is growing too rapidly and is unable to support further growth by debt financing.

"We are enjoying an embarrassment of riches," she states. "Each month we must incur more costs to serve our ever-increasing sales". At the same time, we are increasing debt and must face the fact that we should sell more capital stock." Financial data (stated in thousands) for several years are:

| | 2007 | 2006 | 2005 | 2004 |
|---|---|---|---|---|
| Current assets. | $1,030 | $870 | $720 | $580 |
| Plant assets (net of depreciation). | 3,150 | 1,770 | 860 | 770 |
| Total assets. | $4,180 | $2,640 | $1,580 | $1,350 |
| Current liabilities. | $889 | $550 | $230 | $210 |
| Long-term notes payable. | 1,000 | 450 | 50 | 0 |
| Shareholders' equity. | 2,291 | 1,640 | 1,300 | 1,140 |
| Total liabilities and equities. | $4,180 | $2,640 | $1,580 | $1,350 |
| Net sales. | $9,870 | $4,750 | $3,240 | |
| Cost of goods sold. | $7,930 | $3,640 | $2,380 | |
| Operating expenses. | 930 | 490 | 335 | |
| Interest expense. | 100 | 45 | 5 | |
| Total expenses. | $8,960 | $4,175 | $2,720 | |
| Income before income taxes. | $910 | $ 575 | $ 520 | |
| Income taxes. | 364 | 230 | 208 | |
| Net income. | $546 | $345 | $312 | |
| Additional data: | | | | |
| Average outstanding shares. | 500 | 500 | 500 | 500 |
| Depreciation expense. | $220 | $140 | $60 | |
| Current portion of long-term debt. | $400 | $300 | $50 | $0 |

**Required:**

1. Calculate the earning-power ratios for each year. What is happening?
2. For each year, examine the liquidity and capital adequacy positions. Comment on your findings.
3. Do you agree with the vice-president of finance? Why or why not?

Service

**15–33. Inventory and Accounts Receivable Turnovers.** The president of Oberlin Stores, Annette Boyd, notes that collection of accounts receivable should be improved. She proposes that inducements be given to customers to pay promptly. This, she argues, will increase costs somewhat; but, in the final analysis, the rate of return should increase. Also, she believes that the company is holding a larger inventory than necessary and can improve the rate of return by inventory reduction.

Financial data for last year are summarized as follows along with a budget for next year as prepared by the controller:

|  | Last Year | Budget Year |
|---|---|---|
| Net sales | $4,200,000 | $6,000,000 |
| Cost of goods sold. | $3,000,000 | $4,500,000 |
| Operating expenses. | 500,000 | 650,000 |
| Total expenses. | $3,500,000 | $5,150,000 |
| Income before income taxes. | $ 700,000 | $ 850,000 |
| Income taxes. | 300,000 | 380,000 |
| Net income. | $ 400,000 | $ 470,000 |
| **Average Balances** | | |
| Current assets: | | |
| Cash. | $ 500,000 | $ 650,000 |
| Accounts receivable | 700,000 | 600,000 |
| Inventory | 600,000 | 450,000 |
| Total current assets. | $1,800,000 | $1,700,000 |
| Plant assets (net). | 1,400,000 | 1,300,000 |
| Total assets. | $3,200,000 | $3,000,000 |

**Required:**

1. Find the following relationships for last year and the budget year:
   (a) Return on sales and return on assets
   (b) Accounts receivable turnover and inventory turnover
2. What impacts could you imply resulted from the changes?

**15–34. Measures of Liquidity.** Denny Fink, a member of the board of directors of Egerdal Products, states that the company is becoming overextended in attempting to support a larger operation with insufficient working capital. Vera Amick, president of the company, states that results speak for themselves. Sales volume has increased, profits have increased, and return on shareholders' equity has increased. Financial data for the past three years are summarized as follows:

|  | 2006 | 2005 | 2004 |
|---|---|---|---|
| Net sales. | $4,000,000 | $2,000,000 | $1,200,000 |
| Less: Cost of goods sold. | $3,400,000 | $1,600,000 | $ 900,000 |
| Operating expenses. | 180,000 | 150,000 | 140,000 |
| Depreciation expense. | 50,000 | 40,000 | 30,000 |
| Interest expense. | 80,000 | 30,000 | 0 |
| Income taxes. | 120,000 | 70,000 | 60,000 |
| Net income | $170,000 | $110,000 | $70,000 |
| **Average Balances** | | | |
|  | 2006 | 2005 | 2004 |
| Current assets | $1,930,000 | $1,780,000 | $1,680,000 |
| Current liabilities. | 1,250,000 | 970,000 | 760,000 |
| Long-term debt | 800,000 | 300,000 | 0 |
| Common stock ($10 par) | 600,000 | 500,000 | 500,000 |
| Retained earnings. | 430,000 | 290,000 | 210,000 |

**Required:**

1. Determine these ratios for each year:
   (a) Return on sales, return on assets, and return on shareholders' equity.
   (b) Current ratio, cash flow from operations per share, and earnings per share.
   (c) Percentage of debt to equity and the common equity multiplier.
2. Do you share Denny Fink's concern? Or is Vera Amick's statement of assurance on target? Comment on the trends revealed by your analysis.

## CASE 15A—BAKER, BEG & BALDREE

Judy Baldree, vice-president of sales, has recommended adding a new product line. A market study and cost analyses show that the new line should yield the following annual results:

| | |
|---|---|
| Net sales | $2,800,000 |
| Cost of sales | $1,600,000 |
| Operating expenses | 200,000 |
| Total expenses | $1,800,000 |
| Income before income taxes | $1,000,000 |
| Income taxes (40 %) | 400,000 |
| Net income | $ 600,000 |

Depreciation of $150,000 is included in total expenses. Cost of sales and operating expenses include only direct costs of the new line.

Financial data for last year, considered to be a typical year, are:

| | |
|---|---|
| Net sales | $12,000,000 |
| Cost of sales | $ 7,500,000 |
| Operating expenses | 1,800,000 |
| Total expenses | $ 9,300,000* |
| Operating income | $ 2,700,000 |
| Interest expense | 100,000 |
| Income before income taxes | $ 2,600,000 |
| Income taxes (40 %) | 1,040,000 |
| Net income | $ 1,560,000 |
| Total assets. | $12,000,000 |
| Current liabilities | $ 3,000,000 |
| Long-term debt | 1,000,000 |
| Shareholders' equity | 8,000,000 |
| Total liabilities and equities | $12,000,000 |

\* Depreciation expense included totals $400,000 for the firm.

The investment in additional equipment for the production and sale of the new product line has been estimated at $3,000,000. "The new product line will yield a 20 percent return on assets," Baldree states.

Zeshawn Beg, the vice-president of production, interrupts. "Are you talking about a cash-flow return, Jody?" he asks. "No," Baldree answers. "When depreciation is added back, the cash-flow return will be even greater."

The vice-president of finance, Sarah Baker, asks, "How do you think we should finance the investment?"

"We should be able to issue long-term notes," Baldree responds. "Our debt at the present time is modest. And, with debt financing, we gain the advantage of leverage."

"In your estimate, Judy, you forgot to include any interest cost. It will cost us $150,000 after income taxes to finance $3,000,000," Baker replies.

**Required:**

1.  What impacts will the new product line have on profit measures and cash flows?
2.  Examine and comment on Baldree's strategy to finance the investment. Is it likely that shareholders will be impressed with the investment? Why?
3.  In your opinion, is the investment attractive? Explain your answer.

# CASE 15B—DEB NORTH'S ANALYSIS

Deb North has been doing research on the electronic components manufacturing industry. She has developed the following financial data:

|  | Percentage of Total Assets | | | | |
|---|---|---|---|---|---|
|  | 2003 | 2004 | 2005 | 2006 | 2007 |
| Cash and equivalents. | 6.6 | 6.9 | 7.7 | 7.9 | 8.9 |
| Trade receivables | 30.0 | 29.6 | 28.2 | 29.0 | 27.4 |
| Inventory | 31.7 | 32.9 | 32.6 | 27.8 | 26.4 |
| All other current assets. | 2.5 | 1.9 | 1.2 | 2.3 | 2.2 |
| Total current assets. | 70.8 | 71.3 | 69.7 | 67.0 | 64.9 |
| All noncurrent assets | 29.2 | 28.7 | 30.3 | 33.0 | 35.1 |
| Total assets. | 100.0 | 100.0 | 100.0 | 100.0 | 100.0 |
| Notes payable | 11.9 | 12.7 | 11.6 | 12.3 | 12.4 |
| Trade payables. | 15.3 | 14.2 | 13.3 | 14.0 | 13.6 |
| All other current liabilities | 13.0 | 13.4 | 12.4 | 12.3 | 11.9 |
| Total current liabilities | 40.2 | 40.3 | 37.3 | 38.6 | 37.9 |
| Long-term debt. | 17.7 | 17.4 | 17.6 | 17.0 | 18.0 |
| Equity. | 42.0 | 42.4 | 45.2 | 44.4 | 44.1 |
| Total liabilities and equity | 100.0 | 100.0 | 100.0 | 100.0 | 100.0 |

|  | Percentage of Net Sales | | | | |
|---|---|---|---|---|---|
|  | 2003 | 2004 | 2005 | 2006 | 2007 |
| Net sales | 100.0 | 100.0 | 100.0 | 100.0 | 100.0 |
| Cost of goods sold. | 66.9 | 65.1 | 65.5 | 65.9 | 66.6 |
| Operating expenses | 25.8 | 26.7 | 26.0 | 26.7 | 27.4 |
| Interest expense. | 1.3 | 1.7 | 1.7 | 1.6 | 1.8 |
| All other net expenses (income) | 0.0 | −1.3 | −.3 | −.2 | −.1 |
| Income taxes. | 1.8 | 2.5 | 2.3 | 1.9 | 1.4 |
| Profit after taxes. | 4.2 | 5.3 | 4.8 | 4.1 | 2.9 |

| | Ratio or Percentage Values | | | | |
| --- | --- | --- | --- | --- | --- |
| | 2003 | 2004 | 2005 | 2006 | 2007 |
| Current ratio. | 1.8 | 1.8 | 1.9 | 1.9 | 1.8 |
| Receviables turnover | 6.3 | 6.1 | 6.6 | 6.4 | 6.8 |
| Inventory turnover | 4.0 | 3.9 | 3.6 | 4.0 | 4.6 |
| Times interest earned. | 5.6 | 5.2 | 5.2 | 3.7 | 3.1 |
| Debt to equity ratio | 1.4 | 1.3 | 1.2 | 1.2 | 1.3 |
| Return on equity | 20.1 | 22.1 | 20.9 | 16.5 | 14.3 |
| Return on assets | 8.5 | 8.9 | 8.4 | 6.9 | 6.1 |
| Asset turnover | 1.8 | 1.8 | 1.8 | 1.8 | 1.8 |
| Growth in net sales. | 5.3 | 6.2 | 7.3 | 5.1 | 6.9 |
| Growth in assets | 3.2 | 4.2 | 5.7 | 7.7 | 7.3 |
| Growth in profits. | 5.7 | 8.3 | 6.2 | 5.1 | 3.2 |

Because nearly 300 firms' data are summarized in the preceding numbers, the ratios do not correspond exactly to financial statement numbers of any individual firm.

**Required:**

1. What characteristics appear to cause 2004 to be a high returns year and 2007 to be a low returns year?
2. What do the growth ratios tell Ms. North about the industry?
3. As a potential investor in this industry, identify five key factors you would monitor during the year 2008.

# INDEX

# CHECK FIGURES

## CHAPTER 4

| | |
|---|---|
| 4–1 | Total cost of order #723 = $69.20 |
| 4–5 | 1. $3.00 per hour |
| 4–11 | Applied overhead = $897,000 |
| 4–12 | Direct labor cost = 498,000 shekels |
| 4–17 | Labor hours worked = 22,300 |
| 4–19 | 1. Plant-wide rate = $20.00 |
| 4–21 | Total overhead applied to Brochures = $68,333 |
| 4–22 | Overhead rate per client for Apartment Location = $1,309 |
| 4–24 | 2. Cost allocated to Corporate = $469,778 |
| 4–26 | Overhead rate per labor hour for Concessions = $13.87 |
| 4–32 | 3. Total cost of goods sold in August = $432,800 |
| 4–35 | 1. Cost of contracts completed = $8,905,000 |
| 4–37 | 3. $41,000 |
| 4–38 | 4. Unit cost = $40.08 |
| 4–40 | 2. $20.705 per machine hour |
| 4–41 | 3. (b) Total overhead costs for Alaska = $954 |
| 4–45 | 1. (b) Overhead applied = £222,640 |
| 4–47 | Total overhead costs for P&C = $177,936 |
| Case 4 | 1. Total Civil Dept. costs = $569,000 |

## CHAPTER 5

| | |
|---|---|
| 5–6 | 2. Cost of ending work in process = $13,920 |
| 5–8 | 2. 29,600 equivalent units |
| 5–13 | 2. Cost of units in ending inventory = $48,000 |
| 5–14 | March 31 work in process (total) = $2,588 |
| 5–16 | 1. Equivalent units for materials = 66,200 |
| 5–17 | 1. Total cost of completed units = $51,800 |
| 5–18 | 1. Cost of units completed = $51,734 |
| 5–26 | 3. $145,000 |
| 5–28 | 1. May 31 work in process (total) = $34,000 |
| 5–29 | 1. July 31 work in process (total) = $324,080 |
| 5–31 | 2. Total cost of completed units = $859,017 |
| 5–32 | 1. Cost per unit for materials = $20.9595 |
| 5–33 | 1. Cost per unit for materials = $1.60 |
| 5–35 | 2. Unit cost = $18.31 |
| 5–36 | 2. April 30 work in process (total) = $34,570 |
| 5–39 | 2. Unit cost for overhead = $0.39515 |
| 5–40 | 1. Cost per unit = $14.54 |
| 5–41 | 1. Unit cost for conversion = $4.05 |
| Case 5B | 4. Variable cost per unit = $2.80 |

## CHAPTER 6

| | |
|---|---|
| 6–7 | Overhead cost for white hats = $53,650 |
| 6–14 | 2. Total costs for Streets = $79,750 |
| 6–15 | $61.70 |
| 6–16 | Allocation to Commercial = $18,101,175 |
| 6–17 | $11,800 |
| 6–20 | Per mile cost for Local = $1.40 |
| 6–21 | Overhead cost per unit for Propane = $1,476 |

| | |
|---|---|
| **6–22** | 2. $394,000 debit balance |
| **6–33** | 2. Total for #TK451 = $21,189 |
| **6–35** | Overhead cost with ABC = $11,000 |
| **6–37** | 1. Total for Standard = $253,050 |
| **6–38** | 2. Cost per unit for Y = $19.52 |
| **6–39** | Assigned cost with ABC = $5,842 |
| **6–40** | 3. Total overhead for Gears (ABC) = $3,914,805 |
| **6–42** | Total cost per tour for 21-Day Tour = A$28,847 |
| **6–43** | Profit for Produce = $49,384 |
| **6–45** | 2. Underapplied conversion costs = $10,000 |
| **Case 6B** | Total cost per unit for 1-Bedroom = $2,014 |

## CHAPTER 7

| | |
|---|---|
| **7–5** | 2. Cash receipts increase = £1,280 |
| **7–7** | 2. Cash paid for purchases during February = $2,448 |
| **7–14** | 1. Expected value of net income before tax = $472 |
| **7–15** | 1. Purchases during the fourth quarter = 154,000 units |
| **7–16** | 1. March 31 cash balance = A$30,880 |
| **7–18** | 1. Total cash collections during November = $76,260 |
| **7–20** | 2. Cash available for dividends = $27,000 |
| **7–26** | 3. Maximum sales forecast = 260,000 units |
| **7–28** | 1. January's ending cash balance= $1,000 |
| **7–32** | 2. Labor costs for October = $21,600 |
| **7–34** | Expected contribution margin = $11,902 |
| **7–35** | 2. Expected total cash flow = $1,074,000 |
| **7–37** | 1. Total cost per unit = $26.50 |
| **7–39** | 1. Ending cash balance for June = $351,640 |
| **7–41** | 1. Cost per unit for Red = $10.2333 |
| **7–44** | 2. (a) Manufacturing profits = $5,940,000 |
| **Case 7B** | 1. Balance of loans at end of December = $95,003 |

## CHAPTER 8

| | |
|---|---|
| **8–2** | 2. Unfavorable materials price variance = $4,500 |
| **8–6** | 1. Standard quantity allowed = 1,200 kilograms |
| **8–7** | 3. Actual cost per assembly = $0.912 |
| **8–10** | 2. Unfavorable labor efficiency variance = $6,250 |
| **8–12** | 3. Favorable budget variance = $8,000 |
| **8–17** | Loss on proposal = $61.30 |
| **8–18** | 3. Unfavorable variable overhead spending variance = J$20,000 |
| **8–21** | Total standard cost per workstation = $194.61 |
| **8–24** | 2. Standard cost per unit = $8.80 |
| **8–25** | 1. Actual price = M$8.475 |
| **8–26** | 1. Favorable materials price variance = $7,500 |
| **8–27** | Materials price variance = $276 Favorable |
| **8–29** | 1. Total overhead cost per unit = $0.14 |
| **8–30** | 1. (d) Labor efficiency variance = $80,000 Favorable |
| **8–31** | 3. (b) Overhead capacity variance = $1,100 Unfavorable |
| **8–36** | 1. Break-even point with no learning curve = 25 patients |
| **8–37** | 2. (a) Direct labor cost per order = $44,428.80 |

| 8–38 | 1. Unfavorable capacity variance = 1,600,000 pesos |
| 8–39 | 3. Variable spending variance = $1,460 Favorable |
| Case 8A | 4. Standard cost per unit = $116.41 |

## CHAPTER 9

| 9–3 | 1. Mix variance for Bland weddings = $817 Unfavorable |
| 9–5 | 2. Total revenue mix variances = $80,000 Favorable |
| 9–12 | 1. Profit before taxes = $15,000 |
| 9–13 | Profit after taxes = $165,000 |
| 9–14 | 1. Total unit cost = $30 |
| 9–15 | 2. Profit = $840,000 |
| 9–17 | 1. Total revenue quantity variances = $60,121 Favorable |
| 9–18 | Total interest income rate variances = $1.30 Unfavorable |
| 9–20 | 2. Total revenue price variances = $250,000 Unfavorable |
| 9–21 | 2. Total quantity variances for gross margin = $142,500 Favorable |
| 9–23 | 2. Total manufacturing cost for Rakes = $2.25 |
| 9–24 | 2. Net loss = $90,000 |
| 9–25 | 1. Manufacturing profit for Utility = $920,000 |
| 9–27 | 1. 2005 profit = $22,000 |
| Case 9 | 1. Revenue price variance for Lanes = $14,895 Favorable |

## CHAPTER 10

| 10–2 | Selling price = $24.50 |
| 10–11 | Additional profit from special sale = $800 |
| 10–13 | Variable cost per packet = $2 |
| 10–16 | 1. Contribution margin per service hour for Baker = $30 |
| 10–18 | 2. Maximum amount = $85,000 |
| 10–19 | Direct segment contribution margin = $125,000 |
| 10–21 | 1. Contribution margin per hour for C = $20 |
| 10–22 | Incremental contribution from additional processing = $19,000 |
| 10–25 | Incremental income for Department A = $65,000 |
| 10–28 | 2. Net disadvantage of accepting special order = HK$10,000 |
| 10–29 | 1. Net make advantage = $9,000 |
| 10–35 | Profit is $16,000 higher if Department 2 is kept |
| 10–36 | Net make advantage = $125,000 |
| 10–38 | 1. Net additional profit from special sale = ¥35,500,000 |
| 10–39 | 1. Incremental disadvantage of closing Store 54 = $30,000 |
| 10–40 | 1. Total variable cost per unit = NT$180 |
| 10–43 | 1. (b) Total contribution margin = $2,950,000 |
| 10–46 | 1. Incremental net income for Garden Supplies = $24,000 |
| 10–47 | Variable contribution margin per hour for Iron Frames #10 = $3.50 |
| Case 10B | 1. (d) Incremental profit = $615 |

## CHAPTER 11

| 11–3 | Accounting rate of return = 17.5% |
| 11–5 | 2. Payback period = 3.125 years |
| 11–6 | 3. Net present value = $11,710 |
| 11–11 | Year 5 net cash flows = £140,000 |
| 11–13 | 3. Net present value = $22,436 |
| 11–16 | 1. Payback period for Project 98-G3 = 5.2 years |

| | |
|---|---|
| **11–18** | 1. Net cash inflow after taxes = $18,400 |
| **11–20** | $70,000 |
| **11–22** | Project 3 annual cash inflow = $12,197 |
| **11–25** | 2. Net present value for choice 2 = $4,143 |
| **11–27** | 1. Net present value = $29,258 |
| **11–29** | Case 4: Annual cash inflow = $100,000 |
| **11–30** | 2. Necessary sales volume = 26,541 units |
| **11–33** | Net present value = HK$862,048 |
| **11–34** | 1. Net present value = $247,664 |
| **11–36** | 1. Net present value = $60,197 |
| **11–39** | Net present value = $81,898 |
| **Case 11A** | 2. Annual cash flow = $14,000 |
| **Case 11B** | 2. Profitability index = 0.92 |

## CHAPTER 12

| | |
|---|---|
| **12–6** | 1. Net present value for Alternative 2 = ¥700 |
| **12–7** | Net present value = $30,472 |
| **12–10** | 2. Net present value = $29,424 |
| **12–12** | Net present value = -$3,916 |
| **12–16** | 1. Present value of operating costs for Alternative A = B$337,265 |
| **12–17** | 2. Net lease advantage for Vehicle B = $3,035 |
| **12–18** | Net present value of $130,000 Investment = $17,619 |
| **12–20** | 2. Net present value = $3,584 |
| **12–21** | 1. Annual net cash flow for Machine X = $365,000 |
| **12–22** | 1. Profitability index of X = 1.35 |
| **12–23** | Net present value = -$4,194 |
| **12–24** | 1. Present Value factor = 3.067 |
| **12–28** | 3. Net present value = $520,874 |
| **12–30** | 1. Net present value = $6,626 |
| **12–32** | 2. Net present value = -$35,502 |
| **12–33** | 1. Net present value = $111,497 |

## CHAPTER 13

| | |
|---|---|
| **13–4** | Trois: Imputed rate = 15% |
| **13–8** | 2. $361,600 |
| **13–15** | 1. Profit at 120,000 units = $240,000 |
| **13–19** | 1. Net income = $5,900,000 |
| **13–20** | c. Contribution margin for Marketing = $0.40 |
| **13–24** | 1. Additional contribution margin per unit = 4.6 euros |
| **13–32** | 1. Variable cost per time unit = 18.50 litas |
| **13–33** | 1. Division 1 net income = $1,080,000 |
| **13–34** | 3. Contribution margin for Central = $31,000,000 |
| **13–35** | 2. Cost of buying parts internally = $1,340,000 |
| **13–36** | 1. Present system: transfer price for Order 2 = $450 |
| **13–37** | 2. Variable unit cost = $4.75 |
| **13–41** | 1. Selling Division net income = $1,044,000 |

## CHAPTER 14

| | |
|---|---|
| **14–1** | Internal failure costs = $145,000 |
| **14–5** | 2. Total costs under revised system = £627,000 |

| | |
|---|---|
| **14–8** | $360 |
| **14–14** | 2. 41.5% |
| **14–19** | Total quality costs in 2007 = $591,130 |
| **14–20** | Total costs after installation = $786,000 |
| **14–22** | 1. Total prevention costs in 2005 = $740,000 |
| **14–25** | 1. Target cost = $841,500 |
| **14–28** | 1. Total loss from late shipments = B70,620 |
| **14–30** | 3. First pass yield = 95% |

**CHAPTER 15**

| | |
|---|---|
| **15–1** | 3. Asset turnover = 4.54 |
| **15–3** | (c) Operating cycle = 100 days |
| **15–5** | (b) Dividend yield = 5.33% |
| **15–6** | Average accounts receivable = $67 |
| **15–11** | 2. Dividend yield = 9.375% |
| **15–12** | Net income = $6,000 |
| **15–14** | 6. Asset turnover = 2.0 |
| **15–15** | 2. Return on equity = 6.0% |
| **15–18** | 3. Return on assets after reduction = 9.2% |
| **15–22** | 2. Return on assets for Flexible Conduits = 11.62% |
| **15–24** | 2. Return on sales = 5.0% |
| **15–25** | 2. Times interest earned = 5.5 |
| **15–26** | (f) Gross margin percentage = 33.3% |
| **15–31** | 1. Return on assets for Division 3 = 41.8% |
| **15–34** | 1. (a) 2006 return on assets = 5.5% |
| **Case 15A** | 1. Cash flow rate of return from present operation = 16.3% |